HERITAGE
OF
AMERICAN
EDUCATION

RELATIVITY

Inevitable.
I've heard it's only time
Till we are relegated to the past,
Alive to few but stooped and wrinkled scribes
Who find us in some dry and dusty tome.

I've read of golden Greece who tarnish grew,
And read of Rome, a strong full-bodied brew —
Fermenting slowly, slowly she decayed;
I've read of many more and have been told
That each and all make up our heritage.

I know we cannot be an end ourselves;
As we have built, so we'll be built upon.
One day we'll be allied with Greece and Rome,
In a section marked "Our Heritage"
On the bookshelves of a future race.

CAROL GODFREY

HERITAGE

OF

AMERICAN

EDUCATION

EDITED BY   RICHARD E. GROSS

School of Education, Stanford University

ALLYN AND BACON, INC.   BOSTON, 1962

CONTRIBUTORS

Richard E. Gross, *Editor*
School of Education, Stanford University, Stanford, California

In collaboration with:

Joseph S. Roucek
Departments of Political Science and Sociology, University of Bridgeport, Bridgeport, Connecticut

Dwight W. Allen
School of Education, Stanford University, Stanford, California

Eugene B. Borowitz
Director of Education, Union of American Hebrew Congregations, New York City

William E. Drake
College of Education, University of Texas, Austin, Texas

Robert M. Frumkin
Social Studies Department, State University of New York Teachers College, Oswego, New York

Patricia Grinager
School of Education, Stanford University, Stanford, California

Joseph Katz
College of Education, University of British Columbia, Vancouver

Bernard J. Kohlbrenner
Department of Education, University of Notre Dame, Notre Dame, Indiana

Kenneth V. Lottich
School of Education, Montana State University, Missoula, Montana

Arthur H. Moehlman
College of Education, University of Texas, Austin, Texas

Ray H. Muessig
School of Education, Purdue University, Lafayette, Indiana

CONTENTS

HERITAGE

OF

AMERICAN

EDUCATION

****

HERITAGE OF AMERICAN EDUCATION:
AN INTRODUCTION

Down the stream of centuries, various peoples have brought their singular bequests to civilization. Each tends to be remembered for those gifts that are recognized as epochal contributions to the evolution of modern society. In the West, for example, the Hebrews created seminal religious ideals; the Greeks built philosophy to unequaled heights; the Romans passed on their legal system; and the British developed parliamentary government. For what shall the Americans be remembered? It is our firm belief that objective chroniclers of tomorrow will record — "The American achievement was the fulfilled concept of universal public education." In this book we are concerned with the origins and evolution of this singular attainment.

In the United States a mutual relationship exists in that the extended opportunities for the free schooling of the populace depend upon democratic political principles and, among other factors, economic largess; but these attributes of the society are eternally dependent upon a literate and wise citizenry. The story of America has been explained too frquently without adequate reference to its mighty tradition of informal and formal educative media. On the other hand, it is a serious mistake to attempt to delineate the rise of an educational system if truncated from the social milieu that gives it its very meaning. Thus, in light of its total environment, the evolution of America's educational values and achievements deserves a searching review.

In such an assessment our efforts are centered upon the exploration of the heritage of American schooling. We ask: From whence did it come? How did it develop? What are its outstanding features? In attempting to answer these and related queries, the *Heritage of American Education* documents the educational admixture that has resulted through the centuries, before there was an America, as well as developments in the American story. It reviews in later chapters the more indigenous characteristics of American education and recent developments in cultural exchange by which American influences have been carried abroad. We are concerned with the development of American education but not merely to trace it. The overall goal is to help make education in the United States understandable as it relates to its roots and purposeful in the light of its development.

Through the years only a handful of works in our area have dared to be innovational and it is in this vein that we approached our efforts. Our purpose, however, was not simply to be "different" but to produce a volume that would more satisfactorily meet the emerging needs of teacher education than traditional accounts. We have not presented a chronological recitation of events but, rather, selected studies in the evolution of present-day American education.[1]

Problem of the History of Education in America

From the beginnings of professional teacher education in the United States, work in the history of education was a predominant requirement, and this strong emphasis continued well past the turn of the twentieth century. Albertson cites a study of teachers college curricula in 1914 that ranked history of education second only to practice teaching in those schools' teacher training programs.[2] A survey by Koos and Woody (1917) found teachers listing history of education second only to educational psychology as one of the professional courses that they had taken.[3] However, even in these reports we have the "handwriting on the wall" in the courses listed in each instance in first position; the coming impact of the competence or practitioner approach in teacher education is apparent. The history of education was already failing

---

[1] For a visual overview of the strands of influence in the development of modern education see the diagrammatic presentation by the writer and Lester B. Sands, *History of Education Chart*, Stanford: Stanford University Press, 3rd ed., 1957.

[2] James Albertson, "The Influence of National Inclusive Professional Associations on the Program of Professional Preparation in Teacher Education" (Doctor's thesis, Stanford University, 1957), p. 159.

[3] Cited by Lawrence A. Cremin in *The Role of the History of Education in the Professional Preparation of Teachers* (Ann Arbor: National Society of College Teachers of Education, Committee on Historical Foundations, 1957), p. 4.

in its necessary, interpretive role of revealing how knowledge of the past might serve educational purpose. For many instructors, history of education had become an end in itself and though, as we shall see, there are important values in the general knowledge of events and trends in the history of education, its major role in the curriculum of teacher education should be fixed by the light that it sheds on contemporary professional problems, in being a discipline that relates to present practice and that furnishes the intellectual tools that teachers can use in their work.[4]

Until approximately 1925 the history of education remained one of the most frequently required elements in the professional education of teachers. As with all institutional lag, the reaction to history's impotence did not produce a significant decline in offerings until after 1930. The reaction against traditional history of education courses was part of the ferment that began to mark American society just before 1900 when new forces also appeared in American education that echoed the rather momentous alterations in life in the United States and its growing international contacts. As Cremin has detailed, it was not long until the history of education came under attack, particularly from those who represented the newly emerging concentrations or areas within the field of education.[5] He merges these forces that were jockeying for position in the teacher training program under the heading of the "Scientific and Measurement Movement" in education. Undoubtedly new advances in psychology, our understanding of the learning process, of child development (resulting from the child study as well as the testing movement), new social and educational theories and our growing concerns for special and more individualized education—from preparation for handling the handicapped and the gifted to the vocationally oriented or the delinquent — called for changed emphases and additional subject matter in the education of teachers. Inevitably, in the push for the practical and the new, staid, educational history and courses in arm-chair pedagogical theory were bound to give way.

Traditional historical emphases suffered from the growing impact of new ideas in Western society and scholarship. Historical pre-eminence in the curriculum was jolted by factors such as: pragmatic, cultural relativism; the rejection of the value judgments and "unobjective" interpretations of the older, omniscient historians; the increased interest in sociology and other social sciences that had more contemporaneous outlooks; as well as an accept-

---

[4] See Robert E. Mason, "History of Education and Professional Practice," *Phi Delta Kappan,* March, 1957, pp. 248-249, for an elaboration of this view; Cremin, *ibid.,* and subsequent chapters in that bulletin, present an excellent summary of the issues pro and con on the role of the history of education as held by a number of leaders in the field.

[5] Cremin, *op. cit.,* pp. 2-9.

ance of scientific positivism which rejected anything that could not be proved.

There can be little doubt that the demise of educational history as the central factor in teacher education was also directly related to the sterile, name-date-event, seed catalog approach used by the majority of instructors. There were too few inspired and inspiring professors in the discipline. That this remains a problem to plague the student is evidenced by a questionnaire survey conducted by Moehlman in 1950 of 100 institutions of higher education in which he found approximately one-half of the instructors in history of education to be only partially prepared in the subject, often specialists in other educational areas who had been assigned the course to fill in their teaching load.[6] Even in retrospect, many teachers found the historical offerings to be of little functional value in their own preparation and this attitude was reflected in more recent decades by a rapid continuing decline in the history of education.[7] This has been characterized by a heavy reduction in the number of required courses and by smaller percentages of students enrolled in the offerings. In a number of institutions, the subject has been dropped as a part of the basic program of teacher preparation, although remaining as an elective or in some cases being incorporated into a merged history and philosophy of education course; or into classes such as the introduction to education, educational foundations, social foundations, and those devoted to surveys of elementary and secondary education.

With the growing pressures for emerging aspects of knowledge coming to be deemed essential for teachers, some of the foregoing reductions and arrangements for merger or curtailment were to be expected. It should also be noted that no experimental proof has ever been developed, in spite of over half a century of the attempt to develop a "science" of education, that *any* subject is essential in teacher education; but many of the proponents of newer areas could use an obtuse pedagogical terminology, judiciously interspersed with formulae and statistics, to mesmerize educational administrators as well as the defensive historians themselves into accepting the near elimination of the history of education. Also, with many history of education instructors approaching the subject primarily as a "background" or "liberalizing" element in the professional curriculum, there was every reason for history of education to nearly disappear or to be left to the history department, which would unfortunately bring the same results.[8]

---

[6] Archibald W. Anderson cites this in *The Role of the History of Education in the Professional Preparation of Teachers, op. cit.,* Part Two, p. 43.

[7] Cremin, *op. cit.,* p. 16; in his discussion he details a number of studies that document these conditions.

[8] One of the near tragedies of the research emphases of American historians is the relative void of studies in American educational history. While politics and battles naturally beckon more attractively, the dearth of historical studies by historians of

The survey of teacher training institutions by Moehlman cited previously also revealed that among the schools studied, 87 percent still offered history of education in 1950 but only a quarter required the course.[9] Therefore, depending upon the amount of integration of historical content into other subjects and courses, it is now clear that a majority of educators responsible for shaping teacher education in the United States do not look upon the history of education as an essential foundation offering in the preparation of American teachers. Although we admit prejudice, we suggest that this is a tragedy for teachers must know the story of their own profession. Cicero in *De Oratore* warned, in effect, that to be ignorant of what happened before you were born is to live the life of a child forever. For what is man's life unless woven into the life of his own ancestors by the memory of past deeds? Santayana, much later, cautioned: A nation that does not know history is fated to repeat it. Both of these statements apply equally to the field of education and perhaps we shall return some day, if it is not too late, to the conception that a profession and that a "science" of education can only be built with the help of their history.

Heritage of American Education: Rationale and Orientation

Historians of education are themselves divided on the purposes and proper role of their discipline. We have indicated, however, that most of their published textual works tend to take a similar tack. Some include considerably larger amounts of general cultural history, others include greater or less attention to recent history or to specialized topics within the field. Each writer breaks down his presentation into somewhat varying blocks of subject matter and naturally features certain selections and emphases that reflect his personal concerns and interpretations.

This volume presents format concentrations that move radically from currently available works in the area. We have attempted to meet the growing call, as indicated by criticisms and changes in course offerings and enrollments, for a book that will serve both the needs of courses in the general

---

educational trends and events, educational institutions, and educators leaves a considerable gap in the overall attempt to record and explain America's story. Educators, unfortunately often not well prepared historically, have had to carry out the bulk of the research in this area. Even the Ford Foundation has been moved to offer grants to historians to carry out research in the history of education. See the pamphlet by Paul H. Buck and others, *The Role of Education in American History* (New York: The Fund for the Advancement of Education, 1957). Bernard Bailyn in his *Education in the Forming of American Society* (Chapel Hill: University of North Carolina Press, 1960) also details this condition.

[9] Cremin, *op. cit.*, p. 34.

history of education, wherein American education is increasingly treated, and in the separate class in the history of American education — for it is clear that very few students will ever take both, even where they are offered. The reader who desires more detail than he finds in the text on a topic, either in general educational history or in American educational history, is directed to the footnotes and bibliographical references found in each chapter. The reader will discover that although the focus is upon education in the United States, we have included more material on its backgrounds in the educational developments of other peoples and nations.

The clue to understanding the volume may be best gained by reflecting upon its title, *Heritage of American Education,* and by perusing the list of chapter titles. Such an examination will also reveal the manner in which the book should prove valuable in other courses that have incorporated the history of education or that require such background. It should prove a helpful reference for classes in an introduction to education, the social foundations of education, comparative education, and in educational philosophy. We also believe that the book will bring fresh insights for the general reader who is interested in the progress of education and its continuing problems. A review of the chapters and their emphases shows the topical approach whereby we organize and place the host of developments in the history of education which call for selection and which had to be shaped into manageable and reasonable sections. A number of the chapters do include a basically chronological approach; Chapter IV, for example, traces Catholic education down through the centuries and Chapter VIII covers the great seminal educators, starting with the Greeks and then moving forward in time. Other chapters feature approaches that reflect more directly the title of the volume; Chapter II, for example, does not involve a chronological recitation of developments but, rather, assays Greek and Roman education in terms of their major emphases and fundamental contributions to Western education.

The "heritage" approach to education gave us direction in the difficult task of delimiting and choosing from the vast amount of content that could have been included. It should be understood that this book is not a full history of American education, let alone a complete general history of education — for that matter, what single volume could be so presumptuously comprehensive? Our account is planned to bring a thorough understanding of the backgrounds of American education in attempting to help the reader comprehend education in the United States as it has come to exist today. The writers have aimed at explaining basic educational theories and key educators, curricular and instructional practices, and fundamental aspects of school organization, teacher education, special education, etc., that have characterized the European educational inheritance and that ultimately accrued in, or came to have important meaning for American education.

8

Bettmann Archive

MEDIEVAL SCRIBE AT WORK. WOODCUT, 1493.

The history of America is one with the history of the world. Its present status and its future are part of a global saga without chronological or geographical limits. This inheritance then is our keynote. The details we have included, the emphases chosen, the generalizations drawn, and the interpretations made are all provided to bring understanding of both the direct and the many more indirect forces in general history and in the history of education that came to undergird and characterize education in the United States. We recognize that these gifts have come from diverse sources and that they continue to provide valuable ideas. Therefore, we have reviewed the pertinent highlights of Hebrew and Islamic education in Chapters III and V, as well as the more recent and immediate impact of our neighbors in Canada and Latin America in Chapter X. As the text reviews subjects, for example, the influence of humanistic Renaissance education or the impact of Pestalozzi upon developments in American education, it also introduces supporting evidence and the necessary information about Renaissance education or Pestalozzi to help clarify the situation at that time in the nation, system, or school de-

9

scribed. The volume thereby underscores key elements in the general history of education that also enables us to better understand their impact on the American scene; in this manner the book is meant to serve a dual purpose.

It is possible to "cut the cake" of educational history in many ways, although, as has been shown, in most textbooks the chronological arrangement has been predominant. For our main chapter topics and major sub-emphases, we have chosen to organize in terms of underlying epochal or societal forces that have been prime in shaping the direction of education in the West. Therefore, for example, the treatment of the European impact by national categories in Chapter VII proves a logical and convenient means of controlling content while it parallels the all-important, nationalistic factors in education and the major contributions brought to American schools by peoples from different cultures. Our selection of the Protestant influences in Chapter VI was also based upon those forces which were fundamental in the rise of modern and extended education in Europe and germinal in the foundations of American education.

We also believe, that though men are affected profoundly by environmental and historical factors, the "right" man at the time of crux in the evolution of a society is a prime influence. In the history of education, for example, Luther could never have made his contributions or Rousseau have had his far reaching impact unless their eras were ripe and the following years conducive to the growth of their ideas that ultimately brought significant changes in education. We have not taken a strong biographical approach fetching and colorful as this can be, but we have certainly given key men, who after all do make history, their just due in all of the chapters. One entire chapter (VIII) is devoted to the major theorists of Western education.

The mainstream of American education has been shaped by many forces at home and abroad, and in Chapter IX we have isolated some of these diverse elements, from the educational practices relating to minority groups (as the American Negro) and selected specialized educational contributions from American agriculture, business, and labor, to the important contributory efforts of private business, correspondence schools, the military service academies, and others. This chapter further emphasizes the complexity of the story of American education, its informal as well as formal agencies, and the multiple wellsprings of our traditions and practices.

The volume attempts something unique in its last two chapters, wherein it moves closer to a comparative approach. Chapter XI includes a survey of the educational milestones in the evolution of American education, with particular emphasis upon what the author believes to be the truly indigenous characteristics that have developed as main features of education in the United States. Chapter XII draws the book to its conclusion by reviewing a number of these unique and indigenous features. It attempts to assess their impact upon education in other parts of the world and the means by which these American influences have been carried abroad.

A review of the history of education as presented in this volume should bring the reader to realize that we cannot and should not attempt to bifurcate the history of education completely from the general history of society and that neither can the development of American education, despite its own convolutions, be separated from the history of Western education to which it has been so intimately linked. Although at certain periods the educational exchange was to a considerable extent a one-way passage, recent developments in the world have made interchange, cultural cross-fertilization, ever more essential. It is with these ideas that the book closes, cognizant of a situation in which the history of education in the United States is tied ever more closely to the educational aspirations of our fellows throughout the world. And from this significant development we find further support and direction for having produced a volume of the nature of *Heritage of American Education*.

Purposes of the History of Education

It is now appropriate for us to identify and discuss in some detail the seven major purposes of this volume. Our outlook falls into the realm of the "New History," now no longer so "new," that views history as important, not as an objective, "scientific" study of man's past or as the most accurate interpretation of man's story possible, valuable as such attempts may be. We have rather presented and used frankly selected and segmented aspects of history to uncover and to explain events and trends that have particular meaning for us today. We desire to emphasize and to use those works and interpretations that provide insights into the evolution of American educational history and that should enable the reader to understand recent and current educational problems.

Our approach, then, promises to lead the concerned student to think about educational issues and to analyze related past developments discussed herein or experiences that are part of his own history. This should enable him to formulate appropriate courses of action in his educational endeavors. We believe this no mistaken relativism in approaching history nor is it a capitulation to sociological history or to some of the other charges that are brought against those of us who feel, that in addition to its explanatory, foundational function, we need to employ history to serve educational purpose by helping us meet the challenges of our day. In viewing educational history as an empirical attempt to understand the educational problems of mankind, we believe we have employed an approach that may help resurrect the history of education from the doldrums of its present campus existence.

Some have claimed that history is essentially one of the humanities, primarily concerned with the art of telling a good literary story. This is because the objectivity of history has been questioned as it is written by men who cannot escape their own times and who, in spite of themselves, allow their personal biases to slip into their interpretations. History is also suspect as presenting an inaccurate record of the past since so much of that record is incomplete or forever lost and can never be repeated and observed again. While it is true that history cannot be "scientific" as the natural sciences which can "control" their research, history nevertheless contributes to education through its study of human beings and their institutions. In fact, it offers means of furthering man's knowledge of himself which surpass other fields of learning.[10] In addition, history holds some fruitful approaches in common with the other social sciences. We now turn to our description of the aims of educational history.

PURPOSE No. 1 — *The history of education enables the student to perceive the relationships between a culture and its educational system and to better understand the development of that civilization and of its educational institutions.*

The most commonly cited contribution of history relates to this aim for history tells us how and why our world has come to be what it is and, as we shall see, this is also most important for tomorrow. We are thinking here of the broad aspects of the history of education composed not only of historical but of its philosophical, sociological, and economic aspects. As such, the history of education serves as a valuable link, aiding teachers in bridging the unfortunate gap that seems to exist between their general education in the university and their preparation in professional education.

Education cannot be understood without grasping its ties to the supporting society that it reflects. The study of the history of education emphasizing such relationships can do much to help students perceive the need for an educational program that is closely correlated to the needs of the society it serves. Also, that where this has not been maintained, the society faces the dire threat of extinction or the system of education may be rejected entirely and replaced.[11] This approach, for example, will help the secularly-oriented students in many courses to understand the intimate tie between religion and education that has existed throughout the history of the West. Knowledge of the substantial contributions of religious sects to the development of educa-

---

[10] For a further discussion of these points by the writer, see Richard E. Gross, "History: Stargazing into the Past," *Educational Leadership,* May, 1956, pp. 497-502.

[11] See the interesting examples, according to Toynbee, analyzed by Edward D. Myers, in *Education and the Perspective of History* (New York: Harper and Bros., 1960).

tion — something that may have been largely unrecognized by them until this time — will provide a basis for a much better grasp of many aspects of church-state relations.

One other example of the value of emphasizing such interrelationships can be cited. Students may look upon education and educators as relatively isolated and uninfluential elements in the culture. The study of the history of education in its societal context reveals the close relationship between evolving educational theories and social reform movements. Many radical leaders and reformers in history have either been educators or highly concerned over education. They perceived the uses of education in promoting social change, in instigating reform, and in spreading new ideas just as many of their opponents recognized the value of education in maintaining the *status quo*. Jefferson, Luther, Danton, Rousseau — just to mention four such varied reformers — are not usually thought of as educational leaders, but each with his colleagues and followers had significant educational influence. The student who is given this conception of the role of education may be led to a far more positive attitude toward education and its import in society.

Purpose No. 2 — *The history of education enables the student to become familiar with representative educational thinkers, ideas, practices, and schools.*

We have selected out of the past those elements which help to illuminate our present educational situation. This was previously explained as one of the main criteria for determining what aspects of history would be emphasized in this volume. However, all of these issues have their roots in the past. A major purpose of the book will have been attained if the readers emerge with knowledge of how the continuing educational issues in history took shape and why they have remained with us through the years. Equally important will be the clarification by the student as to where he stands on these issues and the bases for his beliefs. We learn about representative educationists and other aspects of the history of education, then, to help build a foundation for understanding our relationship to similar issues and events.

We have in mind issues as the following, which can give direction to the reader as he familiarizes himself with the essentials of educational history:

Education for an elite clientele vs. education for all
Education for private purposes vs. education for public purposes
Education for the individual vs. education for the society or state
Education for religious aims vs. education for secular purposes
Education for intellectual development vs. education for utility
Education for liberal ends vs. education for vocational goals
Education for knowledge as an end in itself vs. education as a means
Education for what to think vs. education for how to think
Education for discipline, control, and conformity vs. education for freedom

13

Education for adult purposes vs. education for children's needs

Education for training the mind vs. education for applying the mind

Education for former or other societies vs. education for a given people, currently indigenous.

The above continuing issues are not exclusive nor are the answers, as possibly intimated, always either/or. However, these reflect the problems that confront education and that can only be fully understood by a knowledge of their antecedents. We suggest that as the student extends his knowledge of the field, his enlarged educational horizons will enable him to come up with more satisfactory insights and hypotheses for meeting educational problems. Additionally, we would not discount the fact that to be a literate professional in his field, the student must have a minimum acquaintance with the elements of the educational past. Actually he cannot leave this mirror of his past, which is ever intertwined into his present, and it would be folly to attempt to do so. Educational history is both his collective memory and conscience and, therefore, must, to a great degree, influence his planning for the future since we usually tend to act in terms of our experience, and history is a summation of that past experience.

PURPOSE No. 3 — *The history of education enables the student to understand more fully present educational conditions, practices, and problems, and provides a basis for developing attitudes and attributes that mark the intelligent and effective educator.*

As we have indicated above, a knowledge of educational history will help make clear that the strength of any society rests in the social responsibility of the individual members and their competencies in carrying out their social roles. A prime purpose of the teaching of the history of education, as herein conceived, would be to help each student to make up his mind deliberately and intelligently in regard to the educational problems he must face.

Each current educational crisis has its own immediate history. A thorough understanding of the factors back of public resistance to a school bond issue, faculty "coolness" toward a proposed curriculum improvement program, or school board reluctance to establish a democratic policy on the handling of controversial issues can do much to help the administrator map a successful campaign to alter these conditions. In any new educational situation we inherit a history. How much more satisfactorily the homeroom mentor can handle a guidance problem, the new instructor step into the shoes of a very popular predecessor, or the supervisor aid a floundering teacher when they have rather full access to the record of the events leading up to these situations. Much of this we take for granted; but how many ousted administrators, sidetracked "core" programs, and deflated trials in community-centered education might have been saved if only the personnel involved had moved more intelligently

14

following a careful look at the immediate and long-term forerunners of these conditions? Often plain ignorance is the basis of fear and the resulting educational retrogression in instances as these. The provision of sufficient background information could have served to smooth the way for needed educational progress. Again, those involved in such problems might take more prudent steps if they provide themselves with a fuller understanding of the social context in the community that prevents them from carrying out educational leadership.[12] To be effective in education, the attendance officer, the school psychiatrist, the curriculum coordinator, the teacher — all who are involved in the professional field — must use history as indicated above. Unhappy circumstances have too often revealed that we cannot escape history, even should we desire to do so.

Students will benefit from an understanding of educational change, of how it has been brought about and why it has been so slow. In lecture, seminar, and assignment, it would be well for the instructor to emphasize factors that account for the snail-like pace frequently marking attempts at progress in education. Several reasons follow: It is difficult to train teachers to do new and different things, to use practices that they have never experienced; cherished values also persist and parents and those who support education want the children to have what they remember from their own schooling and what they hold to be good; and, people generally dislike experimentation that affects their children's education for they see schooling largely as a preservation and maintenance function rather than an extending experience. Students engaged in research in this area will also soon discover that the control of education usually lies with established, conservative, power sources — from those who dominate the school board to the local taxpayers' association; economic factors enter the picture as every new school service costs money and there is growing competition for the public dollar. The student should also understand the relative infancy of education as a true profession, as well as the newness of its allied sciences (psychology and sociology); this explains why most of the "sure" answers in education still lie ahead and why mistakes have been made that led to entrenchment rather than to further experimentation and change. The need here is to recognize that the school is a custodian of the virtues of our democratic past, is responsible for imparting the essentials for our present, yet still must be flexible enough to prove the hope for our future.

A knowledge of educational history builds a perspective that should enable participants in the educational venture to avoid mistakes of the past and such insights should aid in detecting "fads and frills" and in assessing the "new" educational practices cyclically beleaguering the classroom teacher. Reading

---

[12] Gross, *op. cit.*, p. 498.

about and becoming familiar with the lives of the great educators and the evolution of their schools should also help students to develop some of the important attitudes of an effective educator. A knowledge of the problems that have beset schools in the past and of the reasons for the slow progress in some instances may further the student's patience. Merely an immersion in the sweep of history can promote this needed quality when the student is led to the realization that he lives closer in time to St. Thomas Aquinas than St. Thomas did to St. Augustine, whom the student may view as "contemporaries" in the lengthy period of medieval education! Other attributes that can result from study in this field include openmindedness and the willingness to cooperate and to use critical thinking in attempting to resolve educational problems. Certainly the history of education is replete with examples of the mistakes and the unhappy errors that have resulted from men's unwillingness either to work together or to use reason in the resolution of educational controversies.

PURPOSE No. 4 — *The history of education enables the student to utilize the historical method as he employs the elements of educational history in answering former or current educational problems.*

Unless it includes a problem-type workbook or poses research queries, a typical text in the area of history of education can do little to promote facility with the historical method. This is unfortunate since one of the main reasons for studying history includes experience with and an understanding of the manner in which the historical researcher arrives at his portrayal of a given historical event. Unfortunately, with large enrollments and limited access to the students (Whoever heard of a lab period in history?), the history instructors in the general and even in many of the specialized history courses in the liberal arts school may do very little to build an understanding of how the historian arrives at facts and conclusions. Somewhere in his exposure to history the student needs experience in collecting, sifting, and criticizing data related to an historical issue, for through such endeavors the student is brought to comprehend that objective approach of the historian whereby he earns the right to be called a "social scientist."

A text, however, commonly leaves much unexplained or incomplete that beckons to be explored. These gaps provide numerous opportunities for the concerned reader to follow out his interest and examine more detailed and possibly primary sources, and eventually to hypothesize and draw his own conclusions about the educational question he has studied.[13] Facility with and

---

[13] In addition to general books in historiography that will guide the student in the steps of historical exploration, such as Allan Nevins, *The Gateway to History,* and Louis Gottschalk, *Understanding History,* an excellent guide to research in educational

understanding of the historical method, however, will be best promoted by the instructor who takes time to explain the approach and who assigns problems, papers, or debates wherein the students come to grips with data as they seek reasonable answers or interpretations toward a possible solution to the issue they have been led to examine.

Many libraries, unfortunately, will have but a limited collection of primary sources available on a number of the great issues in education. Collections of readings and source materials can be a help here and certainly secondary sources are appropriate for many experiences in historical research. The instructor who wishes his students to work as much as possible with original sources in such a situation can, however, suggest that the student ferret out records in his own local school or community or on some particularly recent aspect of one of these controversies that has had much public discussion and may be found in readily available journals and papers. It is suggested that the students regularly conduct seminar-type discussions, based upon their own researching of immediate educational questions that usually are related to broader, continuing, national, or international educational issues often reaching far back into history.

Such opportunities present themselves frequently. For example, there may be faculty discussion of increasing teacher education requirements for credentials to a five-year program as is now the rule in a few states. Students can be asked why we now have four years of college and not three or five? There may be a movement to close the local commercial or vocational high school. The teacher may query, "Why did we have such a school in the first place?" Or opposition may appear in an editorial in the local paper to extending the number of junior high schools. When and why were junior high schools added to this community system? Is it true that they grew primarily in response to enrollment problems and financial conditions, rather than because of any dedication on the part of educational leaders to the theory behind their creation? These seemingly insignificant questions actually present excellent opportunities for historical search and can lead to valuable studies not only of the local record but may take the students back a good distance into the past — in the case of the first query, all the way to the University of Paris about 1250 when, we are told, the faculty decided to add the equivalent of a fourth year's course to the university program!

Even a discussion of the physical properties of the history of education

---

history has been developed by William W. Brickman, *Guide to Research in Educational History* (New York: New York University Bookstore, 1949). Readers may also enjoy the more recent general discussion of problems in historical research found in Jacques Barzun and Henry F. Graff, *The Modern Researcher* (New York: Harcourt, 1957).

classroom can lead to historical research. When the instructor points to the ubiquitous blackboard (now, properly, chalkboard) and asks, "Where did it come from?" he has an historical question that can lead a student on a merry chase. The next day one student will volunteer that his source reveals that it all goes back to Pestalozzi's slates; but he will be contradicted by another who will explain that the Irish monks used slates in instruction before 1000 A.D. Now the class is faced with a relatively unimportant quest and in the end they may still find no sure answer. This in itself, however, is one important result of work with the historical method, even if students are attempting to track down some seemingly simple facts such as the correct birth date of W. T. Harris or the location of the first junior college in the United States.

Much current discussion revolves about integration in southern schools. An examination of the sources of segregated schools in the United States can provide some interesting and valuable investigation. The students may discover that such schools first existed outside of the South prior to the Civil War. Or that after the War in several of the southern states, then in Negro and carpetbaggers' hands, under the protection of Union troops, segregated schools were established by the state legislatures in the control of these groups and not by the reactionary forces who later came into power after the election bargain of 1876. Properly, this historical investigation will have led to some answers but to still more questions!

Students and instructors are urged not to neglect the historical method in conjunction with their course and the use of this book. As can be seen, the method is motivating and rewarding; it is one of the best ways to make history serve a purpose; it is history's major contribution to the acquiring of research competencies which mark the scholar; and it is history's way of enabling men to find the truth as best it can be ascertained. Employed adequately and creatively, the method of history removes the discipline from such charges as subjectiveness and antiquarianism, toward a meaningful, objective explanation of the subject of inquiry. It not only "eliminates the nonsense of our wigwams" as Emerson enunciated, but also teaches us "the limits of the possible."[14]

PURPOSE No. 5 — *The history of education enables the student to sense the import and dignity of his profession and stimulates him in his own efforts to carry on and complete the work of past master teachers as he contributes to the stream of educational progress.*

---

[14] See Alan Simpson, "History in Education," *School Review,* Autumn, 1957, pp. 279-286, for an illuminating discussion of how historians can successfully overcome the handicaps to their research.

There is considerable virtue in the exploration of the lives of the great educators who have set the tone for social regeneration through educational progress. Reviewing the life and work of a great teaching personality who loved children and who was vitally interested in education, such as Quintilian, DaFeltre, Pestalozzi, Froebel, Seguin, or Montessori, can do much to help the harrassed schoolman to take heart. Such readings can renew his purpose and pride in carrying on one of mankind's noblest endeavors and they may further inspire him to offer his best efforts to the continuing movement for educational betterment.

Reading and research into the lives of the great educators with certain specific questions in mind can present further experience with the historical method posed previously as being so important. For example, the teacher may ask, "What were the influences that led Horace Mann to be the sort of person and the dedicated and successful educational statesman that he was?" The instructor may point out that if his students could isolate these factors and if it would be possible to reproduce them in the lives of the potential young educators in his class, think of the educational progress that this group might attain! Fortunately most libraries will have a considerable amount of material on Mann from articles in bound volumes in the professional journals and biographies to specialized accounts of some of his specific contributions and his own famous reports as Secretary of the Massachusetts Board of Education. As soon as the students begin to explore these works, they find that they have no simple job. There is no single cause in history and depending upon how they read the record, which pieces of literature are most adequate, correct, or authentic, and upon how much of his story is available, they may well emerge with a many-headed monster. There was the influence of Rebecca Mann, his mother; there is the fact that his father died early in the boy's life; there was the influence of Dr. Emmons, the local Calvinist preacher; and the drowning of his brother Stephen; there was Benjamin Franklin whose library had been donated to Mann's hometown and who thus provided some of the ill-schooled boy's early reading; there was Samuel Barrett, who coaxed Mann to enter Brown; there was Charlotte Messer, his first wife; there was his law school training; and so we can go on and on. At any rate, in following the formative years of a leader like Mann in such a manner, the student is led to better recognize the unbelievably complex story with which he is involved. At the same time, he is led to understand the forces that move men and that ultimately can shape the education of a nation.

We have been particularly careful to try and account for the multiple factors behind many of the developments discussed in this volume, yet realizing the impossibility of assembling the mass of data that is available or that might properly be cited to explain a statement about a given individual. A valuable experience for the students as they move through the course and read about the various personalities that have made educational history will be to watch for opportunities to identify the initiation of an especially important idea or movement in education. At several places in our volume the name of Juan Luis Vives (1492-1540) appears. Here is a good example of a "lost" man in educational history who is seldom credited with many of the key ideas he seems to have initiated — although we would be among the first to admit that a number of his views had ancient forerunners and that we also recognize the principle of independent or simultaneous creation and invention. Nevertheless, the works of certain educators who were Vives' contemporaries or who lived afterwards often reflect his statements so closely that one could be tempted to draw charges of plagiarism.

But even without inveighing such probably unprovable charges and missing the fun of the historical detective work involved, one can still ask, "Why have Vives' contributions been so generally overlooked?" The chart in this chapter includes merely a sample of several of the ideas of seven other educational writers that parallel closely the work of Vives who antedated them. To this list of names we could easily add a contemporary such as Erasmus or Rousseau, Dewey, and a number of other seminal contributors in like columns. The aim here is to reveal the near impossibility of separating or isolating the interlocking web of ideas that have existed in education for centuries and the dangers of historical certainty in stipulating many of the "firsts" and "facts" in the history of education.

The problems evidenced in tracing the relationships of the ideas presented in the chart on Vives and the other educators should not deter the student from attempting historical study or lead him too far down the road of skepticism about the assertions in this volume or in the works of many of the worthy scholars to whom he will refer during the progress of his course. Undoubtedly he will be given some misinformation and will be led to some improper conclusions about certain of the men and events to whom he is introduced. At this point we might inject a word of caution about depending too heavily upon once contemporary and limited, narrow, original sources that are devoted to a given man and his works.

Let us take an example from the medieval field. A well-trained, present-day medievalist with the full and rich record available to him may well produce in a secondary source a much more complete and effective explanation and interpretation of most aspects of feudal education than that which has come down to us from any individual participants in educational endeavors during that era. St. Bernard might give us a highly colorful and pointed, personal view of Abelard but a modern scholar may give us a more well-rounded and unbiased picture of that great teacher. While St. Bede or Alcuin has told us something of isolated aspects of education in their time, that is all, to a great degree, that they could have left us. And they very

20

Ideas of Great Educators Found in the Writings of Vives

Bacon	Comenius	Locke	Mulcaster	Pestalozzi	Herbart	Froebel
Use of the inductive approach to learning.	Use of the object lesson in teaching.	Initial learning to be approached through the senses.	Use of the vernacular in education.	Virtue of the direct study of nature.	Capitalizing upon the interests of pupils.	Education as a drawing-out process.
Reduction of grammar and other less meaningful ancient studies.	Combination of a practical and a spiritual education.	Memory and habit formation should precede reasoning in early stages of training.	Opposition to tutors.	Gradation of materials suited to pupil readiness.	Rewarding effort.	Development through play and self-activity.
Attacked scholastic wrangling as an outmoded teaching method.	The education of girls.	The importance of proper diet in producing a sound mind and body.	The establishment of public schools.	Love and warmth of the family in school relationships.	Relating experience to apperception and generalization.	Understanding of pupil differences.
	A broadened curriculum.		Parent-teacher conferences.		Education as character-building.	Intervals of relaxation in school.

likely would not have understood or used the term "feudal" as we employ it. The modern medieval expert is saturated with a grasp upon 1,000 years of history about which no man who lived from 500 to 1500 A.D. could have known more than a small portion. The ensuing years and the historical investigation therein have brought increasing recognition of many gaps in our knowledge of the Middle Ages and their education; but meanwhile the storehouse of medieval knowledge and interpretation has grown and we have corrected some erroneous earlier views. Therefore, it is very likely that with still improved instruments of investigation and restoration, with the uncovering of presently unknown materials, and with the insights of bright minds yet to come, the synthesis achieved by some future historian in 2022 A.D. will ultimately prove to be the most complete and satisfactory explanation of the medieval panorama, its educational facilities and the scholars who moved upon the scene, that has ever been achieved.

An important fact in all of this is that in sharing the life stories of the great educators and in gaining empathy with their dedicated efforts, the student builds a commitment to his profession. The learnings involved also help the student set the proper direction to his own future educational efforts and ensure thereby the progress of the profession.

PURPOSE No. 6. — *The history of education enables the student to comprehend the background, development, and the interrelationships of his specialized area within the field of education.*

The reader can select most any master's thesis, doctoral dissertation, or, for that matter, any book from the shelf of the education library and he will be apt to find one common feature in each of these works. Although the studies may vary from an analysis of the reading competencies of ninth-grade children taught by a particular method to the assessment of a new type of attitude test, and though the book may be devoted to any topic from democratic school administration to the factors making for nostalgia in foreign students, all will likely contain a chapter or portions devoted to the history of that particular problem or phase of education. As we have intimated before, a specialist working on any project must be familiar with the particular history of his own specialty, of the antecedents of the topic with which he is concerned and the manner in which these are related.

Of course, every specialist in education has the duty to be a generalist and it has been claimed that it is these generalists who have made some of the greatest contributions to the history of education.[15] Certainly, for orientation and backgrounds to all divisions within the field of education, its history pro-

---

[15] See Leighton H. Johnson, "Education Needs Historical Studies," *Phi Delta Kappan,* January, 1955, p. 158, for an exposition of this point.

vides the necessary synoptic overview of relationships between sub-areas which have come to characterize modern educational endeavors. The general knowledge of the history of education provides an invaluable background for reading most of the professional literature in the discipline. We are told today, and rightly so, that a knowledge of statistics is essential for understanding many of the current articles found in the professional journals. What is necessary is that we return to a position that recognizes the similar contribution of historical content, for Demosthenes was right when he explained that, "the time for extracting a lesson from history is ever at hand for those who are wise." It seems to us that much current experimentation and exploration in education could be better planned, more effectively implemented, or even, possibly, eliminated if the researchers had a more adequate knowledge of the history of education and particularly of the roots of their own particular venture!

PURPOSE No. 7 — *The history of education enables the student to understand the implications of the existence of American education — past, present, and future — as part of a worldwide venture and fellowship.*

Fortunately, probably no area of human interrelationships is less limited by boundaries than cultural exchange. This is a Western tradition that goes back to ancient times when a king was accustomed to welcome a seer from a distant land. In early medieval times all scholars in the West used the same language as they moved freely from one monastery or cathedral school to another and the door of welcome was usually open in castle, manor, and rectory to men who were, first of all, brother scholars and Christians and, to a much lesser degree, Burgundians or Castilians. Thus we have established traditions of universal exchange in matters of scholarship that even today transcend Iron Curtains and isolated research laboratories with their electric-eye watchmen.

Of course, the tradition has had a struggle. There have always been those who feared to share or who selfishly believed they must or could keep their ideas and developments to themselves. The rise of nation-states, the growth of economic rivalry, the divisive effects of the advent of Mohammedanism and particularly warring Christian sects, and even bitter personal feuds, among other factors, all contributed to the curtailment of a process already quite inefficient because of limitations in the means of communication and transportation.

This relative isolation of men and their ideas, the very deterioration and collapse of certain cultures and countries with the loss of their records and achievements, plus the obscurantism of many conservative forces, however, still did not prevent the gradual sharing of knowledge, practices, beliefs, art, technology, and the other factors that gregarious man has interchanged.

23

With the commercial and industrial revolutions and their cheap paper, multiple type, navigation instruments, improved transportation facilities, and machines, international contacts were multiplied and many cultures further enriched. Even wars and pestilence in their tragic ways have contributed to the contacts between peoples, from the epochal shock that the Crusades brought to Europe to the emigration by choice and force of scientists and astronauts in the pre and post World War II scene.

We cannot further detail the evolution of cultural exchange; however, cross-cultural interchange is ever more necessary, since the modern world rests increasingly upon a material base of specialism and interdependence. However, from the missionaries and explorers who first tracked her virgin territories to the entertainers and professional journals she now exchanges with the Soviet Union, the history of America has been one with the history of the world.

This fact, unfortunately, had been lost to the minds of many Americans until very recent times. A number of elements in our history from the epic struggle to extend the national frontier to certain of our characteristics such as self-assuredness, righteousness, and exceptionalism have often mitigated against an easy infusion of other ideas. Beck has identified this tendency on the part of Americans as lack of a "sense of historical involvement."[16] For public consumption Americans have often so expressed themselves and frequently foreign ideas were rejected just because they were foreign. But in spite of this, America has been an intimate part of the world.

From our own national birth in one of the first world wars and the impact of Yankee clippers and the China trade to the foundation of UNESCO and the distant launching of weather-predicting satellites, America's story has been an inextricable part of the history of the world. This volume documents in chapter after chapter the educational accumulation that has resulted through the years from what the first European immigrants brought with them to the new world to the international impact of American specialists and technicians who now advise and labor in nearly one hundred different nations.

It seems almost redundant to belabor that America's history and the evolution of its educational institutions need to be taught and explained in terms of their world setting; but in spite of video tape TV productions and mounting daily jet contacts, a look at schoolrooms and schoolbooks in our country reveals a striking need for instruction better oriented to an international frontier.[17] This, however, is not a weakness of education in the United

---

[16] Robert N. Beck, "America and the Hand of History," *Social Education*, May, 1960, pp. 197-199, 206.

[17] Richard E. Gross and Leslie D. Zeleny, *Educating Citizens for Democracy* (New York: Oxford University Press, 1958), pp. 182-184. Chapters 12 and 21 explain this need, particularly in the area of social studies instruction in the secondary schools.

States alone; in fact, if one observes curricula and texts of many other nations, he will see even greater reason for UNESCO's continuing concern for improving international understanding. Many of these programs in other countries are more insular, nationalistic, biased, and far more out of date than their counterparts in America.

Teachers who will use this text cannot help but be oriented towards the global scope of America's heritage, our present status, and our future. Instructors may well support this aim by assigning papers or reports on specific elements of this theme. Students can be asked to look about them in the community or on campus and identify all the ties between past and present and between other cultures and our own that are revealed by so many things from the facades of the buildings to the alphabet used in this book. Krey has suggested how Erasmus would be quite at home in a modern American university,[18] and Salmon wrote two revealing essays — "History in a Back Yard" and "Main Street" — in which she cites hundreds of examples from customs to dress styles that the competent observer can easily note which indicate the unity and the continuity between America and other peoples and nations.[19] Ralph Linton's famous description, in his *The Study of Man*, of the solid "100 percent American" who is almost entirely a product of other cultures is a most striking exposition of a point that even the dean of our frontier historians recognized; for Frederick Jackson Turner also rightly explained that "no country can be understood without taking account of all the past; it is also true that we cannot select a stretch of land and say we will limit our study to this land; for local history can only be understood in the light of the history of the world."[20]

A FINAL PURPOSE. With the above admonition we end our statement of purposes. Together, however, they should make explicit a final overriding role of the history of education that makes it indispensable to any adequate program of professional training or of educational planning. *The history of education is basic in the determination of educational ends.* Too often we tend to forget that schools are maintained by society to promote the ideals that have evolved from the social experience and that these ends are understood because we have a history and comprehend its meaning. History of education serves, then, in providing the insights that enable us to formulate essential educational goals. It also provides clues as to the most appropriate

---

[18] August C. Krey, "What Is American History?" an essay in *History and the Social Web* (Minneapolis: University of Minnesota Press, 1955).

[19] In Lucy M. Salmon, *Historical Material* (New York: Oxford University Press, 1933).

[20] From "The Significance of History" in *The Early Writings of Frederick Jackson Turner* (Madison: University of Wisconsin Press, 1938), p. 57.

accompanying means for attaining society's fundamental, educational aims. The chapters that follow, in addition to their previously stated purposes, also attempt to highlight developments that illustrate the emergence of the ends and the means in our educational heritage.

We have identified the vital roles of the history of education and have tried to motivate the student to read on. With an understanding of the import of the area and a desire to build his own knowledge, the student should now be prepared to learn so that he can effectively employ educational history in his own professional growth and toward the further progression of American education.

Bibliography

Bailyn, Bernard, *Education in the Forming of American Society*. Chapel Hill: University of North Carolina Press, 1960.

Boyd, William, *The History of Western Education*. London: Adam and Charles Black, 1954.

Brubacher, John S., *A History of the Problems of Education*. New York: McGraw-Hill, 1947.

Butts, R. Freeman, *A Cultural History of Western Education*. Second Edition, New York: McGraw-Hill, 1955.

Butts, R. Freeman and Lawrence A. Cremin, *A History of Education in American Culture*. New York: Henry Holt and Company, 1953.

Cole, Luella, *A History of Education: Socrates to Montessori*. New York: Rinehart and Company, 1950.

Committee on Historical Foundations of the National Society of College Teachers of Education, *The Role of the History of Education in the Professional Preparation of Teachers*. Ann Arbor: The Society, 1957.

Cubberley, Ellwood P., *The History of Education*. Boston: Houghton Mifflin, 1920.

Cubberley, Ellwood P., *Public Education in the United States*. Boston: Houghton Mifflin, 1934.

Cubberley, Ellwood P., *Readings in the History of Education*. Boston: Houghton Mifflin, 1920.

Curtis, S. J. and M. E. A. Boultwood, *A Short History of Educational Ideas*. London: University Tutorial Press, 1954.

Eby, Frederick, *The Development of Modern Education,* Second Edition. New York: Prentice-Hall, 1934.

Edwards, Newton and Herman G. Richey, *The School in the American Social Order*. Boston: Houghton Mifflin, 1947.

Good, H. G., *A History of American Education*. New York: The Macmillan Company, 1956.

Good, H. G., *A History of Western Education,* Second Edition. New York: The Macmillan Company, 1960.

Gustavson, Carl, *Preface to History.* New York: McGraw-Hill, 1954.

Knight, Edgar W., *Twenty Centuries of Education.* Boston: Ginn and Company, 1940.

Knight, Edgar W., *Education in the United States.* Boston: Ginn and Company, 1941.

Knight, Edgar W. and Clifton Hall, *Readings in American Educational History.* New York: Appleton-Century-Crofts, 1951.

Mayer, Frederick, *A History of Educational Thought.* Columbus, Ohio: Charles E. Merrill Books, 1960.

Meyer, Adolphe E., *An Educational History of the American People.* New York: McGraw-Hill, 1957.

Mulhern, James, *A History of Education.* Second Edition. New York: Ronald Press, 1959.

Muller, Herbert J., *The Uses of the Past.* New York: Oxford University Press, 1952.

Myers, Edward D., *Education in the Perspective of History.* New York: Harper and Bros., 1960.

Noble, Stuart G., *A History of American Education.* New York: Holt, Rinehart & Winston, 1954.

Peterson, A. D. C., *A Hundred Years of Education.* London: Duckworth and Company, 1952.

Sands, Lester B. and Richard E. Gross, *History of Education Chart,* Third Edition. Stanford, California: Stanford University Press, 1957.

Thut, I. N., *The Story of Education.* New York: McGraw-Hill, 1957.

Ulich, Robert, *History of Educational Thought.* New York: American Book Company, 1950.

Ulich, Robert, *The Education of Nations.* Cambridge: Harvard University Press, 1961.

Wilds, Elmer H. and Kenneth V. Lottich, *The Foundations of Modern Education,* Third Edition. New York: Holt, Rinehart and Winston, 1961.

****

CHAPTER II

OUR DEBT TO THE ANCIENTS
OF THE WESTERN WORLD

The Greek Heritage

Ancient Attica and the Holy Land are tiny parcels unrivaled in their gifts to Western traditions. The Greeks are credited with initiating a number of fundamental ideas that proved key contributions in the evolution of Western education. These beliefs or practices, however, were over 1,000 years in reaching the schools of North America and accrued indirectly. Nevertheless, as the reader considers the educational conditions and issues of his own day, in light of this chapter, he should easily recognize the vitality and the carry-over of ancient views. Reflection upon this material reveals the extent to which we remain indebted to the Greco-Roman creators for much that continues to characterize education in the Americas, as well as in considerable portions of the rest of the world.

There are significant hindrances to the accurate and exact discussion of Greek educational contributions. In many cases scholars must interpret from primary sources as limited as fragments of pottery or shattered friezes. Our earliest extant secondary sources, perhaps a Roman or a medieval manuscript, are often incomplete and liable to errors of copying, conjecture, mythohistory, translation, and expurgation.[1] Except for the works of Plato, this is

---

[1] Some of the Greek educational writings, for example, with hundreds of years and copies in between, were translated by Nestorian Christians into Syriac, then into Hebrew, then into Arabic, and finally, in the 13th century, into Latin, wherein they began to appear in Western educational treatises.

a common problem with the writings of the great ancients. Thus all interpretations and statements of "fact" are in part open to charges of misinterpretation, oversight, error, and contemporaneousness. The viewpoints presented in this chapter reflect generally accepted scholarship, as well as the writer's own opinions and interpretations. It is hoped that interested and critical readers will be led to intensive searches into the more complete volumes cited in the footnotes and bibliography and, where possible, to other basic sources and, ideally, to their own conclusions.

Another problem in identifying "Greek" contributions is the temptation to over-generalize. What do we mean when we use the word "Hellenic"? Do we speak of the simple education of the Homeric period or the relatively mature and complex approaches of the Hellenistic age, so many generations apart? Do we refer to the educational structure of Athens or to the Spartan totalitarian prototype? Are we reflecting the view of one period of time or of one place, or are we citing the position of but one scholar or a given school of thought? When we speak of "Greek" or "Hellenic" education, in many instances it would be more correct to refer to Athenian education during a specific era. With these cautions in mind, we move into our discussion of the Greek heritage.

This was a particularly creative epoch in the history of mankind and it is fortunate that we have the limited records that are available from the 500 years stretching between 650 B.C. and the rise of the Greek city-states to 150 B.C. when Roman forces overran the Peloponnesus. Greek scholars had examined and discoursed upon a wide spectrum of questions, and a variety of creative opinions and theories arose. Considering great limitations as the lack of previous "giants to build upon," the superstitious traditions of obscurantism and mythology, the lack of instruments for study and media for precise observation — we are confronted with an amazing phase of civilization.

Here among a number of near contemporaries were those philosophers most frequently cited — Socrates, Plato, and Aristotle. But we cannot be certain as to just how representative or, perhaps more accurately, unrepresentative they were. There is little question that they exerted a rather minimal influence upon the limited education of most Greeks in their own day. And even in Athens, reflecting a mutual disillusionment with the tragic developments of Hellas and particularly in their own city state, all three urged aspects of education that were not then commonly practiced. But both long before and coeval with this famous trio, we find an intriguing group of scholars who are sometimes not given their just due as seminal thinkers in the development of Western culture.

Among these thinkers we find Thales, sometimes called the "first philosopher" and the father of geometry, who believed that all life arose from water, the earth's basic element, and who first cautioned "know thyself." There was Anaximander who believed that living beings arose from a primitive substance by gradual stages and that man, for example, was once a fish! Also, there was Pythagoras who taught that an understanding of the universe would be tied to unravelling the mystery of numbers. He developed a school of mathematical philosophy and, among other striking observations, claimed that the earth moved and that it was round. Democritus was another of these great theorists and he envisioned a mechanistic universe composed of atoms of eternal matter. Zeno taught that man could discover reason in nature and his followers became known as Stoics, many of them believing in a single, all-powerful God and serving as forerunners of Christianity. Epicuris philosophized on the virtue of pleasant and intellectual pursuits and saw the goal of life in avoiding pain and unhappiness. Xonophone, a student and critic of Socrates, proved a powerful reactionary, who favored the Spartan way and yet has also been credited with initiating ideas, such as home economics education for women. There was Antisthenes who believed that the individual needed to achieve full independence from the outside world to gain the basic good, virtue. He became the father of the cynics. And there was Isocrates who in some ways was the most modern and democratic of these Greek scholars; he believed in education toward service for the state and sought a united Greece. Isocrates came to recognize the futility of war and reached the conclusion that democracies are also threatened from within when they became rich and powerful. Isocrates was also a doer. He opened one of the first rhetorical (secondary) schools in Greece (390 B.C.) and ultimately drew students from the entire Mediterranean world. His school rivaled Plato's Academy, and, although Plato looked down upon him because he accepted tuition fees, certain key features of later humanistic and even modern education are undoubtedly inherited from Isocrates. The belief in putting knowledge to work, in providing opportunities to practice and to test generalizations and principles are all evident in his treatise *On the Antidosis*. He urged a practical education so that a man would give worthy civic service. In this he anticipated the desires of the realistic humanists of the Renaissance and was the opposite of the Platonists who approached knowledge from a contemplative standpoint of attaining the pure absolute. Isocrates also held that man can never know all and that it is wiser to attempt to attain a judicious outlook, explaining that wisdom is best served by "having probable opinions about useful things rather than to attempt to attain exact knowledge of useless things."

A study in depth of Greek educators and Greek culture brings a knowledge of variations and changes that makes statements of any unique characteristics of Hellenic education most dangerous. It poses an equally difficult problem to list distinct contributions of these great Greeks — all read, heard, and discussed one another's numerous multi-faceted and all-embracing views. Also, since we assess Greek education from a vastly different era, we must recognize the constrictions upon our views. Modern technological societies seem to have relatively little in common with practices that served the slave-based economy or the direct democracy of some 40,000 freemen in ancient Athens. Our new mass, international culture is ever farther removed from what was traditionally "culture" among educated Western men. Our present knowledge of human development, the psychology of learning, and our command of instructional media and improved methods would certainly seem to involve the evolution of new theories and effective approaches completely beyond the Greek teacher. Nevertheless, in Greek educational spirit, theory, and practice, there are antecedents that will enable us to better understand our own schools and aspects of their education that remain valuable and applicable. It is left to the reader to decide whether this is true because of Greek wisdom or because man, his needs, and his institutions change so slowly.

Import of Educated Citizens Who Act Intelligently and Responsibly

From the standpoint of education in a democracy the great Hellenic contribution was undoubtedly the idea exemplified in Athens of the import of well-educated citizens. While in Athens it was indeed a highly restricted group and though many of the elements of education were different from those that frequently are held essential today, this concept was fundamental. Athens had no public education as we conceive of it (actually it was Sparta that had a completely subsidized and staffed system of public boarding school education even providing for the education of girls) and few laws related to education until after the advent of the Peloponnesian wars.[2]

The importance of education for citizenship was commonly accepted by the citizen class long before the golden age of Pericles (450 B.C.). This personal learning by observation and practice as provided by responsible parents undoubtedly helped raise a number of generations of able young freemen who were competent in helping extend the powers of the growing citizenship class and who promoted the liberating conditions that enabled Athens to become queen of the Mediterranean world. The germinal idea here was that the State should serve freemen; that men were, to a considerable extent, masters of their own fate; that laws and conditions of living were not immutable;

---

[2] Parents were required to provide instruction in swimming to all young males of the citizenship class and "veterans benefits" were provided for the families of deceased warriors. With the Spartan threat the State became concerned with providing more than free gymnasium facilities for the young men and two years of military instruction and service were required.

and that kings or high priests were expendable and not inherently the possessors of all knowledge or power.

Actual direct State influence in education below the age of 18 probably did not come much before the time of Solon (638?-559 B.C.) when public gymnasia were built where boys from the ages of 15 to 18 carried on a thorough program of physical education under publicly-employed supervisors. This program tended to neglect the intellectual, artistic, and esthetic instruction that they had received previously from their private mentors.

It is unlikely that any compulsory courses in Athenian government or Hellenic history were ever contemplated. The experience the young men gained from contacting the older citizens in the gymnasia and the agora, from attending council or court sessions, and from participating in public ceremonies was recognized as providing appropriate and sufficient political training. At the age of eighteen the worthy young men passed into a final two-year period of "civic" education and in an impressive public orientation ceremony they became cadets and took the famous Ephebic Oath. Now citizens, they were still, however, on trial and spent two years serving in the garrisons on the frontier and carrying out police and military duties. Only with this period completed was the youth looked upon as an Athenian man and accepted into his full role of citizen. The state had completed its formal education. Learning by "doing," however, now continued as the young adult carried on an active role in the life of the city state. The community was a real educational force in the Greek design. Today we have considerably increased public support and regulations affecting the great bulk of the people; but the integration of the life of the school and the life of the community remains a greater challenge than in ancient Greece.[3]

Universal education was but a dream of several philosophers; Greek education has been properly characterized as the "well rounding of the well heeled." However, modern free states might profitably review the Athenian approach and attempt to detemine those emphases and practices applicable in our times that might help build individual responsibility for the welfare and progress of the civic community.[4]

Ultimately, Athenian youth changed as their environment and their state changed. We know the tragic results. Particularly unfortunate was the

---

[3] This problem is discussed in: Richard E. Gross and Leslie D. Zeleny, *Educating Citizens for Democracy* (New York: Oxford University Press, 1958): see Part I, particularly Chapters I, II, and IV.

[4] Several examples of volumes directed at this problem in recent years include *Educating for American Citizenship*, 32nd Yearbook, American Association of School Administrators (Washington, D.C.: N.E.A., 1954) and *Citizenship in a Free Society*, 30th Yearbook of the National Council for the Social Studies (Washington, D.C.: N.E.A., 1960).

disappearance of self-confidence on the part of leaders and youth. When the will to progress is lost, as faith in one's self and society declines, a civilization, according to Spengler, enters the "winter-time" of its history.[5] At such a time, education as well as other key institutions become formalized, artificial, and sterile and there is little likelihood of a coming "spring." Just as the lack of adequate civic education was a fundamental factor in the more cataclysmic decline and fall of the Roman Empire, so were educational shortcomings and the failure to properly balance essential aspects of educational maintenance and change, contributory to the demise of "the glory that was Greece."[6]

The Greeks made a number of other basic philosophical, psychological, and educational contributions that in a chapter of this size it is impossible to cover in depth. Entire detailed books, for example, are available on Greek philosophy. Readers concerned with tracing such developments are referred to the appropriate works in the chapter bibliography. In Chapter VIII, certain of the key ideas in the evolution of Western education that come from Plato and Aristotle are further described. In the next part of this chapter we shall underscore examples of Attic insight and belief that have been entwined in the roots of educational theory and practice ever since Hellenic times.

Philosophical Creativity and the Roots of Psychology and Education

Basic views of the universe, as reflected in the dualism that came to mark Western thinking and in the absolutes or universals that have been the essence and standard for generations of idealistic and realistic thought, are prime contributions of the Greeks. The existence of a real and a temporal, a model and a corporal counterpart, mind and matter or material and immaterial, perfect and imperfect, heaven and earth, body and soul, good and bad — these have conditioned so many aspects of education in subsequent ages that they defy cataloguing.

The complex Christian view of the cosmos underlying so much of our culture arose in a Hellenistic world and was particularly influenced by Platonic conceptions. Randall claims that once Christianity came into prominence, Greek individuals and councils were largely responsible for building its early doctrines.[7] The continuing close tie between religions and education

---

[5] See Oswald Spengler, *The Decline of the West* (New York: Alfred A. Knopf, 1939).

[6] General George C. Marshall, for example, claimed that the "lesson" of the Greek civil wars was an aspect of history that held momentous meaning for Americans and the world in our own day. See his statement "Our Most Serious Military Problem" in *Harper's* magazine, November, 1950, p. 27.

[7] John H. Randall, Jr., *The Making of the Modern Mind* (Boston: Houghton-Mifflin Company, 1940), p. 45; he cites Clement, Origen, Athanasius as such scholars of great influence who served at the famous university at Alexandria.

is documented throughout this volume. Original Greek contributions and later modifications by Hellenistic and Roman scholars left imprints upon Christian philosophy and theology that held material significance in the development of Western education. Many of these aspects are evidenced in later chapters.

The magnificent theoretical creativity of the Greek thinkers was not generally matched in their day by successful application. However, when modern educators operate a school or instruct in terms of the principle of intellectualism (that there is real value in a command of knowledge in itself and that knowledge means power), they act in the Greek tradition. The Greek faith in intelligence is one of our greatest inheritances.

Closely related to the Greek recognition of the need to produce citizens who would function intelligently was the belief that knowledge also leads to goodness. Much of the work of Socrates should be interpreted as an attempt to build a moral philosophy on the basis that right conduct stems from the apprehension of truth. Undoubtedly knowledge can and should lead to proper action; but this transition is not automatic nor has the relationship of intelligence and goodness been proven in the unhappy history of social conflict. This long enduring position also lies back of much of the catechistic fact-cramming and indoctrination of dogmas that has bored and warped hundreds of thousands of captive learners and that in many instances has borne most limited and distorted results. Numerous educators still operate in terms of the principle that insight leads to goodness and that this pursuit also leads to happiness. Modern psychology questions this relationship. The problem is that this is a much more complex process than commonly visioned, affected by varying definitions and values.

The Hellenic scholars also commonly accepted training the mind as an essential function. Drill, repetition, and habit formation were conceived as essentials of education in developing this storehouse of knowledge. These were also deemed important in sharpening the ability of the intellect to function effectively. The idea that form rather than the content of academic material disciplines the mind; that the mind can be trained; and that a primary purpose of formal education is the development of mental power, has held sway ever since the ancient Greeks.[8]

In Hellas, the first to effectively differentiate between the varied fields within Greek philosophy was Aristotle. He established, in his urge to classify, the areas of metaphysics, logic, ethics, politics, and psychology as discrete entities. Naturally, the psychological and learning principles held by a given school or for a given era cannot be understood apart from the overriding

---

[8] Walter B. Kolesnik, *Mental Discipline in Modern Education* (Madison: University of Wisconsin Press, 1958). See Chapters I and II.

philosophical orientations. Just as Greeks held different opinions as to the makeup of the universe, they held somewhat varying psychologies. The word "psychology" itself stems from the Greek word for soul. While Platonic dualism dominated, Democritus, for example, looked upon all physical and natural objects as being only material and taught that even the soul, composed of tiny material atoms, would be dispersed at death. The Sophists claimed human experience to be largely meaningless and many were skeptical of man's

Bettmann Archive

ARISTOTLE AND HIS PUPIL ALEXANDER.

coming to understand the learning process. Murphy implies that a number of Greek thinkers had a tendency toward monism in their search for a prime substance that could help explain the derivation of all else. He indicates that although Aristotle remained true to Platonic universals, which represented the ultimate and the eternally real, his interest in the functions of living organisms and his recognition of the intimate ties between body and soul or mental and physical processes led eventually to the concept that organism and environment are not independent. Rather, these are two aspects of a process

36

defined in terms of interactions and responses.[9] He also credits Aristotle's close study of the senses, of emotions, and of reasoning as providing a basis for the association doctrine of learning. This moved beyond the three main ways that Plato held knowledge to be gained: (1) via reminiscence or recall of the good implanted at birth; (2) through recollection brought about by skilled dialectic questioning; and (3) by contemplation.

The Greek educational method was centered largely in individual instruction. There was undoubtedly some small group work at all levels but most educational experiences involved master and one or several pupils. Where classes did exist, instruction remained essentially individualized and this was often handled by a specialized teacher.

In the lower age bracket a boy spent only part of a day with his grammarian, then possibly moving to the palaistra for physical education where the paidotribes served as masters. Later he would report with his ever-present slave (the pedagog) to the music school for vocal and instrumental (oboe and lyre) lessons. By 300 B.C., teachers of art were sometimes included in the day's tour.

This tutorial type training in the hands of a master teacher commonly involved the lecture and explanation, questioning, and some discussion. The oral emphasis and instruction was accompanied by considerable memorization and recitation. Books were not a common item before the Periclean age but teachers at least had manuscript rolls of basic works such as those of Homer and Aesop. Waxen tablets were the mark of the school boy, even after 400 B.C. when parchment and papyrus became more available. The pupil wrote with a pointed stylus that had a broad top end used to smooth out the inscriptions and to make way for further notes or copying.[10] The 24-letter Greek alphabet also represented the Greek number system, and arithmetic was largely learning how to count on the fingers. With these limitations, Greek contributions in mathematics are surprising. Thus, in primary education, beginning at about age seven, the boy was taught fundamentals in ways that are quite familiar. Girls, except in Sparta, were instructed entirely within the home and family structure and had the much more limited education reflecting their position in Greek society.

Education at the secondary level became distinct during the Golden Age as more advanced intellectual instruction was sought. It soon came to cover a period of about four years between approximately the ages of fourteen and

---

[9] Gardner Murphy, *Historical Introduction to Modern Psychology* (New York: Harcourt, Brace & Co., 1949), pp. 8, 9.

[10] Details of reading and writing instruction and other characteristics of the Greek schoolroom are found in the excellent contribution of K. J. Freeman, *Schools of Hellas* (London: Macmillan, 1922), especially Chapter III.

eighteen, when the youth typically began his two years of military instruction. In addition to expanded physical activities, now often enjoyed in the large public gymnasia, the youth concentrated, it seems, upon advanced rhetoric and mathematics. Those who studied with the Sophists, however, often covered a variety of subjects from astronomy to philosophy. Another mark of growing maturity was the disappearance of the burdensome pedagog.

The Sophists were mainly wandering teachers who came from outside of Athens; they borrowed schoolrooms or taught in the streets or gymnasia. They were attacked by men with established schools, such as Plato or Isocrates, wherein more traditional education concentratiing upon a narrowed curriculum was the rule.

Protagoras and Gorgias were the most famous of the Sophistical teachers, but many of these men became very popular with the rich, upperclass youth who could afford their fees and who were enthralled by their daring approaches. While most of the Sophists lectured formally, their conversations, questions, and aside remarks marked them as unconventional free thinkers. As Athens met dark days in the struggle with Sparta, these instructors lost favor.

A rich and powerful state can afford instructors who question its values and institutions; a state in siege or about to lose a mortal combat will not accept the open or implicit critcisms of those who instruct its youth. The Sophists promoted the idea that the individual was the measure of all things; that laws and traditions were merely handy, man-made conventions. As skeptics who rejected absolute standards, they probed deeply and often did not provide any constructive alternatives while undermining religious and political beliefs. History has given us a black view of these men. However, education in all eras has demanded men who would inquire. Dangerous as some of these street-corner pragmatists may have been, the fact that they made learning exciting and that they caused youth to think should not be overlooked.

Socrates has been called a Sophist and as the self-designated "gadfly of Athens" he personified many of the characteristics of these teachers. He was, however, a native of the city and, in addition, took a more positive position as he continually sought for wisdom. Avoiding the relativism of the Sophists, he believed that ultimate knowledge was possible and that it would bring good men. His moral position was further identified as believing in the existence of a soul. Yet he too suffered the wrath of a jealous opposition and the aroused city fathers. His famous case reflected the fears and disillusionment of a decaying society losing its Mediterranean hegemony. The cup of Hemlock, however, was also symbolic of his own incorruptible search for ultimate answers and of the effectiveness of the method of instruction that he employed. Socrates left us no writings but his students, particularly Plato, brought a full understanding of his approach.[11] The Socratic dialogues found in Plato's works demonstrate this method by which Socrates takes assured but essentially unthinking young men through steps of confusion and dis-illusionment as they see their preconceived ideas punctured, one by one, but then gradually they are led back to an insightful position based upon logic and reason.

Today too few students encounter the exhilarating experience of repeated questioning by a master of dialectic. Even at advanced levels, with the large numbers enrolled, university seminars have largely lost this quality. Great teachers have always strived for the student who knows what he stands for and why, who can explain the logic of his thinking, and who also can and will apply and act in terms of his reasoned conclusions. The Socratic question and answer approach is an admirable means toward this end.

The Greek scholars are credited particularly with bringing the deductive approach to learning. There is little question but that deductive reasoning dominated Greek thought.[12] Aristotelian reasoning is a term frequently ascribed to this practice of organizing facts to fit a stated generalization or to arguing logically from a principle to the particular. Inductive thought, how-ever, is often incorrectly listed as a product of the Renaissance or as emerging even later as a result of the scientific influence of Francis Bacon. Actually this approach from particulars to generalization, wherein principles are drawn in the light of specifics observed and facts gathered, was not common throughout the long medieval period but it was, nevertheless, employed by Greek scholars.

This approach was most evident in the scientific collecting and organizing of Aristotle; certainly Socrates also operated in terms of analyzing varied and specific instances and then attempted to find certain commonalities as a basis for subsequent deduction. In fact, Aristotle credits him as being the father of the inductive method. Another example of Aristotle's employment of this approach was his gathering of a statement of political principles for his *Politics*. He first analyzed some 150 charters, political constitutions, and documents; then he set forth the generalizations that seemed to hold true

---

[11] Scholars differ on how much of Plato is Socrates and vice versa; Herbert J. Muller in his *The Uses of the Past* (New York: Oxford University Press, 1952) points out that the Socrates of the *Apology* would have been the first victim of the state under Plato's *Laws* or totalitarian *Republic*, p. 128.

[12] Interested readers will find much more complete discussions of Greek philosophy and intellectual methods in the various works of Edward Zeller. These have been translated, edited, and brought to date in numerous publications dating from the 1880's. More limited discussions are found in Joseph B. Burgess, *Introduction to the History of Philosophy* (New York: McGraw-Hill, 1939) or Frederick Mayer, *A History of Educational Thought* (Columbus, Ohio: Charles E. Merrill Books, 1960).

about government. Actually it has been a mistake to separate inductive and deductive modes of truth-seeking. Both are used in an intermingled manner in the ratiocination process. When modern day students are involved in problem-solving, they are, therefore, using the indispensable, intellectual tools with which much of Western civilization has been structured. Again, we are indebted to Greek thought.

Among other Greek approaches that are significant for the educational enterprise is one again characterized by Aristotle's attempt to categorize and classify objects in his experience and environment. Aristotle, as stated previously, established clearly separate areas within the broad field of Hellenic speculation. He is better known for his like efforts in biology. However, his interests were so wide that he was the first great encyclopedist.

These collecting and organizing phases of education came to be representative of the Hellenistic period of Greek educational history after the Macedonian conquest (338 B.C.). Actually it was to be expected that the Greek scholars would then turn to such synthesizing activities. The far-flung rule of young Alexander materially increased Near Eastern and Mediterranean contacts influencing Greek life in many ways. Assimilation and reconciliation of new and varied natural and cultural factors was necessary in the expanding Hellenistic world. This emphasis characterized the schools of higher education that had developed in Athens (which remained the educational center of the Western world long into the Roman period) as well as other renowned schools as those at Rhodes, Pergamum, and that most famous Hellenistic scholarly institution — the great museum and library at Alexandria.[13] This cosmopolitan center housed scholars at royal expense and teaching was conducted, as well as the collecting, copying, cataloguing, and varied research. Particularly fruitful was the work carried out in astronomy, geography, and mathematics. Euclid and Archimedes are but two of the many famous names connected with the Alexandrian institution.

Generally, education in the Hellenistic period reflected activities at the Alexandrian center. It was less creative than before and tended to become standardized, more formalized, and perfectionistic as the blending process of cultural admixture went on. All societies undergo altered educational phases and this aspect of Hellenistic life in the emerging Roman and Byzantine world called for a period of sharing and stock-taking. Such phases have characterized other "breathing" and maturing periods in Western culture that

---

[13] These schools are frequently called "universities"; except possibly for the Alexandrian institution, such a designation is largely a misnomer in terms of the modern conception. While there were some loose arrangements between the independent Athenian schools that came to exist during the period of Roman suzerainty over that city, the institutions of higher learning were not even organized as their successors of the medieval age.

have tended to follow great outbursts of originality. It is claimed, however, that if during this era the Greeks and their cohorts could have reduced militarism and strife, developed a more satisfactory economic system, and produced a technology wherein they might have practically applied many of the fundamental ideas that were then available, they could well have had modern civilization within their reach.

The Greek Curricular Influence

Hellenic curricular influence remains to the present. Current debates about the subjects to be emphasized in the school program echo back more than 2,000 years and they promise to be with us for the foreseeable future. What is essential for general education? What are the commonalities basic in citizenship training? Which liberal arts should be emphasized? How shall we conduct schooling in the vocational and applied arts? Which are the fundamental subjects? What content shall be offered for the gifted? The Greeks faced questions like these and many persons today hold the Greek answers. Critics of this bent frequently work with dedication to maintain, extend, or return to programs of study singularly close to the Attic pattern.

Ultimately the educational practices of Hellas tended to bring a unique blend and balance of what had become five essential aspects of learning. There was the intellectual emphasis promoted by the grammarian [14] and at secondary levels in the rhetorical schools and by the Sophistic teachers. Secondly, there was the aesthetic aspect, prompted by the citharist and other instructors of music, and in later years, painting and the plastic arts. The health of the body, of course, was a third major concern emphasized in the palestra and the activities in the gymnasia. Socio-civic responsibilities were built via the legends and literature of the grammarian, the oratory and discussions of the secondary schools, and the music, drama, and poetry of religious or patriotic ceremonies. This fourth emphasis permeated the entire curriculum, reflecting a central concern of education for the citizenship class. Ultimately, with the increased conflicts between city states, many of them initiated a two-year military training program, consisting of one year's drill in or near the city and a subsequent year's service in the outlying forts or in the navy. Particularly during periods of peace, attention to the four previously described aspects of education also found its way into the years of military training.

In spite of the fact that there was no clear-cut system of education, the young male citizens fortunate enough to obtain a full schooling seemed to

---

[14] The term is used broadly; this instructor was responsible for learnings that today would be labeled "language arts" and "communication."

have had a most appropriate education for the roles in society they were expected to fulfill. Late in the Hellenistic period (400 A.D.) the curricular roots of what came to be known as the liberal arts were firmly established. Roman educators reorganized and reclassified these into the famed Trivium, grammar, rhetoric (oratory), and logic; and the Quadrivium, arithmetic, geometry (largely geography), astronomy, and music (theoretical). Here were the beginnings of what during the medieval ages were to become the heart of the "proper" curriculum and of what remained so for centuries. Thus, eventually, built upon a grasp of the fundamentals, much of the content of education of elite Greek freemen became at secondary levels the essential general education for all who were to be educated.

Unfortunately, while Western society has changed immeasurably and more rapidly with each passing century, many educational neo-classicists have rejected concomitant significant alterations in the traditional content and pattern of general education. Inexorably, however, changes have come; no educational program can survive unless it serves a functional purpose. Though American high schools, for example, are now shifting toward more intellectual emphases, their general and civic education programs hold but minimal resemblance to the curriculum of the Greek rhetorical school At college levels the ancient elements of liberal education are more easily identified. Logic remains but is not required; music, largely of a different sort, is available for those who desire it; geography has become separated from geometry; speech competencies are frequently demanded; mathematics, the language arts, and foreign languages may be required. However, even European bastions of traditionalism, where the old and the tried are much more sacred and unchanging than in American society, are undergoing alteration that affects the liberal arts core. This is attested to by the controversy developing over the decision of Oxford and Cambridge to drop their Latin entrance requirements.

It is evident in our time that free citizens in Western society still must have some common unifying elements in their educations in spite of diversified and specialized endeavors. In elementary schools this unity has tended to focus in recent years upon the basic social processes or worldwide human activities,[15] in addition to the fundamental 3 R's. Greater variations have come to characterize secondary and higher education, but in an age that demands increased mutual understanding among all peoples there will undoubtedly be further developments to promote increased communication. The

---

[15] The social processes were forwarded by Leon Marshall and Rachel Goetz in *Curriculum Making in the Social Studies* (New York: Scribner's, 1936) as basic to the selection of school content and emphases. A more recent discussion of these basic human activities is found in Paul R. Hanna, "Social Studies for Today," *NEA Journal,* January, 1956, pp. 36-38.

form and titles of the educational media employed may be unfamiliar, but in a number of instances these will include studies evolved from the Attic heritage but modified in terms of late twentieth century demands.

It is also hoped that modern tendencies toward a revised core of general education may reflect the Greek curricular theory that men who are to live together and forward the welfare of the individual and the democratic state must hold reciprocal values based, with intelligent variations, upon similar knowledge and experiences. Thus, once again a general or a liberal education will include those elements that liberate a man in his time — that enable him to function as an intelligent free individual. One of the tragedies of the Greek story was the failure of the Hellenes to really accomplish this for all through their educational programs.

Another carry-over from the Greek curricular influence has been the attitude that the quality educational program is comprised of the educational offerings taken by the elite. Whatever learnings are appropriate for the upper-classes, the privileged group, or the gifted, therefore carry the appellation of being superior and worth emulating for all.

In the West down through the centuries despite the great extension of educational opportunity and the growing variety of educational needs, there remains a hierarchy in content and discipline. This exists in considerable part because at one time some privileged Greek, Roman, or Renaissance gentleman studied these subjects. Such a belief is reflected, for example, when parents force a small high school in a rural community, beset by all sorts of economic and social problems, to provide three or four years of Latin, no matter the fact that but a handful of the students will go on to college. Such an attitude is also evident in a bitter fight at a university faculty meeting over the approval of a new set of courses in hotel management or some other field of practical or applied science. The young Greek who was educated had no need for what we think of as vocational emphases in his education. His economic and social future was largely assured by his family's position and holdings. His vocation was living the life of leisure for which he was properly prepared through the appropriate liberal arts "vocational" curriculum of his day.

Ever since those times it has been a long and grueling struggle for each of the practical arts to find its way into the school program. While private education could stand firm more easily, even with public education and the increased spread of social demands to be serviced, resistance to curricular additions has been quite unbelievable. Business education, shop courses, and even art and music, as well as physical education, serve as examples of disciplines that have generally, at secondary levels, arisen as extra-curricular or non-school subjects and that found their way only very gradually into the regular program. In many instances the only way such studies could be launched was to create new schools, public or private. The comprehensive

American high school has antecedents in the practical Colonial and European academies but such schools in the United States were often not willing to change. By 1900 it was necessary to establish separate commercial and public trade schools to achieve this education. As late as the early twentieth century, what was not proper for the secondary education of a youth of ancient Greece was still not looked upon by many as appropriate in the program of the American high school. This same resistance to intrusions of new studies has existed on an even stronger basis in the area of higher education. The resistance of scholastically dominated universities of Europe to the subjects demanded by the technological revolution, for example, was responsible for the development of separate technical institutes where much of the scientific experimentation has been carried on. This development was mirrored in the United States by the rise of such schools as Rensselaer Polytechnic Institute (Troy, New York, 1824). However, when Federal funds became available for higher education under the Land Grant College Act of 1862, the practical provisos of this and subsequent legislation helped push American higher education into its present scope and pattern.

The hierarchy and resistances we have illustrated above were also a characteristic of the Greek educational scene. Plato, as other scholars, had his favorite subjects. He deemed geometry the most essential study, though, typically, he frowned upon its being used for earth measurement or base mechanical experimentation. Similarly, such views continue to plague education and outmoded subjects cling on just as the Greek and Roman rhetorical schools continued oratorical emphases long after they served any real purposes for the youth involved. In fact, during the decline of the Roman Empire, at times that called for study and discussion of the vital problems besetting Western civilization, the cream of Greek and Roman youth were mouthing formalized speeches and stylized orations of past eras while their societies crumbled about them. This is a danger of outmoded prestige curricula to any people in any era.[16]

Other Greek Contributions

Although the Romans developed the first clearly integrated system of education, it had its roots in the Greek lower schools, the rhetorical schools and the Sophistical enterprises, and in the higher institutions that evolved. The great centers of learning that dotted the Mediterranean during the Hellenistic period were to serve as prototypes that would develop in Europe 1,000 years

---

[16] The most striking tongue in cheek exposition of this danger is the educational classic of Harold Benjamin, *The Saber-Tooth Curriculum* (New York: McGraw-Hill, 1939).

later. But it is a misnomer to refer to the "University of Athens" during the bulk of the period we are covering. Not till the second century A.D. and the regeneration of Greece under the beneficence of the Roman Emperors Antonius Pius and Marcus Aurelius were the group of schools existing at Athens forged into anything like a university center.[17] The more immediate sources of our traditions of higher education are the medieval universities and their Islamic counterparts. The modern scholar, however, in his philosophy seminar, for example, may trace his viewpoints, the content studied, the means of instruction (such as the Socratic discussion), and aspects of his school's organization back to Greek antecedents.

Among the greatest of the inheritances of the West from the men at Hellas, as indicated previously, are our schools of philosophical thought. Idealists, realists, materialists, and even pragmatists, among others, had their Greek counterparts. Basic positions on ethical and theological questions covering topics from eugenics to atheism can be traced back to Greek thinkers. The philosophical tool, the syllogism, is another legacy.

Other subjects and fields of scholarly endeavor trace their origins to Greece. Mathematics was another of the great areas of Greek achievement and in this realm the Attic contributors set the patterns of study that would hold for 2,000 years. Hellenic scholars also differentiated and extended geographic knowledge. They were among the first political scientists. They probed the areas of biology, anatomy, and embryology. The various branches of medicine also have Greek beginnings. It has been claimed, in fact, that for over 1,000 years the natural sciences could make little progress beyond the Attic achievements until instruments were finally invented and perfected that gave greater scope and precision in observation and measurement.[18]

In poetry, literature, the fine arts, and drama, as in some other fields, the Greek contributions were not made by scholars or artists who taught at institutions of higher learning. Neither were the architectual achievements, the classic sculpture, and even the work of our first historians, the products of men tied to such schools. In the latter case the trio of Greek historiographers — Heroditus, Thucydides, and Polybius — participated actively in the developments of their eras but they held no chairs of history. Yet, Heroditus — the dramatic and biographical historian, Thucydides — the chronological and

---

[17] The traditional four major Athenian schools of higher education are generally identified as: The Academic (Plato); the Peripatetic (Aristotle and Theophrastus); the Stoic (Zeno); and the Epicurean (Epicurius). A thorough discussion of higher education in ancient Attica is available in John Walden, *The Universities of Ancient Greece* (New York: Scribner's, 1909).

[18] Will Durant's *The Life of Greece* (New York: Simon and Schuster, 1939) presents a host of such Greek origins and contributions to Western civilization. See particularly pp. 528-531, and Epilogue, pp. 667-671.

"scientific" historian, and Polybius — the historian who was as interested in his method as much as he was in content and so attempted to write an interpretive universal history — all made singular contributions and can be looked upon as progenitors of various "schools" of historical approach. The same germinal Hellenic influences can be identified in the backgrounds of the majority of our modern disciplines.

An almost endless list of Greek origins can be cited. Our alphabet comes from Greece. We are indebted to the Hellenes for a host of key words and terms, particularly in scientific areas. Every page of the dictionary has its share of these gifts. Although often taking a Latinized form, the language of every scholarly discipline is so indebted. Cicero, for example, in attempting to translate some of the Greek philosophical works, found that the Roman language had no satisfactory counterparts for numerous Greek metaphysical expressions. Thus from Greek beginnings come words such as *cosmos, essence, idea, logic, maxim, principle, mean, category, energy,* and *end.* To use an example from another area, modern schools that have returned to the great Greek emphasis upon sports and physical well-being surround themselves, in their gymnastic and athletic programs, with Attic predecessors. The stadia and the tracks and the training rooms, the sand pits, the games, the races, the body-building contests and activities, as well as many of the instruments of sport, date back to the ancient Greeks.[19]

Educational terminology and pedagogical traditions in large number stem from Hellas. Many of these have already been identified. Perhaps the most unfortunate heirloom is the term *pedagog* itself. This title for the household slave who accompanied the young Greek student in his daily educational travels from home to teachers to palestra and back home again has mistakenly been applied to teachers. The pedagog, of course, was practically forced into learning and teaching. He carried books and tablets, he sat in on the lessons, and he drilled and heard his young charges repeat their homework. Ultimately many of these servants found their way into the teaching ranks and they were in considerable demand as instructors in Italy following the Roman conquest. The history of the profession has paralleled too faithfully over far too long a stream of time the unplanned rise of the pedagog as a mentor. If there is one element in the Greek educational heritage that should be discarded it is the appellation "pedagog" with its sense of servitude and inferiority that has plagued teachers, particularly in the lower schools right to the present day.

Certain contributions to the West, such as coinage, paper, the abacus, navigation instruments, and some of the handicraft arts were actually Hel-

---

[19] An excellent description of these programs is found in H. I. Marrou, *A History of Education in Antiquity* (New York: Sheed and Ward, 1956), Chapter III.

lenic adoptions or adaptations from their Near Eastern and Mediterranean neighbors. These mounted during the interchanges of the Hellenistic period. Many of these and of the pure Greek contributions to our culture were, of course, modified through the centuries by still other peoples. The extent of which we are indebted to the Greeks, however, can become legion if we credit key Roman achievements in government, engineering, and commerce to their Attic antecedents. Although Shelley made a narrow and extreme claim, we can appreciate the implications of his words — "We are all Greeks; Rome would only have spread savagery without Greece."

It is important to maintain a balance in our assessment of the Greek heritage. In the realm of education, Greek gifts were truly comprehensive and significant. However, Greek attitudes and practices in areas of mysticism and superstition, morality, and their treatment of women are unfortunate examples of their culture. So too, have been some of the formalized academic carry-overs from those ancient times. Plato's contributions, such as the belief that the "best" education is intellectual, that certain studies are superior as mind-trainers, and that men of less capability might be "hood-winked" for the benefit of the state, do not ring true with our own modern views. Even in Greece today native educators trained in the United States are attempting, against ingrained practices, to develop a more practical educational program that balances the worthy cultural aspects of traditional education with those emerging subjects and emphases that will serve the needs of twentieth-century Hellas.

In each age of most nations, scholars can identify varying facets of Greek education and life as the prime exemplar of that society. A totalitarian state would look to Sparta and her system of full subjugation of the individual to the community. The authoritarian educational model derived from that city state has served as an archetype on many occasions in the subsequent history of the world, from the Platonic Jesuit theocracy once attempted in Paraguay to the present communal efforts in China. Spartan girls and women received an education and a place of honor almost singular in ancient Greece. However, the civic examination of the new-born, the exposure of the unwanted, the training of boys and girls in military-like packs,[20] the full public boarding school life of the boys from age 12 on into their 30's, the rigorous development of youth, with floggings, rough clothes, and plain diets, the many years of intense indoctrination, military training, and enforced service to the state, and the continuing fitness program that kept men in the army reserve till the

---

[20] It is said that war was declared annually upon the serf-like Helots who lived in the Spartan countryside in order that the young males, whose food supply had been cut, could have actual experience in foraging, stealing, and fighting the enemy!

age of 60 would please a Nietzsche and serve well the educational needs of a Communist or Fascist state.[21]

The Spirit of Educational Freedom

In the West, today, one is tempted to look upon the spirit of freedom in educational inquiry exemplified at times in Athens and by a worthy group of Greek thinkers as the most significant Greek heritage. Indeed, the international outcome of democracy's continuing struggle with totalitarianism may well be decided in terms of the comparative efficiency and success of the conflicting educational approaches employed. No nation that has geared its entire educational program to the single end of war-like supremacy has yet endured as a power over the long pull of history. Equally unsuccessful have been regimes that have tried to shape the individual fully in terms of the total organization of the state. In these points democracy may take some comfort, but democracy has other difficult lessons to learn from the Greek experience.

The outstanding mark of Greek education was its classical humanism, centered upon producing free men primarily through the literature of the great Greek tradition. In a world of limited written communication without satisfactory and inexpensive paper, this education was naturally centered on rhetoric. But rhetorical education included a broad base: the literature expounded included customs, history, law, and a mass of valuable information from many fields. Here also were reflected ethical principles and the all-important teaching of how to think. Greek education was dedicated to producing complete men — wise, beautiful, and good. The most important proving ground for this learning was the political arena where one could persuade eloquently and prove himself a master of debate. Greeks made a mistake in the over-emphasis upon rhetoric but it attained its pre-eminence as a means of building competent citizens. We see the efforts of Protagoras and some of the other Sophists, and those of Socrates, Isocrates, and Aristotle, pointed in this direction.

These men were not devoted primarily to the state or to wisdom for wisdom's sake, but rather toward developing worthy individuals who used and extended knowledge and who managed the state, first of all, for the welfare of the citizens. Protagoras had little time to devote to speculation about the infinite or the nature of the universe; life called him to help produce useful

---

[21] Perhaps one of the fairest assessments of Spartan education, about which there is considerable hearsay, can be found in Ernest C. Moore's *The Story of Instruction,* Vol. 1, The Beginnings (New York: The Macmillan Company, 1936), Chapter 1. He draws extensively, as do most other writers of the topic, from Plutarch's *Lycurgus* that portrays many details of Lacedemonian life.

persons, good citizens who would live worthily and successfully in their time. The much maligned Sophists varied considerably as individuals but as a group were dissenters who led their students to question what others sought to inculcate. As has been explained previously, there was grumbling opposition from local teachers and some citizens who feared the Sophistical influence, but young men who experienced their teaching were led toward independent thought.

Although Socrates and Isocrates both opposed the Sophists, they carried on essentially in the same tradition. Socrates believed that men could discover truth and that goal is reflected as central in his argumentation in Plato's dialogues. Socrates wanted people to think about what they were doing, what they should be doing, and why they were or were not so acting. The clever dialectics were posed to lead men to reason. Isocrates and Aristotle were also both concerned with the application of knowledge and recognized that scholars must be free if they are to attain wisdom. They also held that only a state that upheld such freedom of inquiry would promote knowledge in the widest benefit to all.

In a superstitious and warring world, it is a tribute to Athens and to some of the other Attic city-states that they allowed as much unhampered study, teaching, and expression of opinion as they did. Greek democracy has been overemphasized as have been the glories of its culture. Its democracy and large elements of its culture were missed by the majority of people in an age that was in many ways dark, brutal, and hard. There should be little wonder that Protagoras, who dared to question the existence of the gods, was ultimately banished and suffered one of the first book-burnings in the history of education. Plato and Aristotle left Athens more than once when the political climate became unfriendly. Braver or more foolish Socrates was a scholastic martyr. He was charged with denying the gods and corrupting youth. He did neither, certainly not directly, and his case has served as a source of inspiration to a host of teachers down through the years who have also been forced to taste of the cup of Hemlock because they, too, stood for the pursuit of truth and the right of pupils to learn. Therefore, in establishing the bases for intellectual freedom, the Greeks passed on a precious heritage. And since freedom in education can only be part of a larger climate of democracy, the Athenian experience holds even greater implications.

When a free state feels forced to muzzle instruction and censor the teacher, the proponents of these acts might well look deeper and ponder the question, "Do we strike at the cause or are we rather reacting to the effects of our own follies?" Edith Hamilton explains that the lesson for us in the Athenian experience is that Athenians reached a point where they were no longer willing to carry on their responsibilities as self-reliant free men. Instead, they sought the comfortable life and a modicum of security. As a result they lost all comfort, security and freedom. And then, too late, some remembered that they had not been free because their country was free, but that their country had been free because they had once believed and acted as free men.[22]

Was the spirit of freedom of inquiry and the pursuit of wisdom the most important educational contribution of the Greeks? Some will certainly say "No," pointing rather to the long enduring liberal arts curriculum, to Platonic ideals, or to the traditions of classical humanism. Others would cite the creative ideas basic in the development of their own disciplines. Still others might nominate the striking personalities and contributions of the great individual teachers. Among other possibilities is the intimate bond between mentor and pupil that is essential to learning. Indeed, the impersonal relationships of machine-age mass instruction may prove, in the near future, the greatest threat to true education. We have already suffered tremendous loss in past years as essentially undedicated instructors have attempted to impart learning to hosts of children. Yet, we have been amazingly successful in developing minimal literacy, and a modicum of civic responsibility and character development. But in this grand effort how much real love of learning has been promoted? The ultimate qualities we need for survival and progress may well be best established by the close and profound relationship between learner and teacher that is now threatened at all levels in our expanding educational programs.

Greek education, including the vital teacher-pupil relationship, enabled youth, until the shattering development of civil wars, the Roman conquest, and the enveloping Hellenistic age, to find their secure place in society and to build responsible personalities. What can we salvage for ourselves from this experience? In an international era, far more complex than the confined ancient Mediterranean world, what can we adapt? What must we avoid? What should we emulate? Somehow, in our age of mass culture, we must maintain the essence of the Greek teacher-pupil relationship by which, with the help of our technological wisdom and our machines, we can build democratic men in the full sense of the term. These free men must have standards, a sense of social awareness, a love of learning, a recognition of personal responsibility, and dedication toward extending those values that make life worth living. This, above all else, is what the Greek experience tells us.

Roman Contributions

It is difficult to make a balanced and objective analysis of the impact of Rome upon our Western world, however, the Roman contribution to Ameri-

---

[22] See her article, "The Lessons of the Past" in *Saturday Evening Post,* September 27, 1958.

can education has been significant. In the judgment of some historians, the major nations of the Western world are a series of vast amalgamations derived from the massive Roman inheritance which encircled the Mediterranean and stretched from Hadrian's Wall in Britain to the *Limes* of Southern Germany, from the Pillars of Hercules to the Persian Gulf. There are the physical facts of Roman culture with troops remaining in Britain until the Fifth Century A.D. and the heavy armored cavalry serving as the prototype for the succeeding knights. But also, there are the more persistent, linguistic, mythical, numerical, and other symbols which became a permanent part of Western culture. The Romans had a genius for synthesis and put together what Whitehead called the most effective factor in cultural development, a "massively coordinated inheritance."

Our task is to narrate in brief compass the nature of the Roman contribution derived from many sources, the Oriental world, the Indian and Middle Eastern world, and the Greek and Teutonic worlds. The impact of the *Roman Way*[23] upon our education and culture can be examined by concentrating upon the universal aspects of civilization in sequence: education; language, literature, philosophy, and religion; health and medicine; architecture and art; technology and economics; law and government. Finally, our investigation will deal with certain specific Roman contributions to our schools and colleges, together with some implications of the Roman Way in relation to our culture.

The Development of Roman Education

Roman education changed its scope and direction in the course of its development but there were certain perennial characteristics which Romans preferred even if the force of circumstance often prevented realization of their ideals. The Romans were in pursuit of their own pattern of excellence, emphasizing *mens sana in corpore sano,* or the training of competent men with sound minds and sound bodies who were effective leaders in the field of battle, the law courts, and the public assemblies as well as being responsible heads of families loyal to the state.

The Roman image of the educated man of the upper class or ruling elite was similar to Aristotle's picture of the probable results of the pattern of education outlined in his *Politics*. The desired outcomes were hardy youths, healthy in mind and body, capable of enduring hard physical labor especially in the military field and also educated to be civilized men prepared for the proper use of leisure. The Romans seemed to desire the best qualities of both

---

[23] Edith Hamilton has popularized this term; see her description of Roman life in *The Roman Way* (New York: W. W. Norton, 1953).

the Athenians with their love of thought and beauty, and the Spartans with their training in fortitude and courage; however, the Romans did not attain these ideals for the masses.

Roman education changed and, in fact, was revolutionized by the social pressures paralleling growth of the Republic and the Empire, from the town on the seven hills of the Tiber to its encirclement of the Mediterranean from the Black Sea to the North African coast. From before 500 B.C., for some five centuries, the Roman people developed an indigenous system of education which was centered around the home, and was designed for farmers tilling their own land. The family was the chief educational unit not only during infancy but also to the age of sixteen or seventeen. Fathers taught their sons in book learning, farming, and the duties of life. Mothers taught their daughters the techniques of housework and home management including spinning and weaving. The education was a father-son, mother-daughter type of apprenticeship.[24]

In general, our sources are later writers but the younger Pliny was speaking accurately when he wrote that it was the ancient custom that Romans should learn from their elders, not only through the ear but through the eye, those things which they sould soon have to do and in turn hand down to their successors. Every child had his father for a schoolmaster, and to the boy that had no father such responsibility fell to the oldest and most distinguished citizens in the community.[25] In other words the son was his father's constant companion everywhere around the farm and in the town or city. The Roman child was taught reading, writing, and geometry sufficient to keep accounts and to measure his land. The Roman purpose in education was practical and conservative with the aim of building respect for family and city traditions. Youth was not only taught the daily routine but trained morally in loyalty, self-restraint, and a certain austerity. In addition to the traditions of the farmer family and its virtues of industry, frugality, and severity, the child was also taught the traditions of the Roman Republic, memorizing the fundamental Law of the Twelve Tables.

Naturally, as in Greece, education changed through the centuries of Roman history; yet it retained to some degree its fundamental characteristics of devotion to the family and sacrifice for the state under the control of law and justice. The old education of the Republic made the boy into a man and citizen at about the age of sixteen when he exchanged the *toga praetexta* of childhood for the *toga virilis* of manhood. At this time he was given into

---

[24] This early education is described in somewhat more detail in A. S. Wilkins, *Roman Education* (Cambridge: The University Press, 1905), Chapter 2.

[25] This is documented in Aubrey Gwynn, *Roman Education From Cicero to Quintilian* (Oxford: The Clarendon Press, 1926), Chapter 1.

the care of a tutor who assumed the role of the father, training the young man in civic affairs, oratory, business, and the military life. Roman education began to change with Rome's shift from the status of the chief town in central Italy to a ruling city which absorbed the Greek towns of southern Italy. Furthermore, Rome went on to become a two-language state influenced heavily by Greek culture as she conquered Sicily, Macedonia, and Greece itself by 150 B.C.

In addition, significant Greek teachers came to lecture and instruct in Rome. As early as approximately 250 B.C. a Greek named Livius Andronicus from Tarentum had come to Rome as a slave, gaining his freedom but continuing as a teacher. He used the works of Homer as a textbook and translated the *Odyssey* into Latin. This translation has been regarded as the beginning of Latin literature and was used as a classic text. Suetonius tells the story of another influential Greek teacher who became, so to speak by accident, a pioneer in the teaching of grammar and literature. Crates came as an ambassador to Rome and broke his leg by falling into one of the Roman drains. During his convalescence he began to lecture on Greek literature and grammar with great success.[26] Later many more teachers, pedagogs, philosophers, and rhetoricians came from the Greek areas to Rome. Despite some conservative opposition, the enthusiasm for Greek culture increased. Plutarch said that "it was like a wind sweeping through the city so that people could talk of nothing else."[27] Furthermore, this great change toward emphasis on rhetoric, literature, and philosophy derived from the Greeks coincided with the Punic and Greek Wars. The influx of Greek slaves into Roman households and the occupation of Greek territory made knowledge of the Greek tongue and culture practical and mandatory. However, the Romans did not adopt all elements of the Greek program, such as the athletic and aesthetic emphases, and continued to emphasize some of their own subjects such as the study of law.

Roman education of the Empire beginning with the *Pax Romana* instituted by Augustus after 23 B.C. not only spread the new synthesis of Hellenic civilization throughout the Western world and beyond but also gradually developed an organized structure of education partially controlled by the state. Ultimately, after 300 A.D., Roman emperors extended certain direct controls over schools and universities and expanded the assistance to education with public funds practiced by some earlier emperors. Towns and cities

---

[26] Cited by Paul Monroe in *Source Book of the History of Education for the Greek and Roman Period* (New York: The Macmillan Company, 1901), p. 350.

[27] For some dramatic reading of the life and times of Greece as well as Rome see Plutarch's, *The Lives of the Noble Grecians and Romans* (New York: Modern Library Edition, 1932).

everywhere were Romanized and schools were gradually organized into a system for the education of the upper classes. The rural and country areas and the poorer and lower classes were relatively neglected. The decline of Roman civilization can be directly related to the Roman governmental and educational emphasis upon an urban civilization through which the ancient and obstinate regional rural peoples burst their way in the difficulties beginning in the third century A.D.[28] By this period Roman schools had lost their vitality and were soon on the wane just as the Empire deteriorated.

The Roman school system had developed into a semi-integrated structure of elementary, secondary, and higher education, including: (1) Elementary (6-12 years) known as the *Ludus* or Primary School in which the *magister* taught reading, writing, and arithmetic; (2) Secondary (12-16 years) or Grammar Schools in which the *grammaticus* taught, above all, Greek grammar and literature in a Latin setting; later bi-lingual and Latin Grammar Schools grew to take the place of the original Greek school; (3) Collegiate (16-19 years) or Schools of Rhetoric in which the *rhetor* taught rhetoric, grammar, dialectic, and law; (4) University (19-21 or 25 years), i.e., Greek Universities and the University of Rome in which the *professors* taught such subjects as law, medicine, architecture, mathematics, geometry, and astronomy, as well as grammar, rhetoric, and dialectic.

Rome also contributed to the organization of a liberal arts curriculum and this influence persists to the present day. The liberal arts curriculum was drawn from Greek sources, and modified by the Romans. For example, Varro in the first century B.C. organized a compendium of the liberal arts which could be systematically taught by teachers to students. He added the subjects of architecture and medicine, based on excellent Roman work in engineering and technology, to the Greek curriculum of grammar, rhetoric, and logic (the *Trivium*); and arithmetic, geometry, astronomy, music (the *Quadrivium*), eliminating emphases on gymnastics, and drawing. Varro wrote excellent texts on each of the nine studies which he sought to establish as the liberal education curriculum of the "free man." Varro's nine liberal studies were reduced to the seven liberal arts by Martianus Capella in the late fourth century A.D. in his compendium *The Marriage of Philology and Mercury,* probably one of the worst books ever written. He justified his elimination of architecture and medicine in the interest of retaining only the arts of interest to spiritual and intellectual beings who had no need of the physical and practical. The relationship of this argument to present day

---

[28] Among his other excellent works on Hellenistic and Roman history, see M. I. Rostovtzeff, *A History of the Ancient World* (Oxford: The Clarendon Press, 1927), two vols., wherein this theory of the decay of Rome is presented.

controversies is rather striking as was emphasized previously in the discussion of Greek education.

Roman education was carried on with the handicaps of a lack of printed materials and a scarcity of cheap paper. Methods were characterized by memorization and brutal punishment. The Roman school master tended to be a rather terrifying person, using the rod so that boys might stand up with bravery to their teacher as a Roman soldier faced an enemy.[29] The great defects of this ancient education were the increasing emphasis on rhetoric and the manner of speaking as more important than command of knowledge and nobility of character, and the lack of education for poor children. The Romans continued the tradition of Greek origin in their education for an elite few.

Quintilian and Educational Philosophy[30]

Quintilian, born about 35 A.D., was a Spaniard who became a Roman citizen and a pioneer in teaching. He was a lawyer and noted teacher. The Emperor Vespasian appointed him the first professor of rhetoric in Rome. Quintilian wrote his *Institutes* (93 A.D.) which did much to determine the course of later education. His balance of idealism and objectivity has been of great value to us. In contrast to Rousseau and Locke, he preferred the school as a society in miniature with a group of boys and a teacher rather than the individual student and a tutor. Quintilian thought that the "sympathy of numbers" helped both teacher and student. Quintilian had no illusions about the Roman family of the early Empire. He was a realist who knew that well-to-do Romans already had too much greed for money, love of pleasure, desire for advancement, and ambition, to favor the growth of the young toward a culture including morals and refinement and discipline. Quintilian felt that only a third rate teacher preferred to teach one individual and that the skilled teacher could handle a large group and at the same time give individual attention to each.

Quintilian opposed lenient teaching and believed in firm and basic foundations at an early age. He felt that there were certain fundamentals to be learned and that the young child with his retentiveness and accurate mem-

---

[29] Luella Cole, *A History of Education: Socrates to Montessori* (New York: Rinehart, 1950), has gathered several vivid contemporary accounts of conditions; see p. 62 and p. 87.

[30] Among a number of other sources of Quintilian's works, we are indebted to W. M. Smail, *Quintilian on Education* (Oxford: Clarendon Press, 1938); Robert Ulich, *History of Educational Thought* (New York: American Book Company, 1950); Cole, *op. cit.*; Gwynn, *op. cit.*; Marrou, *op. cit.*; and Monroe, *op. cit.*

ory had great advantages in doing this. He noted, "I would urge that lines which are set as models of copying should not be such as expressed in idle thoughts but which convey useful instruction." Quintilian was perhaps the most successful teacher of his time and he gives us a view from within of the whole process of education as it affected the student. Quintilian was sure that training couldn't begin too early in education. In the old tradition he felt that the parents had a very heavy responsibility and that both should be well educated. He believed that the parents should be very careful to pick the best nurses and servants for the children, especially the pedagogs who, as in Greece, were slaves who followed the children to school, waited there while they were instructed by teachers, and then brought them home again.

Quintilian felt that children should begin learning their letters before the age of seven but that their minds should not be overburdened so that they took dislike to their studies. He wrote, "Let the first instruction be in the form of play, let the pupil be asked questions and be praised for his answers; let him never rejoice in ignorance of anything. Sometimes when he is unwilling to learn let another be taught of whom he may be jealous, let him compete sometimes with others and quite often think himself be victorious." His words reached across the centuries to us; he favored neat and rapid writing, "For since writing itself is the most essential thing in our study and the one thing from which alone springs true and deeply rooted proficiency, a slow pen hinders thought and a badly formed and careless hand is difficult to read." Quintilian believed that competition within the school was healthy, saying, "There is one useful method known to me and which was employed by my own teachers. They arranged us in classes determining the order of speaking according to the ability of the students."

Quintilian insisted upon getting to know the individual student — "Make a study of him to discover his abilities, the standard of his attainments and any other particular mental characteristics which he possesses." His ideas on corporal punishment were illuminating — "As for corporal punishment, though it is a recognized practice . . . I am completely opposed to it, first because it is disgusting, fit only for slaves and undoubtedly an insult . . . in the next place because as a pupil whose mind so well befits a free man's son is not to be corrected by a reproof . . . If you direct the child when he is young by means of blows what will you do when he is a young man who cannot be compelled through fear and has many more important things to learn." Quintilian was an optimist about the student, feeling that each one really wanted to learn and that if they didn't the fault was not the child's but the teacher's. Speaking of the secondary school or grammar school, he interpreted grammar very broadly as the art of correct speaking and the interpretation of the poets.

Quintilian was a great teacher as shown in his maxims on instruction:

It is not sufficient that he should himself manifest severe self control, he must also by the strictness of his discipline control the behaviour of those who gather round him. Let him, then, above all, adopt the attitude of a parent towards his pupils and consider that he is taking the place of those who entrust their children to him. He should be free from vice himself and must tolerate none in his pupils. Let him be stern but not melancholy, friendly but not familiar, lest in the one case he incur dislike, in the other contempt. He must constantly discourse on the honourable and good for the more he admonishes his pupils the less he will need to punish them. He must never lose his temper, yet he will not ignore faults which deserve correction. He must be simple in his teaching, able to endure hard toil, assiduous rather than exacting. He must freely answer questions and put questions himself to those who do not ask them. In praising the recitations of his pupils he must neither be niggardly nor extravagant, for in the former case he will create a dislike for work, in the latter a spirit of self complacency. When he corrects faults he will not be harsh and never abusive; for many are turned away from the studies they have entered upon because some teachers find fault as though they hated the offender.

Many of his maxims are just as pertinent and yet as difficult to follow today as in the era Quintilian wrote them! As is evident, he was modern in many ways, for example, his suggestion that if pupils are to persevere, all must taste success. His sense of ethical responsibility on the part of the teacher is timeless — "I shall have rendered the worst of services to mankind if I forge these weapons not for a (citizen) soldier but for a robber."

The influence of Quintilian declined in the late Empire and in the Middle Ages. The complete text of his *Institutes* was rediscovered, however, in 1416 and greatly affected Renaissance thinkers such as Vittorino da Feltre, Vives, and Erasmus, who not only taught but wrote very popular text books. University teachers of speech and rhetoric in the United States today recognize their debt to Quintilian's emphasis upon excellence of both form and content.

Roman Cultural Contributions[31]

LANGUAGE, LITERATURE, PHILOSOPHY, AND RELIGION. Although the Romans borrowed widely from Greek sources, they eventually produced their own gifts to the Western heritage. Cicero was an eclectic living in the days of conflict between Julius Caesar and his enemies. He was a great man of

---

[31] A much more complete presentation of the broad Roman impact upon many aspects of Western civilization is found in volumes such as: Will Durant, *Caesar and Christ* (New York: Simon and Schuster, 1935) and Frank G. Moore, *The Roman's World* (New York: Columbia University Press, 1936). See also the more recent work edited by Naphtali Lewis and Meyer Reinhold, *Roman Civilization* (New York: Columbia University Press, 1951).

letters, urbanely discussing the problems of the day in splendid prose. Furthermore, he became an orator of the first rank and his *Orations against Catiline* gave a long range of writers a model for forceful and beautiful prose as well as being read by American schoolboys for many generations. Cicero's *Letters* have given us invaluable impressions of life in Roman society. His *De Oratore* helped set the stylistic patterns of Renaissance rhetorical education. Horace was a friend of the Emperor Augustus, living during the days when the Empire was organized. Horace was a great poet, cultivated and satirical, whose *Odes* and other writings exerted tremendous influence over writers of the Renaissance and of more modern days. Again, his influence has been exerted directly upon the schoolboys of the Western world. Virgil's works have had enormous weight in literature, not only his epic *The Aeneid,* a long poem in the meter of Homer tracing the mythical descent of Rome through the hero Aeneas, but also his *Georgics,* describing the beauty of the landscapes and farms of Italy. In the fourth century, Donatus wrote his *Ars Minor* which helped establish the Latin system of grammar that eventually was incorporated into English and still serves to plague students.[32]

The Romans also handed down historical literature of high rank including Julius Caesar's *On the Gallic War* in simple, forceful language. Livy wrote a monumental history of Rome in 142 books which attracted later writers such as Saint Augustine and Dante. Another historian was Tacitus who wrote his *Annals and Histories;* his *Germany,* describing the northern tribes and culture; and his *Agricola,* a fine biography of his father-in-law, and the first full description of the island of Britain. Suetonius produced the *Lives of the Twelve Caesars* while he served as secretary to the Emperor Hadrian. Plutarch wrote his famous *Lives* in the second century A.D., sketching the biographies of twenty-three Greek and twenty-three Roman men of note so cleverly that eventually they became a part of the liberally educated man's library in Europe and the American Republic. These primary literary works of Romans had immense importance in the history of civilization, providing a gateway through which Greek and Roman culture reached the Western World and the United States.

The Roman contributions in philosophy built mainly upon Greek roots. The Stoic school of thought, for example, was advanced both by Marcus Aurelius, an emperor from 161-180 A.D., and the slave Epictetus but its origins go back to the Greek Zeno. The Romans made Stoic philosophy their own and humanized it for their class system. Stoicism was their structure of ethics for difficult times. Its soldierly and practical approach to man as a small figure facing catastrophe in a large world suited the Roman temperament and was well applied in those days of growing difficulty. For example,

---

[32] Cole, *op. cit.,* describes Donatus' contributions, pp. 72-78.

the Marcus Aurelius said, "Don't hope for Plato's *Utopia*: be content if you yourself can make a step forward." He made significant contributions to education and readers will find his views interesting.[33] Another philosophy popular in Rome was the Epicurean, here too, as with the Greek gods they adopted, the Romans were indebted to their neighbors across the Adriatic.

The Latin language was important in the development of the English language and also exerted a significant influence upon form in writing and speaking, as well as on grammar, previously mentioned. Latin became the universal language of Europe's educated classes through the Renaissance. In the realm of religion the Roman Empire served as a seedbed and great nursery of Christianity. Jesus lived and taught in a Roman province and was crucified as a Roman political prisoner. His disciples carried His teachings throughout the empire. The new convert, a Jew named Paul, and a Roman citizen, together with Peter preached the gospel in many communities. The Fathers of the early Christian Church were ultimately to have great impact upon theological thought in the West. Saint Augustine, who lived in the fifth century, wrote his *City of God,* one of the most influential books ever penned, and argued that the Heavenly City represented by the Christian religion fought against the City of Error represented by the evil of man. He set faith above reason and established the medieval philosophical pattern. Saint Jerome also feared the influence of pagan literature and made a lasting contribution in learning Hebrew and then through his subsequent translation of the Old and New Testaments into a fourth century Latin version known as the *Vulgate.* He thus made scriptures available for the curriculum and from this time on they were to share major emphasis with the liberal arts for many centuries of education. The *Vulgate* was the only version of the Bible used in the Middle Ages. It remains the official Catholic Bible in some European nations, and, of course, had its religious impact eventually in the United States.

HEALTH AND MEDICINE. The Romans admired physical fitness and courage, educating for such soldierly virtues despite the decadence connected with the expansion of their empire and its loot in land, wealth, and slaves. The Roman urban civilization created a pattern of public baths and swimming pools, athletic fields and race courses, amphitheaters, and hospitals. The Roman evolution toward professionalized spectator sports such as the gladiatorial games and chariot races provide case examples of a modern problem.

Roman physicians' skills were stimulated by the medical needs of the

---

[33] In their anthology *Prologue to Teaching,* Marjorie B. Smiley and John S. Diekhoff (New York: Oxford University Press, 1959) for example, have included his excellent statement "From These I Learned," pp. 492-494.

Roman Army. The Romans were among the first to build up a far-reaching system of well organized hospitals. One large hospital for the legionnaires on the Rhine had about forty wards, with pharmacies and administration centers. Celsus, living at the time of Jesus, was an outstanding contributor to medical knowledge. His volume *On Medicine* included the definite diagnosis of appendicitis, and a first description of stopping bleeding by ligatures. Galen practiced medicine in Rome and made original experiments on the functions of the spinal cord, kidneys, and arteries. Galenic medicine was handicapped by its limitation to animal dissection; but Galen wrote an encyclopediac synthesis of medicine in 150 books and influenced medieval and later medicine. After Galen, science declined into astrology and alchemy. However, in Byzantium able physicians contributed to medical progress. Paul of Aegina in the seventh century A.D. was a model surgeon showing his skill in operations on tonsils and in obstetrics. Byzantine physicians also developed methods for combating diphtheria, smallpox, and various infections in their crowded and much traversed city. Roman textbooks, practice, and medical institutions exerted a long range influence upon Europe and America.

ART AND ARCHITECTURE. The Roman contributions in art and architecture were extremely important to the Western world and the United States. The eminent Swiss historian of architecture, Geideon, makes a strong case for the Roman Pantheon, built in the first century A.D., as the revolutionary step in the solution of the problem of space enclosure. Its great dome of concrete is 140 feet in height and diameter, and supported by a concrete rim 20 feet in thickness. Many American governmental and public buildings display a grandeur derived from Rome's use of pillared facades and daring domes. The Romans borrowed much from Greek and Hellenistic models, but they created a new and bold architecture expressed in splendid public buildings suitable for serving the great populations of their imperial cities. The Romans used the arch, vault, and dome to create size, strength, and splendor, in their imperial architecture. The Romans built some beautiful temples but their characteristic structures were splendid assembly halls, huge amphitheaters, imposing palaces, great city residences and rural villas, and, above all, superb bridges and aqueducts flung across river valleys and plains — some of which still carry water.

The work in the first century B.C. of the great Roman, Vitruvius, *On Architecture,* had extensive influence upon Renaissance and modern architecture. Both Michelangelo and Bramante were careful students of the work of Vitruvius and extended his influence throughout Europe. The general plan of the Pennsylvania Terminal in New York is distinctly Roman, resembling the Basilica of Constantine and the Baths of Caracalla. The Roman peristyle led to the medieval cloisters influencing American college architecture as in the Romanesque colonnaded cloisters of Stanford University. Many of our capitol buildings throughout the nation were originally inspired by the Roman domes and later models such as the Panthéon in Paris. The Maison Carrée at Nimes, France is a beautiful example of a Roman temple with columns engaged in the walls and mounted upon a high basement and suggested the plan for the state capitol at Richmond, Virginia to Thomas Jefferson.

TECHNOLOGY AND ECONOMICS. The Romans were great builders, technologists, and businessmen. The Roman roads were so well engineered that many lasted through the early Middle Ages. Much of the national road system of Western Europe follows the locations of Roman Roads. The Romans were able to build road bridges and aqueducts with their fine hydraulic cement which defied the tooth of time. Some striking examples include the majestic arched bridge at Segovia, Spain, the Aqueduct at Spalato, Italy, and the Pont du Gard near Nimes. The engineering genius of Rome was expressed in the fine work by Frontinus, *On the Aqueducts of Rome*. The Romans pioneered in great projects of road, bridge, drainage, and harbor construction; their network of over 50,000 miles of excellent roads stands as an achievement to challenge the builders of modern turnpikes and freeways.

The Romans made practical applications of inventions and science beyond the Greeks. Their knowledge of farming and animal husbandry was extensive. The writings of Cato the Elder on agriculture, and later those of Varro exerted a continuing influence upon the development of agronomy and scientific agriculture. The Romans developed the practical use of mathematics and surveying for mining and military works as well as roads. They built the great *limites* or frontier defenses such as the Roman Wall in England stretching west from Newcastle. The Romans invented water wheels for grinding grain; they also engineered accurate tunnels into rock for water supplies and for the mining of minerals.

It should be noted that the Romans set up systems of large scale mass production for metalwares, pottery, and textiles. Roman manufactures from the older provinces were sent out through the channels of trade to the newer lands. The Roman citizens were skillful in commerce and banking, using bills of exchange and all sorts of commercial paper. The red glazed Arretine tableware made in low relief from molds was exported over most of the Mediterranean. The Roman utilitarian spirit and organization of economic life persisted despite the times of trouble in Europe from London to Vienna and especially in the Romanic lands of Italy and France and through Europe to us.

ROMAN LAW AND GOVERNMENT. The political influence of Rome was far reaching. Our governmental terms are largely Roman including *census,*

61

fiscal, salary, municipal, civic, candidate, and others. Roman political thought contributed the conception of the role of the state in protecting its citizens, loyalty of the citizen to the state, the self-governing municipality, checks and balances in the Republican constitution, the jury method of trial, and the representative principle. The principles of separation of powers, and checks and balances in the American Constitution were indirectly derived from the Romans through the writings of Cicero in political theory by way of Montesquieu and Blackstone.

Above all, Roman Law was the primary factor in shaping mankind's legal pattern. Emperor Justinian I of Byzantium provided for the great codification of Roman Law in the sixth century A.D. The method was important. A committee of jurists under the guidance of the famous jurist Tribonian analyzed, rejected obsolete laws, arranged, and stated the laws clearly in sections. They created the *Corpus Juris Civilis* or "body of civil law" setting down the entire body of Roman legal principles clearly and preserving it for the future. The sections were: the *Code* or laws and decrees; the *Digest* or summaries of laws; the *Institutes* or a textbook of Roman Law; and the *Novels* or new laws of Justinian after the second revision of the code. This great codification of legal principles was and is of primary significance in the history of human civilization.

The Justinian Code or *Corpus* was rediscovered in the West by Irnerius in the eleventh century; and the revival of study of the Roman law was fundamental in the twelfth century Renaissance. Gratian composed his *Decretum* or great codification of canon law for the Church in this century, on the basis of the Roman civil code. The *Decretum* became the standard textbook in canon law as did the Justinian Code for civil law in the new medieval universities. The modern jurisprudence of France, Italy, and Spain is essentially Roman and through them French Canada, the Latin American countries, and to a degree Louisiana and the Southwestern United States. English law is particularly indebted to Rome in probate law, equity, admiralty and merchant law. English common law was based on the Anglo-Saxon law written not in Latin but the vernacular. Thereafter, Roman law was grafted upon the basic common law through the Church and the Norman Conquest.

Roman influence was powerful in giving structure and form to English legal documents in the formative period of the common law. As the great English legal historian Maitland put it, Bracton's *Laws and Customs of England,* written in 1259, was English in substance but Romanesque in form. The Roman form and method of teaching and thought persisted as shown in the case of the eminent Sir Edward Coke (1552-1634) who learned his Latin as a boy in the Norwich Free Grammar School. Latin was basic for land owners writing their estatebooks, mariners plotting their voyages, and lawyers apprenticed in their profession. Coke studied Latin and logic at

62

Cambridge University and then was a student of the law in the Inner Temple in London. Later Coke wrote his famous *Institutes* presenting the common law of England in the same style that Justinian's *Institutes* had defined the Roman law 1,000 years before. *The First Part of the Institutes of the Laws of England; or, a Commentary upon Littleton* became best known as *Coke-Littleton* and reached across the Atlantic to help form and teach American students of law — Thomas Jefferson, Patrick Henry, John Adams, John Rutledge, and Daniel Webster. Thereby, Justinian's Roman Code had a long reach into the American future.

Other Roman Contributions to American Education

In the American Colonies of the eighteenth century, the Roman legacy was powerful. The leaders of the country were usually educated men trained in the local Latin Grammar School and then in the college's classical curriculum. There were obvious incongruities between the Latin education and the needs of frontier colonies leading to great shifts and educational revolts in the nineteenth century. However, the system produced a valuable elite. John Adams was trained in the classics, primarily Latin, by his tutor, Joseph Marsh, after being bored to tears by the memoriter methods of the Braintree Latin School. At Harvard College he studied Natural Philosophy with Winthrop and, above all, the classics, Latin, Logic, and Greek with Wigglesworth. He graduated giving his brief oration in Latin. John Adams made a mighty contribution to American independence and a realistic government of checks and balances, a conception growing out of his classically based education and reading for the bar in *Coke-Littleton*. James Madison was another founder of the Constitution who derived much from the Roman legacy whether he was writing the *Federalist* or participating in the great debate on ratification, arguing for justice with a balance between rival interests.

In the nineteenth century, the American secondary schools and the four-year colleges and universities had a classical base that was reflected in the writings and speeches of leaders from this background. The great orators and statesmen, Webster and Calhoun, derived much of their style and content from Cicero and other eminent Romans. They were master logicians in stating their cases and classical craftsmen in their power of oratory. Horace Mann, the pioneer in educational awakening, was a scholar and a lawyer who took the future as his client. His successful fight for universal education insisted upon all youth having access to a liberal education rather than a partial education ending at the onset of adolescence. He used a classical turn of phrase in writing and speaking to help bring America far beyond the Roman Empire's education for only a few. Woodrow Wilson who, with Charles Eliot, Gilman, and others, founded the modern American

University, was a student of the Roman world. Wilson, as teacher, author, and president, wisely used the memory of perils past to guard against dangers to come.

Today, the Roman heritage is part of United States culture. We face similar conflicts between utility and aesthetics or the elite and the masses but are in the process of evolving effective principles and action on a newer and grander scale. In spite of some pressures to the contrary, America moves to an ever broadening conception of general education so as to meet the expanding needs of world participation and leadership. These ideals, the Romans would fully comprehend.

We recognize their positive educational contributions in many areas from the early Roman concept of "education for life is education by doing" to later developments such as the establishment of the principle of matched payments from centralized sources to strengthen local educational efforts. (The Emperor Gratian dispensed imperial funds to municipalities for education on a matching basis between 378 and 383 A.D.) Additionally, the Romans also provided us with several important examples of what *not* to follow educationally.

Probably the most significant educational legacy from Rome is related to the story of Rome's decline. Many reasons are mentioned by scholars for the collapse of the Empire. Probably all were contributing factors — over-extension of hegemony, poor health of the populace, the loss of morals and standards, economic troubles, deterioration of the legions, pressures from the Barbarians, and the others. We hasten to add the failure of the school system (education remained largely in private hands and for the upper classes) to prepare Rome to meet the mounting challenges. As the Empire crumbled around them, young dandies mouthed precise and well modulated orations; they aped Cicero, dead nearly five centuries. This schooling served no purpose in their day. Formal and classical learning in stylized patterns was the tragic educational inheritance from those who shaped schooling in the late Empire period. An impoverished and outmoded curriculum, then, was the unfortunate handicap.[34] In its narrow, humanistic influences, prejudiced against the practical arts and those who so labored, formal education also by-passed large numbers of artisans, skilled workers, and tradesmen, as well as the lower, urban and agricultural classes. Great masses of "citizens" were left uneducated, illiterate, and fully unprepared for the responsibilities necessary for competent citizenship. As the Empire completed its centuries of

---

[34] Toynbee explains the dangerous effects of an old and degenerate school program that is not kept broad and tied to life's problems, as well documented by the Roman experience, in Edward D. Myers, *Education in the Perspective of History* (New York: Harper & Brothers, 1960); see especially pp. 280-286.

collapse, its teachers and school gradually disappeared and Roman fathers even found themselves unable to impart essential knowledge and skills that had once been passed on to them. Western civilization then faced one of its most dangerous epochs, as learning was, in fact, threatened with extinction.[35]

Rome, in all of her grandeur and glory, as the Greeks before, also forgot the underpinnings of her greatness as she unconsciously allowed the means of maintaining and extending her society to disappear. Roman youth were still mastering *The Aeneid* and the words of Cicero but their meaning was lost as Roman leaders had failed in that one basic responsibility which Cicero too had emphasized when he declared, "The very foundation of the whole commonwealth is the proper bringing up of the young." Much of the American story is bound up in the determination to so provide for American children and youth; but Americans can also take warning from the mistakes and failures evident in the story of Greco-Roman education.

Bibliography

Barclay, William, *Train Up a Child: Educational Ideals in the Ancient World.* Philadelphia: The Westminster Press, 1959.

Charlesworth, Martin P., *The Roman Empire.* London: Oxford University Press, 1958.

Clarke, M. L., *The Roman Mind.* London: Cohen and West, 1956.

Cole, Luella, *A History of Education: Socrates to Montessori.* New York: Rinehart and Company, 1950.

Croiset, Maurice, *Hellenic Civilization.* New York: F. S. Crofts, 1925.

Davidson, Thomas, *The Education of the Greek People.* New York: D. Appleton and Co., 1897.

Dobson, J. F., *Ancient Education and Its Meaning to Us.* London: Harrop and Co., 1932.

Drever, James, *Greek Education.* Cambridge: The University Press, 1912.

Durant, Will, *Caesar and Christ.* New York: Simon and Schuster, 1935.

Durant, Will, *The Life of Greece.* New York: Simon and Schuster, 1939.

Freeman, Kenneth J., *Schools of Hellas.* London: Macmillan and Co., 1922, third edition.

Gibbon, Edward, *The Decline and Fall of the Roman Empire.* New York: Modern Library Edition, 1954, three vols.

Gwynn, Aubrey, *Roman Education: From Cicero to Quintilian.* Oxford: The Clarendon Press, 1926.

---

[35] The events and portent of these dark educational days have been well described by A. C. Krey in "The Greatest Educational Experiment," *Social Education,* October, 1938, pp. 457-467.

Lewis, Naphtali and Meyer Reinhold, eds., *Roman Civilization*. New York: Columbia University Press, 1951.

Livingstone, Richard W., ed., *The Legacy of Greece*. Oxford: The Clarendon Press, 1921.

Marrou, H. I., *A History of Education in Antiquity*. New York: Sheed and Ward, 1956.

Monroe, Paul, *Source Book of the History of Education: For the Greek and Roman Period*. New York: Macmillan and Co., 1901.

Moore, Ernest C., *The Story of Instruction: The Beginnings,* Vol. I. New York: Macmillan and Co., 1936.

Moore, Frank G., *The Roman's World,* New York: Columbia University Press, 1936.

Myers, Edmund D., *Education in the Perspective of History*. New York: Harper and Bros., 1960.

Robinson, Charles A., Jr., *Athens in the Age of Pericles*. Norman: University of Oklahoma Press, 1959.

Rostovtzeff, M. I., *A History of the Ancient World*. Oxford: The Clarendon Press, 1927, two vols.

Smail, W. M., *Quintilian on Education*. Oxford: Clarendon Press, 1938.

Walden, John, *The Universities of Ancient Greece*. New York: Chas. Scribner's Sons, 1909.

Wilkins, A. S., *Roman Education*. Cambridge: The University Press, 1905.

****

CHAPTER III

JUDAIC ROOTS OF
MODERN EDUCATION

It is easy for the superficial observer to overlook the Jewish contribution to modern education and American education in particular. Hebraism is not manifest in any special approach to intellectual effort as is Hellenism, nor is it the source of any particular discipline as is Islam. Indeed, for most of the last two thousand years the Jews have never exercised independent control over their own destiny much less that of Western culture. They have been but a minority group, carried by the streams of mankind's history within the currents of both Christian and Moslem development. By all the easy standards of success or dominion the Jews appear a most unlikely group to have influenced significantly the course of man's educational development.

If we must limit our interest to direct and open influence, the role of the Jew has been small indeed though not without significance as will be noted below. Yet Hebraism has made itself felt in a real and tangible if indirect way. Both through Christianity and Islam, the essential Jewish attitude towards education has become, in one form or another, the philosophical foundation and the motive power of much of the education of the Western world. Without the Hebraic cross-fertilization, the Greco-Roman tradition would have developed a far different educational perspective than it did, if indeed it could have survived the Dark Ages at all. Through Christianity and Islam, Judaism brought universal value to the educative process and thereby profoundly shaped the educational aspirations of contemporary man. To be sure, both Christianity and Islam interpreted the basic Jewish commitments in terms of their own religious and cultural genius. The Jewish contribution is thus indirect but still significant.

The purpose of this chapter then is to clarify the Judaic view of education. It was already clearly elaborated in the period before Christianity took on an organized form. This seminal pre-Christian Jewish view is a major concern of this chapter. Yet Judaism did not die with the origins and growth of either Christianity or Islam, hence the picture would not be complete without at least a brief glimpse at the continuing development of Jewish educational practice. During these later periods Judaism concreted its theory and the contributions of Jewish education become more evident.

The Historical Situation

The critical decision in Jewish educational history was reached about the year 450 B.C. It was planned and executed by a religious leader, Ezra, and his political counterpart, Nehemiah. It consisted simply of reading the basic Jewish law, the first five books of the Bible, the Torah, to all the people, and explaining it to them. From this seemingly unimportant act stems a quiet revolution which affects us to this day. To understand its dimensions a brief look at the historical background is necessary.[1]

The Hebrew people became united under a single ruler, King Saul, a little over a thousand years B.C. The monarchy divided into Northern and Southern Kingdoms within a century, and the Northern Kingdom was conquered and lost to history when the Assyrians dispersed its citizens among its empire toward the end of the eighth century. Jewish history is thus the history of the Southern Kingdom, Judah, from which indeed the very word Jew derives.

The Southern Kingdom managed to withstand Assyrian power, but could not long gainsay the Babylonians who soon subdued the entire Near Eastern world. In 597 Nebuchadnezzar's army conquered Judah, and after an insurrection in 586 he not only recaptured Jerusalem and burned the Temple, but he exiled almost all the remaining inhabitants of the land to Babylonia. When the Babylonians were in turn overthrown by the Persians, the Jews were permitted to return to Jerusalem. The Babylonian Exile came to an end about 534 but only a comparatively small number of Jews elected to leave Babylonia.

The group faced formidable difficulties on resettling in their homeland. The general economy of the country had undergone a serious decline in

---

[1] Harry Orlinsky, *Ancient Israel* (Ithaca: Cornell University Press, 1954), pp. 63-141.

the decades following the conquest and exile. Neighboring peoples encroached on what had been Judean territory and sought to keep a new competitive power from arising. And there were all the difficulties of beginning anew in a place that was dear to them but not abundantly blessed in natural resources for an easy practice of agriculture or trade.

For almost a century they appear to have made but little progress economically, politically, or religiously. Then in the middle of the fifth century two dedicated men came from Babylonia to Jerusalem who changed the destiny of this struggling community for lasting good.

Nehemiah, the political leader, had already held the significant position of cupbearer to the Persian King Artaxerxes II. He asked for and was granted a leave of absence to help his Jewish brothers rebuild Jerusalem. He came to them as their governor with the full authority of the Persian Empire behind him complete with funds, building materials and soldiers. His greatest single act was the rebuilding of the walls of Jerusalem, which made it possible for the city once again to serve as the dominant power of the area. Yet tradition has honored him even more as the protector and enforcer of the reforms of Ezra.

The sources report that Ezra was a "scribe," or more literally, "a man of books." Specifically he was a "scribe in the law of Moses" (the Torah) and "he had set his heart to seek the law of the Lord, and to do it, and to teach in Israel statutes and ordinances." No man before him is described in anything like these terms. We hear of priests, prophets, and seers. There is even mention of persons who wrote down the writings of others, but this category of religious leadership, this sort of professional position was totally unknown. Presumably Jewish life in Babylonia, then well over a century old (and destined to continue in the area with great accomplishment down to the end of the first millenium of this era), had produced a new form of Jewish religious functionary — the man who preserved, copied, studied, and taught the traditions of the people. Clearly in the Exile, away from the ancestral home and the traditional centers of religious practice and instruction, the sagas and statutes of the people had become of central importance to them. Ezra was a product of that development.

The religious situation which confronted him in Jerusalem was disheartening in the extreme. The community had succeeded in erecting a successor building to Solomon's Temple some decades before but the level of its religious practice and passion was modest indeed. Even idolatry, that cardinal sin in Judaism, seems to have flourished. Ezra was faced with the need totally to reconstruct Jewish religious life.

Two unusual factors decisively influenced the way in which he determined to do this. First, was the fact that the Jews were not politically independent. They existed as one community of the great Persian Empire. This was in contrast to pre-Exilic Judaism when the Hebrews were an independent nation. In those days religion was a major element of the nation's culture, but it was one factor among many contributing to its continued existence. In post-Exilic days, with national sovereignty gone, religion was a unifying, integrating force in the life of the people — perhaps even the central factor in assuring its continuity. Ezra's determined effort to rebuild Jewish religious life must be seen against this background of social change.

Yet even more important was the influence of the prophetic tradition. From the time of David and Solomon down to the destruction of Jerusalem in 586 and beyond, there had been prophets who had taught that social immorality would eventually bring about social disaster. The burden of their message repeated again and again was that sinfulness could not long go unpunished. There was a power in the universe that made for righteousness, and it would make itself felt against nations who sought to oppose it. The prophetic vision of disaster visiting the iniquitous state had been fulfilled first in the Northern Kingdom and later in the Southern. To Ezra and all the Jews who inherited the prophetic tradition this was not religious theory. It was historic fact.

Nothing could be more important, then, to Jewish religious life and the continuation of the Jewish community in the Promised Land than their action. Unless the level of their religious observance in the full range of ethical and ritual practice could be assured, this settlement too would be doomed.

But how could such universal practice be achieved? What techniques could be devised which would make it as likely as any social organization could, that the Jews would fulfill their religious obligations? An impressive central sanctuary with a professional priesthood officiating amidst great pomp and with great spectacle had not saved pre-Exilic Jewry. And prophetic exhortation, despite its eloquent and vivid denunciation of the abuses of the day, had not helped. A new approach was required. It was here that the genius of Ezra made itself manifest in an event which the sources (the Biblical Book of Nehemiah, Chapter 8) describe for us in some detail as follows:

And when the seventh month was come, and the children of Israel were in their cities, all the people gathered themselves together as one man into the broad place that was before the water gate; and they spoke unto Ezra the scribe to bring the book of the Law of Moses, which the Lord had commanded to Israel. And Ezra the priest brought the Law before the congregation, both men and women, and all that could hear with understanding, upon the first day of the seventh month. And he read therein before the broad place that was before the water gate from early morning until midday, in the presence of the man of the women, and of those that could understand; and the ears of all the people were attentive unto the book of the

Law. And Ezra the scribe stood upon a pulpit of wood, which they had made for the purpose. . . .

And Ezra opened the book in the sight of all the people — for he was above all the people — and when he opened it, all the people stood up. And Ezra blessed the Lord, the great God. And all the people answered: "Amen, Amen," with the lifting up of their hands; and they bowed their heads, and fell down before the Lord with their faces to the ground. . . . even the Levites, caused the people to understand the Law; and the people stood in their place. And they read in the book in the Law of God, distinctly; and they gave the sense, and caused them to understanding the reading.

It is clear — the text emphasizes it several times in a way that we cannot ignore — that this is not a ceremonial reading or a mere ritual act. This is a functional reading. Its purpose is to make the people understand the sacred law in the hope that they will then do it. Ezra has determined that education is to be the primary instrument for the fulfillment of the Jewish religion. He has begun the practice of the systematic study of the basic religious books with the broad masses of the people. He has begun the longest unbroken tradition of study by a whole people known to Western man, and perhaps all mankind.

Ezra's innovation is a revolution in religion. Before this time the sacred books had been the zealously guarded prerogative of the priests. In many a religion it was precisely their knowledge of the holy texts which set them aside from the laity and gave them their sacerdotal power. To be sure even in the early Hebraic tradition the priests were expected to instruct the people, but this was hardly the full disclosure and the systematic instruction that Ezra instituted. Later tradition affirms, and there is little reason to deny, that this first public reading of the Torah was the beginning of the practice of reading a specified section each Monday and Thursday (market days) as well as on the Sabbath. Later Jewish tradition but built on and extended Ezra's institution of the public reading of the law. It gave institutional and technical elaboration to the basic view taken. It never substantially departed from it. Thus in this act, mediated through Christianity and Islam, the impetus for free, public, universal education has begun.

The Philosophical Position

This historical description gives us the sequence of events. It does not make clear the beliefs, the understandings, the values upon which Ezra and the Jewish tradition which followed him based their attitude toward education. Since it is just here, in the philosophy of education, that Judaism made its greatest though indirect contribution to modern schooling, it is important that we make these basic commitments manifest.

71

Judaism views education as a primary value of human existence. To be a true human being, to fulfill the meaning inherent in life, man needs to study and to learn. This elemental commitment to the importance of education stems from the Hebraic view of the universe and man's place in it.

The Bible is one long trembling response to the overwhelming experience of the intelligibility of the universe. The sky, the earth, man himself, are not entirely mysterious or dumb. They may be understood. They reveal both

Bettmann Archive

JEWISH WISE MAN STUDYING THE TALMUD.

facts and patterns to those who would make the effort to attend to them. The world is not, as it is in some ways of primitive religions, either a malicious, whimsical play thing of the gods, or even their inscrutable, unknowable domain which can only be accepted and perhaps controlled. There is not even, to the Hebraic mind, the disorder of many forces continually in conflict. There is rather an underlying unity to all that man sees and participates in, and this controlling, guiding unity is in significant part knowledgeable by man.

There is another half to this basic commitment, that there is something in men, all men insofar as they are men, which responds to that unity inherent in the universe. Somehow, in a spiritual way, man can reach outside himself, into the universe, and understand its movement and direction. This is not delusion, but a genuine correspondence between man's knowledge and the reality of the world about him. He may not understand it all. He may be wrong on occasion and need to learn more concerning it — many of the Biblical personalities spent their lives in such spiritual growth. Yet the knowledge is certain enough and great enough that a man may, and should, build his life upon it.

In the Hebraic view, no other creature in creation commands this power. None but man can make the cosmic patterns the basis of his own existence. More, in knowing them, in subordinating them to his own will and energy, man becomes the master of creation, or in a more traditional Jewish phrase, "a partner in the work of creation." Thus, knowledge and the use of knowledge distinguish man and mark him as that emergence in evolution which is an animal, yet more than an animal. Only when he has exercised his faculty to comprehend and act upon that comprehension is he truly man.

The Hebrews felt this exalted state was reached not in the search of knowledge for its own sake, regardless of its object. As man is distinguished by knowing so he is distinguished by will. He may choose what he will do. He is free to act as he determines. In that freedom is born man's other special gift, his moral character. He can, if he wills it, do the right, the good, the holy act.

This too astonished the early leaders of Judaism, that man had been given not just consciousness, but consciousness of right and wrong. Man could know what he should, what he ought to do in his relations with his neighbors, his community, and even himself. He could reach out into the universe and discern those patterns of behavior, those standards of action, which were as appropriate to man in his freedom as the physical cycles were for the stars and the tides. No other creature shared this talent, for only man of all the animals was free. And only insofar as man exercised this unique kind of knowing and brought it into action was he truly a man and not a beast. Other kinds of knowledge might be interesting and even important for one's daily life. This knowledge of righteousness, this unique human response to the order basic to the universe, was the crown, the summit of one's humanity.

This view is not limited to one man but describes the condition of all men. We share a common lot. We can learn from one another. We can learn from those who went before us. We can transmit what we have learned to

73

those who will follow us. The essential unity which lies behind the changing face of nature guarantees that knowledge can safely be accumulated, that truth will not change from generation to generation though its means of expression may vary greatly. With the passage of time, events and movements occur of profound and lasting meaning. They speak not only to those of their own day but to men of many, perhaps all, generations which follow. It is not just in personal experience, but in the experience of his clan, his tribe, his nation that the moral meaning of the world becomes clear. The Jew saw in the history of his people, its Exodus from Egypt, its journey to Sinai, its entry into the Promised Land, a special dimension of man's understanding of his role in nature. To reject history was to reject a source of truth. To be a man meant to know and learn from history.

That is not all. As there are special moments in history, heavy with truth, so from time to time there arise sensitive souls, gifted in their ability to know that truth and express it to others. Genius is as precious as it is rare, and as little understood. Yet the Hebrews understood that these men spoke truly and enlarged and enriched other men's consciousness of the truth. Lawgivers, historians, poets, sages, they gave their words to their brothers who treasured them. First by memory, and then in writing, these utterances became the heritage of the entire people. No man need be limited by his own powers of intuition or creative imagination. Through the records of his people's geniuses he could make their exalted thoughts his thoughts, their vaulting understanding part of his own. By study he could stand almost equal with the greatest men of the past and thus make of his life more than what it otherwise could have been, and what potentially it should be.

Such a view of education is classical in its tone. It looks to great men and events of the past. As such it can easily become irrelevant and insignificant, an academician's or an archivist's concern alone. But the Jewish tradition was concerned not only with the past. It was pointed toward the future. It saw man's present situation in history as in need of correction. The unity permeating the universe required a similar unity among men, a harmony and integration of their lives. Injustice and oppression must give way to brotherhood and peace. This was the moral direction of history. This was the goal toward which the efforts of men and peoples in history should be directed. The great men and events of Jewish history were great precisely as they illuminated this goal, as they pointed beyond themselves to what must yet be. The Jew was to study the past as a means of fulfilling the future. Hence, while the education was classic in its conception, it overcame the inertia which such a view may easily engender by its dynamic conception of history as a whole.

It went even further. It insisted that the tradition could grow and develop with the times. This was less true in the realm of law and action, for the basic pattern of the cosmos does not essentially change nor does, therefore, man's essential relation to it. Yet even in this realm Judaism stimulated individual study and research as a means of adjusting older practices to new conditions, or of answering previously unasked questions about the way a man should live. Far greater freedom was found in the realm of ideas where Judaism, with the most widespread negative limits, permitted a variety of thought and expression that leaves today's student who is accustomed to look for unity in all fields, gasping with astonishment. Thus, there is no single authoritative Jewish commentary to the Bible. The typical study text is printed with the notes of more than a dozen commentators whose range in time (including the Aramaic translation) is over a thousand years and stems from Jewish communities in the lands of Israel, Spain, France, Poland and perhaps Italy, Lithuania, and Germany, to mention some of the most likely places.

Thus, each generation was called on not only to study the tradition, but to interpret it, to expound its meaning in terms of the questions of its own day. And it had the responsibility which preceding generations had already so well fulfilled, not just to transmit the heritage, but to add to it as well. Education was thus a part of history, not merely a personal affair. It contains a creative, contributive element as well as a strong classical strain.

In all of this it is essential to note that education has not been an end in itself but rather a means to an end. Education is important as a means to living the full, the good, the desirable life. It is essentially life-centered, though it is more interested in the ideal life than in the practical realities of what is now being done. Education has its high value in Judaism because together with prayer and faith (though Judaism talks little about the latter, preferring actions to talk) it is considered a primary means of achieving proper action. Education is then the key by which the Jews have built the ethics of living for God.

In the post-Freudian world there is often considerable doubt as to the efficacy of knowledge in influencing action. So much of motivation is unconscious that rationality seems to play but a modest part in shaping behavior. No one can claim that the older Jewish tradition knew of emotional education or re-education as a primary means of producing the healthy act. As in so many life-centered religions it had its occasional intuitions and insights. Today the psychiatric understanding of behavior is largely accepted within the context of Judaism, as the large number of Jewish psychiatrists would indicate.

Though the efficacy of knowledge has been qualified in our time, it has not been denied. Indeed, psychiatry is the effort to translate the realm of the intuitive and emotional to a rationally ordered form and thus bring it under man's control. To the extent that man is healthy, to the extent that he is man, it is knowledge which is his main tool to guide his purpose. From the Jewish point of view, nothing has changed with its basic affirmation about education, that man must be educated to live as a man; even though the scope of that education or the effective preconditions for rational enlightenment are now differently conceived.

As a matter of fact, the Jewish tradition not only considered study a positive guide, it thought of it also as a form of therapy. The Jewish tradition knows the problem of sin well, not only because of its candor toward its own leaders (as witnessed to by the honesty of the Biblical accounts of the sins of some of its greatest personalities) but because of what the Jewish group has been made to suffer through the sinfulness of others. How can evil behavior be avoided, if not entirely, then in significant part? — through study and knowledge of what the universe calls one to be and do.

This is a form of therapy hardly suited to the deep-rooted ills of our day — but it may say more of what complex industrial societies have done to depersonalize and dehumanize man than it says of the adequacy of education in maintaining the healthy, positive personality in another day. In any case, it is clear that knowledge of the right still has an important role to play in averting the unrighteous deed.

It is no accident that, as yet, there has been no discussion of the education of children or youth. The Jewish view of education encompasses them but it does not begin and certainly cannot end with them. Everything that has been said so far indicates that to Judaism education is a continuing function of being human, not a function of a given age or stage of life. Therefore, education is primarily required by those who claim to be mature. It is they who are supposed to be living life at its fullest; hence it is precisely they who require education the most. Not that it is to preempt all of their life. Education is a means toward living, not life itself, except to the few complete scholars. Yet it must be basic to man's adult existence, an integral part of his way of life.

It can terminate only with life itself. All his life he will read and think and learn and ponder. From the Jewish point of view education never ends. It has no terminal ceremony. Thus one should not really say a man is "educated," implying somehow that he has fulfilled what is expected of him. One would more appropriately say that he is "learned," indicating that he has accomplished much, though not all that he may yet do.

This view is reflected in the popular image of "the good Jew." In countless woodcuts and paintings, and in the minds of many who have known Jews, the "good Jew" is somehow an old man with a book. The continuity of Judaism's view of education, its insistence that one cannot know enough, is thus unconsciously depicted in this highly symbolic figure. And even in the case where the pictures give us a young boy or man, he is almost certain to be a *yeshivo* student, a pupil at the rabbinic academy, beginning to give his life to study. These are the characteristic figures of art with Jewish subjects, and they illustrate Jewish philosophy as well.

This view is reflected as well in the major institutions which Jews created for the purpose of education.[2] Foremost of these is the regular study of scripture as a part of the divine service. Traditional Jewish worship does not exist without the inclusion of strong didactic elements. Even in the briefer services the quotations from the Book of Psalms are as much study as they are adoration and thanksgiving, and the same is even more true of the miscellanies of verses which are often used. Special insertions of post-Biblical study materials are a regular feature of the daily morning service. On the market days of older times, Monday and Thursday, and on Sabbaths, Festivals and Holy Days, the scripture is not only read but expounded. Jewish law goes so far as to say, in discussing the prayers required of the religious Jew, that study may substitute for most prayer.

Study even transforms part of the synagogue. Wherever possible, in the traditional synagogue, there is not only a main sanctuary, but also a somewhat smaller room set aside for the daily service and the daily study. This is the more intimate atmosphere of what came to be known as the *bes ha-midrosh*, "the house of study." It was this room that the synagogue regulars came to know and love as they did their own home. Here were the bookcases filled with the familiar volumes. Here were the study stands or the benches and tables where the study went on. This was not a children's school but an organic part of the synagogue for its adult worshippers and it was a significant center of their lives as individuals and a community as well.

In this environment there grew and developed the *chevro,* the regular group of men who would meet to study even briefly some text that fitted their capacity. Early in the morning before the daily toil, or late in the Sabbath afternoon, the simplest would be reading the Book of Psalms. Others might be studying the basic code of Jewish law or the legends and folklore of the Talmud. Whatever the subject, this was a free association of adults, continuing their study, without professional guidance, in a give and take of knowledge or opinion, for no other reason than that to be a man meant to continue to learn.

The advanced student, anxious to continue his studies with his equals would leave the simple *bes ha-midrosh* and go to a *yeshivo.* The *yeshivo* was a more formalized center of instruction, centering about the great rabbinic personality who was its head. Here there might be young students in great number, but by the standards of the day they were already young

---

[2] Greenberg, Simon, "Jewish Educational Institutions," *The Jews.* Jewish Publication Society, Philadelphia, 1949, pp. 919-925.

men. And the *yeshivo* would be heavily populated with men of varying ages continuing their study as did indeed the head of the *yeshivo* himself.

Education for the child, as Judaism sees it, can only be considered within this context. His education may include vocational education but it must be more than that. It must in essence be education to continue education throughout life. His training may make it possible for him to participate as a good citizen of his society but this in turn implies that he will be able to participate in its continuing educational endeavors. His years of study are but a prelude to more years of study, not a course to be completed so that life may begin. Even historically, as we shall see below, the institutions of adult study preceded those for children.

Nor did this lessen the value attached to the child's study. The fact that there was no proximate goal for Jewish education until very recent times did not make it less important. To the contrary, the fact that this program was to be basic to all the rest of one's life endowed it with a supreme significance which, despite the most radically altered circumstances, it still largely holds today.

This should not be difficult to appreciate even in a culture where education is generally considered a short term means to a degree or a job — and thus freedom from education. In the Judaic view, not just the child's immediate future, but his whole life, is bound up with his education. Not just his livelihood but his destiny is involved in what he does or does not accomplish as a child. On this foundation will his adult life rest, and only upon this youthful study can he hope to erect the structure of his continuing adult learning. The ignorant child may make his way successfully in the business and social world, but that is only the beginning not the fullness of life. By being unable to continue his learning he has cut himself off from a major means of becoming what he was intended to be. His humanity is incomplete.

The child's education is particularly significant to the parents because if man is the educated animal, then the greatest man is the most fully educated. The scholar occupies a uniquely exalted position in the Jewish community. He is, precisely by his scholarship, its leader and commanding figure. Let his scholarship be sufficiently great and, without ecclesiastical organization or sacramental power, he will become the guide and director of Jewish communities far from his own. To be the author of widely read books, to be the head of a highly regarded academy, to be the judge and arbiter of claims and questions sent from distant parts, these are the signs of the great man.

Every child has before him the possibility of such attainment. Though his parents may be of limited education or intelligence there is yet the possibility that he may be something more. No one can tell what he may yet become until he is given the opportunity to prove himself in study. Hence, the education of the child, of every child, may open a whole world to him, whether his parents were part of it or not. No wonder then that this very long range view of education stimulated and aroused the passion to educate the child, though such education was but an introductory step to the more critical education of the adult.

It should also be clear then that since this view of education sees it as required by man as man, it should not be limited to one special group. Education is not the luxury of the wealthy, nor the prerogative of a caste or class. It is a basic necessity for all mankind. It is a universal value. It took some time before this position was fully expressed in institutional form, though by the early days of the Christian Church this was already recognized as an essential goal.

As far as adults were concerned the attitude symbolized in the reading of the Scripture at the synagogue service was easily extended to the adult academies where the great masters taught. Though fees were charged at an early stage, these schools by the end of the first century A.D. were free for all who would attend. There are frequent rabbinic comments bidding the masters take heed of the children of the poor, for from them come great scholars. And great is the disdain for a master who will not freely and willingly teach of what he knows to anyone who would learn.

This does not, as was typical of the Near East and most other cultures until modern times, include women.[3] Their social role may be vital (and there are good grounds for affirming that Judaism gave her a far more positive place in society than most of the contemporary cultures in which Jews have lived down to the nineteenth century) but it is ancillary to that of man. One simply does not think of her in the same terms as man. Her fulfillment is in the family and the home, in serving her husband well. Such education as she requires is to be derived from this attitude, and only in modern times, as part of its emancipation from the ghetto and its entrance into the life of general society, has the Jewish community given equality of status and education to its women. Now, as a logical extension of its commitment to education as a universal value, Judaism has eagerly extended it to its girls and women, though in some areas vestiges of the older tradition remain.

For children it was originally hoped that the family would be the major channel of instruction. Surely almost every father would want his child to develop to the fullest and if this involved study and understanding of the traditions of the people then the father would instruct his child in these as in so much else. Here the natural will was linked with the Biblical command-

---

[3]Nathan Drazin, *History of Jewish Education* (Baltimore: The Johns Hopkins Press 1940), pp. 119-128. This volume covers this ground in the most favorable way but the author cannot overcome his own data.

ment "Thou shalt teach them diligently unto thy children and speak of them when thou sittest in thy house, when thou walkest by the way, when thou liest down and when thou risest up." In theory this should have assumed the education of every child. Yet as society became increasingly complex, as the matters to be studied became increasingly great, the less was the father adequately able to fulfill the role of teacher. The professional teacher and the class composed of many children of different families became the primary vehicle of instructing the young. At first, such instruction was the privilege of the wealthy, but again the commitment to the universal need for education asserted itself and the community saw to it that whenever possible no child should be denied his passage to human fulfillment, but that education should be available to all.[4] Education had become a primary responsibility of the Jewish community, one it has given high priority in unbroken expression down to the present day.

This never, however, became the basis for relieving the family of its own responsibility to educate. To do so would have been in effect to deny the parents their major responsibility for the growth and development of their offspring. This the Jewish tradition would not allow. The community might have its role to play in seeing that all children received an education, but it was a role which was acted out with the families. Thus, the community might regulate the conditions of instruction, the requirements of instructors or the extent of financial responsibility. It may also have established schools for the children of the poor or needy. It did not abolish the system of the instructor who ran his own school and was paid directly by the parent for the elementary instruction of his child. (Advanced study in the *yeshivo* had a far larger measure of communal support though it still retained its essentially private school nature.)

This institutional pattern was matched by a personal commitment. The Jewish family accepted as one of its primary responsibilities the need and importance of educating its children. It is somewhat startling but instructive to observe that, in the prayers read at the circumcision of eight-day-old boys, one is recited which calls for the family to be able to help them enter into "study, marriage and good deeds." So early are the basic values set forth. Though the father increasingly came to leave teaching to the professional, and though community concern for education was greatly increased as the centuries went by, the pattern of primary familial responsibility, with community effort as secondary, remained basic to the Jewish education of children.

---

[4] Nathan Morris, *The Jewish School* (London: Eyre and Spottiswoods, 1937), pp. 42-45. For a touching description of the ceremony of indoctrination to formal schooling that reveals the import of education to the ancient Jews, see *Train Up a Child: Educational Ideals in the Ancient World* by William Barclay (Philadelphia: Westminster Press, 1959), pp. 12-13.

In very broad strokes, this picture of an essentially rational universe inhabited by essentially intelligible men, who have the unique capacity to understand and cooperate with its governing power particularly in its moral requirements, elaborated through history in great events and by great men, made education a universal and highly regarded value. This value each family sought to fulfill for the young under the guidance and encouragement of the community and it remained a continuing life goal for all adults.

The Religious Dimension

The philosophic picture given above may be true to Judaism's intentions. Its language and perhaps even its spirit would be strange to most learned Jews of the past. This exposition has been in essentially secular terms, and despite its diversity of expression and the broad range of its involvements Judaism is a religious phenomenon. It is primarily the relation of the Household of Israel to the God of the universe as expressed in the life of Torah (here not just the constitution read by Ezra, but all the tradition which has followed on it as well). Thus, to speak of education, a critical component of that way of life (indeed so closely bound up with it that "Torah" is often used in the sense of "study" as in the circumcision prayer cited above), without speaking of God would truly be false. Yet it is just this separation of what are essentially religiously derived values from their religious roots which has characterized modern times. It is not the intention of this chapter to abet that movement. Rather, by making this translation of concepts, it is hoped that the origins of much contemporary educational thinking, though it proceeds in other terms may be made clear.

It is necessary to consider Jewish educational thought in the full context of their religious beliefs and man's relation to God — there is a single God for the entire universe (in itself an astounding declaration for the days 2,500 or more years ago) who has created an orderly universe with man as its most extraordinary creature. For God has made man in His image, rational, moral, conscious, so that man can know, understand, and control the universe. He can become God's partner, His co-creator. More, God has revealed Himself and His will to man in general and the people of Israel in particular. He gave His law and instruction to Israel at Sinai and has sent prophets and teachers to guide them in the generations which have followed. Thus, there are books which authentically speak in His name, and each generation since has had its sages who have added to the Torah-tradition. To live in God's image, to know His will, to be enabled to do it, involves education. To be religious, from the Jewish point of view, involves study. The process of learning is a religious duty and education is God's commandment.

For the believing Jew, education is not just a "value" — a term beloved in contemporary discussion primarily because of its abstract apparently objective and dispassionate character. It is rather a matter of his personal, intimate relationship with that God who orders and rules the universe. Study is a means of clarifying and intensifying one's relation with Him. It leads to a greater understanding of what it means to serve Him and thus to live in terms of the divinity inherent within one. Study is itself His service in a way analogous to prayer, and, because essentially rational, almost always available to those who seek Him. Where education becomes service to and communion with the source of one's being and of all being, a profound dimension of personal involvement is added to it.[5] This may perhaps explain the unparalleled devotion of the Jewish people to study over the centuries. In modern times, the absence of faith to ground and integrate the whole has made education useful for life and enriching but still not critical for existence. Education is important but not a necessary personal obligation and irreplaceable part of the good life.

Influence of the Jewish View

Had this attitude toward education remained confined to the Jewish group then this chapter would be interesting as an example of one small people's feelings in this area. But Judaism did not only retain its point of view, it transmitted it to Christianity and Islam. Though each religion in turn transformed this Jewish view in terms of its own individual view of man and God, nonetheless their point of departure and their basic direction seem clearly to derive from their Jewish origins.

The Christian church is not fully intelligible without a knowledge of its roots in the synagogue. Many of the early Christian churches of the Near East grew out of the synagogues which Paul and other missionaries naturally visited on their travels. And the picture of Jesus as a man of the synagogue, reading from the scrolls of the prophets and expounding their meaning, also had its effect. Christianity too was a religion of historical growth. If anything, it was even more dependent upon the historical record than Judaism, for it required the Jewish experience to justify the coming of a messiah and the Christian experience to indicate that Jesus of Nazareth was indeed the Man who fulfilled these expectations. The Jewish practice of knowing and studying scripture was thus renewed and extended, and the church and its schools, as places where scripture was read and expounded, became a per-

---

[5] For a more secular view of the basic Jewish attitude, though one which cannot avoid the religious, see Maller, Julius, "The Role of Education in Jewish History," *The Jews,* Jewish Publication Society, 1949, pp. 897-898.

manent feature of Christianity.[6] It would seem that the development of the life of the sacraments and Paul's view of faith in Christ as basic to Christian existence made possible a different view of the laity's need of education than that posed by Judaism. Still, the basic Jewish commitment to knowledge was in its own way taken over and extended in traditional Christianity.

In another way the same may be said of Islam.[7] Though Mohammed and his earliest followers were not Jews both by birth and training as the earliest Christians were, still the Prophet knew Jews and Judaism and Christians as well. From such knowledge much of his revolution in religion can be traced. Thus the absolute emphasis on the unity of God which so distinguished Islam from anything previously known on the Arabian Peninsula seems part of Judaism's bequest to it. Likewise, its essential scripturalism is Judaism's gift, for Mohammed seems clearly to have recognized the importance of having a religion based on a book. (This lies behind the tradition of his having been the one first to call the Jewish people, the people of the Book.) While study was not made one of the cardinal religious duties of every Moslem, it is the reading of the Koran on Friday which is the high point of the special service in the mosque. And the study and memorization of the chapters of the Koran has been a highly regarded act. Judaism, therefore, sees its scriptural and educational emphasis transmitted through Islam.

The Jewish influence upon Martin Luther and the Reformation as a whole was far from indirect. Yet Judaism can easily see in Luther's emphasis on the study of the Scripture a turn in the practice of Christianity which brings it closer to its own view. Luther's very translation of the Bible into German so that the ordinary Christian might possess the Book and his stress upon preaching the Gospel to the people seem very much like Ezra's own reforms. The emphasis which grew through the Reformation that each man should search the Bible for himself that he might be assured that he had indeed found the road to salvation—an emphasis which was eventually to help create free, public education — is a parallel to the Jewish insistence upon education as a universal value.

It should not be surprising that, having adopted in their own way the Jewish view of the unity of God, of His revealing Himself, and of His presence in history, Catholic Christianity, Islam, and Protestant Christianity, carried on its educational interest.

---

[6] F. C. Burkitt, "The Debt of Christianity to Judaism," *The Legacy of Israel* (London: Oxford, 1927), p. 71ff., though he is inclined to limit the influence as much as possible.

[7] Alfred Giullaume, "The Influence of Judaism on Islam," *The Legacy of Israel* (London: Oxford, 1927), pp. 129ff.

Historical Development

Let us then trace the way in which their own basic view was expressed in the history of the Jewish people. While what can be said here must of necessity be brief and episodic, it will perhaps serve to indicate how a people which has lived under the most diverse geographic and political circumstances for many centuries has yet managed to preserve its educational philosophy and express it in the life of its community. Particular attention must be paid to the fact that for most of its post-Biblical history, the Jews have not been on the land of Israel as part of their own culture but have been widely scattered about the world as a minority group, frequently subjected to oppression and persecution. Yet rather than take on the educational standards of the majority culture, which were less demanding, they clung to their own, which in turn served them as a signal means of preserving their people.

The origins of Jewish educational practice are by now lost to us. The earlier books of the Bible make occasional references to informal, familial and occupational training. One cannot find any explicit references to schools, academies or other formal institutions of instruction. What little we know seems to indicate that the priests were supposed to be the instructors of the people, but we have no data concerning what they did, only an occasional complaint against them.[8]

It is only in the post-Exilic period, particularly after the time of Ezra, that a more overt educational emphasis makes itself felt. The internal motivation has already been made clear. An external factor soon made its effect felt, particularly since it was based upon the expanding economic base of the growing community. This new force was Hellenism, which may be said to have come to the Land of Israel about 333 B.C. with Alexander's march to India. The Hellenistic educational ideal, with its tutors and its schools, with its love of wisdom, was grafted on to the Jewish love of learning, though not without conflict and evaluation.

This newer attitude towards education is epitomized in the Book of Proverbs. Here, for example, are two typical exhortations to learning:

> Happy is the man that findeth wisdom,
> And the man that obtaineth understanding . . .
> Her ways are ways of pleasantness
> And all her paths are peace (*Prov. 3:13, 18*).
>
> Get wisdom, get understanding . . .
> Yea, with all thy getting get understanding . . .

---

[8] Maller, *op. cit.*, p. 898.

I have taught thee in the way of wisdom . . .
Take fast hold of instruction, let her not go;
Keep her, for she is thy life (*Prov. 4:4, 13*).

Some scholars are convinced that the bulk of this book is what the tutors of the sons of the wealthy families actually taught in the Hellenistic period. Thus, while the book itself makes no direct mention of schools and instruction, the imagined setting of the chapters would make this supposition highly likely. Naturally these authorities base their opinions largely on what was transpiring in other communities where the influence of Hellenistic culture was making itself felt in just such ways. The picture is entirely consistent with what else is known to us of the development Judaism underwent in those days.[9]

Not only are the sources silent on the education of youth, they only hint at the growth and development of the class of scribes and teachers which developed into a party in community affairs and gave rise to the academies in which the scholars met to study and debate. There is good reason to believe that by the first century B.C. this advanced level of learning was already well established as a feature of Jewish life. Its primary concern was the exposition of the Torah, the first five books of the Bible, and the "Constitution" of the Jewish way of life. With this there went the discussion and elucidation of the oral traditions which had been handed down from one generation to another. The concern of both aspects of the study was to clarify the contemporary implications of the teaching. And this process of question and answer, of exposition and rejoinder, was open to any of the adult members of the community who wished to devote themselves to this pursuit of knowledge. For this was not an association of professional scholars. Each had his regular secular vocation. They studied because of the value they placed on study and because of its meaning in their lives.

It is within this context of a vigorous, advanced, adult education that we must see the earliest explicit references to an effort to create communal institutions for the education of the young. In what follows, citation is made from that broad variety of writings known as "rabbinic literature." These writings were compiled in their present form primarily between 200 and 500 A.D., though they contain authentic traditions going back several hundred years before. In this voluminous and encyclopedic literature a fully articulated attitude and program is revealed, though nowhere is it presented in systematic or chronological form. While there are numerous scholarly problems in interpreting the citations (particularly in judging whether a rabbinic statement is meant, as so often it is, in a hyperbolic sense, or whether it

---

[9] Morris, *op. cit.*, p. 12.

represents an objective report of things), a reasonably integrated attitude toward education is present.[10]

The rabbis credit Simon ben Shetach, who was at the height of his leadership about the year 75 B.C., with establishing schools for older youths, at about sixteen years of age. While little more is reported to us of this institution, it seems to have been community sponsored instruction analogous to what the sons of the wealthy were receiving at the hands of their tutors. What is significant concerning it is the effort to bring education down from the adult level to that of the youth and the active recognition of the role of the community in aiding the parents who for financial or other reasons could not fulfill the obligation to teach their children.

The next step is reported to us in a paragraph which must be considered the pivotal source for the history of Jewish education for the young:

> Truly that man is to be remembered for good, Joshua ben Gamala is his name, but for whom the Torah would have been forgotten among Israel. Because formerly he who had a father was taught by him the Torah; but he who had no father did not learn it. On what Biblical verse was this based? "And you shall teach them diligently unto they children" was interpreted to mean "and you yourselves shall teach." Then it was arranged that teachers of children should be placed in Jerusalem. On what Biblical verse was this based? "For out of Zion shall go forth the Torah, and the word of the Lord from Jerusalem." Still he who had a father was taken up by him to Jerusalem to be taught; he who had no father did not go up to learn. Then it was arranged that the pupils should be admitted at the age of sixteen or seventeen. But he with whom his teacher got angry rebelled and left. Until Joshua ben Gamala came and arranged that teachers should be placed in every province and every city and that the pupils should be admitted at the age of six or seven.[11]

Here the historical sequence is set forth as follows: first familial instruction; then schools centrally located in Jerusalem; then district schools for the sixteen year olds (the creation of Simon ben Shetach). When this latter system failed because of the maturity of the pupils a further extension was made. Joshua ben Gamala, a High Priest active in the middle and first century A.D., established schools in the various districts of the land for children age six or seven. Again, these are schools sponsored by the community, for any of its children who are not yet receiving instruction. While the year of admission tended to become lower, this became the standard Jewish educational prac-

---

[10] A good summary of the various opinions about the origins of Jewish elementary schools, based on the same data, is to be found in Ebner, Eliezer, *Elementary Education in Ancient Israel* (New York: Bloch, 1956), pp. 38-42. Shortly before the time of Christ, the scribes had come to be called "rabbi," loosely translated as "teacher."

[11] *The Babylonian Talmud,* Baba Bathra, 21a.

tice from that day to the present in unbroken succession. The pattern of free education, made available to all boys by the community, had begun.

The scholars still debate vigorously how universal this education became among the Jews in the early centuries of this era.[12] Yet even those who deny this assertion (on the ground that such education was not compulsory and hence was not truly universal) agree that there was strong social pressure exerted by the community to have children attend and complete the work. The effect was that of universal education. Thus a fourth century scholar could say, "Is it possible to find anyone without an elementary education? Yes, if a child was taken captive and raised among the nations." So too, the late first century historian Josephus, defending the Jews against some anti-Semitic slanders comments:

> Indeed, the greatest part of mankind are so far from living according to their own laws, that they hardly know them; but when they have sinned they learn from others that they have transgressed the law.
>
> Our principal care of all is this, to educate our children well; and we think it to be the most necessary business of our whole life to observe the laws that have been given us, and to keep those rules of piety that have been delivered down to us.
>
> Our legislator (Moses) carefully joined the two methods of instruction together; for he neither left the practical exercises to go on without verbal instruction, nor did he permit the hearing of the law to proceed without the exercises for practice.[13]

Similar comments reflecting the Jewish attitude may be found in the Alexandrian Jewish philosopher of some decades earlier, Philo.

The responsibility of the community in this regard was taken very seriously by the rabbis. Thus, Rabbi Simon bar Yochai, a second century sage could say, "If you have seen communities in the land which were uprooted from their places, know that it happened because they did not pay the Bible and Mishnah (oral legal traditions) teachers." The legal ruling in this regard was that to pay such teachers "a community can impose a tax . . . upon residents who have lived there no less than twelve months." Exaggeration is also encountered in making this point clear. Thus we read, "A scholar is not permitted to live in a town where there are no elementary teachers" and "Any town where there are no schools should be destroyed."

The basic attitude involved here is graphically presented in this rabbinic comment on one's important relationship:

> If a man and his father and his teacher are in captivity, he himself takes precedence over his teacher (for the purpose of being ransomed); his teacher

---

[12] Ebner, *op. cit.,* p. 49.

[13] Josephus, *Against Apion,* Book I, Section 12, and Book II, Section 19.

is to be ransomed before his father; but his mother is to take precedence over all. The sage is to be ransomed before the king. If a sage die, we have no other one like him; if a king die all Israel are fit for the crown.[14]

Rabbi Akiba, of the first half of the second century, who became one of the most influential and seminal figures in the development of the tradition was held up as an example for all to follow:

> What was the beginning of Rabbi Akiba? It is said that when he was already forty years old he had not yet learned anything. Once, when he stood by a well he asked "Who bored out that stone?" So they told him, "Akiba, did you not read (in Job) 'the waters wear away the stone?' The water which steadily falls on it did it." Immediately Rabbi Akiba began to argue with himself, saying "If a soft thing like the water, could hew out a hard thing, like the stone, then the words of the Torah, which are as hard as iron, will certainly bore through my heart, which is only flesh and blood." Then he and his son went and sat before an elementary teacher.[15]

Here the emphasis on education as an adult necessity for all men is clear, as is the importance of an elementary education as the means of reaching the fuller goal.

The general curriculum by which the student progressed has been preserved for us. While it says nothing of what the child may be expected to have learned at home, it is reasonable to assume that he entered upon his studies with some familiarity with Jewish religious observance and some rote knowledge of the blessings said in the home. As for the structure of studies in the school, the statement is made early in the rabbinic tradition: "At five years the age is reached for the study of Scripture, at ten for the study of Mishnah (the oral, legal traditions), at thirteen for the responsible observance of the commandments, at fifteen for the study of Talmud (the advanced discussion of the meaning and application of the Mishnah traditions, both areas which were later reduced to writing and became bodies of literature rather than oral traditions)."[16]

In all probability "Scripture" should be understood here as comprising a broad area of skills and knowledge. Thus the educational development almost certainly began with learning the alphabet and the technique of reading. (Rabbi Akiba goes so far as to remind parents to be certain to teach their children only from correctly copied manuscripts.) There is also reason to believe that it involved the study of the prayer service, since its usage in the synagogue became firmly established in the first centuries of

---

14 *The Babylonian Talmud,* Horayoth, 13a.

15 *Aboth D'Rabbi Nathan,* 6.29.

16 Ebner, *op. cit.,* pp. 74-84, and Drazin, *op. cit.,* p. 88. The quotation is from *The Babylonian Talmud,* Aboth 5.21.

this era. And, as the general name given to this step indicates, to the study of the Bible, with primary emphasis upon the first five books and then on the Prophets and Writings. Schools for this purpose were generally called *"Bes Ha-sefer,"* or in the Aramaic of the later centuries of this period, *"Bes Sifro"* or *"Bes Mikro,"* literally "House of the Book." They are also referred to as *"Bes Ha-kenesses"* (Aramaic *"Bes Kenishto"*), "the House of Assembly." While the former is easy enough to understand, the latter derives from the fact that many of the elementary schools were housed in the synagogue of the community.

The next level was reached in a separate institution called the *"Bes Talmud,"* "the Talmud School." Here the word *Talmud* is used in a very wide sense, for these schools almost certainly dealt mainly with the basic oral traditions called *Mishnah* and only the advanced students continued on to the discussions as to the application of these traditions which was what *Talmud* in its more limited sense referred to. When the *Mishnah* was authoritatively codified about the year 200, the separation of the studies became clearer. In turn the *Talmud* was recorded and that scope of study also became more specifically delimited (though since one cannot study *Talmud* except in relation to the *Mishnah* traditions, the term generally includes both the *Mishnah* and the *Gemoro,* the discussions proper). As communities warranted, separate schools were available for these two levels, or the older students were sent to larger centers for the study of *Talmud.*

The summit of the entire system was the rabbinic academy, in which the adults who reached this level participated in reviewing and clarifying the traditions of the past, particularly in terms of their extension to meet the needs of the present or in the light of specific cases which came before the academies for decision. A somewhat romantic source gives us an approximation of the ratio of persons involved at each of the levels:

> Usually a thousand enter the study of the Bible; of these one hundred proceed to the Mishnah; of these 10 go forward to the study of the Talmud; and only one of the whole number obtains the position of a recognized scholar.[17]

From a number of citations it seems reasonable to assume that thirteen was thought of as the usual age for ending one's studies unless one was gifted. Yet to what extent this was a normal expectation is not known to us.

For those who did not attain the higher levels there was the intellectual life involved in regular attendance at the synagogue and in such of its educational activities for which they had the time and ability. Many probably received training for their occupations since the rabbis highly esteemed labor.

---

[17] *Koheleth Rabbah,* 7.

Unfortunately we do not know much about such education but we do know the emphasis placed upon it. So it is said, "Just as a man is required to teach his son Torah, so is he required to teach him a trade" and "He who does not teach his son a trade is as if he had taught him to be a thief." In this connection it is important to bear in mind that even the scholars of the great academies were not professionals. They too had their trades or businesses but balanced their economic activities with a greater devotion to study and learning.[18]

Women's education was limited strictly to her needs to administer a home. Only one voice is raised among the rabbis calling for fathers to educate their daughters in Torah. (It should be added, the author of that comment was a bachelor.) In general it was assumed that their mothers would teach them what they needed to know for their household and child-rearing role. A typical comment, generous in its praise but precise in its delimitation of woman's role, is Rav's comment to Rabbi Chiyo: "How do women gain merit? By making their children learn the Scriptures in the synagogue and their husbands learn the oral traditions in the house of study."[19]

Another limitation of Jewish educational practice should be noted, its ban against secular studies. There is no question that Greek was widely known and used in the Land of Israel in the Hellenistic period and that access to Greek literature and science was possible for the Jews. A number of rabbis are known to have possessed such knowledge, yet the official Jewish educational program never included the Greek or Latin disciplines. In part this was a reaction to the oppression they suffered at the hands of their Roman masters. It must also have been due to their attitude toward their own tradition. Jewish study was bound up with the ethical service of the one God. The secular disciplines were as intimately involved with idolatry and a pagan outlook on life. Moreover, the Jewish tradition incorporated much of what is called "secular" in its own understanding of what is properly the "religious." Law and jurisprudence, history and poetry, all were part of Judaism. The sciences were important not in their own right, but as instruments for understanding or fulfilling the divine instruction. One cannot apply the Torah to life as the *Talmud* continually seeks to do without being involved in many branches of knowledge ranging from arithmetic to zoology.[20]

By the fourth century Jewish educational patterns for the young were well established. All schools were held in the synagogue and almost every synagogue had its schools. Most of these were operated on a private basis, with parent paying the teacher directly. The community, however, had strict

---

[18] Drazin, *op. cit.*, p. 140.

[19] Ebner, *op. cit.*, p. 35.

[20] *Ibid.*, p. 84ff.

control over the teacher who was considered a public servant. Thus he was invited to come to the city by the community and he could be discharged by the community for neglect. School and synagogue had become the indispensable co-workers in fixing and fulfilling the destiny of the Jewish people through the difficult centuries it has had to face down to this day. Until after the French revolution the basic pattern of Jewish education and its curriculum remained relatively unchanged, so true to its ideals did Judaism consider this educational pattern.

The pattern of adult education was likewise well settled by this time. It centered about the regular reading and exposition of the Torah at the synagogue services. A number of rabbis are highly praised in the literature of the period as teachers on this popular level and an entire literature called the *midrash* (the exposition) grew out of this practice. The synagogue served as a house of study on other occasions as well and the practice of informal groups meeting to continue their study together seems to have become common. Such a pattern was encouraged and stimulated by the presence of a recognized scholar in the community. Often his teaching would provide the basis for the growth of an academy as young students would come to hear him teach the tradition and lead the religious court in deciding the cases brought before it. (Again the term "religious" is used in the all-encompassing sense which has been referred to above.) Occasionally such a scholar in the Land of Israel would become widely recognized as one of the leaders of the generation and his academy would be thronged with both ordinary students and other scholars who would seek to benefit from his wisdom. The highest of all such academies was the one presided by the *Nasi* (the prince) which was recognized as the legitimate successor to the Sanhedrin in the period following the first Jewish rebellion against Rome (in the year 67). This deliberative body was composed of recognized rabbinic authorities who debated and studied Jewish law and ruled authoritatively on it. Significantly, it had its own origins in the academy of Rabbi Yochanan ben Zakkai, for study and life, education and legislation went hand in hand. Though the organization of Jewish adult study changed with time, the essential thrust established in these centuries did not deviate perceptibly in turn until after 1800. This was an essential, unvarying ingredient of Jewish life wherever it might take place.

Perhaps the point can be made most clearly by saying without much exaggeration, there never was a dark age in Jewish history. Though the center of Jewish life moved from the land of Israel to many another land, and though Judaism lived thenceforth as a minority among peoples who considered it peculiar, there was no center without its record of a vigorous intellectual and educational life, without its scholars and its new books. Indeed, before the Renaissance the average Jew could always read and write, which is more than can be said of the ordinary layman of the Middle Ages.[21]

Take for example the Jewish experience in Babylonia from the fifth century on, a dark period indeed in European history. Here the Jewish educational activity known to us from the Land of Israel was continued and in certain ways extended. The sources tell us that it was customary among Babylonian Jewry for the adults to spend two months a year in study, generally at either of the two principal academies. The *Kallo,* as the assembly was called, would convene for a month in the Spring and a month in the Fall, presumably at a time when the largely agricultural population would be expected to do so. Apparently each month was devoted to the discussion of one of the tractates of the *Talmud.* (Some scholars are convinced that it was the preparation of the relevant materials in a given area for these Kallas that sped the transition from the *Talmud* as oral tradition to a written collection.) Since students came from various sections of the country an impetus was thus given to the study of the rabbinic tradition for the rest of the year. The sources report attendance to have been by the thousands. In addition, the sources indicate that special written materials relevant to the Kallas were prepared by the heads of the academies for transmission to communities which could not be represented. It is not clear how long the *Kallo* tradition continued but the chief Babylonian academies produced scholars and guided the course of world Jewry until the eleventh century.[22]

The next major center of Jewish life was in Moslem Spain beginning in the tenth century, building into what has been called a Golden Age and slowly declining from the thirteenth century on. The outstanding feature of this extraordinary era is the relatively full participation of Jews in the cultural life of their day. Though the Christian countries in which they lived had tended to isolate and contain their Jewish communities intellectually (and would do so with ever greater stringency until the French Revolution) the Moslems in Spain had but slight restrictions for their Jewish population. Since this period brought about a glorious flowering of Islamic civilization and there were many points of mutual interest in these two basically Semitic cultures, the Jews likewise rose to a great moment in their intellectual development and literary expression.

Under these happy circumstances the Jewish educational ideal expanded beyond its traditional scope. A number of authors devised programs of education which added to the old program of studies every major aspect of the Arabic-Hellenistic revival, algebra, astronomy, optics, biology, philosophy, and the like. More important, the outstanding Jews of this period were men who

---

[21] Israel Abrahams, *Jewish Life in the Middle Ages* (Philadelphia: Jewish Publication Society, 1896), p. 340.

[22] Maller, *op. cit.,* p. 904.

had gained proficiency in a number of these areas. The poets, physicians, mathematicians, and philosophers were also the defenders of the Jewish faith, its legal experts, and its major Biblical commentators. The multifaceted personality and the man of broad humanistic education became as much a feature of Jewish as of Islamic life, to the enrichment of both.

Yet it must quickly be added that this enlargement proceeded on a personal not a communal basis. As far as our records go no major change in the accepted Jewish curriculum was introduced by any of the Jewish communities of Spain. The continued learning and achieving in the secular disciplines was carried on as a private matter, to which the leaders of Spanish Jewry not only raised no objection but gave considerable encouragement by their own high standards of achievement.[23] Here the Jewish commitment to study and education was given a new form for its expression and Spanish Jewry seized upon it avidly. The older traditions were at the same time carried forward as is shown in this description by Ibn Daud of the scene in the synagogue of Cordova when the learning of Rabbi Moses ben Chanoch was dramatically revealed before the academic assembly. (This is the moment, about the year 950, which marks the transfer of leadership in Talmudic study in the Jewish world from Babylon to Spain, according to the older accounts.)

> The rector of the academy, Rabbi Nathan, was the judge, or rabbi, of the community. He was described as a great and saintly man. Pressing litigants waited patiently in the corridor or courtyard, while he was delivering his discourse before the students in the hall of the synagogue on a complicated subject in the tractate of *Yoma* (the laws of the Day of Atonement). The atmosphere was charged with heated discussion in which the students asked provocative questions and often challenged the opinions of their master. The presence of mature, bearded students excited no surprise or comment. The head of the academy towered above his hearers not by seniority of age or prestige of office but by superior learning; and when he once unexpectedly found a master in a raggedly attired stranger, he proclaimed him, with saintly self-abnegation, teacher and master. He gave up his honored post and declared himself from that day on the pupil of Rabbi Moses, who was forthwith acclaimed rabbi, judge and teacher. With the accession of Rabbi Moses, the Cordova School rose to fame. From all parts of Spain and North Africa students flocked to the lectures of the famed master.
>
> This, in brief, is the historic description of the prototype of the memorable *yeshivos* (academies) in which were to be trained the masterminds of Spanish Jewry.[24]

---

[23] Abraham Neuman, *The Jews in Spain* (Philadelphia: Jewish Publication Society, 1944), Vol. 2, pp. 71-74.

[24] *Ibid.*, pp. 76-77.

It contains, as well, all the essential features of the *yeshivo* of the later centuries.

Spanish Jewry, building on the foundations laid in the Talmudic period, was the first community in Europe to evolve a comprehensive system of "public" education. It was unrivalled in contemporary Christendom and Islam and remained without parallel in the history of civilization until the modern public school era. This was in large measure due to the relatively long period of tranquillity and prosperity which Spanish Jewry had in which to articulate the age-old Jewish educational ideals and programs in concrete social form. It was also due to the way in which community responsibility for such education was accepted and acted upon. One great legal authority of this period, Asher ben Yechiel (thirteenth century) ruled flatly that funds donated to a synagogue or cemetery could be used by the community for the benefit of a school even against the will of the donor, but that educational funds could not be diverted to the use of a synagogue. As late as 1432 a council of Jewish delegates from all the communities of Castile could draw up a statute in the city of Valladolid that provided, "The opening of our words and the beginning of our ordinances are to support those who occupy themselves with our holy law; for it is the Torah which upholds the world; as our sages, may their memory be for us a blessing, expressed it: 'The world is based on three things: Study, Divine service and the practice of charity.' "

This is the unbroken continuity of an educational ideal formulated nearly 2,000 years before. It is given classic expression in the works of Moses Maimonides (twelfth century), the culminating figure of this era, who said:

> Every man in Israel is obliged to devote himself to study, be he rich or poor, of good health or afflicted by diseases, a youngster or a doddering elder; even if he be a beggar living on charity or a father burdened with a family, he ought to set aside time for study by day and night . . . Among the greatest scholars of Israel there were wood-pickers and water-carriers, even blind men, and they nevertheless studied the Torah by day and night . . . Up to what age is one obliged to study the Torah? Unto the day of death . . .[25]

Another unusual period in the continuing development of Jewish educational practice is found in Central and Eastern Europe during the seventeenth, eighteenth, and nineteenth centuries. The social situation here was far different from that of Moslem Spain. The Jews, though once an eagerly welcomed minority, became an unwanted, alien group. Their economic condition, after an early prosperity, seemed continually to worsen though their numbers continued to climb until, early in this century, they had climbed well past 6 million, and were the greatest concentration of Jews the world has ever known.

---

[25] Moses Maimonides, *Mishneh Torah*, Talmud Torah, I, 8-10; II, 1.

One must consider their educational achievements then in terms of two peaks. The first was reached shortly before the pogroms of the middle of the seventeenth century which ended the economic and social well being of Polish Jewry. There followed almost a century of recovery and then another period of achievement. The former peak is characterized by great scholars, authors, and legal authorities who carried the traditions of Jewish law into new and more advanced areas. Their commentaries on the *Talmud* and on the codes of Jewish law became the basis of all advanced study of the *Talmud* down to the present day. The latter peak is noted less for its outstanding individual scholars than for the way in which the entire Jewish culture of the period is permeated by the influence of the *yeshivo*. Here it is the pervasiveness of higher learning, the universality of concern with reaching its advanced levels, the thorough-going involvement of the life of the times with a high level of adult study, that is an extraordinary accomplishment even for Jewish history.

The factors responsible for the earlier success are clear. A surging, expanding economy welcomed Jews and carried its community life forward with it. The crown gave official status to Jewish life and its major institutions. In particular it authorized an extraordinary measure of Jewish self-government and legal autonomy. Jewish communities were organized over comparatively vast areas and these communities joined together in what was called the Council of the Four Lands to exercise centralized, integrated control over Jewish community life including both taxation and education. All these positive factors produced a school system for youth on the traditional model (private payment by all who could afford it, under community regulation of the private schools, and publicly provided education for the indigent). But here the power was provided which could make it compulsory, even to the extent of requiring vocational if not *yeshivo* training at the age of thirteen, the traditional termination date.

It was the *yeshivo,* and the pattern which made of this advanced academy the dominant institution in this time, which was the crown of the achievement. In the somewhat romantic description of the *yeshivo* which was given by a chronicler in the middle of the seventeenth century and which follows, the school that has been seen through the centuries is once more presented, but the unique Eastern European accomplishment is clearly discernible:

> In no country was the study of the *Torah* so widespread among the Jews as in the Kingdom of Poland. Every Jewish community maintained a *yeshivo,* paying its president a large salary, so as to enable him to conduct the institution without worry and to devote himself entirely to the pursuit of learning . . . Moreover every Jewish community supported advanced students (*bochurs*), giving them a certain amount of money per week, so that they might study under the direction of the president. Every one of these

bochurs was made to instruct at least two boys, for the purpose of deepening his own studies and gaining some experience in Talmudic discussions. The (poor) boys obtained their food either from the charity fund or from the public kitchen. A community of fifty Jewish families would support no less than thirty of these young men and boys, one family supplying board for one advanced student and his two pupils, the former sitting at the family table like one of the sons. . . . There was scarcely a house in the whole Kingdom of Poland where the *Torah* was not studied, and where either the head of the family or his son or his son-in-law, or the *yeshivo* student boarding with him, was not an expert in Jewish learning; frequently all of these could be found under one roof. For this reason every community contained a large number of scholars, a community of fifty families having as many as twenty learned men, who were styled *morenu* (our teacher, a rabbi's title) or *chaver* (colleague, a lesser degree). They were all excelled by the *rosh-yeshivo,* all the scholars submitting to his authority and studying under him at the *yeshivo.*

The program of study in Poland was as follows: The scholastic term during which the young men and the boys were obliged to study under the *rosh-yeshivo* lasted from the beginning of the month of *Iyor* until the middle of *Ov* (approximately from April until July) in the summer and from the first of the month of *Cheshvon* until the fifteenth of Shevot (October-June) in the winter. Outside of these terms the young men and the boys were free to choose their own place of study. From the beginning of the summer term until *Shovuos* (Feast of Weeks, occurring late May-early June) and from the beginning of the winter term until *Chanuko* (Feast of Lights, occurring in December) all the students of the *yeshivo* studied with great intensity the *Gemoro* (the Babylonian Talmud) and the commentaries of Rashi and the Tosafists.

The scholars and young students of the community as well as all interested in the study of the Law assembled daily at the *yeshivo,* where the president alone occupied a chair, while the scholars and college students stood around him. Before the appearance of the *rosh-yeshivo* they would discuss questions of Jewish law, and when he arrived every one laid his difficulties before him, and received an explanation. Thereupon silence was restored, and the *rosh-yeshivo* delivered his lecture, presenting the new results of his study. At the conclusion of the lecture he presented a disquisition (*chilluk*), proceeding in the following way: Various contradictions in the Talmud and the commentaries were pointed out, and solutions were proposed. These solutions were, in turn, shown to be contradictory, and other solutions were offered, this process being continued until the subject of discussion was completely elucidated. These exercises continued in summer at least until midday. From the middle of the two scholastic terms until their conclusion the *rosh-yeshivo* paid less attention to these argumentations, and read instead the religious codes, studying with the mature scholars the *Turim* (an early code), with commentaries, and with the (younger) students the compendium of Alfasi (on the *Talmud*). . . . Several weeks before the close of the term the *rosh-yeshivo* would honor the members of his college, both the scholars and the students, by inviting them to conduct the scientific disputations on his behalf, though he himself would participate in the discussion in order to exercise the mental faculties of all those attending the *yeshivo*.[26]

Despite the deprivations wrought by the mid-seventeenth century massacres, the level of study was not permanently destroyed. The Jews retained their autonomy and their numbers, if not their economic condition, continually expanded. The learning of Eastern Europe, particularly in Lithuania, was the glory of world Jewry and formed the immediate cultural background from which came a substantial part of the European Jewish migration to the United States in the late nineteenth and early twentieth centuries. (This migration in turn supplied the parents for an overwhelming majority of present members in the American Jewish community.)

Here autonomy was the key to the elaboration of Jewish educational activity, but autonomy implies separation, isolation, segregation. The Jew was not part of general culture nor did he participate in the general society of the area. As a result his educational goals were entirely those dictated by the tradition over the centuries and it was by these terms that his achievement must be measured.

Jewish life in Western Europe, particularly after the First Crusade, had been similarly cut off from the main stream of cultural development. The ghetto, an Italian invention, spread into other countries and must be considered the symbol of the intellectual as well as the residential situation of the Jew. To this one must add the riots, expulsions, and continual indignities to which Jews were subjected if one would gain some perspective of what the modern period has meant to the Jew. Space prohibits an account of the positive inner response of ghetto Jewry to these circumstances, though the persistence of the Jewish educational ideal through the ages will give the reader some insight into what to expect.

What cannot be omitted from even so brief a survey as this is the effect of the emancipation of the Jew upon his educational programs. Beginning with the French Revolution — though it took the Assembly several years to determine that the Rights of Man included even Jews — the Jews were made a full part of the countries in which they found themselves. They were granted citizenship and rights in their nations, though it took the better part of the nineteenth century for them to win full freedom even in Western Europe and they probably never did receive it in Eastern Europe. (The growth of anti-Semitism as a political instrument and the eventual extermination by the

---

[26] S. M. Dubnow, *History of the Jews in Russia and Poland* (Philadelphia: Jewish Publication Society, 1916), Vol. 1, pp. 116-118.

German Nazi government of 6,000,000 Jews were related factors of this new Jewish status.)

This emancipation proceeded simultaneously with the growth and development of governmentally sponsored public school systems. As far as is known there was no great hesitation on the part of the majority of Jews in meeting this new circumstance. The Jew in the United States, the most advanced country with regard to Jewish freedom, accepted the public school system as the normal instrumentality for the education of his children. It would probably not be too much to say that he did so with enthusiasm. Centuries of segregation had given him an almost unquenchable desire to be part of the world about him, and the American public school system, with its essentially moral and ethical commitment (as seen in its desire to educate all children, equally) was an acceptable means of achieving it. This combination of inner Jewish desire met by a social institution that significantly fulfilled Jewish goals produced the positive relation between the American public school system and the Jewish community at large which persists to this day.

However, the almost universal decision on the part of American Jews to participate fully in the public school system has caused a major change in the customary pattern of Jewish education. It has reduced it to the status of a supplementary program rather than a primary one. It has limited it to the week-end or late afternoon hours, or the summer months, rather than the basic substance of the child's education.[27] To be sure, there was something about the public school that allowed Jews to accept it. In a free society the American Jew, as the Spanish Jew before him, was willing to see the educated Jew in a somewhat broader role than some other Jewries had been able to

---

[27] For a description of the present patterns see Greenberg, *op. cit.*, pp. 929-933. Jewish synogogues and their related schools were initially prohibited when the first immigrant Jews arrived in New Amsterdam in 1654; but by 1731 their first private school opened. This was a forerunner of what has come to be known as the day school. This private, parochial, elementary school tended to combine Hebrew studies and religion with needed secular learnings — often in two different departments and taught by different instructors. During the second half of the nineteenth century with the growth of the common public schools, these Jewish schools diminished in number. Only a handful remained after the First World War. One of the recent striking developments in Jewish education in America is a rapid resurgence of these schools. In the past few years they have grown in number to well over 200. This reflects a Jewish concern for a quality education that meets rising secular demands while at the same time it amalgamates and strengthens the age old goals of Jewish education — to raise up men of holiness and character. Issues surrounding these developments in Jewish education are discussed regularly in articles appearing in *Jewish Education,* the organ of the National Council for Jewish Education. See also aspects of Chapter VII in this text and the *American Jewish Yearbook,* 1960 (Philadelphia: Jewish Publication Society of America) for an excellent summary of current conditions of Jewish education in the United States.

imagine. And they could see the public school educating toward this end. Their hope has been that in their homes and in their supplementary schools they could transmit the unifying, integrating, particularly Jewish elements that are vital to the educated Jew. They have dared to believe that as broad and complex a tradition as Judaism could be made meaningful to each new generation in the hospitable American environment by these new, largely congregational forms of Jewish education.

The problems produced by this commitment have been many and American Jewry stands in the midst of them today. How can one hope to have a profession of learned and respected teachers of Judaism when the opportunity for full-time employment is not available to most of them? What curriculum can hope to transmit an adequate knowledge of Judaism that is yet relevant to the contemporary world, in such a limited time span? What is to be the fate of the Hebraic character of Jewish study through the ages, when language study requires considerable time and significant linguistic mastery takes years of effort to achieve? Can the supplementary Jewish educational program truly cement the ties of Jewish youths to Judaism and provide effective knowledge? These are the problems which confront the community today and which give it a challenge unique in the history of Jewish education.

In a way though, the greatest challenge has been given not at the level of children's education but, what is for Judaism far more critical, on the adult level. Until recent years, the adult American was not thought of as a man who studied. He worked, or if he was fortunate, he also enjoyed himself. Study and learning were for children. Fortunately in our own day there has been a move in another direction. As the level of educational achievement in youth among Americans has arisen, as the economic situation has made leisure activity more widely available, various forms of adult education have become popular though scarcely equivalent to that of recreation. Still, the possibility of including learning as part of the image of the complete American now looms as a realistic possibiilty.

The prospect is important to American Jewry. The Jewish attitude toward education derives from its view of what it means to be a man. Under the influence of the older point of view in this country and particularly because of the pressures on the immigrants to become economically established and to give their children the advantages of American education, the older style of adult Jewish learning has all but disappeared. The advanced academies are schools for professional training. The informal association of adults meeting regularly to study for study's sake is rare indeed. The closest parallel one could find to this ancient passion for learning is the high proportion of Jews involved in graduate work, university teaching, and research. Yet such an essentially secular sublimation cannot long continue without the drive which began with a view of man and his place in the universe. Nor can the tradition which preserved, nurtured and developed that point of view long survive without leadership and enlightened adherents.

The most promising and lively field of Jewish life in the United States today is adult education. The community is a long way from having an advanced academy for the adults of each city. However, adult study and reading has begun on a reasonably serious level in the Jewish community and only time will tell where these strivings may yet lead.

Clearly this is an area where the Jewish philosophy of education can be of great service today. Many a view of education is so limited and narrow that it cannot see the man for gazing so fixedly at the child. The Jewish view does not lose the child for concentrating on the man. Yet it provides a goal which not only heightens the importance of educating the child, it fructifies our view of our society and of man's place in it. Perhaps Judaism can give something of this to contemporary American educational thought, and, characteristic of the unique American Jewish situation, this time the influence can be passed on without intermediates but by Jewish citizens themselves.

We may then summarize the Jewish contribution to modern education as one of *estimate, will,* and *direction.*

The Jew placed learning almost at the summit of his values. He considered it an indispensable part of truly human existence. Because he saw it in terms of human fulfillment and because he saw all men equal before God, he could free education from dependence upon a man's vocation, station, age, or means. Though in practice limited to men in the Jewish community, this commitment to the education of man as man remains the motive source behind the drive for universal education in our time.

This feeling for education was not allowed to remain unexpressed and undeveloped. The Jewish people created institutions which brought this attitude into the life of its communities. The concern for education became not just a private one, but one in which the community shared responsibility with the family. In the history of this development the Western World finds a major source of its own later educational evolution. In this pattern of shared concern it finds the ideal toward which it strives.

The learned Jew was neither a youth nor a technician. Study was a necessary part of his life for all of his life and hence knew no limits. While it included the means of making a livelihood, this was too small a goal for one created in the image of God. Education must be rounded by including man's spiritual dimension, particularly his moral capacity. Thus, only to know could not be a sufficient aim. Even teaching was but part of the living by knowledge that was both the beginning and culmination of study. Today, as man in the Western World seeks to rise above his technical conquests to a vision of the wiser, better, more compassionate man the machines have not yet produced, this Jewish goal may have even greater relevance.

100

Bibliography

Abrahams, Israel, *Jewish Life in the Middle Ages.* Philadelphia: Jewish Publication Society, 1896. Chapter 19.

Baron, Salo, *The Jewish Community.* Philadelphia: Jewish Publication Society, 1942, Volume 2. Chapter 13.

Drazin, Nathan, *The History of Jewish Education, from 515 B.C.E. to 220 C.E.* Baltimore: The Johns Hopkins Press, 1940.

Dubnow, S. M., *History of the Jews in Russia and Poland.* Philadelphia: Jewish Publication Society, 1916, Volume I. Chapter 4.

Ebner, Eliezer, *Elementary Education in Ancient Israel, During the Tannaitic Period (10-220 C.E.).* New York: Bloch Publishing Company, 1956.

Greenberg, Simon, "Jewish Educational Institutions" Chapter 22, Volume 3 of *The Jews,* Louis Finkelstein, Editor. Philadelphia: Jewish Publication Society, 1949.

Maller, Julius, "The Role of Education in Jewish History," Chapter 21, Volume 3, *The Jews,* Louis Finkelstein, Editor. Philadelphia: Jewish Publication Society, 1949.

Morris, Nathan, *The Jewish School.* London: Eyre and Spottiswoode, 1937.

Neuman, Abraham, *The Jews in Spain.* Philadelphia: Jewish Publication Society, 1944, Volume 2, Chapter 15.

Orlinsky, Harry, *Ancient Israel.* Ithaca: Cornell University Press, 1954.

Smith, William, *Ancient Education.* New York: Philosophical Library, 1955. Chapters 9 and 10.

****

CHAPTER IV

THE CATHOLIC HERITAGE

It is a matter of common knowledge that the Catholic Church is engaged in a large educational enterprise in the United States at the present time. There is no section of the country where this is not evident although the extent of the program of Catholic education varies considerably among the various geographical regions. Catholic population is not uniformly spread over the country — where the population that is Catholic is not large, Catholic education is likewise not very extensive. There is, however, something of Catholic education found everywhere in the United States. It is also evident that this religious education exists on all levels of schooling, from nursery schools and kindergartens to graduate schools in universities. Indeed, Catholic education is the largest nonpublic educational system in the nation, largest both in the sense that it contains the largest number of nonpublic schools, elementary, secondary, and higher, and enrolls the largest number of pupils and students outside the public schools. On the elementary and secondary levels this is clear; it is not as evident on the level of higher education.

The statistical aspect of American Catholic education is not the only, nor indeed the most important, aspect of this phenomenon to observe. The magnitude of the undertaking has created many and difficult problems for American Catholics — problems of building, staffing, and financing all the institutions in all the categories. The presence and growth of a large system of Catholic education has likewise raised questions in the minds of many citizens who are not Catholics, questions that have led to public controversy and

103

debate. The fact is that there has never in previous history been developed in any other country as complete a system of independent Catholic educational institutions as in the United States within very recent years. There has always been Catholic education since the beginning of the Catholic Church but its precise form, the institutions in which it is carried on, its relation to the political authority, its curriculum, and its financing — these are particular aspects of its development that are involved in the total cultural and institutional history of which it is a part. Details of organization and structure have varied considerably, especially in modern history when the national states have become firmly organized. Hence, Catholic education in the United States today is what it is partly because of its ancient and continuing religious heritage and partly because it is bound into the current of American history. The intent in this chapter is to indicate some of the major historical continuities of Catholic education and to relate it to some of the most important aspects of the development of American education in general.

Educational Principles and Implications of Christianity

It is important to stress, first, that Christianity is a religion teaching the relations of man and God. Its first concern, therefore, was to make clear its dogmas, to put into effect its sacramental system, and to develop its liturgy. Christianity is a missionary religion and its first leaders had the enormous task of forming its adherents, both adults and children. It had a body of doctrine to teach and this is found in the books of the New Testament and the writings of the Church Fathers. The transmission of this body of doctrine was the obligation of its bishops and priests. It inherited the Jewish tradition of a particular care for children and the function of the rabbi or teacher. Christ declared that He had come not to destroy the Old Law but to perfect it. "I am come a light into the world; that whosoever believeth in me, may not remain in darkness." (*John* xii:46.) His followers were to have the means of eternal salvation in the life and lessons of their Founder. "I am come that they may have life, and may have it more abundantly." (*John* x:10.) And "For this was I born, and for this came I into the world; that I should give testimony to the truth." (*John* xviii:37.) He promised His followers a higher life and taught a scale of values that would distinguish between time and eternity. "For what doth it profit a man if he gain the whole world and lose his own soul?" (*Mark* viii:36.) Also, and more fundamentally, He charged His Apostles to spread to all persons His teachings: "Going therefore, teach ye all nations. . . . and behold I am with you all days, even to the consummation of the world." (*Matt.* xxviii:19.)

Catholicism would thus stress the sacredness of human personality because of its creation by God and its redemption by Christ, the essential equality of all persons before God, the dignity and sacred character of marriage and family, the responsibility of each individual for his own actions (although recognizing both his weakness and the availability of grace), the creation of a whole new body of revealed truth, and the establishment of a teaching Church to spread the "glad tidings" of the Gospel to all the world. Although the commission to the Church to teach is concerned directly with religious truth this truth is so fundamental and has such widespread consequences that it eventually impinges on the entire process of education. The development of this process is the historical account of Catholic education.

Catholic Education in the Greco-Roman World

It is fundamental to note that while the religious background of Christianity was Judaism it arose in a Roman colony. As it spread beyond its original location it came into contact with all the features of the culture of the time in the Greco-Roman world. Its history also was such that it became strongest in the cities, the centers of the contemporary culture. Indeed, the term pagan, which marked the contrast to Christian, originally meant rural. Although writers today often stress the character of Catholicism as both a culture and a cult it must be understood that the peculiarly cultural aspect of Catholicism was very long in developing. In the Greco-Roman world this culture was slowly taking form, particularly in the literary efforts of the first of the Christian writers and in the liturgical developments within the Church. But there was the whole culture of the Hellenistic age surrounding Christianity and it was from this culture that the new adult Christians came. For the primitive Church there were many problems of cultural conflict created thereby but our concern here is more directly related to the educational, in the sense of school, problems that faced the Christians in their world. Although there were individual variations in the solutions proposed by many of the church leaders in the first three Christian centuries, the general pattern arrived at was to make use of the existing schools but to oppose the pagan culture.[1] Although there were harsh judgments made on pagan cultures and schools by many of the Christian Fathers, there is abundant evidence that the existing schools of the Roman world were attended by Christians. There are even many instances of Christians serving as teachers in these schools; although this, too, was frowned upon by some writers, it was never officially forbidden. It is, perhaps, difficult for us today to expect a

---

[1] The best account of this period in English of this complex subject is found in Marrou, H. I., *A History of Education in Antiquity* (translated by G. R. Lamb), (New York: Sheed and Ward, 1956), Chapters IX and X. The present account has drawn heavily on this work.

105

censorious attitude toward the pagan poets, but we should not be surprised that the early Christians were not enthusiastic about the mythologies that depicted immoral gods and godesses; their harmful effect on children had been pointed out much earlier by Plato. But young children could learn their letters even in pagan schools and literary culture was more a concern for adults. The general solution of their problem that was worked out by the Christians involved the use of the existing schools more or less out of necessity and the formation of doctrinal and moral teaching as the obligation of the home and the Church. The training and trying of applicants for admission to the Church was worked out in the organization of the catechumenate. This was not, strictly speaking, so much a school as a system of doctrinal instruction and training in behavior, in preparation for participation in the life and worship of the Church. This preparation for admission to the Church was often prolonged, sometimes to the extent of three years, but it should not be thought of as general education intended to develop literary culture; it was technical training necessary for admission to the Church. Baptism was often postponed until near adulthood. Additional and continuous religious instruction was provided through the preaching and reading that was included in church services. Unbaptized neophytes were excluded from the central part of the Mass, the chief form of Catholic worship. A remnant of this practice is found in the expression "Mass of the catechumens," to designate the preparatory part of the entire Mass. Thus, briefly, the general elementary literary education of the early Christians was provided by the general schools of the time or by family instruction; the specifically religious training was made available through the churches; and the moral formation was a responsibility of both the family and the Church.

How were the clergy prepared for their work? Theological development was provided in the writings of the Church Fathers and precise formulations of belief were incorporated in the creeds (Apostles and Nicene). In some of the more important centers of Christian life advanced theological and philosophical studies were carried on. Such was the work of Clement (c. 150–c. 215) and Origen (c. 185–c. 254) at Alexandria. But, as Marrou points out, such catechetical schools were not the usual means of preparation of priests who learned their theology from personal attachment to a bishop or older priest.[2] There was, however, a growing wealth of writing not only of a theological nature but also devoted to the manner of religious instruction, the selection of a teacher, motivation, and similar pedagogical questions. Mention might be made of the *Exhortation to the Greeks, The Pedagogue,* and the *Stromata* of Clement; the *Catecheses* of Cyril of Jerusalem; the *To Young Men, on How They Might Derive Profit From Pagan Literature,* of

---

[2] *Ibid.,* p. 328.

St. Basil the Great; the *Defense of the Monastic Life,* of St. John Chrysostom; and *Catechizing the Uninstructed,* by St. Augustine. More fundamental Augustinian contributions are found in chapter VIII.

Briefly, then, in the Greco-Roman period the Christians both made use of such pagan schools as were available and put forth efforts to establish new types and forms of schooling. The latter pertained more especially to specifically Christian doctrine and training. For more advanced schooling there was considerable concern about expurgation of pagan works as this literature provided an important segment of instruction. The formulation of creeds led quite naturally to the development of catechetical methods of instruction, a series of specific questions and answers. In the hands of good teachers this would expand into more general considerations and extensions of knowledge.

Medieval Contributions

The historical process involved in the collapse of the Greco-Roman world, including within it the virtual end of classical education, and the beginnings of the Medieval Age was such that there was a great amount of overlapping that might be observed. This was a slow and complex process, and not all of one piece. It is not necessary to go into much detail; it is sufficient for present purposes to keep in mind that all of Western Europe was involved for many centuries with enormous political, social, and economic problems. Although even the dating of the various periods is a matter on which not all authorities agree, for the understanding of educational developments, it might be agreed that the whole range of the Middle Ages can be said to have been a true millenium, from the sixth to the sixteenth centuries. It is obvious that in a period of such length and occurring over such a vast geographical extent, generalized statements of what took place are extremely hazardous. It is a matter of common knowledge, of course, that the general level and quality of education were considerably lower, during the period of the great mass movements of the Germanic tribes in the Empire, in the fourth, fifth, and sixth centuries. But Christianity had at last come out of the catacombs, to be first tolerated by Galerius, in 311, and officially recognized by Constantine as the state religion, in 325. The social and political organization peculiar to the Middle Ages was formulated in the institution of feudalism. The Church had overwhelming tasks in the effort to Christianize the invaders from the north, in crystalizing its own internal organization, and deepening its own life. Eventually peculiarly medieval and Catholic institutions for education took form. Begun slowly and often conducted on a very elementary plane, new life was developed in some of them by the efforts of Charlemagne in the eighth century but in the twelfth and thirteenth centuries there was sufficient original activity in some of the higher schools that the movement has been called the

107

Christian Renaissance, the Renaissance of the Twelfth Century, or the "little" Renaissance, to distinguish it from the Classical Renaissance of the fourteenth and fifteenth centuries.[3]

But before these later developments there had been fashioned several typical medieval educational institutions and practices. There had been inherited from the East, and particularly from Egypt, the practice of solitary individuals withdrawing from the world to live lives of prayer and contemplation. When this ideal developed in the West it usually took the form of a common life of several individuals. This was the beginning of monasticism. In Western Europe this finally was brought to full development in the *Rule* of St. Benedict (c. 525). This outlined in great detail the provisions for the admission of monks to the monastery, the round of duties obligatory upon each monk, and the entire government of the monastery. Two of its chief foundations may be summed up in the expressions "idleness is the great enemy of the soul" and "to work is to pray." In keeping with these two principles each monk was to be occupied every hour of the day and night except for the necessary provisions for sleep. The monastic ideal sanctified work. Originally most of the monks were not ordained priests but lay brothers, the monastery having only enough priests to care for the spiritual needs of the monks. The most characteristic work of the monks was agriculture. The monastery was often purposely located in a most unlikely spot, the choice of such a spot being a challenge to the industry and skill of the monks. They often became very successful farmers but the obligation of reading and the singing of the Psalms was placed upon all monks. The distribution of time among the various duties was accommodated to the seasons of the year, there being more reading required during some periods than others. The *Rule* contained detailed provisions for the training of the young applicants for admission to the monastery. In this manner the monastic schools became established. It is clear that they were intended for the education of those planning on becoming monks but many of the monasteries provided likewise for the education of boys (externs) who would not do so. Similar rules were developed for the communities of nuns and for the preparation of girls who would enter the convents.

A cultural effect of the work carried on in the monasteries and convents was the preparation of copies of manuscripts in the period before the invention of printing. The copying of the handwritten works was especially developed in the monastery founded in Vivarium, in Italy, by Cassiodorus (c. 485–c. 580), but the *scriptorium*, or writing room, that was devoted to this purpose was a feature common to many monasteries. The works most

---

[3] See, for example, Charles H. Haskins, *The Renaissance of the Twelfth Century* (Cambridge: Harvard University Press, 1927).

often copied were the Scriptures and the Psalter but classical works were also copied when available.

The monasteries thus provided for the preparation of the regular clergy (those who lived by *regula,* a rule) but the education of diocesan (secular) priests was the responsibility of the bishop, the head of a diocese. He was usually located in the chief city of his diocese and here he had his cathedral. Hence, the schools that were attended for the training of his priests came to be known as cathedral or episcopal (from *episcopus,* bishop) schools. There were as yet no theological seminaries for this purpose so the bishops assumed the responsibility of preparing young men for their priestly careers. Often the teaching was done by the bishops themselves; at other times the bishop had a *scholasticus* (schoolmaster) for this purpose. The bishop had to determine the standards necessary to ordination of priests and his school was the means to provide the preparation needed.

These two schools, the monastic and cathedral, became the most typical schools of the Middle Ages and it is about them that most is known. Although the range and depth of study that they provided must have varied considerably, depending on the intellectual standards of the abbots, the bishops, and the teachers, a theological and Scriptural preparation was common to all and the general education that came to be provided was formulated as the Seven Liberal Arts.[4] The first suggestion of the organization of studies along this line had been made by Plato, Roman writers had produced textbooks on the subjects, and Christian writers in the Middle Ages produced their versions. The subjects were divided into the group of three literary subjects of grammar, rhetoric, and logic or dialectic (the *trivium*), and the four scientific subjects of arithmetic, geometry, astronomy, and music (the *quadrivium*). It may be assumed that the content of these subjects was very meager in the hands of less able teachers and pupils but more extensive when both teacher and learners were more competent.

There are records coming down from the medieval age that have to do with parish schools but these records are much less complete than those concerning the monastic and cathedral schools. We do know that the Second Council of Vaison, in Gaul, in 529, decreed that parish priests should teach young boys in their charge the beginnings of general and religious education so that they might be prepared for the priesthood. The Council referred in its legislation to the general acceptance of this plan in Italy. The date is interesting coming at about the same time that St. Benedict issued his Rule and when the Emperor Justinian closed the pagan philosophical schools in Athens. Although at this early date the parish schools were regarded as being

---

[4] Paul Abelson, *The Seven Liberal Arts* (New York: Teachers College, Columbia University, 1906).

for future priests, as time went on they took in other pupils not contemplating the clerical life. Later, under order from the Frankish Emperor Charlemagne, who was stimulated by Alcuin, the great mentor of his palace school, parish schools were extended in Western Europe. Monastic schools, however, remained dominant until the late Middle Ages.

In the organization of the Benedictine monastery of Cluny, in France, in the tenth century is found the beginning of a development that led to favorable conditions for the pursuit of education. The distinguished note of the Benedictine monasteries had been their self-containment and independence. In Cluny, however, was begun federation, the central monastery having allied with it numerous other monastic houses. Moreover, the establishments at Cluny were brought directly under the papal authorities. This centralization gave strength to individual institutions and made possible not only improvements in the regulation of monasteries and reform of clerical living but also some relief from the isolation and independence fostered by feudalism and alleviation of the lot of the serfs. More settled conditions were made possible by the introduction, from Cluny, of the Truce of God according to which fighting was reduced in frequency and the lives and safety of travelers and the poor were made more secure. Hence, a more settled life was possible, a life in which learning and teaching might go forward more easily. In the twelfth century more than 300 monasteries came under the Cluniac organization.[5]

If the monastery is regarded as a great source of strength and order in late medieval times making learning more possible than in more chaotic times, that at Bec (founded in the tenth century in Normandy) is regarded as the spark that led to the development of Scholasticism as the characteristic study in philosophy and theology of the later Middle Ages. The term itself indicates its close connection with the schools, and it was largely in the institutions of education that Scholasticism was developed and transmitted. The parallel might be drawn between the development of scholastic philosophy and theology in the later medieval schools of this time and the development of the empirical sciences in universities of our time. Although scientific progress is being made in other institutions, such as independent research centers, it is primarily in the research laboratories of the universities that most of this work is carried on. So, too, the philosophy and theology of the later Middle Ages were being developed at the same time that they were being taught and both activities were carried on by the same persons. The contemporary student finds difficulty in realizing this, thinking that scholastic philosophy

---

[5] W. Kane, *An Essay Toward a History of Education* (Chicago: Loyola University Press, 1935), p. 122. For a general account of the Cluniac movement see, Smith, Lucy M., *Cluny in the Eleventh and Twelfth Centuries* (London: P. Allan and Co., 1930).

and theology are remote from the concerns of the majority of his educational institutions but it is important that we realize that they were in the later Middle Ages subjects of vital concern in the then contemporary society. Lanfranc became the famous teacher at Bec shortly after its founding, in 1039, and to whom were attracted hundreds of students. He later became Archbishop of Canterbury and his students carried his teaching to many other schools.[6] In addition to Lanfranc (1005-1089) many other Scholastic writers and teachers might be mentioned: his successor, Anselm of Canterbury (1033-1109), Peter Abelard (1079-1142), Hugh of St. Victor (c. 1096–1141), Vincent of Beavais (d. 1264), Albertus Magnus (1193–1280), and St. Thomas Aquinas (c. 1225-1274); see chapter VIII, pp. 287-288 for a discussion of St. Thomas' contributions.

The revival of interest in study came at a time when feudal Europe was experiencing a growth of town and city life, and there is probably a causal relation between the two. The rise of cities is, in turn, attributable to the Crusades which brought Western Europe in contact once again with the eastern end of the Mediterranean world, beginning with the first Crusade in 1095. This contact with other cultures led to new stimulation in life and made new works available to the schools and teachers either through the editions of the Saracens or in their original forms. In time the work of the town schools, especially first the cathedral schools and later the universities, eclipsed the former leadership held by such monasteries as Cluny, Bec, and St. Gall.

Now, in the twelfth and thirteenth centuries, was developed a formal organization for higher education. The term for these institutions comes from the Latin *universitas* which is simply the term for a legal corporation. It does not denote a school or an educational institution but it does indicate one necessary feature of higher education, the organization of the two groups, teachers and students, necessary for carrying on higher education. The term also reveals the feudal guild organization characteristic of the Middle Ages. A guild was possible when two groups came together for mutual helpfulness and also protection from each other. In the case of the craft guilds one group would be the master workers in need of young men to assist them and the young would need the master workers to give them the needed training in the craft. The model may be transposed to the field of education with its teachers in need of students and the students in need of teaching. To organize the groups would give each what it wanted and would likewise protect each from the other. Moreover, legal organization would make possible continuity beyond the lifetime of the incorporators. This is the essence of the

---

[6] Frederick Eby and Charles F. Arrowood, *The History and Philosophy of Education, Ancient and Medieval* (New York: Prentice-Hall, 1940), p. 723.

Bettmann Archive

ALBERT THE GREAT TEACHING AT PARIS.

organization of the medieval university which has come down to the present time. While they frequently evolved from cathedral schools, the necessary feature is not found in buildings or campus, however important these may seem in contemporary education. It is evident, likewise, that the universal or near universal nature of what is taught in the modern university does not indicate its medieval origin. The technical term that designated the university as an educational institution was *studium generale,* a school that attracts students from near and far, as against a *studium particulare,* a school of local character. Degrees (teaching licenses) were soon accepted from the former schools beyond the boundaries of the local diocese. Thus, the universities of medieval Europe were international institutions, attracting students from all parts of the continent and Britain. With the rise of the strong national states the universities often lost this characteristic.

The medieval university thus was an organized form of higher education and regulations were drawn up in each for its government according to its basic legal document, the charter that was obtained from either secular or ecclesiastical authority. The regulations covered requirements for degrees, readings for the various courses, fees, student life, and a multitude of other details. Degrees were provided for the first time in the history of Western education, the same degrees as are presently in use, bachelor, master, and doctor, although there is considerable variation in the use of these terms.

112

The full development of the medieval university included four faculties or, as we would say today, four colleges: arts, medicine, law, and theology. Not all of the medieval institutions had all four of these. The term *college* at first referred only to a residence for students but in time the colleges came to be teaching institutions within the universities. In England the colleges eclipsed the universities for a time and they were particularly strong in the seventeenth century when the English colonies in the New World were being organized; this explains why our first institutions of higher education came to be colleges rather than universities. The characteristic method of teaching employed in the medieval universities was the lecture but it should be noted that this meant especially a reading of a text, not a lecture in the modern sense of the term. The lecturer would, it is true, give explanations of the text read but the method centered on a stipulated text rather than on original organization of material for a lecture. In addition to the lectures, there were disputations in which students took part in analyzing and defending propositions. In the colleges the tutorial approach became most common. Finally, at the completion of his course a student was expected to present his masterpiece (again indicating the analogy of the guild organization) by giving a lecture himself. The successful student was given not only a degree but also the license to teach (*ius ubique docendi*). The latter indicates the role of the university in producing teachers. By the end of the Middle Ages there were some 80 universities in Europe, many of which such as Paris, Oxford, Cambridge, and Heidelberg, survive to the present time.[7]

Not only did the guilds, both merchant and craft, provide a model for the organization of the early universities but they were also more directly an educational institution. Primarily, they provided the means for the practical education of workers, usually arranged in the three stages of apprentice, journeyman, and master. All the details pertaining to the organization and administration of the concerns of the various guilds were cared for in the guild corporations, length of training of apprenticeships, wages of journeymen, standards of workmanship, prices, and many similar items. The guilds usually had clergymen appointed to care for their religious needs. Vocational training became the common type of learning available to the common man but the guilds often assumed the responsibility of providing general rudimentary schooling in reading and writing for their own children and sometimes for other children of the town. Some, in time, even extended their instruction to include Latin and thus became secondary schools. The pattern of guild industrial education became so widely followed that, as Monroe

---

[7] The standard work, in English, on the medieval universities is Hastings Rashdall, *The Universities of Europe in the Middle Ages* (Edited by F. M. Powicke and A. B. Emden) (Oxford: The Clarendon Press, 1936), three volumes.

points out,[8] in England Parliament legislated in the Statute of Artificers (1562) and the Poor Law (1601) for a social policy based on the guild system and required the vocational training of the poor. The attitude toward general literary as contrasted with vocational education was then just the opposite of modern society:

> The Englishman of the sixteenth and seventeenth centuries no more thought of the education of the masses as connected with schools and literary training than we now think of it as connected with vocational training in handicrafts and merchandise. But the Englishman of that time did think of education for the masses wholly in terms of the handicraft or vocational training, while we today think of education wholly in terms of book learning.[9]

The English precedent in this regard became extremely important in the original colonies from which the United States was formed.

Another type of late medieval school was the chantry school so named from its being taught by a priest who had received an endowment to chant Masses. It often happened that the guild and chantry schools came more and more directly under the jurisdiction of town and city authorities and hence they are sometimes referred to as burgher or town schools. However, some town schools carried on from Roman times and, especially in Northern Europe, many were established in the growing commercial centers. Instruction remained largely in the hands of clerics. In the late Middle Ages there were also many private individuals who carried on the vocation of school teaching on an individual basis as a means of livelihood. All of these types of educational provision were influential on later times both in Europe itself and in the colonies of the New World.

The Classic Renaissance

All great cultural movements overlap considerably. St. Thomas Aquinas is usually considered the greatest of the Scholastic philosophers and theologians and yet he died only about a generation from the breakup of the medieval age. Dante, on the other hand, is often spoken of as marking the beginning of the new age. He was very influential in the development of the new vernacular Italian but he thought his writings in Latin were the more important of his contributions. St. Thomas died in 1274 and Dante in 1321. The literary and educational lights of the early Classic Renaissance usually listed include Petrarch (1304-1374), and Boccaccio (1313-1375) in Italy; Budé (1467-1540), in France; Thomas More (1478-1535) in England; Jacob

---

[8] Paul Monroe, *Founding of the American Public School System* (New York: Macmillan, 1940), p. 13.

[9] *Ibid.*, p. 20.

Wimpfeling (1450-1528), in Germany; Vives (1492-1540) and Erasmus (1457-1536), in the Netherlands and England. (See also Chapter VIII, pp. 288-290.) Thus, it is evident that the Renaissance extended over a long period of time. During much of this time the interest of the leaders was in the personal and social uses of the new-old learning, rather than the educational or school aspects of the revived classics. The leaders spent much of their time and energy in ferreting out better and more complete manuscripts of the Latin and Greek authors and used them in court and literary circles. Much of the spirit of the earliest period of the Italian Renaissance was frankly pagan and in the works of the pagan authors they found an expression of a philosophy of life that they embraced. But there was a Christian side to the Renaissance also and this had a more prominent place in the schools than the earlier pagan side of the movement.

It is sometimes said that the Renaissance brought Latin back into the schools. This is not quite accurate. Latin had not disappeared from the schools but the Latin that was used in them during the Middle Ages was not only the school Latin but also the Latin in ordinary use at the time, the vulgar Latin as seen in the Latin Vulgate edition of the Bible developed by St. Jerome. This Latin was a living language, subject to change due to use and not, therefore, as pure and polished a language as the Latin of the golden age of Latin letters, the time of Virgil and Cicero. It was the Latin of Virgil and Cicero that the first leaders of the Renaissance sought out in libraries and monasteries and they searched for whole works to replace the partial works that had been available heretofore. This is a period that is often referred to as the period of Humanism, meaning a period devoted to an interest in man and his works of creative power and expression that contributed to social and individual betterment. These were thought to be best found in the literary works of the Greeks and Romans. Italy, as the original home of Latin culture, was the natural location of the earliest of the Renaissance efforts, and Italy also had had the closest contact with Greek culture through the colonizing efforts of the Greeks in Italy and Sicily. Ideally, a Renaissance man would be bilingual but many did not develop fluency in Greek.

There were a few schools in the early Italian Renaissance built on the Christian and classical ideal. The most notable of them was that of Vittorino da Feltre who was commissioned by the Gonzaga family to conduct a school for their children, in Mantua, in 1423. This he did and other children were included in addition to the Gonzagas. This court school, as it is called, was copied by other aristocrats and most of them were excellent but not typical schools in which there was a blending of both Christian and humanistic ideals. More permanently influential were the schools maintained by a religious community, the Brethren of the Common Life, in the Low Coun-

115

tries, from late in the fourteenth century until the Protestant Reformation. In these schools the Brethren promoted the new studies as well as the ancient Christian emphasis on moral and religious development. They had many schools and thousands of pupils, many of whom were later in influential positions. *The Imitation of Christ* by Thomas à Kempis sets forth the high ideals that this non-monastic order sought to extend.

The great school influence of the Classic Renaissance is found in both the aim of education and the curriculum thought best to attain this aim. The best simple statement that might be made concerning the aim of Renaissance education is to say that the purpose of education was to educate man as man; this has usually been referred to as liberal education. This was well defined by Vergerius, a teacher in the University of Padua, when he wrote around 1404:

> We call those studies liberal which are worthy of a free man; those studies by which we attain and practice virtue and wisdom; that education which calls forth, trains, and develops those highest gifts of body and mind which enoble man, and which are rightly judged to rank next in dignity to virtue only.[10]

The influence of social factors is seen in the passage which speaks of free men. Especially in Italy was the Renaissance an aristocratic movement but later times extended the concept of liberal education to include more social classes, and then liberal education could be spoken of as that education which aims to free men from ignorance, from pettiness and limited interests, rather than being the education characteristically obtained only by those in the free social and economic classes of society. In this sense, liberal education is to be contrasted with any type of special education which has a regard for man under only a partial aspect, not man as man. In this sense it is referred to as Christian humanism, or *pietas et eloquentia,* religious formation and intellectual development especially of the abilities to think and express oneself in writing and in speech.

The curriculum thought best for the attainment of liberal education in the Renaissance thus was thought to be one centered on the language and literature of Greece and Rome. Although the emphasis of the early Renaissance was on the content of the literary works, in time this was replaced by a stress on the style of the polished writers. Hence, the use of the term formalism to characterize the emphasis on the stylistic qualities of the classical authors, and the term *Ciceronianism* to indicate the reliance on the works of

---

[10] William H. Woodward, *Vittorino da Feltre and other Humanist Educators* (Cambridge: University Press, 1905), p. 102. An excellent summary of Da Feltre's work is found in Luella Cole's *A History of Education: Socrates to Montessori* (New York: Rinehart, 1950).

116

Cicero as the great model of style. The latter term was also used to character-ize the sterile and artificial emphases that came to mark schooling in the late Renaissance.

Besides the court schools that were established in the early Renaissance, especially in Italy, more permanent institutions for this classical education were found in the grammar schools and the Public Schools (Eton, Winchester, Rugby, and others) in England, the *collèges* in France, and the *gymnasien* in the German States. By far the most numerous and influential of the Catholic schools based on the classical ideal were those organized by the Society of Jesus. This Order was founded by St. Ignatius Loyola, a Spaniard, in 1540. Although the Jesuits have always been active in other types of work, education has from their beginning been an important concern. After much deliberation and considerable experimentation, a detailed plan for the organization and management of their schools was written and ordered used in all their institu-tions in 1599. This is the famous *Ratio Studiorum*. This outlined in great detail the duties of the various teachers and other school officials, the arrange-ment of the subject matter of the curriculum, the methods of teaching to be used, and the control of student life. The Jesuits generally did not work on the elementary school level but restricted themselves to secondary and higher schools. These were referred to as lower and higher colleges, the former com-prising five grades (three of grammar, one of humanities, and one of rhetoric), and the latter being regular universities with a stress on philosophy but in-cluding mathematics and natural science. The grades were not necessarily to be regarded as equivalent to calendar years; they were rather divisions of subject matter arranged in a systematic fashion. Teachers tended to continue handling the same group of boys for a number of years.

The notable success of the Jesuits was due to several factors: special preparation of their teachers, clear organization of the work, firm but mild discipline, careful attention to teaching methods, and the absence of tui-tion fees. An adage of the schools was "repetition is the mother of learning" and in accordance with this, reviews of previously learned material were a prominent feature of the teaching in their schools. Although the or-ganization in the *Ratio* provided for concentration on Latin, its grammar and its literature, teachers were not thought of primarily as narrow specialists as in a strict departmental system. Rather, although special attention was given to literary education, the teacher was responsible for instruction in all the matter related to the selections used. Thus, historical, scientific, and biographical details would be learned in the context in which they were met by the teacher and student. In somewhat modified form, this method con-tinues in contemporary French education in the *explication de texte* whereby the teacher is responsible for a thorough understanding and explanation of literary work with attention given to all the references and allusions found

117

in the text. In addition to the regular class work devoted to classical education, the Jesuit schools, like many of their contemporaries, gave a good deal
of attention to the theatre, the giving of classical plays and the development
of original efforts by the students, and also to declamations.[11] By 1700 there
were over 1,800 Jesuit schools in Europe and they were commonly credited by
non-Catholics as among the best.

Catholic Reaction to the Protestant Reformation

The Catholic reaction to the Protestant Reformation which began with
the posting of theses by Martin Luther in 1517 assumed several forms, so far
as educational consequences are concerned. The Commission on Reform was
appointed by Pope Paul III, in 1537, and gave attention to the ordering of
discipline among the clergy and called for care concerning heretical teaching in
the schools of the time. The Ecumenical Council of Trent was called in 1545
but its final decrees were not signed until 1563. The Council was particularly
concerned with the exact statement of doctrines that had been questioned by
the Protestants and with the preparation of the clergy. It was this Council
that legislated for the establishment of a diocesan seminary for the training
of priests wherever possible. The Council also urged serious attention be
given by bishops and priests to the education of their people, especially
children and particularly in religious matters. The general decrees of the
Council were left to be carried out locally by diocesan regulations and those
local and regional councils regulated educational matters in their jurisdictions,
giving particular attention to Sunday schools and other means of religious
education. Finally, the Council of Trent gave encouragement and support
to the religious orders and societies whose special interest was education.
Among these orders the Jesuits were very prominent, and attention has already
been given to them above. In addition to the Jesuits, special mention should
also be made of the Ursulines. They were founded in Italy in 1535 by
St. Angela Merici. This was the first uncloistered order of women and they
were primarily devoted to the education of girls. They opened schools in
many parts of Europe where there was a Catholic population and they like-

---

[11] There is a vast amount of literature concerning Jesuit education. Some of the
more recent works that are by Americans and that give attention to the American Jesuit
story are: William J. McGucken, *The Jesuits and Education* (Milwaukee: Bruce,
1932). This is concerned with the history of Jesuit secondary education in the United
States and gives a translation of those parts of the *Ratio* that are devoted to the lower
schools: E. A. Fitzpatrick, *St. Ignatius and the Ratio Studiorum* (New York: McGraw-
Hill, 1933). This gives a complete translation of the *Ratio* and Part IV of the *Con*
stitutions; see also Allan P. Farrell, *The Jesuit Code of Liberal Education: The Development and Scope of the Ratio Studiorum* (Milwaukee: Bruce, 1938).

wise founded some of the earliest schools for girls in North America, at Quebec in 1639, and at New Orleans in 1727. There were several other orders also established but the Jesuits and the Ursulines, of all that were founded at this time, were to be the most influential on the development of education in the United States.

Catholic Education and the New National States

The roots of modern national states can be traced back several centuries but the Protestant Reformation furthered this tendency just as it influenced developments in Catholic education. Furthermore, it progressed along rather precise geographical lines, southern Europe remaining largely Catholic and northern Europe becoming mainly Protestant. In the countries that became Protestant (the northern German states, the Dutch Netherlands, and the Scandinavian countries), the churches often became state-established or they became at least an arm of the state. The period immediately after the religious events of the Reformation became one of great struggle over not only religious but also political issues. Religion and nationalism, however, were often joined. The Peace of Augsburg, in 1555, established the principle that religious unity would be secured by giving the ruler the right to determine the religion of his subjects. Thus, there was a great deal more of religious unity than is usually found today. In the highly homogeneous states of the time, with a union of church and state, education came to be regarded as both a religious and political concern but since there was essential unity within the states a harmonious relationship was evolved. Even when there was a tendency to increase the state's concern over educational matters this did not usually lead to friction because of the cultural unity that prevailed. England, unlike the continental countries, did not express a national political concern over education until late in the nineteenth century; before this time it was regarded as a responsibility of the family, the church, the private humanitarian groups. Catholics, however, were placed under civil disabilities and were prevented from obtaining educational opportunities. Here, therefore, Catholic education practically ceased to exist as it did on the continent where the population became almost solidly Protestant. The reverse was true in Catholic countries such as Spain.

In the so-called Catholic countries, education also came more into the hands of the state. Nevertheless, the practical expression of interest in extending educational opportunities was also found in the organization and spread to many religious congregations of both men and women. Mention has already been made of the Jesuits and the Ursuline Nuns. Among others that were founded in the sixteenth and seventeenth centuries and that have been particularly devoted to educational activities there should be listed the Con-

119

gregation of Notre Dame (1598), the Visitation Nuns (1610), the Sisters of St. Joseph (1650), and the Daughters of Charity (1623), all of these being societies of women. Among the groups of men there were the Oratorians (1613), the Vincentians (1625), the Sulpicians (1642), and the Brothers of the Christian Schools (1717). Not all the religious congregations were interested in the general education of children and youth but many of them were. Most of them had to fight against the prevailing notion that schooling was a period of preparation for advanced study, not an activity worthy in itself and to be made available to the numerous poor who had no expectation of pursuing higher education.

The Brothers of the Christian Schools were devoted from their origin to the education of poor boys and concentrated on the first level of schooling. Indeed, to mark their vocation as distinctly concerned with this kind of education, their members were forbidden to teach Latin, a subject indicative of social and economic prestige. Devotion to the education of the poor was so little esteemed at the time by the preferred social classes in France that their founder, St. John Baptist de la Salle, who came from a wealthy family could scarcely realize that he was to expend so much effort on the education of the neglected poor and his family practically disowned him for it. But to his own amazement he persevered in his work through many handicaps and despite much opposition and his congregation became firmly established not only in France but expanded to many other countries. By 1778 they had 420 schools in Europe. To the Christian Brothers are attributed two innovations in elementary education that were to become accepted as necessary for effective elementary education; the organization of pupils by large classes of pupils of similar levels of achievement (the simultaneous method), in contrast to ungraded groups, and the normal school for training the teachers. De la Salle prepared for his teachers a manual that had great influence in organizing the work of not only his group but was widely followed by others interested in organizing elementary education on a systematic basis and preparing teachers for the schools. This was the *Conduite des Écoles Chrétiennes,* 1724.[12]

Since the eighteenth century Catholic education has been on the defensive, even in the predominantly Catholic countries. The period of the *philosophes,* the rationalists, witnessed attacks on the Church as the great enemy of progress and led to a great weakening (in some places a collapse) of Catholic education. The rise of the strong national states in Italy and

---

[12] A good work in English on St. John Baptist de la Salle and his educational activity is: W. Battersby, *de la Salle, A Pioneer of Modern Education* (London: Longmans, Green, 1949); see also E. A. Fitzpatrick, *La Salle, Patron of All Teachers* (Milwaukee: Bruce, 1951).

Germany and the disestablishment of the Church in France in the Revolution were accompanied by anti-clericalism and secularism. The state schools were often the issue of conflict between the forces of religion and secularism. The Jesuits were suppressed in 1773 not to be restored until 1814 but even then not allowed to work in many countries. The French Revolution brought the collapse of all the teaching congregations in that country but they and others returned only to be all forbidden to teach in France in 1904. Since that time there has been continual fluctuation in educational laws and decrees concerning religion in public education and the role of private church schools. Somewhat similar developments have occurred in most of the other European countries, but in none of them, except possibly England and Scotland, has there been developed a system of parish schools along the lines that came to be followed in the United States. Rather, there has been a struggle over the retention of religious instruction in the state schools and the existence of private religious schools. We turn now to the development of Catholic education in the United States.[13]

Catholic Education in the United States

On the elementary school level, the typical school in contemporary Catholic education is that of the parish church. Today the Catholic Church in this country maintains so many parish schools that it is often thought that only Catholics foster this type of school. There are, however, others among the Protestant denominations and this was once a rather prevalent form of school organization in this country. Most historians speak of three general types of school organization in our colonial period: the public school found in the New England colonies, the parish school of the middle colonies, and the private venture school of the southern colonies.[14] It might be argued that perhaps the similarities in these types are so great that they do not represent three distinct forms of organization but all would at least agree that the parochial type was established by many other religious groups besides the Catholics. Most Protestant churches have for many years now abandoned the parish school. Catholic education, however, began in what came to be the United States with other types of schools than that of the parish although

---

[13] For further details on Catholic education outside the United States see the author's article in the *Encyclopedia Americana*, 1959, Vol. 6, pp. 77-81. A survey of the development of national educational systems in the major European countries is found in Robert Ulich, *The Education of Nations* (Cambridge: Harvard University Press, 1961), Part Two.

[14] This is found in Ellwood P. Cubberley, *Public Education in the United States* (Boston: Houghton Mifflin Co., revised edition, 1919), and followed by most later writers.

today it is almost solely the Catholic Church that maintains this type.[15]

Catholic education in the area that eventually became continental United States began with the educational activity of the Spanish and French missionaries in Florida, Arizona, New Mexico, California, and the Mississippi Valley. The theory of the mission system, however, was that it was to be a temporary plan to be followed by the regular diocesan organization under a bishop when settlements became sufficiently large and stable. But even in the English-speaking colonies among the original thirteen the first Catholic educational efforts would be classified as private rather than parochial. Jesuits sailed with the first group of English settlers for Maryland and they set about carrying on educational activities as soon as possible. There is evidence that a Jesuit college was attempted as early as 1640 in Maryland and there were other more or less temporary schools in various settlements in Pennsylvania. The first American diocese with its own bishop was established when John Carroll was appointed bishop of the Diocese of Baltimore, then comprising all of the original States, in 1790. Even before this, however, there had been begun a parish school in connection with St. Mary's Church, in Philadelphia, probably as early as 1767. It should be noted that this school was taught by lay teachers but in time parochial schools almost universally were staffed by members of religious congregations, especially those of women. Ursuline Nuns began teaching in New Orleans in 1727 when that city was still under French control. Along the Atlantic seaboard Poor Clare and Visitation Nuns began teaching in Georgetown, Maryland at the turn of the nineteenth century and Mother Elizabeth Seton opened the first free parish school for boys and girls taught by sisters at Emmitsburg, Maryland, in 1810. This became a pattern of Catholic elementary school organization and in the first decade or two of the century new groups of teaching sisters were organized and opened schools; the Sisters of Loretto, the Sisters of Charity, and the Dominican Sisters were among the first of these groups but were followed by many others. A great increase in Catholic population came in the middle of the century with the migration of thousands of Irish and German settlers and when parishes were organized for them, schools often came to be likewise founded and they were usually staffed by teaching sisters of many orders.

In the meantime some attention was also given to the possibility of establishing Catholic education on more advanced levels. The interest of the Jesuits in college education which had been begun from earliest days of the Maryland colony saw permanent accomplishment in the establishment of

---

[15] This section on the United States follows the author's previous work: James A. Burns and Bernard J. Kohlbrenner, *A History of Catholic Education in the United States* (New York: Benziger Brothers, 1937).

Georgetown College, chartered in 1815 but opened to students in 1791. Bishop Carroll's hope for the establishment of a seminary to prepare priests was fulfilled in the beginning of St. Mary's Seminary in Baltimore, in 1791. Finally, there were opened many schools of a private (as contrasted with a parochial) character by various religious congregations, especially those of women. These would be sometimes referred to as Sisters' schools, convent schools, or academies. A precise pattern for them is difficult to establish; they were Catholic schools but they were likewise independent; they often gave an education that included both elementary and secondary levels, admitting very young pupils and often giving them all the formal education they received. Thus, in the early national period of our history we find under Catholic auspices parish schools, private academies, colleges, and ecclesiastical seminaries. Precise lines of separation between the types and levels of education were not worked out until considerably later.

The pattern of establishing a school in association with every parish and attendance of the children of the parish at this school evolved very slowly. When it was finally established it provided a rather unique organization for Catholic education. Many of the Catholic immigrants had come from parts of Europe where the public schools were responsible for religious education and they had anticipated the same kind of arrangement in this country. But the culture of this country in the eighteenth and early nineteenth centuries was not Catholic and Catholic population was not large until after the great migrations. The public schools began as not only public institutions but they also represented the dominant Protestant culture of the majority of the population. The story of the gradual transformation of the public schools into institutions of nonsectarian education cannot be gone into here but suffice to recall that this transformation did take place in the middle of the last century as part of the vast movement generally referred to as "the common school revival" or "the public school awakening." During this time many Catholic pastors and bishops found themselves unhappy over the education offered in the public schools of the time either because they were forming a kind of general Protestant mentality or, later, a nonreligious or secular outlook on life. They could not, in conscience, approve for Catholic children schools in which Protestant devotions were held, Protestant prayers required of all pupils, the King James version the only edition of the Scriptures read, and textbooks used that promoted an anti-Catholic sentiment. On the other hand, they did not readily see the possibility of providing an entirely separate system of Catholic schools.[16]

---

[16] A recent study of the early Catholic reaction to the character of the public schools is found in Diffley, Jerome E., "Catholic Reaction to American Public Education, 1792-1852," unpublished doctoral dissertation (Notre Dame, Indiana: University of Notre Dame, 1959).

The final general pattern that was evolved, however, called for the establishment of an elementary school in connection with every parish and its use generally by the children of the parish. In the law of the Church each diocese is governed by its bishop; hence, the regulations concerning the establishment of schools and the preferred or obligatory attendance at them by children in the diocese are formulated by the bishop for his diocese. The bishops, however, meet together periodically in councils (provincial councils for areas of the country, and plenary for the entire country) and they have often legislated on educational matters in these meetings. The First Provincial Council of Baltimore was held in 1829. This council expressed dissatisfaction with schooling that did not include religious formation and urged that schools be established where this might be joined with general education. This was followed by the First Plenary Council of Baltimore, of 1852, which took a more definite stand and urgently appealed to the bishops to see that schools "be established in connection with all the churches" of their dioceses, in view of the "very grave evils which usually result from the defective education of youth." Finally, in the Third Plenary Council, of 1884, it was decreed that every parish church should have a school and that children in the parish should attend the parochial school. Exceptions to the general decrees would be granted to pastors and parents, for sufficient reason, by the bishop. The law for the entire Catholic Church is found in the 1918 revision of the *Code of Canon Law*. This decrees the necessity of religious instruction together with general education and obligates Catholic parents to provide a Catholic education for their children. At present, parochial elementary schools enroll approximately one-half the Catholic children of the ages served by those schools.[17] The ideal of a school in connection with every parish and every child of the parish in the school has not been attained, but there are more than 4,000,000 children enrolled in Catholic elementary schools.[18]

As has been indicated earlier, some of the first Catholic efforts in education in this country were exerted on the levels above the elementary. The distinctions between elementary and secondary and secondary and higher were not always as clearly drawn as they are at the present time. It can be generally said that secondary and higher education began together. Georgetown, for example, although classified as an institution of higher education in classical studies in accordance with the Jesuit *Ratio*, gave young boys instruction in English, arithmetic, geography, and other beginning subjects and accepted students as young as eight years of age. In 1860 there were classes in the usual elementary subjects at Notre Dame as well as more

---

[17] Neil G. McCluskey, *Catholic Viewpoint on Education* (New York: Hanover House, 1959), p. 98.

[18] *Ibid.*

advanced instruction, and as late as 1908 a report made then indicated that the colleges for men enrolled many more students of secondary than of higher education.[19] Clearer distinctions between secondary and higher education in the colleges for men were being worked out during the first decade of the present century.

In addition to private high schools sponsored by various religious orders, secondary education is carried on in two other types of organization, the parochial high school and the central or diocesan high school. The parochial elementary school began to expand upward to include secondary grades toward the end of the last century and the first of the central diocesan high schools can be dated at about the same time. It is generally agreed that the first of the latter type was established in Philadelphia in 1890. The separation of secondary from higher education in the colleges led to the separate establishment of private high schools when these grades were taken away from college-level education. Thus, three types of organization for secondary education were developed — the parochial, the diocesan, and the private high school. All three still persist but the tendency in more recent years is to establish secondary education on a diocesan-wide basis, with a greater potential student body from which to draw students and more substantial financial base for support of schools. The number of private secondary schools, however, continues to grow; but these are likely to be college preparatory schools and non-coeducational, whereas the parochial and the diocesan high schools tend to be more comprehensive in their purposes and programs. In 1958-59 there were 1,566 parochial and diocesan high schools, with an enrollment of 500,304 pupils, and 783 private high schools, enrolling 310,464 pupils; slightly more than half of these schools are now coeducational.[20] The majority of these schools should be classified as comprehensive, attempting to meet the needs of both those pupils who plan to enter college and those who will complete their general schooling with the high school. A study made in 1949 found the Catholic high schools classified as follows: Comprehensive, 64.4 percent; academic, 31.6; commercial, 3.8 and vocational, 0.2 percent.[21] The small number of vocational schools is probably due both to a philosophy of education that stresses the intellectual and moral elements, and likewise to the lack of resources that would be needed to establish and maintain an expensive vocational and technical program. A growing recognition of the need to reach and hold adolescents has led some Catholic spokes-

---

[19] Burns and Kohlbrenner, *op. cit.*, pp. 235-237. McGucken gives a detailed account of the transition in the Jesuit institutions, *op. cit.*, Chap. VIII.

[20] McCluskey, *op. cit.*, pp. 100, 112.

[21] Sister Mary Janet, *Catholic Secondary Education* (Washington: National Catholic Welfare Conference, 1949), p. 37.

men to urge a greatly increased program of secondary education even at the expense of traditional Catholic elementary emphases.

In the tendency to establish more opportunities for secondary education, the Catholic effort parallels developments in public education but the reorganization that occurred in public education and led to the establishment of the junior high school was not followed in the Catholic structure. Practically all Catholic education is based on the 8-4 plan. The problem of reducing the length of elementary education for pupils who can proceed at a faster than normal pace has, however, been given a good amount of attention. Even though a six-year elementary school is not the common type in Catholic organization, a number of experiments are being made to achieve this goal if only for selected pupils.

Nor has the junior college become a common institution among Catholic schools. There is a small number of them under Catholic auspices but here also the factor of cost is probably the determining cause of the slow growth. But in this respect the Catholic history is similar to that of all private education because the growth of junior colleges is found in public institutions and the number of those under private control is decreasing.

It is generally agreed that Catholic higher education began with Georgetown, just as this was also the beginning of secondary education, as explained above. From the beginning, Catholic higher education was separately organized for men and women, Georgetown being for men only. From its establishment (1789) until mid-nineteenth century there were forty-one other colleges opened for men.[22] Many of these were in existence for only a short time; mortality among early colleges, both Catholic and non-Catholic was notorious. Among these early institutions are found such contemporary institutions as St. Louis University, Spring Hill College, Loras College, Fordham, Notre Dame, Villanova, Santa Clara, and Holy Cross. Denominational interest in establishing colleges was, of course, very strong, the Presbyterians and Methodists having the largest number of chartered colleges up to the time of the Civil War.[23]

In the last quarter of the nineteenth century many of the Catholic academies for girls gradually expanded and extended their curricula, often designating part of their advanced offerings "post-graduate." Eventually the level of college education was attained in several of them. The distinction between advanced work in the academies and independent college studies is not easy

---

[22] Edward J. Power, *A History of Catholic Higher Education in the United States,* (Milwaukee: Bruce, 1958), p. 255.

[23] Donald G. Tewksbury, *The Founding of American Colleges and Universities Before the Civil War* (New York: Teachers College, Columbia University, 1932), p. 69.

to make but it is generally agreed that the first of the academies for girls to reach the level of higher education was the College of Notre Dame, in Baltimore. This institution organized a full four-year college program in 1895-96 and granted its first degrees in 1899. Trinity College, in Washington, D.C., was the first Catholic institution for the higher education of women that did not grow out of a pre-existing academy. This college was chartered to grant degrees in 1897, receiving its first students in 1900, and granted its first degrees in 1904.[24] As with many of their high schools, separate colleges for men and women under Catholic auspices have remained the typical plan of organization although co-education has come into some of the larger Catholic universities. In some of the latter, co-education is found in all the units of the institutions but in others it is found only in some of the colleges and schools within the universities. In 1959 there were 58 colleges for men, 121 colleges for women, and 32 universities.

Since the Catholic population is not distributed uniformly throughout the country, neither is Catholic education. In some places it constitutes a very small part of the total educational system but in others it enrolls a majority of the pupils available. Catholics have tended to live in the urban centers and in the industrial states and it is, generally, in these same places that Catholic education is a larger enterprise, but there are great differences due to historical and national factors as well as variations in devotion to Catholic education and to leadership in it. In some cities Catholic school enrollment constitutes more than half the total school enrollment but there are dioceses where scarcely a beginning has been made to provide Catholic education. The general historical position, however, is that Catholic educational effort in its origin in this country was part of the traditional pattern of church activity in education but it became a minority effort after the Protestant churches more or less retired from providing religious schools on the elementary level and after the general establishment of the public nonreligious school. These two developments occurred, of course, at about the same time, by the time of the Civil War in the Northern States and by the turn of the century in the Southern States.[25] The general development, therefore, was one that witnessed the gradual lessening of church responsibility for education and a parallel growth of state activity in education.

As Trueblood points out, the decline in Protestant effort even in higher education became so general that it is difficult to determine what is meant today when reference is made to a "denominational" college.[26] Perhaps

---

[24] Power, *op. cit.*, p. 192.

[25] A brief treatment of the decline of Protestant effort in elementary education is found in Curran, Francis X., *The Churches and the Schools: American Protestantism and Popular Elementary Education* (Chicago: Loyola University Press, 1954).

[26] Elton Trueblood, *The Idea of a College* (New York, 1959), pp. 15-16.

all that may be said with certainty is that such a college while it owed its origin to denominational interest and activity, today often has only tenuous relation to a particular church. In contrast to this, all Catholic educational institutions are clearly religious in purpose and program. They constitute a minority but also a growing segment of American education. Their very growth has become a cause for concern and even alarm among some non-Catholics. Throughout its history in the United States Catholic education has experienced many periods of both unconcern by all but Catholics and severe attacks by its bitter enemies. It has been both often ignored and overlooked when it was a feeble effort by a minority of newly-arrived immigrants, and severely attacked when it grew in size and strength. The right of parents to send their children to other than state schools, and hence the right of private, including religious, schools to exist, was tested in the United States Supreme Court in 1925. This was the well-known Oregon school case. The voters of the State accepted an initiative measure which would compel the attendance of all school age children at public schools. The Supreme Court declared the measure unconstitutional as in violation of the Fourteenth Amendment. The decision maintained that:

> The fundamental theory of liberty upon which all governments in this union repose excludes any general power of the state to standardize its children by forcing them to accept instruction from public teachers only. The child is not the mere creature of the state; those who nurture him and direct his destiny have the right coupled with the high duty to recognize and prepare him for additional obligations.[27]

This decision was in keeping not only with traditional American practice but also with Catholic thinking; it has remained the legal defense for the system of Catholic as well as all other private education. This view recognizes the fundamental right of the family to determine the education of the child, and it supports the non-public school as having a right to exist along with the state school. Probably most Americans would agree with the court's decision in the Oregon school dispute but there is a minority view that would suppress non-public schools. The Catholic's answer to this assertion would be, of course, that not only is the private school constitutional but that both the Church and the family have obligations and rights in education that are inherent and may not be assumed by any other institution. Because of particular historical developments in the United States, Catholics felt it necessary to build a system of their own schools. There is evidence that throughout this history many Catholic leaders have thought it unfortunate

---

[27] *Pierce v. Society of Sisters,* 268 U.S. 510 (1925).

that such a separate system was necessary; but in face of, first, the general Protestant character of the early public schools, and later, because of the general secular character that developed, no other solution seemed possible that would provide for religious together with the desired general education. This has been a costly enterprise because Catholic schools receive no public financial assistance. Since Catholics pay whatever they are taxed for the support of public schools even though many of their children do not attend them, they have often felt it an unfair burden imposed on them. But, since most of the states prohibit the payment of public funds for the support of sectarian undertakings, no general public assistance has been received in supporting Catholic education. So called "fringe benefits" in the form of textbooks, transportation, and school lunch programs have been received by pupils of Catholic schools in many states. The defending argument in these cases has been the "child benefit theory," that it is the child who is directly benefited rather than the school which he attends.

The years immediately ahead will undoubtedly see increased debate and efforts on the part of some private and parochial school leaders to gain increased public support. There has been a great growth in the number and enrollments of these schools (recently many other religious groups have moved toward the establishment of their own schools); Catholics have become major blocs in many municipalities and in some states; the cost of good schools has risen precipitously; aids at the college and university level and construction loans to private schools from public sources have increased and are viewed as legal; and, with the promise of enlarged federal aid to equalize educational conditions and opportunities throughout the nation, spokesmen for these schools will stress the securing of additional public assistance.

Certainly new legislation and judicial interpretation and clarification will be necessary to establish the degree of cooperation that is possible between public agencies and private institutions in furthering the education and welfare of American youth within constitutional bounds. Despite the outcomes of this issue, Catholics will continue to find ways to maintain the religious elements of education that they deem so important — be it through new "released time" arrangements, attempting to reach *all* Catholic children in just the primary grades or just in the high school, part-time enrollment of parochial pupils in public facilities for certain aspects of education, the extension of week-end and summer schools, and/or whatever other steps prove necessary and feasible.

Although one may find a number of educational innovations that were introduced or propagated in Europe by Catholic educators, a similar development cannot be found in the United States. This is probably accounted for by the late arrival in this country of a large number of Catholic settlers and by their generally low economic and educational status. Instead of a story of uniquely different educational developments by Catholics, what one finds is rather a record of accommodation by Catholic educators and schools to the prevailing educational practices. Aside from the persistence of the Catholic theory that religious and other education should be integrated and, secondly, the generally conservative character of Catholic education, one finds that Catholic schools are much more like than unlike other American schools. The lack of abundant financial resources probably has been an important factor in the slowness with which many innovations have been incorporated into the system of Catholic educational institutions. Thus, the growth of kindergartens, junior high schools, vocational and technical schools, and junior colleges under Catholic auspices has been very limited. There is some historical irony in the adaptation of Catholic education to the 8-4 plan of division of grades between the elementary and secondary schools, although the Jesuits, who have occupied a very important place in the development of Catholic secondary education in this country, traditionally had provisions for a six-year secondary school. Catholics accommodated themselves, however, to the prevailing institutional organization only to find later that general American educational thought recommended a six-year secondary school. Foreign language instruction in the elementary grades was found in many Catholic schools a generation or two ago only to become suppressed largely on the ground that it was not quite "American" but today such instruction is becoming established in many American schools.

Catholic education is unique in the United States in the fact that it is the most extensive system of Catholic schools in the world that, generally, receive no public support. There are those among the leaders of Catholic education who have questioned the ability of Catholics to provide a complete system of education for the increasing population of the country without some public assistance but there is less disposition among them to question the need for their system or the obligation to extend its services to the largest possible number of pupils.

In conclusion it may be said that in the Catholic view education is of one piece, that the school should support and extend what is taught by the home and by the Church. This does not mean that the only purpose of schooling is specific religious formation for the school has the obligation to give an education which is useful for both time and eternity. Catholic schools attempt to give all the education required on their particular levels, not merely religious doctrine. If this complete education cannot be made available in the public schools, then separate schools will be necessary. The situation in the United States has been such that separate schools are deemed necessary. Ideally, Catholic schools must not be truncated schools because:

> Christian education takes in the whole aggregate of human life, physical and
> spiritual, intellectual and moral, individual, domestic and social, not with

a view of reducing it in any way, but in order to elevate, regulate and perfect it, in accordance with the example and teaching of Christ.[28]

The well-educated pupil does not disesteem civic interests and duties for, as the same authority says:

> The true Christian does not renounce the activities of this life, he does not stunt his natural faculties; but he develops and perfects them, by co-ordinating them with the supernatural. He thus ennobles what is merely natural in life and secures for it new strength in the material and temporal order, no less than in the spiritual and eternal.[29]

Catholic schools have not only continued the traditions of Christian education but, as has already been indicated, they have grown in numbers and size. Nevertheless, they are still a minority movement in American education. In a sense they may be regarded as a protest movement, a protest against any totalitarianization of American education that would suppress alternative systems or deny the right of parents to select the kind of education they wish their children to receive. However, in perpetuating the traditional Christian view of education the Catholic schools have made their greatest contribution to the development of American education. They have continued the effort on all levels of instruction to provide in the same institutions, and in the person of their teachers, the ideal of sound general education informed and directed by Christian ideals and principles.

Bibliography

Abelson, Paul, *The Seven Liberal Arts.* New York: Teachers College, Columbia University, 1906.

Burns, James A. and Bernard J. Kohlbrenner, *A History of Catholic Education in the United States.* New York: Benziger Brothers, 1937.

Eby, Frederick and Charles F. Arrowood, *The History and Philosophy of Education, Ancient and Medieval.* New York: Prentice-Hall, 1940.

Farrell, Allan P., *The Jesuit Code of Liberal Education: The Development and Scope of the Ratio Studiorum.* Milwaukee: Bruce, 1938.

Kane, William T., *History of Education* (rev. by John J. O'Brien). Chicago: Loyola University Press, 1954.

McCluskey, Neil G., *Catholic Viewpoint on Education.* New York: Hanover House, 1959.

McGucken, William J., *The Jesuits and Education.* Milwaukee: Bruce, 1932.

---

[28] Pope Pius XI, *Christian Education of Youth,* Official and Complete English text (Washington, D.C.: National Catholic Welfare Conference, 1930), p. 36.

[29] *Ibid.,* p. 37.

Marrou, H. I., *A History of Education in Antiquity* (translated by G. R. Lamb). New York: Sheed and Ward, 1956.

Pope Pius XI, *Christian Education of Youth,* Official and Complete English Text. Washington, D.C.: National Catholic Welfare Conference, 1930.

Power, Edward J., *A History of Catholic Higher Education in the United States.* Milwaukee: Bruce, 1958.

Rashdall, Hastings, *The Universities of Europe in the Middle Ages* (edited by F. M. Powicke and A. B. Emden). Oxford: The Clarendon Press, 1936, 3 volumes.

Ward, Leo R., *New Life in Catholic Schools.* St. Louis: B. Herder, 1958.

Woodward, William H., *Vittorino da Feltre and Other Humanist Educators.* Cambridge: University Press, 1905.

****

CHAPTER V

ISLAMIC CONTRIBUTIONS TO
AMERICAN EDUCATION

American education has a rich debt to Islam and other Eastern sources that is largely indirect and thus largely overlooked. The high school home-making teacher, for example, uses many words that have an Islamic origin: spinach, syrup, lemon, candy, sherbet, sugar, cotton, mattress, and sofa are but a few examples. An elementary arithmetic teacher, presenting a lesson on the importance of the zero as a place-holder, may not know his indebtedness to Islam from which came the word cipher and many refinements in its use. The secondary mathematics instructor teaches algebra, a word of Arabian origin, and numerous concepts developed by his Middle Eastern predecessors. A university professor in the college of pharmacy "owes his job," in some respects, to the Islamic scholars who were pioneers in this important field. Actually no educators in the West escape Islamic influence. The writers of this chapter hope to redress the typical oversight of this inheritance.

The central purpose of this chapter is to highlight the place of Islamic contributions in the evolution of American education. A historical overview, an examination of the nature and purpose of Islamic education, an analysis of specific aspects of Islamic pedagogy, and an effort to trace given educational contributions from the period of Islamic brilliance to contemporary America, constitute the major sub-emphases.

The Development of Islamic Culture

It is unfortunate that many of the Islamic gifts to the Western World have been obscured by stereotypes which have inhibited understanding and acceptance. There are still individuals who think only of tents, desert sands, swift horses, camels, caravans, exotic perfumes and spices, and nomadic tribesmen when a reference is made to anything Islamic.

Actually, it is erroneous to equate Islamic culture with the nomadic life, occasional oases, and primitive habits; for the Moslems tended the greenhouse of learning during long centuries of chaos and decadence in Western civilization. Reports from those who had had contacts with the Moslems were often distorted or misconstrued. Countless reports were misleading and inaccurate. Moslems were scornfully labeled as "those Saracens," "infidels," "barbarians." Some prejudices, evidences of residual bitterness, and gaps in information still keep individuals and cultures from accepting as facts many of the accomplishments and contributions which were part of this brilliant civilization.

The area which cradled this civilization, the Middle East, comprises those nations between Istanbul and the boundaries of China, especially the nations of Southwestern Asia and, for some purposes, Egypt. The Arab countries lie at the heart of the Middle East. Here are the crossroads of Asia, Africa, and Europe, the center of century-old communication lines and trade routes.

The dominant religion is Islam, the creed established by Mohammed, whose followers are called Moslems. The term Saracen, originally applied only to desert nomads between Syria and Arabia, but later specifically referred to those who accepted the religious tenets of Islam and who were hostile to the Crusaders — not only Arabs, but also Turks, Persians, and others who had adopted the banner of the religion of Mohammed from the eighth century onward.

Racially, the Arabs are of Semitic stock. Their original home is the Arabian peninsula, but their conquests spread them from Spain to Pakistan, as far north as the Black Sea, west along the length of the Mediterranean, south and east along the Red Sea and the Persian gulf. Their language is the mother tongue of the inhabitants of Iraq, Syria, Palestine, Egypt, Libya, Tunisia, Lebanon, Sudan, Mauritania, Algeria, and Morocco. Persia, Afghanistan, Bengal, and Pakistan use Arabic characters for their written communication, and the civilized world now uses Arabic numerals. Culturally, though not radically, Arabs include a great number of Persians, Turks, and Syrians.

Weaver suggests that thirty generations of Arab-speaking peoples kept the seeds of intellect moistened while barbarians ruled the northern part of the Roman Empire. Like America, this region developed as a hybrid society.

134

In the deserts and the mountains and the steamy fertile river valleys, from the Ganges to the Atlantic, these people were of all races and colors and classes, all creeds, all former cultures, all former empires. They included Buddhists, Christians, Moslems, Jews, Hindus, Mongolians, Chaldeans, Assyrians, Armenians, Persians, Medes, Arabs, Greeks, Egyptians, Phoenicians, Hittites, Africans, and hundreds of others whose ancient ancestors had worn the soil to dust before the earliest dawn of history.[1]

We know these regions witnessed the dawn of civilization, that some of the most dramatic episodes in the history of mankind were enacted there. Metal was first discovered and worked in prehistoric times on the southern shores of the Black Sea or the slopes of the Transcaucasian Mountains.

Both Egypt and the Euphrates Valley have been extolled as the early seedbeds of enlightened human behavior. Although the edifices in that latter valley were constructed of mud and clay, we have found the tablets of these ancients and know the proud story of their conquest of the soil. Egypt, with its plates of stone and imperishable pyramids, tells a tale nobler yet in terms of engineering prowess and administrative accomplishment. Ancient history is replete with the great deeds of the Assyrians and Babylonians, who followed in the wake of the earlier Arabs.

Many Islamic historians regard with little enthusiasm these early centuries, the periods of anarchy, captivity or aimlessness. The centuries before Mohammed they term *Djahiliya,* or roughly, the Age of Ignorance or Illiteracy. They have little sympathy with the barbarians who were the victims of Roman might and efficiency. The Christian Bible deals more kindly with the desert sheik-kings of Jerusalem and the "wise men from the East."

Barbarism is a harsh word for the pre-Islamic period though the antiquated Arabian paganism, including moon god worship and cults, in many respects warrants the statement. But there is no doubt that barbarism, however it existed, came to a rapid end when the Prophet Mohammed gave the Moslems a consistent set of moral and spiritual teachings in the form of a book, the Koran.[2]

---

[1] Henry Weaver, *The Mainspring of Human Progress* (New York: The Foundation for Economic Education, Inc., 1953), p. 104.

[2] A convenient date for the beginning of formal Saracenic education would be 650 — at which time, some 18 years after the death of Mohammed, the Koran was compiled from the notes of followers who had recorded them while Mohammed talked. Wilds comments: "It reached its highest development in Spain in the hundred years before 1050 — years during which intellectual Mohammedans (Moslems), because of persecution by orthodox reactionaries of their faith in the East, fled to the more liberal caliphates of western Africa and Spain. It closed its career of phenomenal culture about 1250, by which time the Mohammedan (Moslem) scholars had been driven from Spain before the Christian armies from the north."
Elmer Wilds, *The Foundations of Modern Education* (New York: Rinehart and Company, 1942), pp. 208-209.

Scorned and spurned at first in his home city of Mecca, as has been the case with founders of religions in other times and in other cultures, Mohammed in the first half of the seventeenth century conquered the skepticism of the Meccans from a base at Medina. Wine and gambling were abolished, rigorous spiritual demands imposed and an ideal of an ethical brotherhood established. His teachings were clear enough to have meaning for the most ignorant as well as for the learned and sophisticated.

On the whole, the Romans left few lasting marks upon the Arab world. While Rome itself was Christianized and pacified, the charm of Hellenism remained in the Eastern Mediterranean. As Constantinople grew influential, the efficient central administration was put on the defensive. The Romans won many battles but had not captured the minds of the independent Arabs, many of whom watched with interest the clash between Greek ideals, Roman organization, and Persian might. These wars lasted through the era of Mohammed[3] and are mentioned in the Koran itself.

As these powers wore each other down, the Moslems appeared on the scene with new-found solidarity through the teaching of Mohammed. The Prophet and his successor Abu-Bekr hurled the armies of the Moslems against the once-mighty legions of the Byzantine Greeks and Persians, and trounced them both. Within ten years after Mohammed's death his followers occupied Damascus, Jerusalem, Antioch, and Alexandria; and the Mua'thin called the faithful to prayer in the early centers of Christendom.

> The wave of conquest did not stop after it had submerged the best parts of the Near East. It went as far as India and it touched the shores of the Caspian Sea. From Egypt it spread westward until it was checked only by the Atlantic. Nor was it stayed there. It rushed with vigour across the Gates of Hercules into Spain and gave that Strait its present Arabic name, "Jabal Tariq," (sic) later corrupted into Gibraltar. Northwards the wave broke through the passes of the Pyrenees into France. There it was met by a new and effective opposition. The Franks, under their leader Martel, called the Arabs to a halt — nay, to a round-about-turn. That significant check was at Tours in 732 A.D., a century after the death of Muhammad.[4]

If this empire of the Moslems was greater in size than the Roman's, it was less harsh and more humane. Lane-Poole presents the 700-year occupation of Spain as a prime example of this restraint:

> It must not be supposed that the Moors, like the barbarian hordes who preceded them, brought desolation and tyranny in their wake. On the con-

---

[3] Edward A. Freeman, *The History and Conquests of the Saracens,* 2nd Edition (London: Macmillan and Co., 1876), p. 19.

[4] Khalil A. Totah, *The Contributions of the Arabs to Education* (New York: Bureau of Publications, Teachers College, Columbia University, 1926), pp. 3-4.

trary, never was Andalusia so mildly, justly and wisely governed as by her Arab conquerors. . . . Some of their Counsellors were Greeks and Spaniards, but this does not explain the problem; for those same Counsellors were unable to produce similar results elsewhere, and all the administrative talent of Spain had not sufficed to make the Gothic domination tolerable to its subjects. Under the Moors, on the other hand, the people were, on the whole, contented — as contented as any people can be whose rulers are of a separate race and creed — and far better pleased than they had been when their sovereigns belonged to the same religion as that which they nominally professed.[5]

Religious toleration was generally widespread while the Moslems ruled. Some captives in backward regions earned their ransom by their teaching of reading and writing skills to unlettered Moslems. This is quite revealing in that it shows the reverence Moslems developed for the cultivation of intellect.

When the Goths and other northern tribes had entered Europe, the Latin language fell into decay. The aging civilization shrivelled. Arabic grew as a new shoot to prop up the language of learning and to preserve the lessons of the ages. Arts and sciences were temporarily neglected in Europe until Arabic textbooks were available for perusal. Later, Europe needed the Aabic translations to recall the wisdom of the Hellenes and the oratory of the Romans. The admittedly nationalistic historian, Kheirallah, stated it quite pointedly: ". . . for Greek philosophy had blossomed in the gardens of Arab thought, while it had withered in the stony soil of Rome."[6]

The Moslems did not immediately become the great guardians of information and intellectual documents that they were to be in the ninth and tenth centuries. But time was taken to collect and preserve the classic treasures of earlier empires. Under Harun al-Rashid and al-Ma'mum, father and son, the enthusiasm of Moslems for academic knowledge reached its peak. This was during the late eighth and early ninth centuries.[7] The son, who resisted Christian proselytizing, became a renowned patron of scientists and their studies. On the other hand, Christian ministers, doctors, and academicians were frequently lionized by the earlier caliphs who needed their trained intellects. The Moslems were not above exploiting the knowledge and talents of their subjects.

But the Moslems did not remain mere passive recipients of culture very long. While the Roman Empire fell and the Byzantine Empire limped along

---

[5] Stanley Lane-Poole, *The Story of the Moors in Spain* (New York: G. P. Putnam's Sons, 1886), p. 43.

[6] George Kheirallah, *Arabia Reborn* (New Mexico: The University of New Mexico Press, 1952), pp. 39-40.

[7] Edward Hungerford, "The Rise of Arabian Learning," *The Atlantic Monthly*, October, 1886, p. 544.

a tortuous path, the faithful of Islam established schools and centers for their own study and carried away the books and manuscripts the world would need later. During the later Middle Ages and the Crusades, the contact was even greater than it had been in the eighth and ninth centuries when the internal fever for knowledge ran highest.

While the Dark Ages in Europe may not have been completely dark, they were certainly dull, dreary, and colorless. This period was the result of turmoil caused by invasion, barbarian rule, and adjustment to certain Christian ideals and practices. Many Latin manuscripts were misplaced, stored in musty places to gather dust, lost, or burned. After the furor of the Crusades had subsided and the West was ready to rediscover Greek scientific and philosophical thought, it was in a position where its demand exceeded its supply. It was at this stage of the history of culture that the Moslems were able to render a heroic and noble service. Islamic preservation of Greco-Roman culture through the gathering, storing, translating, and utilization of the best of the ancients' works was a service to culture at large and to Western culture in particular.

The gathering, the borrowing, the utilization of the works of other cultures was not indiscriminate. Von Grunebaum, the Moslem historian, states:

> Islamic civilization seems omnivorous but actually is highly selective. It has admitted, even searched for, such contributions from outside as would help it to keep its identity under changed conditions. So it welcomed Greek dialectics, the method of alegorical interpretation, the psychology of Christian asceticism, as means of broadening its base beyond the limitations inherent in the koranic text. . . . It encouraged foreign skills: the Christian physician, the Indian mathematician, and the Persian administrator and musician could count on appreciation and reward.[8]

If Islamic leaders had drawn their knowledge of classical Western civilization from Syria they dispensed it through two other channels, Sicily and Spain. The Moslems held Sicily (c. 827-1091) before the Normans occupied that gateway to Europe. Even then the Norman Roger II was a patron of Islamic learning; and one of his successors, Frederick II, established the University of Naples which employed Islamic translations of ancient texts, as did the medical school at Salerno. But it was in Spain, "the farthest province of the Mohammedan (Moslem) conquest, that the best results of the intercourse of Arabian, Jewish, and Christian civilizations became apparent. . . ."[9]

---

[8] Gustave Von Grunebaum, *Medieval Islam* (Chicago: The University of Chicago Press, 1946), pp. 320-321.

[9] Sir William Dampier, *A History of Science* (New York: The Macmillan Company, 1936), p. 83.

Spain was conquered early (711-718) and remained subject to the Moors until late in the fifteenth century. Toledo and Cordova were the most fertile fields cultivated by Islamic learning. Michael Scott in Toledo translated some of the Islamic works on astronomy. Others, under the sponsorship of Archbishop Raymon, first translated the algebra (*al-djabr,* the Arabic word) of al-Khwarizmi. And Spain was the avenue from Morocco to Southern France. The victory of Charles Martel at Tours in 732 had "limited the physical invasion of Europe" but the nobler invasion of knowledge continued for centuries.

Perhaps the most valuable contribution was the gift of "Arabic notation," the number system which still enjoys popularity. The ponderous Roman system had made it undesirable and impractical to express the astronomical sums we cope with on occasion. We have also the notion of the "zero" or cipher (both of these Islamic in origin) to express that mathematical limbo between a negative and positive quantity. Though received through the Moslems, our number system is really of Hindu origin. Hindu numerals were also known to the Greeks and Romans, who for some reason rejected them in favor of the so-called Roman numerals. The Moslems used the decimal system, developed trigonometry, measured a degree of the earth's circumference and passed much of this knowledge on to the Europeans. Leonardo of Pisa, author of the *Book of the Abacus* (1202) was the first to expound algebraic and zero concepts for Europeans. Ironically, as has often been the way of history, it was through conquest that this fruit of knowledge was able to be tasted.

Not only did Moslems refrain from pillaging and arson, they planned and built great edifices. Totah enumerates these and asks for proper recognition for Arab designers:

> Those who have visited the Mosque of 'Umar in Jerusalem, the Umayyad (*sic*) Mosque in Damascus, the Alhambra in Spain; the towers, bridges, fountains, mansions, and palaces which still exist in Syria, Palestine, Egypt, North Africa, and Spain, are found to admit the remarkable change which had come over the tastes of those tent-dwellers. To be sure they employed Byzantine artists and utilized Greek talent; but that was not to their discredit, as every individual and every nation must have tuition and guidance in youth.[10]

Islamic fervor carried Moslems to Persia and the Pyrenees, to both ends of the Mediterranean. Mohammed mobilized the missionary zeal of the Moslems They were fired with the desire to discover new learning. Their stamina was fed by their religious inspiration, and their accomplishments were con-

---

[10] Totah, *op. cit.,* p. 5.

tinually nourished and reinforced by their successes. They accepted what they perceived as destiny and began to plough more deeply in the fertile fields of study and research. This passion for learning not only led them to make countless contributions to both educational content and practice; but the desire itself, the attitude, the hunger for learning, served as a living example to those who had taken learning for granted and forgotten its adventure and romance.

But few flowers bloom forever and the petals of Islamic culture fell when Mongols and Mamluks assumed control of major parts of the Islamic Empire. Hitti traces the moral and social forces of disintegration, the "bloodshed and intrigue," the victories of Normans, Genghis Khan, and finally of Ferdinand and Isabella. The cross supplanted the crescent over the towers of Spain and Sicily as Europe rediscovered its might.[11]

Many were the influences of the Crusades on Europe — military, economic, financial and scientific. However, the exchange of ideas and the European appreciation of the role of colleges were to be among the greater benefits of these campaigns. It matters not that Islamic fields of learning lay fallow for many a century while the New World blossomed under the care of Christians; the Moslems made their contribution in an era when their help was needed most, and education is the richer for it.

The Flowering of Islamic Education

No study of the history of an educational idea or system is complete without an examination of certain writings which served as seeds for ideological flowers which blossomed from them. The student of Western education, for example, soon becomes familiar with sources like Plato's *Republic,* Quintilian's *Institutes of Oratory,* Locke's *Some Thoughts on Education,* Rousseau's *Emile,* and Dewey's *Democracy and Education.* One of the heartier seeds in Islamic education is the Koran, the sacred writings of the Moslems which Mohammed gave his followers during a period of approximately two decades prior to his death in 632 A.D.

The word Koran refers to the act of reading, and its derivation (from the Arabic root *qara'a,* to read) has both philological and educational implications, as the Koran became the most direct cause of education in Islam. As soon as Islam began to attract followers and the Koran was recognized as its principal document, a group of readers assumed important roles. Totah states that "the art of reading and writing with the Moslems began in good earnest during the first third of the seventh century A.D." and that the

---

11 Philip K. Hitti, *History of the Arabs* (New York: Macmillan and Co., 1940), pp. 179-203.

Koran "gave charters to the first and to most of the schools among the Moslems."[12]

From its first planting, then, the seed of Islamic education was divinely inspired. The entire educational content and process had an aura of the spiritual. It is not surprising that teachers, students, learning materials, and centers of education had sacred dimensions which transcended the mundane and materialistic.

Both in the West and in the East, the flower of Islamic education was nurtured. Cultural centers like Cordova and Granada in southern Spain provided fertile soil which facilitated educational growth and the healthy reproduction of ideas and achievements. In the East, too, some of the caliphs' courts served as educational hubs. Wilds writes that Eastern caliphs "surrounded themselves with groups of learned Nestorian Christians and Jews, and often themselves became ardent scholars. . . . In connection with these courts, vast libraries were fostered, with manuscripts gathered from far corners of the earth."[13]

Wilds cites the example of one of these courts:

> . . . The caliph Haroun-Al-Raschid (sic) of Baghdad, a contemporary of Charlemagne, and one of the first great patrons of Moslem learning, saw the need for elementary schools and established a school in connection with each mosque, in which reading, writing, simple numeration, and the precepts of the Koran were taught. This custom was handed down and became the pattern for such schools throughout all Moslem domains. . . .[14]

Under al-Ma'mun (Mamun the Great, 813-833), al-Rashid's successor, Islamic education reached even greater heights with the expansion of educational opportunity, endowment of scholars, and increase in various educational facilities like observatories and libraries.

It is interesting that so many Christian countries failed to look over their garden fence for so many centuries at Islamic accomplishments. While Moslems were planting, transplanting, and crossing countless varieties of educational flowers, their Christian neighbors let their old plants go to seed and weed. With reference to the brilliance of Islamic education in Spain, for example, Lane-Poole writes, "For nearly eight centuries under her Mohammedan (Moslem) rulers, Spain set to all Europe a shining example of a civilized and enlightened state."[15] Lane-Poole points out that art, literature, science, mathematics, history, philosophy, and jurisprudence in Spain were truly alive and that those who wanted to grow in their knowledge of these

---

12 Torah, *op. cit.,* p. 12.

13 Wilds, *op. cit.,* p. 222.

14 Wilds, *ibid.,* pp. 222-223.

15 Lane-Poole, *op. cit.,* p. vi.

141

disciplines "flocked from France and Germany and England to drink from the fountain of learning which flowed only in the cities of the Moors."[16]

Aims of Islamic Education

Unlike their Western neighbors, the Moslems were able to achieve a pleasant balance between the real and the ideal, the natural and the supernatural, the temporal and the eternal, the scientific and the theological. While other-worldly concerns, attention to the life hereafter, and the search for salvation channeled and preoccupied Western education, the Moslems accepted the basic ingredients of their faith and added to their study of theology and philosophy countless dimensions directed at experimentation with the observable and the immediate. They did not retreat to their caves in an effort to find personal solitude, salvation, and peace; but they welcomed the exchange of ideas in the open market place.

It is true that Moslems were willing to memorize their Koran and accept the tenets of their faith quite readily, but they left the doors of their minds and laboratories open to study of mathematics, medicine, chemistry, astronomy, geography, and other academic areas. They could enjoy their Aristotelian writings in the fullest sense, while their Western colleagues found acceptance of Aristotle intriguing but difficult, unnatural, and dangerous.

The aims of Islamic education, then, included a balancing of the spiritual, esthetic, and empirical. Islamic education had breadth and depth, continuity and flexibility. It provided for transmission of its heritage but did not rule out practical and functional concerns. It had its pitfalls, its blind spots, its lag between lip-service and practice, its moments of the colorless and meaningless. But it was a petunia in an onion patch when compared with education outside of the Islamic world.

Islamic Pedagogical Works

Islamic educational writing seems to have had its most significant period from about the middle of the ninth century A.D. up through the seventeenth century. The tenth and eleventh centuries were prolific periods for educational concerns which explored: educational objectives, retention, desirable conditions for learning, teachers' salaries, pupil-teacher relationships, the curriculum, and other problems which strike a familiar note today.

Al-Ghazali, who died in 1111 A.D., appears to have been outstanding among Arab educational writers. Of his work Totah writes: ". . . In al-Ghazali's work on education there is originality. . . . His words breathe the

---

[16] Lane-Poole, *ibid.*, pp. vi-vii.

sincerity and earnestness which marked the true teacher. There was nothing hollow about al-Ghazali's theories of education."[17]

Al-Zarnudji is an Arab educational writer who deserves recognition. He lived toward the end of the twelfth century and the beginning of the thirteenth century. His *Ta'lim al-Muta'allim-Tariq at-Ta'allum* (*Instruction of*

Bettmann Archive

BOYS' SCHOOL IN ANCIENT ARABIA.

the Student: The Method of Learning)[18] was written in 1203 and is a compelling piece which points up a variety of pedagogical concerns typical of

---

[17] Totah, *op. cit.*, p. 76.

[18] G. E. Von Grunebaum and Theodora M. Abel (authors of an introduction to this work and translators), al-Zarnudji, *Ta'lim al-Muta'allim-Tariq at-Ta'allum* (New York: King's Crown Press, 1947).

143

the full bloom of Arab educational theory. The *Ta'lim* is quite similar to the earlier work of al-Ghazali though no specific reference is made to its predecessor.

In the *Ta'lim*, al-Zarnudji has something to say to both teachers and learners. He continually emphasizes the importance of a religious commitment which should undergird all education. His respect for the traditional, the enduring, persisting aspects of knowledge is apparent. Al-Zarnudji extolls the virtues of jurisprudence as an academic area, and there is a similarity between his love for jurisprudence and Quintilian's devotion to oratory. One might be reminded of Plato when al-Zarnudji states his belief that knowledge of the ingredients or attributes of the good life such as courage and humility can protect the individual against their evil opposites.

Al-Zarnudji reminds the teacher to be sensitive to the needs and interests of students. He calls attention to the importance of readiness as it relates to learning. He suggests that the teacher who really knows his students as persons can do a better job of guiding and counseling them. He acknowledges the fact that the motivation a student brings with him is crucial in his academic success. He cautions the teacher against seeking shortcuts in education and points out that abiding learning is a slow process. He reminds the teacher to proceed from the familiar to the unfamiliar and to invite discussion, argument, and questioning in order to facilitate understanding and retention.

Students, writes the Islamic educator, should love learning, have a deep respect for their teachers, stick with their studies in a continuous and persisting manner, write things down only after they are fully understood and digested, and be alert to all types of educational opportunities. Al-Zarnudji makes one recommendation to students which too few of them heed even today when he advises them to first choose an area of study and then seek out the most outstanding teacher in this field or the finest institution devoted to this area. His point is well taken as he implies that not every institution is suited to the needs of each individual scholar. A final suggestion of interest is al-Zarnudji's idea that each student should carry writing equipment with him at all times. In this way, the student can capture an idea which he hears in a discussion, forum, or conversation.

While some of al-Zarnudji's ideas are infiltrated by superstitions, biases, and prejudices which were a product of his age and his philosophical orientation, other thoughts still wear well. Von Grunebaum and Abel tell us that the popularity of the *Ta'lim* must have been enduring since three commentaries were written on this work during the sixteenth century.[19]

In educational writing one may not be as impressed with the consistent

---

[19] Von Grunebaum and Abel, *ibid.,* p. 1, footnote.

quality, brilliance, or creativity of the Moslems as he might be in other areas, but Islamic educational writings compare favorably with those of the Western World at this same time even though both had a tendency to center their attention on rather petty details and weary arguments. It is indeed unfortunate that there are so few translations of Eastern and Middle Eastern pedagogical works as many insights could be gained through a study of them.

Islamic Teaching Methods

A close relationship existed between Islamic religion and education, for the mosque was not only the place of worship but, as the Jewish synagogue, was also an educational center. Islamic religious concepts, expressed primarily through the Koran, provided an educational aim and an underlying continuity to the offerings of the agencies of education.

In the mosque, the basic method of education employed to teach children about the Koran and other related customs anticipated Froebel's symbolic play circle or a contemporary reading circle. Children formed a circle around their teacher. The teacher read from the sacred writings, briefly discussed the meaning, and aided the students in learning the material. This was essentially a catechetical method of teaching where there was a primary source, a presentation, memorization, and recitation. One is reminded here of some of the schools of ancient Greece, the Roman *ludus*, various medieval church schools, and the early Lutheran schools of the Reformation. Vestiges of this approach still persist today.

In addition to the learning circle at the mosque, children could attend the *katatib*, an elementary school not connected with the mosque and common by the ninth century, where pupils had their first encounter with basic skills in reading, writing, and other subjects. The Koran was still the major vehicle around which learnings were based and was a model for usage and structure in something of a Ciceronian fashion. Wealthier parents had tutors for their children in their own homes, and these tutors concentrated on character formation. Methods which were employed in the mosque and the *katatib* became so much a part of the system that some of the procedures continued up to the twentieth century. It is alleged that some Moslems could recite the Koran from memory as a result of their continuous exposure to its contents.

With the hours of memorization and recitation, it is not surprising that little Moslem boys became restless and that their teachers resorted to a method with a long, if somewhat infamous, history — corporal punishment. Some limits were placed upon what the teacher was allowed in the administration of punishment, as, for example, a range of from three to ten strokes with a whip for failure to pray. As in the case of ancient Sparta, the boys were expected to demonstrate their courage, ability to bear pain without whimpering, and control in refraining from seeking the intercession of others.

Islamic educators would have found some areas of agreement with the *Ratio Studiorum* of later Jesuit teachers in the insistence upon repetition and drill. One Islamic writer points up the importance of this approach to learning when he comments, "What was learned yesterday should be repeated five times over; that of the day before four times, and that of the day before that three times,"[20] and so forth.

While one might be tempted to express outright criticism for the singleness of purpose and approach in these early schools with their memorization, drill, and punishments, Islamic teachers were dependent upon manuscripts and did not have printed books, so their task of teaching was not an easy one.

While methodology was uniform, routinized, colorless, and inflexible in the lower Islamic schools, the institutions of higher learning presented a different picture. In the universities, the Moslems displayed their real pedagogical virtuosity. Rules were kept to a minimum; there were no standardized programs and no examinations; diplomas and degrees were not granted lest the students get the impression that learning could come to an end with the acquisition of a piece of paper. Weaver discusses the intellectual freedom and climate of learning in this excerpt:

> Classes were held on an open-house basis. Anyone in quest of knowledge was free to wander about and listen. If he decided to remain, he picked a teacher and privately discussed with him what he wanted to learn and what he should study, and they agreed upon a fee. If, after joining the class, he didn't get the knowledge he wanted, he stopped paying the teacher and went to another teacher or another university. When he had learned what he thought he ought to know, he quit school and put his new knowledge to practical test.[21]

The pedagogical writings of Ibn Khaldun are especially interesting and enlightening when one seeks a picture of teaching at the higher levels. Ibn Khaldun's *Muqaddimah* contains a variety of refreshing approaches to methodology. Just as Herbart attempted to systematize the learning process in his famous four or five steps, Ibn Khaldun proposed that the teacher discuss the subject in general, elaborate on various specific points already established, and finally, clarify all points through detailed consideration.

Ibn Khaldun recommended that a student study only one subject at a time; that there should not be prolonged lapses between lectures; that students be invited to ask questions and participate in discussions; and that students be encouraged to disagree with their professors when they could not accept certain conclusions reached by these professors.

---

[20] Totah, *op. cit.*, p. 61.

[21] Weaver, *op. cit.*, p. 106.

Totah informs us that debating was quite prevalent in Islamic education and that various Islamic educators believed that debate would encourage reflective thought which could not be achieved by mere repetition.[22] Lecturing, however, was the primary method of teaching; yet it was not a one-way process. Al-'abdari suggested that the lecturer follow this procedure:

1. The lecturer is to begin by the formula, "There is no power and no might save in God."
2. He is to pray to the Almighty against slips of the tongue.
3. Then he is to present his material.
4. He should give reference to the work of other scholars.
5. He should state his proposition and support it.
6. It is proper to give the listeners an opportunity to discuss.
7. Under no circumstance is he to lose his poise when being heckled.[23]

In addition to the lecture method, various experimental procedures were encouraged in the laboratories; and students were encouraged to acquire certain attitudes of objectivity, reserving judgment, comparing data, viewing certain findings as tentative, and so forth. This scientific methodology preceded the work of Bacon, and our problems approach today is related to Islamic procedures in the universities, laboratories, and observatories.

The Organization of Islamic Education

The early stages of Islamic education were at first slow, informal, unsystematic, and largely private in nature. The individual mosque served as an instructional center. A scholar who displayed competence in a given religious or academic area finally earned the right to teach others and formed a new circle of neophytes around him. They in turn were issued an *ijaza,* or authorization to teach, from their instructor when he was convinced that they were ready.[24]

It was not until the number of converts to Islam increased sufficiently that a more systematic educational program evolved. There was a considerable growth in the number of schools, particularly at the higher levels, throughout the ninth and tenth centuries. The Seljuk Turks in the Mesopotamian section of the Islamic world are credited with the finishing touches of the newer educational system which marked the final stage in the Muslim edueducational pattern.[25] Offerings in some later Saracenic schools were very

---

[22] Totah, *ibid.,* p. 62.

[23] Totah, *ibid.,* p. 60, ft. 8.

[24] H. A. R. Gibb, *Mohammedanism* (New York: The New American Library, 1955) (Mentor Book), p. 111.

[25] Edward D. Myers, *Education in the Perspective of History* (New York: Harper & Brothers Publishers, 1960), p. 202.

comprehensive and well coordinated. Beginning with the Koran, the lower schools expanded their program to include religion, grammar, arithmetic fundamentals, reading, writing, and some science. The scope of the curriculum at the higher levels was indeed impressive and encompassed literature, philology, medicine, surgery, anatomy, pharmacy, chemistry, physics, algebra, geometry, trigonometry, metallurgy, geology, geography, astronomy, history, jurisprudence, and so forth. The Islamic program made the best medieval *trivium* and *quadrivium* look unsophisticated. Another distinct type of school which was founded in the eleventh century was the *madrasa* which helped direct the education of leaders in theology and politics. During this time, scholarships, rations, and pensions for both teachers and learners flowed more freely, and education became more and more a state function.

There were two separate and distinct phases in Islamic education: the initial, informal, and spontaneous organization indigenous to the mosque and the later larger, more carefully organized, state supported institutions which gradually evolved as the Moslems placed increasing emphasis on the process of education.

At the height of Islamic influence, primary schools, some still attached to mosques, colleges, and universities, were spread all over the Islamic world, including Khurasan, Syria, Palestine, Egypt, Northern Africa, Sicily, and Spain. While the largest and finest schools were found in the capitals, provincial towns and villages still had considerable educational opportunity. Any aristocracy which existed in education was an aristocracy of brains — not of material means.

As in Rome, the father had the responsibility of guiding the character of his son and helping him develop skills during his early years. There was a very close relationship between father and son until the son reached the age for more formal education. As a part of this home education, the child was expected to master the prayers by the time he was six.

The primary schools were open to boys and girls of all classes, so every child could have some basic contacts with education. Poorer children might remain for only a few years before being forced by economic necessity to join the labor force, while children with more financial resources could continue. The tutorial system was employed for some of the unusually privileged children. Mastery of the Koran was essential for continued success and acceptance as adults.

At the secondary level, although this stage of education was quite varied according to locale and dependent upon the socio-economic status of the student and his academic aspirations, there were some identifiable institutions which resembled an academy or private boarding school for college-bound students. There were apparently only a few of these privately supported schools. The seclusion of women was a later development and although more girls were educated in the home, there are records of girls continuing to be taught with boys at this level.

Vocational education was also stressed in the Islamic system of education. Technical instruction was given for certain skilled trades and crafts and for some of the professions. While these private technical schools were not large, they became numerous in the eighth and ninth centuries.[26] There was also commercial training, a beginning effort to develop a science of economics and to establish a basis for business and trade.[27]

In the Arab educational organization, there was no provision for an established adult education program, but mosques as in Hebrew prototypes, in the more populous areas, performed an educational function through their lectures, discussion groups, and libraries. Myers explains[28] that there was also an opportunity for the more highly educated adults to join small study groups in various homes. These adult efforts are indeed notable when one reminds himself of the state of affairs in education in the West at this time.

The Movement Toward Universal Education

Perhaps the most profound and vital contribution of the Moslems to educational theory lies in their movement toward universal, free education. Taking the long point of view and looking especially for one of the most direct threads which extends from the Moslems to American education, we should note the efforts of Moslems: to encourage capable boys and girls of all stations of life, to accept teachers of different races and persuasions, to make library materials more accessible to more people, and to spread general enlightenment. Long before Western Europeans like Vives, Luther, Comenius, and Pestalozzi championed the ideal of open educational opportunity, the Moslems were putting this ideal into action in a variety of ways. American Jeffersons and Manns owed more to their Islamic predecessors than they realized or accorded recognition for a knowledge of such Islamic ideals that had been directly introduced into the mainstream of the Western intellectual tradition.

It is true that the Moslems did not have a compulsory system of education; that there was some evidence of socio-economic stratification in education; that an intellectual aristocracy existed; and that girls were not always as welcome as boys in the schools. But the Moslems went a long way toward the realization of a democratic, equalitarian system of education. In various respects, they led Western educational practices by over a millennium.

---

[26] See Myers, *ibid.*, p. 199.

[27] See Wilds, *op. cit.*, p. 215.

[28] Myers, *op. cit.*, pp. 200-201.

The Christian West was behind Islam in democratic practice. Mohammed specifically indicated that the poor and the rich should be equal in the responsibility for the acquisition of knowledge. There are many examples of eminent scholars — al-Djahiz, Ahmad ibn Hanbal and al-Ghazali — who came from humble origins. Financial aid was often available for young men and women who had abilities worthy of recognition, and at the lower levels many children in the more populated areas had open access to basic educational opportunities.

Teachers, Students, and Their Relationships

In the earlier stages of Islamic education before opportunities for schooling were more easily available and before teachers became more numerous, teachers at all levels were viewed with respect and appreciation. Gradually, however, prestige became more and more associated with the level at which one taught. The reputation of the teacher in the lower school dwindled, while that of his professional colleagues in the higher schools expanded. Eventually, teachers at various levels carried different titles based upon their assignment, experience, and preparation. Wages varied according to the teacher's ability to command a better position, and some teachers supplemented their income by provisions for room and board and other means.

The status of the Islamic professor must have earned for him both the respect and envy of his brother teachers at lower levels of education and others in the citizenry. With reference to the prestige which the professor enjoyed, Totah writes:

> He was not a cog in a wheel nor was he a nonentity in the social system. He had personality and standing. Nowadays, education is tempted to worship buildings, equipment, textbooks, and the curriculum. With the Arabs, the professor was, practically, all in all. . . .[29]

Students were drawn from all over the Islamic empire by the professor's personal reputation rather than by the reputation of the institution at which he taught. Classes might contain as many as seven hundred students. The individual professor conferred upon his students their right to teach after they had completed his requirements, and this added to his prestige.

Nor was the position of the student, especially at the university level, without certain prestige and privilege. Certain class and economic barriers were laid aside for the gifted student. The university life was a good one for a student from more lowly beginnings because his lodging and board were often assured. Also, there was a chance to live in the world of ideas, exchange thoughts not on the basis of social standing but on the merit of the

---

[29] Totah, *op. cit.*, p. 88.

idea. The Moslem university was not assigned a dark place in the Islamic cultural closet but a prominent place in the Islamic living room.

An interesting dialogue between two Moslem students in Spain has been preserved for us and indicates that even the rich student was serious in his academic endeavors. This was not a "country club" for him but a serious undertaking. This conversation takes place between a poor student, "working his way through college," and another who had independent means:

Poor Student: I am more ambitious than you are in seeking learning because you study with the aid of a golden lamp while I study by the street lights.

Rich Student: This argument is against you and not for you; because you are studying hard in order to exchange your present condition for one like mine, while I learn for learning's sake in this life and in the world to come.[30]

While relationships between pupils and teachers, students and professors, were formal, they were not without mutual respect and feeling. Totah cites the writings of al-Ghazali as an example of the spirit which he believed should exist between a teacher and his students. In his works, al-Ghazali tells the teacher to:

a. Have sympathy with his students and treat them as if they were his own children.
b. Follow the example of the Prophet and seek no remuneration for tuition.
c. Be perfectly honest with the students and prevent them from presenting themselves as candidates for a degree before they are worthy of it.
d. Exhort them and rebuke them for misconduct.
e. Not revile the subject of a fellow-teacher to a student.
f. Guard against the teaching of matter which is beyond the comprehension of the student.
g. Practice what he preaches lest his deeds belie his words.[31]

Libraries

Today's public school librarian in America has many things in common with the Moslems in their period of brilliance. Here were people who truly respected and loved books; hungered for learning and the insights the printed word could give them; gathered books with a fervor equal to that of a multi-millionaire going after bigger and better holdings; and who valued certain volumes as an informed art collector cherishes his Rembrandt. Some Moslems even went so far as to carry volumes of books with them when

---

[30] Quoted from "Al-Maqqari," Vol. I, p. 33 and found in Totah, *ibid.*, p. 44.
[31] Totah, *ibid.*, p. 63.

they went on extended trips, lest they be parted from their priceless possessions — the books themselves, the thoughts they contained, and later, unfortunately, the symbol of prestige they represented. Others measured their status and success in their literary holdings as some contemporary Americans might tend to judge the measure of their lives by the car or cars parked in their garage.

One of the Islamic leaders who exemplified their desire to gather books, to be close to them and to disseminate their intellectual treasures was the Caliph al-Ma'mun (El Mamoun) in Baghdad. In the early decades of the ninth century A.D., he endowed the first important "House of Wisdom."

> . . . The provinces of his empire were searched for previous manuscripts; his collectors were busy everywhere — in Syria, in Armenia, in Egypt. Governors of provinces had instructions to further the work. Collections of books were taken as tribute. Among the terms of peace with the Greek Emperor, Michael the Stammerer, was the exaction of a series of the manuscripts of Greek authors. Vast numbers of books were brought from all quarters to Baghdad, constituting a library which represented the accumulated learning of the East. . . .[32]

Al-Ma'mun not only collected volumes but also had them classified, transcribed, and translated by competent scholars. Those works which were deemed of value to the students were translated into Arabic so they could be put to use.[33]

Although al-Ma'mun initiated the great library movement with its attending educational influences, he was to be outdone by an even greater enthusiast, al-Hakam II of Cordova. Here was a collector's collector! Although his main library was centered in his palace at Cordova, it is reported that there were seventy other places where his materials were kept in various cities and towns of Spain![34] Various sources report that al-Hakam's collection grew to 600,000 volumes. By way of contrast, Thut writes that the royal library of France was said to have only 900 volumes 400 years later.[35] Though Alcuin is remembered for his contribution to manuscript copying under the sponsorship of Charlemagne, al-Hakam II seems to have operated on a much larger scale both by quantity and breadth of content. An appealing sidelight regarding al-Hakam's literary interests is that he was much more than just a collector in the sense of seeing how many volumes he could gather.

---

[32] Hungerford, op. cit., p. 545.

[33] See ibid., p. 546.

[34] Ibid., p. 549.

[35] I. N. Thut, The Story of Education (New York: McGraw-Hill Book Company, Inc., 1957), pp. 176-177.

. . . Not only did he possess all these volumes, but, unlike many collectors, he is said to have read them all, and even to have annotated them. So learned was he that his marginal notes were greatly prized by scholars of after times, and the destruction of a great part of his library by the Berbers was a serious loss to Arab literature.[36]

The spirit of scholarship which possessed al-Hakam also led him to endow writers and students and to open a number of free schools so children of the poorer families could be exposed to the romance of learning. When one remembers that his rule was during the tenth century, one cannot help but be impressed by his enlightened realization that libraries could be centers of learning, a point of view reflected in America centuries later by Franklin, Mann, and Carnegie.

Importance of Islamic Higher Education to the Western World

Universities in the Western tradition are institutions organized for teaching and research in the branches of higher learning. They grew from Islamic seedlings, Moslem *madariss*. European universities of the Middle Ages were directly modeled after their earlier Islamic counterparts. They grew from church schools, adopted the feature of "nations" or colleges within the university, and encouraged scholarship and travel — all part of the debt Europe owes to the Moslems. Bait al-Hikma, a center of advanced learning in Baghdad, may deserve the title of "having been the first university of the medieval and the modern world, for it bore the torch aloft long before Bologna, Paris, Prague, Oxford and Cambridge. It was on the banks of the Tigris, and not on those of the Seine, Thames, Rhine, and Tiber that the European Renaissance was born," concludes Totah, who translated the name of this early school as the "House of Wisdom."[37]

Only scanty references to this center exist, but it lasted from the early ninth century through the tenth. In modern usage it would probably be more accurately termed an academy rather than a university, but Bait al-Hikma became the most prominent scientific and intellectual center of its day, and prominent faculty went as consultants to other parts of the Mediterranean world. A noted scholar of both astronomy and mathematics served at one time as its librarian. Scholars in all fields came in great numbers to Baghdad to debate widely varied intellectual issues.[38] Although it was

---

[36] Lane-Poole, *op. cit.*, p. 155.

[37] Totah, *op. cit.*, pp. 28-29.

[38] One example was the debate (*Munatharah*) on the use of pronouns, which took place between the grammarians al-Kasa'i and Sibawaihi as cited by Totah (Totah, *ibid.*, p. 27).

the first scientific institute or academy of its period, discounting earlier Hellenistic institutions, it had a very comprehensive library and an astronomical observatory. The reasons for its close remain unclear; Bait al-Hikma might have been suppressed during theological controversies in the eleventh century. At any rate it ceased to exist under that name and was replaced by other institutions.

In the twelfth century an Egyptian college, Dar al-Ilm, developed on the Nile; sponsored by the Fatimites, it lasted for a century and a quarter. Later replaced by a theological school, the college probably stressed medicine, philology, grammar and astronomy and augmented its faculty in a way familiar to modern universities, by inviting visiting professors in such areas as mathematics, logic and jurisprudence.

A chain of *madariss* (colleges) was started by Nizam al-Mulk, who lent his name to these enterprises. Because of the heresies and inter-Islam disputes these *madariss* were instituted as theological and political centers first, and only secondly as universities. They spread quite rapidly, however, and a number of those at Baghdad, Cairo, Damascus, and Jerusalem became quite significant. In Spain, especially Cordova, many were established. Since their founder also provided a generous endowment, it was common to name these schools Nizamiyyahs as they became institutionalized. Myers identifies two distinct divisions of the Nizamiyyah, one the theological school and the other a college for civil service trainees. These "state" schools were government-subsidized and widely copied.[39] Both the curricula and the productivity of work at these centers warrants the title college.[40] Hundreds were founded,

---

[39] Myers, *op. cit.*, pp. 202, 203.

[40] "The Arab-Moslems like to promote the thesis that it was their culture that presented the idea of the university; that the college is the Arabic *madrasa* (hall of learning) with students' quarters attached; that the hood is the Moslem doctor's *tailasan* (cape); that the degree or *license* is only his *ajaza* (written authorization to the student to teach what he had learned)." Footnote: H. A. Gibb, "The University in the Arab-Moslem World," pp. 281-297, in Edward Bradby, Ed., *The University Outside Europe*. (New York: Oxford University Press, 1939). Furthermore, claim the Arab authorities, the Moslem institutions promoted learning on an unprecedented scale even before the European universities; that the college-mosque of El Azhar at Cairo, which was to become the principal educational institution of the Moslem world, was founded in 969 A.D.; in the fifteenth century, there were 155 *madariss* in Damascus alone. These institutions had religion as their core as did the medieval universities of Europe. But the foundation of religious learning in the curriculum consisted of the study of Arabic and the humanities, as represented by Arabic literature, thus providing the linguistic and literary tradition of Arabic; mathematics was also included, and Damascus had three colleges for medical students. The greatness of these institutions was demonstrated also by thousands of textbooks in the early and later medieval periods, and the vast biographical dictionaries of scholars in all fields of learning. (*Ibid.*, p. 282.) See also Roucek, Joseph S., "Education in the Middle East," *Phi Delta Kappan*, Vol. 37, June, 1956, p. 440.

many with one or more specialties and strengths.[41]

Once the state decided to sponsor colleges, financial problems melted away. A nearby source of revenue was designated by the caliphs to help sustain the college, almost always in the form of real estate. Salahaddeen (Saladin), for one, is reported to have endowed al-Madrasa al-Suyifiyyah, in Cairo, with thirty-two shops and a similar college in Jerusalem with a whole street. So these colleges prospered, hundreds of them in all, and dozens in other centers as Baghdad, Damascus, Cordova and Jerusalem. Scholars fought their way to those gardens of learning which were the successors to Athens and Alexandria, the forerunners of Oxford, Cambridge, Paris and Vienna.

The budding university developed in Spain where some of the best Moslem scholars dwelt with the students. Departments or sub-schools such as those for medicine or astronomy, music, navigation and physics were established. From the tenth to the fifteenth centuries Spanish Moslem universities made great contributions in botany, astronomy, mathematics and philosophy, all of which had advanced courses or departments.

A varied curriculum extending well beyond the *trivium* and *quadrivium* included philosophy, art, and history. Officials of the state, professors, lawyers, theologians, all were trained in the Koran, in poetry, law and rhetoric. These became the "intelligentsia" of the Islamic world for four or five hundred years.

It is difficult to apply an objective measure to the contributions of the Islamic universities. A college may train and educate persons willing to learn, but a university as we define it finds its own separate productivity as a source of generation of new knowledge. The Moslems were more than mere transmitters; they transmuted, modified and improved the material they worked with from translations.

Arabic-writing scholars produced works which pioneered in certain fields and opened up new ones, like Djabir ibn-Haiyan (Latin, Geber, c. 775),

---

[41] "Seats of learning were located as the demand for them arose: at Samarcand and Bochara beyond the Oxus, at Balk among its western sources, at Isfahan in Persia, at Baghdad on the Tigris and Cufa on the Euphrates, at Bassora near the Persian Gulf, at Alexandria and Cairo in Egypt, at Fez and Morocco in Western Africa, at Cordova, Seville, Toledo, Granada, Salamanca, and Alcala in Spain, and even in Sicily. Bassora and Cufa originated rival schools of the Arabic language; Baghdad was the literary metropolis of the East, Cordova of the West. Alexandria is credited with more than twenty schools in which philosophy was taught, and about the beginning of the eleventh century there were as many more in Cairo alone, to which crowds of students resorted from all parts of the world, to listen to instructors who discoursed on the philosophy of Aristotle. In Cordova, we hear of not less than eighty schools, apparently of an academical or collegiate order, where professors, influential at home, became renowned in Christian Europe. Besides these, the Kalif El Hakem (*sic*) founded, in the same city, an academy, which grew into fifteen institutions devoted to special sciences. . . ." Hungerford, Edward, "The Rise of Arabian Learning," *The Atlantic Monthly*, October, 1886, p. 547.

who wrote extensively on the then new field of alchemy. The Persian al-Khwarizmi published the first al-Jabr mathematics book. Others such as al-Razi (Latin, Rhazes, 865-925) and Ibn-Sina (Latin, Avicenna, 980-1037) explored the field of contagious diseases. A physician from Dasmascus worked out the idea of a pulmonary circulation well before Michael Servetus.

Persian lore and Greek wisdom blended by the Moslems led into the study of alchemy. They searched for an elixir to prolong life, an acid that would turn stones to precious metals. Gibbon in the *Decline and Fall* admitted that "the science of chemistry owes its origin and improvement to the industry of the Saracens. They first invented and named the alembic for the purposes of distillation, analyzed the substances of three kingdoms of nature, tried the distinction and affinities of alkalies and acids, and converted the poisonous minerals into soft and salutary remedies."[42] Occult art led to sophisticated science, chiefly through the Spanish Moors. The outstanding contributor was Djabir ibn-Haiyan of Kufah, the Latin "Geber" (his most significant treatises are in that language of scholarship now).

Knowledge of chemistry contributed remedies for the treatment of the sick. Moslems were among the first pharmacists and that meant better medicine. They translated Galen's work into Arabic and initiated research in medicine and surgery.[43] "From the Ganges to the Atlantic, they built medical schools and hospitals. While one of these was flourishing at Salerno, Italians a little farther north are credited with doing the first surgical operations ever performed in Europe. Since dissection was forbidden in Europe, the Italians doubtlessly learned their anatomy from the Saracens. Surely no doctor, even in the Dark Ages, would have had the nerve to cut open a patient without some notion of what he was going to find inside."[44] Ibn-Sina (Avicenna) developed the great *Canon* or compendium of drugs and cures, a text most respected by the West. This Persian doubled as an Aristotelian philosopher and helped to publish an *Encyclopedia,* in addition to that medical "bible."

The existence of a body of knowledge permitted caliphs to establish strict requirements for practitioners of medicine so that "quacks" and charlatans were purged. During the ninth century over fifty Christian physicians were in the service of the caliphs. Baghdad had more than 800 men pass the examination in a single year in the tenth century. Hospitals and clinics multiplied and some had libraries and special training programs. The best had separate wards for women, others for the insane, and high sanitation standards.

---

[42] Edward Gibbon, *The History of the Decline and Fall of the Roman Empire* (London: Plummer and Lewis, Printers, 1819), Vol. X, pp. 49-50.

[43] Weaver, *ibid.,* p. 109.

[44] Weaver, *ibid.,* p. 109.

The knowledge that the world was round was gleaned from the Greeks, then passed on to the European scholars who viewed it cautiously. By 1000 A.D. various tables on astronomy and navigation were prepared for sailors. The Arabic numerals, the scientific "zero," algebra, all were contributions to the world of mathematics, although very little was added to Euclid except for trigonometry with sines, tangents and co-tangents.[45] Quadratic equations were developed as an algebraic tool. Philosophical gains were made simply by translating parts of Aristotle and trying to interpret them to the people. All his work on logic, and much of that on physics, psychology, ethics and metaphysics was transported by Jewish scholars but interpreted by Avicenna and Averroes (whose interpretation was condemned in 1270 at Paris).[46]

The garden of human knowledge flourished under Moslem care. Three hundred years of this fruitful labor culminated in Cordova, where there was a direct cross-pollination with Western culture. Euopeans came to the schools of Spain, Sicily, Tunis, and Morocco to study medicine, surgery, chemistry, higher mathematics, astronomy, and philosophy. Their willingness to accept students and teachers regardless of their financial status, nationality, religious persuasions, or other factors and to *accept* rather than to merely *tolerate* differences is a bright spot in the history of higher education. Cordova is exemplary of this open spirit.

> . . . To Cordova came from all parts of the world students eager to culti-
> vate poetry, to study the sciences, or to be instructed in divinity or law; so
> that it became the meetingplace of the eminent in all matters, the abode of
> the learned, and the place of resort for the studious; its interior was always
> filled with the eminent and the noble of all countries, its literary men and
> soldiers were continually vying with each other to gain renown, and its
> precincts never ceased to be the arena of the distinguished, and the repository
> of the true and virtuous. . . .[47]

The impact of Islamic education upon European thought is brought into even sharper focus when we realize that:

> . . . Gerbert (later Pope Sylvester II) studied in Spain; Gerard of Cremona
> sought a copy of the *Almagest* in Toledo; Daniel de Morlai left the Uni-
> versity of Paris for Toledo, and brought thence to England many precious
> books; Michael Scott studied at Toledo, and a monk of Monte Cassino named
> Constantine at Baghdad; Athelard of Bath pursued Arabic science and phi-
> losophy in Asia Minor, Egypt, and Spain; while Arabic textbooks in medicine

---

45 Wilds, *op. cit.,* p. 218.

46 James Mulhern, *A History of Education* (New York: The Ronald Press Company, 1959), p. 242.

47 Lane-Poole, *op. cit.,* pp. 130-131.

157

for a long time dominated the course of instruction given at the celebrated medical school at Montpellier.[48]

To the above list, Roger Bacon, Albertus Magnus, Robertus Anglicus, Daniel Morley, Ramondus Lullus, Arnold Villa Novanus, and other scholars could be added. The influence of Islamic higher education was broad and deep, brilliant and multi-faceted, dynamic and persisting.

Summary

The aroma of Islamic influence on American education is like that of an exotic flower, quite penetrating, but unrecognized as to source. For in the same way we have appreciated the benefits of Islamic civilization, without being conscious of the debt. Our asphalt paving, cotton, ice cream and peaches, spices and fabrics come to us from the Moslems in addition to their many contributions of the intellect. New information is constantly being discovered enabling us to gain a better perspective of that civilization thriving in a millennium once removed.

To assess Islamic contributions to American education is a complex task. Little if any influence comes to us directly. The pedagogical contributions of the Moslems come to us through the stream of the western tradition, as indeed do the contributions of Greece and Rome. They are contributions to our heritage, and one of the primary values in examining the sources of our intellectual hybridization is the value of history itself.

When we talk of the Islamic contributions, we specifically refer to the contributions of the Islamic civilization inspired by the Prophet Mohammed, the extreme dates of which would be 622 A.D., the traditional date of Mohammed's flight from Mecca to Medina and the date marking the beginning of the Moslem calendar, and 1492 A.D., the fall of Granada, marking the end of the reconquest of Spain from the Moors. The height of Moslem influence came between the eighth and twelfth centuries — the heart of the Middle Ages in Europe.

It is possible to develop many alternative schema for cataloguing the effects of one civilization upon another. It is almost a matter of choice, and certainly a matter of judgment, what will be designated "basic" and what will be designated as "secondary." In terms of the eventual impact upon America, one basic ingredient the Moslems consistently evinced, upon which their intellectual posture was predicated, was the power of moral and spiritual teachings. The faith of Mohammed drew together diverse, fractionated, morally decadent, and intellectually dormant people and nurtured them to

---

[48] Paul Monroe (Editor), *A Cyclopaedia of Education,* Vol. I (New York: Macmillan Company, 1915), p. 165.

a productive fruition of culture. This gave them the hunger for learning which sustained important intellectual endeavors for centuries on end. The religious tenets of Islam did not stifle learning, but enabled the Moslems to find a balance between the real and the ideal, the natural and the supernatural, the temporal and the eternal, the scientific and the theological.

The many important contributions to knowledge are of but tangential interest in the examination of the contributions of the Moslems to education. But it is well to recognize those general tenets of civilization which were reflected in their educational theory and practice. Their faith, the faith of Mohammed, gave them free reign of their intellect — a belief in the perfectability of man through fealty to one God, but that this perfectability came through active striving to develop the qualities of the good life such as courage, humility, virtue, and inquiry.

The Moslems refined, perfected, and applied the scientific method and attitude. The dichotomy between innovation and transmission was nullified by the pens of their scholars, the calculations of their mathematicians, the investigations of their scientists, and the practices of their educators. The Moslems delved excitedly into all fronts they encountered: religion, philosophy, economics, technology, jurisprudence, education. In the process they bridged the gap between the classical period of the Western tradition and the Renaissance. The Moslems had the ability to think new thoughts, to dare to be different. They had the ability to unite peoples of astounding differences through religious commitment and education, and obviously improved the lot of those whom they conquered instead of adding to their oppression. Their civilization thrived because they were willing to accept an idea on the basis of its merit rather than its source — Nestorian Christians, Jews, captured scholars and teachers, visiting professors, the legacies of earlier civilizations and their ideas, artifacts, systems, and traditions.

The Moslems recognized that education can change and mold society. Leaders must be enlightened, must study, and must have informed advisors. There was a more valid aristocracy of brains than of material means. There should be a constant search for wisdom, travel, cross fertilization of ideas, and the intercourse of minds. They developed libraries to preserve vital records, manuscripts, documents, and ideas. These libraries were accessible to all of the people as centers where resources could be used, applied, and improved. Each bit of scholarly inquiry, discovery or rediscovery, added dimension to the profile of the flower of Islamic culture.

One of the most significant contributions to education *per se* was the form and structure of the university itself. Historically the Moslems were the first to structure higher education as we know it. Bait al-Hikma, the first Moslem university of which we have a record, was established early in the ninth century — fully three hundred years before the emergence of the European

159

embryonic university at Chartres. The Moslems gave Western European universities the precedent of church affiliation, separate colleges within the university, specialization of universities in a narrow range of subjects, endowed chairs, scholarships for the needy, public financial support, establishment of endowments, auditing of courses, organization of academic disciplines, and student selection of content field and advisor. Islamic universities were of high quality and very numerous, ranging the length and breadth of the Saracen empire. Many Western scholars were included among the students — men who later became Popes of the Catholic Church, Church scholars, university professors, authors, scientists, or physicians. There is no question about the direct fertilization of European scholarship by the Islamic institutions.

The Moslems considered education to be the function of the state. They had a deep and abiding respect for teachers. Ethical standards of teaching were held high, teachers were required to hold licenses before they could teach; but the license was granted by the individual professor after personal assurance of the student's mastery of the subject matter, not as a result of a given series of courses or hours. They recognized the importance of education for all — boys and girls, children and adults, workers and aristocrats. Education was a lifelong process. Adult study groups were established in homes.

The Moslems made a real effort to understand the learning process as such. They were sensitive to the problems of readiness and motivation. They recognized that students had widely differential rates of development and absorption, making uniform instruction ineffective. There were many attempts to organize the process of learning in logical ways. Ibn Khaldun anticipated by centuries the concept, if not the form, of Herbart's theory of the unified lesson. Some educational ideas were purely mechanical. Moslems discovered the process of mass-copying of manuscripts long before Alcuin, who has been credited with the discovery.

The methodology employed in Islamic education was rich and varied. All education assumed a knowledge of the Koran — a firm understanding of the requirements of a moral and ethical life and a comprehensive familiarity with spiritual ordinances. This led to a systematic effort to improve the catechetical method of teaching for younger children. The importance of repetition, drill and review was stressed at all levels; but students were admonished not to write things down, or to try to commit them to memory until they fully understood them. Students were encouraged to study only one subject at a time, reading in depth, discussing it in and out of class, so that real understanding could be gained.

Continuity and continuous study were emphasized as important to the facilitation of learning. Serendipity was eagerly sought — that students be ready to learn at any time, any place, and from any experience. Some writers

160

made the specific suggestion to always have the necessary equipment available with which to record new ideas or experiences.

Variety in instruction was another keynote. Individual teachers had almost unlimited latitude. Classes varied in size from individual tutoring situations to seven hundred or more students in a single group. The importance of a teacher-pupil relationship based upon mutual respect and understanding was prominently noted. Open discussion, exchange of ideas and debates within classes were encouraged. Teachers were told that effective teaching and guidance of a student was not possible unless they understood a student's individual needs, interests, aspirations, and limitation.

Education encouraged cosmopolitan lives. Students from abroad were welcomed, and travel was encouraged. The Moslems firmly believed in the idea of the well-rounded scholar — the "renaissance man," long before the beginning of the Renaissance in Europe.

The Moslems realized that education was a slow, patient process with few short cuts; it takes time to learn. They showed astonishing insights into psychological and methodological processes. They were responsible for some of the first, serious, detailed writings devoted entirely to education, works which were read and used for centuries and which contained many ideas which did not emerge until much later in Western pedagogical writings.

From the too frequently overlooked fruition of Islamic culture came the seeds of many important educational practices which have been sown in our own heritage.

Bibliography

Bradby, Edward (Editor), *The University Outside Europe.* New York: Oxford University Press, 1939.

Brockelmann, Carl, *History of the Islamic Peoples.* New York: G. P. Putnam's Sons, 1947.

Butts, R. Freeman, *A Cultural History of Western Education.* New York: McGraw-Hill Book Company, Inc., 1955.

Dampier, Sir William, *A History of Science.* New York: The Macmillan Company, 1936.

Freeman, Edward A., *The History and Conquests of the Saracens,* 2nd Edition. London: Macmillan and Co., 1876.

Gibb, H. A. R., *Mohammedanism.* New York: The New American Library, 1955.

Hitti, Philip K., *History of the Arabs.* New York: Macmillan and Co., 1940.

Houtsma, M. Th.; Arnold, T. W.; Basset, R.; Hartmann, R. (Editors), *Encyclopedia of Islam.* London: Luzac & Co., 1913.

Jackh, Ernest (Advisory Editor), *Background of the Middle East.* New York: Cornell University Press, 1952.

Khaldun, Ibn, *The Muqaddimah*, Vols. I, II, III (trans. by Franz Rosenthal). New York: Pantheon Books, Inc., 1958.

Kheirallah, George, *Arabia Reborn*. New Mexico: The University of New Mexico Press, 1952.

Lane-Poole, Stanley, *The Story of the Moors in Spain*. New York: G. P. Putnam's Sons, 1886.

Mayer, Frederick, *A History of Educational Thought*. Columbus, Ohio: Charles E. Merrill Books, Inc., 1960.

Moehlman, Arthur and Roucek, Joseph S., *Comparative Education*. New York: The Dryden Press, 1952.

Mulhern, James, *A History of Education*. New York: The Ronald Press Company, 1959.

Myers, Edward D., *Education in the Perspective of History*. New York: Harper & Brothers Publishers, 1960.

Totah, Khalil A., *The Contributions of the Arabs to Education*. New York: Bureau of Publications, Teachers College, Columbia University, 1926.

Thut, I. N., *The Story of Education*. New York: McGraw-Hill Book Company, Inc., 1957.

Von Grunebaum, Gustave, *Medieval Islam*. Chicago: The University of Chicago Press, 1946.

Von Grunebaum, G. E. and Abel, Theodora M., (Authors of an introduction to this work and translators). al-Zarnudji, *Ta'lim al-Muta'allim-Tariq at-Ta'allum*. New York: King's Crown Press, 1947.

Weaver, Henry G., *The Mainspring of Human Progress*. New York: The Foundation for Economic Education, Inc., 1953.

Wilds, Elmer H., *The Foundations of Modern Education*. New York: Rinehart and Company, 1942.

162

****

CHAPTER VI

THE PROTESTANT HERITAGE
IN AMERICAN EDUCATION

When evaluating the influence exercised by religion in creating the foundations of American culture, we are using here the term "culture" as synonymous with what the Romans meant by the word "humanitas" and the Greeks by the word "paideia" — the enlightenment and discipline acquired as a result of mental and moral training, the forces which make for the enlightenment of the spirit and the growth of mind. This is important especially when we remember that the most influential of the American school of historians, Frederick Jackson Turner, has made a definite contribution by stressing the influence of the American frontier in American history. However, this particular stress on geo-economy has tended to neglect the factors which have been concerned with the mind and the spirit, especially religion, defined as "the ultimate passion which determines men's attitudes."[1] Certainly the roots of American educational history cannot be separated from religious history, although the question of separation of church and state has been one of the cardinal issues during the formation of the Constitution and has been debated ever since.

Although all religious denominations, including the Roman Catholic Church, which have adherents in large numbers in the United States, can

---

[1] William W. Sweet, *Religion in the Development of American Culture,* 1765-1840 (New York: Charles Scribner's Sons, 1952), p. 161.

163

point to the contributions made individually to the American heritage, historically, the most definite impact in this respect has been provided by New England's Puritans. Boorstin[2] has emphasized this point, writing in protest against the influence of what may be described as the European school of American historians — those who place the stress on our European origins and the continuing importance of our identification with the European community. It is his belief that the unique character of American democracy is attributable to the peculiar circumstances which governed the European settler's response to the extraordinary opportunities to be found in America, and that the American character of our society was very largely determined by the colonial experience that preceded the Revolution. Nevertheless, American education owes much to European religious antecedents and to the educational policies and programs developed by the various sects once they had become established in the New World. This chapter reviews the highlights of the Protestant contributions. All churches and groups cannot be covered; but the largest and representative sects and forces will be treated.

The Heritage of New England

Ever since Captain John Smith named New England, three and a half centuries ago, that part of the country has been shaping a way of life which in turn has been carried all the way across the American continent by emigrant trains and by Yankee-built ships around the Horn to Hawaii. Wherever its wandering sons have settled, offshoots of its culture have taken roots — schools, churches, voluntary associations, town meetings, and inventiveness applied to new tasks and conditions. This heritage begins with Plymouth, and has shown its importance in its congregational form of church government, the Mayflower Compact, the Fundamental Orders of Connecticut, and the broad tolerance of Rhode Island law under Roger Williams; all were factors shaping American political forms and eventually in forming the Republic.

The appreciations of New Englanders and of the English backgrounds that shaped our nation must not blind us to the fact that, according to the contemporary theory of "cultural pluralism," we should credit the part played in the genesis of the American nation by the elements who did not come from the Anglo-Saxon backgrounds and who were not all Puritans. Modern research shows that there were many "new" immigrants among the founders of the American nation, and that their contributions were also important to the American heritage; furthermore, that the dominant culture pattern has been influenced to a remarkable degree by Protestant sects not related directly

---

[2] Daniel J. Boorstin, *The Americans: The Colonial Experience* (New York: Random House, 1958).

to the Puritans as well as by the Catholics, and that, in addition, the original Anglo-American Protestant culture pattern has been modified by the continued impact of the cultures of the minorities from non-Anglo-Saxon origins.[3] The overall impact made by the Puritans on the American culture pattern cannot hide the fact that, thanks to the massive influx of non-English immigrants, the ethnic framework of the colonies was markedly changed already in the course of some five decades before the Revolution. (It has been estimated that by 1776 possibly as much as one-half of the population of America was of non-English origin.)

Even the first wave of immigration brought elements of diversity to American life, especially those of religious nature. Presbyterianism owes its numerical importance to the Scots and Scotch-Irish; the Germans introduced to this country numerous sects: Lutherans, Moravians, Mennonites, Amish, Schwekfelders, Dunkers, and others. Though most of the Frenchmen were Protestants fleeing the bigotry of Louis XIV, some were Catholics. In fact, this religious diversity was appreciated, by the middle of the eighteenth century, as being peculiarly American. James Reed, a missionary of the Anglican Society for the Propagation of the Gospel in North Carolina, reported to London in 1760 that he was astounded by the "great number of dissenters of all denominations . . . particularly Anabaptists, Methodists, Quakers, and Presbyterians."[4] It is our purpose to place this varied heritage in proper perspective in this survey of the roots of contemporary American education as influenced by various Protestant denominations.

English Separatists, Independents, and Congregationalists

The first English colonies in America were founded by Englishmen — the Puritans, the Cavaliers, the Quakers, the Catholics — and finally the Scotch-Irish; with these came Congregationalism, the Established Church, the Catholic Church, the Baptists, the Friends, and the Presbyterians.[5]

---

[3] Edward N. Saveth, *American Historians and European Immigrants,* 1875-1925 (New York: Columbia University Press, 1948); also "The American School and the Immigrant," pp. 109-116, in George Z. F. Bereday and Luigi Volpicelli, Eds., *Public Education in America: A New Interpretation of Purpose and Practice* (New York: Harper, 1958).

[4] Quoted by Carl N. Degler, *Out of Our Past: The Forces That Shaped Modern America* (New York: Harper, 1959), p. 54.

[5] The Dutch and German elements in the middle colonies were not far behind in influence and in numbers, and out of them came the Reformed Churches, the Dutch and German, and the Lutherans — in addition to the Mennonites, the Dunkers, and the Moravians.

165

The Reformation in England developed along three lines: Anglicanism, Puritanism, and Separatism. The Anglicans held to the old English Church, minus its papacy and the distinctively papal features. The Puritans (including the Presbyterians and some Anglicans) held to a national church but called for a thoroughgoing reformation which would provide an educated, spiritually-minded ministry and would grant the right of the members to a

Bettmann Archive

NEW ENGLAND DAME SCHOOL.

voice in the selection of their ministers, the management of the local church, and the adoption of its creed or confession. They wanted, however, to remain within the Church and thus establish its reformation. The Separatists held that the whole system of the establishment was an anti-Christian imitation of the true church and could not be reformed, and that the only proper thing for a Christian to do was to withdraw himself from it. English Puritanism finally broke into two distinct bodies, the Presbyterians and the Congregationalists; this break came after the great Puritan migration to New England from 1628 to 1640.

The beginnings of American Congregationalism go back to the radical Scrooby congregation of the Separatists under the leadership of John Robinson, their pastor, that fled first to Leyden (Holland), and then laid the foundations of New England and created the model of church government

166

that was later developed by the far more numerous and influential Puritans, the founders of the Massachusetts Bay.

The Separatists hired the famous Mayflower and on November 11, 1620, 102 Pilgrims reached the barren shores of Cape Cod (belonging to the Plymouth Company), although they really aimed to reach Virginia. Since they had no charter, they drew up the famed Mayflower Compact, modeled after the agreement by which they had constituted the church at Scrooby sixteen years before; it became a model for other groups of New England colonists for years to come, and remained the basis of the Plymouth Government until 1691 when the colony was united with Massachusetts.[6]

Historically, far more important than the Pilgrim colony at Plymouth was the Massachusetts Bay settlement. The Reverend John White, a Puritan minister at Dorchester, England, formed a company and received a grant of land from the Council; in September, 1628, the vanguard of the great Puritan migration reached what is now Salem and John Endicott, a rigid Puritan and a member of the company, was named Governor — this was the origin of Massachusetts. In 1629, 26 Englishmen secured a charter for the Massachusetts Bay Company and eventually control passed from the business-minded leaders to those interested mainly in religion. Later the governing body of the company was removed to American soil and it also got rid of the absentee stockholders. The full tide of Puritan migration set in. In 1629 about 900 colonists came to the colony; in 1630, 2,000, and by 1640 some 20,000 had found their way here, although all were not Puritans.

Eventually the churches of the powerful Massachusetts Bay Colony, which originally had no intention of separating from the Church of England, came to be Congregational. In May of 1631 the action of the Massachusetts General Court limited the franchise to church members; Congregationalism became the state church and the government of Massachusetts semi-theocratic. The Massachusetts leaders wanted no religious toleration. "It was not toleration which the Puritan sought, but rather the freedom to carry out his own religious notions undisturbed."[7]

By the middle of the seventeenth century, four Puritan colonies were firmly rooted in New England, in each of which the Congregational Church was the dominating influence. The tendency of Connecticut Congregationalism to go its own way of the Massachusetts churches was especially evi-

---

[6] Among the many pertinent studies covering this period of American history, see Alan P. Grimes, *American Political Thought* (New York: Holt, 1955), Chapter 1, "The Rise of Protestantism," pp. 1-21, and Chapter 11, "Puritan Political Thought," pp. 22-45.

[7] William W. Sweet, *The Story of Religion in America* (New York: Harper, 1950), p. 51. For more on Congregationalist history and faith, see Arthur Rouner, Jr., *The Congregational Way of Life* (Englewood Cliffs, New Jersey: Prentice-Hall, 1960).

denced by the founding of Yale College in 1701, with the hope that the new seat of learning might offset the more liberal and less orthodox tendencies developing at Harvard.

Puritanism, which Americans commonly use in a very loose way, actually means the Calvinist way of life, and "in his ceaseless striving for signs of salvation and knowledge of God's intentions for man, the Puritan placed great reliance upon the human intellect, even though for him, as for all Christians, faith was the bedrock of his belief." Thus also, "the mere emotion of religion was to be controlled by reason. Because of this, the university-trained Puritan clergy prided themselves on the lucidity and rationality of their sermons."[8] Since the use of reason was very important, the Puritans also appreciated education, and a remarkably well-educated ministry testified to the Puritan belief that scholarship was necessary for a proper understanding of the Word of God. The dominant clergy were convinced about the value of the training of the young in a knowledge of the Bible and "other parts of good learning."[9]

The majority of the 21,000 of the first immigrants had some schooling in England, could read the catechism and English Bible, and write in one of the 28 styles, and knew the basic mathematics; between 300 and 400 of them had been educated in a Latin grammar school in England. Among them were some 135 university-trained men.[10] Since Cambridge was the *alma mater* of most of the university graduates in the New World, it was understandable that Newtown, the location of New England's own college, was to be renamed in honor of the English institution. The College, founded in 1636, and soon to be named Harvard, was the only institution of its kind in America during nearly the whole seventeenth century and became "the fountainhead of Puritan learning in the New World."

Since there was a college, it was necessary to create preparatory schools to train the potential students for that institution. In addition, since the society of that period was dedicated to the reading of the Bible, elementary education was more than necessary. Obviously, Puritans favored education for secular as well as religious reasons.[11]

---

[8] Carl N. Degler, *op. cit.*, Chapter 1, "The Beginnings," p. 16.

[9] Louis B. Wright, *The Cultural Life of the American Colonies 1607-1763* (New York: Harper, 1957), Chapter 5, "Zeal for Education," pp. 98-125, and Chapter 6, "Books, Libraries, and Learning."

[10] Gaius G. Atkins and Frederick L. Fagley, *History of American Congregationalism* (Boston: The Pilgrim Press, 1942), Chapter XV, "Concern for Education," pp. 229-230.

[11] Walter Small, *Early New England Schools* (Boston: Ginn & Co., 1914); Alan Simpson, *Puritanism in Old and New England* (Chicago: University of Chicago Press, 1955).

No other colony had such a high proportion of university graduates among its leaders. Within five years of its settlement, Massachusetts Bay had set about founding a grammar school with a basic Latin curriculum like the grammar school of England. They hired Daniel Maude, late of Emmanuel College, to teach; thus started the Boston Latin School which still has an enviable reputation.[12] Other New England towns followed. In addition to grammar schools, with the traditional Latin curriculum, there were writing schools where both penmanship, reading, and arithmetic were taught; these ranged from the most elementary dame schools to slightly more advanced schools where apprentices could learn the rudiments of ciphering and book-keeping. The founders saw to it that the schooling should not be denied to any child because of poverty, and legislation enacted in various New England colonies showed the acceptance of responsibility by the local governments for elementary education. In 1642, the General Court of Massachusetts passed an act requiring the selectmen in every town to make periodic inquiries of parents and masters concerning the training of children and apprentices. This looked forward to universal literacy in the colony. The example of Massachusetts Bay was followed by other New England colonies, and even in Rhode Island local groups and individual benefactors established private schools in considerable numbers. There were also dame schools, either private or supported by the towns. A discussion of subsequent educational developments in New England is found in Chapter XI. It is clear, however, at this point that educational developments in the New England colonies had strong religious antecedents stretching back beyond the motherland to beginnings in Calvin's Geneva.

The textbooks used during the whole period of settlement of this country emphasized the characteristics of the seventeenth century English middle class such as thrift and sobriety and were permeated with piety and religious doctrine. One of the books used in England and imported into the colonies was titled: *The Protestant Tutor, Instructing Youth and Others, in the Compleat Method of Spelling, Reading, and Writing True English: Also Discovering to Them the Notorious Errors, Damnable Doctrines, and Cruel Massacres of the Bloody Papists, Which England May Expect From a Popish Successor* (1715).[13]

The most popular spelling book and elementary reader during the eighteenth century was compiled about 1740 by an Englishman, Thomas Dilworth, *A New Guide to the English Tongue;* he also compiled an arithmetic,

---

[12] Pauline Holmes, *A Tercentenary History of the Boston Public Latin School, 1635-1935* (Cambridge: Harvard University Press, 1935), p. 3.

[13] Clifton Johnson, *Old-Time Schools and School-Books* (New York: Macmillan, 1904), p. 49.

the *Schoolmaster's Assistant,* and other texts. While the children learned to spell and read, they were also taught "Morality," and Dilworth's texts, like later text compilations, spelled out the "morals" of each selection in a sentence called "The Interpretation," a standard technique in elementary reading books.

The longest popularity among the Puritan books was enjoyed by the famous *New England Primer,* published in Boston about 1690. Reprinted, for a century, under different titles and with altered material, it remained grimly Puritan in moralizations and themes. At least three million copies were sold during the eighteenth and early nineteenth centuries, and its imitations appeared as late as the opening years of the nineteenth century.

Educationally, probably the most influential of the early Puritan spokesmen was John Cotton (1584-1652), a famed Boston Minister. He wrote a short catechism for children, *Spiritual Milk for American Babes Drawn Out of the Breasts of Both Testaments for Their Souls Norishment,* which was learned by many generations of children as a part of the *New England Primer.*[14] Therein the child was told that he had been conceived in sin and born in iniquity, his corrupt nature was leading him to sin and transgression of God's commandments, and that the wages of sin were death and damnation. But, at the same time, Cotton stressed that "Honor thy father and thy mother" implied reverence, obedience, and recompense for all his family superiors, as well as in the school, church, and state. Salvation might come only through the sacrifice of Christ, the word of God in the Bible, and adherence to the law of God. Hence, fear, obedience, and discipline were the foundations of the educational method throughout the colonial period; illustrations were used by glorifying outstanding spokesmen of the period and "their views became firmly embedded in the traditional authoritarian attitudes toward the child in the family, the church, and the school. So strong is the tradition that it still survives in much of contemporary life even where the original religious motivations are not so extreme nor so real as once they were."[15]

After the Revolution, patriots began to worry about the royalist and the English slant of Dilworth's and other texts. New England's conservative teachers hastened to provide conservative, Federalist, patriotic, and orthodox texts; Noah Webster, a Yale graduate and schoolmaster, for example, produced his "blue-back speller" that sought to eliminate British forms of spelling, to substitute the native dialect as the standard pronunciation, and soften the Calvinistic appeal. However, Presbyterian and Congregational influences through textbooks continued during the post-Revolutionary period. Jedidiah

---

14 Paul L. Ford, Ed., *The New England Primer* (New York: Dodd, Mead, 1899).

15 R. Freeman Butts and Lawrence A. Cremin, *A History of Education in American Culture* (New York: Holt, 1953), p. 66.

Morse, a Congregational Minister from Yale, published a popular geography, *The American Geography* (1789) and *A Compendious History of New England Designed for Schools and Private Families* (1804). The most famous writer, however, was William Holmes McGuffey (1800-1873), whose *McGuffey's Readers* sold, in various editions, more than 120 million copies. A Presbyterian preacher of Scottish descent, brought up on the Ohio frontier, he attended Washington College in Western Pennsylvania and later preached and taught in Kentucky and Ohio. In 1826 he was appointed Professor of Languages in Miami University (Oxford, Ohio). Later he became President of Cincinnati College and Ohio University at Athens and eventually (1845) he was appointed Professor of Moral Philosophy at the University of Virginia. While at Miami, the Cincinnati publishing house of Truman and Smith signed him to prepare a series of reading books, convinced that the westerners were tired of the doom-and-death motives of the New England primer. McGuffey's compilations remained in vogue for the rest of the nineteenth century. Their influence on American education and literary and moral standards was astounding, combining morality, patriotism, and faith in material progress. They brought into focus middle class ideas and aspirations resembling the ideas expressed in Franklin's Almanacs in the eighteenth century.[16]

Even if the total written output of the colonial settlers is not impressive by our standards, Morison points out vividly the fact that they did preserve, maintain, and sometimes bolster the best of English thought.[17] To them we owe a mighty debt: for transmission of the ancient classics and the mobile instrument of language, for separation of church and state, for compulsory public education, for the form of our colleges with their concept of scholarship aid — and the Congregational Church itself.

Religious Contributions to Higher Education

In nearly all respects, the foundation of America's higher education can be traced to religion, since the colleges rose out of the concern of the various churches for their doctrines. They had their origin in English prototypes mainly because the bulk of settlers came from there, founding charters had to be approved by British officials, their financial assistance came mostly from England, and most of their teachers and organizers had come from Oxford and Cambridge.

---

[16] R. D. Mosier, *Making the American Mind: Social and Moral Ideas in the McGuffey Readers* (New York: King's Crown, 1947).

[17] Samuel E. Morison, *The Intellectual Life of Colonial New England* (New York: University Press, 1956).

At the time of the colonization of America, the Liberal Arts course in England consisted of: (1) six of the medieval liberal arts (grammar, rhetoric, logic, arithmetic, geometry, and astronomy); (2) Aristotle's philosophy (ethics, politics, physics, and metaphysics); and (3) the Renaissance studies of classical humanism (Latin, Greek, Hebrew, and rhetoric). The study of books was the main means of instruction for the historic roots of a liberal education grew out of linguistic and literary studies. These ideas were reflected in the foundation of the American higher institutions.

The leaders of the Puritans had become aware, by the middle of the seventeenth century, that the social order needed to be kept alive by young ministers. Among the Puritan ministers there were several with degrees from English universities who agitated for the introduction of the "new blood." This induced the Colonial Court (colonial legislature of Massachusetts) to grant, in 1636, 400 pounds for the foundation of a college. In the summer of 1638, the first freshmen started to study in a house bought by the Board of Overseers for the use of the college.[18] Somewhat later, John Harvard left to the institution his estate (less than 800 pounds) and his library of some 400 volumes. In recognition of this noble gesture, the name of the college was changed to honor him.

The foundling years of Harvard were difficult; the first head was dismissed for beating a pupil too severely and another for the heresy of "antipaedobatism." Public grants were meager. But the general public of New England helped out with their farm produce, bales of cloth, and small sums of money.[19]

Under Henry Dunster, a Cambridge graduate who was appointed President in August, 1640, the College began to flourish. A course of study was established in the liberal arts, the learned tongues, and the three philosophies (similar in content to the course for the baccalaureate in the English universities). A new building was erected and the first class graduated in 1642. The degree of Bachelor of Arts was conferred after four years' study; the Master's degree after three years' post-graduate study, either in the College or elsewhere. It was in these last three years that candidates for the ministry began their study of theology.

The main goal in maintaining Harvard College (expanded into Harvard University in 1780) was to offer the church graduates for the Puritan ministry, educated in a broad sense for those times. But the college also educated young men for law and statecraft. Latin was the language of instruction

---

[18] Samuel E. Morison, *The Puritan Pronaos* (New York: New York University Press, 1936), p. 89.

[19] Samuel E. Morison, *The Founding of Harvard College* (Cambridge: Harvard University Press, 1935), presents interesting details.

— with much time given to Protestant theology. The Bible was studied throughout the program. Greek was studied so that the New Testament could be read in the original; Hebrew was studied for a year so that the Old Testament could be read. The Bachelor's degree was granted upon the scholar "able to read the originals of the Old and New Testament into the Latin tongue, and to resolve them logically," provided he were "of Godly life and conversation." The "disputations" resembled the metaphysical questions debated during the Middle Ages — such as "Is the voice of the people the voice of God?' or, "When Balaam's ass spoke, was there any change in its organs?"

Harvard's system determined to a remarkable degree the course taken by American colleges and universities. The liberal arts, brought in from England and thus from Western Europe, had retained their influence. The interconnection between religion and humanism has also remained in many American institutions of higher learning and, in fact, retarded the need to consider new economic, scientific, and philosophical currents for some decades; for instance, the Department of Sociology was created at Harvard only in the 1930's.

The foundation of Harvard also established the principle of private and public support of higher education. The gift of John Harvard and the grant of the legislature combined private generosity and public concern toward the cause of higher education. "The colonial college, of which Harvard was the first example, is the parent not only of the modern private university but of the state supported institution as well."[20] This example taught the colonies outside New England the principle that private colleges were entitled to be helped by public funds.

The Harvard example also adapted the English system of Oxford and Cambridge to the American conditions. Cambridge was a federation of many undergraduate colleges, each with one faculty and one course of study. The American system did not adopt the nominal control of one examining body for a number of coordinate colleges of independent foundation, offering, at the same time, practically the same courses of study. When the new schools, departments, and colleges appeared on the American scene, the original Harvard College tended to remain as one general or academic college apart from the specialized professional schools.

Harvard was founded as a theological training seminary and as such it became the battleground of religious cross-currents; Orthodox Calvinism found its spokesman in President Increase Mather, while liberalism was represented by President John Leverett. The orthodox spokesmen of the

---

[20] Edwin E. Slosson, *The American Spirit in Education* (New Haven: Yale, 1921), p. 47.

Church accused Harvard of being too lax in its ideological views, and this led to the formation of Yale.

In 1701 several Congregational ministers donated their books towards the foundation of a college in Connecticut, assuming that a college should start by having a library. During the same year the legislature legalized the erection of a "collegiate school" to train students of "publick employment both in Church and Civil State." Here was a new trend, the charter recognizing not only the needs of the Church, but also of the "Civil State," — that is, the needs of statecraft and public service.[21] The institution was moved from one small town to another until 1720; about that time Elihu Yale, a prosperous merchant, gave the college the proceeds from the sale of three bales of valuable goods amounting to £562. With other donations this amount helped the college to complete a building started in New Haven. In 1745 the College was chartered in honor of its benefactor. In general, Yale resembled Harvard, with its stress on the conventional courses in Latin, Greek, and Hebrew for the study of the Scriptures. The private life of the students was carefully supervised and religious observances rigidly followed. By the close of the colonial period Yale's roster included the names of students from remote colonies as well as from New England; but the founders also succeeded in their original aim — to have the institution stay on the strict and narrow path of Congregationalism.

Before the close of the Revolutionary period the American people saw the rise of six other colleges all growing out of religious or sectarian needs — the only exception being the Franklin Academy which eventually became the College of Philadelphia and later the University of Pennsylvania.

The Episcopalians started the William and Mary (1693) and King's College (later Columbia, 1754); the Congregationalists founded Dartmouth (1769); the Presbyterians are credited for the College of New Jersey (later Princeton, 1747); the Dutch Reformed Church founded the Queens College (later Rutgers, 1766); and the Baptists provided the foundations for the College of Rhode Island (later Brown, 1764).

The dominating influence of the American churches in the rise of American higher education during the colonial era created a framework which was extended to the nineteenth century. Before the Civil War there had appeared such well-known colleges as Oberlin, Wesleyan, Haverford, Wittenberg, Muhlenberg, and Notre Dame. These schools reflected the faith of a variety of sects in the desirability of an extended education for many, as well as their personal interests in guaranteeing the maintenance and growth of their own Christian viewpoints.

---

[21] For more details, see: James T. Adams, *The Founding of New England* (Boston: Houghton Mifflin, 1921).

Later Congregationalism

The gradual decline of Puritan power, even before the Revolution, was due to several causes. Among them was the struggle to maintain the exclusively church-member franchise and the stringent requirements for church membership; there were splits within the ranks and the banishment of Mrs. Hutchinson and Roger Williams did not stop these difficulties. There were outside influences, especially the constant encroachment of other sects on Puritan territory (Quakers especially, and then Baptists and Anglicans). When Anglican England could not force an Anglican establishment on the Congregationalists she revoked the first charter and the tolerationist provisions of a new one (1691) forced the Puritan colonies to allow other sects. Also influential were the cross-currents of the new libertarian doctrines of the eighteenth century and the rising nationalism. Other impacts developed from the consequences of tolerance prevailing in Maryland, Pennsylvania, New Jersey, and New York. As Congregational ministers started to desert the authoritarianism of the older orthodoxy, they had to approach, eventually, the ideological aspects of liberalism, thus providing the foundations of the rise of Unitarianism and Universalism.

A Plan of Union was adopted in 1802 by the Congregational Association and the General Assembly of the Presbyterian Church. This incorporated plans of harmonious cooperation which had been initiated in 1794. The chief motive seems to have been the need for ministers in the rapidly expanding country and the provision of suitable education for the youth of these denominations. Under the Plan of Union and the cooperation which continued with the "New School" Presbyterians, seven colleges were founded jointly: Knox (1837), Beloit (1846), Grinnell (1846), Rockford (1847), Ripon (1851), Milwaukee-Downer (1850), and Pacific University (1854). The plan, as a matter of fact, worked out in almost every instance to the advantage of the Presbyterians and the growing feeling against the Plan of Union by Congregational spokesmen culminated in its unanimous rejection at a national convention in 1852. A year later the American Congregational Union was founded, to unite the energies of the church throughout the country. Among other results was the foundation of Chicago Theological Seminary (1855). The Congregationalists also advanced into the new prairie and mountain states and established several colleges: Washburn College in Kansas (1865), Carlton College in Minnesota (1867), Colorado College (1874), and others in Nebraska, South Dakota, and Washington.[22] However, the first four-year U.S. campus launched in this century is New

---

[22] Atkins and Fagley, *op. cit.,* p. 237.

College at Sarasota, Florida which the Congregational Board of Home Missions plans to open in 1964.

The Congregationalists also founded some of the early academies in the Northwest Territory. Marietta, later becoming Marietta College, was established as early as 1790. The church groups were also very active in the missionary field. In fact, from the very beginning of Plymouth colony, missionary work with the Indians was stressed. In 1826 the American Home Missionary Society was formed. The American Missionary Association, organized in 1846, was especially interested in Negro fugitives and following the Civil War extended its activities into the South. The missionary movement pushed West with the nation. By 1917 the American Missionary Association had Indian missions in Nebraska, the Dakotas, and in Montana, missions among the Chinese and Japanese on the West Coast, and was working in Hawaii, Alaska, and Puerto Rico; in addition to six colleges, it maintained three seminaries and thirty-two secondary and elementary schools for Negroes.

It is evident that Congregational contributions to American education have been considerable. Chapters VII and XI give further attention to other aspects of their influence. Spokesmen of Congregationalism in their history of the Church emphasize particularly the leadership at higher education levels; they claim "No one American denomination has furnished so many distinguished college and university presidents as Congregationalism — and shining constellations of educators in general."[23] Important as this contribution may be, there is little doubt that the most fundamental contribution of Congregationalism has been the general positive spirit toward the promotion of education that has characterized Church members ever since the initial settlements in colonial Massachusetts.

The Presbyterian Church

The Presbyterian Reformed Churches perpetuate the features, doctrinal and governmental, of the Protestant Reformation spread by John Calvin's followers from Switzerland to France, Holland, the Palatinate, England, Scotland, and Ireland. Today these churches, with more than 125 distinct denominations and with a total constituency of at least 60 million, represent the largest Protestant Church group under the same form of government. The doctrinal and ecclesiastical system developed at Geneva, modified somewhat in Holland and in France and transferred to Scotland, became solidified there largely under the influence of John Knox in 1560. Later in England it fostered the development of the Independents who afterwards became the Congregationalists.

---

[23] *Ibid.*, p. 236.

The Presbyterian Churches in the United States trace their origin chiefly to Great Britain. The English and Welsh Presbyterians in the colonies, together with the few French Huguenot Churches, combined at an early date with the Scotch and Scotch-Irish elements to form the Presbyterian Church in the United States of America. Later several groups broke from this organization and, in addition, other Scotch groups appeared in America and ultimately these Churches formed the United Presbyterian Church of North America.[24]

Calvin believed that true faith must be intelligent, that intelligence and not ignorance was the mother of piety and, consequently, that the school was an essential part of any effective church organization. Learning and religion must always operate hand in hand. Upon his return from Strassburg to Geneva in 1541 he announced the foundation of a school system as one of his primary objectives. He urged at least a minimal, universal education for all boys, although not a democratic education as we know it. There were to be two different tracks for the upper and the lower classes or ability groups. He was not able to organize his famous Geneva Academy for the first track until 1559. This was actually a combined gymnasium (copied from the noted German institutions founded by Sturm) and a college. The Academy became a top-flight department of higher education with a number of courses as Calvin had intended that it should become the intellectual center of the Reformed world. The rigorous moral and religious emphasis of the theocratic schools in Geneva have often been recounted, but the thoroughness of the education of those that completed the first ladder cannot be doubted. Hundreds of ministers, theologians, and students graduated and carried the Reformation ideals to many other countries. With them went the model of the Academy, affecting the organization of the universities at Edinburgh, Leyden, Emmanuel College at Cambridge and, eventually, Harvard, among others. As we shall see, it also influenced the formation of the College of New Jersey (Princeton).

Calvin's standards and the strict control of education by the church, the emphasis upon instruction in morals, the careful supervision of learning, and the high Christian qualities demanded of teachers, established standards for Christian education that have been followed by Presbyterians from that day. The Presbyterian Church, early in American history, identified itself in a special way with education; it insisted upon an educated ministry. Near the Presbyterian church there usually stood the school, and not infrequently

---

24 For more details, see: Benson Y. Landis, Ed., *Yearbook of American Churches: Information on All Faiths in the U.S.A.* (New York: National Council of the Churches of Christ in the U.S.A., 1957), pp. 99-102; Wallace N. Jamison, *The United Presbyterian Story: A Centennial Study 1858-1958* (Pittsburgh: The Geneva Press, 1958).

the minister was also the teacher. The word "parson" was derived from the word "person" as he was called originally because of his superior education and leadership.

Scottish-Presbyterians, including the so-called Scotch-Irish, probably influenced early Presbyterianism in America "more than all other groups combined." [25] They brought educational traditions that were particularly important to developments in New Jersey, Pennsylvania, Virginia, and the Carolinas. These traditions go back to August, 1560. At that time the Scottish parliament, under the influence of John Knox, renounced Roman Catholicism and adopted the Reformed faith for Scotland. The Presbyterian Church became the established Church of Scotland, and has remained so to this day. Under Knox's leadership, large provision for Christian education was made in the first Book of Discipline; every church was to have a schoolmaster who was able to teach Latin, grammar, and the catechism. Secondary schools were provided and as capstones to the educational system there were three universities.

Calvinists and Presbyterians were among the very first settlers in colonial America; they came from the various European countries with very similar doctrines. Pilgrims and Puritans were strict Calvinists but the majority believed in the Congregational form of church government. There were some Presbyterians among them and eventually many of their descendants came into the Presbyterian Church. The Dutch began to settle in New York in 1623, and they and their descendants organized the (Dutch) Reformed Church in America. The French Huguenots settled in New England, New York, Virginia, South Carolina, and Georgia. Some entered the Episcopal Church but the majority of them joined the Presbyterian Church. Many Scottish Presbyterians came here directly from Scotland and settled in New Jersey, North Carolina, South Carolina, and other colonies, and participated in laying the foundations of the American Presbyterian Church. The Scotch-Irish (Scotchmen who lived in North Ireland before emigrating) settled in the same colonies and also in Pennsylvania, Maryland, and Virginia. A large number of Germans emigrated between 1700 and 1770 and a goodly number of them were Calvinists. The majority settled in Pennsylvania and helped found the German Reform Church which is Presbyterian except in name.

As the colonial period progressed, the Presbyterians, as other religious groups, worked to promote schools. The Scotch-Irish Presbyterians were especially enterprising in setting up schools in the western counties of Pennsylvania. Zeal for an educated Scotch Presbyterian ministry promoted

---

[25] Francis Miller in DeWitt C. Reddick, Ed., *Church and Campus: Presbyterians Look to the Future From Their Historic Role in Christian Education* (Richmond, Virginia: John Knox Press, 1956), p. 31.

the founding of Princeton and a number of classical academies that preceded it.[26]

Since graduates of Edinburgh, Aberdeen, St. Andrews, and Glasgow were not numerous enough to supply all the colonial pulpits, especially after the Great Awakening revival, candidates for the Presbyterian ministry studied the classics and divinity under some preacher who conducted a little one-man seminary. Most famous of these academies was the Log College at Neshaminy, Pennsylvania, run by the Reverend William Tennent (1727-1742). Although the College ceased to exist after his death, its influence was felt in similar academies or schools founded by some eighteen of his students; among them were Gilbert and William Tennent (his sons) and Samuel Blair who became trustees of the College of New Jersey, and Samuel Davies and Samuel Finley who became its fourth and fifth presidents, respectively. Other Presbyterian ministers conducted schools at Newark and Elizabethtown, New Jersey. The Philadelphia gentry also favored the Presbyterian grammar school at New London (1743). In the South, as the dissenting religious groups gradually won the right to found their own schools, the Presbyterians were quick to seize this opportunity.[27]

The founding of the College of New Jersey (later Princeton) was a landmark in the history of Presbyterian, and American, education. The general religious movement of the early part of the eighteenth century, which manifested itself in England in Methodism, in Germany in Pietism, and in New England in the Great Awakening, found its expression in the Presbyterian church in America largely through Gilbert Tennent who had become convinced of the necessity of personal conversion. When Whitefield came to America in 1739 he found most congenial fellow workers in Gilbert Tennent, William Tennent, Jr., and their associates. Later, in 1746, this group established the College of New Jersey for the purpose of securing an educated ministry. In 1768 the College called John Witherspoon from Scotland and installed him as President and professor of Divinity. He exercised a powerful influence in the colonies and was one of the leaders in the joint movement of Presbyterians and Congregationalists from 1766 to 1775 to secure religious liberty and to resist the establishment of the English Episcopal Church as the state church in the colonies.

John Witherspoon was educated at the University of Edinburgh where he completed his theological studies in 1743. For more than twenty years he

---

[26] Thomas J. Wertenbaker, *Princeton, 1746-1896* (Princeton: Princeton University Press, 1946).

[27] James Mulhern, *History of Secondary Education in Pennsylvania* (Philadelphia: The Author, 1933), pp. 65-67.

179

was one of the most popular preachers in Scotland; but in 1768 he accepted a second invitation to become President of the struggling little college in Princeton. Upon arrival in New Jersey, he identified himself completely with the colonial cause and became one of the stoutest advocates of independence. He converted the parochial College of New Jersey into a cultural center which drew students from the entire eastern seaboard. He added Hebrew and French to the curriculum, provided scientific equipment, organized graduate courses, and set out on a quest for more funds and more students. In due course he took the lead in bringing Presbyterians together in one General Assembly, of which he was the first Moderator. At the same time he headed a local committee of correspondence, organized a military company in the college, was a member of two provincial congresses and of the New Jersey Constitutional Convention, and for five years a member of the Continental Congress. He was the only clergyman to sign the Declaration of Independence. He was also one of those encouraging Tom Paine to write the thirteen papers called "The Crisis," the first of which began: "These are the times that try men's souls. The summer soldier and the sunshine patriot will, in this crisis, shrink from the service of their country." These papers became the most powerful and the most inexpensive propaganda released at that time in America.

Witherspoon's students also exerted their influence. The College of New Jersey had become a rallying point for young patriots before Witherspoon's arrival from Scotland; under his direction the tiny college, with a student body of fewer than a hundred, served the cause of liberty. Twenty-eight alumni served in the Continental Congress, and more than a hundred on local committees of correspondence, in provincial constitutional conventions and congresses, or as officials of newly created state governments. Hundreds of Revolutionary and post-Revolutionary American leaders were educated there; the list is headed by James Madison.

Princeton's graduates also made their mark on the frontier. Fired with missionary zeal for teaching as well as preaching, a number of them went to Southern colonies and were responsible for the foundation of the Liberty Hall Academy in Virginia (which developed into Washington and Lee University), for Prince Edward Academy (which developed into Hampden-Sydney College) and Crowfield Academy in North Carolina (which became Davidson College). Others went to the West setting up schools in places where there had been none before, and the classically trained ministers became carriers to the frontier of Calvinistic theology as well as of classical learning. However, in the nineteenth century, with the rise of the public schools, Presbyterian academies disappeared; a number of them became colleges.

Presbyterians in the American colonies during the last half of the eighteenth century helped to establish colleges in all their principal settlements. In addition to previously cited schools, Presbyterians took the lead in founding the University of North Carolina; in Georgia and Tennessee they started the schools which eventually became the University of Georgia and the University of Tennessee; in South Carolina they established Zion Academy at Winnsboro; and in Kentucky they founded Transylvania College (1783). Southwestern at Memphis, Centre College of Kentucky, and Agnes Scott were to become outstanding liberal arts colleges in the South.

The Civil War destroyed much of the educational program of the Presbyterian Church. In 1865, Southern Presbyterians started the task of rebuilding their shattered educational work by starting King College (Bristol, Tennessee), Arkansas College, and others. One of the most interesting educational institutions was Stillman College, founded in 1873 as a junior college and theological seminary for Negro men; later it was made coeducational. During and after the Civil War the United Presbyterian Church established a Board of Missions that made significant contributions in bringing the rudiments of education to the illiterate freedmen.

In the North during the nineteenth century the Presbyterians took the lead in expanding collegiate education. Migration westward was accompanied by the Presbyterian ministers who more often than not were also schoolmasters. The stress on an educated Presbyterian ministry, one of the universal characteristics of the Presbyterian system, made it necessary that colleges be available to train the Church leaders. Numerous small colleges were founded wherever the Church was established. By 1861 there were 49 colleges and universities, founded by Presbyterians in 21 of the 34 states."[28] The schools founded jointly with the Congregationalists have been identified previously.

The great immigration into the Mississippi basin after the close of the Revolutionary War offered, at the outset, the strategic advantage to the Presbyterians. They were the second largest denomination in America, and had formed a Plan of Union with the Congregationalists — the largest denomination — which provided for the pooling of their resources for evangelizing the West. Because the Presbyterians had the superficial organization, practically all the churches founded in the middle tier of colonies by both Presbyterian and Congregational missionaries and composed of either Scotch-Irish or Puritan stock, came into the Presbyterian Church. In addition, when the great migration began, the Scotch-Irish occupied the strategic areas on the frontier. But while Presbyterians drew ahead of Congregationalists, Episcopalians, and Quakers in occupying the West, they fell far behind both Baptists and Methodists because of a lack of ministers. Baptists and Methodists, who had no educational qualifications, demanding only a genuine

---

[28] Benjamin J. Lake, *The Story of the Presbyterian Church in the U.S.A.* (Philadelphia: The Westminster Press, 1956), p. 61.

religious experience and a desire to preach, had abundant missionaries. Thus the Presbyterians were led to found additional seminaries.

Presbyterian educational interest has remained concentrated at the higher educational levels. As Americans spread to the West, so did Presbyterian schools. Lewis and Clark (1867), Trinity (San Antonio, 1869), Hastings and the College of Emporia (both 1882), Occidental (1887), and the University of Tulsa (1894) are a few selected examples. In the twentieth century, activity declined because of the growing numbers of state institutions of higher learning and the increasing costs of establishing good college facilities. The country had been spanned; but, as with other Protestant sects, new schools continued to be created where populations demanded. Such is the new Florida Presbyterian College at St. Petersburg. Presbyterians by and large have expressed little continuing interest in the promotion of parochial elementary and secondary schools. But the Church believes that the Presbyterian Theological Seminary and the Presbyterian Church-related college are destined to continue to play a major role in supplying an appropriate and carefully defined religious dimension in the public schools.[29] Here as in other areas the contributions of the Presbyterians parallel those of the Congregationalists discussed previously.

The Protestant Episcopal Church

Like the Presbyterian, "the Protestant Episcopal Church has exercised an influence on American life wholly disproportionate to the size of its membership, which is only a fifth of that of the Methodist and hardly more than an eighth of that of the Baptist communion."[30] Up to 1948 the Episcopalians had supplied exactly one-fourth of the 32 men who had occupied the office of the President of the United States (including early illustrious leaders as Washington, Madison, and Monroe). The economic level of the Episcopalians has always been high and hence its membership is conservative; yet this church counts among its members two most radical promoters of the rights of the common man — Thomas Jefferson and Franklin D. Roosevelt. Hence Johnson concludes that American Episcopalianism is "better described as traditionalist than as conservative."

Historically, the Episcopal Church was one of the typically English forces that "enabled the American Revolutionists to effect a transfer of sovereignty

---

[29] General Assembly of the Presbyterian Church in the United States of America, *The Church and the Public Schools* (Philadelphia: Board of Christian Education, Presbyterian Church in the U.S., June, 1957), pp. 17-18.

[30] Gerald W. Johnson, *Our English Heritage* (Philadelphia: J. B. Lippincott Co., 1949), pp. 177-178.

from King to people without an accompanying social upheaval;"[31] after the revolution the members slipped relatively smoothly from the Church of England into the Protestant Episcopal Church. The Episcopalian Church has acted as a bond between the English and American nations. The early political influence was indirect but can be seen especially in the contributions made by the great Virginia dynasty of the early days.

The Protestant Episcopal Church is Protestant as it is divorced from the Roman Catholic hierarchy, and thus free to place the Bible first in its theology and allow its lay members to participate in its leadership; otherwise it remains largely Catholic. The *Book of Common Prayer* is essentially an English translation of the Mass. The parent Anglican Church was identified with the American colonies from the earliest settlements (Jamestown, 1607). In 1789 the Protestant Episcopal Church adopted its present name and became autonomous; it remains an integral part of the Anglican Communion.[32]

The Church had been deeply resented by many as the state religion in Virginia, Maryland, Georgia, the Carolinas, and the environs of New York City during the colonial period. People were required to pay taxes that went for Church support but the Episcopalians were a minority in all these areas except Virginia. Yet in most areas even these taxes did not pay for all the needs of the Church. Help was sent from England by a missionary organization, the Society for the Propagation of the Gospel. Educationally, the Society helped to create the foundations of American popular education by supporting many schoolmasters and founding numerous parochial libraries. It founded schools in Connecticut, Rhode Island, Pennsylvania, New Jersey, North Carolina, and Georgia. The activities were limited to elementary education, though, in one or two instances, it also helped Latin grammar schools. The motive here was religious indoctrination, and pupils were taught to read the Holy Scriptures and memorize the catechism, the prayers, the graces, and familiar Church formulas. They were also taught to write and offered enough arithmetic to fit them for "useful employment." New primers, ABC books, and other texts were sent here from England.[33]

The entire foundation and finance of the Anglicans collapsed overnight during the American Revolution. Except in the South, the Episcopalians were

---

[31] *Ibid.*, p. 179.

[32] Vergilius Ferm, *Pictorial History of Protestantism* (New York: Philosophical Library, 1957), pp. 244-258. See also the chapter on the Episcopal church in Hartzell Spence, *The Story of America's Religions* (New York: Holt, Rinehart and Winston, 1960).

[33] Important documents pertaining to the activities of the S.P.G. in the Southern colonies can be found in: Edgar W. Knight, Ed., *A Documentary History of Education in the South Before 1860: European Inheritances* (Chapel Hill: University of North Carolina Press, 1949), Section III, pp. 62-139.

loyal to George III and Church law required them to pray for the royal family. In London, the missionary society stopped all financial help, and all state Church taxes were abolished. Priests had to run for their lives, many escaping to Canada or England. But the southern Episcopalians contributed materially to the success of the Revolution. On the 56 signers of the Declaration of Independence, two-thirds were Episcopalians, and of the 39 framers of the Constitution, two-thirds were members of the Episcopal Church. In fact, one of them, Charles Pinckney of South Carolina, was the proponent of the clause on religious liberty in that document. George Mason framed the Declaration of Rights in the Virginia Constitution and Patrick Henry's famed "liberty or death" speech was delivered at St. John's Church in Richmond, Virginia (1775).

In the educational aspects of the history of American Episcopalianism we mention here but two examples of the varied contributions through the years by outstanding individuals. Samuel Johnson (1696-1772), born in Guilford, Connecticut, attended the Saybrook Institution and became a tutor when the college (later Yale) moved to New Haven (1718). A Congregationalist, he became a convert to the English Church. In 1754 he became the first President of King's College in New York (now Columbia University). There he introduced a liberal program, in contrast to the narrow theological courses of the earlier colonial colleges; in 1757 he employed a professor of mathematics and natural philosophy and soon afterwards secured "a good apparatus of instruments." He was also the author of the first grammar to be written and printed in America (1765).[34] At a later period an English-born American, William Robertson Coe, who came to the United States in 1883 (and was naturalized seven years later), helped the cause of educational endeavors. He had a lasting interest in American history. After achieving prominence in the business, insurance, and financial world, he financed the Coe Collection in Western Americana, the Coe Chair in American Studies at Yale University, and Institutes of American History or Studies at Stanford, the University of Wyoming, and other institutions.

Between the achievement of American Independence and the close of the War of 1812, the Episcopalian Church saw a period of "suspended animation and feeble growth."[35] Not until large towns and cities began to rise in the Middle West did the Church achieve large growth west of the Alleghenies. By the close of the War of 1812, the Episcopal Church was no longer looked

---

[34] Herbert and Carol Schneider, *Samuel Johnson, President of King's College, His Career and Writings* (New York: Columbia University Press, 1929).

[35] Charles C. Tiffany, *A History of the Protestant Episcopal Church* (New York: Christian Literature Co., 1895, Chapter XIV; W. W. Manross, *A History of the American Episcopal Church* (New York: Morehouse, 1955), pp. 202ff.

upon with suspicion, for many "churchmen" had fought on the American side, while in New England they aligned themselves with the party fight for the abolition of the privilege of the standing order, and they were identified with the rising popular party under Thomas Jefferson.

The Church has founded or controls one university and five colleges. Hobart College (1822) is the college for men in a corporation of colleges which also includes William Smith Woman's College, established 1908. It is an outgrowth of the original Geneva Academy, established 1898, and reflects the interest of the Right Reverend John Henry Hobart, Bishop of New York, in having a center of education related to the Episcopal Church in what was then the West. Originally named Geneva College, it is the oldest college continuously associated with the Episcopal Church in America. Kenyon College in Ohio was incorporated in 1824. St. Augustine College was chartered in 1867 as St. Augustine's Normal School and Collegiate Institute through the joint efforts of the Freedmen's Commission of the Protestant Episcopal Church and a group of clergy and laymen of the Diocese of North Carolina. It is affiliated with the American Church Institute for Negroes, and is coeducational. St. Paul's College was established (1888) at Lawrenceville, Virginia; it is also affiliated with the American Church Institute for Negroes, and is a member of the United Negro College Fund. Trinity College, Hartford, Connecticut, was founded by Episcopal Churchmen (1823) as a college for men of all faiths, and has maintained a close relationship with the Church. The University of the South, Sewanee, Tennessee, located between Nashville and Chattanooga, is owned by twenty-one Southern dioceses of the Protestant Episcopal Church.

The Episcopalian Church has maintained a limited number of elementary and secondary schools down through the years. Many are noted for their academic standing. As of 1958 the Protestant Episcopal Church was reported as controlling a network of slightly over 400 of these schools in the United States. The great majority of these schools were kindergartens and elementary schools attached to parishes; about 140 were high schools.[36] The growth in lower schools has nowhere nearly paralleled the growth of membership in the faith. Episcopalians favoring private education seem to have tended to enroll their children in independent schools rather than to establish their own parochial institutions. As with most other Protestants, the bulk of church members have been inclined to support public education and to send their children to the public schools.

---

[36] A letter of July 14, 1959, by The Reverend Clarence W. Brickman, Executive Secretary, Unit of Parish and Preparatory Schools, Protestant Episcopal Church, Greenwich, Conn.

185

The Baptists

The Baptists who established their faith in America were English Baptists. Like the Pilgrims, the first English Baptists were Separatists who moved to Holland where they organized a church in 1608. They came to America, not as a body but as individuals, and they were frequently persecuted.

The Baptists recognize no human founder, no human authority, and subscribe to no human creed. Perhaps the Anabaptists (known today as Mennonites), who sprang up in the first quarter of the sixteenth century in Germany and Switzerland and insisted that persons baptized in infancy must, upon profession of conversion and in order to gain admission into church fellowship, be baptized again (although they do not always insist on immersion), are the closest to the original ancestors of the Baptists. Some Baptist authorities propound that their denominational history begins with the English Separatists in Amsterdam, Holland. John Smyth, an Anglican priest who became a Puritan and Independent, led a group there in 1609 and accepted the principle that Baptism belonged to believers and not to infants.

The first Baptist Church in America was probably established by Roger Williams, the "Apostle of Religious Liberty," in Providence, Rhode Island in 1639 (although this honor is disputed by the First Baptist Church of Newport, Rhode Island, organized by Dr. John Clarke as pastor in 1638). Williams (1603?-1683), the founder of Rhode Island, was an Anglican, subsequently a Puritan, who came to the Massachusetts colony in 1631, and was banished from it for his dangerous opinions against the authority of the magistrates. He established himself at Providence and soon gathered numerous converts to his faith. These early churches belonged to the Particular, or Calvinistic, branches (which are more numerous than those of the Arminian views who hold that Baptism belongs to believers and not to infants).[37]

With the foundation of the first Baptist church in Rhode Island, Baptist views began to make their appearance in the older Puritan colonies, and among the members of the Congregational Churches. In 1644 the General Court of Massachusetts enacted a statute providing that whosoever "shall either openly condemn or oppose the baptizing of infants, or go about secretly to seduce others from the approbation or use thereof, or shall purposely depart the congregation at the ministration of the ordinances, etc. . . . shall be sentenced to banishment." (The most conspicuous case of this kind was that of Henry Dunster, President of Harvard College from 1641 to 1654.)[38]

---

[37] Harvey Wish, *Society and Thought in Early America, A Social and Intellectual History of the American People Through 1865* (New York: Longmans, Green, 1950), Chapters I and II.

[38] Sweet, *The Story of Religion in America, op. cit.,* pp. 73-74; see also chapter in Spence, *op. cit.*

The first Baptist Church in Massachusetts was formed at Rehobeth in 1663. But as the seventeenth century neared its close, persecution of Baptists was dying out. The new charter of 1691, uniting Plymouth and Massachusetts Bay, granted "liberty of conscience to all Christians, except Papists," but liberty of conscience was so interpreted as to allow the taxation of dissenters for the support of Congregational ministers. It was only in 1728 that an act was passed exempting Anabaptists and Quakers from being taxed for the support of ministers.

The most important Baptist center during the colonial period was in the middle colonies and especially in Pennsylvania and New Jersey. In 1707 the first Baptist Association in America met at Philadelphia with five churches represented. In 1742 this body adopted a strong Calvinistic confession of faith, considered a turning point in the history of that denomination.

The advancement of the cause of the Baptists was slow at first. At the beginning of the Revolutionary War, there were only some 10,000 Baptists.[39] By 1800 they reached the number of around 100,000 and growth in the nineteenth century was phenomenal. Their popularity had been strengthened by their promotion of republican ideals and their opposition to state churches. In many respects, the democratic form of that church mirrored the democratic membership. The softening of the Calvinistic doctrine allowed the Baptists to compete with the Methodists and their "whosoever will" beliefs. This was done by "modifying the tenets of the Presbyterian Church and rejecting tradition," and by having the Baptists believe in "a simplified form of Calvinism which was based on the Bible as their only confession of faith."[40]

The effectiveness of the early Baptist preachers could not have been too well promoted by their illiteracy; "any marked degree of learning was considered by both preacher and congregation as a hindrance. Often they regarded an education as the handmaid of impiety and irreligion, and looked on the education of the Presbyterian minister as being a cold crust which choked his spontaneity and sincerity."[41] Disregard of education had its practical aspects. Since the average preacher was hardly paid enough to stay alive, he had to earn his living in manual labor. Nevertheless, he had to study the Bible and plan his sermons.

The frontier saw frequent clashes between the Methodists and the Baptists, since they were the chief competing religious missionary forces there. "The attractive Methodist doctrine of salvation through works partially explains the tendency of the Baptists to gravitate towards the view of the Presbyterians

---

[39] Walter B. Posey, *The Baptist Church in the Lower Mississippi Valley* 1776-1845 (Lexington: University of Kentucky Press, 1957), p. 155.

[40] *Ibid.*

[41] *Ibid.*, pp. 155-156.

and subsequently accounts for the willingness of the Baptists to accept Calvinism in a rather extreme form."[42] Yet there was no special cooperation between these two sects; they were separated even along the social lines, the Presbyterians deriving their members mostly from the upper classes, while the Baptists (and Methodists) appealed mainly to the lower strata of society.

During this period the Baptist leaders learned the value of a theologically trained ministry and came to support a strong educational program of denominational colleges. "Time also mellowed some of the extreme aspects of Calvinism," and Baptist ministers "took their place alongside those of the Methodist and Presbyterian faiths as the great religious voices ready to defend either church or state."[43]

Nevertheless, the Baptists earned a reputation as opponents of higher education because they fiercely opposed the organization of state universities, especially in the states where denominational colleges were already functioning. They feared state interference in religious affairs. They also frequently opposed the appropriation of public money to parochial and other private elementary schools. Thus they promoted an anomalous position — by advocating state primary education and opposing state higher education.

The rapid increase in Baptists that accompanied the New England revival, especially in Rhode Island, from about 1740 onward, and the appearance of a better educated leadership led to the foundation of educational institutions, the first and chief being Rhode Island College. The idea originated with Morgan Edwards of the Philadelphia Association, who obtained the cooperation of a brilliant young graduate of the College of New Jersey, James Manning. In 1764 the charter was secured.

The liberal intentions of the Baptist founders was shown in the charter which provided: "Into this Liberal and Catholic Institution shall never be admitted any Religious Tests but on the Contrary all the members hereof shall for ever enjoy full free Absolute and uninterrupted Liberty of Conscience." Another provision gave a certain number of Congregationalists, Presbyterians, Quakers, and Episcopalians places on the Board of Trustees. Yet the rules forbade any student assert his disbelief in Christianity, except "Young Gentlemen of the Hebrew Nation." At any rate, removed in 1770 from Warren, New Jersey, as a ministerial training school, to Providence, Rhode Island, this institution became Brown University in 1804, a full-fledged college, comparable to the other colleges of the time.

After the turn of the last century, the Baptists also founded Waterville College (1820) in Waterville, Maine (later Colby College). The Newton Theological Institution was opened in Boston (1825) under the auspices of

---

[42] *Ibid.*, pp. 158-159.

[43] *Ibid.*, p. 159.

ministers and laymen.[44] Along the southern half of the Atlantic Seaboard, Baptist educational activities were more limited, although not entirely dormant. In 1827, Furman Academy and Theological Institution was founded at Edgefield, South Carolina. It took some time to quiet the fears of many members of the Baptist congregations about a learned ministry, but the Mercer University was founded in 1837.

Interestingly enough, the Virginian Baptist ministers had not a single member among them who had been college-educated during the early years of the eighteenth century. It was only in 1831 that the Baptists founded near Richmond a manual labor institute which eventually became the University of Richmond. A year later the North Carolina State Convention bought a farm in Wake County and opened a manual labor school, the Wake Forest Institute which, seven years later, became the Wake Forest College.

During the same period, in states like Kentucky and Tennessee, there arose rather wealthy land owners who were dissatisfied with the old-fashioned type of emotionalized ministers and wanted schools and colleges for both laity and clergy. Among them were leaders like Luther Rice, John M. Peck, and James E. Welch who insisted that education was the key to missionary success. Peck and Welch founded schools at St. Louis and St. Charles, and Peck, after moving to Illinois (1822) eventually started an academy which became Shurtleff College. For many years Baptists were sending their sons to the Transylvania University, the only institution of quality in Kentucky, but controlled by Presbyterians, and it graduated many Baptists as Presbyterian ministers. The need for educated ministers brought the raising of a fund which resulted in the foundation in Scott County of Georgetown College, the first Baptist College in the Mississippi Valley. This school, and also the Western Baptist Theological Institute at Covington, Kentucky, and the Manual Labor Institute near Greensboro, Alabama, all failed. More successful was the Howard University, known later by a less imposing name, Howard College. In Tennessee the Union University at Murfreesboro was founded.

Between 1830-1840, the Baptists were also quite active in Alabama in several educational endeavors. Alva Woods, a Baptist Minister, became the first President of the University of Alabama (1831-1837). His successor, for the next eighteen years, was another Baptist pastor, Basil Manly. In 1832 a Baptist institution appeared at Granville, Ohio, which became (1847) a college and later Denison University. The Baptists also formed state conventions and state educational societies, and the slogan "every state its own Baptist college" was being realized by the foundation of Baptist institutions in most of the older states and the newer ones in the West.

---

[44] *Ibid.*, Chapter 8, "Educational Efforts," pp. 99-114.

Baptists continued through the years to be active at higher educational levels: Baylor (1845), Bucknell (1846), Linfield (1848), Spelman (1881), Stetson (1883), and The University of Redlands (1909) provide several examples. R. H. Conwell's Baptist Temple in Philadelphia adopted institutional features in 1891. Using volunteer teachers he added to social clubs, sewing classes, reading rooms, a gymnasium, and a night school for working people; the school, now non-affiliated, became Temple University. The most famous Baptist school in the United States, although the Baptists have surrendered exclusive control and it is now non-denominational, is the University of Chicago, established in 1890 with a Rockefeller gift of $600,000. At the time of his death some $78,000,000 had been contributed to the institution from the Rockefeller fund.

The present situation as regards to the Baptist position on education was stated by an official of the American Baptist Association:[45]

> ". . . As the name applies, this is merely an association of churches. No church, board, or other group or individual has any authority of any kind over a LOCAL church, each church being absolutely sovereign in everything she does . . . The Association has no schools; however, individual churches do operate schools. . . . There are some dozen such schools in about as many states that are under the control of a local church where the school is located. The purpose of these schools is to teach the Bible and those things directly pertinent to the work of the local church. Preachers and church workers are taught and trained. . . . The position taken by the churches composing the American Baptist Association is a unique one. These churches believe that secular education is a function of the state, and they contend for separation of church and state. . . . It is the opinion of the churches of the American Baptist Association that where the gospel is preached and received into the hearts of people, good citizenship will follow and good government will be a natural result. With good government, we will have good secular schools. . . . As you may know, there are about as many different kinds of Baptists as there are different kinds of weather, or more. The churches of the American Baptist Association contend there is only one group that is right, and that is the group doing things as directed by the New Testament, as Christ and the apostles did things and directed that they be done."

Methodism

At the time when Jonathan Edwards (1703-1758), American philosopher, mystic, and Puritan theologian, and one of the most violent exponents of the doctrines of predestination and the total depravity of mankind, became

---

[45] Letter of Reverend A. L. Patterson, Secy.-Treas., Texarkana, Arkansas, of June 26, 1959, to the author.

prominent in the "Great Awakening," John Wesley (1703-1791) was launching the Methodist movement in England. His fame and that of his younger brother Charles (1707-1788) are interwoven with the early development of Methodism. The two (and later George Whitefield) and others made up a religious fraternity dedicated to a commitment of holiness. This originated with meetings at Oxford in 1729. The group was singled out as being peculiar, receiving such nicknames as "Holy Club," "Bible Moths," and, because of their methodical habits, "Methodists."[46]

Although Methodism arrived in the United States almost 150 years after such denominations as the Congregationalists, they soon outstripped them in numbers; today, with over 10,000,000 members, the Methodist Church is the largest single Protestant body in America. Since it is a church more interested in action than in aesthetics and in preaching simple and democratic gospel, its 23 branches have not quarrelled bitterly over their doctrinal differences. It has had as its spokesmen such diverse personalities as Kansas saloon buster Carry Nation; Bishop James Cannon, Jr., who built the Virginia Anti-Saloon League to power in national politics; and the feminist and educator Frances E. Willard. Its liberality has attracted considerable Negro followers. Its ministers range from the scholarly D. Lynn Harold Hough, former Dean of Drew Theological Seminary and author of some 40 books, to Ozark Mountain faith healers; or from Reverend Dr. Ralph Sockman, whose preachings of the social gospel is known to large radio audiences, to "revivalist" preachers who shout "Halleluja" and "Amen" with true old-style emotionalism.

The remarkable educational accomplishments of the Methodists can be traced to the unusual circumstances, especially since until 1800 not a single American Methodist preacher was a college graduate. (At that time, study and learning, it was felt, interfered with the basic job of soul-saving.)

The Wesleys and George Whitefield, although ordained ministers of the Church of England, soon found themselves excluded from many of the pulpits of the Established Church on the ground that they were preachers of new doctrines, and they were forced to hold their meetings in private houses, barns, halls, and in the fields. As converts were received, they were organized into societies for worship, and as the work expanded class meetings were formed for the religious care and training of members. Then the circuit system was established, by which several congregations were grouped under the care of one lay preacher; itinerancy came into existence, as the lay preach-

---

46 For more details, see such works as: U.S. Department of Commerce, "Census of Religious Bodies, 1936," *Methodist Bodies: Statistics, Denominational History, Doctrine, and Organization* (Washington, D.C.: Government Printing Office, 1940); Richard M. Cameron, *The Rise of Methodism: A Source Book* (New York: Philosophical Library, 1954); and William W. Sweet, *Methodism in American History* (New York: Abingdon Press, 1954), pp. 11-112, and bibliography, pp. 440-441, and pp. 208-210.

ers were transferred from one appointment to another for greater efficiency; and, finally, in 1744, the annual conference was instituted in which Wesley met all his workers. Thus the principal distinctive features of the Methodist organization grew out of the necessities of the work.

The doctrinal position agreed, in the main, with that of the Church of England, and the Articles of Religion were largely formulated from the 30 Articles of that church, although no formal creed was accepted save the Apostles Creed. The stricter doctrines of Calvinism, predestination, and reprobation were put aside, and the milder emphasis on Arminianism, on repentance, faith, and holiness were accepted. (The acceptance of Arminianism caused a divergence, though not a permanent breach, between the Wesleys and Whitefield.)[47]

Although the Wesleys died in full ministerial relations with the Church of England, serious differences arose between them and the church. When the Bishop of London refused to ordain ministers for the Methodist societies in America, which were left by the Revolutionary War without the sacraments, Wesley in 1794 appointed or ordained men and gave them authority to ordain. He thus ordained Thomas Coke, D.C.L. (who was already a presbyter of the Church of England) to be superintendent of the Methodist societies in America, and set apart for a similar purpose in Great Britain Alexander Mather who had not been episcopally ordained.

In America, the first interest of the Wesleys was connected with a philanthropic movement started by Governor Oglethorpe in Georgia in 1733. He invited them to come as spiritual advisers to the colony. Both accepted, and John remained until 1738. It was chiefly through the preaching of Whitefield, whom Wesley later sent over, that the revival spread through the colonies. (Whitefield made seven visits to the colonies.) His sermons appealed to the plain people in a crude environment, with their simplicity, directness, and sincerity; his stress away from dogma and empty ceremonials to the inner life and personality produced a host of followers. Others followed; for instance, Robert Strawbridge came to Maryland in 1759, built a log house, preached, formed circuits, and inspired others to preach. In 1771 Wesley sent Francis Asbury (1745-1816) to America; when he arrived, there were but a dozen Methodist preachers in the country, and when he died there were nearly 700. The first Protestant bishop in America, called the "Foreign Minister of Methodist," was LL.D. of Oxford; Thomas Coke (1744-1814), was a scholar and voluminous writer. He and John Wesley ordained Richard Whatcoat and

---

[47] George Whitefield (1714-1770) was the powerhouse of early Methodism. Born in Gloucester, England, he studied in Pembroke College, and found his conversion after a tumultuous experience in 1735. Regeneration to him was an experience, not a doctrine, and in his enthusiasm he became a near fanatic.

Thomas Vasey as presbyters for American assignments. Coke and Asbury called themselves "bishops" over the protests of John Wesley; but thus began the organization of the Methodist church. In 1784 the famous Christian conference met in Lovely Lane Chapel and the series were given the name "Methodist Episcopal Church."

From the beginning the growth of the church has been remarkable. In 1799 there were 272 itinerant ministers and over 60,000 communicants. In 1812 the number of ministers had increased to 688, and the membership to 195,357; and in 1831 the ministers numbered 2,010, and the membership 513,114. By 1920 there were 4,680,741 members and 20,439 ministers.

The largest unification movement ever to take place in the United States has been between three Methodist bodies — the Methodist Protestant, the Methodist Episcopal Church, South, and the Methodist Episcopal Church. A general plan of unification was officially adopted in 1938 and this was approved by a Uniting Conference in Kansas City on April 26, 1939. The new Methodist Church — the word "Episcopal" was omitted from the name of the new church — contained nearly 8 million members.

Although today the Methodists support more colleges than any other Protestant denomination in America, at the death of Francis Asbury (1816) there was no single educational institution above the grade of academy under Methodist control. Among the things discussed by Thomas Coke (the first Protestant Bishop in America) and Francis Asbury, a "General Superintendent of the Methodist Societies in the United States of America," in 1785, was the advisability of founding a literary institution for the education of the sons of the preachers and others. Asbury wanted a school; Coke, with his L.L.D. from Oxford, wanted a college. The conference of the Church voted for Coke's plan and founded a college called Cokesbury in honor of the two superintendents.[48]

The institution was located in Abingdon, Maryland, 25 miles from Baltimore, and opened in 1787; but in 1795 the college building burned down, "which was to Asbury an indication of Providence that it was not the duty of the Methodist Episcopal Church to found and operate colleges."[49] So convinced, he favored the founding of lower grade (district) schools. The results were: Ebenezer Academy in Brunswick County (Virginia), Bethel Academy in Jessamine County (Kentucky), Cokesbury School in Yadkin County (western North Carolina), Wesley and Whitefield School (Georgia), and Union Seminary, Uniontown (Pennsylvania). But not a single one of them founded by Asbury survived; they were established in out-of-the-way places so that the students could be shielded from temptations, and then the

---

[48] Sweet, *Methodism, op. cit.,* pp. 11-112, 208-210.

[49] *Ibid.,* p. 112.

Methodist members were indifferent to education and were generally poor.

An important step was taken in 1820 by the General Conference when it recommended the establishment of literary institutions and provisions to permit the Bishops to appoint traveling preachers as officers and teachers in colleges, a practice till then frowned upon by the church. There followed numerous efforts of Annual Conferences to establish colleges, and the great college-building era was the period of two decades between 1820-1840. First came Augustana College (Kentucky, 1825-1849), the joint product of the Ohio and the Kentucky Conferences. In 1841, Transylvania University at Lexington (Kentucky) was offered to the Methodist Episcopal Church. The Madison College (1827-1830), just like Augustana College, did not survive.

The first permanent institutions were seminaries (academies), the ranking place having been taken by Wesleyan Academy (Newmarket, New Hampshire in 1817, and removed to Wilbraham, Massachusetts in 1825). Other seminaries came into existence in rapid succession. Cazenovia was founded by the Genesee Conference in 1824 as a school for both sexes, then an experiment in education.

One of the ironies of history is that Methodist circuit riders have often been caricatured as the enemies of learning, and Peter Cartwright, a representative circuit rider, is frequently cited as an opponent of education. Yet during his lifetime he helped found McKendree College, Illinois College for Women (now MacMurray College), and Illinois Wesleyan College; as a member of the Illinois Legislature, Cartwright introduced a bill to establish a state university. The list of great Methodists in the field of education includes such pioneers as Martin Ruter, Wilbur Fisk, Stephen Olin, John P. Durbin, John Emory, Braxton Craven, and Ignatius A. Few.

Ruter was admitted to the New York Conference, on trial, at the age of 16. Through self-study he became one of the best educated men of his day, and knew Hebrew, Chaldee, Syrian and other ancient languages, and was the first Methodist preacher in the United States to receive the honorary degree of Doctor of Divinity (from Transylvania University of Lexington, Kentucky). In 1815 he became the principal of Newmarket Academy, New England Methodism's pioneer educational adventure. He was elected President of Augustana College. Later he became first President of Allegheny College, and laid the foundations for Southwestern University (Texas).

The success of the seminaries and the election of Andrew Jackson (1828) gave a new impetus to the movements making education accessible to more people. The first permanent Methodist institution of college grade was the Wesleyan University (Middletown, Conn., 1831); in 1832 the Randolph-Macon College (Virginia) was founded, while Dickinson College became a Methodist institution in 1833 (although chartered as a Presbyterian College fifty years before). Allegheny College dates from 1834. The oldest Methodist College west of the Alleghenies was at Lebanon (Illinois), which opened as Lebanon Seminary (1828) and became McKendree College (1834). In 1837, the Indiana Conference founded Asbury University (now DePauw University) at Greencastle (Indiana). (Indiana Asbury University was transformed into De Pauw University in 1884 as a result of large gifts and larger promises on the part of Washington C. De Pauw, a glass manufacturer and an influential Methodist layman.) During the 1830's there also appeared Emory College (Georgia) and Emory and Henry College (southwestern Virginia).[50]

Although the Church was active in founding academies and colleges from 1822 on, there existed for many decades a strong prejudice against college-trained ministers, especially in the West. However, during the twenty years following 1840, a number of educational institutions were founded: Ohio Wesleyan University (1844); Northwestern University (1851); Trinity College (Duke University, 1851); Iowa Wesleyan (1854); Wofford College (Spartanburg, South Carolina, 1854); Central College (Fayette, Missouri, 1855); and Baker University (1858).

By 1840 there were at least 28 academies, seminaries, and manual-labor schools under Methodist auspices, well distributed throughout the country. The Mississippi Conference in 1840 was sponsoring Elizabeth Female College, Emory Academy, Vicksburg Academy, and Woodville Female Academy; the Georgia Conference had under its control Emory College, Georgia Female College, Georgia Conference Manual Training School, Collingsworth Institute, and Wesley Manual Labor School, while the North Carolina Conference was supporting Randolph-Macon College (a female institution at Greensbury) and two academies.

The period following the Civil War was one of greater educational advances. The program of the Centennial celebration (1866) called for the foundation of a Centenary Educational Fund; the strengthening of the two Biblical Institutions in existence and the founding of the new Biblical Institutes in the Eastern Middle States, in Cincinnati or vicinity, and on the Pacific Coast. Daniel Drew, a wealthy New York layman, offered $6 million for the establishment of a theological seminary at Madison, New Jersey; the Drew Theological Seminary opened its doors in 1867 under the Presidency of Dr. John McClintock, the "most universally accomplished man

---

[50] A. W. Cummings, *The Early Schools of Methodism* (New York: Phillips & Hunt, 1886); H. M. Du Boise, *A History of Methodism* (Nashville, Tennessee: Smith & Lamar, 1916), especially Chapter XXI, "Schools of Southern Methodism"; Paul N. Garber, *The Romance of American Methodsm* (Greensboro, North Carolina: The Piedmont Press, 1931), Chapters VIII, "Educational Contributions," and IX, "Training the Preachers."

American Methodism has produced."[51] In 1869, Boston University was chartered; Syracuse University started operating in 1871 with an endowment of $300,000.

The Church South tried to establish a real university but could not raise the adequate sums until Cornelius Vanderbilt of New York gave half a million dollars which he increased later to one million, and his son, William H. Vanderbilt, added $250,000. Vanderbilt University (1875) was the first true University the Methodists built in the South, with six departments (including the first theological school of the Southern Church). Some years later, George I. Seney, a Methodist layman of New York, gave $260,000 to Emory College and Wesleyan Female College of Georgia.

In 1880, the Methodist Episcopal Church controlled eleven theological seminaries and institutes; forty-four colleges and universities and 130 seminaries and women's schools, with a total enrollment of 21,000 students and property valued at $11,560,100.[52]

At the same time, the administration of the Methodist colleges began to come under the control of laymen. Prior to the Civil War, these institutions were controlled by annual conferences; the Presidents were ministers and formed a majority of the faculties. But in the later decades with the hope that they might contribute to the institution, wealthy laymen were invited to take places on boards of trustees. The influence of money is exemplified by the withdrawal of Vanderbilt University from the control of the Methodist Episcopal Church, South. Originally established by the Annual Conference of the Church South, the University was transferred in 1898 to the control of the General Conference. After a court battle, ending the church contol and bringing about an alliance between Vanderbilt University and the funds under the control of the Peabody Foundation, the General Conference had to accept the decision of the Supreme Court of Tennessee (1914) — and immediately took action authorizing the foundation of Southern Methodist University (Dallas, Texas), changing Emory College (Oxford, Georgia) to a university, and founding a theological school at the Southern Methodist University. The Methodists also gave special attention to Negro needs; it is estimated, for example, that over fifty percent of the Negro doctors now practicing in the United States have been trained at Meharry Medical College at Nashville.

The list of graduates of Methodist schools who have influenced American public life is imposing. One of Cokesbury's students, Charles Tait from Georgia, became a U.S. Senator and he introduced the bill to admit Alabama

---

[51] Sweet, *Methodism, op. cit.,* p. 318; Halford E. Luccock and Paul Hutchinson, *The Story of Methodism* (New York: The Methodist Book Concern, 1926), Chapters XX to XXIV.

[52] Sweet, *Methodism, op. cit.,* pp. 333-334.

to the Union with its provision for a state university. Abel Bliss, also a student of Cokesbury, was one of the founders of Wesleyan Academy in Massachusetts, and Wesleyan University (Middletown, Connecticut). Augusta College in Kentucky gave to the church Randolph S. Foster, first President of Northwestern University and later a Methodist Bishop;; John G. Fee of Augusta College founded Berea College; Holland N. McTyeire of Randolph-Macon founded Vanderbilt University; General Fisk of Albion College founded Fisk University; and Leland Stanford of Cazenovia Seminary founded (non-denominational) Leland Stanford Jr. University. John O. Gross, President of Kentucky's Union College for many years, has recently sparked the continuing drive to establish Methodist colleges from Alaska to Hawaii.

With the founding of Andover Theological Seminary (1808), many theological seminaries came into existence. The election of John R. Vincent (1868) as secretary of the Methodist Sunday School Union and editor of the Sunday school literature of the church, produced far-reaching results. He revolutionized Sunday school teaching by teacher-training classes, teachers' institutes, and regular training courses for teaching. His Uniform Lesson system, approved by the International Sunday School Convention (1872), popularized Bible study.

The Board of Education was originally the agency charged by the General Conference with the promotion and supervision of the educational interests of the Church (since 1868). Its first large responsibility was the administration of the Student Loan Fund; by 1935, this fund, formed by the annual Children's Day offerings of Methodist Episcopal Sunday schools, had an aggregate of more than $3 million. The work of the former Board of Education is now administered through the Department of Educational Institutions. At the close of 1935, there were five universities, under the auspices of the Church, 36 colleges, 7 junior colleges, 20 secondary schools, 5 theological schools, 3 training schools, and 15 colleges and secondary schools for Negroes.[53]

Today the Methodist Church in varying degrees controls some 136 schools. Included are: 9 universities, 12 seminaries, 21 junior and 76 senior colleges (including such institutions as the American University, Boston University, Duke University, the Nebraska Wesleyan University, Lincoln University, the University of the Pacific, Syracuse University, University of Denver) and supports 168 Wesley Foundations at state and independent college and university campuses and some 350 other organizations of the Methodist student movement in America.[54]

---

[53] Census of Religious Bodies, 1936, op. cit., pp. 16-17.

[54] See the Directory of Educational Institutions of the Methodist Church U.S.A., 1959, Leaflet No. 1073-E1, Board of Education of the Methodist Church, Nashville 2, Tennessee; See also Time, "College Building Church," Feb. 3, 1961, pp. 48-49.

Another important development in the general field of education, brought about by Methodist influence, was the introduction of the Chautauqua Assemblies, which started as a Sunday-school teachers' assembly, and eventually developed into an elaborate national institution, with regular courses of study covering many fields.

In 1864 some Methodist preachers interested in a camp-meeting site found a spot on Chautauqua Lake in southwestern New York. John Vincent (1832-1920), an editor of the Sunday school publications of the Methodist Church until his election as Bishop, established here with Lewis Miller a Summer Assembly to train Sunday school teachers. Eventually he also adopted the winter Lyceum idea.[55] The famed Chautauqua institution heard and saw the foremost and frequently the best platform performers. The camp developed into an interdenominational summer resort. In 1878 it began a program of education, a "school out of school," and a liberal arts college course.

The idea became extremely popular throughout the country. "Little Chautaquas" popped up on lake shores from Maine's pines to the Florida panhandle to California's big trees. A dapper young man, Keith Vawter, placed the Chautauqua under a camp meeting tent and sent it out like a traveling carnival to small towns. With expenses guaranteed and whooped up by local sponsors — and on a possibly higher plane than the air-waved and kilocycled sights and sounds that have displaced it — "Chautauqua week" was the most important six or seven days of the year in hundreds of American communities. "The most American thing in America" was the superlative given it by Theodore Roosevelt. In 1878 the Chautauqua Literary and Scientific Circle offered a four-year reading course in literary, social, scientific, and religious studies. But the idea was killed by the radio's vacuum tube and the movies' sound track, and this vanished institution is now only one of the fragments of American history and of the experiments in adult education.

Johnson evaluates the impact made by the Methodists on American culture as follows:[56]

> . . . part of the pattern of American life set by the English through the Methodist church is an affirmation of the dignity by asserting the responsibility of the individual. . . . they were strongly influential in giving the sanction of religious faith to the political theory of democracy. They are still exercising that influence so powerfully that they have come near to incor-

---

[55] John H. Vincent, *The Chautauqua Movement* (Boston: The Chautauqua Press, 1886); Edgar W. Knight, *Fifty Years of American Education: A Historical Review and Critical Appraisal* (New York: Ronald Press, 1952), Chapter 5; more recent and complete is Joseph E. Gould, *The Chautauqua Movement* (New York: University Publishers, 1960).

[56] Gerald W. Johnson, *op. cit.*, pp. 175-176.

porating democracy in religion. This is one part of the patterns set by the English that thus far exhibits no tendency to fade.

It was to be expected that the Methodists would be strong supporters of public education; they have so proven down through the years.

The Society of Friends (Quakers)

Quakerism is a familiar name for members of the Society of Friends, an evangelical religious body having no definite creed and no regular ministry, founded in England by George Fox between 1648 and 1650. Fox turned early against the insincerities of contemporary religious practices and social behavior, and experienced a conversion in 1646. Evangelistic in temper, he boldly espoused his convictions and buffered persecution for his preaching, was accused of blasphemy and disturbance of the peace, and was imprisoned eight times. It appears from his *Journal* that the Quakers first obtained the appellation (1650) from the following circumstance: "Justice Bennett, of Derby," stated Fox, "was the first to call us Quakers, because I bade him quake and tremble at the word of the Lord." He drew on smaller sects and so-called "Seekers" to his cause. For the Friends the "inner voice" is the source of the positive beliefs, and man himself may personally appropriate the will of God and does not have to be bound by any creed. The Scriptures are the instruments for an inner experience and a personal witness. As a reaction to the formalism of the church, the Society stresses simplicity of life and commitment to truth as one sees it.

Persecuted, the Friends went to the New World. William Penn (1644-1718), a member of the Society of Friends, is known to American history as the founder of Pennsylvania who superintended the laying out of Philadelphia. He envisioned a colony where religious freedom and equality should prevail, having in mind the persecution of his own faith. In 1682, he sailed with a hundred immigrants for his province of Pennsylvania (named in honor of his father by the King of England). He played fair with the Indians and his colony grew rapidly.[57] The first Quaker missionaries had reached

---

[57] Penn authored many books, some of them in prison, in which he dreamed of international federation. He also prepared charters for New Jersey (1676) and Pennsylvania (1683) in which he applied many of the devices of Harrington's *Oceana;* these constitutions were considered models and were expected to be permanent. Pennsylvania, especially, acquired great fame in Europe, and Voltaire and Montesquieu wrote of it in terms of high admiration. The experiments were, however, failures, although the belief in property qualifications, the concept of civil and religious liberty, and the idea of a written constitution survived. See: C. O. Peare, *William Penn* (New York: Holt, 1958); Elbert Russell, *The History of Quakerism* (New York: The Macmillan Co., 1942); William C. Braithwaite, *The Beginnings of Quakerism,* rev. by Henry C. Cadbury (Cambridge: Cambridge University Press, 1955).

America in 1656; they started a systematic movement which had touched all the English colonies by 1660. By the time of the American Revolution Friends were found throughout Anglo-America; in fact, by that time they had dominated the colonial governments of Pennsylvania and Rhode Island and were influential in New Jersey and the Carolinas.

Although the Puritan morals are always quoted as being most oppressive in Amerian history, actually the early Quakers were more rigorous than Puitans in enforcing simplicity of dress and of speech and the banning of sports, cards, dice, plays, dancing, intemperate drinking, the reading of fiction, instrumental music — and even whistling. "It is one of the ironies of history that the nineteenth century romantics and their disciples should have succeeded in fixing in popular usage the contemptuous epithet *Puritan* upon a rigorousness of personal asceticism that to the true Puritan mind was but one consequence of sectarian fanaticism."[58]

The Quaker, in his religious affirmations, was, like the Puritan, a seventeenth century Protestant, enticed by the experience of regeneration through the agency of the Inner Light, the Seed, which was God's presence in the soul of the believer. For the Quaker, his mysticism cultivated his religious experience not only by direct contact with the divine spirit within but also by the light that it shed on his everyday problem. The Quaker differed from the Puritan in believing that man was morally depraved but could be perfectly regenerated. The final distinguishing feature of Quaker religion was its voluntarism, that ultimate responsibility for salvation or damnation rested with each individual.

In application, Quakers took over from the Puritans the theory of congregationalism in ecclesiastical organization and in practice. This implied not only the complete autonomy of each congregation but also the rigid separation of church and state; no formal clergy with authoritative powers to interpret the Word of God was necessary. "In short, Quaker sectarianism presupposed a pluralistic, tolerant, flexible form of society precisely the opposite of the seventeenth century Puritan theocracy or the Twentieth Century totalitarian state. . . ."[59]

The Quakers were among the first Protestant groups to enter systematically into missionary activity and they were banned in Massachusetts. The Quakers were the first to introduce universal manhood suffrage in America, in William Penn's Constitution of 1682. Equalitarianism was another consequence of Quaker practice. Women were guaranteed complete equality with men. Their scrupulous dealings with the Indians were well known and their pioneer opposition to Negro slavery is praiseworthy.

---

[58] Stow Persons, *American Minds: A History of Ideas* (New York: Holt, 1958), p. 64.

[59] *Ibid.,* p. 66.

The seventeenth century Puritans hated and feared the Quakers.[60] They differed in their doctrines, one stressing the community obligation based on responsibility, subordination, cooperation, and leadership, and the other on self-sufficing independence. No effort was made by Puritans to propagandize among the Quakers and hence the Quakers held the initiative.

Fox, in 1668, about twenty years after he started to preach, advised the setting up of two schools: one for boys and one for girls. Before the end of the seventeenth century many Friends, some of them ex-clergymen who could no longer preach, had opened privately owned schools. Some of these offered advanced teaching, including Latin. By 1700 the policy of sending Friends' children to their own day or boarding schools was well established. Beginning with 1690, London Yearly Meetings were held to establish schools and advised against the training of Friends' children by non-Friends.[61]

The history of Quaker education in America can be divided ito four stages, each stage representing the rise of a certain type of school which has survived to the present. Earliest came the elementary school (during the seventeenth and eighteenth centuries); next the academy and boarding school (during the first half of the nineteenth century); third the college (during the second half of the nineteenth century); and fourth the center for study of adults (initiated during the twentieth century).[62]

Believing, as the Protestant sects in New England, that each individual should read and interpret the Bible for himself, the Quakers, next to the Puritans, pursued zealously the goal of educating the common man, and from the very beginnings of their settlements in Pennsylvania, New Jersey, North Carolina, and other colonies they founded schools for the children of their congregations.[63]

Pioneer Quaker communities established schools soon after setting up meetings. The London advices of 1690 and later, concerning the education and apprenticeship of Friends' children, had a strong influence in the New World. The first schools were in homes or meeting houses. In some communities a log cabin school house was built close to the meeting house. In the early eighteenth century, many meetings in Rhode Island, New York,

---

[60] Perry Miller, *The New England Mind: The Seventeenth Century* (Cambridge: Harvard University Press, 1954); Miller, *The New England Mind: From Colony to Province* (Cambridge: Harvard University Press, 1953); Alan Simpson, *Puritanism in Old and New England* (Chicago: University of Chicago Press, 1955); Clinton L. Rossiter, *Seedtime of the Republic* (New York: Harcourt, Brace, 1953).

[61] Howard H. Brinton, *Quaker Education in Theory and Practice* (Wallingford, Pennsylvania: Pendle Hill, 1949), pp. 23-27.

[62] Brinton, *Ibid.*, p. 27.

[63] Thomas Woody, *Early Quaker Education in Pennsylvania* (New York: Columbia University, 1920).

New Jersey, Pennsylvania, Maryland, Virginia, and the Carolinas recorded educational concerns. In Philadelphia, a Quaker schoolmaster was first engaged by the Provincial Council in 1683 in 1689 George Keith was put in charge of a school designed to meet the needs of rich and poor. In 1701 Penn granted a charter to this school for teaching "the rich at reasonable rates and the poor to be maintained and schooled for nothing." In 1779 there were five schools in Philadelphia under the "Overseers of the Public School," a Quaker committee set up by Penn's charter. In 1770 a school for Negroes was set up. In 1750 there were about forty Monthly Meeting schools in Pennsylvania and by the end of the century as many as seventy, with about half as many more in New Jersey.

Quaker influence dominated education in colonial Pennsylvania. An early law required parents to have children taught reading and writing; but this statute was not enforced and no "public schools" were established. Penn's first Frame of Government ordered the governor and Council to erect public schools. Although these authorities never founded a public school system free to all comers, they established schools free for those unable to pay — although they did not make education a matter of public concern as did Massachusetts Bay.[64]

The Quakers stressed practical education as opposed to classical learning; they emphasized less the classics and more English, mathematics, and such "useful studies" as bookkeeping and surveying. They did not, however, oppose the traditional Latin grammar schools. The Friends Public School, founded in Philadelphia in 1689, eventually became the William Penn Charter School (still in existence), an aggregation of schools, headed by the Latin School, which had the Latin School as the apex of the educational hierarchy; it was open free for poor children but those able had to pay. The religious character of the instruction was carefully supervised.

The Quakers had zeal for elementary education but were comparatively indifferent to the college (although a number of Quakers were graduates of English universities), as they did not believe that the clergy was an order of men set or trained apart from the community. This very attitude tended also to make their schools to become denominational. This in turn prevented the foundation of any general system of education in Pennsylvania, along with the fact that the colony was settled by various denominations none able to dominate it and impose its system on the rest.

Interestingly enough, the Quakers' ideal of "public" education resulted in

---

[64] In his *Address to Protestants,* William Penn proclaimed: "If we would preserve our government, we must endear it to the people. To do this . . . we must secure the youth." See: William Penn, "Address to Protestants," in a *Collection of the Works of William Penn* (London: Assigns of J. Sowle, 1726), vol. 1, pp. 738ff.

one of the opening wedges for the concept of parochial education. Many Pennsylvanians of other sects were openly antagonistic to the Quakers' trying to enforce any general educational requirements. As Penn's relations with the Anglicans and Presbyterians became progressively worse, eventually the Quakers had to give up this goal. While they formerly had made the state the trustee for their youth and ordained the foundation of schools and the instruction of youth, they granted the right, by The Charter of Privileges (1701), to all "religious societies or assemblies and congregations of Protestants . . . to purchase any land or tenements for . . . houses of religious worship, schools, and hospitals."[65]

Quaker elementary education east of the Allegheny Mountains reached its peak between 1800 and 1810. Then came the decline due to divisions within the Society and the growth of public schools; in fact, many Quaker schools became public schools.

As a result of the transfer of elementary schools to the care of public authorities, the Friends turned to academies and high schools. There are still a number of elementary schools; however, where Friends have elementary instruction, it is carried on mainly as lower-divisions in secondary schools. Most of them are in Pennsylvania, then in New Jersey and California. The academy (seminary or higher school) has often retained the elementary school out of which it developed. The leading type was the co-educational boarding school. These came to present wide variations in the subjects taught. Often they overlapped the college. With the exception of Fair Hill Boarding School, Maryland (1819-1865), Stavanger Boarding School, Iowa (1891-1913) and Spring River Academy, Kansas (1881-1915), these schools survive or have become colleges. Among them are: the Moses Brown School (formerly Friends' School in Providence, Rhode Island), Oak Grove Seminary in Maine, Westtown School in Pennsylvania, and Guilford College (evolved from New Garden Boarding School in North Carolina). These are all controlled by the Yearly Meetings, except Pickering College and Friends' Academy at Locust Valley, Long Island. The Western academies had an interesting history. They were "important focal points for intellectual life in the Society of Friends,"[66] as students came from long distances and lodged in dormitories or private homes, and eventually became loyal alumni. In the South there were also Quaker academies, most of them under Quarterly Meetings.

In the early colonial days colleges existed mainly for the education of the clergy. Since the Friends conceived preparation for religious service as a

---

[65] Cited in Francis N. Thorpe, *The Federal and State Constitutions* (Washington, D.C.: Government Printing Office, 1909), Vol. V, pp. 307ff.

[66] Brinton, *op. cit.*, p. 35.

life-long individual development rather than an institutional program, they felt no need for colleges. Thus the first Quaker colleges were founded only in the later part of the last century. Several began as a more advanced type of boarding school which maintained a religious education: Haverford School at Haverford, Pennsylvania (1833) became a college in 1856; Guilford in North Carolina, founded in 1837, became a college in 1889; and Earlham at Richmond, Indiana, founded in 1847, became a college in 1859. Then came: Swarthmore (1869), William Penn College, Iowa (1837), Wilmington College, Oregon (1871), Pacific College, California (1885), Nebraska Central College (1899), and Whittier College (1901). Some individual Friends have founded colleges through endowments: Joseph Taylor endowed Bryn Mawr College in 1855; Johns Hopkins in 1873 endowed both the hospital and the university in Baltimore which bear his name; Ezra Cornell endowed (1868) Cornell University; Moses Brown helped to found Brown University. However, "Of these, Bryn Mawr College was the only one intended by its founder to be fully included in the actual Quaker tradition."[67]

The fourth stage of Quaker education in America was the rise, in the present century, of centers of study for those who had completed their formal education. This stage of education started with the Haverford summer schools of 1900 and 1904; other such sessions were held later at Swarthmore. The biennial meetings of the Friends' General Conference, which started in 1902, are also educational in character. Pendle Hill, a new school for religious and social study, inheriting the assets of Woolman School (1918-1927) was set up at Wallingford, Pennsylvania, in 1930; its summer school of 4 weeks allows many Friends short course studies in current thought on religious and social problems. Work Camps, initiated in 1934, together with the Institutes of International Relations, represent another modern development. The work of the Friends and their American Friends Service Committee has also been an important contribution in promoting international understanding. The exchange program for students and other aspects of their experiment in international friendship have been particularly valuable.[68]

Some hundred years ago the ideal of Quaker education was stated as follows: "By education we ought to understand whatever has a tendency to invigorate the intellect, to train the mind to thought and reflection, to mould aright the affections of the heart and to confirm us in the practice of virtue."[69] The early Friends were "called off" from music, painting, the drama, and artistic poetry as being dangerous diversions. This has left a marked effect

---

[67] *Ibid.,* p. 38.

[68] David Hinshaw, *An Experiment in Friendship* (New York: Putnam, 1947).

[69] Dorothy L. Gilbert, *Guilford, a Quaker College* (Greensboro, North Carolina: Guilford College, 1937), p. 77.

upon educational stress in Friends' schools which stress more natural science than literature or languages. "In general, Quaker talent as developed in Quaker schools has shown itself in science rather than in liberal arts," claims Comfort.[70]

The control exercised by committees appointed by the Monthly or the Yearly Meetings is justified, according to Comfort: "The reason for all this investment in elementary and secondary education is the same as that of the Catholic Church in America: the desire to insure a certain control, not of the curriculum, but of other character-forming influences."[71]

Since the seventeenth century days of their founder, George Fox, the Quakers had helped their neighbors in peace and war — but as small individual groups. Then during World War I, for the first time, this pacifist sect offered its help to a government at war. In conscience the Friends could not fight, but they could feed the hungry, clothe the naked, and find homes for the homeless. It was in the late summer of 1917 that 100 young men in Quaker-gray uniform sailed for France. This was the beginning of a wave of Friendship which swept around the world. During the next three decades the Quakers had dispensed $6 million in funds and an additional $10 million in goods; only about six percent of the money was spent in administrative expenses. Approximately 6 million people in 22 countries received material aid under this program.

The activities of Herbert Hoover, perhaps the outstanding Quaker in American history, are shining examples of Friends' concerns in this area. Thoughout his long career of public service, he has made a number of direct educational contributions.[72] To cite but three varied examples: he called a famous White House conference during his period as President, from which came the influential "Children's Charter"; he led the drive to establish the well known Institute of War and Peace at Stanford University; and later in his career gave unstinting efforts to the promotion of the Boys' Club of America for Underprivileged Youth.

Between the two wars the American Friends demonstrated a concern for the unfortunate in their own country. They recruited young people to work in detention homes, settlement houses, and migrant work centers. They also showed coal miners in depressed Pennsylvania and West Virginia how to supplement their incomes by crafts and farming. At the end of the Second

---

[70] William W. Comfort, *Just Among Friends: The Quaker Way of Life* (New York: The Macmillan Co., 1941), Chapter V, "Quaker Education," pp. 111-130, and bibliography, pp. 207-210.

[71] *Ibid.*, p. 120.

[72] A thorough discussion of Hoover's educational contributions will be found in: Raymond H. Muessig, "Herbert Hoover and Education" (Doctor's thesis, Stanford University, 1959).

World War, with the withdrawal of the United Nations Relief and Rehabilitation Administration from most countries, a tremendous responsibility was again placed upon volunteer groups like the Quakers who, during the war had served overseas in various Samaritan capacities. While many of these deeds were not directly educational, there can be little question that such contributions do have considerable educational implications.

The impact of the Friends has been far greater than their number in the world would seem to warrant. There are less than 150,000 Friends, of whom 120,000 are Americans. But through their quiet strength and "inner light," the Quakers have inspired thousands of other persons to help them in helping others.

Moravians

Moravia is a province of Czechoslovakia. The Moravian Brethren or United Brethren (Unitas Fratrum) were named after this province, although they are also known as the Bohemian Brethren. The formal organization of this sect dates from 1467, when the episcopacy was conferred on a small band of the followers of John Hus by the Waldensians (an evangelical organization that had led a religious life independent of Rome). During the thirteenth and fourteenth centuries, the Roman Church sent crusading armies against the Waldensians and other non-conformist sects in Christendom; large numbers of French and Italian Waldensian exiles found refuge in Bohemia, where they were welcomed by the nobles resenting the antagonism of Rome to their use of the national language in religious worship. As the Waldensians claimed independent existence since apostolic times, they bestowed the episcopacy upon the new Bohemian sect.

The Bohemian Brethren became a powerful ecclesiastical organization, although in no sense a national church, and at the beginning of the Thirty Years' War its membership exceeded 200,000. They were banished from Bohemia and Moravia after 1620, fleeing to Saxony, Poland, Hungary, and eventually to America. Missionaries were sent throughout the world — to Greenland, Labrador, North America, the West Indies, Tibet, Africa, and the East Indies.

The foundation of the Church is a Trinitarian belief in God, the Son, and the Holy Spirit. The Apostles' Creed is used as representing the oldest and simplest general beliefs. The Holy Scripture is regarded as the only rules of faith and conduct, and is the basis of all teaching. A special confession, based on the one compiled by Martin Luther, is recited on great Church holidays. From its inception the Moravian Church has been famous for its church music sung by the congregation. Because the foundation of the Church is the Bible, the children received early training in reading so as to understand and appreciate the Scriptures. The orders are strictly Episcopal, since only Bishops can ordain, but the local government is Presbyterian. The Synod meets every six years and is the supreme court of the Church and controls the funds of the Church.

The Brethren came, after 1620, as refugees from Bohemia, to the estate of Count Zinzendorf in Saxony, a Pietistic Lutheran, who at first tried to lead them to accept the Pietistic principles. But the Moravian Church began gradually to emerge and a Bishop was consecrated for the Herrnhut group in 1735 and two years later Zinzendorf himself was consecrated a Bishop.

The formation of the Herrnhut ("The Lodge of the Lord") Moravians into a separate church brought persecution upon them, and Count Zinzendorf took steps to obtain a refuge for some of these persecuted people. In 1733 he received a promise from the Georgia trustees of land and a free passage but for another Protestant group known as Schwenkfelders. However, they changed their plans and proceeded to Pennsylvania instead. Zinzendorf then secured the Georgia tract for the Moravians; in April 1736 a company of nine, under the leadership of Spangenberg, reached Georgia. The next year twenty additional colonists arrived. On the shipboard with this group was John Wesley, coming out as Chaplain to General Oglethorpe, who has left us in his *Journal* a memorable account of his impressions of the Moravian Brethren. But the Moravian colony in Georgia failed to prosper and antagonized the authorities since it refused to bear arms in the war with Spain. In 1740, George Whitefield offered them a free passage on his sloop to Philadelphia and the first American Moravian colony was transplanted to Pennsylvania. They settled at Bethlehem, Nazareth, and Lititz.

Although they numbered by the time of the Revolution only about 2,500, they already were known for their religious and educational activities. Their missionaries to the Indians were especially successful, and they provided religious education to many frontier settlements.

Of all non-resistant groups, the Moravians suffered most in the American revolution, though they rendered great service to the American cause. Their buildings at Bethlehem were used as a general hospital for the American Army during several years of the war; they cheerfully responded to numerous requisitions for supplies. But their greatest service was rendered through their Indian missions, and they frequently persuaded the Indians to turn back from their planned war paths, and on several occasions warned settlements of scheduled raids.

The Moravians also suffered for a number of years after the Revolutionary War by the domination of the governing board from Germany and by the continuance of the use of the German language in their worship, while the laymen had no voice in the management of the church affairs. There was also a lack of well-qualified ministers.

The Moravians not only cleared the forests, developed farmlands, and carried the Gospel to the American Indians, but wherever they went they promoted education. John Heckewelder, David Zeisberger, and Christian Friedrich Post were among the Moravian missionaries who were intimately connected with the early history of white settlement in the Ohio country; Zeisberger translated religious books and hymns into the Delaware Indian language, and his group promoted churches and mission schools wherever they went. "The courage, endurance, self-sacrifice, and humanity of the Moravians in colonial times constitutes one of the finest chapters in the history of colonial beginnings in America."[73]

The remarkable educational work of the Moravian Brethren is rooted in the ideas of one of the greatest educators of all times, John Amos Comenius (Komensky), and a lesser known educator, Count Nicholas Louis von Zinzendorf. Comenius (1592-1670), the last Bishop of the Moravian Brethren, is not only revered in his native country (now Czechoslovakia) but throughout the world under the influence of Western civilization.[74]

Without going into details, it is sufficient to note here that many of his educational ideas are commonplace today (such as the concept of universal education and of coeducation) and have been incorporated into the basic ideas of what is known as "progressive education." He exerted influence on such modern educators as Francke, Rousseau, and Pestalozzi. Actually UNESCO is dedicated to his idea of seeing education as the only solution for bringing about universal peace.

His basic ideas have been summarized as follows: (1) Education should start early. (2) Education should be practical, not theoretical. (3) Children ought to be taught in their native tongue. (4) Education should be universal and an equal opportunity should be granted to rich and poor. (5) Education should be granted to all. (6) Education should be based upon sense experiences — the use of realia, objects, and pictures. (7) Education should be natural and logical, not artificial. (8) In addition to more traditional fare, students should have a broad education, including, for example, geography, history, natural science, physics, economics, political science, physical education, etc. (9) Artisans, peasants, and women also need education, so that they would have something to occupy their minds, know how to direct their actions, and endeavor to see God everywhere. (See also Chapter VIII, pp. 291-293.)

---

[73] Carl Wittke, *We Who Built America: The Saga of the Immigrant* (New York: Prentice-Hall, 1946), p. 79.

[74] There are numerous studies of the influence of Comenius; see, for example: W. S. Monroe, *Comenius and the Beginnings of Educational Reform* (New York: Scribners', 1900); Matthew Spinka, *John Amos Comenius: That Incomparable Moravian* (Chicago: University of Chicago Press, 1943).

From Comenius, the Moravian Brethren inherited these ideals of education, and wherever they went they organized schools, academies, and other educational institutions, and "the world owes these zealous Christian teachers a large debt of gratitude for the improved school systems which their labors made possible."[75] Comenius is also acclaimed as "The Father of the Graded Method." He advocated and practiced the grading of hymns, prayers, and of Bible reading. He is said to be the first to use a shortened Bible, adjusted to the age of the pupil. Many a parent of today is impressed with the attractively illustrated textbooks which our children use; it was the *Orbis Pictus* of Comenius that was one of the first picture-books ever written for children. It is also seldom known that Comenius is the "Spiritual Father" of Masonry.

Count Zinzendorf (1700-1760), a Saxon nobleman of great celebrity, lived in the house of Francke for six years while a student in the Halle *Padagogium*. He set up on his estate a religious community composed of the refugee Moravian Brethren, known as *Herrnhut*. Following the example of Francke, he founded a number of orphanages and schools. But his most important contribution was the foundation of Moravian colonies and schools in Pennsylvania. These communities were semi-Communist in character and the schools were institutions in which to live a well-ordered life. They had nurseries in which the young children were kept, boarding schools for boys and girls, and secondary boarding schools for adolescents. In addition to the religious and regular subjects, vocational training was also offered. Liturgies and hymns played a prominent part in the educational plan for children, as well as adults. The singing of hymns received a creative impetus widely felt throughout Protestantism today. Zinzendorf, like Comenius, developed a shortened form of the Bible for children, as he believed that many passages, such as those referring almost exclusively to Jews, were of little interest or concern for them. He also translated the Bible at many points into the familiar idioms of his time. In fact, he wrote much for children. Far ahead of his time, he advocated that children be "brought up from infancy so as never to think otherwise than that they are the children of God."[76]

From Zinzendorf's point of view, the most important feature of his scheme of religious education was the "choir" system; the whole community was divided into groups on the basis of sex, age, and marital status. There were eight groupings for children and young people, and three for adults. A program of Christian education was developed on the basis of the particular needs of each choir. The annual festival day of each choir was a feature of this plan.

---

[75] Will S. Monroe, *The Spell of Bohemia* (Boston: L. A. Page & Co., 1910), p. 462.

[76] Raymond S. Rauper, *Pioneers in Moravian Education: John Amos Comenius and Count Nicholas von Zinzendorf* (Winston-Salem, North Carolina: Interprovincial Board of Christian Education, Moravian Church, 1957).

The ideas of Comenius and Zinzendorf were imported to America by the Moravian Brethren who practiced them in their parochial schools, especially the concepts of education for all, kindergartens, teaching in the vernacular, nature teaching, and the use of the physical senses in learning. In the Moravian communities, education was of primary importance to the community. The schools were free, and they were opened to both boys and girls. The stress was on religious training, but the teacher's aim was a well-rounded Christian character. The early curriculum included English, German, mathematics, astronomy, and history; instrumental music, vocal music, and drawing were also a part of the curriculum. The girls were also taught spinning, needle-work, and embroidery.

The early schools were established at Bethlehem in 1742 and at Nazareth in 1743. In 1742 Count Zinzendorf started a school for girls at Germantown, Pennsylvania, the first boarding school for girls in the thirteen colonies; it was later transferred to Bethlehem, where it continued as a seminary and college for women. A decade later, the Moravians established an excellent boys' boarding school at Nazareth. In recent years the Moravian College and the Moravian College for Women have merged into the new corporation, Moravian College, which operates a liberal arts college for men and women and a professional graduate school of theology, Moravian Theological Seminary. Altogether the Moravians founded ten educational institutions in Pennsylvania.[77] The Winston-Salem settlement of the Moravians became as important in the South as Bethlehem was in the Northern states. The music developed by the Moravians in both their churches and schools was probably more highly developed in their communities than in any other colonial communities, and Winston-Salem is even today noted for the Easter services conducted by the Moravian Church. Bethlehem, in fact, became the musical center of the colonies during the eighteenth century, and it has remained a center of the Bach cult in America.

In general, certain definite principles of the Moravian Brethren have made an impression on the cultural and educational history of America. The strong stress on education, the importance of nursery schools, the accent on teaching in the vernacular, the emphasis on character and vocational education which must be stressed in the early years of school, and the belief in peace and democratic principles can be traced to them. The Moravians also brought with them a profound philosophy that all men are equal and that the purpose of all education is to make each man like his Maker. It is true that they were small in number and shared these beliefs with other groups and

---

[77] Joseph S. Roucek, "The Moravian Brethren in America," *The Social Studies*, Feb. 2, 1952, pp. 58-61; Mabel Haller, *Early Moravian Education in Pennsylvania* (Nazareth, Pennsylvania: Moravian Historical Society, 1953).

educators; but their attempt to live their ideals made a profound impression upon those who came into contact with them.

Lutheranism

In recent years, authorities point out, an extraordinary transformation has been rapidly changing the character and size of the Lutheran churches and synods of America.[78] For the past three centuries most of the Lutheran churches in America could be identified by their European origin — as German, Swedish, Norwegian, Danish, Slovak, and Finnish. But that is not the case today. Throughout the country Lutherans are shedding their foreign characteristics and are rearing many new edifices in which the worshippers are as polyglot in background as the nation itself.

Only the highlights of the development of Lutheranism can be sketched here. Luther, the son of a miner in the Harz mountains, after completing a course in the study of law at the University of Erfurt, abandoned his plans to become a lawyer and entered an Augustinian monastery. But try as he might to satisfy the rules of the order, he could not satisfy himself that he had won salvation. Finally in despair he turned to a careful rereading of the Bible and the works of St. Augustine and became convinced that no one could attain salvation through good works but only through faith in God. This doctrine, that man is a miserable sinner, incapable of good works, whose only hope is to throw himself on God's mercy, is known as "justification by faith" and is the central doctrine of Luther's teaching. While professor of theology at the University of Wittenberg, Luther worked out the details of the doctrine and began teaching it to his students. He first drew attention to himself through a dispute about indulgences. In 1517 Pope Leo X proclaimed an indulgence to raise money to rebuild St. Peter's at Rome. Luther believed that claims as to the efficacy of indulgences were being made which were not justified, and accordingly he wrote out ninety-five theses or statements to debate about indulgences which he posted on the church door at Wittenberg. Their translation from Latin into German and extensive circulation revealed the current discontent with the church. Eventually, Luther reached an open break with the Pope and the church. For his heretical doctrines, Luther was excommunicated in 1520, but he had won so many friends that the bull of excommunication made little practical difference to him. Even the edict of the Diet of the Holy Roman Empire, meeting at Worms in 1521, had no

---

[78] Henry E. Jacobs, Ed., *The Lutheran Encyclopedia* (New York: Scribners', 1899); Abel R. Wentz, *The Lutheran Church in American History* (Philadelphia: United Lutheran Publishing House, 1923); U.S. Department of Commerce, Census of Religious Bodies, 1936, *Lutherans: Statistics, Denominational History, Doctrine, and Organization* (Washington, D.C.: Government Printing Office, 1940).

more effect. Luther remained in hiding under the protection of his friend, the elector of Saxony, devoting himself to the translation of the New Testament into German, still one of the classics of German literature.

The reaction to Luther's ideas in Germany varied widely with different groups. In 1529 a group of rulers who had accepted Lutheranism drew up a protest declaring that the Emperor's order (that no one should preach against the Mass or be prevented from attending it) was in violation of the ruling of the Diet of Speyer (1526); thus the name "Protestantism" originated. In 1530 the Emperor ordered the Protestants to draw up a statement of their beliefs to be presented to the Diet in the hope of arriving at some compromise. The statement, known as the Augsburg Confession, still exists as the creed of the Lutheran Church. Thus the Lutheran Churches of America believe that the canonical books of the Old and New Testaments are given by inspiration of God and are the perfect and the only rule of faith and life. They believe that the three general creeds — the Apostles', the Nicene, and the Athanasian — exhibit the faith of the Christian church, in accordance with the Holy Scripture. Justification by faith alone in Jesus Christ is held to be the central doctrine of the Word of God according to which all other doctrines are determined and developed. The preaching of the Word of God, rightly divided between law and Gospel, occupies a prominent place in accomplishing repentance and faith. The Lutheran Church is a firm believer in thorough Christian indoctrination and education, and insists upon catechical instruction preparatory to confirmation.

Lutheranism also spread to the Scandinavian lands. The Reformation in Norway, Denmark, and Sweden followed much the same course as in the German states, the rulers taking the lead and establishing national churches directly under the control of the state, though here the episcopal system was retained.

Lutheranism was introduced into the United States by Dutch colonists on Manhattan, later by Swedes on the Delaware, by Palatines in Pennsylvania and New York, and by Salzburgers in Georgia. Throughout the colonial times, Pennsylvania was the chief home of American Lutheranism. The Swedes settled first in Delaware and New Jersey in 1638 (the colony having been originally projected by Gustavus Adolphus in 1626); at the end of that century, their settlements totalled about one thousand families. German Lutherans found their way in considerable numbers to New Netherlands, Delaware, and New Jersey. But heavy immigration began with the settlement of Germantown in 1685, a result of Penn's visit to Germany and his liberal offers to colonists. All in all, at the time of the Revolution, the German element composed the bulk of population in New York and Pennsylvania, with large elements in Maryland and the other southern colonies. Most of the Germans were nominally Lutherans; the same applied to the Swedes and a number of the Dutch. Some joined the German Reformed, the Dutch Reformed, and the Episcopal Congregations. By 1773, the Colonies had an estimated 100 Lutheran churches, with a confirmed membership of 10,000; in 1798 nearly 300 churches, with 20,000 members; and in 1823, 700 congregations with approximately 38,000 communicants.

The first Lutheran school on American soil was Swedish (1638). When the Salzburgers came to Georgia (1734), they immediately established schools; John Adam Truetlen, the first Governor of Georgia, was a product of one of these schools. In fact, Lutheran parochial schools of Scandinavian, German, and Dutch origin flourished in New York, Pennsylvania, Delaware, New Jersey, Maryland, the Carolinas, Virginia, and Georgia in early American history.[79] In fact, "The Lutheran school systems established in the original Colonies and States before the enactment of public-school laws comprised without doubt the largest and most extensive system operated on a purely parochial basis within a particular denomination," reports Beck, with "more than 400 schools having been established and maintained during this early period."[80]

When the Germans started settling in America in large number during the eighteenth century, they at once provided for the schooling of their children. Every German sect had its parochial school. Wherever a community established a church, it also immediately started a school. The ministers were often the school teachers. But some schools had professional educators who soon became the leading spirits of their colonies.

In methods and organization, the early Lutheran schools in Pennsylvania preserved many of the traditions peculiar to their fatherland. Almost without exception they were appendages of the church, and the master was a church official. Like the Dutch schoolmaster, he was usually an assistant to the pastor. The curriculum was similar to other schools of the time. Catechism, recitation of the scriptures, memorization and singing of hymns, reading, writing, spelling, and arithmetic were taught. The German tongue was the vernacular. And like the other types of education of the time, Lutheran education was universally cold and bleak.

---

[79] William A. Kramer, "Christian Education," pp. 207-215, in Erwin L. Lueker, Ed., *Lutheran Cyclopedia* (St. Louis, Missouri: Concordia Publishing House, 1954); W. H. Beck, *Lutheran Elementary Schools in the United States* (St. Louis: Concordia Publishing House, 1939); Lutheran Education Association, *One Hundred Years of Christian Education* (River Forest, Illinois: The Association, 1947); F. V. N. Painter, *Luther on Education* (St. Louis: Concordia Publishing House, 1928); A. C. Stellhorn, *The Meaning of Lutheran Education* (St. Louis: Concordia Publishing House, 1928); William A. Kramer, *Religion in Lutheran Schools* (St. Louis: Concordia Publishing House, 1929).

[80] Beck, *op. cit.*, p. 10; we have drawn extensively upon this valuable work here; unfortunately it is now out of print.

By 1750 there were at least 40,000 Lutherans in Pennsylvania. One of the big difficulties was the need to get enough teachers and pastors to serve the congregations. This was a serious problem. As a result, the Lutherans had to resort to the employment of "fly-by-nights" and other undesirables. When some of the children started attending Catholic schools and a Moravian competition sprang up in Pennsylvania, action had to be taken. Heinrich M. Muhlenberg was sent from Germany. This marked a turning point in Lutheran history.

Meanwhile the ranks of the Lutherans had been strengthened by continued immigration. Later they pushed into the Midwest. In 1839 Saxon immigrants settled in Missouri. The Scandinavians came later in large numbers — and a Norwegian Synod was organized in 1853, a Swedish Lutheran church at New Sweden, Iowa in 1848. Most Lutheran Church groups then came to be identified by their European origins.

Heinrich Melchior Muhlenberg (1711-1787), "Patriarch of the Lutheran Church in America," was born in Einbeck, Hanover, Germany. He entered the University of Göttingen in 1735 as one of its first students. After his graduation he taught for one year at the Halle Orphanage and was pastor in Upper Silesia (1739-1741). Dr. Francke of Halle persuaded him, in September, 1741, to accept a call to the "United Lutheran Congregations" in Pennsylvania. By preaching and pastoral and missionary work, he soon succeeded in establishing well-organized churches in eastern Pennsylvania. He organized the Pennsylvania Ministerium, the first Lutheran synod in the United States, in 1748. He also extended his influence from northern New York into Georgia. He married an Indian and became the founder of an illustrious family.[81]

His firm hand united scattered Lutherans into a strong organization; he built parish schools, secured more teachers from Europe, and finally set up a school to train local ministers for the ministry. It resembled a German gymnasium and its curriculum was composed of Latin, Greek, Hebrew, and other classical subjects. Muhlenberg also set up a code for schoolmasters. In 1787 he was honored by the legislature of Pennsylvania; Franklin College was founded at Lancaster for the specific benefit of the German population and Muhlenberg was appointed its first President.

The congregational character of the Lutheran churches placed all matters of school practice and administration directly under the control of each congregation. Separate school codes were frequently drafted, patterned after the *Schulordnungen* common in Germany since Luther's Day, and they were

---

[81] See: W. J. Mann, *Life and Times of Henry Melchior Muhlenberg* (Philadelphia: Frederick, 1887); "Muhlenberg, Heinrich Melchior, and Family," pp. 720-722, in Lueker, *op. cit.*

administered by the early pastors and were usually graduates of German universities. Typically, before being engaged, the schoolmaster was examined by the pastor. He taught, usually, five or six hours a day, granting a recess of one hour at noon. The schoolmaster was not to entertain any complaints from parents or employers, but to direct them to the pastor and vestry. On Saturday the schoolmaster instructed only in the morning, and in the afternoon cleaned the church and helped with the divine services. The schoolmasters were to receive their stipulated salaries semi-annually, from the contributions of the congregations and the tuition-fees from parents, proportionate to their means.[82]

The subjects taught were the usual ones instructed in during that time, but special stress being laid upon instruction in Catechism, recitation of the Scriptures, memorization and singing of the hymns, reading, writing, spelling, and arithmetic. One of the outstanding features of Lutheran educational work has been the emphasis upon music that Luther valued so highly. The German language was the common medium of instruction; English was taught only, as a general rule, after 1790. Textbooks were not used, except catechisms, Bibles, and devotional books imported from Europe. Christopher Saur and Benjamin Franklin issued several German readers, and later such publishers as Billmeyer in Germantown, Zentner in Philadelphia, and the Henkels in New Market, Virginia, published several German A-B-C books of various grades, containing reading and spelling exercises, portions of the Catechism, multiplication tables, and geographic notes.

Lutheran pastors generally called themselves *Lehrer* (teacher), rather than *Pastor;* hence the term teacher was seldom applied to the school. Teachers usually were designated as *Schulmeister.* Most of them had come from Germany and had been fairly well trained. But the high standards made it difficult to secure an adequate number of them. Hence the pastor had to spend much of his time in the classroom when teachers were not available or the congregation was unable to support one. Many of the early teachers had the status of "catechists," those who taught school during the week and delivered a discourse on the Lord's Day; they also visited the sick and officiated at funerals. As more qualified teachers were engaged, they were given a higher status and considered "licensed" preachers.

In addition to the teaching duties, schoolmasters had to serve also as sextons, organists, or cantors, for which services they were sometimes paid extra; they were expected to keep the records of the congregation, and even sometimes baptized children. Congregations usually paid only from 2 to 25 pounds a year; these salaries were augmented by tuition-fees, donations of food, fuel,

---

[82] Drawn from the code drafted by Muhlenberg in 1750 for the school at Trappe, Montgomery County, Pennsylvania; partly reproduced by Beck, *op. cit.,* pp. 50-51.

and clothing. In the country congregations, schoolmasters were usually provided with a house and land for tillage, frequently occupying part of the schoolhouse. Collections for them were taken up at various times such as church festivals.

A school term ran from three to ten months. In the rural schools it was usually divided into summer and winter terms, the older children coming in during winter and the younger ones in summer. In some areas the school was open only during the winter. It was customary to terminate the school year with the confirmation exercises on Palm Sunday or Easter, and the school year began after the harvest in late October or in November.

According to Beck (whom we have drawn upon here), the development of the Lutheran parochial school can be divided into two distinct periods.[83] The first period began in the earliest colonial days and was carried on in the Eastern colonies and states by several regional Lutheran synods and reached the peak by 1830 when some 400 schools had been established. The second period started in Ohio about 1818 and has continued in the Midwest to the present day. The Ohio Synod and the Missouri Synod established schools in Ohio, Missouri, Wisconsin, Iowa, Minnesota, Michigan, and New York; schools were also established by the Norwegian, Augustana Swedish, Danish, and the Slovak Synods. By the end of the century there were more than 2,500 schools. In 1939 the system still included some 1,500 schools, maintained by the Missouri, Joint Wisconsin, Norwegian and Slovak synods, and the Negro missions, with some thirty schools remaining in the American Lutheran Church (the Ohio, Iowa, and Buffalo synods). Most were known as Christian day-schools.

The Pennsylvania legislature donated 5,000 acres of land to the free schools for the Lutherans in Philadelphia in 1791. But generally speaking, the development of the parochial schools in the eighteenth century was seriously interfered with by the revolutionary war and the internal conflict regarding the use of the vernacular. In 1795 a demand began to grow in Pennsylvania and other areas for the use of English in the schools. The new generation considered German a coarse language, and since the newspapers were written in English, they wanted to speak English. The arguments within the congregations, or even the families, became bitter. Most of the ministers and older generation people resented the idea of English being used in their schools, because the primary purpose of the school was to teach the children the German tongue which was the official language of the church. However, thereafter it was a losing battle. When the Pennsylvania education law of 1834 was passed, a rapid decrease in Lutheran schools followed. Although the law granted aid to free schools, it is not known to what extent Lutherans

---

[83] *Ibid.*, pp. 407-416, and bibliography.

applied for it. Public school districts were permitted to take over school buildings erected by the church; public schools thus became schools run by the congregation and the local school board. The teaching of religion continued and the Lutheran minister frequently visited the schools, but the church was gradually losing out, especially in regard to the use of the German language.

After the Napoleonic wars in Europe, increasingly large numbers of immigrants sought their fortunes in America. Many of the new Lutheran congregations were established with schools but this tendency slowed down after 1820 because of the agitation for public schools and since neighborhood subscription schools could be found nearly everyhere. The Germans of Pennsylvania were especially opposed to the Pennsylvania school law, fighting its adoption in 1834 and not cooperating with it too well after its adoption. The opposition was not against education but against the change of responsibility which involved no longer the supervision and control by the Church. The Lutherans simply wanted to maintain their own schools and did not want to have their children considered paupers by being educated at public expense. The Lutherans were supported by the Friends (Quakers) who maintained an extensive school system in the southeastern section of the state. But the efforts to revive the program of elementary education was not effective and it remained for the newer synods in the Middle West (the Ohio, Missouri, Iowa, Wisconsin, Michigan, and Minnesota synods, as well as to several Norwegian and Swedish bodies) to give a new impetus to the movement, which resulted in the establishment of the present extensive system of Lutheran elementary schools.

The number of German immigrants during the four-decade period before the Civil War had passed a million and a half; in the quarter-century following it the number reached about 3 million. From 1820 to 1892, the number totaled almost 5 million. Next to the people from England and Ireland, the Germans represented the largest group from an individual country. There were but few Lutherans among the immigrants from countries other than Germany and the Scandinavian countries.

The earlier immigration had been caused by the dissatisfaction and unrest caused by religious persecutions, interference with religious liberty, and the political upheavals of 1830 and 1848. Later, the glowing advertising propaganda of steamship companies, and the tales and rumors of possible wealth and the prospects of unbounded liberties and opportunities, induced thousands more to forsake the Fatherland. The Church had the task of assimilating the many immigrants crowding in from all sides. There was initiated an even more vigorous program of activity in missionary and educational endeavor, and every effort was made to promote the welfare of the schools. The majority of the Lutheran schools were of a rural, one-teacher type, since a large proportion of the membership of the synods lived in rural areas. But there were numerous larger schools, particularly in the cities (St. Louis, Chicago, Milwaukee, St. Paul, Omaha, Kansas City, New Orleans, Fort Wayne, Cincinnati, Cleveland, Toledo, Detroit, New York, and many smaller cities in the Midwestern States), with four, six, and nine classes, and with an organization and program fully equal to the public schools in these communities. But nearly one half of the schools were taught by the pastors themselves because of the shortage of trained teachers.

Around 1890 the decline of the parochial schools began. Various substitutes were resorted to in order to solve the perplexing problem. Saturday schools became quite common, serving chiefly the purposes of German-language instruction as long as that was the language of congregational worship. In other instances, classes for such language instruction were held on various week-days, after school hours, with evening classes for older children and adults. Kindergartens appeared for a time to be a successful means of getting the children for the school. Saturday or Monday schools were carried on until World War I. But even the plan for part-time or week-day religious education was neglected until it was revived after 1930, when the movement began within many denominations, as the Protestant churches in general came to the belated realization that the full education of the child could not be effected and complete without a thorough and intimate connection with spiritual and moral values.

World War I came to be of more far-reaching effect upon the Lutheran Church than upon any other Protestant denomination. The American churches were subjected to much of the bitter propaganda and persecution thanks to their German background and close ties with the church in Germany. The effects often divided the loyalties of the membership, brought the closing of numerous smaller schools which never opened again, and the replacement of German by English in worship and education.

The movement to prohibit the use of a foreign language in the elementary schools, public or private, had begun already before the war. By 1913 seventeen states had already adopted laws requiring that English alone be the medium of instruction in the public elementary schools; during and after the war some 21 States enacted such legislation. Opposition, however, developed in some States. Several Lutheran bodies (especially in Missouri, Wisconsin, and Iowa) officially protested. On December 26, 1919, the Nebraska State Supreme Court upheld the right of the parochial schools to teach religious subjects in other languages than English. Thereafter some Lutheran schools taught courses partly in German (chiefly religion) after or before the regular school, while others continued as before in teaching such courses for whatever time was considered best. The complete victory for the Lutheran claims came by the U.S. Supreme Court decision of June 4,

1923, which declared several state laws unconstitutional. But the antipathies of the public had their effects. Virtually all congregations which had carried on chiefly in the German language in time became bilingual; English and German services were held on the same Sunday or alternated; all Sunday-school work became English. Many of the smaller schools were closed.

The Lutheran Church in America, like the other churches, at first looked to Europe for its ministers. About the middle of the eighteenth century, it became evident that this source of supply was inadequate. The beginning of the home training was made by appointing certain men as theological instructors, authorized to prepare young men for the ministry; these candidates were then examined by the clergy in convention. The first training school was established in 1797 when representatives of the estate of the Reverend John C. Hartwick (1714-1796) resolved to establish a "theological and missionary seminary."[84] In 1815 this seminary was located at Hartwick, New York, but it was not an official seminary of the Church. In 1826 a school was opened at Gettysburg, Pennsylvania, the first official Lutheran theological seminary in the United States. In 1830 the Capital University at Columbus, Ohio, was opened, together with the Lutheran Theological Southern Seminary at Columbia, South Carolina. In 1830 the Saxon immigrants to Missouri founded a classical college and school of theology. Since then sixteen Lutheran seminaries have been established.

When, in the nineteenth century, the Eastern colleges gradually transferred their management from church control to independent and self-perpetuating bodies, and religious curricula were replaced by non-religious courses, the Lutherans, like other denominations, founded their own colleges. The large number of schools reflects the multiplicity of synods. Among many others Muhlenberg was founded in 1848, Gustav Adolphus College in 1862, St. Olaf (1874), Dana College (1884), Concordia College (1891), Upsala (1893), and Pacific Lutheran (1894).

Today there are wide differences in the stress placed upon Christian education in the various Lutheran Church bodies, and upon the agencies and means whereby Christian education is to be achieved. In addition to the Sunday schools and vacation Bible schools, some Lutheran bodies maintain practically no schools except for ministerial training schools and foreign mission schools. Others emphasize a complete system of Lutheran education, including elementary schools, high schools, and colleges.

Lutheran elementary schools, now centered primarily in the Midwest,

---

[84] R. L. Kelly, *Theological Education in America, A Study of One Hundred Sixty One Theological Schools in the United States and Canada* (New York: George H. Doran, 1924); C. V. Sheatseley, *History of the First Lutheran Seminary of the West* (Columbus, Ohio: Lutheran Book Concern, 1930).

are usually maintained by individual congregations (though some are inter-parish schools). Lutheran high schools are usually maintained by associations of congregations. The seminaries, teachers colleges, and preparatory schools are maintained by synods, and the Lutheran University at Valparaiso, Indiana is maintained by a Lutheran association. All Lutheran synods carry on active mission work, especially in South America, India, China, Japan, Africa, Madagascar, and New Guinea, as well as among the Negroes, Indians, and Mexicans in North America. They also maintain a variety of schools for orphans, the crippled, feeble-minded, and deaf children.[85] The work of the last mentioned special schools has been particularly important, wherein the Lutherans have led other Protestant groups.

During the nineteenth century several of the synods helped sponsor secondary schools patterned after gymnasium-type private education but all these Lutheran academies and high schools were closed by 1900. The relatively few secondary schools that are now maintained are of more recent vintage and there appears to be today two diametrically opposed views of the American Lutherans on high school education. In June, 1959, the 600,000-member Augustana Lutheran Church came out in opposition to any extension of the Protestant parochial system on the high school level. A report approved by the church's 100th annual convention asserted that "there appears to be no need or desire" on the part of the denomination for church-supported high schools of either the parochial type or the boarding academy type.[86]

This view is the opposite of that held by the Lutheran Church-Missouri Synod, 2,300,000-member sister denomination of Augustana. The Missouri Synod operates more than 250 parochial schools in various sections of the nation, including some high schools. Other Lutheran bodies that support secondary schools include the Joint Synod of Wisconsin, the American Lutheran Church, the Evangelical Lutheran Church, and the United Lutheran Church.

Today the Lutheran denomination ranks fourth in size, behind the Roman Catholics, the Baptists, and the Methodists in the United States. The American Lutherans are divided into sixteen separate bodies with a total membership of over seven million. In spite of differing opinions among the Synods, the Lutheran Church remains the chief Protestant supporter of the parochial schools (80% of which are operated by the Missouri Synod); in addition, it supports 32 senior colleges with 32,338 students, plus high schools and junior colleges enrolling 12,058, and 23 theological seminaries with 3,344 students.

---

[85] For details, see: Beck, *op. cit.*, Chapter XIII.

[86] George Dugan, "Church Opposes High School Plan," *New York Times,* June 19, 1959.

SCANDINAVIAN LUTHERANS. Immigration from Norway and Sweden and Denmark reached but minor proportions before the Civil War, as compared with the two decades following it. The Swedes had first settled on the Delaware in 1638 (under Peter Minuit, a former director at New Amsterdam). Together with a few Finns, these settlers maintained an independent colony on the Delaware for sixteen years. Their specific contribution was the establishment of the Lutheran Church in the Delaware Valley and the introduction of the notched-log construction in housebuilding. "To the Swedes, and perhaps later to the Germans, the American frontiersman owed the model of the log cabin that would become the easiest type of house to build in the woods to the West."[87]

The influx of about a million Norwegians and as many Swedes reached its high-water mark in the early eighties of the past century when the "American fever" had become even stronger in these countries than in Germany and elsewhere. Betwen 1870 and 1919, 1,750,000 Northmen came to American shores. The total number of Scandinavians was considerably smaller than that of Germans and British, but it was relatively large in proportion to the population of their countries. The underlying causes were: hard times, crop failures, stringency of money, unemployment and low wages, dissension from the policies and practices of the Lutheran state church, dissatisfaction with the unfair social system, plus the results of propaganda, rumors, and the glowing letters from those who had found in America the realization of their hopes. Danish immigration began about 1864 at the close of the war with Germany. Many of the Danes affiliated with the Norwegian congregations.

Minnesota became the chief home of these immigrants, and by 1900 had a Scandinavian population of more than 1 million. But the American Lutheran synods were divided and not prepared for the problem presented by the immigrants and a large majority were lost to the Lutheran Church; only seven percent of the Danes joined any church, not more than twenty percent of the Swedes, and less than thirty percent of the Norwegians.[88]

There was a marked similarity in the educational background of the Norwegians, Swedes, and Danes. In all three countries the principles and ideals of Lutheran education had been introduced during the era of the Reformation, and the establishment of the Lutheran Church as the state church put

---

[87] Louis B. Wright, *The Cultural Life of the American Colonies,* 1607-1763 (New York: Harper, 1957), p. 51. For the details on the Scandinavian immigration, see: Oscar A. Benson, "Swedish Americans," pp. 73-77, B. J. Hovde, "Norwegian Americans," pp. 66-73, and Paul M. Gustafson, "Danish Americans," pp. 77-83, and respective bibliographies, in Francis J. Brown and Joseph S. Roucek, Eds., *One America* (New York: Prentice-Hall, 1952).

[88] Sweet, *op. cit., The Story of Religion,* p. 340.

the school systems jointly under the control of the church and the state. The school systems developed were basically of the parochial type, and the stern religious tenets of the church obligated the Scandinavian immigrant to give the proper instruction of his family in the Catechism and the Scriptures in the mother tongue. Interestingly enough, many of the early leaders among these immigrants were teachers of parochial schools rather than preachers as there were few regular pastors among the immigrants since at home they had lifetime appointments as state officials.[89]

So, while the clergy favored the parochial school, few of the Scandinavian pastors were willing to follow the example of their German Lutheran brethren in being active in establishing a school or in teaching it when other helpers were not available. On the whole the clergy was not prone to put itself too much on a level with the laity.

Hence the full-time parochial schools did not come to flourish among the Scandinavians as they did among the Germans; those that were established were usually short-lived and soon developed into part-time summer schools. The public schools came quickly into popular favor among the Scandinavians and they were attracted by the American, free, democratic, publicly-controlled school system. Even the problem of language did not loom up as important to them as it did to the Germans. Full-time schools developed more among the Norwegians than among the Swedes, since the Norwegians came into closer contacts with the German synods maintaining such schools.

The program of the Scandinavian schools followed, to some extent, that of the native folk-schools, stressing especially the rudiments of catechetical and Biblical knowledge and of the mother tongue. The memorization of hymns and tunes was stressed; English language and reading, arithmetic, geography, and penmanship completed the course of the full-time schools. School terms varied from three to ten months, depending upon the community. In some sections one or two teachers served each school in each parish for a number of weeks, making circuit, and hence resembled in many respects the "moving" schools of the American Colonial era. Most of the schools of the Scandinavian bodies had by 1890 lost their essential character as elementary schools and were conducted chiefly for the purpose of teaching religion in the language of the respective churches. These were largely the week-day or vacation type of religious schools, with only a few regular elementary schools mainly within the Norwegian synod remaining. Most of these regular schools were discontinued during World War I.

Although the Danish folk high school movement (discussed in Chapter VII) has been a widely praised organization, it had only varied success among the Danes in America. Many of these schools were short-lived, reflecting

---

[89] Beck, *op. cit.*, pp. 133-160.

possibly the rapid rate of assimilation, even in rural America. Today there are only a few in existence operating on a somewhat curtailed basis, generally in summer. However, many of the principles of adult education had their beginnings in this movement and are mirrored in such aspects of American education.

The Scandinavian synods traditionally gave greater attention to higher education. They developed a number of outstanding Lutheran colleges, some of these having been noted previously. At this level as at lower levels, Lutheran bodies have come to maintain the principle of the separation of church and state. The Scandinavian Lutherans have generally supported high standards of public education and they worked hard to get good schools for their children through these media.

Luther himself had recognized the need for public support of church-sponsored education. In his day and place it was essential if the new principles of Lutheran education were to be nurtured and disseminated. However, in still another land and in a new era the Lutherans eventually found the public schools the most satisfactory means to achieve their founder's insistent demand that every man be both literate and a thinker.

Indigenous Religions

Indigenous religions in America have made some valuable educational contributions. Although the roots of certain of these churches can be traced back to older sects, groups as the Unitarians, the Disciples of Christ, the Holiness Churches, Christian Scientists, Mormons, and Seventh Day Adventists are among the sects usually classified as indigenous. Just two of these groups will be considered in this chapter, the Mormons and the Seventh Day Adventists, not because they are representative, for there is great variation in these sects, but because they have had a greater educational impact than the others.

Mormons

In June, 1844 an Illinois mob murdered the Mormon prophet, Joseph Smith, while he was confined in jail; this cowardly act set in motion the greatest single organized migration in United States history. Thousands of Mormons, led by Smith's successor, Brigham Young, headed west by foot, wagon, and horseback from the Mississippi River toward the Great Salt Lake. At their abandoned capital in Nauvoo, Illinois, the Mormons left behind an expensive temple, hundreds of homes, and thriving farms. But they took with them 30,000 cattle and an amazing capacity for disciplined work that quickly built a great new city, a self-sustaining agricultural empire, and laid the foundations for the modern beehive state.

223

The church was envisaged as a monopoly of power in commerce as well as in spiritual matters and had a very intriguing beginning, the details of which can only be sketched here. The term "Mormons," derived from the *Book of Mormon*, is a nickname that has been accepted by the members of the Church of Jesus Christ of the Latter-Day Saints. The sect was founded in 1830 by Joseph Smith, following earlier revelations that he claimed he had from the Father, the Son, John the Baptist, and the angel Moroni. Smith stated that he was directly empowered to found the new church and he gradually collected a small group of converts in the New York-Ohio area. He maintained also that he was directed to proclaim its truths to the world and to help perfect the lives of those who joined. Three other books besides the Bible were accepted as containing the revealed word of God and a cornerstone of the faith is the belief in continued revelation. While there is no formal Creed, the *Articles of Faith,* written by Smith in 1842, state the basic doctrines. There is no clergy class (all men who desire and are worthy may become priests) but the church is centered in and governed by the President and the self-perpetuating high priests.

The Mormons eventually settled in Missouri but found the social climate inhospitable and moved to Illinois. They built the thriving city of Nauvoo (1840) which soon had a population of 20,000. Again, for political and economic reasons more than for deviationist religious practices, they became targets of jealousy and fear. Following Smith's martyrdom they moved into barren Mexican territory, but within a year of settling in Utah they found themselves again within American boundaries as a result of the annexation of the area by the United States following the Mexican War.

The first Mormon trek to the West reached its peak in the Spring of 1847. It was followed by more every year; some 80,000 "Saints" made their way across the plains before the transcontinental railroad was built. Many were poor converts from abroad who had no horses or oxen, so they walked and pulled their belongings with them in twin-wheeled carts. The inspiring story of the great migration is detailed in a number of general works and in biographies of Brigham Young.[90]

Educational contributions of the Mormons to America's educational history in the West have been significant. Believing in schools because of their value in directing the religious training of children, the Mormon leaders started to establish schools on their arrival in Salt Lake Valley. The village life of the Mormons was a strong help in school development (the same way that the village life of the Puritans helped the genesis of schools in Colonial

---

[90] See: *Among the Mormons,* ed. by William Mulder and A. Russell Mortensen (New York: Knopf, 1958). See also: Kenneth V. Lottich, "Indigenous Religions in the United States: II. Mormonism," *The Social Studies,* March, 1955, pp. 93-98.

New England). The tie between the church and the schools was kept until Utah was admitted into the Union as a State in 1896. Schools were first under the direction of the University of Deseret, founded in 1850 (later to become the University of Utah) for its tasks as a center of higher learning as well as a body administering all education. The Office of Territorial Superintendent of Common Schools was established in 1851 to handle the administration of the educational program. While the early Mormon schools were tuition schools, the nature of the Mormon tie between education and religion promoted a high degree of attendance and literacy.

In 1865 the Utah legislature passed an act giving each school district the right to assess and collect a tax of two percent for the payment of qualified teachers' salaries and to secure suitable textbooks where two thirds of the taxpayers of the districts had so voted. In 1868 the legislature defined schools as those organized by the direction of the board of trustees of the respective districts and classified them as common schools. In 1874 the levying of a territorial tax was legalized, qualifying the help for each district which operated "a good school at least three months in each year." This law created the foundations for the modern state school system of Utah.[91] With the granting of statehood in 1896, public education was further stimulated.

The earliest Mormon schools offered secular as well as religious education.[92] Later, the church tended to welcome secular institutions since, with the bulk of the populace being Mormon, there would be little chance of church-state differences. With the advent of state aids the Mormons tended to largely eliminate elementary and high school education from their system of church schools. The Mormons also established for religious instruction a number of church academies and some of these included elementary as well as higher education; these appeared between 1875 and 1911 in a number of Western states as well as Canada. Some advanced to the college stage (Weber) and Brigham Young University serves as the church-maintained center of higher education in Utah. In addition, nearly 200 seminaries or institutes have been maintained near high schools and colleges to offer religious instruction for Latter-Day Saints youth attending these schools.

The Mormons took seriously their maxim "A man is saved no faster than he gains knowledge." They worked zealously to foster schools and reached the point where Utah had the highest ratio of college students to population in the United States. The Mormons take pride in the Thorndike study that

---

[91] John C. Moffitt, *The History of Education in Utah* (privately printed), 1946.

[92] Milton L. Bennion, *Mormonism and Education* (Salt Lake City: Department of Education, Church of Jesus of Latter-Day Saints, 1939); Roya A. Cheville, *The Role of Religious Education in the Accommodation of a Sect* (Independence, Missouri: Herald Publishing House, 1942); E. T. Clark, *The Small Sects in America* (Nashville, Tennessee: Cokesbury Press, 1937).

listed Utah, in proportion to its population, as the state that had contributed the largest number of outstanding Americans.[93] A Mormon educational leader has explained the reason for this in that the Mormons accept the point of view presented by John Dewey when he claimed, "Education has no end beyond itself. It is all one with growing." This is so because, as far as the Latter-Day Saints are concerned, education is all one with growth toward temporal and spiritual salvation and, therefore, education and salvation are synonymous expressions.

Seventh-Day Adventists

This evangelical denomination traces its origins to the movement begin-ning with William Miller in the 1830's and '40's that practiced the observance of Saturday as the Sabbath.[94] The church was not formally organized until 1863. Its tenets include: the belief in a literal creation accomplished in a literal week as the source of this world; in the fall of man as told in Genesis, and thus in the importance of redemption; that history is the working out of God's plan; that man is mortal and may have eternal life only through belief in the atoning sacrifice of Christ; and that Jesus is coming imminently once again in a cataclysmic event that will end man's earthly existence. For the Seventh-Day Adventists, therefore, education must serve as an agency to prepare man for maximum happiness in this life and for the eternal satis-factions of the after-life.[95]

The adventists did not give serious thought to creating their own schools until some time after their children began to have to bear the ridicule for the mistaken expectations of their parents, who had accepted the view of Miller that the world would come to an end in October, 1844. Parents also were concerned about the number of children dropping their faith and they blamed this upon the general influence of non-church public school youth. The children also were criticized for their practices — such as the rejection of pork as a food and for their cereal diet. With the advent of Darwinism, church elders moved to establish their own schools. A college for training ministers had been opened at Battle Creek, Michigan, and later it was moved

---

[93] See the list of many of these educators and scientists in *The Encyclopedia Ameri-cana*, Vol. 27 (1957 ed.), p. 614.

[94] For a description of the Millerite beginnings, see: Kenneth V. Lottick, "Indi-genous Religions in the United States: IV. The Seventh Day Adventists," *The Social Studies*, April, 1957, pp. 130-135.

[95] The writer is indebted to Dr. V. H. Koenig, Principal of the Mountain View Academy, Mountain View, California, for information on the Seventh Day Adventist religious program presented herein. See also: Ellen G. White, *Education* (Mountain View, California: Pacific Press Publishing Association, 1903).

to Berrien Springs where it operates as Emanuel Missionary College. Later Pacific Union College was founded and between 1880 and 1910 a total of seven colleges were established in the United States.

Elementary schools were organized next, generally appearing as a room or a part of the church building, and in some more populous areas several churches would join together to conduct a combined school. Over 1,000 elementary schools have been established in North America since the first schools of the 1870's. Secondary schools, often including boarding arrangements because of the rural environs of many Adventist groups, now number about 70 in North America. The Adventists are also noted for their work in medical education and for the emphasis upon industrial education as a part of their regular school offerings.

The Adventists would find many who approve of their approaching education as an expression of God's purposes and there are those who have been influenced through their contacts with Adventists who would accept the following nine principles which have been established as guides for Adventist education:

1. The building of character is the first and greatest work of a Christian school.
2. The Bible must be the foundation of every course.
3. Regular courses in Bible should be taught in all schools. Every college should have a ministerial curriculum.
4. Adventist schools should be in a rural environment. They should be close enough to settled communities to enable students to do missionary work, but far enough away so that students will live in school homes.
5. Industrial and agricultural training should be combined with scholarship.
6. Stress must be placed on labor and missionary work, instead of upon sports or entertainment.
7. The scholastic training should be thorough.
8. The school administration should be democratic, not autocratic.
9. The school should produce men and women who not only know what is right, but who will so act.[96]

Conclusions

An understanding and appreciation of the dynamics of the educational influence of religious doctrines and bodies in the United States requires consideration of the background against which the religious groups developed.

---

[96] Archa O. Dart, et al., *The Story of Our Church* (Mountain View, California: Pacific Press Publishing Association, 1956), p. 400-401. See also, for details on this denomination: *Seventh-Day Adventist Yearbook* (Washington 12, D.C.: Review and Herald Publishing Association, 1958).

This also requires some understanding of their relationship to one another in American history and to the society of which they have been a part. Historical forces evolved so that English civilization exerted the most influence in American history. It also provided the strong religious character and the religious roots for the beginnings of education in America. As we have seen, there was great complexity in the British religious patterns established in colonial America, and this was extended as Lutherans, Moravians, Dutch and French Reformed churches, Roman Catholics, Jews, and others moved into the New World. While Protestantism laid the basic pattern for the American educational genesis, ultimately the rights of other churches to establish their schools were also guaranteed. As America developed, indigenous sects such as the Mormons and the Adventists were led to establish their own private schools. Large numbers of American children have always been enrolled in private and parochial schools, at all levels, and tradition, legislation, and court decision, as well as the deep beliefs of many of these people, have helped to maintain these institutions in spite of the great growth of American public education.

From the details presented in this chapter it is evident that although the separation of church and state has been an agitating factor in the educational policies of the states, especially in regard to the role of religion in the public schools, the religious heritage of the American educational background has played a considerable and continuing role on all levels of the American educational scene. Church groups have made material contributions to American education in many ways. We have, for example, given only limited attention to their auxiliary organizations and activities, such as the Methodist Youth Fellowship, the American Friends' Service Committee, Sunday Schools, summer encampments, educational conferences, and like programs that have had considerable impact. Additionally, churches and related organizations have played a fundamental role as "moral stewards" in the evolution of American society. From the anti-slavery movement to the temperance crusades, religious societies have promoted causes and forwarded educational programs that have aided Americans in moving closer to realization of their great ideals.[97]

Even though the common public school system, rising rapidly and extensively in the nineteenth century, replaced many church schools, American education has never become thoroughly secular. The historic influence of religious values has been so strong that many interesting accommodations have been worked out between parochial and public education — such as

---

[97] See the activities of churches and their affiliated groups as detailed in Clifford S. Griffin, *Their Brothers' Keepers* (New Brunswick, N.J.: The Rutgers University Press, 1960).

the state aids to private schools permitted in Louisiana and several other states. But even where the schooling is almost entirely public, the fundamental religious beliefs of teachers, parents, and pupils are constantly revealed in their mutual relationships, let alone in the school curriculum or extra curriculum. A leading Catholic educator, for example, has outlined seven religious fundamentals that should be taught in the public schools. (Many like-oriented Protestants would agree.) These are: the existence of God; man's condition as a creature dependent on his Creator; God, the source of the inalienable rights of man; the fundamental purpose of our laws and protection of these God-given rights; the basic equality of men under God; the dignity of man and sacredness of human life; and man's responsibility to the moral law as formulated in the ten commandments.[98]

In spite of recent local, state, and national publications on the need for moral and spiritual emphases in the public schools,[99] there are considerable differences of opinion on the specifics of suggested programs. Protestants find themselves far apart on such issues as released time for religious education, state transportation of private school children, etc. In fact, in approximately one-half of the states any sectarian religious reference or activities are forbidden in public schools, while in the other half of the states, Bible use, Scriptural readings, and the like are either required or permitted! This reflects the divided feelings that Americans have about the relationships between their basic religious beliefs and education. Another revealing factor here is the recent increase in growth of private schools, even among Protestant groups, and the N.E.A. has estimated that by 1965 approximately one child in six will be enrolled in a private or parochial school. Now, some ninety percent of these, over 4 million children, are concentrated in Catholic schools. (See chapter IV, pp. 123-125.)

Undoubtedly the differences that exist on the issues of religious education will continue to be resolved as they have in the past, by time, by compromise, and by governmental action. The basic principle of the American way that guarantees the freedom to believe has also been interpreted to guarantee the rights of parents to educate their young according to their conscience. As

---

[98] The St. Louis Archdiocesan Superintendent of Schools, cited in *Scholastic Teacher*, Dec. 1, 1955, p. 1.

[99] See, for example, Educational Policies Commission, *Moral and Spiritual Values in the Public Schools* (Washington, D.C.: National Education Association, 1951; *Tentative Guide to Teaching Moral and Spiritual Foundations in American Democracy* (Tallahassee, Florida: State Department of Education, November, 1956); *Guide to Moral and Spiritual Education in Elementary Schools,* Part I (San Diego, California City Schools, 1953). Two recent journals that have given thorough coverage to questions of religion in education are the issues of the *Phi Delta Kappan* for April, 1955 and May, 1959.

long as certain churches fear the domination of the material or secular spirit in the public schools, and as long as some of these hold strongly to the ideal that their first loyalty is to God rather than to the state, sectarian education will continue to exist in the United States. In addition, the Judaic-Christian heritage of democratic, ethical, and spiritual values that have permeated much of our culture will continue to characterize and influence American public education for the forseeable future.

Bibliography

Beard, Charles A. and Mary R., *The Rise of American Civilization, 1: The Agricultural Era.* New York: Macmillan, 1927.

Beck, W. H., *Lutheran Elementary Schools in the United States.* St. Louis: Concordia Publishing House, 1939.

Bennion, Milton L., *Mormonism and Education.* Salt Lake City: Dept. of Ed., Church of Jesus of Latter-Day Saints, 1939.

Brinton, Howard H., *Quaker Education in Theory and Practice.* Wallingford, Pennsylvania: Pendle Hill, 1949.

Brown, J. Howard, *The Elizabethan Schooldays: An Account of the English Grammar Schools in the Second Half of the Sixteenth Century.* Oxford: Basil Blackwell, 1933.

Brown, Nicholas C., ed., *The Study of Religion in the Public Schools, An Appraisal.* Washington, D.C.: The American Council on Education, 1958.

Cubberley, Ellwood P., *The History of Education.* Boston: Houghton Mifflin, 1920.

Dunn, William K., *What Happened to Religious Education? The Decline of Religious Teaching in the Public Elementary School, 1776-1861.* Baltimore: The Johns Hopkins Press, 1958.

Educational Policies Commission, *Moral and Spiritual Values in the Public Schools.* Washington, D.C.: National Education Association, 1951.

Eggleston, Edward, *The Transit of Civilization From England to America in the Seventeenth Century.* New York: D. Appleton & Co., 1900.

Kandel, I. L., *History of Secondary Education: A Study in the Development of Liberal Education.* Boston: Houghton Mifflin, 1930.

Leach, Arthur F., *English Schools at the Reformation, 1546-8.* Westminster, England: Archibald Constable & Co., 1895.

Luxcock, Halford E. and Paul, *The Story of Methodism.* New York: The Methodist Book Concern, 1926.

McCluskey, Neil G., *Public Schools and Moral Education.* New York: Columbia University, 1958.

Morison, Samuel E., *The Founding of Harvard College.* Cambridge: Harvard University Press, 1935.

230

Nettels, Curtis P., *The Roots of American Civilization: A History of American Colonial Life.* New York: Crofts, 1938.

Noble, Stuart G., *A History of American Education.* New York: Rinehart & Co., 1954.

Nottingham, Elizabeth K., *Methodism and the Frontier: Indiana Proving Ground.* New York: Columbia University Press, 1941.

Parrington, Vernon L., *Main Currents in American Thought.* New York: Harcourt, Brace, 1930.

Price, J. M. et al., *A Survey of Religious Education.* New York: Ronald Press, 1959.

Seyblot, Robert F., *The Public Schools in Colonial Boston,* 1635-1775. Cambridge: Harvard University Press, 1935.

Small, Walter H., *Early New England Schools.* Boston: Ginn, 1914.

Smith, James W. and A. L. Jamison (Editors), *Religion in America's Life,* Princeton: Princeton University Press, Vols. I and II, 1961.

Spence, Hartzell, *The Story of America's Religions.* New York: Holt, Rinehart and Winston, 1960.

Stephenson, George W., *The Puritan Heritage.* New York: The Macmillan Co., 1952.

Sweet, William W., *Religion in the Development of American Culture, 1765-1840.* New York: Charles Scribner's Sons, 1952.

Updegraff, Harlan, *The Origin of the Moving School in Massachusetts.* New York: Teachers College, Columbia University Press, 1908.

Weeden, William B., *Economic and Social History of New England, 1620-1789.* Boston: Houghton Mifflin, 1890.

Wertenbaker, Thomas J., *The First Americans, 1607-1690. A History of American Life, II.* New York: Macmillan, 1927.

231

****

CHAPTER VII

THE EUROPEAN IMPACT UPON
AMERICAN EDUCATIONAL HISTORY

Although there are today definite differences between English and American educational institutions, we must acknowledge that it was initially the English who gave origin and form to a number of aspects of American education. At higher education levels, for example, the sons of Emanuel and of other Cambridge colleges were the founders of the first American college, Harvard. The names of William and Mary were later given to the infant institution in Virginia and its charter was signed by these two sovereigns. Then came the founding of Yale and other colleges, all with English antecedents. In these schools English traditions in curriculum, academic government, and methodology predominated until the outbreak of the Revolution. Secondly, the attitude of the Puritans toward education resulted in the Massachusetts laws of 1642 and 1647 that established precedents for standards, for compulsory support, and laid the groundwork for public education. Later, these New Englanders carried these ideas to practically all of the new Western States.

This English heritage must not, however, prevent us from appreciating the impact made by others, such as the Scotch and the Dutch, on American educational history. Also, the Revolutionary War led to a repudiation of British religious and intellectual thought in America and thereafter French influence in literature and philosophy, as well as in government, grew. A great name here, reflecting French views, was Thomas Jefferson who represented some of the best native educational thinking of the time and who with others of his bent helped further to mold education in the United States.

A decline of French influence came with the downfall of Napoleon. There was, however, no enthusiasm in America for registering at Oxford or Cambridge or for moving toward other British practices, thanks mainly to the memories of colonial history and the struggle for independence. During this next era there was, however, a growing interest in German literature and Prussian schools. After the first group of enthusiastic American students returned from Germany and took academic posts in strategically important American educational positions and institutions, the influence of German education, particularly of their universities, became profound in the United States.[1] It should be pointed out also that the structure of our emerging school programs during the nineteenth century tended to reflect the influences of the German *Gymnasium, Realschule, Volkschule,* and Kindergarten.

The influences from England, France, and Germany have made the major foreign impressions upon all levels of the American educational structure, not to mention the other deep impressions they brought to American intellectual and artistic life. Furthermore, within the historical stream, these areas have produced important individuals, either foreign-born or first-generation native Americans, who have served as influential bearers of the European heritage. In this chapter we will consider the British and continental influences, both those that came with the stream of settlers as well as the programs and practices that reflected great European schools and educators.

We will also go a step further than stopping with the contributions to the American pattern from the English, the French, and the Germans. We accept here the theory of "pluralism" and its premise that the stress on the important role played by the educational backgrounds in the major Western European nations should not blind us to the contributions stemming from other countries and somewhat lesser known individuals. In every area of American cultural life, from colonial times to the present, we find traces of the influences and legacy brought by foreign nations and their emigrants from all regions of the world.[2] Education, for instance, would be different and definitely poorer in the United States if it were not for men who have come from these other European areas. Poland has sent such noted scholars as the anthropologist Malinowsky, the semanticist Korzybski, and the sociologist Znaniecki. From Czechoslovakia came Hrdlicka, another noted anthropologist. Sorokin, world-famed Harvard sociologist, came from Russia, and from Scandinavian backgrounds came such noted thinkers as Veblen, the economist;

---

[1] John A. Walz, *German Influence in American Education and Culture* (Philadelphia: Carl Schurz Memorial Foundation, 1936), p. 51.

[2] See Francis J. Brown and Joseph S. Roucek, Eds., *One America* (New York: Prentice-Hall, 1952), Part Five.

Hegge, the educational psychologist; and Rockne, the famous Norwegian who used Polish boys to make the "Fighting Irish" the national football power. Such a list, if extended to scientific and other fields, would be endless, and the above, although mainly representative of the later periods of emigration, are but a few of the many leaders, teachers, and administrators who might be cited. When we add to those who came from Europe the impact of theories stemming from men and women who stayed in their homelands or made but brief visits to the United States, such as Pavlov, the Russian "behaviorist" psychologist, the Czech-born but Austrian resident Freud, or the Italian mentor Montessori, our recognition of such influences is further broadened.

While during the seventeenth century the religious and economic discontent in England induced people to migrate to the colonies, the economic troubles in Ireland and Germany in the early eighteenth century introduced the first leaven of Scotch-Irish and Germans into the English stock in America. Between 1820 and 1920 the greatest waves of Europeans flooded America and in that single century 38 million came to the United States.[3] But between 1902 and 1914 over half a million immigrants reached this country every year and in the space of those 12 years the total number of immigrants far exceeded all the new arrivals of the 1820-1880 period which had been the peak for all immigration. A final surge of important immigrants, although considerably reduced in number, came with the advent of Fascism and Nazism before the outbreak of the second World War and then during the unfortunate post-war period of "cold war" and displaced persons. In total these persons have brought to America and its ways one of the most diverse, colorful, cosmopolitan, and progressive cultures in the history of civilization.[4]

---

[3] For details, see Carl N. Degler, *Out of Our Past: Forces That Shaped Modern America* (New York: Harper, 1959), Chapter X.

[4] We show in Chapter VI how these immigrants, especially as groups, have made their educational contributions through the operation of their native and New World-modified institutions, especially as religious and parochial schools, for in that chapter we attempted to highlight the relationships between Protestant religions and American education. Certain topics covered in that chapter might be included herein — such as the treatment of the rise of higher education, but it was felt that this was tied more intimately to religious backgrounds than it was to other aspects of these national cultures. Thus, for a fuller view of the European legacy both chapters need to be considered in total. This chapter can, of course, only highlight some of the selected foreign cultural contributions, and the ramifications and breadth of these influences are so great and in many ways inseparable from other aspects in the background of American life, that the reader is referred to the following publications that are available on the valuable heritage from foreign sources. Details on the contributions of immigrants to Americal life are found, for example, in Oscar Handlin, *The Uprooted: The Epic Story of the Great Migrations That Made the American People* (Boston: Little, Brown, 1951) and Francis J. Brown and Joseph S. Roucek, Eds., *Our Racial and National Minorities: Their History, Contributions, and Present Problems* (New York: Prentice-Hall, 1936).

The British Heritage

The settlers of the Thirteen Original Colonies were chiefly English-born and English-educated. Although recent evidence shows that the percentage of English in the colonial population was not so overwhelming as formerly believed, with a considerable admixture of Swedes, Dutch, Germans, and

Bettmann Archive

COLONIAL CLASSROOM.

French in the early population, the fact remains that these non-British elements, though important locally, were much less influential in molding the dominant cultural pattern of the colonial settlements.[5] The main honor is reserved to the British whose traditions, customs, and language together with their ideas on religion, government, and education made the major im-

---

[5] According to *American Council of Learned Societies Report of the Committee on Linguistic and National Stocks in the Population of the United States* (printed in the *Annual Report of the American Historical Association for the Year 1931* (Washington, D.C.: The Association, 1932), pp. 103-441, an analysis of the first federal census of 1790, employing linguistic techniques in the analysis of family names, shows that of the total white population of 3,172,444 in America: 60.9% were English; 14.3% were Scotch and Scotch-Irish from Ulster; 8.7% were German; 5.4% were Dutch, French, and Swedish; 3.7% were South Irish; and 7% were miscellaneous.

pression on the emerging American character.[6] The British were indissolubly connected with the rise of America in all areas. It was English capital that supplied the means for much of the early American beginnings of commerce and manufacturing. George Washington was the great grandson of a Yorkshireman (subsequently nearly two-thirds of the American presidents were entirely or partially of English blood) and from this great man on every chapter in American history is studded with British names. As stated in the previous chapter, the influence of English religious groups was profound in determining the future development of American education. Johnson summarizes the English religious influence in American history:[7] "In religious affairs . . . the pattern that the English set is one of interwoven figures — through the Baptists, respect for the individual; through the Methodists, respect for tradition; through the Presbyterians, respect for learning; and through the Episcopalians, respect for England. . . ."

The origin of the American public school is historically ascribed to New England but not because the colonists were the first to found such an institution there. Virginia and the New Netherlands can claim this distinction. Nevertheless Massachusetts and Connecticut formed the educational laws which became models for the Southern and the Western States. Most of the first textbooks used throughout the Union and its territories came from New England publishers, and the graduates of Harvard and Yale and the other New England colleges sent their graduates all over the settlements and to the frontier.[8]

In the history of American education the seventeenth and the first third of the eighteenth centuries can be described as a period of transplanting and of transitional schools. The period from Andrew Jackson's presidency to 1850 is often called the period of the common school. British influences were strong in both periods; but far the most influential during the initial era.

Often having come to America to secure religious freedom, it was only natural that the perpetuation of their faith by means of education should have been one of the most pertinent matters engaging the attention of the Puritans soon after building their homes and establishing their civil government. Being deeply imbued with theocratic Calvinistic ideas, they desired to

---

[6] For details, see Gerald W. Johnson, *Our English Heritage* (Philadelphia: J. B. Lippincott, 1949); Stuart G. Noble, *A History of American Education* (New York: Rinehart & Co., 1954), Chapter I; Edward Eggleston, *The Transit of Civilization From England to America in the Seventeenth Century* (New York: D. Appleton and Co., 1900); and Thomas J. Wertenbaker, *The First Americans* (1607-1690) (New York: Macmillan, 1927).

[7] *Johnson, ibid.*, p. 181.

[8] Edwin S. Slosson, *The American Spirit in Education: A Chronicle of Great Teachers* (New Haven: Yale University Press, 1921), pp. 1-2.

found in America a religious commonwealth, the cornerstone of which would be religion and education. In education at first English precedents were followed; home instruction, quite common in England among the Puritans, was initially employed on a large scale to teach the children to read the Bible and to train them to participate in family and congregational worship. The English apprentice system was also early established and masters gave their apprentices similar basic instruction. Since more of the elements of the educational history of colonial New England are covered in Chapters VI and XI, we will merely list the features which were largely transplantations from England but which became integral aspects of American education. The English settlers brought with them particularly the Dame school, the village reading and writing school, the Latin grammar school, the charity or pauper school, apprenticeship education for orphans and paupers, and the English college. Growing out of these institutions that made the pattern of New England education were four principles that became generally accepted in American educational structure: (1) the state could require all children to be educated; (2) the state could require towns to found schools; (3) the government could supervise and control schools by public officials and (4) public funds could be used for the support of public schools.[9]

Apprenticeship and Vocational Education

It is important to note that the churches and the governments of colonial America were interested in the education of underprivileged and poor children and that the steps they took in respect to that problem were to become a foundation of what is now America's public school system. The idea that education was a basic contractual obligation was an essential element of the concept of apprenticeship.[10]

More specifically, the apprenticeship agreement was generally written between a child's parents and a tradesman and bound the youth as an apprentice for a period of generally seven years, with no pay. During this period the tradesman was required to furnish food, clothing, and lodging, plus being responsible for teaching him his trade and the rudiments of reading and writing. Apprenticeships were looked upon as contracts binding both parties and many cases were brought before the courts for breaches of contract. The courts took quite seriously the failure of tradesmen to teach their apprentices the fundamentals. It is also important to remember that professional men, as lawyers and doctors, were trained largely in such a manner well into the

---

[9] R. Freeman Butts and Lawrence A. Cremin, *A History of Education in American Culture* (New York: Henry Holt & Co., 1953), p. 103.

[10] Paul Monroe, *Founding of the American Public School System* (New York: Macmillan, 1940), p. 34.

eighteenth century and hence the enforcement of adequate training was looked upon as of considerable importance by colonial settlers. British laws of 1562 and 1601 had shaped apprenticing into a national system; they attempted to provide some protection and reasonable wages (where they were paid) and required church wardens and overseers to apprentice poor children (boys until the age of 24 and girls until 21 or to the time of their marriage).

This system was transferred to the American colonies and in 1641 the General Court of the New Plymouth colony recognized the principle of the English Poor Law of 1601 — that poor children were a public responsibility. In June, 1642, the Massachusetts Bay colony legalized the requirements that parents and masters teach their children "to read and understand the principles of religion and the capital laws of the country" and provided fines for those failing to report on these matters when required; local officers were also authorized to apprentice those children whose parents were unable or unfit "to employ and bring them up." In each town an officer was responsible for a certain number of families.[11] Fom these beginnings the principle of responsibility by the local governments for elementary education grew and took further shape by the famous Massachusetts law of 1647 discussed in the previous chapter and in Chapter XI. These laws were copied in Connecticut in 1650 and later in New Hampshire, when it became independent of Massachusetts, and ultimately all of the New England colonies except Rhode Island followed the principle that the state had the authority to promote education as an important civil matter.

Later the British settlers also laid foundations for vocational education through day and boarding charity schools that reflected the English schools of industry. Here poor boys and girls were sent who were to enter domestic service and various trades. These schools taught the fundamentals along with vocational training. They were usually attached to a business establishment and were in some cases partially supported by public funds. These schools were also designated as workhouse schools. They often reflected the religious resurgence of the eighteenth century in that they were supported by philanthropic and school societies. These schools, of course, gave only the basic rudiments of education but the students often emerged with at least a trade and minimally literate. Such schools were urged for the masses, for example, by John Locke who thought they were an answer to the unemployment problem, the debtors' rolls, and the overcrowded jails. The interest in these schools reflected the middle class British ideology that stressed the virtue of

---

[11] For details, see: Edgar W. Knight, *Education in the United States* (Boston: Ginn, 1951), pp. 100-101; M. W. Jernegan, "Compulsory Education in the American Colonies," "The Educational Development of the Southern Colonies," and "Compulsory Education in the Southern Colonies," *School Review*, January, May, June, (1919); and W. H. Small, *Early New England Schools* (Boston: Ginn, 1914).

industry; this gospel of work was set forth as the doctrine that the surest way of serving God and reaching happiness in this and the coming world was by working diligently in an honest trade. This ideology was accepted by the Puritans and the Quakers and was stressed particularly in schools of this type in New England and Pennsylvania. Instruction in writing and ciphering, for example, was offered to poor boys so that they would be able to keep accounts as secretaries and bookkeepers; orphan girls were taught embroidery, sewing, and subjects that would be of value to them as household servants.

The Dame School

Another thoroughly British importation was the Dame school. It appeared from the very first years of the colonial settlements and reflected the rural English situation where the young people in the community were again provided with at least some rudiments of the fundamentals, commonly in a situation where there was no other school to serve their needs. However, in some communities the Dame school paralleled the village writing school or served children who were under age for the town or parish school. The children were usually gathered in the kitchen or the living-room of a local woman with at least some erudition, but possibly with more willingness to give some time and energy to imparting the essentials to the group gathered in her home. These schools rightly had a poor reputation; but many children in the early colonial period had their only exposure to formal education in the limited atmosphere of such a situation.

The Latin Grammar School

In addition to establishing the village writing schools that ultimately evolved into the familiar district school of the post-revolutionary period but which stemmed from laws as the Old Deluder Satan Act of 1647, this law also required every town of 100 families or more to appoint a schoolmaster to give instruction in Latin grammar to prepare boys for college. Latin grammar schools followed the British example and were early established in all the colonies except Georgia. They were the only secondary school unit in the colonies until the rise of the academy in the late eighteenth century. Their origin in the United States dates to the foundation of the Boston Latin grammar school in 1635, probably under the prodding of John Cotton.

Since the grammar schools were conceived mainly as preparatory institutions, whose graduates were usually to take up the ministry, college requirements detemined the curriculum. The pupils started to study Latin at the age of eight, completing the course at about the age of fifteen. They learned little except Latin and the related fields of religion and English and the literatures therein. The school day was long, there were no extracurricular activities, the textbooks were dismal, and most work was assigned in the Bible and the classics, with practically no social, scientific, artistic, or physical education in the program. The specific deadly details of the work involved have been described by several authors.[12]

These institutions were not public schools as we understand them today. In New England they were founded by state authorities under the domination of the Puritan Church; in Virginia and Maryland they were under the supervision of the established church. In other cases they were private institutions. The parents had to pay tuition fees and, although some had income from the state or from various endowments and some were actually termed "free schools," this was more in line with the British concept of "public school" in that the schools were open to any who could gain entrance and the actual "free" concept applied to only a few poor students who were awarded scholarships.[13] These institutions flourished in compact settlements and in college towns, mainly in New England. By the end of the eighteenth century most had withered away. As with many other institutions of a given setting, it is difficult to graft them into a new environment and often the graft does not last for long. However, the Latin grammar schools that were transplanted remained generally true to their classical heritage. As America grew and changed, the Latin grammar school did not suffice and would not provide what was wanted in the way of curriculum. The more practical dual purpose academy rose to take the place of the Latin school and this, too, had British antecedents.

The Academies

The academy was a product of the realistic movement; it was founded in opposition to the formalized grammar school with its narrow classical program. The academies stressed the vernacular, the sciences, the social studies, more modern foreign languages, and offered many practical courses. Often these institutions were controlled by the church and in these instances they tended to mirror more closely the Latin school than the more secular private academies which seemed to be more democratically inclined; some even opened their doors for the education of women. These latter schools were frequently sponsored by the rising mercantile and manufacturing classes, being found more frequently in the larger cities and towns.

---

[12] Butts and Cremin, *op. cit.,* discuss the elements of these programs, pp. 122-123; for a more complete description of the unhappy conditions in the typical British grammar schools of the period, see Luella Cole, *A History of Education* (New York: Rinehart & Co., 1950), pp. 277-284.

[13] Pauline Holmes, *A Tercentenary History of the Boston Public Latin School* (1635-1935) (Cambridge: Harvard University Press, 1935) and Elmer E. Brown, *The Making of Our Middle Schools* (New York: Longmans, Green, 1903).

The Scotch-Irish Presbyterians frequently receive major credit for initiating and promoting these institutions in light of the nonconfirmist academies in Britain that they had founded to offer a broader and more practical training in keeping with the emerging needs of that group. John Milton published his *Tractate on Education* in 1644 and the school plan he outlined became the basis for a number of excellent Puritan academies in Britain. However realistic Milton's plan may have been, in his broad program of studies, he gave heavy emphasis to the classics and the American academies that emerged tended to go beyond Milton's recommendations in terms of vocational-type courses.

It is customary to give credit for the rise of the academy movement in America to the foundation of Franklin's Academy in Philadelphia at the middle of the eighteenth century; actually the historical record shows that they had existed before this period. For instance, such a Free School was founded in Charleston in 1712 and the Public School of New York (1732) was of a like nature. Products of their own age, they satisfied the need to offer education beyond the Dame School, the Southern Oldfield schools, the reading and writing school, and the charity schools. By meeting the rising educational demands which the Latin grammar school did not, the academies were eventually favored by local and state authorities. They were exempted from taxation, allowed to run lotteries, and were even granted the receipts from the sale of confiscated lands and certain fees collected by state offices.[14] The academy, however, proved an example of an institution that was to be merely a transitional school, until we developed the high school.

Infant Schools

Another somewhat later importation from England during this formative period of American history reflected a form of humanitarianism and was called the Infant School. Its most ambitious proponents were Robert Owen and Samuel Wilderspin.[15]

Owen was an English manufacturer who sensed the social impact of the rising factory system and tried to ameliorate its effects. He became convinced that he had discovered the true principles of human nature and the proper mode of social organization and he did not spare himself and his wealth to put his ideas into effect. He converted a factory town in Scotland into a model community and founded the Utopian settlement in New Harmony,

---

[14] Newton Edwards and Herman Richey, *The School in the American Social Order* (Boston: Houghton Mifflin, 1947), pp. 270-273.

[15] See Arthur E. Bestor, Jr., *Backwoods Utopias* (Philadelphia: University of Pennsylvania Press, 1950) and Alice F. Tyler, *Freedom's Ferment: Phases of American Social History to 1860* (Minneapolis: University of Minnesota Press, 1944), pp. 200ff.

Indiana in the United States. Owen felt that most of mankind's troubles could be solved by education and in 1809 he opened a free school at New Lanark, Scotland for children from five to ten years of age. This idea was carried to London and in 1824 the Infant School Society was founded with Wilderspin as agent. In 1826 the Glasgow Infant School Society was founded under the leadership of David Stow. These schools became popular in Eastern American cities where small children were usually not accepted in the few available free schools. In 1818 Boston granted $5,000 to make the Infant School a part of its city system; the school was to be opened the whole year round and run by women.[16] Similar institutions opened in New York, Philadelphia, and Providence and eventually the Infant School became part of the public school system and was absorbed as the primary grades.[17]

The Lancastrian Monitorial Movement

One of the interesting innovations of the early nineteenth century was the "system of mutual instruction," a movement rooted in poverty and the growing urban centers, that was promoted by philanthropic efforts to make education more universal. The basic idea was to instruct the younger and less competent children through the use of older, brighter, and more advanced students under the supervision of a master teacher.[18]

The idea is credited to Andrew Bell (1753-1832) who obtained it from schools in India. Joseph Lancaster (1778-1838) conceived a similar plan somewhat later. Both men developed materials for use in schools working under this plan. With the support of several of the British school societies many schools were established, using the monitorial system, in England and Wales.

Although the system enabled a somewhat improved and extended education for many children, it had many defects. It was mechanical; there was the lack of the important direct contact between pupils and master teacher; and the monitors were not paid for their work. However, it is easy to see how the system became popular in the United States as a means for handling the rapidly expanding number of children at a moderate cost. It was introduced in New York in 1806 and spread widely to the Mississippi. When Lancaster visited America in 1818 he was received with honors and adulation; DeWitt Clinton, the admiring Governor of New York, hailed Lancaster as a "benefactor of the human race." However, when the defects of the system

---

[16] Adolphe E. Meyer, *An Educational History of the American People* (New York: McGraw-Hill Book Co., 1957), p. 124.

[17] Vera M. Butler, *Education as Revealed by New England Newspapers Prior to 1850* (Philadelphia: Majestic Press, 1935).

[18] Edwards and Richey, *op. cit.,* show little appreciation of the idea, pp. 185-186.

became apparent — superficial teaching, mechanical administration, militaristic organization, and the appeal to wrong motives — it declined rapidly.[19] But the experience brought some contributions; Americans came to recognize that universal education might not be too expensive and actually the many schools built for Lancastrian classes served as an excellent beginning for the rising public school system in many cities.

The Sunday School Movement

In 1780 Robert Raikes opened a school at Gloucester, England on Sundays for poor children. A type of charity school, reading, writing, arithmetic, and spelling were taught along with hymns, the catechism, and the Scriptures. The idea became popular and the Society for the Establishment and Support of Sunday Schools Throughout the Kingdom was organized in 1785. The Methodists and Baptists particularly supported such schools and later they gave up the secular emphasis and concentrated on religious education.

In the United States such a school was organized by Bishop Asbury in Virginia in 1783 and the first such society appeared in Philadelphia in 1791. By 1820 all leading denominations were fostering these schools and the large number of children in attendance undoubtedly stimulated interest in universal education.

British Personalities

English teachers, from the famed Ezekiel Cheever who held forth for many years at the Boston Latin school to the learned Presbyterian ministers who founded schools and colleges throughout the colonies, were of immeasurable influence in seventeenth and eighteenth century America. A number of these men, as the Anglicans, responsible for schools such as King's College and William and Mary, and the Congregationalists, Quakers such as Penn, Methodist leaders, and the contributions of a host of others, have been documented in Chapter VI. Many an unremembered man, such as the Scottish teachers and private tutors who helped civilize isolated regions, deserve attention. The peripatetic Scottish teacher and the circuit-riding Scotch Presbyterian minister, for example, often provided the only means for frontier children in localities without organized schools to obtain a bit of education.[20] It is important to remember that without the dedicated efforts of English teachers

---

[19] A discussion of why these schools failed is found in H. G. Good, *A History of American Education* (New York: The Macmillan Co., 1956), pp. 136-140.

[20] Louis B. Wright, *The Cultural Life of the American Colonies 1607-1763* (New York: Harper, 1957), p. 70.

from Georgia to Vermont, in many localities there would have been little, if any, education.

There is no question that American life and its educational institutions are primarily indebted to the initial British tradition that shaped and molded them. Johnson particularly credits the British for our heritage of "brain and character" tradition that comes fom the English as a basic foundation of our democracy.[21] He points out further that Americans are much more English than they think and that from this source come such prime attributes as our exaltation of economic power and the trader, the valuable concept of gradualism, the faith in our own ability and in progress, and many aspects of our basic philosophies.

Certainly in the field of education we are indebted to Locke's empiricism, his *tabula rasa* theory of learning and teaching, and his views on government. (See also Chapter VIII, pp. 293-294.) In addition to the impact of others we have mentioned, British influences resurged following the work of Darwin and his exponents, such as Huxley and Spencer (1820-1903). Spencer's sociological-scientific emphasis was largely rejected in his own country but his essays such as "What Knowledge Is Of Most Worth?" made further dents in classicism and helped promote the idea of a more practical education. His views on "Education for a Complete Living," that called for an emphasis upon physical well-being, vocational education, education for parenthood, citizenship education, and education for the worthy use of leisure, were amalgamated into the recommendations for improvements in American education in the early twentieth century. At present some critics of education in the United States are again particularly interested in superior aspects of British education, so that the British example and British influences promise to remain.

Continental Influences

The French and the Dutch

When surveying the influence of France in the genesis of American educational history, the name of Thomas Jefferson is usually recalled as the representative spokesman of the era when French academic influence was most pervasive in American life. This French largess was particularly related to higher education in the United States between Yorktown and Waterloo, but it certainly affected education at other levels and later at the beginning of the twentieth century Rousseau's views were especially powerful in helping shape modern American elementary education. Before dealing with the impress of French ideas we will note a few facts about the French men and

---

[21] Johnson, *op. cit.*, p. 242.

women who came to the American shores and made their contributions to the progress of American culture.

The people of French descent were never a large group when compared with those of English or German stock, but people of French ancestry have been active in American history from the days of the explorers down to our own time. Certain main groups can be distinguished. First there were the explorers, trappers, and settlers who came for the love of adventure and in hope of building a "New France" in the new world; later the French Protestants (Huguenots) fled to the English and Dutch colonies to escape religious persecution at home; ever since the founding of the new nation, French Canadians, descendants of settlers in New France, have been attracted to the United States by opportunities for economic betterment and many smaller groups have emigrated, such as the Alsace-Lorrainers who have settled in California, the Basque shepherds working in our Western mountain regions, and individuals such as businessmen and chefs who have come to our urban centers.[22]

Although Britain and France fought each other throughout most of the eighteenth century, the French Huguenots and other French refugees found new homes in British America coming particularly via England, Switzerland, or Holland. They settled in all the colonies; but most went to South Carolina, Virginia, Pennsylvania, and New York. The greatest non-Huguenot influence came later from the French who settled in Louisiana. From the late seventeenth century to the end of the colonial period, efforts were made to import the French as prized immigrants by land speculators and promoters, for the French brought with them an industriousness and a diversity of skills and accomplishments. Their intelligence and adaptability helped many of the second generation to achieve positions of distinction in American life. Frenchmen were soon found in many key business and professional positions. Names such as Girard, Hillegas, Fanueil, Bowdoin, DuPuy, Jay, and Revere speak for themselves.

Many of the French became teachers of the arts, the social graces, the classics, the sciences, navigation, and other subjects. Their widespread dispersal and the multiplicity of their activities made them a potent force in the

---

[22] For details on French contributions, see: Carl Wittke, *We Who Built America: The Saga of the Immigrant* (New York: Prentice-Hall, 1946), Chapter 3; Howard M. Jones, *America and French Culture, 1750-1848* (Chapel Hill: University of North Carolina Press, 1927); Harvey Wish, *Society and Thought in Early America: A Social and Intellectual History of the American People Through 1865* (New York: Longmans, Green, 1950), Vol. I, Chapter 10; Donald C. McKay, *The United States and France* (Cambridge: Harvard University Press, 1951); and Oscar W. Winzerling, *Acadian Odyssey* (Baton Rouge, Louisiana: University of Louisiana Press, 1955).

cultural progress of the colonies.[23] Many served as tutors or established private schools. In New York, for example, the colony was settled not precisely by the Dutch but rather by the Huguenots under Dutch supervision. The Huguenots, most of them French-speaking Walloons, had emigrated to the Netherlands to escape persecution. They were refused permission to establish settlements in the English colonies so they applied to the Dutch and comprised the first batch of emigrants to set foot in New Netherlands. Peter Minuit was a Walloon and for three generations the French he initially led were greatly involved in the affairs of New York. All official documents were printed in Dutch, French, and English.

Let us turn our attention to Dutch influences. The immigrants from Holland who were Dutch were mainly traders working under the Dutch West India Company, the agency which founded New Netherlands to organize trade with the Indians. The company tried to establish schools in several towns along the example of the New England colonial schools under the influence of the Dutch Reformed Church that was related through its Calvinism to Puritan concepts of education. As early as 1637 one Adam Roelantsen, a schoolmaster, was listed among the salaried officials of the Dutch West India Company. The earliest schoolmasters usually were also sextons of the church, precentors, and comforters of the sick — the last being a peculiar office to the Dutch Reformed Church, which, with the West India Company, shared the responsibility for licensing, hiring, and supervising teachers.

The school headed by Roelantsen became known around 1647 as the Collegiate School and is still in existence. The Dutch founded schools in Brooklyn, Flatbush, Flatlands, Bushwyck, and Harlem — among other places. Generally the Dutch seemed to show more interest in education than the Anglican-led leaders who replaced them in authority after the English took final control of the colony in 1674. The Dutch elementary schools gave instruction in reading, writing, arithmetic, and catechism; but religious instruction was always stressed above all. The Bible, the catechism, and the psalm book were the chief readers used. Girls and boys went to these public schools (some tuition was also charged) but the girls sat apart from the boys or were instructed in a separate room. When English rule was established it was impossible to enforce a common religion through the public schools so the Dutch schools became church schools, maintaining instruction in Dutch, and often concentrating primarily on religious instruction. With the exception of the Collegiate School, the Dutch parochial schools gradually closed with the rise of increased numbers of public schools in the early decades of the nineteenth century, although some survived for a while as private academies.

---

[23] Wright, *op. cit.*, p. 57.

By 1740 leaders of the Reformed Church had come to the definite recognition that they had to provide their own form of higher education in America if they wanted to maintain their traditions. After some internal dissension a faction went ahead and secured a charter for a college in New Jersey (1766) which was given the name Queen's. However, it remained only on paper until 1774. After the Revolution it was renamed Rutgers in honor of one of its benefactors, but eventually its control passed to the State of New Jersey. The Reformed Church subsequently founded a number of other seminaries and collegiate institutions and cooperated in the development of others such as Union College.

The Dutch remained for a long time a distinct cultural element in New York City and environs and up the Hudson Valley. They influenced the government and many other aspects of life in New York. Their contributions in architecture, customs, and geography still persist; but the Dutch mingled with other strains in America and the specifics of any group contribution dwindled after the Revolutionary period.

The French in Louisiana, New Orleans and the surrounding territory have never lost their French stamp. Two universities provide educational facilities in that area and reflect French influences — Tulane, founded in 1884 by Paul Tulane, an American of French extraction, and Loyola founded by the Jesuits in 1913. Attached to Tulane is Newcombe College, founded by Louise Lemonnier, which offers higher education to women. French religious orders are particularly active in Louisiana and instruct many thousands of pupils. In addition to the Creoles and Cajuns, it is estimated that some 50,000 Negroes in Louisiana speak the French that their ancestors learned from their former masters.

By far the largest group of Americans of French extraction is made up of those who come from Canada; it is estimated that there are almost a million and a half French Canadians in New England. About two-thirds of them live in closely knit communities where they speak French and maintain their own churches and schools; 21 centers in New England have French-speaking populations of more than 10,000 persons. Four factors give the French-Canadian communities of New England a high degree of solidarity; these are: their religion, French language press, private organizations, and schools. There are over 425 French-Canadian Catholic parishes in the area; with the church came schools. A recent count listed almost 90,000 students in French-Canadian institutions in New England attending a total of 207 elementary schools, 55 high schools, one college, and a few boarding schools.

Historical Impact. French writers and thinkers, such as Montesquieu, Condorcet, and Rousseau had great impact upon a group of erudite Americans at the end of the eighteenth and early nineteenth centuries when the ideas of the Enlightenment became popular. The views of these Frenchmen about natural rights, government, secularism, progress, reason, and citizenship have considerable educational implications. When the surge of liberalism ran over in France, it was Danton, the revolutionary, who cried, "After bread, education!" A Frenchman living in the United States at this time, Samuel du Pont de Nemours, belonged to a group of educational writers who, after the Revolution, offered a number of plans for a system of public schools that would create a uniform system of public education which would preserve and extend liberty, democracy, and citizenship. Du Pont favored a national board of education which would create a uniform system for the whole country and help unify the heterogeneous peoples of the Republic.[24]

French influence can also be seen in the university organization and programs in the United States. This was reflected especially in New York where in 1784 the Board of Regents of the University of the State of New York was founded to keep an eye on secondary and higher learning. Since that date all the States have followed through with varying procedures and powers established for their state departments of public instruction. The system in New York resembled that created by Napoleon in his scheme of organization which compressed all of the higher institutions, *lycées* and *collèges,* into one corporate body called the University of France.

Although Franklin made no small contribution to American education with his *Poor Richard's Almanac* that helped educate many thousands of farmers and tradesmen, his academy, his sponsoring of public libraries, and his foundation of the Discussion Junta that was to become the American Philosophical Society, he was not influenced by the French as greatly as was Thomas Jefferson.

Jefferson (1743-1826) accepted the view that, since men were naturally endowed with reason, the tools of learning handed to them through education would enable them to use the power of reason to free themselves from the religious and social indoctrination to which they had been subjected. He insisted on freedom of inquiry and expression and relied, above all, on the force of reasoning. He felt that no special instruction in morality was needed because man's mind, freed from its chains of indoctrination, would recognize and accept the truth to be found in the teaching of Jesus and the other great philosophers. Hence Jefferson's desire for public education and for a state university with his wish to abolish chairs of religious instruction which appeared to him to have mainly provided courses in indoctrination.

---

[24] Bessie G. DuPont, *National Education in the United States of America by Du-Pont de Nemours* (Newark, Delaware: University of Delaware Press, 1923), and Allen O. Hansen, *Liberalism and American Education in the Eighteenth Century* (New York: The Macmillan Co., 1926).

His own epitaph reflects his views as to what were his prime contributions. It does not mention his inventions, his governorship of Virginia, his work as a congressman, his period as minister to France, his role as Secretary of State and Vice President, or even that he served as third President of the United States. The tombstone reads:

"Here was buried Thomas Jefferson
Author of the Declaration of American Independence
Of the Statute of Virginia for religious freedom
And Father of the University of Virginia."

The last two of the above items were directly related to education. In 1779 Jefferson attempted to get a state system of education launched in Virginia but failed. If accepted by the legislature, his plan would have provided a three-year common public school education free for all citizens. The plan was organized to subsequently promote the most worthy scholars at state expense on a narrowing basis through the hierarchy of schools in the State. Ultimately a few from each class would graduate from William and Mary as elite leaders in Virginia. The founding of the University of Virginia and most all of the provisions that Jefferson stipulated in connection with its curriculum and organization reflected French influence. For example, he urged the introduction of the elective system that was then unknown in the United States.

Jefferson's most important educational contribution can be credited only indirectly to French democratic theory. This was his role in getting the educational provisions written into the land ordinances of 1785 and 1787. The former provided that the 16th section of every township surveyed in the new Western territories would be set aside for educational purposes; the Act of 1787 set aside two entire townships for the establishment of future state universities in those areas.[25] Of course, when Jefferson urged a "crusade against ignorance" or claimed to "swear eternal enmity against any tyranny over the mind of man," he revealed the extent to which he believed education to be essential in the furtherance of democracy. Although he did not urge extended universal (Jacksonian) public education, the American people cherish the memory of the man who stated unequivocally "I know of no safe depository of the powers of society but the people themselves; if they are not enlightened enough to exercise their control with discretion, the remedy is not to take power away from them but to inform them by education." French roots existed for his faith in the ability and goodness of the ordinary

---

[25] The most authoritative work on Jefferson's educational views has been Roy J. Honeywell, *The Educational Work of Thomas Jefferson* (Cambridge: Harvard University Press, 1931); a new collection is Gordon C. Lee (ed.) *Crusade Against Ignorance: Thomas Jefferson on Education* (New York: Teachers College, 1961).

man, his belief in the possibility of improving human life by reform in government, law, and education, and his conviction to the cause of human freedom.

Butts and Cremin emphasize the French influence during this early period of United States history and give particular credit to the French for the conception of centralized state systems of education, the heritage of universal public education for national ends, freedom of thought, and the emphasis upon secularism as "the very heart of this French influence."[26] When British religious and intellectual thought lost its dominance during the period of the Revolutionary War, it was replaced by such French ideas as deism and rationalism that received favorable reception in America and were particularly popular in some American colleges for several decades. But once French Revolutionary armies were no longer marching over Europe and Napoleon was deposed, America was influenced by the rise of German and British romanticism and transcendentalism that strengthened the forces of spirituality at the expense of French naturalism. French educational influence declined except that a number of American travelers to Europe brought back particularly striking reports about the effectiveness of French teacher training and our normal schools ultimately took their name from like French institutions.

ROUSSEAU AND LATER PERSONALITIES.   The heritage of Rousseau's educational ideas were not to blossom forth till the late nineteenth and early twentieth centuries. By this time America had reached a stage of development wherein she was ready to apply a number of the key ideas that Rousseau (1712-1778) had urged in his famous Émile.[27] Rousseau had reminded educators that nature would have the young be children before they are men; that the child learns actively, individually; that the learning experiences of children should be in harmony with their physical and mental development; that reason is not the key approach, particularly in elementary education; that the place of the teacher is in the background; and a number of other equally striking generalizations that finally became part of the central core of the progressive education movement in the twentieth century. Rousseau held many erroneous ideas and preached some dangerous half-truths, but he was a powerful regenerative force. Education in the United States and throughout the world is indebted to this man who exalted natural development and interests over austere and unreasonable discipline, freedom to learn purposeful and practical subjects rather than to submit to the absolute authority of the

---

[26] Butts and Cremin, *op. cit.*, p. 243.

[27] Chapter VIII of this text carries a further discussion of Rousseau; his contributions are objectively assayed in Frederick Eby, *The Development of Modern Education, Second Edition* (New York: Prentice-Hall, 1952), Chapter 13.

older generation and the right of the individual learner over the inert pressures of the outmoded past.

French influences have also been great in the area of the education of the exceptional child. Meyer points out that as early as 1760 a Frenchman was attempting to teach the deaf, and following earlier explorations Louis Braille (1809-1852) developed an effective method of teaching the blind. Schools using these ideas spread in various cities in the United States and Thomas Gallaudet brought the sign method for teaching the deaf from Paris in 1817 and introduced the first such school in the United States.[28]

Later, Edouard Seguin (1812-1880), a French physician, became interested in the problem of educating idiots. He developed a school in Paris and ultimately sent out a number of teachers, some of whom founded schools in America based on his approaches. He emigrated to the United States in 1848 and ultimately became head of the Pennsylvania Training School for Idiots. His lecturing and consultant work, as well as the teaching materials he developed, such as form boards, made a considerable contribution toward providing the training whereby these poor unfortunates could carry out routine tasks and to a limited degree care for themselves. His influence upon sensory education in the kindergarten and primary schools was also important. Alfred Binet (1857-1911) was the director of the laboratory of physiological psychology at the Sorbonne in Paris. His main work was in the direction of determining individual differences and in 1904 he was asked by the French ministry of public instruction to help find a method of identifying subnormal children so that they could be removed from ordinary classes. In 1905 with the help of Theodore Simon, working with children in Parisian schools, he developed the first scale of a test to identify imbeciles. These tests were revised in later years to apply to higher levels of intelligence and to normal children. In the United States Binet's test was shaped into the now familiar IQ test by Lewis Terman's 1916 Stanford Revision of the Binet-Simon scales. Binet recognized the importance of determining the aptitudes of children as the "greatest business of instruction and education" and that teaching needed to be individualized and based on a proper foundation of experimental psychology.[29] The work of these Frenchmen is of inestimable import in providing the heritage of special education for the handicapped to which America is now dedicated on a large scale, as well as providing the related beginnings of the mental testing and guidance movement that are also outstanding characteristics of American education.[30]

---

[28] Meyer, *op. cit.*, p. 311.

[29] The work of Seguin and Binet is recounted in Cole, *op. cit.*, Chapter XIX.

[30] Frank Freeman, *Mental Tests: Their History, Principles and Application* (Boston: Houghton Mifflin, 1939).

Many other Frenchmen could be identified who have made their mark upon education and whose ideas and approaches have found expression in American schools. Michel D. Montaigne (1533-1592), the French Renaissance essayist, contributed to the realistic humanist position that ultimately took root in the United States. His opposition to memoriter education, bookishness, and verbalism, his emphasis upon utilitarian pragmatic education for social adjustment, and his promoting the development of the student who is an independent thinker, all have a familiar ring. Jean Baptiste de la Salle is discussed in the chapter on Catholic education but serves as an example of the French educators and Orders that have contributed to the stream of educational improvement. The Christian Brothers operate over 100 schools and colleges in the United States today.

Later, such French thinkers as the father of modern sociology, Auguste Comte, and the social philosopher, Emile Durkheim, did much to influence the evolution of sociology and educational sociology in the United States. American education in the twentieth century has been criticized as being overly child-centered (an inheritance from Rousseau); it is interesting that some of the basic balancing ideas of relating education to the conditions and needs of society also have French roots. However, without the further parading of names, it should be clear that American education is indebted to and far richer because of its French inheritances.

Germanic and Swiss Influences

Although there was no Germany as such until Bismarck's creation of 1871, Germanic peoples formed by far the largest number of non-English speaking settlers in colonial America.[31] It has been estimated that at the time the Declaration of Independence was signed, almost one-tenth of the population of the new nation was composed of people of German blood with the largest single group living in Pennsylvania. Interestingly enough, religion and economics were just about equally responsible for the beginning of this great migration of the German people to the American Colonies, attracted there especially by William Penn's effective advertising of his great proprietorship of Pennsylvania, his liberal land policy, and his promise of religious freedom.

The trail was blazed by the Mennonites, who, today, number about 20,000 in Lancaster County, Pennsylvania. Another small sect, the Church of the Brethren, followed; these groups, with the Schwenkfelders, have preserved what is known today as the Pennsylvania Dutch culture. But by far the

---

[31] For details, see: Wittke, *op. cit.*, pp. 66-97, and Frank Spencer, "An Eighteenth-Century Account of German Emigration to the American Colonies," *Journal of Modern History*, March, 1956, pp. 55-65; also Walz, *op. cit.*

largest immigrant group was composed of German Lutheran or German Reformed background, who came primarily for economic reasons.

The first body of German immigrants came to America in 1683; their leader, Franz Daniel Pastorius, had bought a tract of land from William Penn and had established the first German permanent settlement here, only two years after the founding of Philadelphia. This Germantown became the distributing center for the large and continuous German immigrations throughout the eighteenth century in the colonies surrounding Pennsylvania. South Carolina also received a large contingent of German settlers, beginning about 1735. A map of the frontier settlements of 1775 reveals that the German colonists were spread along the entire length of the frontier line from Maine to Georgia, as shown in the names of their settlements, from Mecklenburg in the Carolinas to Rhinebeck in New York.

Steady German immigration continued until the mid-nineteenth century when, between 1845 and 1860, a flood of over a million and a quarter Germans arrived in the United States. Usually well supplied with resources, they went to the farms of the Old Northwest and into Missouri and Iowa; their skilled workers and intellectuals went to the growing central western cities (Cincinnati, Milwaukee, St. Louis, Buffalo, Cleveland, Detroit, Chicago, and the smaller cities of the Northwest). There was even talk of forming separate German states (Illinois, Wisconsin, and Missouri)! There, for three generations, they attended their German churches, parochial schools, Turnvereins, musical clubs, picnics, and beer gardens. Coming to the "raw new West they introduced the seeds of artistic appreciation, and their respect for education influenced the rising new state universities."[32]

The last phase of German immigration started in the 1870's and continued up to World War I. This immigration outnumbered all others; from 1870 to 1910, 3,750,000 Germans reached our shores. To a larger degree than the previous immigrants they were industrial workers, and although many took up lands in Kansas, Nebraska, and the Dakotas, they moved more and more to the cities.

Germans, just like other immigrant groups, have made distinct contributions to American civilization, especially in the fields of arts, science, business, and industry — in addition to their remarkable contributions to education.[33] For example, in the industrial history of the nineteenth century in America, the Germans dominated all those branches requiring technical

---

[32] William W. Sweet, *American Culture and Religion* (Dallas, Texas: Southern Methodist University Press, 1951), p. 20.

[33] See Wittke, *op. cit.*; Walz, *op. cit.*; and Henry A. Pochmann and others, *German Culture in America, 1600-1900: Philosophical and Literary Influences* (Madison: University of Wisconsin Press, 1957).

training (since technical schools had not yet been founded on any scale in the United States) and became the leading engineers. In America the Germans also led in the chemical industry, drugs, pianos and musical instruments, optical instruments, machinery manufacturing, lithography, brewing, and food and meat product processing.

GERMAN IMMIGRANTS. Germans made a host of cultural and educational contributions to American life. One of the earliest teachers was the noted Pennsylvania schoolmaster, Christopher Dock. He wrote one of the first books printed in America on education, *Schulordnung* (1770), which dealt with many aspects of school keeping. In 1743 Christopher Saur printed the complete Lutheran Bible in the German language, the first European language Bible produced in the American Colonies. German Quakers in Germantown immortalized themselves by their formal protest against Negro slavery in 1788, the first time such action was taken in America. Peter Zenger, founder of the independent *New York Weekly Journal,* was tried for libel in 1735 and made the first great fight for liberty of the press in America. Before the end of the colonial era David Rittenhouse had achieved the distinction of being the greatest mathematician and astronomer in the Colonies and succeeded Franklin as president of the American Philosophical Society. Henry Muhlenberg achieved the distinction of becoming the father of American Lutheranism and organized a system of schools among the German Lutherans in Pennsylvania.

The German liberal movement in the first half of the eighteenth century was rooted in the universities in student groups and in adult patriotic organizations known as the Turnvereins devoted to preparing for the coming struggle for a unified republican Germany in which liberty and freedom would prevail (a program resembling the sokol movement among the Slavs). However, the ill-fated revolution of 1848 forced many German exiles who were members of these organizations to seek refuge in the United States. Among the wave of emigrants were many intellectuals. Karl Follen, a fugitive student leader, had earlier introduced the German gymnasium in Boston and began instruction in his mother tongue at Harvard. Francis Lieber, another early refugee, undertook shortly after his arrival in 1827 the preparation of the *Encyclopedia Americana* and instructed in subjects from political science to physical education at a number of American colleges. Karl Beck and Franz Joseph Grund also became distinguished professors at Harvard; along with other German leaders, they helped popularize the idea of physical education as a requisite base for the well-rounded cultivation of the mind. Among the many radical reformers and revolutionaries who came to America after 1848, perhaps most outstanding was Carl Schurz (1829-1906) who rose to prominence in the Republican Party, was a Civil War hero, served as a cabinet member, was United States Senator from Missouri, and a noted writer including the editorship of the *New York Evening Post*. By the late nineteenth century, however, German contributions to American education were already being absorbed into the stream of the American public school. We shall now review some of the educational activities of Germans who came into the United States previous to this time. The reader is reminded that a thorough discussion of the Lutheran contributions to education in the United States was presented in the previous chapter.

GERMAN SCHOOLS.   In America the German element was usually interested in education "partly because of a genuine interest in a sound school system, partly because of a sincere desire to maintain the German language in a new environment by having it taught to their children in the schools, and partly because some German-American leaders in the middle nineteenth century believed that American culture was at such a low ebb that a German scheme of education was essential to raise its level."[34]

Before the Civil War many private German schools had been set up. The bulk were parochial schools of the Lutheran churches, but others were supported by various German societies. The German settlements tended to organize a *Schulverein* that hired the teachers, often from Germany. Many Germans served as private tutors and as music teachers. Some of the private institutions they organized in New York, Baltimore, St. Louis, Cincinnati, and Milwaukee exerted considerable influence on educational progress in those communities.[35] Germans were also active in the public schools and men such as Theodore Bernhard, who is credited with organizing the school system of Watertown, Wisconsin that included the first system of free textbooks in that state, and George Bunsen, noted superintendent of schools in Belleville, Illinois who promoted Pestalozzi's methods, are examples of leadership in this area.

The insistence of preserving the German language amidst the more or less "hostile English" environment was a persistent problem for the American Germans from colonial days and the matter of language periodically interfered with "the peace and progress of both the churches and the schools."[36] With the gradual waning away of German-American private schools that came with increased attendance of German youth in American public schools and

---

34 Wittke, *ibid.*, p. 232.

35 Wittke, *ibid.*, p. 233.

36 Walter H. Beck, *Lutheran Elementary Schools in the United States: A History of the Development of Parochial Schools and Synodical Educational Policies and Programs* (St. Louis, Missouri: Concordia Publishing House, 1939), p. 67; see also the previous chapter of this text.

because of the liberal influence of the free thinking "Forty-Eighters," many second generation German-Americans, who wanted to preserve German *Kultur,* pressed for the introduction of the German language in public schools. In Massachusetts and Ohio, for example, thanks to the help of Horace Mann and Calvin Stowe (whom we shall see subsequently had been quite impressed with the high qualities of the Prussian system of education), German was introduced in the schools in their States. Wittke explains that at a time when Prussian schools were regarded as models in education and the German vote in many States was large enough to be a deciding factor in elections, it was not difficult to secure the addition of German to the public school curriculum.[37] In fact, a Pennsylvania statute of 1837 and an Ohio law of the same decade not only allowed the teaching of German in public schools, but even permitted instruction in the German language when there was a demand for it. By 1885 a national organization of German teachers numbered nearly 5,000. German remained in the curricula of the public schools of many States until the first World War.

One of the main goals of German Lutheranism was always the preservation of the German language, second only to the preservation of uncorrupted Lutheranism. Under the attacks of the Methodists, Presbyterians, and Baptists, with their experiences in evangelizing the frontier, "Old Lutheranism" consolidated its forces in the nineteenth century by founding the Concordia Seminary in St. Louis; it has remained the heart of the Missouri Synod, dedicated to the promotion of German learning, art, and religion in the New World. Its graduates went to the seaport towns, erected immigrant houses, and tried to shepherd the recent arrivals into the fold of the true church; they stressed the importance of the parochial schools and insisted that the instruction in Lutheranism be in the German language. They fought radical, socialist, and agnostic Germans as the sworn enemies of religion, property, and the family; but it was a losing cause.

During World War I, Ohio and Nebraska passed laws prohibiting the right to conduct schools in a foreign language. However, in Robert Meyer versus the State of Nebraska case (1923), the U.S. Supreme Court declared all state laws prohibiting the teaching and use of German in private and parochial schools as unconstitutional. The decision came too late; German language instruction never recovered from the blows of two World Wars.

In recent decades, the German educational institutions have suffered severely — as all other immigrant institutions of this type. Possibly most successful was the work of the Turner movement. The first Turner societies were opened in the fall of 1848 in Cincinnati, and soon were organized in other American cities, with the instructors from Germany who had received

---

[37] Wittke, *op. cit.,* p. 233.

their physical training in their homeland. George Brosius of Milwaukee was able to open, in 1875, a normal school for training teachers of physical education, with large numbers of pupils attending. He later became Superintendent of Physical Training for the public schools of Milwaukee. Graduates of his school were able to ask for the introduction of organized work in light gymnastics in the public schools of many cities. Meanwhile, the work of the Turnvereins provided a core of adult education in nearly every German community and included parades, pageants, concerts, balls, public addresses, theatrical performances, and exhibitions of drills and gymnastics.

While the pioneer work was done by the Germans in the area of physical education and the Germans in America strongly supported vocational training, the kindergarten is the most unique and lasting of the German contributions to American education. The idea was imported to the Middle West, where, in 1855, Mrs. Carl Schurz, a former pupil of Froebel, founded the first kindergarten in the United States in Watertown, Wisconsin. In 1860, the first English-speaking kindergarten, a private one, appeared in Boston under Elizabeth Peabody; and some eight years later a special training school for kindergarten teachers was founded there. In 1873, St. Louis opened the first kindergarten in a public system in America. From there they spread rapidly into all corners of this country, although kindergartens are still not recognized as a part of the regular school system in many States.

Fredrich Froebel (1782-1852) provides an excellent example of the German who never left Europe but whose thinking had tremendous impact upon American education. John Dewey, among many others, was indebted to this man who did so much to promote the instruction of pre-schoolers. A disciple of Pestalozzi, Froebel believed that guided self-activity in terms of their budding interests and needs was the key to teaching young children. He fostered the view that play was a natural and appropriate educational experience for children. He developed his famous teaching materials ("gifts" and "occupations") that included the then rare blocks, balls, cylinders, tablets, corks, sticks, sewing cards, and the memorable pantomime Mother Play Songs. Froebel's play-circle, symbol of unity and source of identification of self with others, as a first taste of the social interdependence that man must perfect, remains today a place of morning assembly and greeting for hundreds of thousands of kindergarten five-year-olds. (See also Chapter VIII, pp. 305-7.)

Froebel was also one of the first to employ women teachers on a large scale (he could not get men to bend to such instruction). He felt that these young women would do much to develop the warm environment he believed to be so necessary for learning at this level. Certainly as we review these factors in the light of recent and current American education, it is easy to ascertain that the Froebelian influence reached far beyond the kindergarten. What nation has more fully provided an educational program with a way of learning that meets the quotation on Froebel's tombstone "Come, live for your children."

FURTHER GERMAN AND SWISS INFLUENCES. When dealing with the German contributions to the genesis of American education we must remember that the influence was not only direct, but also, as evidenced above, of derived relationships. Froebel developed some of his key ideas while working in Switzerland. The impact from Germany on the American educational field can be seen from the lowest to the highest rung on the educational ladder. Features from the kindergarten to important aspects of the American university are German importations. However, the educational theories coming from Germany are deeply interwoven with those applied throughout Europe and thus they found their way into American education in diverse ways.

An example of the latter type of influence would be the ideas of Johannes Sturm (1507-1589), whose classical humanistic program at his famous Lutheran gymnasium at Strasbourg was copied throughout Europe. His program was adapted by Calvin for his Geneva academy and thence spread through Europe and the New World as a Swiss, Dutch, or Scotch Presbyterian institution. Sturm's ideas have survived in the European gymnasium and are reflected in concepts of college preparatory education that marked American secondary schools for generations.

Undoubtedly the most influential of the continental educators was Johann Pestalozzi (1746-1827) who was born in Zurich, Switzerland. He was probably the most famous teacher in the history of education and key aspects of his work are evaluated in Chapter VIII; however, the means by which his approaches spread and were modified serve as a revealing example of the movement of educational ideas in a cross-cultural manner.

Pestalozzi, like Froebel, was greatly dependent upon Comenius, Locke, and especially Rousseau; but he accomplished what Rousseau could never do. He taught magnificently in his orphanage and in his schools at Burgdorf and Yverdon (1805-25). Here he demonstrated his use of direct sense experiences in learning and developed his famous object lessons. Starting with the emerging interests of children and their growing motor development, he launched an activity school by which he hoped to set an example of how society could ultimately be regenerated by the proper education of the individual. He taught the total child, stressing a combination of intellectual, physical, moral, and vocational training. The use of realia in lessons, the teaching of geography via field trips, the learning of arithmetic by solving actual problems that concerned the pupils, the procedure in instructing from known to unknown and from the concrete to the abstract, the broadening of the elementary school curriculum to include nature study, geography, art, and music, and the preparation of teachers based primarily upon an intimate knowledge of the child and of its development — all of these were to have prime significance a half-century later in educational developments in the United States.

In the story of how Pestalozzi's ideas reached and influenced American education, we meet the dual example of Germans coming to America and of the growing importance of the increasing numbers of Americans who were to receive their education in German schools or who visited there with the purpose of studying achievements, particularly in Prussian education. Pestalozzi's principles were used by many American teachers, therefore, who had them inculcated in their teacher training experiences and also by German educators who came to the United States and helped spread his ideas.

Some of the most important American results of Pestalozzi's work came from the visits made to his outstanding school. William Maclure, William Crawford, John Griscom, William Woodbridge, editor of *The American Annals of Education,* and later others, as Mann and Barnard, all popularized the story of his experiments. Maclure brought one of Pestalozzi's teachers, Joseph Neef, to Philadelphia in 1806 to conduct a Pestalozzian school. Woodbridge visited Pestalozzi several times between 1820 and 1829 and was especially interested in geography and music, and as a result of his contact with Pestalozzi he published several much used textbooks in geography that made a significant contribution to improving instruction in that subject which up to that time had not always been included in the regular school curriculum. Woodbridge's enthusiasm for the Pestalozzian method also carried over to the teaching of music. He aroused the interest of Lowell Mason (1792-1872) who developed music (one of the neglected fields of Puritan education) as an important aspect of the programs in the rising American public schools. In 1821 Warren Colburn published his *First Lessons in Arithmetic* which became widely used and were based upon acquaintance with Pestalozzian principles. William Russell founded the *American Journal of Education* which published many articles on Pestalozzian teaching and he was also responsible for importing Hermann Krusi, Jr., son of Pestalozzi's noted assistant, to teach in his normal school at Lancaster, Pennsylvania. Edward Sheldon (1823-1897), Superintendent of Schools at Oswego, New York, learned of Pestalozzi's work through an exhibit of the materials and object lessons; he employed a British Pestalozzian teacher to introduce the work at Oswego where he developed a training school. She was followed by Hermann Krusi, Jr., who continued the work for 25 years. Thereby Oswego became the center of Pestalozzian influence in the United States and hundreds of teachers trained there carried these practices throughout the entire country.[38] The foregoing examples serve to reveal the varied and multiple

---

[38] Cole, *op. cit.,* presents very sympathetic treatment of the highlights of the contributions of both Froebel and Pestalozzi; see Chapters XVI and XVIII. Interested readers

manner in which Pestalozzian approaches were brought to America.

More credit than is usually given should be granted to Philipp Fellenberg (1771-1844), one of Pestalozzi's disciples, whose idea of manual labor schools to teach practical agriculture and hand work by sort of an apprentice system was adopted in America in a modified form after 1820. This stress was also introduced into a number of reform schools. In some of the academies, colleges, and theological seminaries the manual labor system was used to allow students to earn their way and, in the absence of athletics, to provide physical exercise. The movement also influenced the growing interest in agricultural education and there appears to be a resemblance between Fellenberg's ideas and cooperative education plans developed at the University of Cincinnati, Western Reserve, Oberlin, Wabash, Berea, Antioch, and other colleges.

AMERICAN CARRIERS. German educational ideas continued to be promoted by the report of Americans abroad and by the growth of American educational publications that provided a medium for the extension of these influences. In 1835 the Cousin report on German education was published in New York. Victor Cousin had been commissioned by the French government to study Prussian schools; his *Report on the Condition of Public Instruction in Prussia* appeared in France in 1832. This work was extensively circulated, particularly in Massachusetts and Michigan. "No other work had such powerful influence in the field of higher education. The University of Michigan and the public school system of that state are deeply indebted to this work."[39]

In 1836 Calvin E. Stowe (husband of the well-known Harriet Beecher Stowe) was commissioned by the Ohio legislature to study the Prussian system of education and his report was also influential in bringing educational reforms in the United States. A professor of Greek at Dartmouth, he was a leading Hebrew and Biblical scholar. Stowe was impressed with the education of teachers in Prussia and urged a similar policy in the United States. He was also actively interested in the improvement of common schools and regarded this as one of the greatest needs of the young West.[40] Stowe's report was circulated by the legislature of Ohio and reprinted in other States. It

---

are referred, of course, to the writings of the great educators themselves; see, for example, Froebel's *The Education of Man* (New York: D. Appleton, 1891) and Pestalozzi's *Leonard and Gertrude* (Boston: Heath, 1897).

[39] Frederick Eby and Charles F. Arrowood, *The Development of Modern Education, in Theory, Organization, and Practice* (New York: Prentice-Hall, 1946), p. 733.

[40] See Dumas Malone's article in *The Dictionary of American Biography* (New York: Charles Scribner's, 1936), Vol. XVIII, p. 115. *The Dictionary of American Biography* is recommended reading for brief but complete and well-written biographies of American educational leaders.

contrasted educational conditions in Ohio with those of Prussia and other German states, with particular reference to the primary schools and the organization and thoroughness of instruction therein and with the need for teachers' seminaries wherein neophytes could be properly taught the art and science of teaching. The meager elements of the Ohio elementary schools were contrasted with the enriched programs in Prussia and the Pestalozzian method was also heralded.

Another outstanding report on German educational systems came from Alexander Bache who studied conditions in Europe under a grant from the trustees of Girard College, an institution for the care and education of orphans. Bache was the first principal of Philadelphia's Central High School and built a three-track curriculum that reflected the realschules and gymnasiums he had observed.[41] Included was a two-year terminal program, a four-year classical Latin curriculum, and a four-year practical academy program. Here was revealed the amalgam that was ultimately to emerge as the American comprehensive high school. Interestingly enough, the fact that the German educational successes were performed within the framework of an absolute monarchy did not seem to bother these educational reporters. If anything, these men implied that the free American government should be much less progressive and permissive in educational matters and copy Prussia, that most autocratic of European governments.

Perhaps the most definite cross-cultural influence was extended by Henry Barnard (1811-1900), secretary of the Connecticut Board of Education and later the first United States Commissioner of Education (1867). Barnard, after his first visit to Europe, became the most vocal proponent of the introduction of the best of European organizations and practices into America's schools. One of the most prolific writers on educational problems, he vividly described foreign educational systems.[42] Barnard, of course, became acquainted with Pestalozzian approaches and devoted much space and effort to familiarizing American educators with these ideas and Froebel's. Barnard was remarkably successful also in creating an efficient centralization of educational administration and control, in securing more financial support for the schools, and in inspiring an abiding faith in public education. Following his work in Connecticut and Rhode Island, he became President of the University of Wisconsin and then of St. John's College; it was from there that

---

[41] Alexander Bache, *Report on Education in Europe, to the Trustees of the Girard College for Orphans* (Philadelphia: Lydia R. Bailey, 1839).

[42] In addition to his notable reports as State School Secretary in Connecticut and Rhode Island, he published state school journals, and the *American Journal of Education,* 30 volumes, 1855-1885, contains a great collection of historical and biographical material; see also Richard Thursfield, *Henry Barnard's American Journal of Education* (Baltimore: Johns Hopkins University Press, 1945).

he was called to Washington to become first U.S. Commissioner of Education.

Horace Mann (1796-1859), known as the father of the American public school, should be credited, with Barnard, for establishing workable public education at the state level, where these systems of education became models for other states. Both are rightly honored as pioneers in the struggle to found a system of free schools for all the children of all the people.

Without going into details about his great accomplishments,[43] it is sufficient to note that he left the presidency of the state senate to become secretary of the Massachusetts State Board of Education; he published his famous series of annual reports dealing with a variety of educational problems and, of particular importance historically, following his European visit, Mann's classic seventh report (1843) was devoted to describing the schools in Great Britain, Belgium, Holland, Germany, and France. Mann also established the *Massachusetts Common School Journal,* worked hard for better teachers, higher teachers' salaries, an enriched curriculum, improved school buildings, school libraries, better administrative procedures, and non-sectarian schools. He was particularly impressed with teacher education in France and Germany and perhaps of all the improvements that Mann set underway, his role in helping found normal schools was perhaps the most far-reaching. Mann believed that the common schools would not prosper without teacher training institutions, claiming, "As well might we expect to have coats without a tailor and houses without a carpenter or mason, as to have an adequate supply of teachers without normal schools."

Another distinguished educator who provided education with a philosophy that bridged for Americans their traditional ideologies to new actualities, without having them lose their sense of identity with older values, was William T. Harris (1835?-1908).[44] Harris was a leading member of the St. Louis movement in philosophy which began at the close of the Civil War and lasted until about 1885 when most of its leading members had left St. Louis. Although a typical American movement, it was inspired from Germany and founded by a German-American, Henry Brockmeyer; the movement eventually merged with Emersonian idealism and the Concord school of philosophy.

---

[43] Two of the best volumes on Mann are B. A. Hinsdale, *Horace Mann and the Common School Revival in the United States* (New York: Charles Scribner's Sons, 1898) and E. I. F. Williams, *Horace Mann, Educational Statesman* (New York: The Macmillan Co., 1937); interested readers are urged to refer to his 12 reports which have been republished by the Horace Mann League and the Hugh Birch-Horace Mann Fund of the NEA. See also Chapter XI of this text.

[44] Merle Curti, *The Social Ideas of American Educators* (New York: Charles Scribner's Sons, 1935), Chapter IX, is devoted to Harris; valuable interpretations of other leading American educators' thoughts will be found in this volume.

An ardent student of Kant, Fichte, and above all Hegel, Harris, who had studied in Germany, influenced American education by his able administrative leadership and his writing in the field of educational philosophy. Believing that man possesses the capacity for infinite culture, he saw in the public school movement means of bringing the people into harmony with the advancement of knowledge; his emphasis on the education of the self and the role of reason in the life of the individual related Emerson's transcendentalism and the experimentalism of John Dewey. This Yankee from Connecticut carried an important weight on educational circles, he was about the most frequent speaker at NEA sessions. He was a noted teacher, superintendent of schools in St. Louis, U. S. Commissioner of Education (1889-1906), and above all a social philosopher. Harris, as editor of *The Journal of Speculative Philosophy,* introduced and popularized Hegel's philosophy in the United States, and this was the first metaphysical journal in America voicing German idealistic philosophy. Wesley reports that Nicholas Murray Butler of Columbia University credited Harris with doing more than "any single person, living or dead" to construct the curriculum on the basis of a sound philosophical discussion.[45] The movement, together with the Kant Club, formed a rallying point for a whole generation of rising young teachers and thinkers — Peirce, Hall, James, Royce, and Dewey, among others.[46]

GERMAN PSYCHOLOGICAL FACTORS. Although the United States subsequently fought Germany in two World Wars, the impact of German scientific contributions from psychology and sociology to physics and rocketry continued to grow. Inseparable from the impact of psychology upon education is the scientific movement in education, a proposition introduced by Herbart but which did not achieve prominence until the end of the last century, particularly under the influence of Wilhelm Wundt. Wundt (1832-1920) proposed that psychology be made a science,[47] and he attracted students to Heidelberg and Leipzig from all over the world. He was a physiologist and a philosopher, as well as an experimental psychologist.

Among the students who worked under Wundt was William James, a young medical student from Harvard who founded his laboratory-psychology in America at Harvard and inaugurated Harvard's first course in psychology. His *Principles of Psychology* (1890) dominated American psychology for at least a generation and had a great influence on the rise of educational psy-

---

45 Edgar B. Wesley, NEA: *The First Hundred Years* (New York: Harper & Brothers, 1957), p. 190.

46 Pochmann, *op. cit.,* p. 313. Further influences of Kant are treated in Chapter VIII of this text.

47 Edwin G. Boring, *A History of Experimental Psychology* (New York: Appleton-Century-Crofts, 1929).

chology in this country.[48]   His main theme, the "Stream of Conscious Thought," was digested and further developed not only by educators and psychologists but by sociologists, historians, and anthropologists, so that the germ planted in Wundt's laboratory flowered in the contributions of James McKeen Cattell, Edward Bradford Titchener, and G. Stanley Hall, among others.

G. Stanley Hall founded America's first university laboratory of analytical psychology (1883) and later as President of Clark University he pioneered in the growing child study movement. In 1887 he founded the *American Journal of Psychology*. To the generation of Hall belongs Cattell, a former assistant of Wundt who used laboratory and statistical methods in his psychological research. His *Mental Tests and Measurements* (1890) marked a milestone in the field and his student, E. L. Thorndike, was destined to become the most outstanding proponent of educational statistics. Out of their work, and that of Binet, Goddard, and Terman, discussed previously, grew the testing movement. The so-called intelligence test soon became a popular and inseparable aspect of American education. Additional contributions to the field were made by Charles Judd, another disciple of Wundt, who promoted his views at the University of Chicago while Thorndike was a member of the faculty at Teachers College, Columbia University. They, in turn, produced a long line of followers who have contributed to the growth of such periodicals as *The Review of Educational Research, The Journal of Educational Research, The Educational Measurement Review, The Encyclopedia of Educational Research,* and similar important publications.[49]

In recent decades the German influence in psychology, which had been somewhat paralleled by sociological influences that can be traced to Max Weber and Karl Mannheim, reappeared in the form of Gestalt psychology. Introduced in Germany by Max Wertheimer in 1912, it was popularized in America after World War I. Its approach stressed that every experience has a definite and intrinsic pattern or configuration. Further advances in this field made by American psychologists attacked the older positions of the behaviorists and the stimulus-response connectionists; they influenced American education by their contributions to a better understanding of perception, learning, development, intelligence, and personality.[50]

Another continental contribution came from the psycho-analytical views

---

[48] William James, *Talks to Teachers on Psychology* (New York: Henry Holt, 1899).

[49] A recent study of Judd's influence in shaping secondary education in America is Margaret W. Clark, "Charles H. Judd: Educational Leadership in American Secondary Education" (Doctor's thesis, Stanford University, 1960).

[50] For more details of the scientific movement in American education, see: Meyer, *op. cit.,* pp. 281-284.

of Sigmund Freud who stressed the role of the unconscious in explaining the vagaries or abnormalities of human behavior. Freud's theories were over-hauled by Alfred Adler and Carl Jung who relied less on sex than Freud and depended more on psychological types. American educational theories and practices, without being too willing to acknowledge it, have been con-siderably influenced by Freudian beliefs about instincts and Adler's contribu-tion of the inferiority complex.

THE GERMAN UNIVERSITY. Many of the German influences that have been documented in this chapter stemmed from the German university. While English universities gave origin and initial form and development to higher education in America, the intellectual nourishment for American scholarship in the nineteenth century was largely a result of contacts with German universities.[51]

The history of this impact is also a history of a grand international and intercultural migration of students and scholars. Although Germany was far more remote to most Americans than either England or France and the Ger-man language more of a foreign tongue than the French, almost 10,000 Americans studied at German universities during the last century. Through them, through the scores of Americans who came to know Germany, through publications and/or visits, and through German expatriates teaching in American institutions of higher learning, the methods and the ideals of the German university were imported into the United States.

America did not, however, copy the German system bodily; it simply took from German sources that which fitted her needs and which could be accul-turated within the social framework. The first men to pioneer in this academic venture to Germany went to Göttingen. This was well before 1850 when larger numbers followed the trail to Germany. In this early group were Edward Everett, George Ticknor, George Bancroft, and Joseph Cogswell; they all became important men in American educational history. While Everett failed to transform Harvard into the German pattern, Bancroft and Cogswell succeeded at the Round Hill School which they opened in North-ampton, Massachusetts, as a model of a gymnasium of the more liberal type and which attracted during its first eight years 293 students from 19 States. Ticknor became the first professor of modern languages at Harvard; George Bancroft was to be a shining light in American historical scholarship. Ralph Waldo Emerson studied at Göttingen in 1824 and Henry W. Longfellow in 1829. Up to 1850 some 100 Americans enrolled at Göttingen, Berlin, Halle, and Leipzig. The possession of a German degree became the passport

---

[51] See Charles F. Thwing, *The American and the German University: One Hundred Years of History* (New York: The Macmillan Co., 1928).

into American academic circles. Thwing explained how these men upon their return to their native land profoundly influenced American education.[52] He particularly emphasized the spirit of freedom in learning and in teaching, together with the keen appreciation of scholarship. The German schools inspired their students to independent research and thought and they provided a sense of understanding of the deep need for proper scholastic tools, such as laboratories and libraries.

As mentioned previously, these men, and others, were joined by a group of Germanic scholars of renown who joined the faculties of American universities — such as Charles Beck, Francis Lieber, and Louis Agassiz. Another group who studied in Germany and who became presidents of American universities, thereby influencing a number of important changes in American education, were: Henry Barnard (Wisconsin), Henry Tappan (Michigan), William Folwell (Minnesota), Andrew White (Cornell), Daniel Coit Gilman (California and Johns Hopkins), G. Stanley Hall (Clark), James Angel (Michigan), Charles Eliot (Harvard), and Edmund James (Illinois). Probably the most enthusiastic was Henry Tappan, President of the University of Michigan from 1852 to 1863, who was fortunate enough to be called upon to head the institution by the founders who had read the report of Victor Cousin on German schools. Under Tappan's guidance, the University of Michigan took the lead among the younger state institutions, widely imitated in the West. Of similar stature was Charles W. Eliot, President of Harvard from 1869 to 1909, who directed the expansion of the small New England college of the traditional type into a powerful undergraduate college, surrounded by a large number of professional schools of the highest caliber, plus a first-class graduate school. Cornell and Johns Hopkins also both featured the German system, especially the cultivation of experimental sciences and the creation of great libraries.

In higher education, Germany helped introduce to America the elective system, the lecture, the seminar method, the mushroom growth of the sciences, the development of graduate studies, the support of scholarship and research activities, and a deepened sense of liberty in learning and teaching.

OTHER GERMAN PERSONALITIES. We have undoubtedly overlooked a number of Germans who contributed to the heritage of American education. Four more, however, will serve as concluding examples of the varied and important carryover of German ideas to American educational institutions.

August Herman Francke (1663-1727) has been called the "noblest example of the practical Christian educator of Germany."[53] As pastor of a Lutheran church and professor at the University of Halle, he developed a series of

---

[52] Thwing, *ibid.*, pp. 321-322.
[53] Eby, *op. cit.*, p. 247.

educational institutions that became noted throughout Europe. Included was an orphanage, an elementary school, a Bible institute, a Burghers' school, a Latin gymnasium, and his Padagogium (for children of the nobility). In addition, he ran two teacher training institutions at the University. In spite of an overriding, pietistic, religious emphasis in his school programs, he offered a very broad and practical school curriculum. His influence reached beyond Prussia and ultimately to the United States, and this has been described in the sections on Moravian and Lutheran education in the previous chapter. One of Francke's students was Johann Hecker (1707-1768) who founded one of the first realschules providing a second-track secondary education of a terminal nature for boys who were not going to go to the Latin gymnasium. This was established in 1747, very close to the time of the rise of a similar practical institution (Franklin's academy) in America. Hecker's influence also reached America through the work of Zinzendorf and Muhlenberg who carried Francke's ideas into the New World. Hecker wrote the general code for Prussian schools in 1763, and, as we have seen from the previous discussion, this system, with modifications through the years, came to be highly praised and aspects were adapted in the United States.

Johann Basedow (1723-1790) was the greatest and most interesting of the eighteenth century German school reformers; he breathed new life into continental schools and in many ways anticipated Pestalozzi. He was a sense realist, taken with Rousseau's ideas, but a skillful eclectic who, going beyond Rousseau, recognized the need for teacher training and the great lack of children's literature and who built a school and provided materials that attained the aims of many of the great educators before him. His *Elementarwerk* (1770), became the most famous educational work of its time and it contained an amazing variety of valuable information that Basedow claimed included all the content and methodology teachers needed to educate the young. At his experimental school, the Philanthropinum, he and his excellent teachers demonstrated many advanced theories of education. The system of scholarships, the school spirit, the individualized attention, purposeful projects, summer camp, group work, correlated instruction, student aides, learning games, student government, and "modern" content including sex education and current affairs instruction marked the school as an amazing institution. Basedow's teachers wrote a number of influential textbooks and novels, and his instructors in physical education were instrumental in forwarding their ideas through the Turner movement. The latter ideas reached America with German immigrants in the early nineteenth century, but the bulk of Basedow's contributions did not appear until many of them were incorporated into the progressive education movement.[54]

---

[54] Very little is available in English on Basedow; Cole, *op. cit.*, Chapter XIV, reviews a number of interesting details of his school.

Johann Herbart (1776-1841) became a noted German educator at the universities of Göttingen and Koenigsburg where he succeeded Immanuel Kant. (See also Chapter VIII, pp. 304-5.) Herbart was concerned with developing educational principles and a system of instruction that would be based upon a sound psychology of learning. At the time of his death he realized that he had not progressed very far toward these goals with any certainty, but his followers in Germany spread his ideas until his philosophy and psychology of education were dominant forces in shaping the curriculum and instructional method. Herbart was able to shape Pestalozzi's theories into a usable system and these ultimately were stated in the famous five steps of preparation, presentation, association, generalization, and application which provided guidelines for a successful act of teaching and learning. Herbart saw the need for lesson plans and has been called the grandfather of the unit method. His ideas became very influential in the United States in the latter half of the nineteenth century with the stream of American students returning to these shores. Herbart's views have now been replaced largely by more advanced psychological and educational knowledge, but the championship of his methods by Charles De Garmo and Charles and Frank McMurray brought the five steps of teaching to the ken of most teachers trained in the United States at that time. To forward the scientific study of education, these men helped organize the National Herbartian Society (1892) which changed its name in 1902 to the National Society for the Scientific Study of Education. American educators soon moved ahead and turned from slavish adherence to Herbartianism, wherein unfortunately many teachers had allowed helpful means of instruction to become sterile ends in themselves.

This survey of Germanic influences has revealed the extent to which Americans are educationally indebted to these peoples. The influence came later and was not as fundamental as the British origins; but should someone seek to marshal all the evidence, he might well present a strong case for German contributions as being the most important factor during the adolescent period of United States education when it reached towards maturity and prepared to make its own unique impressions upon the world.

Other Continental Influences

Russian and Scandinavian Factors

It is not commonly known that in addition to the influence exerted from Russia by Pavlov on American psychological behaviorism (which reached its zenith early in the 1920's), portions of one other aspect of American education — industrial arts education — can be traced to Russia.

In 1880 Calvin M. Woodward, professor at Washington University, laid the beginnings of industrial arts education as an organized enterprise by opening the St. Louis Manual Training School. The courses of shopwork were based upon those developed by Della Vos in the Imperial Teaching School of Moscow, Russia.[55] An exhibit of the results of that famed institution were displayed at the Centennial Exposition at Philadelphia (1876). The samples of metal and woodwork attracted the attention of John Runkle, President of the new Massachusetts Institute of Technology, who had been searching far and wide for ideas which might be integrated in the work of rising M.I.T. His eulogistic reports on the exhibit provoked an interest in manual training as well as discussions on the nature of education in general. His address delivered in St. Louis some two years later led to the establishment of America's first manual training high school.

This "Russian system," modified for American conditions, and developed by the St. Louis Manual Training School, became the standard example of educational shop courses in the secondary schools of America for several decades. These courses were built of carefully graded series of exercises, or "models," based upon detailed analyses of tool processes. Accent was placed upon accuracy and correctness of procedure, as well as upon the general educative (as contrasted with the specific occupational-training values) of the work.

The system became popular almost immediately, especially in other privately supported schools, and within two years of the start of this experiment in St. Louis, manual training tended to become popular in the public elementary and secondary schools. Under the leadership of Woodward, in contrast to other technical instruction, this program stressed a general education in and systematic study of the motor skills associated with common tools, as general preparation for later specific technical activity; furthermore, he believed that manual training helped the development of intellectual capability as much as symbolic material improved and directed motor activity.

After 1888 the Swedish "sloyd," as developed by Otto Salomon (1849-1907) in Sweden and by Gustaf Larson (1861-1919) in Boston, began to impress America's manual and industrial education.[56]

In the second half of the last century, Sweden's home industries were hard pressed by competition of the rising factories. The government believed that a remedy could be found in manual training, and in 1872 manual training (sloyd) was introduced into the Swedish schools; by 1877 the movement had been absorbed by the Swedish Folk Schools. Salomon, a Swedish schoolman, after touring neighboring Finland, started to remodel his country's program

---

[55] Charles A. Bennett, *History of Manual and Industrial Education 1870 to 1917* (Peoria, Illinois: The Manual Arts Press, 1937), Chapter I.

[56] Bennett, *ibid.*, Chapter II.

of manual training on that example, especially on the theory that the student was to do his own work from beginning to end, that what he made should be useful as well as ornamental, and that the modeling be based on real objects rather than patterns.

In 1888 a special Sloyd Training school was founded in Boston; the moving spirit of the enterprise was Gustaf Larson, its first Principal, who was born in Sweden and educated in the Swedish Normal School of Sloyd. Over 400 teachers of arts and crafts were sent out from the Boston institution, and ten subsidiary centers were founded as far away as in Mexico and India. This type of manual training was interested not only in accuracy and disciplinary procedures, but also in "the utility of the models in the home or to the children personally," and the "development of the sense of form and beauty." These two elements were vital to a continued development in industrial activities in the new schools and, combining them with the establishing courses of manual training, placed these courses on an "enduring foundation of a phase of general education."[57]

In the 1870's and early 1880's Danish agriculture was hard hit by foreign competition in the European grain markets. Wheat fell in value and at that time the chief product of Danish farms was corn. The Danish peasantry successfully turned for a remedy to technical improvements and an altered production program, rather than to protection, and soon were exporting butter and bacon rather than grains. This adaptability is one example of the work credited to the Folk or People's High Schools and to the new group of leaders of the peasantry who organized the new agricultural program and who, for the most part, were graduates of the Folk High Schools.

In the background was the influence of a small body of disciples of N. F. S. Grundtvig (1783-1872), noted pastor, poet, historian, and educational reformer. It is claimed that what Arnold of Rugby did for England, Grundtvig, in another sphere of education, did for Denmark.[58] He was inspired by the idea of liberty and the power of wisdom, and with his followers (chief among them Christian Kold, 1816-1870) founded the People's High Schools. These Folk Schools gave the essence of a liberal education to farmers' sons and

---

[57] C. P. Coates, *History of the Manual Training School of Washington University* (*the St. Louis Manual Training School*) (Washington, D.C.: U.S. Bureau of Education, 1923), Bulletin 1923, No. 3, p. 605; for more details on the evolution of manual training and vocational education, see A. B. Mays, *The Determining Factors in the Evolution of the Industrial Arts in America* (Milwaukee: Bruce Publishing Co., 1924) and W. P. Sears, *The Roots of Vocational Education* (New York: John Wiley, 1931).

[58] For the best survey, see: Holger Begtrup and others, *The Folk High Schools of Denmark and the Development of a Farming Community* (London: Oxford University Press, 1949); also see: Olive Campbell, *The Danish Folk School* (New York: The Macmillan Co., 1928).

271

daughters and to young adults as well. They also built an effective spirit of cooperation and problem-solving. The humanities were central in the schools but, nevertheless, the programs did not breed traditional intellectuals. Between 1860 and 1880 the Folk Schools are credited with working a miracle in the culture of the Danish countryside. The spiritual growth of the students was also not neglected and the schools became excellent examples of the combination of cultural studies with practical social needs.

The idea soon spread to other Scandinavian countries. Later, at the end of the nineteenth and early twentieth century, in the United States and Canada some Folk High Schools were founded in the mid-continent and western regions where there were centers of Danish immigration. However, only a few of these schools are still active, usually on a curtailed summer basis. Nevertheless, some of the main features of modern adult education (part-time classes, enrollment age 18 and over, instruction at hours and times convenient to workers, applicatory cultural offerings, practical courses, limited homework, etc.) had origins in the ideas employed in the Scandinavian Folk Schools.

While it can be seen that the main Scandinavian influences have been of a vocational nature, it should also be reported that they have made definite contributions with their handicraft orientations, especially when applied in the field of occupational therapeutics. Their skills in arts and crafts have been particularly important not only in aiding mental recovery but in promoting the rehabilitation of the crippled and the handicapped. A number of leaders in the United States in these areas of work are of Scandinavian extraction.

Italian Contributions

This relatively brief survey of foreign and immigrant influences would be incomplete if we did not note the impact made by Maria Montessori (1869-1952) of Italy. The first woman to receive an M.D. from the University of Rome, Madam Montessori worked initially with mentally deficient children and developed special didactic materials for training them through the use of each of the senses. When some of her children outshone normal children in their learnings, she became interested in extending her work. After further graduate studies in pedagogy and anthropology, she opened, in 1907, her first *Casa de Bambini,* a school for children between three and seven in a remodeled tenement building. These spread in Italy and meanwhile she developed a program for the entire elementary grades. As early as 1911 the Montessori system was established in Swiss schools and her children's schools became popular in Great Britain. She visited the United States in 1917 and later circled the world, starting Montessori Societies and classes to spread her ideas and approaches. By 1916 there were over 100 Montessori classes in the United States, most of them established in private schools.

Madam Montessori was, of course, greatly indebted to Pestalozzi and Froebel and operated in terms of three basic principles: learning through the senses, individualized self-learning, and freedom in learning. Like Pestalozzi, she showed that properly motivated children can learn much and work for sustained periods of time, even at a very early age. She was particularly effective in developing reading competencies, arithmetic ability, an under-standing of nature, and good health habits, as well as having amazing success in teaching little children to burst spontaneously into script writing as a result of her kinesthetic method of instruction.[59] Among other contributions, she showed the virtue of flexible time schedules, of well planned instructional periods, of adapting the curriculum to fit local needs, and she introduced the anecdotal record.

Her classes were closed by the Fascists in Italy in 1933 and she set up new headquarters in India. After the second World War she returned to Europe and lived in the Netherlands until her death. While Montessori schools exist in these latter areas today, in the United States almost all have disappeared. However, again, many of her approaches have been absorbed, with modifica-tion, into regular school programs and debate continues as to the virtue of attempting to achieve some of the things she claimed could and should be accomplished with small children.

Giovanni Gentile and Benedetto Croce were Italian thinkers who had impact upon European thought but their educational views are little known in the United States.

Summary

The main contributions from abroad were felt during the early periods of American educational history. Even throughout the nineteenth century it has been stated that "the best in American pedagogic theory was of alien origin."[60] However, as has been evidenced, the carryover of foreign influences into the twentieth century remained significant in many areas from the primary years to the graduate school.

In the late nineteenth century a native pedagogy began to rise in the United States, thanks to several first-rate men whose theories and premises are still valid. Outstanding among them was Francis W. Parker (1837-1902), who, true to the fashion of the day, had studied in Germany. On his return to

---

[59] Madam Montessori presents a complete description of her philosophy, materials, and methods in *Montessori Method* (New York: Frederick A. Stokes Co., 1912).

[60] Meyer, *op. cit.*, p. 245.

America he tried out the ideas of Pestalozzi, Basedow, Herbart, and Froebel. He was, however, no mere imitator and as superintendent he launched a revolutionary program at Quincy, Massachusetts, that soon drew national attention.[61] Parker was called to head the Cook County Normal School at Chicago and became involved in working with John Dewey who was professor of philosophy and education at the University of Chicago. With Parker's death, Dewey succeeded him as "father" of the progressive education movement then evolving. Dewey belonged to the same philosophical group as William James, the founder of Pragmatism, and of Charles Peirce, the coiner of the word. Dewey derived his ideas from a number of great educators (this is discussed in Chapters XI and XII), but many of his contributions were looked upon as being original American educational theories and practices and were passed into public learning through the progressive movement.

The emerging twentieth century educational theory in America, although rooted abroad in its historical development and indebted there for certain seminal ideas, was influenced minimally by the then contemporary European education. This became particularly true following the period of the first World War.

The only direct foreign influences of any moment in the history of American education are traceable to European backgrounds. In this respect the most dominant, the British, made their more definite impression in colonial times. The foundation of American culture was laid by the English peoples, although it must be stressed that from the beginning this was a process of acculturation rather than of exact transplantation. The concepts of apprenticeship, the compulsory principle of education, vocational education practices, and the Latin grammar school, for example, grew from British ideas. For all their variety and number (now more than 1,200) the four-year American college leading to the bachelor's degree is also a native adaptation of the English idea of higher education. Taking their origins from the seventeenth century collegiate schools of New England and Virginia, the colleges spread like a prairie fire across the land. Even in the post-revolutionary period of awakening, efforts to experiment with ideas imported from England continued. For example, academies expanded and the Lancastrian Monitorial Movement and Infant Schools were introduced.

In any consideration of eighteenth-century America, the Scots deserve some special attention since they were such an important group in the cultural development of the colonies. The heritage brought by Scottish teachers and private tutors helped in the civilization of the isolated regions. Their greatest cultural contribution was their insistence upon a learned ministry and the

---

[61] Parker wrote very little. He described "The Quincy Method" in the *American Journal of Sociology,* VI, 1900, pp. 117-124; see also his *Talks on Teaching* (1896) and his *Talks on Pedagogics* (1894), published by E. L. Kellogg and Co., New York.

necessity for a classical education. They founded schools, academies, and colleges in all areas of America, their major monument being Princeton which had great influence on education on the early frontier. English and Scotch influences declined with the development of the United States, but today many aspects of American education continue to reflect the British heritage — be it the Sunday school movement, the church-maintained liberal arts college, or the educational program of the Y.M.C.A.

France represented, after England, the second dominant international influence that helped to form education in the United States. French ideas were at the base of the foundation of the University of Virginia and affected its representative spokesman, Thomas Jefferson. The French Huguenots made distinguished contributions to the rise of intellectual and artistic life and the French in New Orleans and surrounding territory have left an important economic and social heritage. French influence can also be seen in the university organization in the United States and the whole conception of centralized state systems of education had French origins. The heritage of universal state education for national ends, of freedom of thought, and of secular learning is also indebted to French beginnings. In more recent times we can discern the influence exerted by Comte and Durkheim on the rise of American educational sociology, together with the psycho-sociological theories of Tarde and LeBon. Also from French beginnings came successful efforts in the education of the feeble-minded, the blind, and the origination of the mental testing movement.

Various German sects, the largest composed of German-Lutheran or Reformed backgrounds began reaching the shores of America during the colonial era. During the nineteenth century German immigration outnumbered all others and they contributed individually and collectively to the fields of arts, agriculture, business, science, and industry in addition to their remarkable ideas in the field of education. The German university was a particularly strong force in shaping American educational history, particularly through students and visitors who brought back educational practices that affected all levels of public and private education. The ideas of Sturm, Pestalozzi, Froebel, Herbart, Fellenberg, and others were accepted and interpreted by American followers, and developments from the kindergarten to state normal schools can be traced to such German origins. In addition, many German scholars and expatriates came to the United States and further improved and shaped our educational institutions.

Although Russia, before the rise of the Soviet system, had been under pressure from some of its leaders who were trying to westernize its culture, there was a minimal educational interchange between it and the United States. However, Pavlov's concept of behaviorism and Russian practices in industrial arts education made a definite impact on American education.

Scandinavian experiments in home industries impressed America's manual and industrial education and their Folk High Schools provided examples of wise practices in adult education.

In recent times the influences from abroad have not been so direct but the international cross-currents of Western European ideas remain evident in American education and reflect the contributions of Freud, Binet, Wundt, Montessori, and others. Perhaps the most important developments of the twentieth century reflect a reversed turn in the major direction of flow of educational ideas and practices. Educational theories and approaches have always crossed the Atlantic in both directions and will so continue, but more recently there has been a mounting increase in the flow from America to Europe and the rest of the world. This overdue return by America for its rich inheritances has set European education in a flux of revisionist activities. From Britain to the Soviet Union there is ferment in education of all kinds and at all levels. At long last the circle of influence has turned back and a number of these contributions are identified in Chapters XI and XII wherein American modifications and creations in education are highlighted.

Bibliography

Brown, Francis J. and Joseph S. Roucek, Eds., *One America: The History, Contributions, and Present Problems of Our Racial and National Minorities*. New York: Prentice-Hall, 3d ed., 1952.

Butts, R. Freeman and Lawrence A. Cremin, *A History of Education in American Culture*. New York: Henry Holt & Co., 1953.

Cole, Luella, *A History of Education*. New York: Rinehart & Co., 1950.

Cubberley, Ellwood P., *The History of Education*. Boston: Houghton Mifflin, 1920.

Curti, Merle, *The Social Ideas of American Educators*. New York: Charles Scribner's Sons, 1935.

Degler, Carl N., *Out of Our Past: Forces That Shaped Modern America*. New York: Harper, 1959.

Eby, Frederick, *The Development of Modern Education,* Second Edition. New York: Prentice-Hall, 1952.

Eggleston, Edward, *The Transit of Civilization From England to America in the Seventeenth Century*. New York: D. Appleton & Co., 1900.

Good, H. G., *A History of American Education*. New York: The Macmillan Co., 1956.

Handlin, Oscar, *The American People in the Twentieth Century*. Cambridge: Harvard University Press, 1954.

Johnson, Gerald W., *Our English Heritage*. Philadelphia: J. B. Lippincott, 1949.

Jones, Howard M., *America and French Culture, 1750-1848*. Chapel Hill: University of North Carolina Press, 1927.

Kandel, I. L., *History of Secondary Education: A Study in the Development of Liberal Education*. Boston: Houghton Mifflin, 1930.

McKay, Donald C., *The United States and France*. Cambridge: Harvard University Press, 1951.

Meyer, Adolphe E., *An Educational History of the American People*. New York: McGraw-Hill Book Co., 1957.

Noble, Stuart G., *A History of American Education*. New York: Rinehart & Co., 1954.

Pochmann, Henry A. and others, *German Culture in America, 1600-1900: Philosophical and Literary Influences*. Madison: University of Wisconsin Press, 1957.

Sands, Lester B. and Richard E. Gross, *History of Education Chart,* Third Edition. Stanford, California: Stanford University Press, 1957.

Thistlethwaite, Frank, *The Anglo-American Connection in the Early Nineteenth Century*. Philadelphia: University of Pennsylvania Press, 1959.

Thwing, Charles F., *The American and the German University: One Hundred Years of History*. New York: The Macmillan Co., 1928.

Walz, John A., *German Influence in American Education and Culture*. Philadelphia: Carl Schurz Memorial Foundation, 1936.

Wittke, Carl, *We Who Built America: The Saga of the Immigrant*. New York: Prentice-Hall, 1946.

****

CHAPTER VIII

KEY IDEAS FROM GREAT FOREIGN
EDUCATIONAL THINKERS

We are concerned in this chapter with the key ideas from great foreign educators and thinkers that have had a particularly lasting effect upon thought and practice in American education. Since limitations of space demand a high degree of selectivity, we will be omitting both men and ideas that others would include by right of personal choice. This is unavoidable, and the best that we can hope for is that our choices are intelligent ones, wise in the sense that they give us a keener insight into the fundamental meanings and values which we attach to the American educational program. Also, other choices of theorists the reader might select may well be discussed in other chapters.

To accomplish our purpose it is necessary that we have some idea of both structure and time. First, it is recognized that American education is a part of Western culture and that therefore the educators and thinkers with which we are concerned are a product of that culture. Second, in so far as our educational heritage in terms of ideas is concerned, there is a great division of thought between the old order and the new which occurs at the time of John Locke (seventeenth century, A.D.). There is therefore a body of ideas which we shall designate as Classical-Christian which developed prior to 1600 A.D. and which profoundly contributed to America's educational heritage. In developing these ancient and medieval ideas we shall identify them with two great classical thinkers, Plato and Aristotle, and two great Christian writers, St. Augustine and St. Thomas Aquinas.

Our second pattern of ideas which began to develop around the seventeenth century will be considered transitional in character, as best identified with the period of the American Revolution and the nineteenth century, and as pointing to the significance of the individual as contrasted with the prior emphasis on the divine order in the educational process. These ideas will be keynoted in the contributions of four men, John Amos Comenius, John Locke, Jean Jacques Rousseau and Herbert Spencer.

Education in America during the twentieth century has been profoundly influenced by a number of ideas coming from another group of European writers and scholars of the late eighteenth century and nineteenth century. These writers point toward a third pattern of ideas which involves a socio-psychological concept of the learner and the learning process as a part of the movement to reassess the role of meaning and value in the life structure. These new ideas are best represented in the contributions of Immanuel Kant, Jean Heinrich Pestalozzi, Johann Friedrich Herbart, and Friedrich Froebel; and are further extended in the writing of numerous scholars among whom are Charles Darwin, Sir Francis Galton, Alfred Binet and Wolfgang Köhler. They constitute the background of thought out of which much of American educational practice of the twentieth century has developed, and are especially identified with the thinking of John Dewey.

Key Ideas from the Classical-Christian Heritage

As explained in previous chapters, it is from the classical cultures of the ancient world of Greece and Rome and from the religion of the Hebrew and Christian peoples that we derived the key ideas on which Western civilization was built and operated until the eighteenth century. Our problem here is to identify these ideas as a part of America's moral and intellectual heritage.

Colonial America of the seventeenth century has been rightly referred to as a medieval civilization tempered by rationalism. This is said not without due recognition of the challenge of frontier life and the everyday demands of the new world. What we are concerned with here is the life of the mind, with level of insight and intelligence of the people who first colonized the new world, with their meaning and value structure. From an ideological standpoint the mind of seventeenth century colonial America was a closed mind in which all things were viewed in terms of status and absolutes. There was that pervading belief that everything good was handed down from on high whether from God or the Crown. God existed in his heaven, on his throne, above the earth, while Satan abided in regions below amidst hellfire and brimstone. Neither the concept of democracy nor that of individualism had as yet come into practice on any significant scale. There was as yet no realization of the idea of progress or the potentiality of scientific knowledge.

The magic of prayer was still thought to ward off evil and to bring rain. Witches still lived and often cast their evil spells upon both old and young, while in the slave markets men were sold as beasts of burden.

Regardless of what aspect of colonial American life we consider, whether economic, political, social, cultural or religious, we see the same pattern of knowledge as that which had prevailed in Europe for more than 1,000 years. As yet, the colonists show no evidence of having heard of Copernicus or of the revolution in science which was to follow. Their most marked characteristic was their Protestantism, which, while violent in its opposition to the central authority of the medieval world, was, at the same time, medieval in spirit and obsessed with the problems of sin, grace and salvation. Also, there was a fierce devotion to the medieval ideal of uniformity of faith and a general intolerance of dissent.[1] This blind allegiance to another-worldly order of superstition and brutality is borne out in the first best seller in the New World, Michael Wigglesworth's *Day of Doom* (1662) and in *The New England Primer* (1690), the first real elementary school reader used by the colonial child.

If the program of education found in the elementary schools of the colonies reflected most strongly the moral purpose in Christian education, a program well illustrated in the Old Deluder Satan Act (1647) of the Colony of Massachusetts, instruction provided at the secondary and college levels truly emphasized an almost complete reliance upon the contributions of classical Greece and Rome. While it is important to recognize that the languages of greatest importance in the several colonial church colleges were Greek and Latin, it is of even greater importance to point up the key fundamental concepts, and their creators, around which the colonial culture pattern of meaning and value was structured. See Chapter XI for more details on the above conditions.

In a very real and genuine sense, education as viewed from the Classical-Christian point of view was a process of preparation or of getting ready for a life that was to come. The eternal life, and thus the good life, was not that in which man lived as a natural being, but rather that life which followed in a supernatural order of soul being. Socially this was carried out so that there was no such thing as education for childhood, only that of preparation for adult life. This raises the fundamental question of whether or not an education which emphasizes the possibilities of life after death can, at the same time, contribute to the full development of present natural life possibilities. Judged by the record of the time, the old order of being, in this respect, surely failed. There was indeed a peculiar contradiction between the edict of

---

[1] Herbert Muller, *The Uses of the Past* (New York: Oxford University Press, 1952) p. 268.

"change or die" which confronted the adventurer in the new world and the formal religious and educational affirmation of defense for the status quo.

Yet, as one looks back to the origin of the basic ideas around which the classical and medieval Christian educational programs evolved one is struck both by their positive nature and their continuing significance for our present program of American education. It would seem that their key significance lies in that larger understanding of the nature of being, of the relation of the knower and the known. Without that larger insight which comes from the key ideas implicit in the foundations of Western culture our present educational program would be like a picture puzzle with more than half of the pieces lost. Viewed in this light American education would be much the poorer if there had been no Plato, no Aristotle, no St. Augustine, and no St. Thomas Aquinas.

Platonic Ideas

It is in the writings of Plato (427-347 B.C.) that we find the first clear-cut recognition of the significance of theory, of ideas or concepts about the world which make up the nature of the mind of the individual. To Plato, these ideas were "perfect realities," the highest of which was the Idea of the Good, or his supreme God. A good illustration of Plato's "perfect realities" would be the assumption that the "idea" of a chair is eternal whereas the chair itself is only temporal and of passing significance. While the material world was knowledgeable by sense perception, the real world, or world of ideas, was knowable only by contemplation, intuition, or communication with the supernatural world which lies above, beyond, and outside the natural world. This is the essence of the Platonic doctrine of innate ideas that ruled the Western World until the eighteenth century.

Societies before Plato's time had been founded on custom and belief, but Plato would have them founded on the truth of an idea. Thus, stated another way, Plato was the first of the world's great educational philosophers. His belief that only through education could the world be made a better place in which to live is among the most profound ideas in the history of Western culture. It is an idea which is not only more alive today than in any past century, but is probably the source of man's best hope for the future. Real meaning and value came to man as he struggled to attain the ideal community, not as he sought to defend the status quo with its injustices in the world around him.

Plato's deepest concern is with the problem of justice, another key idea which he affirms is most clearly seen in the social and political relations of man. In analyzing the individual approach to the problem of justice, Plato finds such an approach deficient because it is always based upon personal self-interest. Justice could not be based upon what an individual thought was due him or upon the interest of the stronger, because such narrow self-interest could never produce harmonious relationships between individuals. It was the harmonious relations developed between the three classes which made up society, and which expressed the virtues of wisdom (ruling class), courage (fighting class) and temperance (working class), that produced the ultimate of social good, or the cardinal virtue of justice. Note that in this connection the problem is seen as not being one which singularly involves the relation between the knower and the object but rather that of the quality of relationship which exists between one class and another. As we speak of democracy today the emphasis would be on the quality of the relationship existing between individuals rather than Plato's assumed social realities.

There is profound importance in the Platonic idea that those who rule over the people should be the best educated of the people. The significance of this concept is illustrated in the intellectualizing of the leadership of both Catholic and Protestant Churches, in the enlightened despotisms of Europe, in the high quality of leadership found in the government of the British empire for the past 200 years, and in the crying need for more intelligent administration in the local, state and national governments of the United States.

Writing in the *Republic*, Plato had this to say about intelligent, responsible political leadership:

> Until philosophers are kings, or the kings and princes of this world have the spirit and power of philosophy, and political greatness and wisdom meet in one, and those commoner natures who pursue either to the exclusion of the other are compelled to stand aside, cities will never have rest from their evils, — no, nor the human race, as I believe, — and then only will this our State have a possibility of life and behold the light of day.[2]

This is the same point of view expressed by Thomas Jefferson in his "A Bill for the More General Diffusion of Knowledge" which he submitted to the Legislature of Virginia in 1779. Plato, unlike the other Ancients, would have accorded the opportunity to become such an intellectual leader to women, whose education, in theory, he favored.

One other key idea of Plato which is deeply rooted in our heritage is that of education as a redirection of the soul; for the child at birth was turned in the wrong direction. To save the soul from self-deceit and disillusionment it must be cleansed of the lie that is implicit in its birth. One can reject the assumption that the child at birth has any such spiritual essence, evil or otherwise, and still affirm the concept that moral education is the logical

---

[2] Book V.

foundation of any sound educational system. As a living, developing entity, Plato saw the soul as needing protection against the evil forces which might well overtake it. To accomplish this end there must be much state supervision and control, even censorship. Only through right training beginning in the nursery could the soul of the child be directed to that love of excellence which was a necessary part of a perfected manhood. Moral sensitivity to the welfare of one's fellow man would seem to be the ultimate positive product which has come out of this aspect of the Platonic heritage.

Christianity provided the first medium through which the key ideas of Plato, especially that of moral education, could come into being. In building on the Platonic heritage, St. Augustine (354-430 A.D.) modified and added on to the original Platonic ideas, for St. Augustine, more than any other thinker of his period, brought about a fusion of "ancient culture with the Christian religion."[3] With the coming of the Renaissance, during the fifteenth century, and the movement toward humanism in Western culture, Plato's ideas, as a part of the revival of interest in classical culture, found a new birth in philosophy, politics and education. Before pointing up the key Christian ideas found in the writings of St. Augustine and St. Thomas Aquinas, however, we need to identify these classical ideas to which Aristotle (386-322 B.C.) directed our attention. (See also Chapter II.)

Aristotelian Ideas

In many respects Aristotle's ideas on education are only an extension of those of Plato, but, even so, there are certain key ideas which we particularly identify with him. Aristotle, as contrasted with Plato, emphasized the need for facts before coming to a conclusion. Thus Aristotle was the first of the great scholars to organize and to classify knowledge in the various respective areas upon which both the medieval and the modern universities built their programs. In this respect, he could be considered more scientific than Plato and to have had a more paramount influence on the educational process. No one single scholar in all the history of Western civilization contributed more greatly to that profound sense of a need for knowledge, for understanding, before making a policy decision. Aristotle certainly was the key intellectual figure in the medieval university and in its colonial American counterpart, the church college.

Aristotle's form-matter hypothesis is the key idea around which the people of the Western World organized their thinking about the nature of the world in which they lived, and of the meaning and value of life. His dynamic

---

[3] S. J. Curtis and M. E. A. Boultwood, *A Short History of Educational Ideas* (London: University Tutorial Press, 1953), p. 70.

conception of the universe begins with a concrete thing whose nature is determined by both form and matter. First-matter according to Aristotle is not describable because description comes only with form, and without form there is no meaning, no knowledge. All this, when thinking of the tree in relation to the acorn, points to first matter as potentiality and form as actuality. It was Aristotle who formulated the idea of the fixity of species, a theory which served the Christian world until modern times as a basis for understanding the nature of man, an idea which stands in striking contrast to the modern concept of evolution.

While both Plato and Aristotle treat of education in relation to politics, it is in Aristotle's *Politics* that we find the most detailed elaboration of the idea of the state as a primary institution. Since the state is the institution through which the common good is to be realized, politics in Aristotelian thought is supreme among the arts, for in politics man can best find use for all the arts. Concerning the relation of the citizen to the state Aristotle had this to say:

> But matters of public interest ought to be under public supervision; at the same time also we ought not to think that any of the citizens belongs to himself, but that all belong to the state, for each is a part of the state, and it is natural for the superintendence of the several parts to have regard to the superintendence of the whole.[4]

Education is the most important of the subordinate arts for it is through education under the control of the state that a man acquires the necessary intelligence and character for good living. Hence the present day tendency of making the state the supreme authority over the education of the child is an Aristotelian rather than a democratic idea.

Aristotle also forwards the view that there are two kinds of goodness, that of character which is for all the people, and that of intellect which is for the few. Here not only is the justification for Plato's idea of the rule of the few who are intellectuals but for the right of the control of education exercised by the European and Colonial American aristocracy. Only the few who rule can discover right for themselves. The great mass of people must be trained to follow. Since the happiness of man ultimately depends upon the intellect, leisure time is only for those who can engage in pure intellectual activity. While this idea also was used for centuries to support a class-conscious society, it nevertheless was the foundation of the great liberal arts program of the universities and the felt need for intellectually responsible state leadership.

---

[4] Aristotle, *Politics, Chapter I,* Rackham translation (Cambridge: Harvard University Press, Loeb Classical Library Series).

Augustinian Contributions

St. Augustine, operating from within the Christian Church and as a product of one schooled in Platonism, made such significant contributions that his key ideas on education were built into the framework of Christian dogma. Their universal significance for us lies in their time, in their utility, and in their functional worth, not in their affirmation of absolute truth. It should be observed that, in this respect, the solutions at which St. Augustine arrived on many questions dealing with the process and meaning of life are in direct contradiction to those ideas found in the writings of modern scholars from John Locke to John Dewey.

St. Augustine's most basic and key idea on education is that the single source for teaching man knowledge is God. By this he meant that ideas do not come from some external agency such as a sense experience, or through the medium of language, but rather they exist in the mind itself (Plato's innate ideas). Since only words are exchanged between teacher and pupil, according to St. Augustine, the true function of language is to awaken that which is already in the mind. A teacher can help explain or define an idea in words, but he does not create the idea. Since the teacher learned the truth that was in his own soul, a light that proceeds only from God, all he can do is to help his pupil do the same. St. Augustine used the term "Divine Illumination" as a kind of metaphor in which the activity of the mind in thinking is compared with the eye in vision.

Closely related to St. Augustine's basic idea that the single source for teaching man knowledge of God, is his key idea that all universal truths grasped by the mind are Divine ideas. Actually, he saw these universal truths existing in two forms, first and originally in the mind of God, and second in the physical world where they provide the only reality that the world possesses, giving it both order and purpose. In Augustinian thought, the mind of man is only an instrument more or less capable of grasping the Divine ideas which have been revealed in the Holy Scripture. On this point a distinction is to be made between what is to be enjoyed as an end in itself and that which is to serve only as a means to an end. Christians needed to know the liberal arts (Aristotelian influence) because they provided the best words, signs, and books through which the will of God could be declared to men. In this way St. Augustine helped greatly to modify earlier views about the content of Christian education.

A good illustration of St. Augustine's thinking is to be found in his analysis of the relation of good and evil in his *Treatise on The City of God*. "How then can a good thing cause an evil will? How, I say, is good the cause of evil? When the will, turning from the better of two alternatives, chooses the worse, it becomes evil; not because that is evil to which it turns, but because the turning itself is vicious."[5]

St. Thomas Aquinas and the Active Intellect

From the time of St. Augustine (430 A.D.) until that of St. Thomas Aquinas (1225-1274 A.D.) no significantly new educational ideas came out of Western culture; and just as St. Augustine reflected the mind of Plato so did St. Thomas Aquinas reflect the mind of Aristotle. From the point of view of Aquinas you do not talk about your experience with God first and then about how you know Him, but rather you take under consideration the arguments for the existence of God.[6] The recovery and translation of Aristotle's works through the Arabs had provided the basis for the new thinking, at first condemned by the Church, but soon to provide for a widening and enrichment of the intellectual life.

Of the key ideas coming out of the writings of St. Thomas Aquinas, none was more significant for Christian education than his conception of primary matter (Aristotle). Matter was not coexistent with God in eternity for God created matter out of nothing. From this primary matter the universe and all things in it were made, an act of creation which involved the giving of definite forms to different objects. As defined by St. Thomas, primary matter was "being in potentiality," not something having an existence apart from God, and, strangely enough, a concept easily related to the new physics of modern times.

Another key Thomistic idea, and one closely related to that of primary matter, is the idea of Divine existence, where rational understanding on the part of the individual of the experience of God takes priority over that of his everyday experience. In considering the arguments for the existence of God, Aquinas started with the external world we see around us, a world made up of objects each distinct from the other according to its unique qualities. The one common thing in all this variety of essence is existence, which in Aristotelian terms has been defined as the "ultimate efficient cause," or the Unmoved Mover.

A third key idea stemming from Thomistic thinking is that an insight into the design and purpose of the world is possible only as we identify the existence of God with an Active Intelligence. Each existent object in the world has its own design, its own entelechy, indicative of a complexity which could only be a result of great design and not of chance.

Since Thomistic thinking, in strict Aristotelian fashion, separated *natural theology* from *supernatural theology*, there was a growing separation of phi-

---

[5] Hitchcock, F.R.M. translation (New York: Macmillan Co., 1922), pp. 80-81.

[6] Butler, J. Donald, *Four Philosophies,* (New York: Harper & Brothers, 1957), p. 396.

losophy, and later science, from religion. Revelation was a fact which philosophy was made to accept, and in so doing philosophy and theology could not conflict when dealing with the same questions.

A study of the educational systems in the Western World since the fifteenth century graphically indicates the extent to which the thinking of Aristotle and of St. Thomas Aquinas has pervaded our culture; although in recent decades the separation of scientific and religious thought has seemed to serve as a barrier against our further social progress. To Aristotle we are especially indebted for the organizing and stucturing of secular knowledge, and to St. Thomas Aquinas we owe a debt for defining and intellectualizing Christian thought. Living in the twentieth century, it is difficult to appreciate the extent to which Aristotle's ideas on the state and the nature of the universe ruled the Western World for 2,000 years. But even more important is that respect and need for appreciation of the role of intellect in man's progress toward the good life. In opposing the teaching of St. Augustine that knowledge of the natural world was unimportant, St. Thomas Aquinas not only gave further stimulus to the demand for enlightened government, both in the church and in the state, but also he helped advance the cause of natural philosophy.

In his reconciliation of the rediscovered pagan thought and Platonic scholasticism of the medieval period, St. Thomas did not turn from faith as the supreme source of truth and as the means for knowing truths not evident from exploring the realm of natural philosophy. But the important contribution here was his establishing the propriety of an inductive (Aristotelian) approach to discovering truths about conditions in the temporal world. From this time on man would move ahead in an ever more amazing restructuring of his conception of his universe and in the ways of studying and learning about it.

The Transition to Naturalistic Individualism

Western education was only to take considerable strides after the developments of the Enlightenment in the eighteenth century. The ferment of the seventeenth century's age of transition, to be discussed later, was foreshadowed, however, by some of the educational theory of the Renaissance period. Considerable progress in implementing certain of the worthwhile principles understood by Greek and Roman educators and forwarded by the position allowed by St. Thomas in the late medieval period were reflected in practices and in the writings of fourteenth and fifteenth century educators.

An outstanding school, for example, was established by Vittorino da Feltre (1378-1446) in northern Italy not far from Venice. Although atypical it is worthy of note. Several of the most enlightened princes of the subsequent

288

period in the history of Italian city states came out of this school. In its atmosphere, its curriculum, its methodology, and in its head teacher it exemplified the best of ancient education and the humanistic ideals of Renaissance life.

The writings of Renaissance educational thinkers, such as Juan Vives (1491-1540) and Desiderius Erasmus (1467-1563), also heralded better practices to come. Realistic humanists, these men attacked the hang-over of Medieval scholastic thought as well as the blind acceptance and emulation of the rediscovered ancient education that was becoming popular during their era. The typical school of the age, unlike Vittorino's, tended toward a superficial concern over the husk of learning rather than on the meaning of the kernel. Erasmus challenged these sterile emphases that prompted meaningless echoing of ancient orations that came to be known as Ciceronianism. Vives also wanted the classics used but to serve purpose in his day. The ancients were not to be studied merely for the sake of a command of classical knowledge or style in themselves but to "forward the good of mankind." Vives, incidentally, made important initial contributions toward the development of the psychology of education, the education of women, the broadening of the curriculum, the use of the vernacular, and recognized both the individual and social purposes that should be served by schooling.

These Renaissance educators wanted a combination of antiquity's man of the world with the character of the Christian gentleman. How far they might have pushed improvements in education will never be known for the spirit of light and progress to which they gave promise was soon nearly extinguished by the unfortunate developments of the Reformation. In this period of considerable educational retrogression, wherein nearly all parties turned their backs on improved educational vistas promised by the Renaissance, they returned to an authoritarian, Augustinian conception of training in which religious dogmas held full sway and brooked no deviation.

Education in seventeenth century Europe was marked by spiritual and intellectual unrest as well as by vast social change. The discovery of new lands in the preceding two centuries, accompanied by a vast commercial revolution, had led to the shattering of the old medieval order, initially set asunder by the results of the Crusades, and the rise of a new and more aggressive middle class. One is struck by the growth of urban centers, by the shift in population from an illiterate, complacent, agrarian peasantry to a restless, poverty-stricken but adventurous laboring class. While the mental outlook of the great mass of common people was slow to change there was much ferment in all areas of human endeavor. Evidences of the struggle are found not only in the economic, political and social phases of life, but equally as well in the religious and the intellectual.

Side by side with the emphasis on classical humanism, there was a growing emphasis upon and an intellectual interest in the natural world and man's relation to it as contrasted with the previous theological and supernatural centered outlook. In a sense it can be said that the greatest contribution of the period was science and the accompanying birth of a new mind. While the universities were enslaved by a worship of Aristotelianism and the churches were persecuting those who taught the Copernican theory, numerous societies were being organized by those who were interested in conducting experiments in physics, chemistry, anatomy and mechanics.

Special recognition in the trend toward an emphasis upon scientific endeavor is due Francis Bacon, who, in his *New Organon* (1620), made a detailed analysis of the scientific method and its relation to the new theory of knowledge. As contrasted with Platonic idea-realism, it was now held that the only realities were natural things and the laws of the universe which governed them. Bacon admonished men that they should clear their minds of the preconceptions and prejudices concerning the nature of being if they were to achieve the great desired human ends. The philosophical reverberations of this trend are to be found in the movement toward rationalism and empiricism, but it is in the latter that we find the most significant developments for American education.

While American education in the twentieth century continues to reflect many of the key ideas of the classical and medieval Christian thinkers, it also points up the contributions of those European scholars who made significant contributions in the transition from the supernatural and metaphysical world of Plato and Aristotle, and their Christian counterparts, St. Augustine and St. Thomas Aquinas, to the natural and everyday world of temporal man. By means of the controls over nature which the new science provided, man would be better able to combat the deficiencies of his existence. Scientific knowledge would make possible the obliteration of famine through the mass production of foods, of disease through the advancement of medicine, and of poverty through an abundance of economic goods.

It is in the emphasis upon the significance of the individual, however, that we find the beginnings of what we have identified as the democratic approach or point of view in education. Such an approach, it must be recognized, carried with it strong negative as well as positive ingredients. The attack on the old order was surely warranted because of its tyranny and brutality, and because of its enslavement of both the body and the mind of man; but in making the past a total evil and a total error there was a tendency to defy both reason and freedom and to exaggerate the worth of man in the raw. In the United States the positive element was pointed up in the glories and achievements of the American Revolution.

In both England and the American colonies there was a major shift in human values during the latter part of the eighteenth century. The progress

290

of representative governments had elevated the concept of social change into a major principle[7] which was to displace the traditional concept of status quo. Societies were no longer what they were because of the will of God, but because men had made them that way. Through enlightenment (new knowledge), and a vision of the future, the old order could be made over into a new society where man could live in peace with his fellow man. Of those who made significant educational contributions in this transition toward an emphasis upon and concern for the welfare of the individual, John Amos Comenius deserves our first consideration.

Comenian Thought

In many respects John Amos Comenius (1592-1671) was a medievalist. He strongly held to such medieval ideas as that of man being at the center of the universe, the essence of a thing being its purpose not its activity, and the idea that all nature has a purpose. On the other hand he stood for certain key ideas which greatly contributed to basic reforms in modern education. (See also Chapter VI, pp. 208-9 and footnote 74.)

Comenius will be remembered for his insistence that the materials used in the classroom must be adapted to the interests and abilities of the pupils. It was his belief that there was a right order of learning, of the presentation of materials, and of teaching. The problem for the educator was to discover the laws of learning and to adapt the curriculum and teaching methods to them. Under the Classical-Christian ideology, emphasis was upon the commandment, the law, the rule, the principle or the word. Emphasis was upon the outside in and not the inside out. Comenius would change all of this by placing an emphasis upon method as well as upon words, an idea which is related to another of his key ideas, that an individual learns better through his senses than by memorizing a list of words which convey little or no meaning.

Training of the senses according to Comenius was fundamental to the moral education of the individual as well as to the development of his intelligence. It was through the senses — seeing, hearing, feeling — that the memory and the imagination could best be fostered. Books, universal books, were important, but it was best to proceed from the perception of the senses rather than to rely upon Augustinian intuition. Comenius, like St. Thomas Aquinas, saw the need for intelligence and insight into the natural order of things, but he went beyond Aquinas in applying this principle to all men. He urged, therefore, a system of universal education. Comenius did not originate

---

[7] (The) *Forty-First Yearbook of the National Society for the Study of Education,* (Part I, Philosophies of Education), (Bloomington, Illinois: Public School Publishing Company, 1942) p. 18.

Printing   *Typographia.*

The Printer
hath Copper Letters
in a great number

put into Boxes. 5.

    The Compofitor 1.
taketh them out
one by one, and
(according to
the Copy,
which he hath faftened
before him in a
Viforum 2.)
compofeth words

Typographus
habet *æneos Typos,*
magno numero,
diftributos
per *Loculamenta.* 5.
    Typotheta 1.
eximit illos
fingulatim,·
& componit
(fecundum *Exemplar*
quod *Retinaculo* 2.
fibi præfixum habet)
verba

INTERIOR OF A PRINTSHOP. PAGE
FROM AMOS COMENIUS' TEXTBOOK
ORBIS SENSUALIUM. PIDUS LATIN
EDITION, 1654.

the idea of group education but he was a strong believer in the value of group teaching.

Another of the key ideas of Comenius is revealed in that he wrote one of the first illustrated books for children, an extension of his idea of learning through the senses. In the first series of pictures found in his *Orbis Pictus,* the objects shown are those which make a noise such as the lamb bleating, the baby crying, and the grasshopper grating. Among the values attributed by Comenius to the picture-book were those of: (1) better impression of objects on the mind; (2) enhancement of pleasure to be derived from reading books; (3) aiding learning to read; and (4) providing a pleasant introduction to language study. The impact of this one key idea has been deeply imbedded in American educational practice for a century.

Finally, it is from Comenius that we have inherited the idea that learning can not be forced, but comes only when there is genuine desire on the part of the learner to learn. This idea, like his other key ideas, is a part of the Comenian theory of learning through the senses. Comenius was not opposed to punishing a child when necessary, but he held that such discipline should never be associated with the learning process. Creating a desire for learning was a major responsibility of the teacher, for a pleasant atmosphere was necessary for good motivation of the child.

Key Ideas from Locke

John Locke (1637-1704) is significant for us not only because he marked the beginning of the movement away from Platonic thought but because he provided much of the thought which helped lay the foundations for a democratic way of life in America. By and large, much of the thought that went into the American Declaration of Independence is found in the writings of John Locke. It is true that his thinking reflects much of the influence of Aristotle, and his social outlook is that of a seventeenth century English aristocrat; but as a transitional thinker Locke is important, for he marked the beginning of a new approach to the problem of knowledge as well as the opening up of new avenues for individual freedom. It was Locke who provided the key ideas on which the new era of naturalistic individualism was to be built.

It was John Locke who first during this period came forth with the idea that both reason and knowledge were derived from "experience." In his own words he stated that the child did not come into the world "stored with plenty of ideas . . . [Platonic]. It is by degrees that he comes to be furnished with them."[8] To Locke the mind at birth was a blank sheet of paper.

---

[8] *An Essay Governing Human Understanding* (Ed. H. C. Fraser) (London: Clarendon Press, 1894) Vol. I, p. 9. For more on Locke's educational views, see *The Educational Writings of John Locke,* (London: Arnold, 1912).

Knowledge of the external world came first through the activity of the sense organs. Reflection followed as the mind perceived such operations as thinking, reasoning, and knowing. Locke's assertion that ideas were representations rather than the actual presentation of things in a world external to the mind is just the opposite of the classical point of view.

Another major idea contributed by Locke lies in his assumption that since it is man's understanding that determines his attitude and achievements, his mind must be carefully trained. Understanding on the part of the people in a democratic society is more important than the will of the people since it is understanding which determines the quality of the ideas and images of the mind. Also, it is understanding which determines our sense of need for studying the real differences between individuals and the factors which determine the processes of our insight. This idea is the justification for the assumption that Locke marked the beginning of the movement which has culminated in that body of knowledge now known as the science of psychology.

It is to Locke that credit is due for the idea that children should be treated as rational creatures. This was a part of his larger idea that we should not put into a child that which was "to sway and influence his mind." If we were going to have individuals who were rational we must treat them as such. To accomplish this end Locke held that both the body and the mind needed to be "hardened," but in doing so he did not imply the dangerous or the foolish act but rather the persistent, regular and vigorous activity. Only through such a hardening process could the individual gain that true education of self-control.

The Naturalism of Rousseau

In many respects Jean Jacques Rousseau (1712-1778) represents the extreme opposite of the classical point of view. As such, it is no wonder that he has been so closely identified with the causes of the French Revolution. Where the classical tradition emphasized discipline and authority, Rousseau emphasized freedom and personal choice. In the mind of Rousseau, evil and tyranny were in the world, not because of the nature of man's birth but because of the corruption of society and enslavement of man by his fellow man. From the standpoint of education Rousseau can and should be considered as the father of progressive movement. (See also Chapter VII, pp. 251-2.)

One of the several key ideas found in the writings of Rousseau, particularly in his *Discourse on the Arts and Sciences,* is that of mis-education. This could be taken as an attack on formal education as compared with informal education. Rousseau saw the education of his day as a major source of corruption of the mind, especially the mind of the child. Through formal education man had departed from nature, the source of his natural freedom. This idea is further amplified by Rousseau in his *Social Contract* where he affirms that man in giving up his natural liberty should have gained civil liberty, but he had acquired only the bondage of slavery. We may well protest against the extreme negativism of a point of view which in wholesale form condemned all of man's social inheritance, yet we must admit that in doing so Rousseau undermined the practice of blind submission to an order created not by the will of God as it was so generally assumed, but according to Rousseau, rather by the hand of greedy, brutal, and sinful men.

Rousseau more than any other one thinker is given credit for the key idea of discovering the child. There is that well known statement of his in which he affirms that "Nature wants children to be children before they are men. If we deliberately pervert this order, we shall get premature fruits which are neither ripe nor well flavoured, and which soon decay." The ancients had placed nearly all emphasis upon preparation for adult life, upon the job to be done, and little or nothing upon the person who was to do the job. The child was to know his subject but no one was to know the child. In Rousseau's time little if anything was known about the nature of the child, physically or mentally. In shocking the world into a realization of its ignorance of childhood, Rousseau may be said to have initiated the major revolution in education in modern times.

Along with his key idea of childhood, Rousseau introduced another bombshell into the educational world, that of "free activity," an idea around which a verbal war has developed in twentieth century American education. This idea was an outgrowth of Rousseau's rejection of the doctrine of original sin and its replacement with his theory of natural goodness. Following from this premise Rousseau deduced that all man-made discipline for children was bad and therefore should be discarded for the discipline of natural consequences. For formal education, which he associated with adult tyranny, Rousseau substituted free activity wherein the child could make full use of his senses, and where he would not be the victim of "words, words, words" which had no more meaning to the child than that of a dead language. Here was the beginning of the modern "learning by doing" theory which has erroneously been attributed to John Dewey, for with Rousseau, words should be used only when doing was impossible.

A panel of distinguished educators has adjudged Rousseau's *Emile* (1762) the world's greatest classic in the history of education.[9] Although, in addition to the impact of the above ideals, it contains many half truths and errors (he opposed the use of reason with the young, he did not espouse the use of books in learning, he accepted a recapitulation theory of human development,

---

[9] George W. Pieper, "The Educational Classics," *History of Education Journal*, Vols. 3-4, 1951-1953, p. 79.

etc.), it also reflects his other epochal writings and marks him as one of the greatest regenerative forces in eighteenth and nineteenth century society.

The Individualism of Spencer

In many respects Herbert Spencer (1820-1903) was much like Rousseau, especially in his naturalism, in his individualism and in his opposition to the key ideas implicit in classical culture, but he was very much unlike Rousseau in his allegiance to science both as a discipline and as a body of practical knowledge. In good scholastic form he held that although "language familiarizes with nonrational relations, science familiarizes with rational relations. While the one exercises memory only the other exercises both memory and understanding." [10] Spencer's impact on American education, however, was more directly related to secondary education and to the shift from a classical culture centered curriculum to one of practical utility.

Spencer's key idea of practical utility is exemplified both in his lack of sympathy for art and literature and in his antagonism toward classical studies. He speaks of trying to read Plato's dialogues and of putting them down with the belief that Plato was mistaking "words for things." Classical literature was only ornament and decoration for it contributed nothing to the economic well-being of the great majority of the people. Only those subjects which contribute to self-preservation, securing the necessities of life, raising children, maintaining social and political relations and enjoyment of leisure, says Spencer in his treatise on *Education: Intellectual, Moral and Physical,* are worthy of our consideration.

From his idea of practical utility, Spencer deduced a second premise, namely, that the scientific studies, especially those dealing with self-preservation and good health, should take priority over all other subjects. As a leisure time pursuit, literary studies were placed at the bottom of the scale. Of the study of history, he was equally as critical, especially that history which was concerned only with kings, queens and court intrigues. Of rote memory he was equally as critical. He would have been much more sympathetic to the modern social science approach in the high school.[11] Spencer believed in formal discipline but only the subjects of practical worth were to be so used. In arguing for the principle of proceeding from the simple to the complex, he does not make it clear that such is applicable only as we take into consideration the age and mental development of the child.

---

[10] Herbert Spencer, *Education: Intellectual, Moral, and Physical* (New York: Appleton-Century-Crofts, 1920) p. 78.

[11] Richard E. Gross, in "Education's Centennial Dilemma: What Knowledge is of Most Worth?" *School and Society,* February 13, 1960, pp. 66-69, points out that the issues raised by Spencer 100 years ago are far from settled.

Spencer was not blind to the nature of the development of the child, for he deserves much credit for the idea that it was the prolonged period of infancy which made it possible for the individual to acquire the learning necessary for the little animal to become a human being. In addition to the nourishment, adult guidance, and mental nurture provided by the adult, the long period of growing up made it possible for the child to educate himself in great measure. This building of perceptions and establishing relationships came through the child's use of his senses, his eyes, ears, literally his whole body. There was a natural rhythm in this development and education needed to be attuned to it. And in the new world arising youth would need instruction in such overlooked subjects as hygiene, sex education, and education for use of leisure.

One final key idea of Hebert Spencer's is worthy of our attention, that of the nature of being or of reality. As an evolutionist he defined evolution as the "integration of matter and concomitant dissipation of motion" in which matter passed from an incoherent homogeneity to a coherent heterogeneity.[12] This concept of motion involved the basic assumption that while we could not know the true nature of reality, we do know that it embodies the element of motion, of process or force. This emphasis upon force or process is an important aspect of American pragmatism, democracy being defined in terms of a way of life rather than an end product. Stated otherwise the note of the power of method has become a significant element in our understanding of the nature of the educational process.

The trend toward naturalistic individualism which had been demonstrated in the ideas of Comenius, Locke, Rousseau, and Herbert Spencer emphasized the significance of knowing self as contrasted with the ancient emphasis on the external world. This trend, which is observable in philosophy, religion, and education, stands in striking contrast to developments in the field of the natural sciences. Here the motivating factor was found in discovery of the natural laws, first in the realm of the physical sciences and second in the field of the biological sciences. On this point the key ideas of Francis Bacon (1561-1626) were especially significant because of their impact upon those educators whom we shall identify with the ideas embodied in the socio-scientific movement, the third of our pattern of ideas. Particular reference is made in this final section to the experimental approach to knowledge and to the felt need for understanding the child's nature.

Before discussing a number of the key ideas which have contributed to the socio-scientific impact upon American education we need to add a note of clarification concerning the problem of defining the nature of the indi-

---

[12] Herbert Spencer, *First Principles of a New System of Philosophy* (New York: D. Appleton, 1896) p. 396.

vidual. Insofar as the classical tradition is concerned, it is a truth that the individual, when considered from the point of view of naturalistic individualism, was distinctly secondary to the eternal values and primary social institutions, especially as they have been represented in the writings of Plato, Aristotle, St. Augustine, and St. Thomas Aquinas. When dealing with the ideas of Comenius, Locke, Rousseau and Spencer the problem, however, is of an entirely different nature.

There is a deep underlying difference between the point of view taken by Comenius and Locke and that taken by Rousseau and Spencer in regard to the individual and to man's social heritage, and, as such, each had a decidedly different influence on American education. Both Comenius and Locke were realists; and while each was in universal opposition to the injustice and cruelty of the old order, each was convinced that the errors in the knowing assumptions were generated by errors in the methodology of knowing. Both Comenius and Locke believed that there was an external world, but that it could be known only through the intelligent use of the senses. The psychology of Comenius was not much better than that of any other scholar of his day, but he did not commit the fatal error of identifying the order of God with the slave-discriminating social institutions of his day. Of greatest significance, however, is the fact that both Locke and Comenius emphasized the identification of the role of intellect with that of a free society. Leaders of the American Revolution, especially those responsible for the work of the American Philosophical Association (Franklin and Jefferson included), were consistently intellectual in their point of view, and are to be identified in their concept of the individual and his educational needs with the outlook of Comenius and Locke.

In the case of Rousseau and Spencer the issue is entirely a different one, for each in a fundamental sense was both negative and anti-intellectual. Rousseau's concept of government was clearly anti-constitutional and as such was vested in a will to power based on majority rule. Such a policy could hardly protect the rights of the minority or the individual whom he pretends to cherish. Spencer was a strong devotee of the sciences, so much so that he would substitute science for the whole of the Classical-Christian heritage. Herein Spencer affirms the kind of laissez-faire capitalism which so markedly characterized the Western World of the past century, that is a free-wheeling profit system without moral underpinning or government control.

During and following the era of Jacksonian democracy in the United States the concept of the individual took on the same strong overtones of individualism such as those defined by Rousseau and Spencer. The strong anti-intellectual trend of the mass public education program was noted by Ralph Waldo Emerson in 1841 in the following manner:

The cause of education is urged in this country with the utmost earnestness — on what ground? Why on this, that the people have the power, and if they are not instructed to sympathize with the intelligent, reading, trading and governing class; inspired with a taste for the same competitions and prizes, they will upset the fair pageant of Judicature, and perhaps lay a hand on the sacred muniments of wealth itself, and now distribute the land.[13]

The low level at which the public schools were financed, along with a matching low level in teacher qualifications, tends to confirm Emerson's convictions. Later in 1897, Jane Addams, writing on the same theme, said:

The business man has, of course, not said to himself: "I will have the public school train office boys and clerks for me, so that I may have them cheap," but he has thought, and sometimes said, "Teach the children to write legibly, and to figure accurately and to be prompt, to obey, and not question why; and you will fit them to make their way in the world as I have made mine."[14]

One final note on the effect of the individualistic interpretation of the nature of the individual is deserving of comment. The development of the sciences of physiology and biology came to be used by many to confirm an individualistic interpretation of the democratic process. Further confirmation of the assumption that the individual was an entity in himself was sought in bio-physical behavior psychology where all the individual was or could hope to be was bound up in biological evolution. Study animal nature and you would find the secret of human nature. This was the point of view taken by E. L. Thorndike in his doctoral dissertation on "Animal Intelligence" at Columbia University, 1898. Also, this point of view took deep root in the educational psychology courses taught in the teacher training institutions across the country. The dichotomy between the so-called scientific point of view here expressed and that of the Christian concept of the nature of the individual was such as to create only a pattern of confusion in the mind of the teacher.

Present day overtones relating to the entity concept of the individual found in naturalistic individualism are being widely reflected both in the wholesale attack upon progressive education, and, conversely, in our lack of a comprehensive social intelligence. This latter deficiency has been frankly stated by a vice-president of one of our leading universities:

Democracy is defined by such a large number of our citizens as to have significant repercussions in the chaos of the day, in terms of freedom from

---

[13] Ralph Waldo Emerson, *Nature Addresses and Lectures* (Boston: Houghton Mifflin Company, 1929) p. 320.

[14] Quoted in Merle Curti, *The Social Ideas of American Educators* (New York: Charles Scribner's Sons, 1935) p. 203.

compulsion, and freedom from the direction of certain individuals, groups, or mores. Democracy is to these citizens protection from powers which have become personally distasteful. Such an interpretation led in the not too remote past to the brand of rugged individualism of the frontier and the West. Today it leads to deadly social confusion in the form of a negative philosophy. This is seen most pointedly in teenage gangsterism, in racism, in anti-religious bigotry, in certain states' rights movements, in labor union irresponsibility and counter-proposals to curb union powers, and in isolationism and widespread clamor against the United Nations.

A similar view of democracy in education is held by many administrators and teachers. Trustees and presidents invoke democracy to free their hands of legislatures and pressure groups within the constituency. Instructors cry, "Undemocratic," when their board, faculty, or president takes action not to their liking. Students ask in the name of democracy for fewer rules and regulations upon their educational and social conduct and activities.[15]

In pointing up the limitations of naturalistic (scientific) individualism there is no desire to ignore or de-emphasize the positive contributions of the key European thinkers of this era. From the standpoint of American education it is more than important to emphasize the prominence which method gained in the era of individualism as contrasted with the centuries-old classical emphasis on subject matter. This is not to say that method did not have a place in the old order of things, but that method herein had nothing to do with determining the nature of truth for man. Since to John Locke mind had qualities but not essence, as in the case of Plato, method took on special significance for the learning process. It was Rene Descartes, however, who in his "Discourse on the Method of Rightly Conducting the Reason" elevated "method" to a position of major philosophical concern. In this respect he was ably supported by the writings of Sir Francis Bacon, Gottfried Wilhelm von Liebniz and Sir Isaac Newton.

By the close of the eighteenth century the significance of method in modern philosophy had been fully established thus paving the way for the development of a science of education. Method so understood has not one but a variety of contextual meanings.[16] It pertains to a way of gaining new knowledge rather than the mere demonstration of a truth already known. It is general rather than particular in that it deals with procedures which can be applied to any problem worthy of consideration. It can be applied to matters both ethical and political in nature as well as those involving the physical and the biological sciences. Finally, and of very great importance, is the

---

[15] Donald Faulkner, "Democracy in Higher Education" *AAUP Bulletin,* Vol. 45, No. 2, p. 235.

[16] James E. McClellan, "Dewey and the Concept of Method," *The School Review,* Charles Scribner's Sons, 1935), p. 203.

assumption that method is related to the very essence of being, an expression of the rationality of the human soul.

Socio-Scientific Foundations

In a very real sense the key ideas advanced under naturalistic individualism were in direct contradiction to those which had contributed to the foundations of the Classical-Christian heritage. In undermining the Platonic doctrine of innate ideas Locke had not been able to replace them with a solid and positive foundation for an acceptable belief. Rousseau in his ideas had graphically pointed up the limitations and evils of the "ancient regime," but the sum total effect of what he offered was foundationally negative. Spencer had come forth with new key ideas that gave much support for the build-up of the sciences and social studies in the curriculum, but the effect even here was to posit one body of knowledge against another, thus creating, in the language of John Dewey, a contradiction in meaning and value for the educational process. In seeking a synthesis of this Hegelian thesis and antithesis the solution seemed to lead in the direction of bio-social man or some form of contextualism.

Key Kantian Ideas

Immanuel Kant (1734-1804) marked the beginning of the movement toward a resolution of the impasse in which the Western World found itself following the attack which both Descartes and Locke had made upon the classical intellectual tradition. The fundamental epistemological problem had resolved itself into the relation of the knower and the known. The Cartesian assertion "I think, therefore I am" had raised the crucial issue of whether or not what the individual knew was all from the inside out as against the classical tradition of knowing from the outside in. Could man really know his world, the things in it, or was knowledge all a matter of projecting the self upon the world? In resolving this issue to his own satisfaction, Kant wrote three key studies, *The Critique of Pure Reason* (1781), *The Critique of Practical Reason* (1788) and *The Critique of the Judgment* (1790).

In terms of everyday education, Kant may be thought of as seeking to resolve the issue that had been raised over whether or not the child centered school is more important than the subject matter centered school or vice versa. In a metaphysical sense it can be said that he did not resolve the issue for he accepted the classical assumption of an external reality along with the individualistic assumptions set forth by the naturalists. What he did do was to reconcile these two assumptions into an epistemological frame of reference. This in itself was a germinal idea for it laid the foundations for the more thoroughly developed twentieth-century concepts of contextualism, field

301

theory, and gestalt. People in general, however, still talk in terms of the old dualism and seem to be unaware of the nature of the newer educational concepts.

Among Kant's significant ideas none was more important than his belief that through education human nature would be continually improved until man was brought to a condition worthy of his creation. Kant was sympathetic with Rousseau's assumption concerning the animal nature of the child, but, instead of the child being a noble savage, he was a candidate for humanity. "Man can only become man by education."[17] Education was the most difficult of all problems faced by man, for man's insight depended upon education just as his education depended upon his insight. This is saying that man's ultimate moral freedom is dependent upon his intellectual freedom. By the nature of the situation education was a slow process, for each generation depended upon the preceding generation for its store-house of knowledge and in turn added something to it. Of special significance in this process was the need for developing a more adequate theory of education.

Although Kant did not attempt to work out a theory of education, he did formulate the basic concept that the world of reality for man was only a world of phenomena, a synthetic world, and that man's judgments were all of a synthetic character. In support of this position he held that there were three aspects of experience: (a) *subjective states,* which were only haphazard streams of associated ideas; (b) *things-in-themselves,* outside of all sense experience and beyond knowledge; and (c) *phenomena,* that which existed between the individual and the world around him and which represented the knowledge which was the common possession of mankind. The significance of this key idea lay in the fact that it provided a basis for a socio-psycho-logical concept of mind and of education. Kant rightly observed that there was more to man than just a capacity to think, and that man was a creature of both action and judgment. To the classical emphasis on morality and intellect Kant had now added the psychology of the act.

Pestalozzian Contributions

In dealing with the fundamental contributions of Johann Heinrich Pestalozzi (1746-1827) we are aware of the fact that many of his ideas had found limited expression from the time of Comenius in the efforts of certain scholars and teachers, but it remained for Pestalozzi to give them the kind of significance which made him the outstanding educator of his time and a pioneer in the socio-scientific movement in education. Also, it is important to emphasize that Pestalozzi opposed Rousseau in his separation of the task from

---

[17] Immanuel Kant, *Education* (Trans. A. Churton) (Ann Arbor: University of Michigan Press, 1960) p. 6.

the natural desire; that is, he saw the problem of authority versus freedom as aspects of the same situation.

In his study on *Investigations into the Course of Nature in the Development of the Human Race* (1797), Pestalozzi came forth with one of the first of the sociological evaluations of education. Herein Plato's idea of education as a means of salvation for mankind takes on a new and modern form. Man's advance toward a higher level of humanity depended upon the intelligence and goodness of his education; for while morality was at heart a matter of individual effort, it was, at the same time, the foundation of progress. The beginnings of such effort were to be rooted in a good home in a good community. Using education as a means of social reform carried with it the idea that society would assume the responsibility for helping each individual develop his maximum ability and that good schools were necessary to such an end.

Also, Pestalozzi should be recognized for his discovery of the experimental method in the teaching of science. This he did through the experience of teaching his son. Examples were found in the use of snow and in the study of the effects of both voice and attitude in instruction. Such a method had implicit in it the idea of learning through directed activity, of object teaching, and of nature study. The teaching procedure concerned involved the formation of worthy ideas by first naming the object, investigating and naming its parts and formulating a worthy definition. The child was continuously to describe what he saw, felt and heard in order to acquire satisfactory language construction. The same rule was to be applied in the study of other subjects such as arithmetic and geography.

The significance of Pestalozzi's social and experimental ideas is best illustrated in the way in which they tended to break the iron grip which subject matter held over instruction in the classroom. Since subject matter in itself was thought to define the nature of reality in the Classical-Christian tradition, there could be little or no improvement in the work of the school until the fallacy of this assumption could be demonstrated. Pestalozzi saw only too well that there could be no social regeneration of humanity until reality was defined in more fundamental social terms. This implied not only that the "know what" needed to be defined in terms of the "know how," but that there was a need for continuing experimentation if individual development was to be assured. The basic shift in fundamental ideas is thus a shift from the subject matter to that of individual development in a social context.

Finally, there was primary significance in the Pestalozzian idea and effort to show the world that it was possible to secure teachers in large numbers through a scientific training procedure. This idea stands in striking contrast to the classical idea that teachers were born and not made, and its significance for American education is attested by the efforts throughout the history of the public schools to secure teachers in ever larger numbers for the increasing school population. But the issue is far more than a matter of numbers, it is based upon the larger idea that human nature can be changed and changed for the better. The beginnings of this new program of teacher education in the United States is well marked in what is now recognized as the Oswego Movement (1865). Unfortunately for many teachers, it has not as yet been extended beyond the level of a narrow surface methodology which seeks to bridge the gap between the classical point of view on subject matter and the naturalistic-individual concept of the child. (See Chapter VII, pp. 259-61 and footnote no. 38 for more details on Pestalozzi's influence.)

Herbart and the Psychology Movement

It is necessary here to note and to emphasize the changing conception of the nature of the individual and of society that came over the Western World in the latter part of the eighteenth century and the early part of the nineteenth century. This changing point of view which was expressed in the key ideas of Kant and Pestalozzi found further and more extensive expression in the work of Johann Friedrich Herbart (1776-1841). (See also Chapter VII, p. 269.) What is particularly important about the ideas of Herbart is that they supplemented the thinking of Kant and Pestalozzi by pointing toward and laying the foundations for a social psychology of education. The idea of a science of education was implicit in the thinking of Comenius, as we have already indicated, but the world of Comenius was dualistic, separating the spiritual or eternal soul-self from the world of nature, whereas Herbart would resolve this dualism in a social reality.

Applying psychological principles to the teaching-learning process was without doubt the key idea in Herbart's educational thinking. Starting out with the assumption that body and soul existed at birth, but not mind, Herbart developed the concept that mind was a result of the sum total of the impressions that entered into one's consciousness in the course of a life cycle. These impressions were a product of a kind of interaction between the soul and its environment and were designated as an "apperceptive mass." It was the teacher's responsibility to direct this apperceptive process in which new experiences were always to be interpreted in terms of old ones. Thus, for Herbart, the teacher was the creator and builder of the child's mind, a created social mind. In emphasizing this point we need to add that Herbart was a social realist who would form the mind of the child in accordance with determined social realities.

Herbart's concept of the created social mind called for a new and revolutionary teaching procedure, the logical lesson plan. In the process of instruction the teacher needed to go through a definite procedure involving four fundamental steps: (1) presentation of materials in such a way as to prepare the child's mind for reception of new knowledge; (2) association of materials by observation or comparison so as to produce a general idea or ideas; (3) synthesizing and supplementing of the materials by the teacher; and finally, (4) application of the knowledge gained to varied human experiences by way of exercises and illustrations. Such careful instruction was possible only through well thought out lesson plans. Of special importance was the follow-through and integration so as to produce a matrix of connected ideas, or a unified mind.

Also, Herbart gave new meaning to the concept of discipline, substituting the idea of discipline as instruction for the traditional idea of discipline as punishment for disobedience. Under the idea of discipline as the will to do what was good, Herbart would ban cruelty to children, for such cruelty only produced antagonism. What was needed was a carefully planned program of directed instruction which led to an acceptance on the part of the child of his share of responsibility. When punishment was applied it should always be logical, uniform, consistent, and applied without emotional involvement on the part of the teacher. While external control needed to be stronger when the child was very young and had not as yet developed a sense of responsibility, it was of little value to restrain the undesirable act unless replaced by a preferred one. Mere passive obedience was not the way to develop character.

Herbart's concept of discipline is closely related to another of his key ideas, that of interest as motive power. In this respect interest was not an incidental or superficial factor in learning but an outcome of apperception, the main outcome in human behavior. It was interest which directed the human will toward that most fundamental purpose in education which was individual "virtue." Only through many-sided interest could a man achieve the highest of moral character. Actually, Herbart used the word "interest" in a two-fold sense, as a force which facilitated the apperceptive process and as a feeling of pleasure resulting from the completion of a successful act. Interest here was not something which welled up from within the child but rather something which was produced by the teacher in order to enhance the growth of character as well as the mastery of subject matter.[18]

Froebel's "Law of Human Growth"

Friedrich Froebel (1782-1852), a German educator of the early nineteenth century, profited greatly from his associates and his general cultural environment. Developments at Jena, where the philosophical center was under the

---

[18] For an illustration of the continuing influence of Herbart in Western education see Otto Willman, *The Science of Education* (trans. F. Kirsch), 2nd ed., (Latrobe, Pa.: The Archabbey Press, 2 vols., 1930). See especially the introduction.

supervision of Goethe, were especially significant. Here Fichte, who contributed so greatly to the rebirth of the German national spirit after the Napoleonic wars, chose to interpret Kant in such a way as to make the individual ego the creator of the universe. Fichte held that the ego in creating and affirming itself came to recognize the existence of the non-ego or the external world. By so doing the ego and the non-ego assumed the relation of the knower and the known. This theory concerning the nature of the individual, plus the influence of Schelling, who accepted the idea of the importance of the ego but rejected the assumption that it possessed the power of creation, regarding it only as an inner force, had much influence on Froebel's general thought pattern and, in particular, upon his key educational ideas.

One of the most fundamental of these key ideas is that of functional or "inner unity." True value and meaning came not by an exclusive concern with sense perception, but by interpreting nature in terms of one's own inner wholeness or self. It was not enough for the individual to act as an agent for the transmission of the knowledge and values of the past, for the basic elements to be conveyed were implicit in the individual not in an external tradition or books. Education of necessity must bring about unity and freedom through the mutual expression of both the physical and the mental attributes of the individual. True education for the individual could be achieved only when the relation of education to all of society was understood. The individual could not hope to maintain his unity except as he was a part of a larger unity. In a religious sense this, according to Froebel, called for that highest unity which was unity with God, the original organism.

Froebel's educational theory was grounded, also, in the idea that each individual was possessed of an internal drive which caused him or her to develop along certain definite lines. Each organismic unity, plant or animal, operated according to some universal creative force which, although functioning within a well-defined structure, was possessed of unlimited possibilities for change and variation. Within this process of unfolding, or of evolution, there was bound up the reasoning power of man, his moral and ethical nature as well as his physical development. This process, lying at the heart of man's creation, called for maximum superior effort in fostering its potentialities.

The ideas of "functional unity" and of "unfolding" according to a universal law are fundamental to Froebel's assumption that at all stages in the education of the child there must be an abundance of opportunities for creative self-expression. *Darstellung*, as Froebel named it, called for the widest variety of opportunities possible so that the innate drive of the organism could achieve its potential for a fuller life. The impulses of the pupil must find expression, or better, be lived out in natural constructive activities which were purposeful and meaningful. Opportunities for learning, materials and methods provided by the teachers, were not to be imposed upon the pupil, for such practice would be contrary to his personal needs. Pupils should find opportunities for creative self-expression, activities involving dancing, painting, constructing, gardening, story-telling, numbers games, play-acting, drawing, writing, singing, both individually and in groups. To help achieve this end Froebel devised a series of wooden blocks which he called "gifts," and which to him represented the universal forms in nature and art—sphere, cube, cylinder, triangle, square, ring and stick. If properly developed, work in the ideal society would become play and play would become work.

To exalt the interests and spontaneous activities of the child Froebel created the "Kindergarten," a place for pre-school children ranging from one year to eight. Here the child was to discover his true self for "what yet is to come out of mankind, what human nature is yet to develop, that we do not yet know, that is not yet the property of mankind; and still human nature, like the spirit of God, is ever unfolding its inner essence."[19] (See also Chapter VII, pp. 258-259.)

The socio-scientific ideas are a fundamental part of the newer social concept of the individual and of democracy which has been replacing the nineteenth century free-wheeling individualism. This defining of democracy in social terms has sought to provide for not only a larger degree of individuality, but, equally as well, for greater social responsibility. In defining the individual, the concept of a classical spiritual entity has been replaced with that concept which sees the individual as being derived from an organism interacting in a pattern of environmental forces. There is that viewing of democracy as a total quality and way of life, not just a political instrument in which individuals balance their powers against each other. Right education is that kind of education which contributes maximally to this process.

Other Ideas Contributing to the Socio-Scientific Movement in American Education

In concluding our presentation of the key foreign ideas which have made American education what it is we propose to discuss briefly (1) the concept of evolution, (2) the statistical method, (3) the gestalt, and (4) psychoanalysis.

While each of these ideas has made an imprint upon our educational practice, none has been more revolutionary in its influence than the concept of evolution.

---

[18] Friedrich Froebel, *Education of Man* (Trans. W. N. Hailmann), (New York: Appleton-Century-Crofts, Inc., 1910) p. 4. The most well known modern exponent of Froebel's approaches, who developed her own successful modifications, was the famed Italian educator, Maria Montessori (1869-1952).

THE CONCEPT OF EVOLUTION. From the standpoint of education the social creative significance of the concept of evolution is equally as important as that of biological mutation. As long as the nature of society was believed to be determined by either divine or natural law, the only kind of education possible was that of discover and conform. This was true under the Classical-Christian tradition as well as under the naturalistic concept of creation derived from Newtonian physics. In this old order of being we have the foundation of the disciplinary theory of education, about which we continue to hear so much today, along with the deification of the memoriter method.

When Charles Darwin came forth with his *Origin of Species* in 1859, he almost sealed the fate of the Classical-Christian tradition and that of naturalistic individualism and of socialistic communism as well. Naturalistic individualism, growing out of the eighteenth century, as reflected in the thinking of Rousseau and Spencer, had negated the worth of the social order, while socialistic communism, growing out of Newtonian physics and Hegelian thought had, from Marx and Engels, created a social absolute to replace the absolutes of the medieval tradition. It is true that when the evolutionary principle is limited to the field of biology it tends to support an individualistic approach in education, as already indicated, but when it is elevated to the level of a metaphysical promise, man's social order becomes a part of the natural creative process. Thus educational psychology in America has been developed both from a bio-physical and from a bio-social frame of reference, with the bio-physical approach still tending to dominate in our teachers' colleges and schools of education.

The concept of social evolution, which has found full expression in the philosophy of John Dewey, is primarily significant in that it would make of the school a primary social institution rather than an institution of secondary significance as has been largely true in the tradition of Western culture. Pragmatism, the personification of the socio-evolutionary concept, unlike realism or idealism, approaches education as basically a bio-social process, as a means by which society renews itself, and as " process which in its inner essence is social, embracing individuals who, while they are separate and distinct physical and psychical entities, are at the same time society cast into individualistic forms."[20]

In a metaphysical sense the concept of evolution not only defines reality in terms of a creative universal process, but makes man at his highest level a part of the creative act. Darwin's contribution was only a link in the development of this broader and more penetrating insight into the nature of being. There is bound up in the theory of evolution the idea that if man, all animal life, and all plant life were obliterated from our earth, out of the creative

---

[20] J. Donald Butler, *Four Philosophies* (New York: Harpers, 1957) p. 480.

evolutionary process there would likely come again and again if necessary more plant and more animal life, but not necessarily in their present forms. Man's creative contribution, his ability to create his civilization, began with the dawn of consciousness, which itself was a derivative of experience, and which marked the birth of mind. An improvement of the quality of man's experience has become the major task of the school, for in the realm of the quality of man's mind rests the final issues of man's progress or annihilation.

THE STATISTICAL METHOD. In applying psychology to statistics we have the beginnings of the foundations of a numerical and quantitative approach to the problem of the education of the individual. The origins of this idea can be found first in the work of Sir Francis Galton (1822-1911), for it was in his work on eugenics and that of Karl Pearson that James McKeen Cattell and E. L. Thorndike of Columbia University got their first insights into the significance of the statistical method.

American interest in mind measuring, however, is more directly related to the work of two Frenchmen, Edouard Seguin (1812-1880) and Alfred Binet 1857-1911). Seguin's contribution was the teaching of the idiot through motor education, and it was only after careful study of the causes of such conditions that he opened his school for the training of idiots in 1839. The detailed explanation of these ideas is found in Seguin's study on "The Theory and Practice of the Education of Idiots" (1842). It was through motor education that he was able to bring the uncoordinated movements of the body under control, a method which is now universally applied in the testing of young children. Also, it was Seguin who opened the door for Binet, whose basic contribution, with the help of Simon, was that of the measurement of the degrees of intelligence. In doing so Binet worked out an exact scale; and, although first published in 1905, it was continually improved upon over a period of the next six years. Operating on the assumption that the higher functions of man, such as intelligence and comprehension, varied more than what we define as motor functions, Binet and Simon set to work to devise a second measurement series testing the higher functions of mentality from ages three to twelve. Today this idea, and the improved procedures which have flowed from it, have found universal acceptance.

THE GESTALT. This, meaning form, figure, pattern or configuration, is an outgrowth of a psychological movement which found its beginnings in Germany in 1912 when Max Wertheimer stated its fundamental propositions. The basic idea or ideas here expressed were in direct conflict with those of William Wundt, a well established leader among the German psychologists. This configurational view is that parts of a given situation are not seen in isolation but as an integrated whole; whereas, in the thinking of Wundt

309

the approach was based upon the study of specific or particular aspects of a situation.

Actually, gestalt psychology was based upon two fundamental weaknesses in the psychologies of structuralism and behaviorism, those of elementarism and associationism. Elementarism, in holding that mind was only a mere collection of elementary units, erred in that it violated the fundamental principle of unity or wholeness and left the more important aspect of mind, that of insight, untouched. Associationism, which was supposed to supply the mental glue which held the elements together, was equally as inadequate as that of elementarism and erred for the same reasons. From the standpoint of gestalt the elements themselves were artificial, thus undermining the foundation on which the pillars of the old psychologies had been built. The problem of gestalt psychology has been defined as that of "determining the intrinsic nature and organization of the psychophysical field"[21] and of studying the relation of this field, to a geographical environment and the resulting behavior.

According to the gestalt theory every experience is said to have some kind of intrinsic pattern; or, stated otherwise, every environment seems to have some kind of totality. Such a pattern or totality does not necessarily remain permanent, as for example, a change in purpose. While gestaltists did most of their original work in the area of perception, they have, in recent years, concerned themselves with such educational matters as growth, intelligence, personality, feeling, thinking and learning. Much criticism has been made by the gestalt psychologist of the S-R bond theory, especially its reference to the significance of tension in behavior as contrasted with neural connections. Statistical averages in the final analysis, it has been argued, can tell us very little about what makes an individual tick in a given situation.

It was not until after World War I that there was any evidence of interest in the gestalt psychology movement in the United States. This came with the publication of Wolfgang Köhler's *The Mentality of the Apes* in which it was demonstrated that the responses of the apes were not random acts but rather were a result of some kind of mental process.

PSYCHOANALYSIS. As our society becomes more and more urbanized, and as the problems of youth mount, provision for the school guidance counselor has become a must in the well administered school system. The key idea for this movement is traceable back to the work of Sigmund Freud and his development of the method of studying the psyche which he called psychoanalysis.

---

[21] Fred S. Keller, *The Definition of Psychology* (New York: D. Appleton-Century, 1937) p. 89.

310

As we know it today psychoanalysis is essentially a method of medical practice which enabled the trained doctor to interpret, ferret out and treat the appropriate mental disorders. These disorders are discovered in the realm of the psyche, or mind, and a readjustment is made by means of analysis, or of getting the individual to face up to the causes of his disorder. Freud discovered this process mainly through the use of hypnosis but in doing so he learned that the hypnosis process was not completely satisfactory. Better cooperation could be achieved with the patient if he remained completely conscious and in control of all of his faculties. Frequent interviews and working slowly with the disturbed individual, through the free association technique, produced far better results. Nervous disorders of a mental rather than those of a purely physical, anatomical character tend to define the limitations of the method.

In developing his method of psychoanalysis Freud saw the psyche as possessing three distinct entities, (a) *the id,* the instinctive and the unconscious, (b) *the ego,* the rational and predominant conscious, and (c) *the superego,* the moral conscience. The id represents man's primordial urges, the foremost of which is the sex impulse. Impulses generated from the erotic instinct, unless directed toward the creative in life, become fixed, as illustrated in the mother fixation or the infant's "first love." When integrated these impulses make up the Oedipus complex which is found in every individual, and which comes out in the open, as in dreams, when the guard is down. Later modification of the Freudian concept by Jung and Adler tended to put greater emphasis on psychological types in determining the role of personality; but it is particularly in the problem of the disordered mind that the use of psychoanalysis has proven of greatest significance. In this respect the case study technique has come into wide use and is being applied now in our better schools.

American education is now embroiled in testing, debating, and modifying the implications of the new science and of recent psychological and quantitative understandings and approaches described above. These are in too early a stage of development and the fundamental, "reservoir" disciplines still so tentative in their hypotheses and knowledge, that the ultimate educational applications cannot as yet be assessed. It can only be ventured that in an age of increased international communication and mutual interests, American education will continue to be enriched by fertile ideas from abroad.

In summary, it is clear that American education is deeply indebted to a host of foreign educators and thinkers of whom it has been possible to identify only a few in number. It has been demonstrated that the pattern of American education adds up to a kind of Hegelian thesis-antithesis-synthesis pattern, the thesis being represented by the Classical-Christian pattern of intellectual and moral concepts, the antithesis by those concepts identified with naturalistic

311

individualism, and the synthesis by those concepts making up the socio-scientific movement. It has been demonstrated thus that more than anything else the problem of upgrading American education lies in the realm of concepts of intellectualizing and reconstructing our experiences. Such up-grading is mandatory if our democratic way of life is to survive in the twentieth century. It is hoped that this analysis will contribute to that process.

Bibliography

The writings of the men who contributed the key foreign ideas are the best possible supplementary material for this chapter. Books of special significance are Plato's *Republic* and *Laws*; Aristotle's *Politics* and *Ethics*; Augustine's *Confessions* and *De Magistro*; Aquinas' *Summa Theologica*; Comenius' *Didactic* and *Orbis Pictus*; Locke's *An Essay Concerning Human Understanding* and *Thoughts in Education*; Rousseau's *Emile*; Kant's *Critique of Pure Reason* and *Critique of Practical Reason*; Spencer's *Autobiography* and *Education: Intellectual, Moral and Physical*; Pestalozzi's *Leonard and Gertrude* and *How Gertrude Teaches Her Children*; Herbart's *The Science of Education* and *Outline of Pedagogical Lectures*; Froebel's *The Education of Man*; Darwin's *The Origin of Species*; Köhler's *The Mentality of Apes*; and Freud's *Introduction to Psychoanalysis by Teachers*.

The following secondary source materials are suggested:

Butler, J. Donald, *Four Philosophies*. New York: Harper's, 1957.

Butts, R. Freeman, *A Cultural History of Western Education*. New York: McGraw-Hill, 1955.

Cole, P. R., *A History of Educational Thought*. London: Oxford, 1931.

Commager, Henry Steele, *The American Mind*. New Haven: Yale University Press, 1950.

Counts, George S., *Education and American Civilization*. New York: Teachers College, Columbia University, 1952.

Cowley, Malcolm and Bernard Smith (Editors), *Books That Changed Our Minds*. New York: Kelmscott Editions, 1938.

Curtis, S. J. and Boultwood, M. E. A., *A Short History of Educational Ideas*. London: Universal Tutorial Press, 1953.

Drake, William E., *The American School in Transition*. New York: Prentice-Hall, 1955.

Lodge, R. C., *Plato's Theory of Education*. London: Reegan, Trench, Trubner, 1947.

Mayer, Frederick, *A History of Educational Thought*. Columbus, Ohio: Charles E. Merrill, 1960.

Monroe, Will S., *Comenius and the Beginnings of Educational Reform*. New York: Scribner's Sons, 1900.

Randall, John Herman, Jr., *The Making of the Modern Mind*. Boston: Houghton-Mifflin, 1926.

Rusk, Robert, *Doctrines of Great Educators*. London: Macmillan, 1918.

Shaw, Charles Gray, *Trends of Civilization and Culture*. New York: American Book Company, 1932.

Stocks, J. L., *Our Debt to Greece and Rome — Aristotelianism*. Boston: Marshall Jones, 1925.

Taylor, H. O., *The Medieval Mind*. London: Macmillan, 1930, 2 vols.

Thut, I. N., *The Story of Education*. New York: McGraw-Hill, 1957.

Trattner, Ernest, *Architects of Ideas*. New York: Carrick & Evans, 1938.

Ulich, Robert, *History of Educational Thought*. New York: American Book Company, 1950.

****

CHAPTER IX

WHAT DO WE OWE TO
OUR AMERICAN NEIGHBORS?

Introduction

Many are unaware of or overlook influences from the other Americas upon education in the United States. Maintaining his broadly conceived interpretation of "contributions" and undaunted because he recognized the many obscure, nearly hidden or forgotten and indirect forces that have marked this cultural intercourse among the Americas, the editor persisted in finding two writers who could portray such Canadian and Latin American sources. The authors of this chapter have succeeded in delineating these influences and connections, combining the factors of time, space, people, and institutions with original research that results in two unique and insightful presentations.

The Canadian Contribution to American Education

Basic Political Perspectives

The way in which the educational theories and practices of one nation affect those of another is dependent in no small measure upon the total of social, economic, political, and religious forces at work in the societies under consideration. However similar these societies may be, there are nevertheless differences which manifest themselves in a multitude of ways. The two

315

societies may have similar traditions, and have drawn their mores and social institutions from more or less similar backgrounds, yet the way in which these work out will be different. In the case of the United States and Canada the relationship though geographically and historically close has developed in such a way as to give evidence of significant differences, and this is especially true of education. Education is so much an integral part of the life of any nation, so deep a part of the warp and woof of the life of every one of its citizens, that to attempt to unravel the threads which have gone into the weaving of the national cloth, the shaping of its institutions, is to require first a consideration of the forms and forces which have been at work in and through the societies.

Nationalism, liberalism, and democracy are the three major social and political forces which have entered strongly into the shaping of Canada and the United States — forces which enter into the educational thinking of both peoples. Though both nations had their beginnings in the eighteenth century, the nationalistic forces which had been playing their part in Europe in the seventeenth century contributed to the ideals and ideas of many of the people who ultimately helped shape these nations. The Revolution of 1688 in Britain, the socio-political concepts which had preceded the French Revolution in 1789, had both contributed to what was to happen in Canada and the United States. Though the Declaration of Independence in the United States, and the British North America Act in Canada were respectively eighteenth and nineteenth century documents, the social and political principles which shaped their liberal and democratic institutions (including the educational) derived from the forces of nationalism and rationalism extant in Europe in the seventeenth and eighteenth centuries.

The period following feudalism in Europe had seen the advent of monarchies strong enough to change the individualistic tendencies of the former period to group identifications involving language, custom, ethic, and sympathy. These changes had paved the way for nationalistic tendencies which helped shape the revolutions that ultimately introduced republican principles into the governments of many peoples. By the time Canada and the United States entered the community of nations, liberalism and democracy were forces clear enough to identify. So clear were these that the concept of public education emerges in this period quite sharply. Nevertheless, there was no uniformity in the way in which liberalism and democracy reached the two countries, for Canada was called upon to compromise two distinct concepts of government in French and English traditions, whereas the United States, though drawing also from France and Britain, drew from a different period in each. Too, whereas the United States was born in revolution, it was compromise which gave Canada its constitutional being. Interestingly enough, a similar pattern is reflected in the way in which the educational systems have

316

developed. Thus, Canada and the United States, though both democracies, and possessing fundamentally similar institutions, differ in respect of the roles played by citizens in these social institutions, and this difference in roles is to be found particularly in the universities and colleges of the two countries.

The Canadian and United States forms of democratic government, though both drawn from British and French traditions, manifest differences in the conception of democracy. Canada, from the moment of her birth, has felt the weight of empire and of the commonwealth, a weight which threw the balance against the individual, and placed authority on the side of the government. The United States, by contrast, eschewed empire and common-wealth, choosing rather to add stars to its flag, thereby focusing the attention of individuals upon internal matters, and ultimately suggesting the importance of his unquestioned right to influence, form, and shape the government. Though both the United States and Canada may subscribe to the principles of the Magna Carta, the Bill of Rights, the Petition of Rights, and of Habeas Corpus, the direction these principles have taken since being first adopted has diverged in line with the conceptions of the weight to be given to the individual in revealing his role of responsibility within the body politic. It is this aspect of the role of authority and its relevance to the role of responsibility which, for example, has influenced university personnel in Canada to leave for positions in the United States.

This is well demonstrated in the differences to be found in the two public school systems on either side of the border. In Canada, by and large, schools follow a more prescriptive and restrictive type of program than in the United States where programs are left far more frequently to the responsibility of the school and of the individual. Again it is to be found in the difference in administrative organizations in Canadian and United States universities. Whereas, for example, presidents and deans, and to a large extent professors in Canada may enjoy life-long tenure, this is less true of their colleagues in the United States. Furthermore, the administrative power to be found within offices of the university in Canada differ in some instances quite markedly from similar power allocated to similar offices in the United States. These differences are far from superficial in their effect upon the climate of learning in educational institutions as they are also far from insignificant in the life of the judiciary, business and industry. It is perhaps because of this difference in the role of responsibility accorded individuals that in the United States the frontier was always considered a challenge for the individual, whereas in Canada this challenge became more a matter for the group to deal with. In somewhat the same way a latter age has accorded the individual a more significant role in the development of new social, economic, scientific, and industrial frontiers. Canada to this extent is suffering from a conservatism which to a degree belies the historic liberalism of her institutions.

The Southern Horizon — Geographical Factors

The end of the Seven Years' War in 1763 had left Great Britain a world power in a position to devote her attentions to the problems which beset her on the American continent. The "northern wastes" she was able to save; not so the American Colonies which, with the Declaration of Independence in 1776, opened up a new democratic frontier. Only the beginnings of each nation had been established, for it was not until after at least another century and a quarter that the present geographic boundaries were to have been hammered out on the fur trail, and around the treaty table. In the process, both Canada and the United States came to appreciate the role of their legal and constitutional powers in establishing the limits of country and of citizenship. The boundaries which came to denote their several countries not only separated the lands which had heretofore been travelled in common by all, but came to separate the idea of a Canadian from the idea of an American. What had been natural lines of travel north and south came suddenly with the establishment of the 49th parallel to be walls beyond which one was no longer the same citizen, but in effect, an alien. The call of empire had swung the two chief partners of the American continent a full 180 degrees to look East and West, rather than North and South. However, whereas clime and culture beckoned the American colonist North and West, the Canadian settler was slower to respond, since for the most part only the West beckoned, and even this was hampered by a thousand miles of rugged, unopened territory. This change of direction in the horizon of colonial aspirations laid the foundation for educational developments in each country that reflected the difference in these aspirations.

The continental territory of the United States (except Hawaii and Alaska), stretching as it does from below the thirtieth parallel to the forty-ninth, differs from that of Canada whose territory reaches from the forty-ninth to the Arctic Circle. Where those living in the United States can move freely and rapidly from one part of the country to another, not so in Canada, where for a portion of the year, even in its southernmost reaches, inclement weather restricts mobility. The geography of the United States, characterized by a wide variety of climates, and topography, has been able to attract peoples from widely scattered regions seeking comparable areas of living though escaping social and political conditions inimical to their welfare. The distribution of regions in the United States being greater than in Canada, and more richly productive, has of necessity attracted more people in a shorter time. The more than twenty degrees of latitude of the United States as against the less than ten cultivable degrees of Canada dramatically demonstrates the difference in their productive potential. The range and variety of climes and topographies has, furthermore, made for wide distributions of large populations in the United States, concentrations which in Canada are extremely rare. These richer geographic potentialities for people living in the United States have of necessity attracted educational personnel as well as others. Thus the United States from the very beginning has possessed those geographic features which have proved attractive and productive in the lives of people everywhere.

Allied to this geographic attractiveness was the nature of the economy and of world trade when the United States was rising to power in the eighteenth century. European economies were then seeking not only raw materials for their own machines, but markets for their products. With the change in the mercantilist theory of trade which came about in this period, the United States was in a position to benefit from its own productive potential. At the same time academies were developing which were called upon to train individuals in the procedures of business, a line of educational development which gave the American educational scene a distinct edge over the Canadian — however, not before a great deal of exploration had taken place. By contrast, Canada also opened up her territories by way of exploration, but her industrial potential was delayed in its development. The result of this difference was to give the United States a magnetic power which Canada has not been able to match. This difference in economic development was matched by a difference in educational development; for example, where the United States tended to emphasize education for the world of business, Canada tended to emphasize agricultural colleges.

The Canadian-American border stretching from the Atlantic to the Pacific provides not only a line of separation, but a line of thought. Canadians and Americans move freely across this border, themselves and their goods and chattels.[1] Over the years families have been separated by this line but not with any feeling of having moved a great distance or into an alien culture. Customs regulations may interfere with complete freedom, but these are not so onerous or so restrictive that they make themselves unduly obvious. This north-south flow of people and goods is accompanied by the flow of ideas. Nevertheless this movement is somewhat characterized by the principle of osmosis, in that the movement is predominantly from the less dense to the denser medium. The same border has, of course, not been arrived at without travail, for one war and many disputes intervened between definition and settlement.

The idea of the border is essentially a political one. The border separates one flag from another, one kind of English from another, and one kind of democracy from another. It does not separate the ethical character of its people; it does not separate the roots of the institutions which have taken

---

[1] An interesting report on this border is found in C. Mydan's article, "A Long Border that Peace Built," in *Life,* V. 49, Sept. 12, 1960, pp. 44-51.

shape in each society. The peoples today move readily from their occupations on one side of the line to similar occupations on the other side of the line without feeling that the technical sides are significantly different. Politically institutions differ in respect of their greater freedom in the south; socially the rate of mobility is greater; ethically there is a greater complex of mores to the south; morally there appears to be greater freedom also. The movies, the television programs, the newspapers, the magazines, and the periodicals all conspire to make of the border more of an imaginary line than anything else, in this respect tending to bring Canadian patterns of behavior more in line with those found in the United States. Though this tendency is evident, it does not quite come off, for the roots of home, of Commonwealth, and of geography (especially climate) are still weighty enough to redress the balance. The border exists as a political convenience, as a reminder that no two nations exist side by side, and that anyone moving from one side to the other should not forget he has done so, however easy it may be to do so.

Social Osmosis

American institutions have assumed a character partaking of the complete identification of its peoples with the American dream. This is to be recognized in the political organization, in literary contributions, in social activities, in economic arrangements, in school and college curricula, and in almost all phases of its life. The same may not be said of Canada, with the exception of Quebec where the "Canadien" has established institutions unique to the North American continent. When one contrasts, for example, the American with the Canadian forms of government one finds not only a difference in organization, to wit, the responsibility of the Prime Minister and his cabinet to the House of Commons, but a difference in the temper with which the people's representatives assume responsibility for their constituents. Whereas the American President and his cabinet may have both houses in opposition to a policy, and would not be required to resign, this is not the case in Canada. Somewhat similar differences in definition of responsibility are to be found in schools and colleges, differences which, again, partly explain why Canadians have sought to enter the American educational scene.

In the field of literature Canada has lagged well behind the United States. American literature may claim authors of the international stature of T. S. Eliot, Faulkner, Lewis, and the like. These have been recognized in Europe, and from the very beginning of its history, men of the caliber of Jefferson, and of Emerson, have caught the American scene and given it a universal meaning. Canada, whether because of a lack of spirit, of people, or of the yeast which gives rise to great literature has only recently begun to feel its way toward the great Canadian novel. Though painting and music have had their interpreters, and their practitioners, no truly great compositions have emerged to provide a guiding light to later and other generations. To say that Canada is a young country, too young to have produced anything significant in the arts, is to beg the question in the light of the performance of the United States. Rather, it has been claimed, the social and intellectual climate of those who possess the reins of government and of social institutions in Canada have stifled imagination and creativity by supporting only that which looks to return a profit in dollars and cents. Evidence for this is to be found in the paucity of monies made available for the arts and for education by the napoleons of business and industry in Canada. When compared with what their American counterparts do, the poverty of the performance is indeed magnificent! Canadian educators interested in the exciting social scene for material for literature and the humanities have naturally been attracted to the wider opportunities which the American society provides. What these Canadians have contributed has been imbedded in the American genre.

Both Canada and the United States have English as the main language of discourse. Here, as elsewhere, there is a significant difference in the way in which the language has developed. American English has been mapped and documented, as witnessed by the work of H. L. Mencken,[2] and the unique character of this form of English has become universally recognized. Not so in the case of Canadian English which only at the moment of writing is being traced in respect of its form which makes it unique. People do recognize that there is a unique quality to Canadian English, but the documentation has still to come.

The cultural complex of a people may also be explored by way of the forms of its food, shelter, and clothing. In this respect Canadians and Americans do not differ too much, but they do in terms of the varieties of each available to them. Americans enjoy a much broader scope when it comes to choosing food, shelter, and clothing, if for no other reason than that there is a greater zest for experimentation in their nature and outlook. Because a food is different, or exotic, or strange, does not condemn it in the American food mart, as it will, in all probability, in the Canadian. The same may be found in the case of clothing, especially women's apparel, for which many Canadian women are thankful. Too often Canadians bow to tradition in matters of food, as they do in matters of clothing. To be different in Canada is to invite comment of a nature which is not always complimentary. Fear of criticism is another indicator of the way in which Americans and Canadians differ, and matters of food, shelter, and clothing are only a few examples of this

---

[2] H. L. Mencken, *The American Language; An Inquiry into the Development of English in the United States*. New York: Knopf, 4th ed., 1937.

321

trait. While the American is conscious of criticism he will nevertheless go ahead and experiment. Not so the Canadian; he will refrain from acting until the opportunity passes, and probably make do with what he has found in the past to be safe, and sound, and "sensible." This zest for experimentation in the United States has attracted those Canadians who are so minded, and Canada, especially in the fields of science, industry, and education, has contributed scholars who were and are interested in opening up new frontiers of knowledge in each of these areas.

In quite another realm of the social scene, mass media, one finds vast differences between the American and Canadian worlds. The American press is characterized by a wide variety of reporting, all the way from what can be called yellow journalism to the stately, scholarly columns of the *Christian Science Monitor*. The press in the United States is accorded freedom of communication and the responsibility of ensuring that the public will be fully informed, thus able to act as intelligent citizens. Though to a very great extent the Canadian press operates under these same principles, it is nevertheless governed by the prevailing conservatism and tends to maintain a middle-of-the-road standard without providing anything like the other two extremes. In somewhat the same way Canadian television and radio are less dramatic and less flamboyant than their American counterparts. For one thing, Canadian television and radio, through the Canadian Broadcasting Corporation, have been largely dependent upon government subsidies and have had to submit to government controls, a condition which does not hamper the American free enterprise system of communications to the same extent. The attempt on the part of the Canadian government to foster a Canadian culture through television and radio, and lately through the monies given the Canada Council, has been a laudable effort, but, it has demonstrated the fact that there are not in Canada either those forces or those people who feel it worthwhile enough to do so on their own. Canadians, particularly through their government, have been attempting to resist the incursion of American cultural forms and forces in the way of programs, publications, and plays, but the attraction of these lies not so much in their arriving in Canada to impede development as they do in representing a society that has found itself in its culture and has given this culture a universal appeal, of which Canada is but one element. What Canadians fear from American culture is not the forms it presents, but the deficiency in Canada it reflects. One has only to consider the appeal of the American stage, the American publisher's market, the American zest for trying out new forms of communications to recognize that this display of national curiosity on a grand scale makes its appeal to the youth of Canada as its own conservative staidness cannot possibly do. In the realm of communications Canada is an old country despite its historic youth, and this especially by contrast with the United States, that has managed to retain the zeal and the zest of its youth for modern frontiers.

The foregoing examination of only a few of the institutions common to Canada and the United States is revealing of the way in which a more or less common heritage has developed in different ways to separate two societies, though at the same time, holding many things in common. These several forms of their cultural patterns highlight a staid conservatism on the one hand, not necessarily explained by vast uninhabited distances or by inclement, frigid climates, and by a vital, driving, dynamic society on the other. The verve and energy displayed by American society not only provide evidence of a youthful exuberance, but provide an irresistible attraction to youth and youthful people in Canada. The contrasts between Canada and the United States are not to be reckoned in quantities but rather in qualities, for it is this which in the end provides the magnetic forces for Canadians. For these reasons Canada has contributed youthful energy and vigor with its active imagination to the realm of American education.

Academic Aspirations

The educational history of a land is a history which reflects its social, economic, and cultural development. This is true for both Canada and the United States. In both countries four periods of educational development may be discerned, though of necessity there are differences in timing, distribution, pace, and rate. These periods are the colonial, the agricultural, the industrial-commercial, and the social-technological — in this last period both countries are now to be found. The colonial period, understandably, is one in which the movement of peoples from one country to another and the many common elements allow little differences to be discerned. The second period, the agricultural, is characterized by a cataclysm of major proportions, the American War of Independence, following which several thousands of persons, later called Loyalists, moved to Canada because of their anti-revolutionary feelings, and pro-British sentiments. These bodies settled in the maritimes, mainly New Brunswick, and in Upper Canada, and brought with them pro-British sentiments which went a long way toward influencing the emphasis to be given to education in Eastern Canada, at least. In the third period, the commercial-industrial period, both Canada and the United States moved forward to developing the resources of their respective economies with this important difference — that the United States moved much more rapidly and along a broader front. Though the Civil War had almost rent the nation in two, one result was to hasten the productive capacity of the economy with a further result in hastening the need for new formats in education. The fourth period has seen Canadian and United States institutions affected by the social and technological revolution which has accompanied the latter half of the present century. The four periods, of necessity approximate in their delineation, suggest that common historical precedents and common geographical factors have helped shape two countries with much that is similar.

Though the two economies have had somewhat parallel developments over time, several elements have gone into the separation of their social and technological development. In the social sphere, the United States has succeeded in creating an "American" who feels he is a citizen of the United States, has his roots in its soil and in its history, and is a part of all of its institutions. In the technological sphere, the United States has set itself to accommodating every mode and variety of invention and ingenuity with the result that the outlets for human imagination and creativity have always been legion. By contrast, the land to the north, perhaps more phlegmatic because more frigid, has in its social development been far more conservative. In part this may be attributed to the presence of two cultures — the French and the Anglo-Saxon, the latter modified by the advent of many mid-Europeans — who have had to compromise in order to remain together. In addition, the peoples who inhabit Canada have been late in coming to any feeling of nationhood, to any real sense of identity with its soil and its ethics. Too many see no necessity for a flag, preferring to owe silent (and often vocal) allegiance to a symbol whose history and tradition lie outside Canada. There is not to be found in Canada the kind of ethos which permeates the American social sense. To be a Canadian is not as important to a Canadian's individuality as is being an American to a citizen of the United States. On the technological side, Canadian science, business, and industry have lagged behind the United States. Where these have developed frequently it has been with funds from the United States or Britain. The fact that the human resources of Canada have never been fully appreciated by Canada goes beyond the fact of Canada's having ample natural resources, the development of which would challenge her people. Instead, Canada has been satisfied with extracting and shipping the raw unprocessed products of her farms, forests, and mines. The inevitable result has followed. Whereas the processing of a product from a raw to manufactured stage involves several people, these people have tended to move to the large manufacturing centers, and that has meant to the United States. Besides, Canada has furthered this kind of thinking by restricting immigration to such an extent that a circle is set up — few people, few internal markets, few internal opportunities. Over time these two strands, the social and the technological, have accelerated, but at such different rates, that Canada is lagging sadly behind the United States — lagging largely because of a lack of imagination, and of people. As a result of this complex of economic and industrial forces young Canadians interested in furthering both themselves and their economy have moved south to opportunity and development.

The two educational systems have reflected the pattern of development to be found in the social and technological phases of Canadian and American societies. Whereas Canada has tended to retain the character of education usually associated with the traditional conception of the academic life, the United States has gone on to adapt its educational system to the needs of its dynamic society. The United States, too, from the time of Jackson has subscribed to the conception of mass education whereas Canada has adhered to a more austere interpretation of this conception, preferring to tailor its educational provisions to the needs of the few who could benefit from its academically oriented offerings. The vocational and technical demands made on the school systems of the United States by business and industry have been met to a greater degree than in Canada, though at times the American educational machine has had to sacrifice some of its intellectual emphases in order to do so. On the other hand, the readiness to adapt in the United States has broadened the base and extended the height of the educational pyramid. One important result of this process has been to give the United States an educational system, which, because of its sensitivity to public demands, has required many more professional people of all degrees of interest to maintain the establishment. A wider variety of professional capacities has been accommodated in the educational system of the United States than is considered in Canada. This process has been particularly true at the American college and university level, and it may be discerned at the high school level as well, where one finds, for example, in addition to the comprehensive offerings, that commercial courses have a wider scope, and vocational and technical education a broader coverage. So far as the junior college provisions are concerned, the United States long has been well in advance of Canada in taking care of the needs of its young people.

Historical Perspective

Before moving further into a comparison of the Canadian and American educational systems it would be well to take a brief glance at the historical development of Canadian education. The first school in Canada is supposed to have been established at Three Rivers, Quebec in 1616 by the Recollets, and was followed by one in 1639 in the city of Quebec conducted by the Ursuline Sisters. Such schools as were established in the remainder of the century continued to be denominational in character and reflected French patterns of education on the continent. Nevertheless, though settlements were few and far between and interest in education continued to be low, toward the end of the century training in practical arts was being provided in some schools in addition to the meagre offerings of the three R's.

With the advent of the eighteenth century, and largely as the result of an increase in the number of communities and expanding populations, interest

325

in education increased. Following the military and political settlement of 1763 when the Seven Years' War was brought to a close, the British educational tradition was added to that of the French. Phillips in tracing the development of Canadian education in this period identifies church, parish, charity, Sunday, and infant schools as providing the elementary education of the period, although some seminaries and convent schools also appeared.[3] The British tradition showed itself in the establishment of schools conducted by the Society for the Propagation of the Gospel in Foreign Parts, and by the further establishment of Latin grammar schools such as that found in St. John's in 1799.

Although the denominational aspects of public and private educational establishments continued to predominate, the eighteenth century was a period during which British and French educational traditions helped shape the pattern of the future. The nineteenth century witnessed a rapid expansion of educational facilities along both religious and secular lines with the latter coming under more and more legislative controls reflecting an increase in organized community interest in education. Among the more interesting developments in this period was the appearance of the Monitorial school designed to provide education for the masses at low cost. Nevertheless, the Grammar Schools Act of 1811 did indicate in the same period continuing adherence to traditional European concepts of the role of education in the community. Despite the increase in the number of schools, however, and increase also in the legislation governing schools, the programs still seldom lasted longer than six months in any one year and the educational fare was correspondingly limited.

Several acts in this period attest to the mounting public interest in education. In Quebec, the Act entitled Royal Institution for the Advancement of Learning appeared in 1801. In 1807, in Ontario, the Public School Act provided provincial funds limited to secondary grammar schools indicating the tenor of the times by according these schools a more important place in the hierarchy of the social and political economy of the day. In 1824, the Fabrique Act of Quebec centered the control of church shools in the parish, and in 1829, in Ontario, legislative provision was made for elected school board members. By the time the British North America Act appeared in 1867, the principle of provincial control of education had been established assuring also the continuance of separate denominational schools where these were in existence at the time of the union. The clearest evidence of this pattern is to be found

---

[3] Instead of frequent footnotes in this brief survey, the reader is referred to the selected volumes in the chapter bibliography for details of the development of Canadian education.

today in the province of Quebec where two systems of education operate side by side, the French Catholic and the English Protestant system, both under the administration of a secretary of education.

The twentieth century saw the rapid expansion of the schools of Western Canada influenced largely by the principles established in Eastern Canada, though modified to some extent by American ideas. The early quarter of the twentieth century saw Canadian schools everywhere add agricultural, commercial, vocational, and technical education courses to the already existent classical and traditional curricula. The period between the first and second World Wars was one in which the local administrative unit gave way to the larger unit of administration, and in which a clearer Canadian pattern emerged distinguishable from its earlier French, English, and American components.

College and university development in Canada was in some respects similar to that in elementary and secondary education. All began with some kind of denominational affiliation which was either maintained or dropped depending upon the extent to which the locale of the institution made it possible for them to sustain enrollment denominationally or required a loosening of the religious regulations. Thus, the history of King's College, of Dalhousie, of Queen's, of Victoria College, and of others, all fall into this category. Later, others like the University of Alberta, of Saskatchewan, and of British Columbia were established as provincial non-denominational institutions. The denominational influence, however, has not been without its effect upon even these institutions, for in several instances denominational colleges are affiliated with them. Here, too, French and British traditions are to be found playing their part as distinct from American traditions. Although colleges and universities in Canada have since World War I been influenced by American educational concepts to a greater degree than was formerly the case, this influence has not been as marked as that in the elementary and secondary schools. A greater conservatism has been manifest throughout higher education, one reason being the tendency of these institutions to import instructional personnel from Britain and Europe, another reason being their autonomy.

Even a brief sketch of Canada's educational history would be incomplete without some reference to those individuals who helped shape it over the first three centuries, and who in some instances continue to do so. It is significant that the eighteenth century emphasized religious orders rather than individuals for in this early period educational services were shaped by the Recollets, the Jesuits, the Ursuline Sisters, the Sisters of the Congregation, and by the Brothers of the Christian Schools. The nineteenth century witnessed the provincial departments of education beginning to shape and sharpen their individual programs.[4] It remained for the twentieth century to initiate a developing awareness by the people of the need for greater inter-provincial cooperation and for a national image, preferably through the Federal Government's assumption of some measure of financial responsibility. In this period, too, the importance of an international dimension was recognized.

This international dimension took form early in the thirties when Canada became aware of the need for markets. However, it was not until later, in 1944, on the suggestion of the American Council on Education, that a Canada-United States Committee on Education was established. One of the first projects completed by this committee was "A Study of National History Textbooks Used in the Schools of Canada and the United States." The work of this committee also helped lay the basis for Canadian and American exchanges of personnel in education, a practice which has contributed to Canadian educational views finding their place in the American system. Unfortunately, the extension of the work of this body is hampered by a lack of Federal interest in its objective. Nevertheless, the increase in the number of educational personnel who continue to visit and study in American institutions contributes to mutual appreciation and understanding.

The church-state relations of Canada differ markedly from the situation in the United States. Whereas in the United States there is a clear separation of church and state that is so defined in the Constitution, such is not the case in Canada. The British North America Act of 1867, the instrument which is the Canadian counterpart of the American Constitution, was not written until long after French culture and traditions had taken root in the Province of Quebec, and in the maritimes; the provisions for education had to take this into account. One result was the provision in the B.N.A. Act for the educational rights of religious minorities and for the continuance of those educational systems already in existence at the time of the writing of the Act. This last provision explains the existence in Quebec of a provincially supported Catholic school system, as well as the continuance of the minority Protestant system. In most of the remaining provinces of Canada there is some form of separate or denominational schools, though in the main without

---

[4] The major educational advances in Canada in the nineteenth century are associated with Jean Baptiste Meilleur, J. O. Chauveau, and Daniel Wilkie of Quebec, with E. I. Rexford, John Strachan, Robert Strachan, and Egerton Ryerson of Ontario; and, with T. H. Rand, John McNeill, Alexander Forrester, J. W. Dawson, and Thomas McCulloch of Nova Scotia. In listing these people from Nova Scotia it is well to note a Canadian phenomenon — that the maritimes, essentially Nova Scotia, Prince Edward Island and New Brunswick, have for years been contributing more than their proportionate share of educational leadership across Canada. Without doubt the Scottish tradition which has played so large a part in both secondary and higher education in Canada, has stemmed from this region.

financial support by the province. This should be qualified to the extent that in Ontario, for example, parents may allocate their taxes to the school system of their choice, and a similar provision is also to be found in the province of Alberta.

Exactly how much influence the example of Canada, and particularly of Quebec, in partial or whole support for denominational education has had on educational thinking in the United States is difficult to determine, since no direct evidence of such influence is readily available. Certainly the continuing pressures for state and Federal support of education are recurrent themes in American educational discussions, and these pressures undoubtedly derive part of their impetus from the examples north of the border. Nevertheless, there appears to be developing, even in Quebec, a body of thought cognizant of some of the losses suffered by splitting up the community's educational dollars and efforts. This, in full recognition of the spiritual values implicit in the purpose of such institutions, is spearheaded in part by certain Catholic religious and lay leadership.

Canadian and American Educational Systems

The Canadian and American educational systems are alike in many respects. In general the provincial control of education in Canada is matched by the state controls to be found in the United States. Too, the organizations of the systems are similar in that a six-year elementary is followed by a three-year intermediate, a three-year high school, and finally a four-year university program. This single ladder scheme holds generally in Canada, with two major exceptions: Quebec differs in retaining the seven-year elementary, and has also the classical college — an educational institution unique on the continent. The United States, on the other hand, has a quite comprehensive junior college system, an idea that has not made any appreciable headway in Canada.

The most important difference between Canada and the United States in the realm of education is to be found in the regional accrediting associations which govern the standards maintained by schools, colleges, and universities. These are absent from the Canadian scene with the result that the power exercised by provincial departments of education is largely exclusive of any kind of check or balance such as exists in the United States. The effect of this almost singular control is to vest in provincial authorities a measure of control that removes it from the salutary criticism of both professional and lay public. Although the Canadian institution of Royal Commissions helps periodically to appraise the operation of the educational system, this tends to be somewhat too peripatetic to keep the educational machine in line with social and other changes in the society. What has been said thus far affects

329

the public school systems in the main, there being relatively little control of private institutions.

One other aspect ought to be borne in mind. Although both the United States and Canada have respectively state and provincial administrations, there is in the United States federal representation at cabinet level, a seat which does not have its counterpart in Canada. The United States Office of Education, limited as it is to the assembly of information and the dissemination of the results of its studies, does provide a national platform for the consideration of any educational problem, a framework that is absent in Canada. When to this federal office is added the number of national organizations such as are subsumed under the National Education Association, or the American Association of Colleges for Teacher Education, or the many others, one can begin to appreciate the attention possible for any educational question on a national scale. There has recently developed in Canada the Canadian Conference on Education, and it is possible that this will develop a purpose and function consistent with Canada's needs. In the meanwhile the lines laid down for education in Canada in the British North America Act of 1867 continue to impose a provincialism on the educational machine which is serving as a brake on adequate progress.

The universities in Canada, however, generally operate under separate provincial charters, and by tradition enjoy exclusive autonomy with respect to academic matters. Nevertheless, the provincially supported universities, as their American counterparts, are dependent upon an enlightened legislature as to the state of their financial solvency. Since the legislatures are in several instances prone to consider university funds alongside of the funds necessary for more politically profitable ventures such as sewers, roads, and bridges, the universities are often held back from developing along the lines which sound educational policy would dictate. Insofar as the private universities are concerned, they are confronted by the same problems as their American counterparts. In general the internal administration of Canadian universities follows the pattern of American with the singular exception that tenure plays a much stronger role. A second difference to note is that there is a more authoritarian complexion to Canadian internal university administration, with staff members playing a much lesser role in the definition of policy or of curriculum. This factor has frequently militated against the best atmosphere for the productive work of scholars. Too, there has been a tendency for Canadian universities to emphasize teaching as against research and service, although in this last respect the agricultural, horticultural, ichthyological, and silvicultural branches have done trojan work in servicing the fundamental industries of the country. Notwithstanding the apparently greater freedom enjoyed by American institutions, Canadian professors do enjoy academic freedom in the sense that they are not subjected to the indignity of loyalty oaths or to gross interference by outside bodies as can happen in American institutions.

The educational systems of the United States and Canada, up to and including the university, are essentially not too different one from the other. In one important respect, however, they do separate quite markedly, and that is at the post-graduate level. Here the American universities have funds and facilities which Canadian universities do not have in anything like the same degree. When one considers, too, the variety of opportunity available for post-graduate study, one begins to perceive the dimensions of the problem confronting Canadian institutions which are seeking to retain their best and most productive students. In addition to the great number of scholarships, aids, and fellowships available for post-graduate studies, there are in American institutions also a great many athletic scholarships and bursaries for undergraduate students, and this provides still another attraction to the Canadian student who does not find the same appreciation of his talents north of the border.

Canadian universities continue to be leavened in their educational philosophies and practices by a steady influx of Commonwealth personnel, mainly from England and Scotland, though Australia and South Africa also contribute. As a result, Canadian institutions, having as they do Canadian and American personnel as well, find themselves with quite a broad range of viewpoints, sometimes a broader range than is to be found in American institutions. This breadth, however, is attended by a slowing up of decision-making since so often several viewpoints have to be reconciled before any kind of action may be taken. The homogeneity of educational viewpoints to be found in many American institutions does make for readier action.

Canadian Educational Contributions

The foregoing examination of the historical, geographical, cultural, and educational constructs of Canada and the United States provides a backdrop for a closer look at what have been and are Canadian contributions to American education.[5] Against this backdrop one can perceive Canadian conservatism contrasting with American experimentalism. More of the frontier has remained in the American way of life than has remained in the Canadian. Too, there is evident a more virile energy in the American scene, the result not only of a greater population, but also of wider horizons to be found in a more prevalent urbanization. Despite Anglo-Saxon and French contacts maintained by Canadians, Americans have maintained a closer liaison with both

---

[5] The author wishes to acknowledge the signal contribution of the several hundred Canadians now resident in the United States who responded so ably to his inquiries concerning Canada's contribution to American education. Their perspective was as invaluable as their perspicacity was insightful.

Europe and Asia, a liaison which inevitably has led to broadening and deepening the American culture. The social process at work in the United States when contrasted with the same process at work in Canada is revealing of the way in which the two systems have set up what we have called a cultural osmosis whereby movement is from the less dense Canadian medium to the denser American medium.

This cultural osmosis, of course, works in two directions: ideas and processes move from the United States to Canada, and people move in the main from Canada to the United States. This two-way process is best illustrated by the words of F. E. Whitworth, Director, Education Division, Dominion Bureau of Statistics, who wrote in 1959:

> There are not too many statistics available but we find, for example, that in 1957-58 there were 812 students from the United States, 91 from Mexico, 70 from the West Indies, and 44 from Central America enrolled in the private colleges outside of Quebec and since the majority of French-speaking and Catholic students would be found in Quebec, I rather fancy that there might have been from 800 to 1,000 there. For the same year there were 1,773 students from the United States enrolled in Canadian universities and colleges. Again there were some 5,271 Canadian students enrolled in the colleges and universities of the United States, and almost as many full-time graduate students in the United States universities as there were American students in Canadian universities. While it is impossible to evaluate the effect of this migration for education, there is little doubt that Canadian ideas will permeate American students and American ideas will affect Canadian students. Again it is likely that our students in American universities have considerable influence on the thinking of American students with whom they come into contact.[6]

Certainly the movement of students is in two directions, but as the figures reveal, the predominant movement is from the north to the south. With people, of course, go ideas, and though these may not always be of an order to invite public attention or acclaim, the cumulative effect of many viewpoints personally expressed may be considerable. That this cumulative influence goes beyond what may be found in academic circles alone is attested to by the fact that the 1950 United States Census showed approximately a million Canadian-born residents of the United States out of a total population of roughly 151 million people. Of these million Canadians some quarter of a million were French-speaking Canadians. If to these influences are added those of art, literature, and painting, and again those of TV, radio, and the movies, one can begin to perceive something of the order of the front along which cultural osmosis is taking place.

---

[6] From a personal letter to the writer.

332

A survey of Canadians engaged in educational pursuits in the United States reveals that their services and offices cover an exceedingly wide range. Canadians, resident as long as twenty and thirty years in the United States, have become presidents and heads of university faculties or departments, are in several instances directors of research, have reached the office of vice-president or president in several national organizations, and have assumed the chairmanships of many committees of local, regional, or national bodies. Canadians have even reached positions of signal responsibility in the United States Government service, and in several instances have served or are serving on Presidential Advisory Committees. Canadians are to be found as editors, as American representatives on foreign missions, as representatives of American educational bodies at international congresses, and in one instance as a curator of a famous American museum. Although only a few Canadians are represented in the aforementioned samples, it is nevertheless revealing of the influence they are exerting on American education insofar as position or office may provide opportunity for such influence.

The same sample indicates that Canadians are located predominantly in the upper echelons of the American educational system. A very large number of Canadians are to be found in various kinds of agricultural departments such as dairying, poultry husbandry, agronomy, soil conservation, plant pathology, cereals, milling, and the like. They are also to be found in business administration, psychology, genetics, education, mathematics, economics, marketing research, aviation research, geology, radiology, rubber research, seismological research, physics, biology, and in archaeological research. American medicine has attracted many Canadians and here we find them not only practicing their calling, but also engaged in instruction and in research. In the latter instance radiology, bacteriology, and physiology are but a few of the areas in which specialization has been manifested.

As is to be expected, these people, engaged as they are in research and writing, have been exceedingly productive. Although all have been productive in the several callings and fields, publications of research run to over 100, 150, or 200 separate papers for several of them. In addition there are the publications of books and pamphlets. From the number of talks, speeches, and addresses these Canadians have been called upon to give, it becomes more than ever evident that their influence is of a considerable order.

The specific nature of the Canadian contribution is quite another matter to identify. Since all of these Canadians are engaged in work alongside of their American colleagues the contribution they may make will blend perceptibly or imperceptibly with that of the others. Again, a Canadian, once a member of a staff or research team, will not think of himself as either a Canadian or American, nor will he be thought of by his colleagues in one or another sense, but rather will be recognized for his professional competencies. For these reasons, to identify specific Canadian contributions to American education is to highlight an aspect of the contribution which in one sense is inconsistent with the ideas usually prevailing in any community of scholars. Only insofar as is possible to identify people who are Canadians as distinct from contributions which are Canadian is it possible to give credit where it is due. Nevertheless the real and substantial contribution which Canada makes to American education is significant. In effect, this is the extraordinary contribution: Canada is subsidizing American education by educating many Canadians, then letting them leave Canada for the many obvious opportunities which await them in the United States. Every now and again some one or other Canadian statesman or publisher will draw attention to this steady draining away of some of the best brains, the most virile and experimentally-minded young people, but that will be as far as it goes. Without demonstrable action, Canada will so continue to subsidize American education, if only by default and neglect.

Canadians involved in one or another section of American education are appreciative of the opportunities they have been accorded in the United States. Their comments signify, too, an appreciation of the quality of the society which has provided such opportunities. On the other hand, these perceptive observers of the Canadian and American educational scenes are not without their critical appraisals of the situation. In no instance is there evidence of their regretting a move south, nor of disparaging the work in which they are engaged or the conditions attaching to this work. Nevertheless their appraisals do give Canada, and Canadian leadership a drubbing, at the same time showing evidence of the way in which American education could benefit further from Canadian experience and thought. Among the more interesting comments are the suggestions that opportunities for women in the educational field are greater in the United States, especially where positions of leadership and responsibility are concerned. Some go on to say that American education could learn a lot from Canadian education if Canadian educators "would stop trying to ape American practices" and hold more to their own principles of development. A significant number believe that Canadian high schools provide a better education than their American counterparts, though this could be affected by the fact that fewer students go on to high schools in Canada than do in the United States. Some of the Canadians in the United States are critical of other factors; for example, they believe the holidays granted are too long for the good of the students. Such criticism of local educational practices made by Canadians in the United States can constitute a contribution.

On the other hand, Canadian educators in the United States have levelled significant criticisms of the conditions surrounding education in Canada. These criticisms, arising as they do out of their own personal experiences, and out of their vantage point overlooking two cultures, are constructive and realistic. According to the views expressed there is a lack of appreciation on the part of the management of Canadian companies of the worthwhileness of research in industry. The significance of the role of research has been apparently often lost upon management, with the consequence that the liaison between industry and the universities is far less adequate in Canada than it is in the United States. One result of this has been to turn a great many young, research-minded Canadians to research institutes in the United States. American professors appear to sense a greater challenge in their work than do Canadian professors in theirs; either this, or the conditions in universities foster a better balance among research, service, and teaching. Whatever the main reason or combination of reasons, Canadian professors in American universities seem to find a broader scope for their interests and pursuits. Apparently there are few comparable opportunities in Canada, not only as regards the variety of positions available, but also as regards the scope within job situations. Another aspect of Canadian views is that those Canadians who do move to American institutions are less parochial in their outlooks and seek a professional environment that is characterized by a more international outlook. It would appear from the foregoing that Canadians are helping to shape the international character of American education, and to foster a breadth of outlooks in their special fields.

In general, the graduate of a Canadian university seeking post-graduate training in many fields, including education, is often forced to seek opportunities in either Britain or the United States. Even though there are provisions for post-graduate research and study in certain areas in Canada, the facilities provided by Canadian universities are relatively poor when compared with those available in the United States. As a consequence, these post-graduate students will migrate to the United States, and once in a program are soon caught up by the machine. The contribution which these post-graduate students make to American education is not without its importance, for though as yet learners, the level of their learning is such as to warrant their active participation in many significant research projects on the way to completion of their work. In so doing their contributions take the form of pushing the bounds of knowledge still further.

The Canadian contribution to American education, though primarily concentrated in university personnel, and in Canadians engaged in private and public research organizations, is nevertheless also made by personnel in TV, radio, and the press. Canadians are also found in the teaching ranks of the elementary and secondary schools, and their contribution here would be that share of their experience and training which they could bring to bear upon the solution of problems met with in the course of their work. The extent to which the Canadian contribution may be said to be greater in the field of

335

education than in other fields is limited by the paucity of qualitative and quantitative statistics available. That the proportion of Canadians in senior positions of education in the United States is as great as it is, however, is significant of the contributions they are making to American education.

Another way in which the Canadian makes his contribution to American

UNIVERSITY OF SASKATCHEWAN, CANADA. SASKATOON CAMPUS.

education is by way of the theories and practices of administration which he takes with him from Canadian to American institutions. Although the more conservative practices of Canadian institutions may not appeal to the Canadian educational migrant while in Canada, once within the American setting he finds values in former practices not earlier realized and attempts to introduce ideas with which he was formerly acquainted, thus tending to influence administrative practice. In part, these ideas concerning administrative practice are shaped by British and European patterns with which the Canadian is usually more familiar than his American counterpart.

Canadians make their contributions to American education in still another way. Many Canadian educators are members of American educational organizations and take an active part in their proceedings and conferences. One

336

reason for this participation is to be found in the fact that only in recent years have national organizations in the field of education appeared on the Canadian scene. In many instances these are still in the formative stages. As a result of the professional interests of Canadian educators they have had to find an outlet in American organizations. In one instance, at least, American organizations have had branches established in Canada, a practice which finds its parallel in many areas of business and industry. Along with participation in American organizations, Canadian educators contribute widely to American professional periodicals. Again, although there are several professional outlets in Canada, these by no means provide the pages necessary to carry the publications of Canadian educators.

The teacher and student exchange programs are yet another means whereby Canadian educational theories and practices exert an influence upon Ameri-

UNIVERSITY OF MEXICO.

can education. The largest proportion of exchanges takes place between Canadian and American elementary and secondary teachers and these provide for a two-way communication. Canadian public school practices and programs, particularly at the elementary level, are shaped by American ideals; nevertheless, Canadians going to the United States are able to take with them some of the more conservative approaches they utilize in their own system, and bring these to bear in their American situations. While the

337

number is not large, American students trained in Canadian institutions of higher education return to the United States with insights into Canadian viewpoints. In 1958-59, 1,983 such students were enrolled in Canadian under-graduate and graduate facilities.[7] As has been explained previously, the predominant influence in numbers and ideas flows in the opposite direction; but often the American-trained Canadians return again to the United States with their modified but basically Canadian outlooks.[8]

The measure of the Canadian contribution to American education is somewhat difficult to assess by virtue of the fact that there are so many in-fluences upon Canadian education coming from the United States. Canadian educational ideas are not yet so distinctive as to be clearly separable from those in the United States. Yet even though a Canadian may have been in-fluenced by American conceptions in Canada, there is nevertheless a Canadian residue which he has been able to take with him into the American educa-tional scene. In the final analysis, the Canadian contribution to American education results from the cumulative influence of many Canadians in the schools, colleges, and universities in the United States. This influence has manifested itself especially in medicine and agriculture, and in the main in the sciences as distinct from the humanities. There seems, however, to be little question but that in the years ahead Canadian education and that in the United States, at all levels, will be drawn into greater and more satisfying compass.

Latin American Antecedents and Implications for Education in the United States

Our educational relationships and heritage south of the Rio Grande have been and remain different from the Canadian interchange. Our discussion of Latin American factors takes, therefore, a varying tack, as it pushes much further back, yet looks even more to the future. This heritage provides the anomaly of a rich past that remains largely to be uncovered, appreciated, and applied in the years ahead that promise to bind the Americas, from the arctic Canadian Provinces to distant Patagonia, ever more closely.

---

[7] Cited by F. E. Witworth, Director, Education Division, Dominion Bureau of Statistics, Ottawa, in a letter to the editor.

[8] Canadian contributions to American culture could well be materially extended if schools in the United States did more to promote interest in and knowledge about Canada. Some of the problems involved, suggested emphases, and bibliographical refer-ences are traced in two interesting articles: "Teaching About Canada in the American Schools," by E. L. Daniher, *Social Education,* April, 1954, pp. 164-168; and "Canada, Still the Unknown Country," by R. W. Winks, *Social Education,* December, 1958, pp. 381-383.

In this section of the chapter the writer also attempts to reveal the advantage to historical interpretation and toward an understanding of contemporary education that accrues from an anthropological orientation. Just as sociological factors are emphasized in Chapter IX, the following exposition should indicate the extent to which our understanding of an era or area can be enriched by the insights and approaches of another of the social sciences. Anthropology, along with geography, political science, economics, psychology, and the other related disciplines, adds dimensions to the historian's portrayal that enable him to reach a more complete and satisfying analysis and at the same time brings us a more adequate and well-rounded knowledge and appreciation of our educational scene. With these introductory remarks we turn to the Latin American heritage.

Latin America consistently defies attempts to neatly classify it. Historically, the term was once more appropriate than today when France alone, of all the Latin governments, exerts even minor influence. Linguistically, it has never been strictly correct since more than half of the inhabitants speak languages bearing no resemblance whatsoever to any of the Latin tongues. For the purposes of clarity only, then, let us limit our definition of Latin America to the self-governing republics of Argentina, Bolivia, the United States of Brazil, Chile, Colombia, Costa Rica, Cuba, Ecuador, El Salvador, Guatemala, Honduras, Mexico, Nicaragua, Panama, Paraguay, Peru, Uruguay, and the United States of Venezuela.

The word American by itself, however, implies non-European. In this sense, the exact American part of our heritage might justifiably be suspected as being Indian. To begin to comprehend our educational heritage in these terms calls for a complete re-orientation of traditional thinking. We must deliberately wrench ourselves out of comfortably familiar frames of reference to wrestle with evidence recorded very differently than the revered papyrus and paper-printed tomes that come to us via Europe and points East. Various institutions of higher education have been sending out archaeological expeditions to what they call Nuclear America (Mexico to Peru) for more than fifty years now in an on-going attempt to bring back to light our Indian civilizations which are as old, as magnificent, as any in Europe; to resurrect and to piece together again the distinctly American side of early man's global wanderings which lead back beyond written history into the depths of prehistory itself. Strictly speaking, then, by nicknaming the two continents in this hemisphere the New World, fifteenth century Europeans merely admitted that it was a world new to them.

Archaeological Exploration Leads to New Knowledge

Far from being underestimated as sometimes was the Roman, these civilizations have been all but forgotten, even denied, for what the work of nature

339

hasn't done to obliterate them, well-intentioned, though often mistaken, man has. Today, painstaking archaeologists patiently metamorphosize grass-grown slopes to great white temples. In some places these newly unveiled skylines stretch for six miles. Ghost cities reveal themselves in photographs taken from airplanes. Bush-burners clearing ground report new ruins as do highway construction crews, bridge and dam builders. Scores of known sites, packed with ruins, haven't been touched. Still others have been only partially examined. The educational heritage that comes to us through these restorations and excavations presents itself in 3-D, in audio-visual aids par excellence, rather than in the written forms with which we are more accustomed. We learn about social organization through analyzing settlement patterns. The arts, economics, religion and medicine through funerary memorabilia. Science education, through testimony of knowledge of astronomy, metallurgy, mathematics, calendrical systems, and graphics. Engineering education through road, aqueduct, pyramid and city construction, the re-direction of rivers, and the formation of floating gardens. Agricultural education through the awesome presence of an amazing variety of plants; plus impressive evidence of soil renewal and reconstruction. Home economics education, through pottery and weaving techniques that haven't been excelled or even equalled since.

In the late 1940's eight universities, collaborating under the name of the Institute of Andean Research, concentrated on a single river valley on the northern coast of Peru to unearth one of the longest unbroken histories of civilization known to date.[9] The record commences with fishing, gathering, and hunting nomads; moves on to early farmers; temple and town builders, pyramid and city planners in which all the arts accumulating from the past flowered and flourished; then catapults into fusion of this civilization with others through conquest and warfare; to be absorbed finally into the empire of the mountain Incas who ruled benignly in the area when the Spanish arrived. Experts don't agree on the dates yet but some have ventured the guess that a span like this easily covered 6,000 years, with the earlier epochs lasting always the longest.

Nomads Establish Unity

The learning environment for the fishing, gathering and hunting nomad extended as far as his eye could reach: out into the flat Pacific which sheltered succulent sea food; across endless sands and up mountain slopes where spare fruits and roots might be gathered and small animals killed or caught. His motivation was survival. Transmission of skills or culture was passed

---

9 William Duncan Strong, "Cultural Epochs and Refuse Stratigraphy in Peruvian Archaeology," *American Antiquity,* April 1948, pp. 93-102.

down from one generation to the next pragmatically; that is, one learned by experiencing, by doing in a real life situation. Education was action, practical and meaningful; reinforcement, immediate. It took place within the protection of primary kin, with relatives for teachers to guide and direct. Both young and old acquired new skills through transfer in observation or imitation of nature itself. The individual personality merged itself in a group personality; the group personality, into an earth or world personality.

> . . . the truth that intensity of life, beauty in the human relationship, happiness, and amplitude of personality are not dependent on complexity of material culture or on that "security" which . . . has come to be a controlling objective. The essential goods of life were had by man — were created by man — and there are groups of men here and now who know and prove that these essential goods were and are, and how they were and are and can be created and sustained.[10]

Many anthropologists have written about this steadfast, spiritual poise of the Indian but few as beautifully as John Collier, formerly United States Commissioner of Indian Affairs. Edgar L. Hewett, who taught school from the grades to college before he graduated into archaeology, eulogized this view of man and the universe which summarizes the spiritual unanimity of all American Indians,

> . . . the mode of the life of the American aborigines was primitively framed after one sociological principle on the whole American continent and that consequently the culture of the American Indian has varied locally only in *degree* not in *kind;* that the religious principles were fundamentally the same and that physical causes more than anything else have lain at the bottom of local differences in culture. No single fact concerning any race has been more firmly established than that of unity in the American . . . That America has been capable of implanting such traits in the human species should be to every American, aboriginal or intrusive, a matter of pride and hope.[11]

Early Indian Agricultural Accomplishments

No one knows, really when or how man stumbled into agriculture. It is not difficult to see how a gatherer automatically spreads seeds. The concept of saving them and planting them in one place deliberately prepared for the purpose, however, might easily have taken a millennium of accumulating

---

[10] John Collier, *Indians of the Americas,* Mentor Edition, (New York: New American Library, 1951) p. 20.

[11] Edgar Lee Hewett, *Ancient Life in Mexico and Central America* (New York: Bobbs-Merrill Co., 1936) p. 346.

separate perceptions. As a fisherman, the fertilizing value of parts of seafood dropped in with the seed as it is planted lingers on today. As a hunter, too, his capturing and raising of young animals whose mothers he had killed might easily have disclosed in time the soil enrichment qualities of manure. Indeed, to the ethnobotanist, a scientist who studies botany in its cultivated beginnings, the prehistory of man is written in the incompleted story of plants. When we consider, even with all our expensive modern laboratory equipment and highly trained personnel, that not a single radically new botanical specimen of more than incidental consequence has been created in the last several thousand years, our debt to the unheralded research experimentations and continued applications in genetics through the ages of these Indian farmers of nuclear America skyrockets. They solved the problems of their survival by developing the avocado, lima and kidney beans, cacao, cassava, corn or maize, the papaya, peanut, pineapple, squash, sweet potato, potato and the tomato! Inedibles included such economically important items as balsa wood, Indian cotton, curare, rubber and tobacco. Indeed, we should either admire them for their patience or their brilliance. If nothing basically new has been added to the plant world since 3000 B.C.[12] we are forced to admit that agriculture had prodigiously earlier beginnings, weighted in proportion to what they nurtured into domesticity compared to what we haven't. All told, they innovated from twenty-five to fifty percent of the plant domesticates of the world. Most of us, however, ignorant of their bounty, do not acknowledge this debit with so much as a grateful passing thought when we consume these gifts to all humanity as they appear on school picnics; in field-trip lunchbags; on scholarly banquet or school cafeteria tables.

A fragmental example in this legacy took place near the mouth of a river in the Peruvian valley where the Institute of Andean Research focused its activity. Junius Bird of the American Museum of Natural History plotted strata lines with nails and string along the side of a large mound there called Huaca Prieta. Back in the United States a fellow scientist, of a school of archaeology which concentrates on ceremonial sites where the work is less back-breaking and more glorified, had discouraged his investigating this mound by insisting, "You'll be wasting your time. I've been all over that site and it isn't worth the trouble." Nonetheless, for the next seven months he and ten assistants sifted everything dug out between those two lines. They unearthed evidence of sea and bird life; thousands of stone flakes, too coarse for arrow heads but usable as fishing weights, firestones or hand axes. Since the mound stood a few meters above the ground water table of the area, perishable matter that would have decomposed in a million other sites

---

[12] Edgar Anderson, *Plants, Man and Life* (Boston: Little, Brown and Co., 1952), pp. 133-134.

was retrieved almost as intact as the day it had been left there. They procured cotton, gourds, aji peppers, beans and local tubers already developed to the same perfection that they are today. They unearthed patches of cotton cloth that differed either in color or weaving technique or both. There were pieces of matting woven with cotton cords going one way and reeds the other. Baskets of different styles, imaginatively fashioned with varying thicker and thinner strands. They excavated no leatherwork, no weapons, no land mammal bones, no garments, no ornaments, no hearths, no pottery. For at least ten centuries, fishermen farmers unwittingly built up that mound by living there and letting the refuse of their lives lie where it fell when they dropped it. For ten centuries, judging by the garbage (more picturesquely sometimes referred to as kitchen midden) at least forty generations repeated the identical pattern of their existence. Education, then, was sustained enculturation within the primary group that the majority of our children experience to a lesser degree before they enter nursery school. Skills were transmitted through practice influenced by motivation and readiness. Their religion, a psychological, continuing union with their fishing-gathering-hunting forefathers, left behind no tangible cult artifacts. Material enrichment and aesthetics show up in the variety of weaving techniques in both cloth and basketry. No one knows for sure whether weaving was a specialty of certain people for only certain occasions or the spare time activity of everybody.

According to the number of houses which appear toward the top-most levels of the mound, no more than 100 people ever lived on Huaca Prieta at any one time. These dwellings lay underground, about the shape of Eskimo igloos, as roomy as telephone booths. Stones from the beach, cemented into place by a paste made from mixing ashes, dirt and broken sea shells with water, line the walls. Short beams of wood and bone interspersed with stone and twigs comprise the roofs which come up to the ground level. Literally pockets in the earth, these shelters are too small to lie down in comfortably. In the native language of the people of the area today, the word for "to live" is the same as "to till the soil." Since early plant domesticators virtually organized their lives in behalf of their small garden plots, it is highly possible that the two words were the same even then. That their "home life" was not spent in these pint size habitations in the earth but rather out on the land itself which required constant and careful tilling, reclaiming, renewing to bring sustenance forth from the desert. "So much is the delight and gratification they got and still get out of their fields, that because of them they forget every other pleasure, as if their fields were their final goal and ultimate happiness," reported an ancient Spanish chronicle.[13]

---

[13] Cited by Sylvanus G. Morley, *The Ancient Maya* (Stanford University Press, 1956), p. 52.

That's all there is to Huaca Prieta, but, by this bit of amazing detective work, Junius Bird exhibited an example of healthy self concept in action for an age that deplores, "We do not teach them how to think." I refer to that predisposition to find out for oneself; to persist patiently through drudgery when need be, in order to follow that finding-out through. In the face of others ready to dismay him or discount his efforts, he toiled on to present to the world's growing body of organized knowledge a thousand year, uninterrupted record of the peacefully complete, everyday life of ancient agricultural researchers.

Interrelationships of Education and Culture

William Duncan Strong of Columbia University dug into a similar mound across the river at Guanape. This site was further in from the coast and closer to the mountains but about the same farmable land distance from the river as Huaca Prieta.

He found signs of corn, pottery, and a religious symbolism centering on a cat god art motif. The jigsaw puzzle piece for where these originated remains one of the hundreds of pieces slowly being fit into place through the manpower and money furnished by institutions of higher education on both continents. Be that as it may, after a millennium of staying put on one hill as a tiny world turned in upon itself without the invigoration of ideas or trade articles that come in from contact with other persons and places, visitors arrived and settled down.

In the more or less 2,000 years that follow we can almost watch a sedentary farming region, always retaining its agricultural emphasis as a supportive substructure, evolve into a prosperous, populous valley state of temple and town builders. Here is an opportunity close at home and in our own past to study the influence of acculturative forces on society, on education. Briefly, everything burgeoned.

Here is a chance to diagnose in detail the myriad interrelationships of societal demands on educational resources as the former becomes more complex and the latter more specialized. Simple primary group transmission sufficed for farming people all through the years but only specialists who apprenticed their own successors as early as five years of age had the time or the training for temple ritual; intricate pottery design arts; mathematics; astronomy; architecture; irrigation engineering; trade with jungle, mountain and coastal peoples; military science and defense; government; and graphics that haven't yet been translated. Without the ethnocentrism of traditional documentation, here nuclear America provides a geographical and historical stage unique on our planet for the objective study of the rural-urban-rurban sequence of almost any social science. Each separate scene for the different sub-dramas of development from a population of one hundred to one hundred thousand is set. All that is missing are the monologues of the participants.

Fusion of This Civilization With Others

A series of neighboring peoples overran this valley from 300 A.D. to the time of the Spanish conquest in the early 1500's. The Mochica who lived in the same coastal vicinity, descended first. Strange as it may seem, these people recounted the autobiography of their culture almost entirely in pottery forms. With nothing but clay as a medium, they portrayed the ethnographic details of their way of living with such stark realism and photographic exactitude that one Mochica pot is worth "a thousand words." There are portrait mugs so lifelike that one could recognize the living model on the street. Like pages in a book, a series of pots graphically depict symptoms and remedies for the complete range of known diseases or anatomical discrepancies; care and training of animals, of plants, of children; household arts; sexual practices; treatment of criminals, war captives; family life; games and recreational customs; navigation. These pieces of pottery come in shapes and sizes that disorient our preconceptions of what a pot or a vase should look like. Nevertheless, for educators of this century who search for mediums of universal communication amidst a multiplicity of mutually unintelligible linguistic survivals from outdated insular speaking groups, Mochica pottery extends enthusiastic encouragement. Art educators take heart in the realization that the American Indian managed to blend his humanities and his sciences by expressing his spiritual and practical life in visible aesthetic forms. This knowledge, too, is pregnant with insights for the rest of us who strive toward making any learning more meaningful.

Practically nothing is yet known about the Tiahuanaco, a mountain people from the south, who pushed right up the coast of Peru, conquering valley states, building roads before them as they progressed which are in use today. In the words of William Duncan Strong, these people "just play with stone" with methods that are currently lost to our heritage though possibly retrievable at some future date. They carved bowls, furniture, and rooms out of solid rock. With what? No one knows. How? No one knows. Why? Rock is a medium as available in the mountains as clay is on the coast. When the missing chapters of the Tiahuanaco history are finally complete and as we consider their reputation for engineering know-how in moving boulders the size of armored tanks up 8,000 feet of mountain height, to fit them into place without mortar in a stronghold that shows signs of lasting forever — skills fifty years ago attributed to the Incan civilization may be questioned. Indeed, since the early chroniclers generalized all Indians in Peru as Incas, this might be simply another carry-over of initial ignorance masquerading as assumed fact, as was our being called the New World.

345

The Chimu, whose story too needs to be untangled, are believed to have come down by sea from an island off the coast of Ecuador. In any event, they took over eight valleys from the Tiahuanaco and built the first true cities in the Western Hemisphere — cities divided into sub-cities with hand carved public walls, brightly colored buildings. Techniques of conquest were combined with techniques of administration until eight valleys were incorporated under one central control.

By the time that Columbus was walking around Spain asking for money for his first trip, the Incas had emerged masters of the Kingdom of Chimu after a campaign of conquest that stretched from Ecuador to central Chile. The Incas took the best ideas, the most artistic skills of the separate states that came under their command, adapted them to their way of life and material culture, then spread them throughout the empire. Inca leaders married into the ruling families of those whom they conquered. Royal young people from the far reaches of the land were educated together in schools provided for the purpose in the capital so that as leaders later they always had that "old school tie." Both the wealth and the work of the empire was divided equally among all the people so that there was no want anywhere. By such means, they are credited with having created one of the most ideal social governments of all mankind. When we are ready to learn in detail how they did it, perhaps this, too, will become part of our heritage.

Opportunities for Inter-Cultural Empathy and Identity

We have presented here a mere facet of the whole: the story of a single river valley in Peru. Our knowledge is so little; our ignorance, so great. In the geographical setting of Latin America, however, ruins of the Chibcha, the Aztec and the Maya, to name but a few, bespeak long and intense human occupation. These cultures were not transplanted here. They developed indigenously here, in this hemisphere.

But, even so,

> . . . in the ruined cities of Egypt, the stranger knows the story of the people whose vestiges he finds around him. America, say historians, was peopled by savages; but savages never reared these structures, savages never carved these stones . . . There are no associations connected with this place, none of those stirring recollections which hallow Rome and Athens. But architecture, sculpture, and painting, all the arts which embellish life, had flourished; orators, warriors, and statesmen; beauty, ambition and glory had lived and passed away, and none knew that such things had been, or could tell of their past existence. Books, the records of knowledge, are silent on this theme.[14]

---

14 John L. Stephens, *Incidents of Travel in Central America, Chiapas and Yucatan* (New Brunswick, New Jersey: Rutgers University Press, 1949), p. 80-81, vol. 1.

346

Our ignorance of these peoples exemplifies channeled knowledge. Granted, the heritage colonial forefathers brought forth across the broad Atlantic is rich and wonderful, but somewhere, in the process, there has been a blind pulled down to blot out the vision of our own native heritage so completely that we do not even suspect its absence. Like the other side of the moon, we haven't thought of it. If some purposes of living and learning today are to broaden horizons and to add perspective, then the heritage (once lost, now being found) of Indian civilizations in Latin America taunts our patterned concepts. How wide will we permit our horizons to be? How much perspective are we going to let in?

While we hesitate to answer, educational leaders everywhere grow increasingly aware of our responsibility in training toward intercultural empathy. Three out of four alive in the world today are not white. At the time of the Inca conquest, eight million persons spread over an area of 1,200,000 square miles lived under one government in peace and plenty and beauty. Not one of them was white. European contact "deprived the Indian of his leadership, of his learned men, of his old idols and old priests, of his men of science, of his government, of his faith in himself as a man."[15] Then, in devilish alliance with their own preconceptions, Europeans described the posterity of this and other conquered kingdoms as uneducable, unclean, apathetic and incapable of rational judgment. From a natural laboratory of race relations, however, distant enough in both time and space to eliminate or at least lessen emotional reactions, archaeologists bring in renewed proof of the Indians' superior pre-colonial heredity. So perhaps we might more objectively evaluate his post-colonial environment. To this end our sister America provides us with a fertile field close to home for comparative historical study in which to better prepare our young people for their part in an even more intimate relationship with those in the world whose skin contains more melanin.

In closing this section, we might ask ourselves, "Why do institutions of higher education send archaeologists out to poke around in ruins that are not bothering anybody?" Often, burdened with backache, insects and dust, laboring with pickaxe or whiskbroom, the archaeologist might conceivably ask himself, "Why do I do it?" Part of our national character was forged on the frontier with each man most interested in here and now, and what he physically could do about it. Today, we are developing an international character, facing frontiers that are more subtly concerned with theres and thens that need to be tackled more mentally and emotionally than physi-

---

[15] Frank Tannenbaum, "Toward an Appreciation of Latin America," in *The United States and Latin America* (The American Assembly, New York: Columbia University, 1959), p. 16.

cally. Universities, by sponsoring the archaeological study of the Americas, strengthen bonds of friendship between the two continents at the same time that they project frontiers of knowledge back into prehistory, thus extending our traditions. For many reasons, as individuals and as scientists, archaeologists strive to rescue their fellow human beings across the ages from oblivion. Where man's books are silent, Mother Earth, eternal female that she is, holds closely guarded secrets. In sum, these excavations in Latin America have restored to the American Indian his historical identity. In doing so, they have bequeathed us aspects of our identity as Americans, for we too, as Americans, belong to these ancients. Yet it remains a heritage that still, in the main, beckons to be claimed.

Spanish-Colonial Heritage

Columbus carried letters of introduction to the Great Khan in Asia when he headed westward from Spain. Until his death in 1506 he probably still fancied the territories he'd touched upon in his four different trips (Central and South American mainland, and the Caribbean islands) were Oriental outposts. He had wishfully referred to them as "The Indies." After two voyages down the coast of South America, however, Amerigo Vespucci criticized this notion in writing. In 1507, geographer Martin Waldseemuller published a map of the world depicting Asia in somewhat the same form that we know it with the addition of a bulky, elongated extension on the Pacific side. He called this annex "America." Nearly a century passed before the term caught on. Considering how we have seemingly monopolized it, however, it is significant to note that the name originally applied only to what is now South America.[16]

Within a short forty years after Columbus' death, swashbuckling Latin adventurers had ranged inland as far as Eastern Kansas and had sailed up the coasts to Oregon and Nova Scotia. They "blitzkreiged" across the entire region of Mexico, Central and South America in an eager rush to have and to hold either El Dorado or the Fountain of Youth in one form or another. Most of them set forth from the aged, cultured university city of Sevilla in Spain in creaky boats that often held no more than fifty men. As much as a third of the population of Sevilla, to list but one town, hastened to America in an intoxicating, expansive people's movement from medieval Spain and Portugal to vulnerable Indian kingdoms where anyone had the chance to get rich quick. Pizarro, for example, who won Peru, could neither read nor write. Although born a swineherd, he died a marquis.

With characteristic directness, seeing no reason to depend entirely on the

---

[16] William L. Langer, Ed., *An Encyclopedia of World History* (Boston: Houghton Mifflin Company, 1948), p. 368.

mother countries for culture or education, *conquistadores, adelantados,* clergy and commoners together built cities as beautiful as those they came from on top of the Indian capitals they razed. Almost immediately, they began establishing schools and colleges. Cortes, who conquered Mexico, endowed schools during his lifetime and provided for more in his will. Both the Universities of Mexico City and San Marcos in Lima date from 1551. In Peru, they grafted a national postal service on the Inca *chasqui* messenger system. They hauled a printing press into Mexico City as early as 1537 and more than 100 books were printed there in the sixteenth century. Later, the famed mission builder Junipero Serra (1713-1784) established the first library in California. Musuems, theatres, art galleries, palaces, bookstores and cathedrals, meanwhile, quickly appeared across the continent. Buenos Aires, Rio de Janeiro, Mexico City, Lima, Bogota, Santiago, Quito and Panama were all flourishing cities laying plans for their centennials when the Pilgrims landed at Plymouth. From the frame of reference of American education, this story, too, as that of the earlier Indians, albeit unrealized heretofore, belongs to our heritage.

Education of the Converted Indian

From 711 A.D., dark skinned non-Christian Moors had dominated the kingdoms of Spain. After centuries of battle, the Moors' last stronghold finally fell in 1492. That same year, the victorious Spanish Catholics determined to expel both the Moors and the Jews from Spain. Hence the reason for the legend that Isabella promised to pledge her jewels to finance Columbus lies in the fact that money was being spent for these other pressing religious issues.

Another consequence of the events surrounding the year 1492 explains in part the ethos behind the beginning of colonial mission schools. Like the Moors, the Indians were dark skinned non-Christians. According to the climate of the time, non-Christians were as socially welcome as patients suffering from acute cases of advanced tuberculosis or typhoid would be with us today. Therefore, the colonists were confronted with the "sincere if fanatical desire to kill or convert them."[17]

Acculturative Aims of the Teaching Clergy

The church and the crown together controlled education. By law at least, individuals of Indian blood were not allowed in holy orders. Similarly, only members of holy orders were permitted to teach. At the start, then, all edu-

---

[17] Preston E. James, *Latin America* (New York: The Odyssey Press, 1950), pp. 14-15.

cators in the colonies were clergy, men or women who had been imported from the mother country. They aimed to hispanify the savages by converting them into Catholic Christianity and by ennobling them through instruction to the rudiments of European civilization. Due to the lack of a common language, the church utilized the educating-by-entertainment potential of music and drama to communicate these primary objectives.

Methodology

An immemorial lifestream secret of the Indian people is their grouphood, their mutual blending of individual wills so the larger total personality of everyone combined intensifies the meaning of each individual part. By choosing drama as a means of conveying the faith, the mission fathers brilliantly created functional learning experiences out of what would otherwise have been insurmountable difficulties. This took flexibility, imagination, patience and perhaps some luck. The spirit of "The play is the thing" made more sense to the Indians initially than a completely new religion could. Nuns and friars taught children and young people to sing, to dance, to act out the stories of the gospel in pantomime. Then they performed for their parents who gradually found here a substitute for their temple rituals of old by watching the "many mysteries put to them as sights so they stay staunch."[18] Conceived to acculturate them away from ancient beliefs, these dramatic productions became so impressive that churches and monasteries competed with one another in the training of their native actors and stage effect producers, in the size of their repertoire.

The Curriculum

Religious education centered around the two testaments of the Bible. Zealous friars in city and outpost missions learned native languages in order to compile dictionaries and translate Latin or Castilian Bibles into different tongues. The first book printed in this hemisphere by Europeans (the Aztecs had had a library of their own in Mexico City) was a bilingual Spanish-native prayer book. Threatening admonitions regarding moral behavior according to Christian standards supplemented the holy word. "Here in this world we travel by a very narrow, steep and dangerous road . . . on either side is a great gulf without bottom, and if you deviate from the path you will fall into it."[19] The compromise that was ultimately reached allowed for relapses during fiestas.

---

[18] Salvador deMadriaga, *The Rise of the Spanish American Empire* (New York: The Macmillan Co., 1947), Chapter 10.

[19] William H. Prescott, *The History of the Conquest of Mexico: The History of the Conquest of Peru* (New York: The Modern Library, undated), p. 716.

The amount of time varied from place to place but agriculture was taught at least an hour per day because of the natives' obvious enjoyment of it as well as for its practical value. Priests and their pupils in school gardens attached to missions planted the first figs, bananas, lemons, limes, mangoes, olives and oranges to grow on American soil. Ancestral agricultural arts, however, unknown to the teaching faculties, lay neglected and forgotten in the colonial curriculum except in places too remote for contact.

Similarly, priests intentionally employed art education to further the word of the Christian Lord. In contrast to the rich, pristine Indian art tradition, only Spanish arts and crafts fitted this goal. Since both peoples shared a common aesthetic sensitivity, transfer seemed to take place with happy success. In most Indian post-Columbian art work, however, no matter how Christian the motif, some glimpse of ancient tribal symbolism superimposes itself as unobtrusively as the lines of sunburst on the cross to the discerning eye.

Classical education, on the other hand, was not Spanish at all but Latin or even Greek. Armed with a saber-toothed curriculum twice removed, undaunted friars not only attempted but frequently succeeded in teaching one unknown by means of a second unknown! Here and there, Indians with mother tongues as far removed as Nahuatl or Quechua mastered Greek through instruction from Spanish speaking teachers as well as logic, Aristotelian science, Euclidian geometry and philosophy. Some composed poetry and expounded with learned Spaniards on Thomas Aquinas. But, no matter how apt any became in forming percepts ordinarily meaningless into concepts educationally meaningful, the inferior social position of an Indian condemned him to the frustrating limitations of personal inferiority.

Organization and Administration

The Spanish colonial government in Latin America endured longer than any other historical instance of European colonization. For three centuries, the King in Spain and the Pope in Rome conscientiously supervised education in the colonies jointly. Their overall emphasis regarding the Indians as people was humane and benevolent. A papal bull reminded the colonists that the conquered were human beings with souls inside them and children of the same God as they. Nonetheless, the long list of royal *cedulas* indicates by their numbers that the directions from the main offices in Madrid and Rome somehow got lost on the way to the innumerable branches across the sea. Separated from each other by mountains second only to the Himalayas in height, with communication so difficult that messages took months, even years to get through, those locally in charge acted in accordance with their own passions so that the actual shape of the Indians' education varied from valley to valley.

351

Evaluation and Summary of Period

A broad generalization might be safely made that the earlier mission fathers were on the whole more selfless and dedicated men than any of their successors. The seemingly boundless natural and mineral resources of the New World, whose largess upset the economy of sixteenth century Europe, also managed, as the gilded years spun by, to turn the heads of saints. There came a point where few padres practiced what their predecessors taught and instruments of kindly acculturation were somehow distorted into instruments of selfish oppression. In too many places, religious instruction dwindled into speedy recitations of unintelligible trite formulas. Religious holidays degenerated into miserable mechanisms for extracting exorbitant offerings from the powerless for the powerful.

Even though the details of the Indian heritage itself were systematically bypassed in education, the dramatic, the religious, the agricultural, the aesthetic and the classical emphases of the colonial curricula did not make enough of an impact. The everyday life of the typical newly conquered Indian, therefore, remained much as in the past. As the tempo of the times looked to more money, labor, and land, however, kindly mentors metamorphosized into greedy masters. The value of the Indian as a mind or a soul was mislaid and replaced by a command of his muscle power as a readily available human animal. In answer, millions of inarticulate Indians closed in on themselves in a kind of passive forbearance which their self-ordained proprietors inwardly dreaded but outwardly manipulated to their own exploitive gain. Yes, the Indian was exploited in the mission schools as in the *haciendas* and the mines. To the extent that he was exploited, in his gentle way, he exploited his avaricious superintendents in turn by demoralizing them.

This account does not propose to lay blame or to make excuses. Men like Father LasCasas in Venezuela and Santo Domingo preached with spoken and written word against the slavery system here and abroad but the momentum was such that there was no stopping to listen at the time. Our task now is to drag these and similar skeletons out of their educational hiding places in the history of every land on earth; to scrutinize and to become acutely aware of them so as to be that much better fortified against the temptations of repeating them in the teaching-learning contacts with other peoples in the international era ahead of us.

Education of the Elite

The gulf between the upper-uppers and the lower-lowers during colonial times spanned an unbridged social chasm with no middle class anywhere between. The two lived in mutually unfathomable, separate worlds: conquered and conquerors. Later, the descendants of conquerors claimed privilege and position befitting their families' illustrious names and pure blood. As in the homeland, one had to prove his Spanish blood to study in a university, college, seminary or academy as well as for subsequent admittance into the clergy, the government or the military. At the same time that the elite made a monopoly of themselves in the New World, they kept tight ties with Europe by sending as many children as they could afford to back there for their education. Generally, we hypothesize that the schools in a country mirror that culture. Education for the upper-uppers, in this case, mirrored a culture that had not changed in a thousand years. Ultimately, this situation affected the number of schools that were not built in Latin America as well as the mental tone of those that were.

Enculturative Aims, Products and Methods

Characterized as the training grounds for the leisured class, the institutions of higher education that did exist aimed to train "noblemen for holy orders" or Christian scholars and gentlemen. Methods included reading or listening to lectures for memorization; discourse and debate; the taking of examinations "not for life but for the event." Quite naturally, the social distance between students and professors was minimal and either was "always able to express himself on general subjects but never able to tackle the real problems of his environment."[20] Salvador deMadriaga aptly described these educated gentlemen as being like nicely combed wigs that looked good but had no roots.

Consequently, the Golden Age in the Indies never glittered as brightly with its own ideas as it did with other peoples'. Both gentlemen and ladies kept abreast of European intellectual thought through books, which were admitted duty free. Although the period coincided with the Inquisition, travellers of the day reported well-stocked libraries which included the so-called prohibited ones, despite climatic conditions that made the upkeep of collections difficult. The mania for persecuting books or people, as with the witchhunts in our country at the same time, was part of the overall cultural environment to be taken in stride. In fact, some suspected that the best propaganda for a book was for it to be put on the *Index.* Upon the issuance of "licenses to read," (since even reading was a class privilege), forbidden books were owned, read and lent by both clergy and lay persons.

Curriculum in Humanities and Sciences

Vives, who remained a popular import throughout the period, recommended in his writings that the humanities be used as foundations for

---

[20] M. B. Laurenco-Filho, *Yearbook of Education* (London: University of London Institute of Education, 1959), p. 214.

wisdom rather than for literary style. Literary style, however, appealed to the leisurely-paced splendor of the epoch and even viceroys wrote drama. The classical sources that monopolized the humanities were two: Greek by way of the Moors and Roman through the Christians. By disregarding Spanish and/or New World history, letters, art and grammar, Latin America unwittingly failed to create a truly Spanish-American culture with which the people as a whole could identify.

Heavily theological, the classical outlook stifled the sciences and their improvement by underestimating the progressive values inherent in practical techniques. Future engineers, for example, learned a superficial physics by discussing the writings of Aristotle; and budding doctors, anatomy through Ptolemy.[21] Linguists whose prestige traced directly back to the renowned Arabic-Latin translation center in Toledo[22] translated Indian languages into Spanish in order to rewrite the Bible in native tongues.

As the age became more literally golden, colleges and universities degenerated into "monuments of imbecility designed to keep men from true science."[23] Regulations slackened, standards declined, techniques deteriorated, mechanical and useful subjects were abandoned. Well satisfied with society as it existed, college graduates with average capacity and mediocre moral outlook attained success by avoiding real effort.

Cultural Contrasts Between the Americas

Once again, this account does not attempt to lay blame or to make excuses. Persons of really high ability raised their voices in written and spoken protest but the milieu was such that there were no ears for listening. Its value as a part of our American educational heritage, however, lies in the object lessons it presents for comparing the essential differences in the material, intellectual and moral historical development of the Americas so as to further equip us with a broad background for real understanding as we take up our role in today's educational frontier where social psychology is writ large, and is writ ever more, internationally.

From the beginning and even unto this day, both Americas tend to turn more toward Europe than either does toward the other. Together, we inherited the scars of family feuds between our mother countries on economic, military, political and religious issues that were burning points over a century ago. On these separate continents, too, non-European contact differed com-

---

21 Laurenco-Filho, *ibid.*, p. 218.

22 W. H. Cowley, *An Appraisal of American Higher Education* (School of Education, Stanford University, mimeographed, 1956), p. 185.

23 Jose Lastarria, cited in Crawford, R. W., *A Century of Latin American Thought* (Cambridge: Harvard University Press, 1945), p. 61.

pletely. The transplanted Europeans in one America simply exterminated or pushed Westward most of the relatively few Indians they encountered; while the other transplanted Europeans, in lower America, ran into populous Indian kingdoms whose survivors, population statistics being as poetical as they are, still equal or exceed in number their ancestors of 1492. Here hides, also, a partial explanation for the social class systems that grew up in the two places with all the integrated repercussions that each person differentiates according to what he wants to see.

Spanish America had two social classes: the lower-lower indigenous groups reminiscent of the serfs and the upper-upper Latin noblemen of court, church or army who lived like feudal lords of old (who came over here attracted by almost unbelievable affluence and prided themselves on their illustrious names, their royal families and large supportive kin connections). In contrast, the forerunners of our middle class came over here because they were dissatisfied with the way things were back home. They were attracted by the opportunities to build their world new. They prided themselves on their own sturdy individualism.

Colonial Latins spoke of the "holy sacrament of conversation"; life was a matter of style, of leisure in which to enrich the art of living. For the North American settler, however, it was "never mind the style, let's *make* a living." The Hispanic Americans sought to enjoy the fuller life for themselves; immigrants to New England sought to increase their economic capacity. Such a comparative list extends as far as one wants to go with it, but always the qualities of one area dynamically counterbalanced those of the other.

In the light of Latin America's current lack of material development, their people probably overdid their leisure. In the light of our current developments in automation on the other hand, we have to learn all over again what to do with ours. The great educational challenges of each America today are diametrically opposed: south of the Rio Grande, to raise their standard of living through learning; north of that boundary, to raise our standard of leisure through learning. Like Yang and Yin, the educational heritage of each fulfills the discrepancies of the other.

Revolution and Recent Heritage

So far as we now know, both North and South America, except for a few unknown adventurers, lay isolated from the rest of the world until 1492. During colonial times the enforcement of anti-foreign trade laws, initially designed to maintain monopoly of economic relationships between each colony and the respective mother country, succeeded, but for the New England-West Indian trade, in disassociating the two continents within the hemisphere. The revolutions for independence that raged across Latin America after 1810 jolted us into realizing that Africa was not the only dark continent. Today, over a century since, the "average educated and articulate Latin American is far better informed about the United States than is the comparable North American about Latin America,"[24] even though "we are unanimous in our conviction that no area in the world is of more importance to us than Latin America and that no other area matches us in our importance to the future of (it)."[25] At least part of our profound public ignorance lies in the fact that, with characteristic haste, we seem to ferret for reduced terms to describe an area two and one half times the size of the United States as a single unit. By doing so, we limit our chances for understanding any of the nations themselves.

Separated from each other by a mad geography that holds the world's record for extension of mountain barriers and tropical forest areas, our Southern neighbors are regionally proud of their individual differences. These "disunited" States of Latin America are as different from each other as India and Indiana in terms of geography, size, and political, economic, and social progress. The countries of Latin America do, however, show continent-wide resemblances in their current bold re-thinking of education as a means of human resource development.

Here on our own doorstep, in our own lifetimes, individual Latin American republics are injecting a time capsule dimension into our educational heritage. They are helping their peoples to join in and take advantage of the waves of rising expectations that are surging forward in the underdeveloped regions of the world "with the noise and shine of waters gushing from their ancient sources."[26] After 450 years of living that each generation began and each generation ended, ill clothed, ill fed, ill housed, and illiterate, innumerable natives are timorously coming to sense that a new conception of life is theirs for the learning. Watchwords such as, "To educate is to redeem!" "Land and books!" "Learn to read better to live better!" tease the millions in rural districts away from their habitual resignation in what bodes fair to evolve into the Hispanic-American counterpart of a worldwide renaissance.

The Constitution of the United States nowhere mentions education. In contrast, at least twelve of the independent Latin American republics, confronted with the terrific challenge of educating everybody everywhere, variously define education as a fundamental duty of the state and Panama even gives it priority in the official budget. Although education is conceived in the broadest way, constitutionally free at all levels up to and often through

---

[24] Edward W. Barrett, and Penn T. Kimball, *The United States and Latin America* (The American Assembly, Columbia University, 1959), p. 82.

[25] Milton S. Eisenhower, Report to the President, 27 Dec. 1958, *United States and Latin American Relations* (Dept. of State), p. 16.

[26] John Collier, *op. cit.*, p. 15.

college, and compulsory in childhood, it is no more than an ideal until the social context makes implementation possible. Quite frankly, with the fastest growing population as well as the fastest changing social structure in the world today, Latin American school systems lack everything but pupils. We never had a situation like this since our educational universe grew by gradual accretion. They must create an entire educational system all at once.

Education for Well-Being

Because of the subsistence standard of living everywhere prevalent, however, a new term, fundamental or integral education is adding to the magnitude of educational theory by acknowledging in practice the blunt fact that improved physical well-being must necessarily precede the 3 R's. Traditional, taken-for-granted classical school subjects are relinquishing their time-honored monopoly to curricula about soap and seed selection; vaccinations and ventilation; vegetable gardens, cooking, and pure drinking water. Dewey's idea of learning by doing, or the action type school (*Vitalismo*), has taken hold, too, at the same time that it has freed impoverished schools from the necessity of much formal educational equipment.

The Nucleo School

The nucleo school was initially established in Bolivia with help from the United States. A team of our technicians, working closely with the Ministry of Education, purposefully concentrated on a few typical rural schools in different vicinities rather than attempting to work with each and every one. They transformed them into experimental stations with curricula adapted to the local customs to serve as a nucleus to which both teachers and students from surrounding schools came to see demonstrated how economically and socially useful new ideas on education could be. Ordinary occupation skills of the Indians as weaving, farming, ceramics, animal husbandry and the making of clothes were taken as the base points for instruction. Then, by modifying the technology alone, they subtly prepared young people to be incorporated into the overall economic growth of Bolivia. In place of the slow and patient weaving of a blanket by ancient methods, for instance, youngsters learned to weave the same thing with the same designs and skill on modern looms. They were also encouraged to make the intellectual jump that is needed to comprehend such concrete concepts of today's living as the internal combustion motor, DDT, tractors, preventatives against disease and sewing machines.

Simultaneously, the nucleo schools conduct workshops for the in-service training of teachers. No reliable national statistics exist on the profession of education, but it is estimated that as high as 80% of rural teachers are neither

357

adequately trained nor experienced. The most promising trainees are sometimes sent to universities in the United States on paid scholarships for study in elementary education as applied to rural teaching situations. They come back, welcomed by an excited press, to conduct nucleo schools themselves.

The whole project represents United States beginnings in overseas assistance through education which has now grown to worldwide proportions. Originally greeted with open skepticism as a "foreign outfit," despite the relationship with the Bolivian government, the program has been highly successful regionally. But, unfortunately, these efforts, to borrow a phrase from Bolivar, meet the mass needs of the continent no more than if they were ploughing the sea.

Cultural Missions

The cultural missions are mobile schools that come to Indian primary groups in their natural settings on request with teams of different kinds of teachers (that vary with the needs of any one area) to work together with the entire community for a "classroom." In small societies that place a high premium on cooperation and mutuality of purpose, a kind of learning experience that emphasizes these qualities is the only one that attracts them. Besides instructors to guide them in mastering such separate skills as carpentry, masonry, midwifery, nutrition, soil improvement, etc., there is usually a recreation leader along to teach games, handwork and songs, to draw out the sleeping artistry of their ancestors. In some nations these missions follow ox cart trails cut by theatrical troupes of colonial times; in others, they courageously penetrate remote areas, where no roads lead, by jeep, mule or river boat.

Adult Education

Adult education corresponds somewhat with the cultural missions except that we will here differentiate it as a step up from the acquisition of the skills of physical well-being, to a stress on the 3 R's. Adult education in Latin America can and does take place at any level; primary, intermediate, or higher, rural or urban. This is a partial reflection of the fact that the landed aristocracy who survived the revolutions restricted initial literacy laws to children so as to continue slave labor. Consequently, in the middle of the twentieth century, at least one-half of the adults in Latin America cannot read. A military urgency can be sensed in the language used in the adult education programs. Literacy corps conduct campaigns instigated by emergency laws, with councils on literacy set up to organize details. Each person who learns to read is drafted to teach another. Some countries pay for this, others require it by law. In like manner, illiterates who are given the chance to learn to read are legally ordered to do so. Some adults, eagerly desirous of the prestige and the opportunities that reading ability brings, have formed clubs on their own initiative to help each other overcome the handicap from lack of teachers. The chief difficulty so far is the absence of primers which are simple enough for beginners but interesting enough to hold adult attention. Chile imaginatively solved the problem with an easy-to-read encyclopaedia which serve both as a primer and as a beacon to further learning, while Cuba reported that more teachers in her schools were writing their own primers. Teaching machines, too, predict the opening of promising new avenues in this direction from reading readiness to literature. In the meantime, governments strive to keep up with the demand for those limited materials that are available.

The Teacher in Training

On the state and local level certain resistances invariably frustrate progress. One of these, shared by some of our own traditions, stems from a negative cultural notion regarding the educability of females. Sarmiento in Argentina almost 100 years ago and UNESCO today see the education of the female as the fulcrum for raising standards of living. In her role as wife and mother, she is the one most intimately concerned with the health of the family which bears direct relationship to the probable success or failure in the education of anybody. But each year the girls' line grows shorter than the boys' line as children file up in front of the primary schools of the land because the missing girls have been pulled away for such family tasks as tending sheep. Similarly, women have the reputation for being universally the most inaccessible group in rural adult education.

For the role as teacher-in-training there are far too few for the jobs to be done. As with us, also, families from the upper lower class often take the first moves into the middle class when one of their members chooses teaching as a career. The families of women graduates of teacher-training institutions, however, unwittingly accentuate the delicate mutual balance existing between a society and the education it is able to provide by discouraging their daughters from taking positions in rural districts. Often two days away by truck from the nearest outpost of civilization, primary and secondary schools necessarily have boarding-in arrangements. But the teachers who live in these quarters, male or female, soon discern that they are not only set off geographically from their familiars back home but psychologically within local neighborhoods themselves. Nine times out of ten, the vernacular is not native to the teacher so that they sound like "foreigners" when they try to teach in it. Because of this language obstacle, sincere efforts are being made by dedicated teachers-of-teachers to take even the training schools out to the rural areas so that instructors from now on can be native speakers of the local tongue.

An added challenge in teacher training calls for a many-sided competence that scoffs at the current North American penchant for increasingly narrower angles of specialization. On top of being able to instruct in the 3 R's, the teacher in training for rural education must become something of a social service worker who has also familiarized herself with details about sanitation, agriculture, tools, nutrition and medicine.

New Developments in Mass Education

In the meantime, techniques in mass education through radio and television are already revolutionizing old-fashioned notions about the neighborhood of a school. When the "school" becomes a radio or television station, its influence is felt no longer only in the neighborhood of this or that place, but in a neighborhood of a nation; in the neighborhood of a continent. Educational television particularly, when the inadequacies of electrical installation are overcome, cancels the previously almost insurmountable obstacles of material, building and teacher shortages with one fell swoop. Through the truly universal language of photography, it abates linguistic differences at the same time that it enriches the variety of educational fare by making expert teachers available to everybody. In regions where governments have already installed sets in village centers for collective viewing, television has become a unique teacher around which the villagers gather together. There is no personal element of strangeness on the part of either "teacher" or student. A simple box with a picture tube on one end, viewed together in the protection of the kin group, artfully inculcates ideas, along with its very physical newness, for that breath of the wider world. Television brings with it an eventual end to existences locked in the vicious circle of ignorance, poverty and lack of opportunity. This movement is global. Here again, this heritage we share with our sister America enables us to more completely encompass all parts of the multiple and varied approaches to international progress through education now being desperately employed.

Latin American Educational Thinkers

Just as we affirm the importance of international progress in education, so also might we profitably ponder on the hospitality toward international understanding within our own educational system that is enhanced by the presence of another America. By candlelight, for instance, versatile intellectuals composed many of the remarkably twentieth century aims for education that were subsequently written into the constitutions of Latin America: education for personality, for patriotism, for humanity. But the North American stereotype as the man-of-action is not typically as fond of thinking for its own sake as the Latin American stereotype or the man-of-thought. At least, judging by a comparison of their popularly attributed nicknames, they

360

are not condoned as such. Persons in our culture with scholarly inclinations equivalent to *los pensadores*, or men who meditatively contemplate, are characterized irreverently as egg heads who are, if anything, slightly un-hatched. For those of us on this continent who delight in adventuring into the realms of thought, then, both the writings and the lives of the pensadores in the land below the Rio Grande guarantee rare inspiration and reverie.

Plato's vision of a world in which philosophers became kings and kings, philosophers, has literally come true in Latin America in a number of in-stances. For example, Dom Pedro II, (1825-1891), Emperor of Brazil 100 years ago, discovered a comet and founded the Brazilian Institute of History and Geography. He personally financed the overseas study of scores of Brazilian students as well as the visits of noted intellectuals of the day to Brazil. Possessed of an insatiable thirst for knowledge, he was an omnivorous pencil-in-hand reader who spent several hours of each day all his life in purely intellectual pursuits. "If I were not Emperor," he often mused, "I should like to have been a teacher. I know of no nobler calling than that of directing young minds and preparing the men of tomorrow."[27]

Domingo Sarmiento, (1810-1888), a self-educated poor boy, experienced both the real and ideal life of Dom Pedro II. As a young man his "pity for ignorance and love of the truth" led him into education which he conceived as the supreme blessing of mankind. He recommended or built schools for women, for workers, for prisoners, for teachers. In 1868, on the platform, "We must make the whole republic into a school," he was elected President of Argentina. As the schoolmaster president, one of his greatest pleasures was the knowledge that the importation of paper for books increased during his administration from 12,000 to 200,000 reams. An embarrassingly large number of our most modern ideas on education, by the way, can be found in his writings.[28]

The Challenge — Rediscovering a Heritage

The more one trails off into the ramifications that surround the present and the past of Latin America and the more one becomes captivated by the sparkling thought of its political, educational and literary intellectuals, the less one is able to find in our reference books and in our libraries. Just as information about our Indian predecessors was shut out from our ken until archaeologists unremittingly brought so much evidence to light that we were finally jarred into realizing what we were missing only because it had almost

---

[27] Hector Lyra, in *The Green Continent,* Germain Arciniegas, editor (New York: Alfred A. Knopf, 1944), pp. 285-305; see also Mary W. Williams, *Dom Pedro The Magnanimous* (Chapel Hill: Univ. of North Carolina Press, 1937).

[28] Leopoldo Lugones, quoted in *The Green Continent, ibid.,* pp. 337-354.

been deliberately hidden, so too, has information about Latin America been cunningly deprived us due initially to the fact that our colonial mother countries were not ardently friendly. When one has become attuned to these inherited discrepancies, the differences in the amount of space devoted to British items and to Spanish items in our encyclopaedias, biographical dictionaries, textbooks and the like arouse either fascination or frustration, depending upon one's personality syndrome. A similar comment might also be made for the slant with which most of these items are written. In spite of a number of recognized area study programs at the level of higher education, there are few if any completely rounded centers of research or training on Latin American studies in the United States today.

As for mass media, Latin America does not carry as much prestige as an overseas assignment for newspapermen as does Europe and less news is daily sent to the syndicates from there. Small town newspapers generally weed out all of this for space reasons and only the larger or largest tabloids print enough quantities regularly enough to build up and sustain reader interest and to kindle the social interaction that comes from familiarity with the same news stories. In like vein, even the major United States polling agencies minister to the conspiracy of silence by compiling relatively little data concerning the level of interest or of information among North Americans concerning Latin American affairs.[29]

This concerns all who are sensitive to the undercurrents of the era, who look with a long range view both backward and forward in time as well as to the present, because they are assigned to educate and to transmit the fullest possible heritage to youth who are destined to carry on our civilization. We justifiably wonder, "Where can we learn about Latin Americans as they themselves see themselves? As they see us?" A self-perpetuating circularity, set off in history and continuing on its momentum, doesn't have room for questions like these that aren't ordinarily asked. Here again, there has been a blind pulled down to blot out the view of part of our own heritage as Americas so completely that we seldom suspect it is there.

A purpose of living and learning today is to broaden horizons, to add perspective. Through chapters such as this, our horizons once again spread out from the shores of both Americas to the rest of the world. Our deepened perspective insistently stretches back into prehistoric time when a spiritual unity pervaded the ancients of the entire hemisphere. In subsequent centuries others discovered and then segregated the two Americas. Transplanted alienation took tenacious root. Through mutually dedicated efforts contemporaries of the sister continents now face the challenge of re-discovering one

---

[29] Edward W. Barrett, and Penn T. Kimball, *op. cit.,* p. 89.

another.[30] The Good Neighbor Policy takes new and broader meaning as we launch President Kennedy's *Alianza Para Progresso* — the success of which depends upon educational elements in both continents.

Canadian Bibliography

Althouse, J. B., *Structure and Aims of Canadian Education*. Toronto: W. J. Gage and Co., Ltd., 1949.

Andrews, J. H. M., and Brown, A. F., *Composite High Schools in Canada*. University of Alberta Monograph in Education No. 1. Edmonton: The University of Alberta, 1959.

Bissell, C. T., ed., *Canada's Crisis in Higher Education*. Toronto: University of Toronto Press, 1957.

Brown, George S., *Building the Canadian Nation*. Toronto: J. M. Dent and Sons Ltd., 1942.

Canada, Bureau of Statistics, *The Canada Year Book*. Ottawa: Queen's Printer.

Canadian Education Association, *Canadian Education*. Toronto.

Carter, G. Emmett, Very Rev., *The Catholic Public Schools of Quebec*. Toronto: W. J. Gage Ltd., 1957.

Clark, S. D., *The Social Development of Canada*. Toronto: University of Toronto Press, 1942.

Education — A Collection of Essays on Canadian Education. Toronto: W. J. Gage & Co. Ltd., 1957.

Katz, J., *Canadian Education Today*. Toronto: McGraw-Hill, 1956.

La Zerle, M. E., *Teacher Education in Canada*. Toronto: W. J. Gage & Co., Ltd., 1951.

Lower, A. R. M., *Canadians in the Making: A Social History of Canada*. Toronto: Longmans, Green & Co., 1958.

McInnis, Edgar, *Canada a Political and Social History*. New York: Rinehart & Co., 1947.

Morton, W. T., *The Canadian Identity*. Madison: University of Wisconsin Press, 1961.

Park, Julian, ed., *The Culture of Contemporary Canada*. Toronto: Ryerson, 1957.

Percival, W. P., *Across the Years*. Montreal: Gazette Printing Co., 1946.

---

[30] The teacher concerned with building personal background as well as promoting student knowledge of Latin America's past and present is referred to the selected volumes in the chapter bibliography; additionally, see the survey of references and excellent suggestions in "Latin America" by Ellis A. Johnson and Ralph A. Brown in *The Social Studies*, October, 1959, pp. 177-184, and also the special issue of *Social Education*, November, 1958, that was devoted to teaching about Latin America.

Percival, W. P., *Should We All Think Alike?* Toronto: W. J. Gage & Co. Ltd., 1952.

Phillips, C. E., *The Development of Education in Canada.* Toronto: W. J. Gage & Co., Ltd., 1957.

Stewart, F. K., *Interprovincial Cooperation in Education.* Toronto: W. J. Gage and Co. Ltd., 1957.

Swift, W. H., *Trends in Canadian Education,* Tenth Series of Quance Lectures in Canadian Education. Toronto: W. J. Gage and Co. Ltd., 1958.

Latin American Bibliography

American Council on Education, *Latin America in School and College Teaching Materials.* Washington, D.C.: The Council, 1944.

Anderson, Edgar, *Plants, Man and Life.* Boston: Little, Brown & Co., 1952.

Anguilera, Francisco, ed., *Handbook of Latin American Studies,* No. 20 (Annual). Gainesville: University of Florida Press, 1958.

Arciniegas, Germain, ed., *The Green Continent.* New York: Alfred Knopf, 1944.

Bannon, John F. and Peter M. Dunne, *Latin America, An Historical Survey.* Milwaukee, Wis.: Bruce Pub. Co., 1958 (rev. ed.).

Barrett, Edward W. and Penn T. Kimball, *The United States and Latin America.* New York: The American Assembly, Columbia University, 1959.

Collier, John, *Indians of the Americas.* New York: New American Library, 1951.

Crawford, R. W., *A Century of Latin American Thought.* Cambridge: Harvard University Press, 1945.

deMadariaga, Salvador, *The Rise of the Spanish American Empire.* New York: Macmillan, 1947.

Follett, Helen, *This Way to Latin America.* New York: Horace Mann-Lincoln School of Teachers College, Columbia University, 1943.

James, Preston, *Latin America.* New York: The Odyssey Press, 1950.

Perkins, Dexter, *The United States and Latin America.* Baton Rouge: Louisiana State University Press, 1961.

Rippy, J. Fred, *Historical Evolution of Hispanic America.* New York: Appleton-Century-Crofts, 1945.

Stephens, John L., *Incidents of Travel in Central America, Chiapas and Yucatan.* New Brunswick: Rutgers University Press, 1949.

Strong, William D., *Cultural Stratigraphy in the Viru Valley Northern Peru.* New York: Columbia University Press, 1952.

UNESCO, and the International Bureau of Education, *International Yearbook of Education,* Vol. XIX, 1957.

UNESCO, *Interrelations of Cultures, Their Contribution to International Understanding.* Paris: UNESCO Press, 1955.

Wilgus, A. Curtis (ed.), *Readings in Latin American Civilization.* New York: Barnes and Noble, 1946.

****

CHAPTER X

CONTRIBUTIONS FROM MINORITIES, ELITES, AND SPECIAL EDUCATIONAL ORGANIZATIONS

The general purpose of the volume in which this chapter appears is to describe and interpret the heritage that has made education in the United States what it is today. Many types of groups and organizations have contributed to this heritage. It is the purpose of this particular chapter to illustrate the influences stemming from such diverse factors as the education of ethnic and racial groups, occupational groups, special educational organizations, social class elites and professional elites, and to explain the implications therein for education in general. In addition to these more formalized forces, we should not overlook the contributions, derived less formally, from family and community, that since early colonial times have had continuing impact and frequently unrecognized roles in the education of Americans.

Definition of Significant Terms

Minority Group

Perhaps the most widely accepted definition of a minority group is that proposed by Schermerhorn: "Minorities are subgroups within a culture which are distinguishable from the dominant group by reason of differences in physiognomy, language, customs, or culture patterns (including any combination of these factors). Such subgroups are regarded as inherently different and 'not belonging' to the dominant group: for this reason they are consciously or unconsciously excluded from full participation in the life of the culture."[1]

According to the above definition, the following groups, whose contributions to the American educational heritage will be considered, are minority groups: Orientals (Chinese and Japanese), Mexicans, certain European ethnic groups, Jews, and Negroes.

Elite Group

An elite group is one whose members have high status and prestige, power, and influence, by virtue of favorable definitions ascribed to them in the past and/or present. Thus, recognized members of the upper classes in American society are part of an elite group. Likewise, persons in highly esteemed professions represent elite groups, e.g., clergymen, lawyers, physicians, and professors in first-class colleges and universities. All of these elites will be dealt with in this chapter.

Special Educational Organizations

All major social institutions in complex societies attempt to educate members of the groups they serve. A special educational organization is here defined as an association instrumental in inculcating the particular values and encouraging the particular behaviors which support the aims of one or more of the major social institutions in our society. Thus, social institutions of all kinds have their adult education programs, military institutions their military education programs, and business and labor institutions their worker educational programs. Special educational organizations serve these major institutional aims.

Education of Immigrants

Students of American immigration distinguish three fairly distinct periods in the general history of American immigration. Before 1882 most immigrants were from Northern and Western Europe. In the 1790 Census, the first U.S. Census, it was estimated that 60 percent of Americans were of English origin, about 18 percent of Scotch and Irish descent, and the remainder German and Dutch. From 1850 to 1882, the absence of Federal restrictions led to an influx of numerous Chinese immigrants.

During the second period, 1882-1923, there was a declining immigration from Northern and Western Europe, and an ascendancy of immigrants from Southern, Central, and Easten Europe. Italians, Russians, and Poles were

---

[1] Richard A. Schermerhorn, *These Our People* (Boston: D. C. Heath, 1949), p. 5.

especially conspicuous during this period. Most Japanese immigrants came during the 1890's.

In the third and last period, from 1924 on, there have been few immigrants from any source, but quotas have favored immigration from Northwestern Europe. During this last period there has been a large body of refugees, mostly Jewish, admitted to the country.[2]

The great immigration of Mexicans to this country occurred during the second and third periods described above, specifically between 1910 and 1930 when more than a million Mexicans crossed our borders.[3]

Students of Jewish immigration to America distinguish five periods or waves of immigration: (a) During the colonial period, most Jewish immigrants were from Spain, Portugal, or Holland; they were Sephardic Jews. (b) From 1850-1881 there was a large influx of German Jews. At the close of this period it was estimated that there were about 230,000 Jews in the United States. (c) The greatest wave was stimulated by the pogroms after 1881 in Russian Poland and the Ukraine. Jews from these areas and other parts of Eastern and Central Europe came in large numbers, particularly Jews from Hungary, Rumania, Slovakia, and Bohemia. This great wave lasted until World War I. (d) Another large immigration occurred after World War I, from most of the same areas as (c) above, the peak coming in 1921, and reduced greatly after 1924 due to immigration quotas. (e) The final wave followed the beginnings of Nazi persecution and World War II. This group included mostly Jews from Germany and Austria, and a small number from Poland and Central Europe. It is estimated that about 2.5 million Jews came to the United States from 1881 to 1942.[4] Today there are approximately 5.5 million Jews in the United States.

Educational Values of Selected Immigrant Groups

The Values of Orientals

It has been pointed out that both the Chinese and Japanese place high value on education. In the past, scholarship was one of the most important requirements for membership in the Chinese upper classes.[5] A recent study in

---

[2] Clyde V. Kiser, "Cultural Pluralism," *Annals of the American Academy of Political and Social Science,* March, 1949, pp. 117-130.

[3] Ruth Tuck, *Not With the Fist, Mexican-Americans in a Southern City* (New York: Harcourt Brace, 1946), p. 56.

[4] Schermerhorn, *op. cit.,* pp. 387ff.

[5] Al-Li S. Chin, "Some Problems of Chinese Youth in Transition," *American Journal of Sociology,* July, 1948, pp. 1-9; also, Bradford Smith, *Americans From Japan* (Philadelphia: Lippincott, 1948), p. 119; and Francis Hsu, *Americans and Chinese* (New York: Schuman, 1953), p. 135.

Berkeley, California, indicates that Oriental youth were more studious than youth in other ethnic groups.[6]

The Values of Mexicans

The poorly acculturated Mexicans have an apathetic and indifferent attitude toward education. Only a small minority of Mexicans, the fairly well acculturated, seem to appreciate the values of formal education.[7]

The Values of European Ethnic Groups

The majority of ethnic groups from Northern and Western Europe, since they immigrated to America early in our history, have become highly acculturated and assimilated, and have accepted the American stress on the values of formal education. This is not generally so for those European ethnics from Southern, Central, and Eastern Europe. First of all, these latter groups have arrived largely since 1882 and so are not as well acculturated and assimilated into the American cultural patterns. Hence, many ethnics in this group do not fully appreciate the value of formal education.[8] This is, in considerable part, due to this latter group's strongly peasant and low socioeconomic status origins in which formal education was viewed as impractical and because of the kind of employment that many came into upon entry in the United States.

Jewish Values

Jewish history is full of references to the high values Jews have traditionally placed on education and intellectualism. In America, Jewish group survival is dependent upon education and Jews have achieved high social class status, even though a minority group, through largely educational routes.[9]

---

[6] Davis McEntire, *Leisure Activities of Youth in Berkeley, California* (Berkeley: University of California Press, 1952), p. 10.

[7] John H. Burma, *Spanish-Speaking Groups in the United States* (Durham, North Carolina: Duke University Press, 1954).

[8] Handlin, Oscar, *The Uprooted* (Boston: Little, Brown, 1951).

[9] S. N. Behrman, *The Worcester Account* (New York: Random House, 1954); also Robert M. Frumkin, "Science and the Jewish Ethos," *Ethos*, IV, Spring, 1959, pp. 19-25; Wirth, Louis, "Education for Survival: The Jews," *American Journal of Sociology*, 1942-1943, pp. 682-691; Pope, Liston, "Religion and the Class Structure," *Annals of the American Academy of Political and Social Science*, March, 1948, pp. 84-91; see also Chapter III of this book.

Education as Acculturation

Acculturation refers to the process by which an out-group acquires the culture of an in-group.[10] Here we are concerned with the acculturation of Orientals, Mexicans, European ethnic groups, and Jews. Since formal education, in particular, is concerned with the transmission of cultural values, it is a significant force in the acculturation of immigrant groups with foreign cultural patterns.

Oriental Acculturation

While both Chinese and Japanese have placed a high value on education and made excellent records in American schools and colleges, discrimination in employment, public places, and in social contacts prevents these Orientals from first-class citizenship in spite of the fact that most second generation Orientals have become "Americanized," that is, fairly well acculturated. Thus, even American-born and acculturated Orientals have generally been denied opportunities in occupations and professions for which, by training and education, they are well prepared to engage in.

Mexican Acculturation

Mexicans came from a peasant cultural background in which formal education was not regarded as practical. In the United States, Mexicans have suffered the same kinds of caste discrimination that Negroes have experienced, that is, segregation and quasi-segregation in education, housing, and discrimination in employment. Of the immigrant groups considered here, the Mexicans seem the least acculturated. Mexican children have a real difficulty in obtaining more than an elementary grasp of English, since Spanish is generally spoken at home and little opportunity is found to speak English outside the home because of various forms of segregation and discrimination.

These Hispanic Americans include a major portion of our migrant workers. Along with the educational lacks and issues surrounding the schooling of American Indians on the reservations, the problem of educating the children of migrants provides one of the historically darkest and least satisfactory aspects in the story of education in the United States.

---

[10] See *inter alia*, Henry P. Fairchild, Ed., *Dictionary of Sociology* (New York: Philosophical Library, 1944), p. 3; also, Robert Bierstedt, *The Social Order* (New York: McGraw-Hill, 1957), pp. 154-156.

Acculturation of European Ethnic Groups

Unlike the Orientals and Mexicans against whom a color and/or racial barrier has been erected, the European ethnic groups have not found it as difficult to become Americanized and assimilated into the American pattern of life. Second and third generation members of ethnic groups who formerly looked at formal education as impractical now see that education is the key to upward social mobility in our society.

Jewish Acculturation

Jews throughout history have had favorable attitudes toward education and learning. In America acculturation generally has proceeded with great ease in spite of discrimination in employment, housing, and higher education. The advantage Jews have had as an immigant group is that they have not had to overcome any color or racial barrier and their stress on education had made acculturation less difficult. While Orientals have had a favorable attitude toward education, color or racial barriers have been strongly against them. Mexican immigrants have been at a disadvantage because of both a color or racial barrier and a peasant cultural background. The Central, Southern, and Eastern European ethnic groups have had the initial disadvantage of "Ghetto" and isolated living as well as unfavorable attitudes toward education but no racial or color barriers. Studies of social class position of these various ethnic groups suggest that the Jews have been the most generally successful of the ethnic groups, Mexicans the least successful in achieving American arete,[11] that is, values highly prized in our culture.

The American School and the Immigrant

American agencies are more efficient and extensive than the immigrant institutions when modifying the cultures of minorities. Chief among these is, of course, the public school. Its influence is not limited to those in attendance, whether they be foreign-born adults in night schools or Americanization classes, or foreign-born children and native-born children of foreign parentage in day schools, but extends though them to others in the family or groups. Not all transmission of culture is from adults to children; frequently in acculturation the influence is greater in the opposite direction. Among other agencies helping the adjustment and modification may be noted social settlements,

---

[11] For a definition of the concept of arete see Walter Goldschmidt, "Values in the Field of Comparative Sociology," *American Sociological Review,* June, 1953, pp. 287-293.

unions, immigration commissions, international institutions, various immigrant welfare societies, and social agencies specializing in ciitzenship help and in programs for the foreign born and their children.

The story of the immigrant and the American public school dates well back into the last century. However, starting with 1880, numerous immigrants from Central, Eastern, and Southern Europe began to reach the United States. Sheer numbers helped make prominent their distinctive cultural characteristics, different from the dominant American pattern. It became popular to blame these "hordes" for the problems of poverty, slums, corruption, etc., and demands arose requesting the education of the immigrant.[12]

The census figures of 1900 showed that in the American native white population of ten years of age or over, 4.6 percent were illiterate, as compared with 12.9 percent in the foreign-born white population.[13] Yet, aside from patriotic purposes, before World War I few were concerned over immigrants' becoming Americanized, as many Americans wished them to help build America for the profit of those employing them. The school, in fact, took little special account of many of them. Neither were the immigrants anxious to change or transform themselves. For that reason, the easing of the burden of acculturation was provided by the ethnic colony, the settlement house, the church, and various ethnic organizations. But at the same time most Americans then also had little sympathy for the immigrant's need to hold on to part of his past.

The public school tried, half-heartedly, to teach the immigrant the rudiments of the English language. But not many aliens made use of the offers of the school. At the same time, the public school treated the immigrant children as natives, disregarding entirely their cultural backgrounds and judging their performance by American cultural standards. This, in turn, led the children to break with their family traditions, to regard their fathers' backgrounds as definitely inferior. A considerable number of such children made up, as a result, America's delinquent and criminal groups.[14]

Just before World War I, the American school began to be more interested in the immigrant. With the increasing number of immigrants and with

---

[12] See Ezri Altzman, "The Educational Programs for Immigrants in the United States," *History of Education Journal,* Spring, 1958, pp. 75-80; also, Joseph S. Roucek, "Education of the Refugee in the United States," *International Review of Education,* 1958, pp. 374-380; also, Morris I. Berger, "The American School and the Immigrant," pp. 109-116, in George Z. F. Bereday and Luigi Volpicelli, eds., *Public Education in America* (New York: Harper, 1958).

[13] *Reports of the Immigration Commission, Abstracts of the Immigration Commission* (Washington, D.C.: Government Printing Office, 1911), p. 157.

[14] See *inter alia,* Frederick M. Thrasher, "Are Our Criminals Foreigners?" in Francis J. Brown and Joseph S. Roucek, Eds., *Racial and Cultural Minorities* (New York: Prentice-Hall, 1937), pp. 697-710.

their entrance into industry, the American employers had learned the need for more educated immigrant employees, preferably able to understand the English language, since the efficiency of the laborer depended upon his familiarity with English. The knowledge of English also helped to reduce industrial hazards and to curb the tendency toward accidents and larger production costs.

During World War I, this mercenary aim became transformed into an ideal of so-called Americanization, relating the teaching of English to instruction in the Constitution and forms of American Government. This instruction, however, was only given, in the evening schools. The course of World War I intensified this effort because of the experience of the immigrants during the war as soldiers and workers in industry. In turn, the immigrant learned the value of such learning in terms of increased income, extended opportunities for work and wages, and rise in status. The enthusiasm for this type of "schooling" went on for several years after World War I, and was focused on the broader lines of civil understanding and social adjustment. Such evening courses even offered special instruction in the household arts or in the requirements of healthful living. Yet, the public school paid little attention in its curriculum to the needs of immigrant children with a totally different cultural background; in fact, this situation in numerous cities continues to the present, the fundamental stress being on subjects appropriate to children with an American cultural heritage.

Gradually the concept of acculturation introduced by the sociologists had its effects; its proponents started to ask for better teaching methods and more appropriate content for the immigrant. Schools began to give up the idea that America had one uniform culture, and educators came to accept the concept of cultural pluralism — a theory favoring the retention of the immigrant cultures but permitting immigrants to make contributions to the overall pattern of a "One America" culture which would be the end result of many cultures.

In this new perspective, immigrant education was conceived as a total way of life, and the notion that Americanization was rooted in the mere mastery of the English language was rejected. Also rejected was the concept of producing Americanization by law, of forcing knowledge and the use of the English language. A respect for the newcomer was featured rather than rejection and contempt, with the accent on the idea that American culture was a mutual process, a process of give and take. Recognition grew that the values, experiences, and spiritual riches of the immigrant's national life would strengthen America's culture.[15] After World War I immigrant education

---

[15] U.S. Bureau of Education, *Proceedings, Americanization Conference,* Washington, D.C., May 12-15, 1919.

became broadly conceived as social education, that all aspects of the immigrant's life had to be appreciated and nurtured rather than merely his ability to read, write, and speak the English language and know the rudiments of the American Constitution.

These ideas had a definite impact on the tasks assigned to public education. The school could now operate successfully by becoming a community center — the public forum, the meeting place, the social center, the evening school, the neighborhood house, the place where formal and informal educational processes could be discharged.[16]

Before World War I, the theory of cultural pluralism was studied only more or less academically in several institutions of higher learning. At the same time, while the immigrants as a group were left to their own devices, their more ambitious and competent sons had "escaped" from their foreign backgrounds by graduating in ever growing numbers from the best American institutions of higher learning. World War II intensified this process in another direction. While in World War I the Armed Forces were acutely aware of many "foreigners" unable to read and speak English, during World War II the "illiterates" were mostly native-born (especially from the isolated regions of the South).[17]

Contributions From the Education of Immigrants

The "melting pot" philosophy in American society and the various programs of "Americanization" reflect a general desire to assimilate ethnics, to have them shed their alien cultures. This desire for homogeneity is the assimilationist point of view.

On the other hand, there is a smaller minority, mostly intellectuals, who decry the assimilationist point of view, and instead ask that we preserve these ethnics, preserve our heterogeneity. This is the pluralist point of view.[18] Those who adhere to this viewpoint, like Adamic, state that diversity is the

---

[16] Actually this was not a new idea, since it was propounded by social settlement workers in the 1890's. In fact, settlement houses should be evaluated more definitely as being experimental institutions between 1890 and 1920 for vocational training and guidance, kindergartens, community center programs, and as international houses; see Morris I. Berger, *The Settlement, the Immigrant and the Public Schools, a Study of the Influence of the Settlement Movement and the New Migration Upon Public Education: 1890-1924*, unpublished Ph.D. thesis (New York: Teachers College, Columbia University, 1956).

[17] For details, see *inter alia*, Eli Ginzberg and Douglas W. Beay, *The Uneducated* (New York: Columbia University Press, 1953); also, Eli Ginzberg et al, *The Ineffective Soldiers*, 3 vols. (New York: Columbia University Press, 1959).

[18] On the assimilationist and pluralist points of view see Brewton Berry, *Race and Ethnic Relations* (Boston: Houghton-Mifflin, Second Edition, 1958), pp. 14-17.

source of American strength and that a vigorous policy of assimilationism could destroy that strength.[19]

Both the assimilationist and pluralist points of view have been reflected in the education of immigrants. The former point of view has been promoted by civil authorities in their efforts to Americanize immigrants. The latter view has been promoted largely by the immigrants themselves, sometimes with the help and encouragement of social workers and sociologists, through sectarian groups connected with the church, various kinds of clubs, parochial schools, and ethnic centers.

Of the various ethnic groups, there is increasing evidence that the Jews are the most acculturated, Americanized, but still one of the least assimilated. They have achieved high social status through learning American values and the English language but they have one of the lowest rates of exogamous marriages. There is a very close inverse relation between assimilation and ethnic endogamy, that is, the higher the rate of endogamy, the less the assimilation. The education of Jewish immigrants suggests that an ethnic group could be acculturated and not yet fully assimilated and still make a worthwhile contribution to American society. In short, it demonstrates the strength of the cultural pluralist position in favor of a heterogeneous America. The case of the Mexicans and Orientals indicates, however, that too little assimilation prevents ethnic groups from making their full and potential contribution to American society.

The pluralist influence is found to some degree in many public schools in the metropolitan New York area. For example, the public schools of Newark, New Jersey, provide courses in the language and culture of the ethnic or minority groups which they serve. Thus, at the Weequahic High School, in a predominantly Jewish district, there is a course in Hebrew Language and Literature; at the West Side High School, in a predominantly Italian district, there is a course in the Italian Language and Literature; at East Side High School, in a Polish district, there is a course in Polish Language and Literature.

Many colleges and universities follow a similar course. At the University of Buffalo, which serves a large number of Polish students (mostly native-born of Polish-born parentage), there are courses offered in the Polish language, Polish history and culture, and there is an active, extracurricular Polish Arts Club. Many non-Polish students at the University of Buffalo take such courses and gain a greater appreciation of Americans of Polish ancestry.

---

[19] Louis Adamic, *A Nation of Nations* (New York: Harper, 1944). The point of view expressed here is also variously called "cultural democracy," "cultural pluralism," etc.

The recent emphasis on the study of foreign languages and cultures in our schools and colleges comes about, in part, as a result of what American educational policymakers have learned from attempting to assimilate and acculturate the immigrant. We are finding out now that we must teach native Americans not only to appreciate America's ethos but also that of other peoples of the world as well, many of whom have made America the vigorous nation

Bettmann Archive

AMERICN NEGRO SCHOOL, CIVIL WAR PERIOD.

it is. If world peace and brotherhood are to be a reality, we must not foster assimilation at the expense of cultural pluralism; we must not foster nationalism at the expense of internationalism. This, we think, is the great contribution from the education of the immigrant — from improved approaches to educating the foreign-born and their children we are building educational programs for all Americans that will make them more understanding and effective citizens of the world.

The Education of Negroes

No label of nationality other than American describes our Negroes, yet Negroes constitute a minority group in American society. Today, about one in ten Americans is a Negro.

375

It was in 1619 that the first Negro slaves were brought to the American colonies. By 1750 slavery was recognized by law in all of the colonies. At the time of the first U.S. Census in 1790, Negroes constituted nearly 20 per cent of the population. Largely stripped of their African culture, the characteristics of the American Negroes are understood mostly in terms of their low caste-like status deriving from slavery and the consequences of that status. The education of Negroes in the United States, therefore, is closely related to continuing efforts of some whites to preserve the low caste-like status of the Negro and the efforts of Negroes and other whites to change that status.[20]

Effects of Caste-like Status on Negro Education

The formal education of Negro Americans may be said to have had its beginnings with the founding of the first schools for Negroes in the South during and following the Civil War.[21] Most of these were private institutions, created by a combination of Northern philanthropy and Northern zeal. Church missionary groups, the Freeman's Bureau, and the Union League all now attempted to build the literacy that pre-war Southern laws had forbidden.

The tortuous road that the Negro had to travel from the Reconstruction period to the recent advances was stormy. For several decades after the Civil War, a debate was carried on over industrial education of the Negro, which, for some people, meant "practical" public education, and for others, "industrial training."[22] Booker T. Washington's influence on the rise of the industrial school movement was important, as we shall see later, but actually this form of education was too often limited in public schools to learning about cooking and menial services, and "vocational training" for Negroes as a result was "little more than a slogan to cover poor, cheap, and ineffective Negro education."[23] Fortunately, for the most part, this movement evaporated in the subsequent decades, due to the gradual reduction of Negro illiteracy, the realization on the part of the public and philanthropic foundations and Negroes themselves that they needed the same varieties of education as the

---

[20] For an account of the ideological aspects of Negro-white relations in the United States and their meaning for Negro education, see Robert M. Frumkin and Joseph S. Roucek, "The Relationship of Major Ideological Premises of Whites and Negroes as Manifested in Political and Social Policy Changes to the Present and Future Education of Negroes in the United States: A Social Scientific Analysis," *Journal of Negro Education,* July-October, 1959, pp. 141-57.

[21] Charles Johnson, *Growing Up in the Black Belt* (Washington, D.C.: American Council on Education, 1941), p. 63.

[22] Gunnar Myrdal, et al., *An American Dilemma* (New York: Harper, 1944), p. 897.

[23] George E. Simpson, and J. Milton Yinger, *Racial and Cultural Minorities* (New York: Harper, 1953), p. 551.

white man. But the general antagonism of the South to the more educated Negroes fitted into the need of the region to keep Negro labor cheap. This attitude began, however, to be modified at the turn of the present century when the larger industrial concerns (especially those in the coal and iron business in Alabama) started to elevate Negroes slightly in the socio-economic scale. But the situation in the rural districts remained miserable; there a close relationship existed between the operations of the Negro schools and the agricultural system. The dates for the opening and closing of the school in the cotton belt were, in fact, decided upon by the landlords watching the crops, and the internal school program had to accommodate itself to the farming needs.[24]

From the initiation of Negro education after the War between the States, segregated Negro education has generally followed the patterns of education developed by the whites; but it has been inferior in all aspects. This problem affected both whites and Negroes as, for years, the section with one-third of America's children was forced to attempt to educate them in a dual system with less than one-sixth of the national income.[25]

Ever since the Reconstruction period, Negro education suffered from the handicap of starting from nowhere. Literacy was estimated at about 5 percent among Negroes in 1860; by 1890 nearly 60 percent were still illiterate; by 1910 illiteracy had been reduced to 30 percent. While a few lower schools in four or five Southern States had been opened on a mixed basis by the Negro-Carpet Bag governments of the immediate post-war era, most of the Southern States established separate schools for whites and Negroes. For many years there were no local school taxes in the South, the funds being distributed from state sources to counties on a per capita basis; thus the heavily populated counties with large numbers of Negroes received more money than those counties with smaller Negro populations. White groups in smaller counties were angered by these provisions but it was not long before funds due to Negro schools were being diverted in various ways to white schools throughout the South. By 1930 Negro schools were still on the average getting only 37

---

[24] See Myrdal, *op cit.*, pp. 897-899; also Johnson, Charles, *Patterns of Negro Segregation* (New York: Harper, 1943), p. 21.

[25] The history of Negro education is well documented. The following paragraphs are drawn upon these volumes: Harry S. Ashmore, *The Negro and the Schools* (Chapel Hill: University of North Carolina Press, 1954); Horace M. Bond, *The Education of the Negro in the American Social Order* (New York: Prentice-Hall, 1945); E. F. Frazier, *The Negro in the United States* (New York: The Macmillan Co., 1949); Edgar W. Knight, *Public Education in the South* (Boston: Ginn & Co., 1922); Truman M. Pierce et al., *White and Negro Schools in the South* (Englewood Cliffs, New Jersey: Prentice-Hall, 1955); and Carter G. Woodson, *The Education of the Negro Prior to 1861* (New York: G. P. Putnam's Sons, 1915).

percent of the amount due to them on a per capita basis. In the 1890's and early 1900's, as a result of Negro sympathy with the unsuccessful Populist movement in the South, the Negroes were punished by further deprivations of civil rights on all fronts. Having no political voice, being a particularly weak economic force, and remaining largely uneducated, Negroes were the unfortunate victims of one of our greatest national tragedies and blights.

Although a considerable amount of aid was given Negro education by private foundations during the late nineteenth and early twentieth centuries (Peabody, Slater, Jeanes, Rosenwald, Carnegie, Phelps-Stokes funds and the General Education Board), they made only a limited dent, important though it was, in the local morass. By 1900, according to a report of the United States Commissioner of Education, out of over 1,000 public high schools in the South, less than 70 were provided for Negroes. It has been claimed that possibly the private funds may have only supported the Southern white rulers in their failure to live up to their public educational responsibility for their second-class citizens; however, these funds were particularly helpful in providing essential rural elementary education and teacher education for Negroes. The years of the Great Depression further strained Negro education as increased thousands of Negro youngsters, squeezed from the labor market, bulged the schools. Generally in the South, the Negroes still had ramshackle buildings, more poorly trained teachers, near starvation salaries, and "benefited" from discarded white school desks, books, and decrepit buses.

Some white leaders were, nevertheless, driving against the general inertia to improve the Negro's lot. Educated Negroes themselves, with leadership, for example, from their growing "A and M" colleges and organizations such as the N.A.A.C.P. (founded 1909), were pushing for their Constitutional rights. Meanwhile the Federal Government had poured over $200 million in school construction funds (P.W.A. and others) into the South, but again, as had been typical, only eight percent went for Negro schools.

Several key factors brought the long overdue improvements that have marked the recent history of Negro education. World War II and the subsequent economic and population boom brought a changing South where whites had less to fear from Negro competition, where the Negroes had much more money to spend, and where increasing numbers of whites were finally awakening to the simple truth stated so long before by Booker T. Washington, to effect, that a man cannot keep another man down in the gutter without staying down with him! Additionally, under continuing pressure from the militant N.A.A.C.P., the South was moving toward providing more nearly separate but equal conditions. Several court cases had resulted in Southern States being forced to allow Negroes into public white graduate and professional schools because there were no equivalent facilities for Negro citizens. The logical next step would be the frank recognition that segregated lower

378

schools were abysmally unequal. Despite the hurried spending of millions (a number of Southern States had long paid much more proportionally on their two sets of school systems than richer states with integrated programs), there was no staving off the inevitable. In 1953 the United States Supreme Court spoke and the still long road ahead was opened towards attaining the education promised to Negroes by the Fourteenth Amendment 85 years before. Chapter XI discusses this latter development.

The Washington-DuBois Controversy

In September, 1895, Booker T. Washington became a new leader of the American Negroes after delivering an important speech at the opening of the Atlanta Cotton States and International Exposition. It was in this speech that he spoke of the future dreams of the Negro and the present need for practical and realistic measures to lift Negroes from their illiteracy and ignorance. He urged educational facilities which would help the Negro rise from the bottom organically rather than artificially from a point equal to the white man's position. He felt honestly that the Negro was not yet ready for equal status with the white. To the whites concerned about the Negro's desire for political power, Washington assured them that the Negro was now mainly interested in industrial education and economic gain only. One statement he made prepared the way for the separate but equal doctrine (1896, the case of Plessy v. Ferguson) which became an established principle for Negro-white relations for almost 60 years: "In all things that are purely social we can be as separate as the fingers, yet one as the hand in all things essential to mutual progress." Many whites accepted this statement as Washington's approval, as representative of American Negroes, for keeping the Negro "in his place." In essence, Washington wanted Negroes to prepare for jobs which were open to them. This, Washington apparently believed, was the realistic road to equal status sometime in the future. The Negro must first become literate and learn skills which might help him to be economically independent. Then, perhaps, he would be ready for political and social equality with whites.[26]

Dr. W. E. B. DuBois, a Negro sociologist and educator, attacked Washington for accepting the Negro caste position and for remaining silent and asking other Negroes to remain silent in the face of injustice. In effect, he suggested that Washington had been a kind of traitor to the Negro people and had sold out to the whites. DuBois and his associates demanded no less than equality of opportunity in education at the higher levels as well as in elementary and vocational training.[27] They argued that, in the struggle for

---

[26] Booker T. Washington, *Up From Slavery* (New York: Doubleday, 1901).

[27] W. E. B. DuBois, *The Souls of Black Folk* (Chicago: McClurg, 1928).

equality, training for inferior positions will not be of much help. What was needed was a large number of highly literate and capable Negro leaders who could only come into existence if equal opportunities in higher education become a reality.

Hampton Institute

Hampton Institute opened its doors in April, 1868, in the gloomy day of the Reconstruction Period. Its early aims were those suggested later by Booker T. Washington, one of its early graduates. Negroes were to be trained for the kind of jobs that were open to them. Hampton became the chief source of Negro industrial education in the United States. The kind of education which W. E. B. DuBois advocated came later. Today Hampton is rated as a Class A college by the Southern Association of Colleges and Secondary Schools. It offers a Bachelor of Science Degree in the Departments of Agriculture, Business, Home Economics, Nurse Education, and Divisions of Teacher Education and Technology. It also offers a Master of Science Degree in Education. While it might seem that a general or liberal education as advocated by DuBois has been superseded by vocational education, this is not the case. Beginning with a basic core of subjects required of all freshmen, a general or liberal education program is concentrated in the first year but also continues, in decreasing proportions, throughout the student's course of study.

An excellent feature of the Hampton program is its emphasis on teaching the student to communicate effectively. Hampton has an excellent Communications Center. The Center was designed to do three important jobs: (1) to help all students to read, write, speak, and listen effectively (language deficiencies have been one of the major handicaps with which Negro students enter higher education); (2) to assist all students in understanding and appreciating the literary heritage of the world; and (3) to identify, encourage, and train young people who show promise of being superior teachers, graduate students, writers, actors, speakers, or speech correctionists.[28]

One of the authors of this chapter, formerly a faculty member at Hampton Institute, could objectively testify to the fact that Hampton Institute is a living resolution to the Washington-DuBois controversy. In the Newport News-Hampton, Virginia area, Hampton Institute is the cultural and intellectual center, the place where any person, regardless of race, might find the facilities and programs and the kinds of persons which might help him satisfy his thirst for knowledge. In short, Hampton Institute is living proof that vocational and liberal education are not necessarily antagonistic but can be complementary forces in the progress of the Negro toward first-class citizenship. Other such schools of higher education that were essential for developing

---

[28] See the *Hampton Bulletin,* January, 1952.

380

Negro teachers and leaders so badly needed in the post-Civil War period were Fisk, Howard, and Tuskegee.

Contributions From the Education of Negroes

The greatest single contribution from the education of Negroes is that finding which comes from an examination of the Washington-DuBois controversy, a controversy in some ways similar to the assimilationist-pluralist controversy in the education of immigrants. Booker T. Washington stressed the idea that the Negro must first be economically independent before he could be ready for political and social interaction with whites on the level of the whites. W. E. B. DuBois disagreed with Washington, stating that such a position prevents the Negro from ever being literate enough to fight for the social justice which will make equality a reality. What actually has happened is that the progress of Negroes has come through adherence to *both* suggestions. Simultaneously, the Negro has increased his socio-economic status and educational status. Greater economic independence made possible by industrial training has made possible higher education for Negroes. Greater opportunities in higher education in turn have prepared Negroes for the kind of leadership that has led to the tremendous gains toward the realization of first-class citizenship that our nation and the world are now witnessing.

In addition to the sad lessons accruing from 85 years of segregated education, the great contribution of Negro education to the American heritage is, therefore, the finding that for first-class citizenship, regardless of race, one must have both a liberal education and an education that prepares one vocationally. Current controversies concerning school and college curricula center on this very old but crucial issue of the liberal versus the vocational education. From the education of Negroes it is now known that in a democratic society, for full and responsible citizenship, for a full and happy life, people need both kinds of education. In general, we realize today that for American education as a whole we have not, until now, realized that vocational and liberal educations are complementary and not antagonistic.

Education of Workers

THE LABOR MOVEMENT AND WORKERS' EDUCATION IN THE UNITED STATES. A labor movement refers to a continuous association of wage and/or salary earners for the purpose of improving their economic and social well-being. Its principal purpose is the improvement of the status of employees (workers) *as* employees. Its appeal and challenge is based on the premise that employees can and should share in the good things of life while remaining employees; that economic well-being and its accompanying social prestige and privileges need not be solely contingent upon becoming an employer or self-employed businessman.[29] In America the earliest labor organizations were established in the skilled handicraft trades. But today labor organizations include many kinds of salaried workers — for example, teachers. The history of the labor movement in the United States is an exciting and important chapter in man's quest for the good life but beyond the scope of this chapter.[30] We are concerned here with a description and analysis of labor's contribution to American education.

Workers' education is not a generic term but rather a specific one. It is a special kind of adult education designed to give employees a better understanding of their status, problems, rights, and responsibilities as employees, as union members, as consumers, and as citizens. While vocational and professional educations are designed to train persons for individual advancement, workers' education is largely concerned with group advancement and the solution of group problems. Cultural and recreational features are often included in workers' education programs but these features are peripheral to the central theme: the employee's status in the work, community, and world situations.[31] A more specific definition is given in a recent bulletin from the U.S. Department of Labor: "Workers' education. . . . attempts to fulfill the educational needs of workers which arise from their membership in a trade union. That is, its function is to provide instruction designed to help union members toward a better understanding of, and closer and more effective participation in, their union, their community, and the society in which they live, and to train potential union leaders."[32]

In these definitions of workers' education we see the reappearance of the Washington-DuBois controversy, the problem of the vocational versus liberal education. For full status in a democratic society, a person must have both kinds of education and the employee is no exception. An employee must not only possess vocational competence; he must understand his role in the work situation, in the community, and in the world. Workers' education, in short, seems to be designed to supplement vocational education with a liberal edu-

---

29 This is a slight modification of the definition given by Florence Peterson, *American Labor Unions* (New York: Harper, revised edition, 1952), p. 3. The modification has been the addition of salary earners along with wage earners, since salary workers are continuing to play a more significant role in the labor movement than they have in the past.

30 See, *inter alia,* Harold U. Faulkner and Mark Starr, *Labor in America* (New York: Harper, revised edition, 1949); Peterson, *op. cit.*

31 See Peterson, *op. cit.,* p. 137.

32 U.S. Dept. of Labor, Bureau of Labor Statistics, *A Guide to Labor-Management Relations in the United States* (Washington, D.C.: U.S. Government Printing Office, 1959), BLS Bulletin No. 1225, Chapter on "Workers' Education," pp. 1-13.

cation, to help provide the complete kind of education necessary for full participation in a democratic society.

A fairly comprehensive picture of workers' education programs has been drawn by Starr from a survey of union education conducted by the Fund for Adult Education. Information in this survey was obtained from such labor-education bodies as the American Labor Education Service (ALES), the AFL Workers' Education Bureau (WEB), and the CIO Education and Research Department, as well as universities and colleges. The programs include the following kinds of activities: week-end institutions and conferences; workers' evening classes; one-week and two-week resident full-time training institutes and labor schools, as well as a one-year program of full-time study leading to employment by the union upon successful completion of the theoretical and practical work; use of filmstrips, films, and other audio-visual aids; field trips; participation in community projects; and a host of other activities with educational implications.[33]

Since 1914 the International Ladies' Garment Workers' Union, one of the oldest and most progressive unions, has been a leader in the field of workers' education. It maintains educational activities on three levels: (1) *mass education,* which includes lectures, excursions, and visits to museums, art galleries, and other places of interest, and other types of recreational and cultural activities; (2) *classroom education,* which provides new members' classes, and courses in union history, current events, labor problems, languages, journalism, parliamentary law, and public speaking; and (3) a *training institute* for members likely to assume positions of responsibility in local unions. The union, at a recent accounting, had 24 full-time educational directors in the larger population centers, as well as a staff training institute and a varied program ranging from individual counseling to mass meetings of area membership.

Programs intended for the rank-and-file members include:

A. New members' classes. In some areas, attendance is compulsory. Ranging from a single lecture to a series of four to six planned talks, these classes cover such topics as rights and responsibilities of new members, why members pay dues and what they get in return, welfare agencies available to union members, etc.

B. Cultural and recreational classes in handicraft, art, music, dramatics, and choral singing. An annual Spring festival exhibits work done by students in sculpture, painting, and ceramics.

C. A special course, English for Hispanics, which grew out of the large influx of Puerto Ricans into the garment industry. The specially de-

---

[33] Mark Starr, "Union Education Survey," *Labor and Nation,* VII, 1951, p. 57.

veloped textbook and homework assignments are built around trade union and shop experiences.

D. Organized tours of the United Nations building. These have become increasingly popular in locals surrounding the New York City area.

E. In Pennsylvania and Massachusetts, musical reviews produced by the union are presented to raise funds for local charitable and relief agencies.

Programs for local officers include:

A. Officers' qualification course. This is carried on mainly in the New York metropolitan area where completion of the 17-week, two-nights-a-week course is a prerequisite for new candidates for full-time office. The course includes such subjects as ILGWU history, trade union techniques, economics of the garment industry, etc.

B. Refresher courses for shop stewards, usually conducted at local level, weekly or in week-end institutes.

C. One-day, week-end, seven- and ten-day institutes for officers and active members. Some 45 such institutes were carried on in 1955. Some are conducted in conjunction with a university labor program. Included in these programs are economics, political action, and labor and international affairs.

D. Spanish language course for business agents and staff — mainly in the New York City area.

The ILGWU training institute puts approximately 25 qualified students a year through a 12-month full-time study-work training program. Qualified applicants are ILGWU members or members of other unions; some come from outside union ranks. Those successfully completing the course are offered staff jobs in the ILGWU.

Divided into five periods, the students' training includes an initial 12-week study period at the Institute in the union's headquarters in New York City followed by a period out in the field on an organizing drive or working in a local union. Another 12 weeks of study at the Institute leads to a second period in the field followed by a final period of study at union headquarters.

The curriculum includes history of the ILGWU, labor history, labor law, economics for workers, structure and operation of the ILGWU, economics of the garment industry, problems in organizing, comparative labor movements, comparative economic systems, and local union administration. In addition, skills in mimeographing, leaflet writing, operation of film projectors, etc. are developed in workshop sessions.

General services of the education department include: extensive publication of pamphlets, books, outlines, songs and records, a film library with 60 items available to union and community groups (including the widely used ILGWU-produced film *With These Hands*), a book sales division, packet mailing service of education aids to education directors and committees, and a lecture program at Unity House, the union's summer vacation center.

The national Education Department spends much time on talks and film showings to foreign labor delegations and public school groups visiting the union's headquarters. It provides speakers for schools and religious and community groups. Monthly meetings of education directors in the New York City area serve to discuss new ideas, coordinate programs, preview new films, and develop new materials.[34]

Many universities and colleges have been cooperating with labor in workers' education. For more than a quarter of a century, the University of Wisconsin School for Workers has been one of the most outstanding schools of its kind in the nation. Selected groups of laborers attend a variety of enlightening courses during special short sessions. In a recent report Schwarztrauber, whom we paraphrase below, described the objectives of the School's program by comparing them with the service programs of regular university departments. He explained that all are related to one vital problem — how a going concern can dispose of its goods and services at a fair price. He points out that the chief problem of laborers closely parallels that of a farm or a business concern. The worker like the farmer or the employer seeks to sell his product (his labor) at a fair price. This labor is highly perishable; it must be sold today or it is gone forever. He cannot save it nor can he effectively sell his products in competition with other individuals like himself. As an individual seller he is helpless to a great extent. But if the same worker bargains with his employer along with the power of a thousand other workers, together they will probably meet with considerable success.

It is at this point that the worker, in his group relationship with his employer, needs educational services. The School for Workers functions in such situations to help laborers achieve an intelligent and informed approach to their problems as a basis for collective bargaining. Thus the School for Workers does for the laborer what the School of Commerce does for the businessman and the School of Agriculture for the farmer in their extensive activities — it meets his educational requirements at the point of most vital need.

In addition to this prime function of substituting industrial government for industrial warfare, other implicit purposes exist in programs such as that of the School for Workers. One of these is to enable organized labor to come to recognize its place in industrial society — that it must take an active part in the social and civic, as well as in the economic life of the community and

---

[34] U.S. Department of Labor, BLS Bulletin No. 1225, *op. cit.*, pp. 4-6.

nation. Workers should learn to serve as members of city councils, school boards, and to carry on other activities in which citizens are engaged. The laborers should be instructed so that they can assume responsibilities in the various agencies, national and international, that play a role in directing world affairs. Until recently these citizenship responsibilities have been largely the monopoly of middle and upper class members of society. This situation cannot be allowed to continue if democracy is to grow in meaning and if it is to endure as a true characteristic of our social order. Therefore, the School for Workers is an example of a labor education program as vital as life itself "for there is no real life for the individuals of any society unless each individual in it is given a place of dignity and respect equal to any other."[35]

At the Second Constitutional Convention of the AFL and CIO in 1957, in Resolution 159, it was urged that the AFL-CIO support a Labor Extension Service in the Department of Labor to provide services and material comparable to those provided to farmers and businessmen through federal agencies. It suggested that the program be administered at the national and state levels through advisory boards made up of representatives of organized labor and cooperating institutions and agencies.[36] This resolution is a clear indication of the recognition by labor leaders of the continuing need for labor education. In modern industrial society, as their earlier efforts such as English language and orientation-to-America classes and schools decline, the labor movement will replace these with more sophisticated efforts, such as the development of Schools and Colleges of Labor as integral units of higher educational institutions.[37]

Contributions From the Education of Workers

If we might for a moment imagine that non-unionized workers (or employees) are like underprivileged immigrants or minority group members in our society, we might begin to see what contributions the labor movement has made to the heritage of American education through what is known as workers' education. The immigrant has suffered because of a lack of acculturation as well as assimilation. The minority group member has likewise suffered for reasons similar to those of the immigrant as well as from the lack

---

[35] Ernest E. Schwarztrauber, *The University of Wisconsin School for Workers* (Madison: University of Wisconsin School for Workers, no date), pp. 20-22.

[36] *AFL-CIO Resolutions on Education* (Washington, D.C.: AFL-CIO, 1958), p. 6.

[37] For two good sources on universities and workers' education, see Jack Barbash, *Universities and Unions in Workers' Education* (New York: Harper, 1955) and Joseph Mire, *Labor Education* (Madison, Wisconsin: Inter-University Labor Education Committee, 1956).

of the right kind of education which is due, in part, to minority group status. Thus, the non-unionized worker is very much like an immigrant or minority group member in the industrial society — he is at the mercy of the dominant group, management, because he is essentially illiterate and feels strange in this industrial world. When a worker joins the union he is no longer a member of an underprivileged minority group, he is no longer a kind of immigrant in a culture unfamiliar, he is no longer a member of a subservient group. As a union member he is a partner to members of management, a partner in an industrial society. A union member can talk man to man with a member of management, with the employer. More and more union members are being provided with a liberal education with a "major" in the field of labor and industrial relations; here he learns the role of a union member, of a worker in a democratic society.

The non-unionized employee is like an alien in an industrial culture. He is in it, but not a part of it. Like the immigrant he must learn the ways of the new culture he enters, he must learn the language and customs of labor and industrial relations. The non-unionized member is like the Negro or minority group member in American society. He must have vocational skills but these skills can only provide him with a wage or salary. To have first-class citizenship the laborer needs a liberal education so that he can understand his role in society and secure the social justice that the democratic foundations of our nation promise all citizens.

The contribution of workers' education to the American educational heritage is precisely that it, through the labor movement, has recognized that workers (or employees) must have more than a vocational education to be first-class workers and citizens in American society. Drucker has recently pointed out that we have become an "employee society," a society in which a man's status is almost directly related to his employee status and that status alone.[38] Since we are a society in which the overwhelming number of persons in our labor force are employees, the fact that this large segment of the population is becoming aware of its role and responsibilities in a democratic society is of the utmost significance.

From its beginning, organized labor has recognized that universal public education is essential for the achievement of equality of opportunity by the children of the United States. Organized labor, thanks to the influence of workers' education programs, takes pride in the fact that a growing number of trade unionists are members of school boards and are otherwise giving active support to the educational needs of all our people. In short, workers' education is helping unionists to become first-class citizens in our industrial society,

---

[38] Peter Drucker, "The Employee Society," *American Journal of Sociology*, January, 1953, pp. 358-363.

and to assume the social responsibilities only persons with a liberal education are prepared to accept because they understand their role in our democratically oriented society.

EDUCATIONAL INFLUENCES OF AMERICAN BUSINESS.[39]   Lest it be thought that workers' education was only the concern of unions, it should be explained that down through the years, from the initial general education of indentured servants and apprentices to the many large-scale present programs, employers have provided education of considerable variety. Some have stressed fundamentals so that their employees were more literate, able to carry out their quantitative duties adequately, or work more effectively with the public or the consumer. Special education directly related to the job has had a continuing emphasis and has grown in recent years as employers have realized not only the value of a liberal education but the fact that their own vocational training programs, attached to plant or office, can often develop more satisfactorily necessary special skills other than learnings provided in the public schools, business schools, or colleges. In addition, from health and safety education campaigns, civic and patriotic lectures and short courses for the employees (and often their families) to special brush-up programs or advanced college work for their key employees and administrators, American business spends many millions each year on educating members of its own families.

The greatest national educational contribution of American business has undoubtedly come through the media of advertising. Though we may be highly critical of many of the attempts and the results, the billions spent each year on radio and TV, newspapers and magazines, and other media, from calendars to billboards, have certainly in a sense educated America and much of the world! In light of the complaints of geographers as to the limited geographic knowledge of the American people, perhaps they should credit the hundreds of thousands of free road maps distributed each year by the oil companies for most of the national geographic understanding the people do exhibit!

When we see colorful magazine advertisements on school bulletin boards that highlight the comments of great personalities or portray major events in

---

[39] In recent years American business has come to recognize its essential stake in education. A variety of aspects of this stake were reported in the special issues of the *Saturday Review* (Jan. 19, 1957) devoted to "Education and Business: New Partners," and (Nov. 14, 1959) on "Are We Really Educating Our Business Leaders?"; see also: John K. Norton, "The Common Interests of Business and Education," *The Science Teacher*, Dec., 1951, pp. 277-279, 300, and Harold C. Syrett, "American Business Enterprise and the Mass Mind," *Social Education*, Jan. 1948, pp. 13-18, for two earlier discussions of the evolution of this idea.

American life, observe students reading excellent pamphlets from insurance companies or banks on a host of topics from inventions to health or when we note teachers instructing from business-prepared kits on the functioning of the stock market, foreign trade, atomic structure, or conservation, we begin to recognize the contribution that American business is now making in public education. Although much of this passes as advertising rather than public service, most companies hold the "sales pitch" to a minimum and students can view an excellent free film supplied to the school or an exhibit at a science fair with merely an unobtrusive trademark to show the source of the material. Naturally all materials provided have to be used with care and slanted or unfair propaganda exposed or balanced.

Only since 1900 and particularly since World War I has business entered the field of education on a grand scale. Much of the early educational work was an attempt to parry the rising tide of progressivism and the socialistic influences that business began to fear so deeply following the bitter strikes of the late nineteenth century and the liberal reform movement that characterized much of American life during the first third of the twentieth century. Chambers of Commerce, the National Association of Manufacturers, and organizations like the American Bankers Association and the National Electric Light Association urged and carried out an extensive campaign of publicity and poured out millions of words via newspaper broadsides, pamphlets, and the airwaves to improve the public's understanding of our economic system and to promote a favorable attitude toward American business.

Much of business' concern over education has been at a level above advertising or propagandizing. Corporations cooperate with schools in sponsoring field trips and in providing resource visitors and speakers for school classes and programs. The scholarships and awards resulting from honors records, contests, and essays have been a real aid to families and individuals hard put to continue a gifted student's education. In recent years these financial aids have been extended to thousands of teachers in many workshops, special summer conferences, and school courses paid for by individual companies or business-sponsored organizations. Science teachers, for example, have benefited materially from the multiple opportunities open to them. The Joint Council on Economic Education is just one example of a business-supported organization that has done much to improve social studies instruction and the economic backgrounds of social studies teachers through its comprehensive program of workshops and publications.

The Ford Foundation and its widespread activities dwarf other such organizations of greater vintage; but again we must realize as with the Carnegie and Rockefeller Foundations, the millions spent have come from business and have made immeasurable contributions in many aspects of education from sponsoring the exchange of foreign scholars and building libraries to educating minorities and promoting experimentation for strengthening teacher education. Recently, many corporations, as well as the foundations, have moved into the support of research in the universities and institutions (now hard-hit by the disappearance of the great individual donor, because of income and inheritance tax laws) which have benefited materially from such grants and subsidies. The Internal Revenue Service estimated, for example, that in 1956 such business-sponsored research in the universities amounted to over $100 million.

It is easy to overlook the contributions of American business and industry to education. Many of these, as has been shown, are hidden, indirect, or unpublicized; but the businessmen of today are far removed from their plutocratic ancestors of the last century. They now openly recognize that a well-educated manpower is just as essential to American business as it is to the perpetuation of society. Recent activities evidence the realization of a sense of responsibility that goes far beyond superficial good will of business-education days. Business men have also come to realize that satisfied, mentally well-adjusted employees are just as important to their enterprises as those who are skilled and economically literate. Since the free economy is a basic part of the American way, educators and business men have come to recognize the need of teaching the relatedness of freedom and responsibility in all aspects of American life.

Education of Adults

The term adult education is a rather fuzzy one. Essert defines it as voluntarily selected educational experiences by persons whose major concern is no longer going to school or college.[40] Any kind of education for adults which does *not* grant a degree, issue a certificate, or give academic credit — that is, informal education for adults, constitutes another definition.[41] For the purposes of this chapter we modify Houle's[42] definition of adult education as the formal and informal means by which adults, voluntarily or involuntarily, acquire new or improved skills, knowledge, attitudes, understandings, and appreciations which enrich their lives through providing socio-economic rewards (i.e., occupational advancement, opportunities, adjustment, higher standard of living, etc.) or psychological satisfactions (i.e., greater happiness,

---

[40] Paul L. Essert, *Creative Leadership in Adult Education* (New York: Prentice-Hall, 1951), p. 5.

[41] Henry Pratt Fairchild, Ed., *Dictionary of Sociology* (New York: Philosophical Library, 1944), p. 103.

[42] Cyril O. Houle, et al., *The Armed Forces and Adult Education* (Washington, D.C.: American Council on Education, 1947), p. 8.

sense of accomplishment, etc.). Informal education includes all kinds of educational experience for which degrees, academic credit, or certificates are not generally objectives. Formal education includes all kinds of educational experiences for which degrees, academic credit, or certificates are generally objectives, and/or for which training, vocational education, is acquired. Generally speaking, informal education is concerned with the attainment of non-material goals, that is, greater understanding, appreciation, greater knowledge for its own sake. Formal education is usually of a utilitarian nature — that is, formal education usually is concerned with providing the learner with special skills which directly or indirectly aid in vocational training and advancement. Many programs are mixed, however, so that classification into formal or informal is difficult or impossible. Another problem lies in defining an adult; many youth no longer in school participate in adult education.

The 1950 rough estimates of the number of persons engaged in adult education activities as students were as follows: Cooperative Agricultural and Home Economics Extension Service — 7,000,000; Commercial College and School Radio and Television — 6,000,000; Public School Adult Education Programs — 3,000,000; Library Adult Education — 1,500,000; Private Correspondence Schools — 1,000,000; University College Extension Services — 500,000; Armed Forces Education Programs — 250,000; and others (includes Alumni Education; Forums; Lyceums and Chatauquas; Parent Education; Workers' Education; etc.) — 10,000,000 or more.[43] Thus, about 30,000,000 or more adults are engaged in adult education programs each year.

It is the purpose of this part of the chapter to describe several of these adult education programs and indicate their contributions to American education.

Informal Adult Education

LIBRARIES. Perhaps the chief agency for informal adult education in America has been the public library. Johnson suggested that the public library could be our permanent center of adult education — it could be a "people's university."[44] It has been shown that some libraries have achieved this aim. The Louisville, Kentucky Public Library is, in fact, such an institution, a far cry from the collection of books begun by Benjamin Franklin in a room in Philadelphia in 1731 which marked the beginning of the public library movement in this country.[45] The Louisville Public Library, among

---

[43] Essert, op. cit., p. 37.

[44] Alvin Johnson, The Public Library (New York: American Association for Adult Education, 1938).

[45] See Karl Detzer, "They Pushed Out the Walls," Saturday Review of Literature, July 7, 1951, pp. 8-10. The Encyclopedia Americana, Vol. 17, 1957, has an excellent summary of library history, pp. 318-357a.

other services, operates a 14-hour-per-day radio station, supported by tax-payers, which serves purposes of recreation as well as cultural advancement. Such public libraries also sponsor community discussion programs, art, music, and museum activities, and reading clubs.

Some libraries are serving adult education by promoting or cooperating with a "great books program." Adler has made a case for such a program, claiming that the great books deal with the continuing basic problems, both theoretical and practical, of yesterday, today, and tomorrow. He believes that the ideas contained in these volumes are "the ideas all of us have to think about and think with. The great books represent the fund of human wisdom, at least so far as our culture is concerned, and it is this reservoir that we must draw upon to sustain our learning for a lifetime."[46]

The goal of the library becoming a people's university and center of learning was realized in the life of the now famous, well-educated man with no formal schooling — Eric Hoffer. Here is the story of a poor man whose university was comprised of the nation's public libraries. Here is the story of a man who gave himself a liberal education simply by making use of our public library facilities.[47]

Y.M.C.A. AND Y.W.C.A.   These organizations have as their chief purpose the task of ministering the spiritual, intellectual, social, and physical needs of young men and women in particular, but also persons of all ages. Any person of good, moral character, regardless of race or creed, may become a member of the organizations and enjoy their privileges.[48] A development of the urban growth following the industrial revolution, the "Y" movement was imported from England in 1851. The Y.M.C.A. is known as one of the largest and most effective organizations for promoting sound physical education for large segments of the public; but certainly the "Y" programs go far beyond the provision of physical education in their stated objectives and offerings. Thus, the directing committee of the adult education program of the Central Y.M.C.A. of Chicago includes among its services and activities formal and informal classes, fellowship clubs, special interest groups, forums, institutions, exhibits, and publications which meet a variety of adult needs.

---

[46] Mortimer J. Adler, "Adult Education," *Journal of Higher Education,* February, 1952, pp. 67*ff.*

[47] See Eric Hoffer's refreshing book entitled *The True Believer* (New York: Harper, 1951). The extent to which libraries serve the public is also dramatically evidenced in the example of the great New York City Public Library as presented in *Time,* June 2, 1961, p. 34.

[48] Howard C. Hopkins, *History of the Y.M.C.A. in North America* (New York: Association Press, 1951); see also Pence, Owen E., "Young Men's Christian Association," *The Encyclopedia Americana,* Vol. 29, 1957, pp. 653-663; and Sims, Mary S., "Young Women's Christian Association," *ibid.,* pp. 665-666.

Implementing its objectives, the Central Y.M.C.A. of Chicago recently sponsored the following courses for men and women: Rapid Reading, Photography, Public Speaking, Painting and Sketching, Starting Your Own Business, Salesmanship, Writing for Business and Pleasure, Vocabulary Building, Contract Bridge, Psychology and Personality, Current Events, Enjoying Music, Successful Marriage, Social Dancing, Gardening, Real Estate, as well as a Day High School and an Evening School.[49] The same Y.M.C.A. has sponsored excellent forums at extremely reasonable prices. A recent winter forum included the following series of topics for white collar workers: Finding a Place in Today's Changing World; Housing for Everyone; The Cost of Living; Ending Racial Tensions; Education for Real Living; Making Marriage Work; Constructive Use of Atomic Energy; Making Their Opinions Count. Among the speakers in this forum were Norman Thomas, Horace R. Cayton, and other distinguished persons.[50]

In short, the Y.M.C.A. and Y.W.C.A. have been conducting significant "out of school" education, particularly in urban centers. In addition, they cooperate with schools in Hi-Y Clubs, Tri-Hi-Y projects, etc.

CHURCH PROGRAMS. Most churches among the major religious groups in the United States provide some kind of adult education program. While all of the churches include courses about religion, many contain non-religious offerings as well. A description of a few of these programs should help to clarify their major characteristics.

In Yankton, South Dakota, one spring program of the First Methodist Church included these courses: Moral Problems of Today — Why Be Good?; Science and Religion; Making the World Christian; Religion in Drama; Personalities in Church History; The Book of Life — The Bible; The Methodist Discipline; Outwitting Our Nerves. The Council of Churches of greater Portland, Maine, in their adult education program during one term had courses as follows: Jesus and Present-Day Living; The Family in Modern Life; My Philosophy of Life; Four Problem Areas in World Life. A three-week adult education program was held by the Evanston (Illinois) Unitarian Church on the topic: World Government: Why and How? During the three weeks there were discussions, forums, and lectures on world government at the Church and at the homes of members. On the final day of the project the students were so enthusiastic about world government that they formed an Evanston Chapter of the United World Federalists which meets in the

---

[49] Malcolm S. Knowles, *Informal Adult Education* (New York: Association Press, 1951), p. 207.

[50] *Ibid.*, p. 162.

church.[51] The Catholic Christian Family Movement and other church study clubs provide discussion and action programs for the resolution of social problems.

In some religious communities the leaders are so erudite that every weekly sermon is like a brilliant lecture by a world famous scholar. Temple Israel in Columbus, Ohio has in Dr. Jerome D. Folkman this type of leader. Dr. Folkman, in addition to his religious training and degree, has a Ph.D. in sociology and an honorary D.D. from the Hebrew Union College. His command of the English language and his scholarship led to an event quite unprecedented in the history of the Ohio State University. He was requested to and did deliver the main address at his own graduation on the day he received his Ph.D. degree.

Clergymen today are being trained, as we shall see, to be competent in many roles. One of these new roles is that of a leader in adult education. It is estimated that the amount of knowledge has doubled since 1930; the schools cannot possibly handle this themselves in their basic programs. Therefore, other institutions responsible for continuing education, such as the churches, will be called upon in the years immediately ahead to provide increasing amounts of adult education.

Museums. Typically, in museums of art, natural history, science and industry, etc., the emphasis in educational programs is on tours, exhibits, and lectures. A few museums offer organized courses.

The Cleveland Museum of Art one autumn offered some of the following courses (6 meetings, no fees): Comparative Aesthetics; Saturday Afternoon Sketch Club; The Collecting and Care of House Plants; Portraits and Figures in Water Color; Pictorial Photography; Art Appreciation; Music Appreciation; and The Dance as an Art Form.[52] Nature hikes are sponsored by the Buffalo Museum of Science. Adults spend many invigorating Sundays studying plants, insects, birds, and other aspects of nature besides getting plenty of exercise, fresh air, and making new friends.

Other agencies of informal adult education can be identified from the Great Decisions discussion groups sponsored by the Foreign Policy Association to the host of trips, speeches, programs, and publications sponsored by community groups as varied as a county historical association and a local businessmen's service club. Throughout American history the influence of informal forces for education has been substantial. From family to state organizations, such as a social welfare board, they have been responsible for an immeasurable amount of education. Such forces are often overlooked in

---

[51] Knowles, *ibid.*, pp. 160-161, *et passim.*

[52] Knowles, *ibid.*, pp. 154-155.

history of education textbooks that concentrate upon formal educational institutions. It is, for example, very possible that the total picture of education in America during the colonial period was much brighter than often portrayed when the influences of church, family, tavern, workmen's groups, social clubs, and almanacs and newspapers are considered.

Formal Adult Education

CORRESPONDENCE SCHOOLS. More than a million persons each year take courses from correspondence schools. Contrary to popular opinion, in studies of students who take advantage of college level correspondence courses, it has been found that these students tend to do considerably better work than the average classroom student. It is estimated that about 80 percent of the students taking correspondence courses do so for vocational reasons. A large proportion also comes from rural areas where school and college classoom studies are not so readily available. The main criticisms against correspondence teaching are that it: (a) reduces the personal element in the teaching process; (b) paves the way in unsupervised institutions for fraud; (c) contributes to the maladjustment of those who are inadequately prepared to take courses and fail in them; and (d) absorbs 30 to 80 percent of the fees in selling costs, so that instruction purchased with the remainder is inferior. This last criticism applies more specifically to private schools than it does to public ones where fees are generally low and quality of instruction is very high. With the public institutions from 12 to 53 percent never complete courses started, but as high as 94 percent drop out in certain private correspondence schools.[53]

In recent years, correspondence schools, particularly private ones, have been more closely controlled by the National University Extension Association, the Federal Trade Commission, and by state agencies. Correspondence schools appeared in large numbers after the Civil War and met the rising need for specialized studies, as well as appealing to the self-educated lower classes who could use the school services to build competencies for better employment by night study while holding down a full-time job. Many an American has owed his opportunity for advancement and for technical training, as well as for other study opportunities, to such schools — be they the famous International Correspondence School founded at Scranton, Pennsylvania in 1891 or one of the rash of TV and electronics schools that appealed to veterans after World War II. If the current popularity of correspondence-type courses on television networks is any sign of the future trends,

---

[53] Gladys A. Wiggin, "Correspondence Teaching" in Harry N. Rivlin and Herbert Schueler, Eds., Encyclopedia of Modern Education (Philosophical Library, New York, 1943), pp. 194-195.

then the future should see both an increase in the quality and quantity of correspondence schools and courses and in the number of adults taking correspondence courses.

COMMERCIAL AND BUSINESS EDUCATION. Private business schools have existed since antiquity. Scribes taught shorthand to employees of commercial entrepreneurs in ancient Egypt. Business education has had to be largely private because it did not evolve as a respected part of the liberal or general education program deemed proper for citizens since Grecian times and because it was tied to the crass vocational needs of apprentices. Gradually with the commercial revolution there was a growing need for bookkeepers, accountants, and office clerks that was difficult to satisfy through apprenticeship, and the backgrounds and skills were also not provided by traditional private education or even in the rudiments of public education then appearing. The private schools and academies that developed in the late colonial period in America, therefore, came to offer a variety of courses that met practical needs of navigation, surveying, bookkeeping, correspondence in modern foreign languages, etc.

Private schools continued to dominate the field of business education throughout the nineteenth century. With the great expansion of business in the United States and the early resistance of high schools to such offerings, there was a burgeoning of commercial schools. This growth was further stimulated by the development of the typewriter in the late nineteenth century and the employment of women. The shortage of male workers at the time of the first World War also contributed to the enlargement in the scope of programs provided by private business schools which were now offering courses from salesmanship and window decoration to advertising and personnel counselling. Some of the schools such as the Golden Gate College in San Francisco became actual colleges offering general education as well as two-year and four-year business degrees and certificates. However, since the 1920's the number, the enrollment, and the influence of private business schools have declined. This was due primarily to the belated acceptance of business-type subjects into the public school day and evening programs in the emerging comprehensive high school, as well as to the fact that large vocational and commercial high schools had appeared in many areas. In addition, on-the-job training arrangements between businesses and the public schools materially reduced the need for commercially oriented students to attend private schools. A third factor in the decline of the business school has been the upward shift in job training since the depression years. This brought more and more youth into junior colleges and colleges wherein they have received appropriate instruction in the expanding programs of these institutions. Another factor in the decline of the commercial school has been the technological advance in office machines that has reduced the need for certain types of employees and increased the call for some more highly trained specialists who are best provided through programs in public colleges or, on an increasing basis, in the internal program maintained by the employing companies.

Many G.I.'s used private schools after the second World War and the Korean War to build their special education needs. The scope and impact of business education schools and related private instructional institutions (as special schools for mechanics, industrial design, electronics, etc.) have never been fully assessed; but we must recognize the gaps that these schools have filled for hundreds of thousands during the many years that public education did not meet these demands. Often these schools have provided basic and advanced general education, as well as specific vocational competencies, and they have played a material role in the advancement of American life.

AGRICULTURAL PROGRAMS. Only several examples of the vast web of agencies and groups involved in agricultural education can be cited. The cooperative Agricultural and Home Economics Extension Service is a joint undertaking cooperatively administered by federal, state, and local governments. It has been so successful that it has gained international recognition and has become the largest tax-supported adult education program in the world.

The scope of this program is indicated by the following information assembled in the 1950 annual report. About 4,600,000 families changed one or more agricultural practices as a result of extension activities. More than 3,300,000 families were influenced to change homemaking practices. Extension agents worked with about 340,000 young men and women between the ages of 18 and 30. It is estimated that about 7 million farm families are reached every year by the extension program.

Agricultural extension programs in the early years after the passage of the Smith-Lever Act (1914) were narrowly conceived of as instruction in vocational agriculture only. In recent decades, however, liberal changes in these programs have permitted the introduction of subjects in the social sciences and in the arts. Today, agricultural extension programs constitute, de facto, a kind of gigantic, rural people's university. The history of these programs provides our most convincing evidence that social change toward established goals can be brought about by a program concentrated on the adult citizens of the community.[54]

---

[54] See inter alia, Paul H. Sheats et al., Adult Education (New York: Dryden, 1953), Chapter 5, "Agricultural Extension," pp. 98-119; Edmund de S. Brunner and E. Hsin Pao Yang, Rural America and the Extension Service (New York: Teachers College, Columbia University, 1949).

Although the cooperative movement in the United States has never approached the size of the program in Britain and Scandinavia, it has influenced the education of many Americans, particularly the farming population. Both consumers' and producers' co-ops have sponsored a variety of educational programs for their members: lectures on economics; publications and advice on home-making, conservation, child care, and canning; scholarships and educational awards; teaching materials for the public schools as the kits provided by the Cooperative League of the U.S.A.; forums on politics and international affairs; cooperative nursery schools; and income tax and insurance instruction. These are representative services provided to the better than 30 million members (1950) of the American co-ops and their friends and neighbors.[55] In addition, the indirect educational implications, for example, of credit unions and rural electric co-ops, that have provided needed monies and brought radio and telephones to thousands of isolated farmers, can never be measured.

UNIVERSITY EXTENSION PROGRAMS. It is estimated that more than a half million persons take advantage of university extension programs in the United States each year. These offerings have moved far beyond their agricultural genesis. By university extension we mean the variety of ways of extending the educational services of higher institutions of learning to the general population, including correspondence courses and class instruction on or off the campus for persons not registered as resident students of the institution. State universities and institutions in large metropolitan areas have been particularly active in the establishment of off-campus centers of instruction.

An example of a university extension program is that offered by the Cleveland College of Western Reserve University not too long ago. The courses ran eight weeks and cost a nominal fee. The program included some of the following courses: United Nations and World Government; History of Russia; Reading Poetry; Modern Piano Music; Remedial Reading; Needlecraft; Practical Farm Management; and many other interesting classes.[56]

SPECIAL SCHOOLS FOR ADULT EDUCATION. Two different schools will serve as examples of the kinds of practical and enriching opportunities open to

---

[55] In addition to contacting the Cooperative League of the U.S.A., Chicago 4, Illinois, see the following for information and bibliography on educational phases of the cooperative movement: D. L. Beran, "Cooperatives in the School Curriculum," *Social Education,* May, 1950, pp. 215-217; and *Cooperatives in School and Community* (New York: Bureau of Publications, Teachers College, Columbia University, 1947).

[56] Knowles, *op. cit.,* pp. 146-147; Good, Carter V., "University Extension," in Rivlin and Schueler, *op. cit.,* p. 871.

mature persons in urban areas — the Cooper Union and the New School for Social Research, both in New York City.

In 1859 Peter Cooper endowed the institution that carries his name, the Cooper Union, and that has developed into a renowned educational center and technological institute. His purpose was "to provide free courses of instruction in the application of Science and Art to the practical business of life" without restriction as to sex, race, or creed. The school has drawn on leading practitioners in the New York metropolitan area for its instructional staff. It developed extensive day and evening course offerings, ultimately awarding baccalaureate degrees in various areas of engineering and certificates in applied arts such as design, architecture, interior decoration, and fashion. The evening program of extension courses and forum lectures appeals to the varied needs of many urban dwellers and furthers Cooper's purpose of broadening the general education of workers, as well as helping them to improve vocationally.

The New School for Social Research is unique and an excellent example of its kind of education.

> The New School conceives of education as a continuing process, at every stage related to life, and of learning as an experience that begins with exploration, goes on to acquiring knowledge and eventually to the formation of judgment. Such learning is a common enterprise of student and teacher. It depends on self-discipline more than on regulations. Its rewards are the enjoyment of intellectual effort and the satisfaction of mental growth rather than certificates and credits.

> The New School uses a combination of methods. While kept on the university level they range from discussion panels to thorough scientific research and from courses meant to popularize difficult disciplines to seminars using the strictest academic methods. They deal with topics that appeal to the individual who seeks to understand himself better, but also with techniques for citizenship participation and political action.

> The New School provides opportunities to mature students to find more than themselves by exploring science and the arts and by probing beyond the finite through philosophy and religion. It keeps its curriculum and its program flexible in response both to the interests of students and to the needs of the changing times. It is ever "new."[57]

An example of the kind of courses the New School offers is that called the *Wisdom of Life*. This course attempts to take advantage of the life experiences of persons, who, from different vantage points, seem to have understood, at least partially, their own experiences and the implications. In each of the eight monthly (1959-60) sessions one of the following noted persons

---

[57] *New School Bulletin*, September 7, 1959, p. 2, *et passim*.

399

presented that wisdom of life they have gained: Richard Schüller, economist, cabinet minister; Alvin Johnson, teacher-educator, social scientist; Lillian Gilbreth, engineer; G. Bromley Oxnam, clergyman; Dorothy Day, publicist and social worker; Robert M. MacIver, social philosopher and social scientist; Learned Hand, judge; and Robert Frost, poet.[58]

The faculty of the New School reads like that of a Who's Who in the academic world, in public affairs, and in the arts. Among the current faculty members are some stellar lights: Chaim Gross, sculptor; Horace Kallen, social philosopher; Hans Kohn, historian; Margaret Mead, anthropologist; and Saul K. Padover, historian.

Any adult who lives in a metropolitan area near such schools as the Cooper Union and the New School for Social Research is missing extremely valuable opportunities for personal growth if he fails to take advantage of such offerings.

PUBLIC SCHOOL ADULT EDUCATION PROGRAMS. A recent estimate is that around 3 million adults attend some kind of public school adult education program in the United States. At the turn of the century and until about 1920, adult education in the public schools consisted mostly of Americanization and vocational classes. Since 1920, however, the scope of adult education includes virtually every field of human learning. There has been a recognition that learning for all should help continue to solve the problems of adult life.[59]

The courses offered at the Caldwell Adult School, New Jersey, are typical of those offered throughout the country. They include some of the following courses: The Contemporary Theater; Psychology of Personality; An Analysis of World Affairs; Better English; First Aid and Home Safety; Contract Bridge; Social Dancing; Flower Arrangement; Creative Writing Workshop; Chess; Conversational Spanish; Typewriting; The World's Outstanding Films; etc.[60]

The recent development of the junior or community college in many states has been directly related to the post World War II enrollment boom in higher education. These schools, whose history began well before the turn of the century, even though not designated as "junior colleges," have only grown considerably in number since 1900. It is estimated that there are now about 600 in the United States. These schools have helped to take the great pressure off the state universities and state colleges and many now

---

[58] *Ibid.,* p. 15.

[59] *Public School Adult Education,* National Association of Public School Adult Educators, Washington, D.C., 1956.

[60] Knowles, *op. cit.,* pp. 151-152.

serve primarily as two-year prep schools catering to students who either cannot attain entrance or cannot afford the costs of living away from home at a four-year institution. One of the main reasons cited by the promoters of the movement for instituting such schools was to free the universities of the demands of lower division students and instruction. With the great demand for a higher education presently growing, these colleges may yet serve this purpose. However, many of these schools came to provide an extended two-year program of terminal general education. In California, which has led in the movement, the junior colleges are legally thirteenth and fourteenth grade extensions of the public school system. Junior and community colleges have come to serve a third purpose of meeting the demands of citizens for vocational programs and extended evening offerings. As with the special adult schools discussed previously, they cater to a growing variety of needs and their bulletins list as heterogeneous a fare as Vector Analysis and Fundamentals of Engineering to Anthropology for Laymen and Cake Decoration. In some urban centers the evening and adult education offerings threaten to dwarf the regular day program.[61]

Contributions From the Education of Adults

The great contribution of adult education to American education is the fact that it has destroyed forever the myth that education is something only for children and adolescents. It has shown that adults can continue their education after adolescence, that they can and are taking advantge of educational opportunities open to them at all levels of adulthood. Moreover, adult education has proven that such education brings the kinds of positive results upon which a democratic society depends for its perpetuation. Best of all, the adult education movement has stimulated programs of informal self-education. In summary, adult education has helped American educational objectives to reach full maturity — to recognize that education is a lifelong process which never ends, which continues from the cradle to the grave.

Education of Military Personnel

A recent edition of the *Army School Catalog* lists the current schools and courses. A total of 54 geographically separate schools are named in it and these schools offer 278 separate courses for officers and an additional 294 for enlisted men.[62] The Navy and Marines, the Air Force, and Coast Guard

---

[61] See Leland L. Medsker, *The Junior College: Progress and Prospect* (New York: McGraw-Hill, 1960).

[62] Ivan J. Birrer, "Education of Army Officers," in Lloyd E. Blauch, Ed., *Education for the Professions* (Washington, D.C.: U.S. Government Printing Office, 1955), p. 253.

also have numerous schools and courses for officers and enlisted men.[63] It is enough to say that thousands of men and women, as military personnel each year receive a great many educational services from some branch of the military forces in the United States. In this chapter we shall discuss a few of these educational facilities that have made contributions to the American educational heritage.[64]

Militarism has been defined as: the predominance of the military class or prevalence of their ideals — the policy of aggressive military preparedness.[65] Nativism is closely allied with militarism. The hero of the nativist is the patriot-warrior. He believes that war proves the quality of man and nation. In war only the fittest will survive and so prove the power of one's state.[66] Despite the recent messages in the press concerning changes in the curricula of our national military academies toward a liberal education which will help preserve peace on earth and good will toward men, the basic programs of the academies generally support the ideologies of militarism and nativism. Their basic orientation is simply that of preparing good officers to win wars, to master the arts and sciences concerned with war.

The entire curriculum at West Point is prescribed except for a choice of one of five languages. Emphasis in the program is on scientific-engineering and military-professional courses. These courses take up more than two-thirds of the curriculum, while less than one-third of the program is concerned with social-humanistic studies.[67] While at Annapolis there is currently much talk about changes, the curriculum is still one heavily dominated, as at West Point, by militaristic vocational education.[68] The only requirement which leads, in part, toward a liberal education is the requirement, both at West Point and Annapolis, that a foreign language be mastered. This is supposed to be done in what is approximately equivalent to 10 semester hours of course work.

---

63 Homer C. Rose and D. W. Fisher, "Education of Naval and Marine Corps Officers"; James C. Shelbourne and Charles H. Connelly, "Education of Air Force Officers"; and G. F. Hicks, "Education of Coast Guard Officers," in Lloyd E. Blauch, Ed., *ibid.*, pp. 261ff.

64 For an excellent unique work on military education see John W. Masland and Lawrence I. Radway, *Soldiers and Scholars* (Princeton, New Jersey: Princeton University Press, 1957).

65 *Webster's Collegiate Dictionary*, 5th Edition (Springfield, Mass.: G. & C. Merriam Co., 1936), p. 633.

66 For a good discussion on nativism as a value orientation see H. Otto Dahlke, *Values in Culture and Classroom* (New York: Harper, 1958), pp. 51-54, 64.

67 *Catalogue of the United States Military Academy, 1959-1960* (Washington, D.C.: U.S. Government Printing Office, 1959).

68 *Course of Instruction at the United States Naval Academy*, Annapolis, Maryland, 1957-1958.

Of the various military academies, the U.S. Air Force Academy, begun in 1955, is the one with the most flexible program. It prescribes, relatively speaking, the broadest and largest number of social science and humanities courses and has a curriculum enrichment program to allow for individual differences in the ability of students to progress in their studies. The enrichment program, as it applies to the academic phase of the curriculum, permits the cadet to take special courses as substitutes or additions to those that are prescribed. It enables the cadet to concentrate in a subject area or to broaden his understanding by taking extra courses in several areas. Thus, at the Air Force Academy a cadet could get a Bachelor of Science degree with a major, something not presently offered at the other academies. He may earn a degree with a major by taking 17 additional hours of specialized subject matter in addition to the prescribed courses in the area chosen as his major.[69] But, in spite of this fine program, there are missing those courses which provide a true liberal education — that is, there are no courses offered in the fine arts, philosophy, sociology, anthropology, logic, scientific method, basic psychology, and the like. This is not only true for the Air Force Academy but the other academies as well.

While a semblance of Athenian democratic ideals can be seen at the Air Force Academy, all of the major military academies in the United States are still very much Spartan in their value orientation. In short, the military academies are what they have been since inception — vocational training centers for patriot-warriors.

There are numerous specialized schools and programs for officers and enlisted persons in the armed forces. We shall deal with several of these schools — United States Army Command and General Staff College, the United States Navy Hospital Corps School, and the United States Armed Forces Institute.

U.S. ARMY COMMAND AND GENERAL STAFF COLLEGE. The purpose of this Army college, located at Fort Leavenworth, Kansas, is to prepare selected officers of all components of the Army as commanders and general staff officers. For those officers who attend, this college is the keystone of their military education. It is the Army tactical school and the only academic institution devoted to the operation of all the combined arms and services in combat. In essence, this college teaches the Army in the field and how it fights. The motto of the college is unequivocally *Ad Bellum Pace Parati* — to prepare in peace for war. Its ideology is the militaristic-nativistic value orientation because it suggests that the way of preserving peace is to be prepared for war.[70]

---

[69] *United States Air Force Academy Catalog, 1959-1960,* USAF Academy, Colorado.
[70] *United States Army Command and General Staff College Catalog, 1959-1960.*

A psychologist who spent a year assisting with the instructional program at the Command and General Staff College has these observations to make: "At Fort Leavenworth an extraordinary amount of time and effort is spent in developing instructional materials; an extraordinary amount of time is devoted to a study of these materials by those who 'put on instruction.' Also, examinations and other forms of evaluation receive special attention. In a word, everything is done in a systematic, orderly manner. Nothing is left to chance. Objectives are formulated very carefully (they are easy to formulate in an institution of this type) and the examinations are designed to measure the extent to which the objectives are attained. Two abilities are stressed: *Comprehension of information;* and the *ability to apply knowledge understood.* A student must meet both of these requirements for graduation."[71]

However, the above psychologist who provided us with this information suggests that this college as well as most service schools operate along mechanistic lines — that is, these schools operate on the basis of the behavioristic theory of learning: they regard the learning process as fundamentally a mechanistic type of habit formation. Some of the exponents of this orientation have been Thorndike, Watson, Skinner, and Hull. In this atomistic approach, trial and error, exercise, and elimination of faulty responses are the principal means of learning.[72]

Perhaps the most dramatic aspect of the service schools is their use of the latest and finest audio-visual aids and other instructional materials. An examination of the Command and General Staff College's classrooms and/or auditoriums makes most ordinary civilian college classrooms and auditoriums seem prehistoric by comparison.[73] The college at Fort Leavenworth shows, therefore, what many educators have known for a long time, that amazing things in education can be done if the money could be raised to support modern educational programs.

U. S. NAVY HOSPITAL CORPS SCHOOL. The civilian program for the training and certification of practical nurses takes usually about one year. The U.S. Navy Hospital Corps Schools do the job in less than three months.[74] During this time the students take the following subjects: Nursing and

---

[71] From a personal letter by a psychologist who had spent time at the college and whose anonymity the writers wish to preserve.

[72] S. Stansfeld Sargent and Robert C. Williamson, *Social Psychology* (New York: Ronald Press, 1958), pp. 207*ff*.

[73] W. C. Washcoe, "Audio-Visual Aids: Effective Weapons on the Educational Battlefield," in Lionel C. McGarr, Ed., *Keeping Pace With the Future* (Ft. Leavenworth, Kansas: U.S. Army Command and General Staff College, 1959), pp. 182-197.

[74] New York is one of the many states which license U.S. Naval Hospital corpsmen as practical nurses.

Dietetics, First Aid and Minor Surgery, Anatomy and Physiology, Chemistry, Hygiene and Sanitation, Chemical Warfare Nursing, Bacteriology, Materia Medica and Toxicology, Medicine and Pharmacy.[75] Because students are highly motivated, have a good high school background in the physical sciences, are carefully selected, and have a general interest in medicine, they do an excellent job in their assignments after graduation. Hospital corpsmen have such good records in civilian hospitals that many civilian hospitals prefer them to civilian trained practical nurses. These Hospital Corps Schools demonstrate the fact that good results could be obtained in a short time with well selected, highly motivated students, high quality of teaching, and practical field experience under critical supervision. This is equally true of some of the service foreign language schools.

USAFI: The World's Finest and Largest Correspondence School. USAFI, the United States Armed Forces Institute, has frequently been called "The School with the World Wide Campus." The campus is wherever the soldier, sailor, airman, marine, or coast guardsman happens to be. This may be in any of the more than 70 foreign lands where our Armed Forces are serving. It has been estimated recently that since 1942 over 4,200,000 military personnel have enrolled in USAFI courses.

A form of adult education, USAFI provides opportunities for military personnel to continue their education while they are on active duty with the Armed Forces of the United States. To this end USAFI supplies instructional materials, including courses for individual correspondence study and for group class work, and tests and examinations. USAFI aims constantly to develop these educational materials in conformity with the highest civilian standards.

Over 200 courses may be taken directly from USAFI in elementary, high school, college, and vocational-technical subjects. For an initial fee of $5.00, a student may enroll in his first USAFI correspondence course. He may thereafter continue to take other USAFI courses at no further cost as long as his progress is satisfactory.

In addition to the courses offered directly by USAFI, more than 6,000 correspondence courses are available through USAFI from the extension divisions of 44 leading colleges and universities. These correspondence courses are offered at reduced prices to military personnel under the terms of contract agreements between the Federal Government and the educational institutions.

Permanent records of all courses taken with and through USAFI and of all tests and examinations, with the exception of elementary level work, are

---

[75] *United States Navy Hospital Corps School Catalog*, Bainbridge, Maryland.

maintained by USAFI. All USAFI test results are automatically reported to the military services. Upon request, official reports of these records are sent to schools, employers, and other civilian agencies.

USAFI, with headquarters at Madison, Wisconsin, is the principal servicing and supplying agency for all the overseas branches — Alaska, the Caribbean, Europe, Hawaii, and Japan. It is the responsibility of USAFI, Madison, to distribute to branches the courses and tests developed by USAFI. The USAFI organization around the world is ready to serve military personnel wherever they are stationed and whatever the level of educational requirements.[76]

Contributions From the Education of Military Personnel

It has been recently estimated that more than 80 percent of the national budget is a war budget. The truth is that the American economy is overwhelmingly tied to war.[77] The numerous Armed Forces schools and colleges are primarily vocational training institutions, training men and women in skills necessary for modern warfare. While many of the skills are useful in civilian life and for peaceful purposes, the real purpose is to prepare for the successful management of a war. What little liberal education is given in preparation for peace is given, if at all, generally on a voluntary basis. USAFI, for example, offers liberal education courses for those interested in correspondence study. There is no question concerning the way in which the Armed Forces select and train specialists, at all levels, for the complex division of labor needed in preparing for and engaging in modern warfare. Good teaching methods, teaching materials, well selected students, and critically supervised, practical experiences are among the characteristics of service schools which suggest some possible directions for changes in civilian schools.

All the mechanistic competence of the Armed Forces schools does not alter the fundamental fact that ideologically these schools are, for the most part, militaristic. This, of course, is to be expected; so is their vocational emphasis; so is their honor of the patriot-warrior. Some will wish for broader curricula at these institutions so that leaders trained there may better understand and represent the total heritage and ideals of the American way. On the other hand, observers of military schools might benefit from an examination of the academies and the worthwhile means by which they attain high

---

[76] *USAFI Catalog*, 10th Edition (Washington, D.C.: U.S. Government Printing Office, 1959), pp. 7-8; see also, *Bibliography of Published Materials Concerning the United States Armed Forces Institute*, June, 1959. Both items are available from USAFI, Madison, Wisconsin.

[77] Paul B. Horton, and Gerald R. Leslie, *The Sociology of Social Problems* (New York: Appleton-Century-Crofts, 1955), pp. 462-463.

motivation, efficiency, spirit, dedication, and devotion — qualities ever more important for our society and its schools.

Education of the Upper Classes

Generally speaking, the higher the social class position of an individual, the more and the better education he receives. It has been claimed that education is primarily a means whereby social class positions are stabilized across the generations, that only secondarily is it significant in aiding social mobility.[78] The one deep experience that distinguishes the upper classes from the merely rich and those below is their schooling, and with it, all the associations, the sense and sensibility, to which educational routine leads throughout their lives.[79] This learning, however, is more than formal schooling. It begins with the informal kind of education sociologists call socialization — that is, it begins in early infancy and continues through a variety of channels.

Ideologically the upper classes are conservative — they are satisfied with the status quo.[80] They need not strive for status; they already have it. It is ascribed to them. Family loyalty, stability, more and better education, excellent occupational opportunities — all these things tend simply to insure a status which persons in the upper class inherit. Because this status is inherited there is an almost magic quality attached to heredity — that is, there is a strong belief that upper class social psychological and cultural characteristics are acquired through "good blood." This "good blood" is preserved through careful marriage selection. Upper class marriage is class endogamous, marriage outside the class being considered a threat to the survival of the "good blood," and, of course, all of its obvious advantages.[81]

There seems to be an ideal among many in this stratum to spend as little time as possible in business affairs and as much time as possible in leisure and recreational activities. Generally, the upper classes have tended to pursue forms of leisure and recreation which, because of expense and exclusiveness, are presently denied to classes below them.[82] For example, polo on Long Island, yachting along the Atlantic seaboard, cricket in Philadelphia, etc. Much time is simply spent socializing with persons of similar status in exclu-

---

[78] Bernard Barber, *Social Stratification* (New York: Harcourt, Brace, 1957), p. 395.

[79] C. Wright Mills, *The Power Elite* (Oxford University Press, 1956), p. 63.

[80] It should be understood that by upper class we mean what Warner has called "upper-upper" or the "old aristocracy." See W. Lloyd Warner, *Social Class in America* (Chicago: Science Research Associates, 1949).

[81] See *inter alia*, August B. Hollingshead, *Elmtown's Youth* (New York: John Wiley and Sons, 1949), pp. 84ff.

[82] Thorstein Veblen, *The Theory of the Leisure Class* (New York: Macmillan, 1899).

407

sive clubs — the Somerset in Boston, the Pacific Union in San Francisco, the Knickerbocker in New York, and so on. Generally, many upper class persons feel it an obligation to support the fine arts and, thus, belong to the boards of directors of art museums, or symphony and opera associations. Their style of life is always in the "best taste." On the whole upper class individuals seem most interested in reading history and biography, and are well acquainted with the traditions of their families to whom they are deeply indebted for their status and their style of life.

In many ways, therefore, the style of life of the upper classes is that of a subculture within American culture. It is a different culture. And if one is not socialized in that subculture one is likely to feel quite uncomfortable in it.[83]

THE PRE-COLLEGE UPPER CLASS PREPARATORY SCHOOLS. In modern industrial societies, like America, there are publicly supported schools for all social classes, but the upper classes have established for their own children certain, more or less exclusive private schools that train these children for upper class occupations and the upper class style of life.[84]

Until the age of four the upper class child is usually under the care of nurse and mother, after which he or she is under the daily care of a governess who often speaks French as well as English. At about the age of six or seven, he or she will then go to a private day school or away to a boarding school. Generally the boys will go away to boarding school at an earlier age than the girls. The girl may go to any one of such finishing schools as St. Timothy's, Miss Porter's, Westover, Foxcroft, Brearley, Miss Chapin's, Spence School, Rosemary Hall, etc. The boy will go to St. Mark's, St. Paul's, Choate, Groton, Andover, Lawrenceville, Phillips-Exeter, Hotchkiss, Middlesex, etc. It is fairly agreed among the social class experts that the one clue to unity of the upper classes in America would best be the exclusive schools which upper class boys and girls attend. These schools are a unifying influence, a force for the "nationalization" of the upper classes. They are also the admission tickets to the upper class cliques and clubs at the college level and beyond. In short, these exclusive pre-college schools are significant agencies working for the preservation of the upper class subculture.[85]

---

83 See *inter alia,* Milton M. Gordon, "Kitty Foyle and the Concept of Class as Culture," *American Journal of Sociology,* 1947, pp. 210-217.

84 In upper class circles the schools for boys are called prep or private schools; the schools for girls, finishing or boarding schools. There is a rigid separation of the sexes. Upper class schools are characteristically unisexual.

85 See *inter alia,* Barber, *op. cit.;* Mills, *op. cit.;* and Ferdinand Lundberg, *America's 60 Families* (New York: Vanguard Press, 1937).

Of the private preparatory schools for boys of the upper classes, the Groton School is one of the most famous examples. Its founder, the Reverend Endicott Peabody, early acknowledged that he was a patrician, believed in patricians, and that his school was modeled directly after the upper class English "public school," and was, therefore, for the upper classes.[86] When Franklin D. Roosevelt attended Groton it was estimated that over 90 percent of the boys were from families in the social register. At Groton, Roosevelt had a liberal education — studied Latin, Greek, Mathematics, English, French, German, History, Science, and the like. From there he went on to Harvard. Most upper class boys go to Harvard, Yale, or Princeton after attending such a school as Groton.[87]

For the upper class male, "It is the prestige of a properly certified secondary education followed by a proper club in a proper Ivy League college that is the standard admission ticket to the world of urban clubs and parties in any major city of the nation. To the prestige of the voice and the manner, constructed in such schools, local loyalties bow, for that experience is a major clue to the nation-wide upper class that is homogeneous and self-conscious."[88] There is much evidence, already cited, that the upper class individual gets a better quality of education than his social class inferiors. Upper class young men will generally go to one of the Ivy League universities. Upper class young women will generally go to Vassar, Smith, or Radcliffe. These colleges serve, consequently, more to perpetuate the upper classes than as a channel of upward social mobility.[89] Upper class educational institutions, therefore, provide upper class youth with the intellectual and social skills necessary to maintain and perpetuate upper class culture.

Contributions From the Education of the Upper Classes

The education of the upper classes demonstrates that while the amount and quality of formal education is generally related to socio-economic status in America, the quality of that education is *not* the key to upper class perpetuation but rather the result of upper class status itself. To be upper class, in terms of our definition, means simply to be born into the upper class. Since the upper class is, in essence, a subculture, this subculture perpetuates itself by both informal and formal means of socialization. However, what is sig-

---

[86] Frank D. Ashburn, *Peabody of Groton* (New York: Coward-McCann, 1944).

[87] Edward D. Baltzell, *The Elite and the Upper Class in Metropolitan America*, unpublished doctoral dissertation, Columbia University, 1953; also, Barber, *op. cit.*; Mills, *op. cit.*

[88] See Mills, *op. cit.*, pp. 67-68.

[89] Ernest Havemann and Patricia S. West, *They Went to College* (New York: Harcourt, Brace, 1952).

nificant about the education of the upper classes is the implications it has for the education of the middle and lower classes. It shows quite dramatically that given the advantages of higher status, more and better education, one can actually make greater achievements and contributions to society.

Lazarsfeld put the point very succinctly: "The underprivileged youth has seen less, read less, heard about less, has in his whole environment experienced fewer changes than the socially privileged, and he simply knows fewer possibilities."[90] For that reason, if the underprivileged youth is ambitious, intellectually able, and talented, he still is likely to dissipate his energies in more or less blind alleys because he does not understand or know that his eventual achievement is due, in large part, to his initial class status. Warner states essentially the same points in a more direct way: ". . . our understanding of the principle of social status tends to be implicit and to be learned obliquely and through hard and sometimes bitter experience. The lives of many are destroyed because they do not understand the workings of social class."[91]

In a study of Nobel prize winners, a study of the world's intellectual aristocracy, the researcher notes what, in essence, is the point of this whole section on the upper class: ". . . one first fact must be noted: it is that the social origins of the Nobel prize winners are never 'humble.' The fathers almost always are of very high social position."[92]

The contribution to American education by the upper classes is its demonstration that high achievement is likely to be a product of more education of a better quality from the very beginning of life. This initial advantage is, for the most part, undemocratically, mainly the privilege of the upper classes. This is, as Jefferson long ago noted, a waste of precious talent, a waste of America's greatest resource — its able youth who because of the accident of being born into underprivileged social classes get both less education and a poorer quality of education.

Education of Professional Elites

In the 1850 census, persons in the professions constituted 1.9 percent of the working force in the United States population. This percentage increased to 3.8 percent in 1900 and to 6.4 percent in 1950. With increased specialization in our occupational division of labor has come a tremendous increase in the number and proportion of professional personnel in the population.[93]

---

90 Paul F. Lazarsfeld, *Jugend und Beruf* (Jena, Germany: Fischer, 1931).

91 Warner, *op. cit.*, p. 5.

92 Leo Moulin, "The Nobel Prizes for the Sciences, 1901-1950," *British Journal of Sociology*, September, 1955, pp. 246-263.

93 "The Professions in the United States," in Blauch, *op. cit.*, pp. 1-8; also, Samuel A. Kramer, "Appendix — The Professions in the United States Census," pp. 292-296, *ibid.*

Professional education too has changed. The change has been in the general direction of longer and better programs and a careful selection of students seeking admission into professional schools. In the elite professions the increasing cost of education generally often means that only the well-to-do may enter these professions.

THE EDUCATION OF CLERGYMEN. In the spring of 1947 the National Opinion Research Center interviewers examined a nation-wide cross-section of Americans to determine how they evaluated 90 different jobs at all occupational levels. The occupation minister ranked 14th among the 90. It is an occupation with high prestige.[94]

Like most elite professions today, the education of clergymen reflects the current trend toward depth and breadth in the pre-professional and professional education. There is a recognition that today's world demands that the minister have a liberal as well as vocational education. His education is far different from that of his colonial counterpart — that is, he must study the behavioral sciences in order to better understand human nature; clinical psychology and psychiatry (sometimes collectively called pastoral psychology) to help solve some of the personal problems of those who seek his aid. These changes have been made necessary, in large part, by the ever expanding functions of modern urban churches. Thus, in addition to public worship services of the traditional sort, the time-honored ministrations to the sick and bereaved, and the giving of religious instruction, churches now sponsor some of the following activities in which the minister has a major or minor role: adult education, athletic activities, summer camps, premarital and marital education, Boy and Girl Scout troops, forums, picnics, parties, and numerous other activities. Some of the churches are now so large in membership and activities that they require, in addition to a pastor or head minister, several full-time assistants and an executive director to handle some of the many non-religious functions which many ministers today are expected to assume.[95]

THE EDUCATION OF LAWYERS. In the previously cited nation-wide study of the prestige of 90 occupations, lawyers ranked 18th.[96] They too have high prestige in American society.

---

[94] National Opinion Research Center, "Jobs and Occupations: A Popular Evaluation," *Opinion News,* September 1, 1947, pp. 3-13.

[95] See *inter alia,* Seymour Siegel, "Theological Education: Jewish," Oren H. Baker, "Theological Education: Protestant," and James E. O'Connell, "Theological Education: Roman Catholic," in Blauch, *op. cit.,* pp. 230ff.; also, Jerome F. Carlin and Saul R. Mendlovitz, "The American Rabbi," in Marshall Sklare, Ed., *The Jews* (Glencoe, Illinois: Free Press, 1958); Samuel Blizzard, "The Minister's Dilemma," *Christian Century,* 1956, pp. 508-510; and J. D. Donovan, *The Catholic Priest,* unpublished doctoral dissertation, Harvard University, 1951.

[96] National Opinion Research Center, *op. cit.,* p. 4.

The American Bar Association, through its section on Legal Education and Admissions to the Bar, is generally recognized by public authorities as the accrediting body for law schools. Today, of the 167 law schools in operation, 126 are on the approved list of the American Bar Association (ABA). In all law schools approved by the ABA, three years of satisfactory college work is required for admission, except in several schools which have established a four year law curriculum and may admit students on the basis of two years of college credit. Most law schools, however, have a three year program. In any event, at least six years of college and law school credit are necessary to obtain the Bachelor of Laws degree in a full-time school or seven years or more in a part-time school.

There seems to be a growing emphasis in law schools to encourage students to get a liberal, pre-legal, college education in which there is thorough training in English and the social sciences. A number of law schools now require the law school admission test which is administered by the Educational Testing Service, Princeton, New Jersey, and several schools give their own aptitude tests.

As has been recognized in other professions, there is often a gap between formal professional education (what might be called the theoretical aspect of education) and practice. Law schools have been trying recently to bridge this gap by the introduction of practice and moot courts, by emphasizing careful legal writing and draftsmanship and the like. A promising device developed by some law schools is the legal-aid clinic in which students may, under supervision, work with actual clients and problems.

Another important development in recent years is the emphasis on making provisions for continuing legal education for lawyers. A lawyer, regardless of age and experience, needs professional education beyond his own practice if he is to keep abreast of the development of modern law. Toward this end programs have been sponsored by state and local bar associations, usually with cooperation from law schools. At any rate, the need for continuing education has been recognized and steps have been taken to make such education a reality.[97]

THE EDUCATION OF PHYSICIANS. Physicians ranked second among the 90 occupations evaluated in the study previously cited. But with relation to the professional occupations, physicians ranked first.[98] Thus, physicians have greater prestige than any other professional group.

---

[97] Joseph A. McClair, "Legal Education," in Blauch, *op. cit.,* pp. 109-120; also, Albert J. Harno, *Legal Education in the United States* (San Francisco: Bancroft-Whitney Co., 1953).

[98] National Opinion Research Center, *op. cit.,* p. 4.

412

Since 1953, it has become mandatory for students entering approved medical schools to have a minimum of three years of college work. However, the Council on Medical Education of the American Medical Association strongly recommends that, in order to acquire a broad general education, a liberal education, premedical students take the full four year college course. Since that time, more than 70 percent of the students entering medical school have had bachelor's degrees. While candidates for admission to medical schools must meet certain subject matter requirements (which include as a minimum the completion of a satisfactory course in English, physics, biology, inorganic chemistry, and organic chemistry) some medical schools have additional specific requirements in scientific and nonscientific subjects. The recent trend has been to encourage premedical students to get a liberal education and discourage overemphasis on the premedical sciences.

The basic medical course leading to the degree of Doctor of Medicine has been four years in length. Traditionally, the first two years of medical school have been devoted largely to the study in the laboratory of the basic or preclinical sciences which include anatomy, physiology, biochemistry, pathology, pharmacology, and bacteriology. The last two years are devoted to the clinical subjects — medicine, surgery, pediatrics, psychiatry, obstetrics, public health, and the various medical and surgical specialties. The modern medical school, however, is breaking with this tradition. Western Reserve University's School of Medicine is one which has led in the revolution in medical education.[99]

The dramatic changes at Western Reserve have been reported by Caughey.[100] Emphases in medical school are to be upon a broad four-year program of general education in medicine with specialties to be taught at the graduate level. The aim is to help the student develop appropriate attitudes toward his professional responsibilities that have not always accrued from traditional programs. Content is taught in a correlated manner by interdepartmental teams. Much free and elective time is allowed for student exploration. Grades have been changed to "S" and "U." There are a number of approaches to eliminating traditional medical school "cramming" and a climate of friendly relationships has been established to promote communication and learning between faculty and students. A clinical-experience program is featured in which the student works with a family about to have a baby and follows through the subsequent year with infant care. In the third year the student has one-half day a week office practice and assumes a family doctor role with the selected patients.

---

[99] Donald G. Anderson, "Medical Education," in Blauch, *op. cit.*, pp. 130-143.

[100] John J. Caughey, "The Medical School Phase of the Education of a Physician," *American Journal of Mental Deficiency*, July, 1958, pp. 42-44.

The University of Buffalo Medical School has also pioneered in the study of its educational program and techniques. This has served to revitalize the instructional program at that institution. Medical schools at Harvard, Stanford, and the University of Colorado are among others that are making fundamental alterations in their programs.[101] These programs promise to revise centuries of tradition in medical education and to produce more effective physicians. Treated like mature individuals, students are encouraged to think rather than merely to memorize and to behave as sympathetic and rational human beings. These programs are also indicative of the valuable cross-fertilization of educational ideas that are now moving from one professional school to another in our educational institutions.[102]

The Education of Teachers

The first teacher training in the United States was carried out in a private school in Vermont, established in 1823 by the Reverend Samuel Hall.[103] Slowly, first in the Northeast, public (1838 in Massachusetts) and private normal schools appeared. The relatively weak and unsatisfactory two-year academic and pedagogical program of the typical normal school, frequently including associated laboratory school experience, had beome the major instrument of teacher education by 1900. Most students enrolled, however, did not complete the program and although there were over 300 such schools in the United States by the turn of the century, the bulk of teachers were still entering the ranks by direct entrance from high school, academy, or college, or through meeting local requirements, such as enrolling in training institutes or by passing a district examination. As long as the reward for teaching remained so low and so many "transient" individuals were a major source of personnel, it was impossible to build a profession.

Gradually the public came to recognize the import of properly trained instructors. The States began to develop certification requirements. Teachers associations, led by the N.E.A. (established in 1857), influenced and improved professional standards. The idea of establishing agencies to accredit teacher training institutions took hold. Ultimately, liberal arts colleges and

---

[101] For a description of one of these programs and a helpful bibliography, see: Lyman M. Stowe, "The Stanford Plan — An Educational Continuum for Medicine," *The Journal of Medical Education,* November, 1959, pp. 1059-69.

[102] See Stephen Abrahamson, "The Professional Educator and Medical Education," *Journal of Higher Education,* January, 1960, pp. 38-41.

[103] For details on the past and future of teacher education, see: Elsbree, Willard S., *The American Teacher: Evolution of a Profession in a Democracy* (New York: American Book Co., 1939); Stiles, Lindley J., *et al., Teacher Education in the United States* (New York: The Ronald Press, 1960); Lieberman, Myron, *The Future of Public Education* (Chicago: University of Chicago Press, 1960).

private and state colleges and universities moved into the teacher education field and they became the main source of high school teachers. The normal schools had declined greatly in number by 1920 but this was a decline largely in name only. The expanding school population at all levels was demanding even more teachers and most of the normal schools had been incorporated into state teachers colleges. In recent years the vogue has been to drop the name "teachers" and these expanded institutions remain a major source of American teachers. Some of the state colleges along with their major private contemporaries, such as Teachers College, Columbia University and George Peabody College for Teachers, have provided significant leadership in the field. Teachers College, Columbia, in fact, has been a singular force in teacher education in the United States and in recent years has borne the brunt of the attacks and charges against programs in effect throughout the nation. Along with such exceptional schools, the bulk of experimentation and professional leadership in education, however, has fallen to the graduate schools of education in the major universities.

In recent years these institutions have sponsored a host of interesting trials of new approaches to teacher education. Much of this stemmed from the efforts and funds provided by the Ford Foundation wherein certain leaders wanted to test present balances between professional courses and subject-matter preparation. The inconclusive state-wide Arkansas experiment in teacher education was an early large-scale trial in this area. As many of the subsequent plans, the attempt here was to substitute "on the job" or apprenticeship-type training, summer schools, and special workshops for the typical sequence of professional education courses. Since present teacher training programs are relatively lately evolved over a period of only 75 years with very limited experimentation, most educators have recognized the tentativeness of current practice. There had long been a feeling that more creative and different approaches might well turn out more effective neophytes. Therefore, as the Ford fund opened its coffers in this field, many universities and top teachers colleges drew up proposals that are now in the early stages of testing and development. Most of the millions of dollars that have been granted are being used to check a variety of intern and teacher-aide arrangements that frequently carry state certification and/or the master's degree for students who complete the program. Some of the schools are also working on such vital problems as: extending the competencies of elementary teachers in the broad fields that they need to master, finding financially realistic ways of extending teacher education to five or even six years, and involving the public school systems in greater responsibility for the pre-service education of their prospective teachers. With adequate evaluation there is hope that these programs will reveal strengths of present approaches and yet redirect certain emphases in teacher education so that the same revitalization that stirs

415

other professional fields will also characterize coming alterations and practices in the structure of teacher education in the United States.

Contributions From Professional Education Programs

If one wants to achieve any kind of eminence in the academic world, it has seemed to be preferable to have the following items attached to one's *curriculum vitae*: white, Anglo-Saxon, Protestant, male, and undergraduate and graduate degrees from major universities or outstanding liberal arts colleges, with the favored terminal graduate degree being a Ph.D. There have certainly been many striking exceptions to this categorization but persons of other backgrounds may find the path to academic success as elusive as K. found life in Kafka's *The Castle*.

Caplow and McGee state, for example, one aspect of the matter quite frankly: ". . . the initial choice of a graduate school sets an indelible mark on a student's career. In many disciplines, men trained at minor universities have virtually no chance of achieving eminence."[104] They also explain how men trained in minor departments and those who stop too low on the prestige ladder in their early job seeking may be seriously handicapped. An examination of the backgrounds of the past presidents of the American Sociological Association and the American Psychological Association confirms the point made above. Only a few out of all these eminent academicians earned their terminal degrees at institutions which were not outstanding. As Havemann and West put it: the fellow from Princeton has a decided advantage over the one from "Podunk." The man from the better school gets a better education, better opportunities, and, consequently, makes greater achievements in the long run.[105]

It is fitting, in many ways, that this section is the last one in this chapter. The education of professional elites ties up the seemingly unrelated sections of our contribution. The dynamic nature of American society makes it necessary that *all* citizens have a liberal as well as a vocational education. The ferment and broadened scope evident in current aspects of evolving professional education bode well for this balance in general and vocational preparation. So do the improved methods. This education of professional personnel is also worth considering because it points up the need for various educational institutions and agencies to apply the very best of man's accumulated knowledge to help in the education of persons for positions of great responsibility and for positions which require the utilization of high level skills.

---

[104] Theodore Caplow and Reece J. McGee, *The Academic Marketplace* (Basic Books, New York, 1958), p. 225.

[105] See Havemann and West, *op. cit.*, Chapter 15, "Princeton Versus Podunk."

416

If human brotherhood and democracy are to be a reality, the education of men must, in addition to all we have mentioned, contain an ethical imperative — it should be directed toward enhancing man's dignity and happiness. For, if man does not soon follow this imperative, the education of man may no longer be a question of concern to us, since man might be extinct.

Conclusions

The assimilationist and pluralist points of view have been reflected in the education of immigrants. Civil authorities have generally promoted the assimilationist position. Immigrants themselves have largely promoted the pluralist viewpoint. From the education of immigrants we have learned that we must teach all Americans not only to appreciate America's ethos but also that of other peoples of the world. If world peace and brotherhood are to be a reality, we must not foster assimilation at the expense of cultural pluralism; we must not foster nationalism at the expense of internationalism.

The great contribution of Negro education to the American educational heritage is the finding that for first-class citizenship, regardless of race, one must have both a vocational education (as advocated by B. T. Washington) and a liberal education (as advocated by W. E. B. DuBois). From the Washington-DuBois controversy we have learned that vocational and liberal educations are complementary and not antagonistic. We need both in a democratically oriented society.

A non-unionized employee is like an alien in an industrial culture. He is in it, but not a part of it. Like the immigrant, he must learn the ways of the new culture he enters, he must learn the language and customs of labor and industrial relations. The non-unionized member is like the Negro or minority group member in American society. He must have vocational skills but these skills can only provide him with a wage or salary. To have first-class citizenship one needs a liberal education so that one can secure the social justice that the democratic foundations of our nation promise all citizens. To live above and beyond the pig-level of existence, as Plato put it, to live as a human being, one must have an understanding of one's role as an employee in the modern industrial society in which one lives. The contribution of workers' education to the American educational heritage is precisely that it, through the labor movement, has recognized that workers (or employees) must have more than a vocational education to be first-class workers and citizens in American society. In short, workers' education is helping unionists to become first-class citizens and to assume the social responsibilities only persons with a liberal education are prepared to accept because they understand their role in our democratically oriented society. Equally important and

417

broadening in the education of Americans have been the multiple and consequential efforts of American business.

Adult education has destroyed the myth that education is something only for children and adolescents. We have reviewed the contributions to broadening and enriching American life, from private schools, agricultural agencies, special adult schools, the junior college, and other sources. It is clear that these agencies have helped American educational objectives reach full maturity and have led the great bulk of Americans to recognize and participate in education as a life-long process.

We have reviewed education of various elites. While our early military leaders like George Washington relaxed with works of Voltaire and Locke, Eisenhower read cowboy tales and detective stories.[106] The contribution from the education of military personnel is the reminder that the goals of education are as important as the means. A successfully mechanistic vocational education does not necessarily prepare one for peace. A liberal education is indicated as serious for all persons but particularly for leaders of this elite who seem to be gaining more important positions of responsibility in our society.

What is significant about the education of the upper classes are the implications it has for the education of the middle and lower classes. It has shown quite dramatically that given the advantages from the very beginning of life of a higher status, responsible attitudes, more and better education, that one may more likely attain greater achievements and make increased contributions to society. The education of professional personnel points up the need for educational institutions and agencies to apply the very best of man's accumulated knowledge to help perfect the education of persons for positions of great responsibility and for positions which require the utilization of high level skills. Some modern professional schools have begun to create such programs. These programs promise to provide those seeking professional training both a thorough liberal and vocational education, to encourage an attitude of dedicated social responsibility, to recognize education as a continuing, ever-to-be-improved process, to integrate the theoretical and applied aspects of knowledge, and to treat the student like a human being instead of some inert raw material to be stamped out on an assembly line.

In summary, the seemingly unrelated materials in this chapter point to the following contributions to the American educational heritage which have come from the education of immigrants, Negroes, adults, workers, military personnel, upper classes, and professional elites: a democratically oriented society demands for its perpetuation that every citizen, in order to be a responsible citizen and productive person, must be guaranteed a liberal as well as a vocational education; must be exposed to the kinds of learning experiences

---

[106] Mills, *The Power Elite, op. cit.*, p. 350.

which encourage education as a continuing, lifelong process; must be permitted to get as much education as he can profit from and the best quality of education available, regardless of his race, ethnic background, religion, social class status, age, sex, or other characteristics; must be taught to integrate theoretical with practical knowledge; must be treated like a human being so that he does not turn out to be like an inhuman robot; and, finally, must be provided with humanistic, altruistic goals so that his knowledge will be used not to destroy or exploit or dominate man but to help raise man to levels of dignity and happiness which, at present, still remain too remote and utopian for many Americans.

Selected Topical Bibliography

The Education of Immigrants

Barron, Milton L., Ed., *American Minorities*. New York: Knopf, 1957.

Brown, Francis J., and Roucek, Joseph S., Eds., *One America*. Englewood Cliffs, N.J.: Prentice-Hall, 1952.

Burma, John H., *Spanish-Speaking Groups in the United States*. Durham, North Carolina: Duke University Press, 1954.

Hsu, Francis L. K., *Americans and Chinese*. New York: Henry Schuman, 1953.

Schermerhorn, Richard A., *These Our People*. Boston: Heath, 1949.

Sklare, Marshall, Ed., *The Jews*. Glencoe, Illinois: Free Press, 1958.

The Education of Negroes

Ashmore, Harry S., *The Negro and the Schools*. Chapel Hill, North Carolina: University of North Carolina Press, 1954.

Butcher, Margaret Just, *The Negro in American Culture*. New York: Mentor Books, 1956.

Frazier, E. Franklin, *The Negro in the United States*. New York: Macmillan, 1957.

Ginzberg, Eli, et al., *The Negro Potential*. New York: Columbia University Press, 1956.

Myrdal, Gunnar, et al., *An American Dilemma*. New York: Harper, 1944.

Suchman, Edward A., et al., *Desegregation*. New York: B'nai B'rith, 1958.

The Education of Workers

Barbash, Jack, *Universities and Unions in Workers' Education*. New York: Harper, 1955.

Commission on Educational Reconstruction, *Organizing the Teaching Profession*. Glencoe, Illinois: Free Press, 1955.

Faulkner, Harold U., and Starr, Mark, *Labor in America*. New York: Harper, Revised Edition, 1949.

Fitch, John A., *Social Responsibilities of Organized Labor*. New York: Harper, 1957.

Peterson, Florence, *American Labor Unions*. New York: Harper, Revised Edition, 1952.

Wilensky, Harold L., *Intellectuals in Labor Unions*. Glencoe, Illinois: Free Press, 1956.

The Education of Adults

Brunner, Edmund deS., and Yang, E. Hsin Pao, *Rural America and the Extension Service*. New York: Teachers College, Columbia University, 1949.

Essert, Paul L., *Creative Leadership of Adult Education*. New York: Prentice-Hall, 1951.

Hopkins, Howard C., *History of the Y.M.C.A. in North America*. New York: Association Press, 1951.

Johnson, Alvin, *The Public Library*. New York: American Association for Adult Education, 1938.

Knowles, Malcolm S., *Informal Adult Education*. New York: Association Press, 1951.

Medsker, Leland L., *The Junior College: Progress and Prospect*. New York: McGraw-Hill, 1960.

Public School Adult Education. Washington, D.C.: National Association of Public School Adult Educators, 1956.

Sheats, Paul H., et al., *Adult Education*. New York: Dryden Press, 1953.

The Education of Military Personnel

Ekirch, Arthur A., *The Civilian and the Military*. New York: Oxford University Press, 1956.

Ginzberg, Eli, et al., *The Ineffective Soldier: Lessons for Management and the Nation*. New York: Columbia University Press, 1959, 3 volumes.

Masland, John W., and Radway, Lawrence I., *Soldiers and Scholars*. Princeton, New Jersey: Princeton University Press, 1957.

McGarr, Lionel C., Ed., *Keeping Pace with the Future*. Fort Leavenworth, Kansas: U.S. Army Command and General Staff College, 1959.

Millis, Walter, *Arms and Men*. New York: Putnam's Sons, 1956.

The Education of the Upper Classes

Barber, Bernard, *Social Stratification*. New York: Harcourt, Brace, 1957.

Cuber, John F., and Kenkel, William F., *Social Stratification in the United States*. New York: Appleton-Century-Crofts, 1954.

Havemann, Ernest, and West, Patricia S., *They Went to College.* New York: Harcourt, Brace, 1952.

Kahl, Joseph A., *The American Class Structure.* New York: Rinehart, 1957.

Lundberg, Ferdinand, *America's 60 Families.* New York: Vanguard Press, 1937.

Mills, C. Wright, *The Power Elite.* New York: Oxford University Press, 1956.

Veblen, Thorstein, *The Theory of the Leisure Class.* New York: Macmillan, 1899.

Warner, W. Lloyd, et al., *Social Class in America.* Chicago: Science Research Associates, 1949.

The Education of Professional Elites

Blauch, Lloyd E., Ed., *Education for the Professions.* Washington, D.C.: United States Government Printing Office, 1955.

Caplow, Theodore, and McGee, Reece J., *The Academic Marketplace.* New York: Basic Books, 1958.

Conwell, Chic, *The Professional Thief.* (Annotated and interpreted by Edwin H. Sutherland.) Chicago: University of Chicago Press, 1937.

Elsbree, Willard S., *The American Teacher: Evolution of a Profession in a Democracy.* New York: American Book Company, 1939.

Ham, Thomas E., "Current Trends in Medical Education," *Journal of Medical Education,* March, 1958, pp. 297-309.

Lieberman, Myron, *The Future of Public Education.* Chicago: University of Chicago Press, 1960.

Stiles, Lindley J., et al., *Teacher Education in the United States.* New York: The Ronald Press Company, 1960.

****

CHAPTER XI

WHAT IS INDIGENOUS
IN AMERICAN EDUCATION?

Our Forest Commonwealths

Here on the edge of the forest, a little more than three centuries ago, in an unparalleled geographical situation, a transplantation of European cultures occurred that was, within the brief span of 150 years, to change the course of the world's social and political history. The very incidence of these borrowed cultures, imported yet dependent for their life upon the clearer air of the New World, entailed the swift inception of fresh and countervailing tendencies in politics, society, and, eventually, education. Nor was the significance of his forest setting lost upon the "new man" who developed here; although it has been debated for the last three-quarters of a century to what extent he directed his own destiny or whether the frontier was in control.

The colonization of British North America represented a movement far more significant than the popular idea of a search for local religious liberty, important though this concept was to the later development of American individualism. Moreover, with the exception of Maryland and the Quaker settlements, the New England colonies were the only ones making even a pretense toward theological justification for their founding. Even in New England, Massachusetts Bay, Connecticut, and New Haven were established only nominally for religious reasons, economic and social motives being dominant. Maine and New Hampshire later split from Massachusetts; the state of Vermont arose from the efforts of the Puritan pioneers of the Connecticut valley. But under no circumstances can these be considered primarily religious in origin.

Only Plymouth and Rhode Island can withstand a strict test of the religiosity connected with their foundings. Of these, Plymouth (although intrinsically or symbolically the most significant of all) actually remained relatively unimportant in the determination of the New England tradition. In fact, Plymouth was absorbed by Massachusetts (Bay) in 1691. While we may assume that Congregationalism acted as a leavening agent on Boston's intransigence, the New England ethos came to be Puritan rather than Pilgrim and this domination epitomizes the Calvinistic influence in the shaping of the tradition. Rhode Island was a most turbulent factor in New England civilization but had relatively little effect on the course of American history.

The Sections

In the plantation colonies to the south the ideal was that of the Greek democracy based on slavery and the aristocracy of means. It was here that the great estates flourished with the erection of splendid manor houses such as Mulberry, Westover, Carter's Grove, Brandon, Berkeley, and Gunston Hall. The principles of the Anglican Church dominated and it was not particularly interested in education. In the back country and the Piedmont, however, the Scotch-Irish Presbyterians held sway and their influence contributed materially to the development of Southern culture. It is hardly necessary to add that, from this western section, came Jefferson, Calhoun, and Woodrow Wilson.

The middle colonies were composed of a welter of nationalities as well as religions. This great region, stretching from Chesapeake Bay to the Hudson River, was too fragmented to allow the hegemony of any one culture, to say nothing of a common educational system. The early control by Dutch autocracy and the feudal-minded Penns did little to encourage the development of democratic ideals or a society immediately reflecting its New World potential. Education in the middle colonies, following the lead of the Reformation, which had indeed brought the majority of its settlers to these shores, although their reasons for coming were many and various, was largely parochial. Even charity school work, for example, was carried out by that arm of the Episcopal Church known as the Society for the Propagation of the Gospel in Foreign Parts.

Consequently, to Puritan Massachusetts and Connecticut go the laurels for the fabrication of the dominating principles of American culture and civilization. What the Puritan did was to inaugurate a fusion of Congregationalism, economics, and social structure. His "way of life" was exclusive,

424

hierarchical, and oligarchical. Moreover, Puritan acumen quickly saw the possibilities of "education" for the perpetuation of his system. The harshness of the regime was modified by an internal mobility, which although immediately offering opportunity only for the "elect of God," was eventually to become democratic and to be superseded by a more representative order. Puritanism forged the machinery of a new government, social order, and educational system; it remained, however, for other hands to more democratically steer their leviathan.

While the stronghold of Puritanism was the Massachusetts Bay region, a refined variety of this religio-economic plutocracy penetrated westward to the river towns of Hartford, Windsor, and Weathersfield, and around Cape Cod to New Haven. Here theocracy, far from being extinguished, took on a new lease of life on Long Island Sound and in the Valley of the Long River. Religious liberty being equated with theocracy, the stage was set for the development of the first important strain in the American ethos — that peculiar combination of religion, politics, localism, and education, which paralleled in Europe developments arising from the wars of religion.

In New England the development was most unique. Wertenbaker judges that:

> . . . the founders of the Massachusetts Bible State confidently expected it to endure forever. To them it was no social and religious experiment, but the carrying out of God's commands. . . . (with) congregations whose autonomy was derived from a covenant with God, a civil government in which only church members participated and an educational system designed to buttress the orthodox religion. . . .[1]

Parrington believes that Thomas Hooker (leader of the Connecticut migration) was the architect of New England democracy as well as New England Congregationalism. The very polity of Connecticut Congregationalism became, for the elect, a refined Puritanism in which, while the church was equated with the state, the government of both was an instrument placed in the hands of all believers. Hooker's design, as elaborated in his *Survey of the Summe of Church Discipline,* indicates his "Ecclesiastical Policy," which he asserts "is a skill in the ordering of the affairs of Christ's house, according to the pattern of his word."[2] Congregationalism was the church of the "Visible Saints" who, confederating together to walk in the fellowship of the faith, chose officers through a process of "election of the people rightly ordered by the rule of Christ."

---

[1] Thomas J. Wertenbaker, *The Puritan Oligarchy* (Vol. III, *The Founding of American Civilization*) (New York: Charles Scribner's Sons, 1947), pp. 339-345.

[2] Quoted from Vernon L. Parrington, *The Colonial Mind* (Vol. I, *Main Currents in American Thought*) (New York: Harcourt, Brace and Co., 1927), pp. 60-61.

Nevertheless, the old Puritan drive and surety was not absent from Connecticut Congregationalism. Ralph Barton Perry's estimate of Puritanism may well stand as a general appraisal of the other side of Hooker's shield for it, says Perry:

> . . . tended to theocracy. It was intolerant to other creeds — in this resembling its God, who might be merciful but was not tolerant. It was disposed to make its own creed all pervasive, and to perfect, after the scriptural model, all the aspects and social relationships of life. To achieve this end it did not scruple to employ the full force of the civil authorities, to limit citizenship to members of the church, and to identify its religious ideal with the public policy.[3]

It is certain that the uniqueness of Hooker's Puritan system could not fail to influence the development of his state domestically as well as in the colonial efforts of her migrants.

Burning brightly for almost 100 years, the religious fires of New England were gradually and persistently quenched by the rising tide of commerce and mercantilism. Vainly did Jonathan Edwards attempt to spike the rafters of the house of Calvin. For the urge to economics which had been a crystallizing force in the birth of Protestantism now threatened to shake the very foundation of its edifice. The rise of higher levels of capitalism proved to be the almost insurmountable obstacle to Puritanism. The church of the Pilgrims as well as King's Chapel in Boston went Unitarian although Congregationalism lingered longer in Connecticut.

Political and Economic Factors

The growing commercial success of New England and other parts of the British Empire led Parliament to a realization that a general overall mercantile structure for the empire was an economic, if not a political, necessity. Legislation proceeded. Resentment aroused as a result of these trade "restrictions" began the creation of a local focus on embryonic nationalism both in New England and elsewhere throughout the colonies. The swing from Puritanism to Unitarianism was to be duplicated in a new orientation of loyalties in the political sphere. New terminologies followed this shift in basic allegiance. Their origins may be found in the potentiality for democracy in the State religions of New England.

The political break between thirteen North American colonies and Britain is spoken of as the American Revolution, although actually this "revolution" had slowly been taking place for over a century — a century bounded by

---

[3] Ralph B. Perry, *Puritanism and Democracy* (New York: The Vanguard Press, 1944), p. 115.

the Trade Acts of 1660, nourished by an Era of Salutary Neglect, and fulfilled in the "repressive" measures after 1760. Actual warfare obtained between 1775 and 1781 and several decades of "cold war" in the northwest followed the peace treaty of 1783. A partial settlement of the northwestern problems was effected in 1794 by General Wayne's rout of the Iroquois and Wyandottes at Fallen Timbers but a definitive adjustment waited until after the War of 1812 had driven the British from this area permanently.

Meanwhile, the "United States" had experienced three governments: first a *de facto* regime under a "Congress" composed of representatives of various colonies of the "original" thirteen; secondly, after 1781, by a "Confederation Congress," with a nominal presidency, rotated annually; thirdly, in 1787 a Constitutional Convention had established a system of "checks and balances" and a quadrennial executive independent of Congress, thus assuring a stable and an aristocratic government for a period of 40 years. At the conclusion of this era, the early class distinctions had been so whittled away as to permit the selection of a "democratic" president from the western frontier state of Tennessee.

The achievements of the Confederation Congress are probably as remarkable, for a given period of time, as those of the government which followed it. For it made peace, sent its ambassadors forth, and enacted the famous northwestern acts of 1784, 1785, and 1787. Collectively these represent the colonial policy of the United States and the later success of the new nation in settling and nationalizing a large area of the North American continent is to a great degree built upon this formula for state development which may easily be traced to the old New England policy for the creation of a new town. And indeed one can well argue that it was upon Maryland's insistence that the land claims of the States be placed in the general domain that the new government was able to implement the policy for statehood.

Moreover, the fountainhead for subsequent educational legislation and state practice may be found in the Land Ordinance of 1785 and the Northwest Ordinance of July 13, 1787. The first of these set the foundation for the public land system and included the grant of the sixteenth lot in each township for the people of that town for the maintenance of public schools. The second provided for the government of the Northwest Territory and its formation into States, with the declaration that "schools and the means of education shall forever be encouraged." Both documents are significant in that they preconceive an emphasis on education and schools in the new country which was to be on much the same basis as that which had obtained in that part of the United States in which public education first flourished — New England. (For European and religious antecedents of subsequent developments traced below see Chapters VI and VII.)

Our Debt to the Devil

It is a strange but true fact that the Devil made his home in Massachusetts. No doubt he sallied forth, but not for long; in the Puritan ideology his presence was a virtual requirement. The threat of his iniquity served as an excellent spur that was used with telling effect by minister, magistrate, and magister. His presence likewise served as a catalyst to literature and to the reams of scholarly exegesis on the fall of man so dear to the New England divine. He was responsible for the "blue laws" of Connecticut and for the school code in both the Bay State and Connecticut. Indeed, one may irreverently place him next to God in the Puritan pantheon; sometimes it seemed that he even oushone the Deity.[4]

Although, for the Puritans, religion itself was education, it had occurred to them conveniently early that formal training too was a necessary ingredient of statecraft — state and church equated as they were in the Puritan-Congregational system. The founding of Boston Latin School in 1635, the fear of an illiterate leadership that led to the establishment of Harvard College in 1636, and the famous acts of 1642 and 1647 all serve to confirm the necessity of education if their wilderness Zion were to prosper.

Indeed the latter act — the so-called "Old Deluder Satan Act" — spelled out the requirements for the inception of the perfect society: (1) that each citizen should be proficient in reading and knowing the Bible, for it was reasoned that all truth (especially theirs) was locked in "Holy Writ"; and (2) that all could be able to read and understand the capital laws of the colony (whereby allegiance and conformity to the established order should be secured). It had been, of course, the Devil's doing that reading was difficult; and that "tongues" were essential for a clear interpretation of the Scriptures. Agencies of formal education thus could render Satan's schemes null and void.

The schools themselves, with the exception that they were public and that towns were commanded to provide them, were not unique. The dame school had existed for many years in England, the reading and writing school was an importation, the Latin Grammar School was copied from the "public" schools of the mother country, and Harvard too was but a replica of Emanuel College at Cambridge, from whence had come a goodly number of the Puritan leaders. Nor were these saints alone in their fear of the Devil. Martin Luther write of "his cruel spite" and alleged that "on earth there is not his equal."

---

[4] See Henry W. Holmes, "Our Debt to the Devil: How the Puritan Belief in Satan Helped to Establish Public Education in America," *School and Society*, March 27, 1948, p. 233.

The Puritan System

Yet the Puritan system was unique (if totalitarian); and the comprehensive view of an educational pattern which could provide not only the highly trained and educated leaders for their society, but an educated commonality and laity as well, was distinctive. It also proved proto-democratic in that, once the ecclesiastical control had been shorn away, the public features, themselves worthy of emulation, when operated under republican auspices, were to set a standard for the provision of a state or national organization of schools.

Significant too were the methods of support. For example, the Boston Latin School was financed through (1) voluntary contributions; (2) income from town property; (3) income from the rental of islands in Boston Harbor; (4) income from the rental of a tract of land in Braintree; (5) income from other town lands, docks, ferries, and house rent; and (6) general town taxation. From 1635-1789 the school was supervised by the *selectmen* of the town, chosen by the citizens of Boston at the town meetings. The debt to the Congregational and Presbyterian form of church government is obvious. After 1789 the school committee plan was used — a device presently controlling the destinies of the more than 100,000 local school districts in the United States.

In order to emphasize the contribution of the Boston school to the development of education in general it may now be stated that, in the colonies as a whole, it was first (1) to be organized as a secondary school; (2) to be supported by general taxation; (3) to be controlled by its own town — through the *selectmen*; (4) to break the use of the imported seven-year course; and (5) to make provision for the education of girls in the public writing and reading schools during the summer months.[5]

Although there is not the space to detail the methods of instruction or much of the curriculum for the student, the goal of Puritan education was what now would be known as "character education." It was expected that schooling would serve as the developer of honesty, diligence, industry, frugality, sobriety, patience, perseverance, will-power, and Christian piety — Calvinistic virtues all.

The Puritan man or woman should be obedient, punctual, reliable, thorough, trustworthy, and have no vices to excess. He could be known as one favorable in the sight of God because he would be energetic, vigorous, physically fit, and quite capable of engaging in manual labor with no thought of class stigmatization. The reader immediately will turn his mind to Ben-

---

[5] Pauline Holmes, *A Tercentenary History of the Boston Public Latin School, 1635-1935* (Cambridge: Harvard University Press, 1935).

jamin Franklin and his famous system of moral bookkeeping for, although Franklin is not here classified with the Puritans, the qualities mentioned above came to be considered the ideal American virtues.

In many ways the noble Puritan resembled the Pharisee. When he took counsel from Moses rather than Christ he was, in all, consistent; and when he strove to uphold the letter of the law rather than its spirit he only followed his own natural bent. So it was with his observance of the school law and thereby came that most unique of all American educational practices — the decentralization of school policy and control.

New England School Organization

The Old Deluder Satan Act required each town of 50 families to establish a reading and writing school, each town of 100 households to operate a Latin Grammar School for those who would be fitted for Harvard or Yale. Tax levies were permitted and fines likewise were prescribed for failure of performance. It is a sad duty to report that there were towns that found it less costly to pay the fine than to operate their school; nevertheless, they fulfilled the letter of the law.

There was yet another subterfuge. As is perfectly well known, except to some dwellers beyond the Hudson River, the New England town represented a geographical entity of from 25 to 40 square miles. The village where the school was first located certainly served only a proportion of the population. This, of course, was legal but quite inconvenient for parents who chanced to live at the edge of the town. Imagine that our town is Dover. As the population grew, in addition to Dover Village one might expect to find South Dover, West Dover, North Dover, and perhaps Doverport.

When the citizens of these outlying centers arose in town meetings (at Dover Village) they demanded schools for their localities. And because they voted together they succeeded. Thus school might be held for six weeks at the Center, then moved to South Dover, and so forth. Obviously, the children were cheated, but it all was strictly legal. And when eventually the patrons had had enough of this they demanded a proration of town funds so that they could conduct their own schools (although, for lack of adequate funds, they would be mercilessly short). Each location was called a district and so the unique system grew. At first informal, the creation of districts was legalized in Connecticut in 1766; in Massachusetts, in 1789.

This was, of course, the school of the 3 R's, the Little Red School of song and story, the "District Skule." While much that is unflattering might be said about its teachers, interference by the local community or by prominent locals, its iron-clad discipline (or the lack of it), these things are too well known to suffer repetition. Indeed they too became parts of the American school tradition.

It is significant that these schools were public, and to a large degree tax-supported. They lent support to the principles made famous by the North-West Ordinance — "religion, morality, and knowledge." The schools and this accent was carried wherever the New Englander went, especially west of the Appalachians.[6] These schools were the embodiment of the Puritan virtues and a legacy which survived the decay of Puritanism as a state religion.

Other Areas

The contribution of the South and the Middle Colonies must not be ignored. While in the South education was largely in private hands, there were the "old-field schools" (cooperative family enterprises), charity schools subsidized by the Anglican Church and, in the Scotch-Irish region, parochial schools of a high quality. On a somewhat higher level were the so-called "finishing schools" and the private venture establishments of all kinds. But education was not public, nor was it in the Middle Atlantic States where parochial type schools dominated.

Nationalism and Education

The problem of an education, elementary in scope and depth, in a setting which, although nationalistic, was both democratic and only slightly stratified (because many of the class distinctions had either been removed or re-oriented by the Revolution) occurred as early as 1790 to Noah Webster, the apostle of nationalism and public education. The new objectives, unique to American life, demanded new schools for the people rather than for those of wealth and privilege. Webster indicated the necessity for an enrichment of the curriculum and a change in content for the realization of these new goals. He demanded also a change in method more in harmony with democratic institutions; he thought that to "continue the form of education that had largely prevailed while the States had been colonies under a monarchial form of government (that bred aristocracy and class divisions) was to miss the spirit of the Declaration of Independence." On this point he commented:

> . . . This appears to me a most glaring solecism. The constitutions are republican and the laws of education are monarchial. The former extend the civil rights to every honest and industrious man; the latter deprive a large portion of the citizens of a most valuable privilege.[7]

---

[6] See Kenneth V. Lottich, "Culture Transplantation in the Connecticut Reserve," *Bulletin of the Historical and Philosophical Society of Ohio,* July, 1959, pp. 155-166.

[7] Quoted from Webster's *Essays,* 1790. In Oscar A. Hansen, *Liberalism and American Education* (New York: Macmillan, 1926), p. 235.

Webster was not the first to speak for the democratization of education. Franklin, too, had observed the growing disproportion between the curriculum of the Latin Grammar School and the College and the developing American way of life. Together with Francis Alison and others he was instrumental in securing the establishment of the Philadelphia Academy on January 7, 1751.[8] The philosophy of the new school is summed up in Franklin's *Proposals:* "As to their studies, it would be well if they could be taught every Thing that is useful, and every Thing that is ornamental: But Art is long, and their Time is short. It is therefore proposed that they learn those Things that are likely to be most useful and most ornamental. Regard being had to the several Professions for which they are intended." [9]

While this academy failed to become the completely secular and practical school that Franklin had envisaged, it did add new subjects to the curriculum and set a standard for the creation of such institutions throughout the colonies. But before the story of the academy can be told, we must turn to a unique development in higher education.

The College of William and Mary, second in the American colonies (first in its antecedents which go back to the College proposed at Henrico in 1619) was chartered February 8, 1693. For this institution many "firsts" may be claimed, the most significant centering around 1779 when Thomas Jefferson became governor of Virginia. As a matter of pride in the America of the Revolutionary period, it should be noted that William and Mary was first to become a University; first to introduce the elective system of study; the first college to adopt the honor system; first with a school of modern languages and first with a school of municipal and constitutional law. In 1784 William and Mary became the first to teach political economy and as early as 1803 organized a school of modern history.[10]

Jefferson, likewise, offered a plan for more democratic education in Virginia. His *Bill for the More General Diffusion of Knowledge* did not pass in 1779; nor did it when reintroduced 40 years later. Nevertheless, although the plan is remembered chiefly for its Platonic scheme for developing an aristocracy of brains and talent, his bill did have a democratic underpinning; all children (girls as well as boys) were to be allowed to attend the primary school at public expense for a period of three years. Outstanding students were then to be skimmed off and given advanced education by the state.

---

[8] For a full account of the founding of "Franklin's" Academy see: James Mulhern, *A History of Secondary Education in Pennsylvania* (Philadelphia: Published by the author, 1933), pp. 174-216.

[9] *Proposals,* p. 11; as quoted in Mulhern, *ibid.,* p. 178.

[10] From photographic representation of a plaque placed at Williamsburg in 1914. In the *Bulletin* of College of William and Mary in Virginia, April, 1959, facing p. 1.

That Virginia still refused to agree to this in 1817 as they had rejected it in 1799 clearly shows that New England's priority in public education represented an unusual dedication, analyze its purpose as you will.

Yet, at the close of the revolution, new ideas in education were already abroad. Although one might not be completely happy with the New England district school system, it was public and did represent a grass roots movement toward free and universal education. The development of the academy represented another phase in purveying a more practical form of schooling than that of the Latin Grammar School. The modernity of the curricular and administrative changes at William and Mary suggested an eventual popularization of higher education and probably foretold the advent of state universities.

Two principles had already appeared that were very much in harmony with Webster's concept of the necessity for developing new schools for an educated citizenry. These were: (1) acceptance of the idea of public taxation for the basic education program (at least in New England); and (2) national dedication to the public school idea as shown through the grant of Section 16 in the Northwest Ordinance and in the provision for the establishment of universities through the grant of two or more townships for the same in the new Western States.

The Popular Academy

Meanwhile, as though the people were impatient of the fulfillment of these ideals, the private academy flourished. At first glance, it may seem strange that such widespread allegiance should be given an institution which demanded tuition and which offered a curriculum in which the old subjects of the grammar school were so subtly compounded with those of the newer dispensation: navigation, surveying, mensuration together with modern languages and nautical astronomy.

There are two prime reasons for the popularity of this institution. First, although the academy was a subscription school, its rates were low, and in a peculiar way it was *public* to the degree that no one was excluded. This met the urge for democracy. Secondly, the very multiplicity of its offerings satisfied; one could become "cultured," technically trained, or prepared for college. The curriculum was not snobbish. When one could join the ranks of the "educated" with the expenditure of a few months' time or a few paltry dollars, why hesitate? This too was in keeping with the developing American tradition and its pragmatic features require little elaboration. What America had done was phenomenal: independence from a leading world empire, the creation of the first really representative government in the history of the world, the winning of the West and its eventual translation into states equal in all repects to those established a century or longer on the seaboard. All things were possible. This is indeed what the academy signified: education to further progress.

Carl Russell Fish in a commentary on the intellectual development of the early national period speaks of the part played by those imbued with the new fervor:

> Its belief in education, its opportunities, the thrill of its renaissance were wonderful to behold. The influence of this New England element varied in the different sections. In the Lake region its members at once took the lead in educational affairs, and strongly influenced the region through education and example, in its attitude toward life.[11]

New Englanders are mentioned here but they were not the only groups involved. And in many ways the academy stressed those virtues associated with the early Puritan, earnest effort, intellectual struggle and moral discrimination.

W. W. Boyd, who made a study of the development of higher education in Ohio, the first State to be cut from the Northwest Territory, concludes, however, that the influence of the population origins in the various settlements in Ohio was responsible for the development of secondary education in the form that it took in each. He maintains that "in sections of New England people, the classical and literary ideal found expression in the new academy course." In other sections the influence lay on the development of a "practical education" or in "finishing schools." [12]

An English traveler in the United States of the early 1800's noted the prevalence of the academy in the new west and wrote with some astonishment of the comprehensive program he saw:

> . . . Besides District-Schools, however, there are what would be called in England, Academies, in the villages of the Reserve (northern Ohio), where the young people finish their education. I had the pleasure of attending an Examination of the High-School (academy) at E., which contained about eighty students of both sexes, most of whom were above fourteen years of age, and many of them one and twenty.[13]

Nor was the curriculum lacking in either classical or scientific subjects; and, as indicated above, the school was co-educational, a rather surprising development to Griffith:

---

11 Carl R. Fish, *The Rise of the Common Man* (New York: Macmillan, 1929), p. 226.

12 W. W. Boyd, "Secondary Education in Ohio Previous to the Year 1840," *Ohio Archaeological and Historical Quarterly,* January, 1916, pp. 133-134.

13 D. Griffith, Jr., *Two Years Residence in the New Settlements of Ohio* (London: Wesley and Davis, 1835), pp. 85-86.

The young gentlemen passed a very creditable examination in Latin, Greek, mathematics, etc., and the young ladies in grammar, geography, chemistry, etc. The young ladies too were dressed uniformly for the occasion, everyone wearing a black silk gown with a white handkerchief about her neck, her hair braided with a garden herb called hemlock, and her left sleeve ornamented with a white bow. . . . such publicity for the young ladies falls rather below the English standard.

Newspapers also played their part in the popularization of the new academy. Through their columns can be traced the desire and aspirations of the people they strove to serve. Thus, Boyd reports the premiere of a new institution in the village of Akron:

. . . M. and A. C. Joyce respectfully inform the inhabitants of Akron and vicinity that they have opened a school in South Akron where they will instruct a few young ladies in Arithmetic, Orthography, History, Composition, Natural Philosophy, Astronomy, Botany, Rhetoric, Chemistry, Drawing in Color, Mezzotinting, Pencil, India Ink, Japanning, Flower Painting, etc. Terms made known on application.[14]

The Western Herald and Steubenville Gazette of August 15, 1818 heralded the opening of an "English and Mathematical School" by one J. Wampler. The subjects announced were spelling, reading, writing "grammatically," arithmetic, bookkeeping, geometry, trigonometry, surveying, navigation, mensuration, and practical geography with the use of globes and maps.[15]

In addition to the *public* feature identifying the academy, it usually was non-sectarian. This tendency was in keeping with the new American nationalism of the 1800's and the aftermath of the Revolution which generally succeeded in disestablishing religion in the various colonies. Mulhern reports that in Pennsylvania, a State early subject to parochialism, "while the charters are generally silent on the question of religious control, many of the incorporated institutions, by the provision of their charters, were non-sectarian. Occasionally, one sect may have come to exert undue influence in the management of an institution, as was probably true of the Presbyterian group in the case of Bucks County Academy, but this seems to have rarely occurred." [16]

Education for Women

Another significant feature of the academy was the admission of women. Indeed, this period was remarkable in that female emancipation makes its

---

[14] Quoted from the *Akron Journal*, May 20, 1836. In Boyd, *op. cit.*, p. 132.

[15] In Carl D. Washburn, "The Rise of the High School in Ohio" (Unpublished Doctoral Dissertation, The Ohio State University, 1932), p. 57.

[16] Mulhern, *op. cit.*, p. 233.

slow start, especially in the area of education and frequently coeducation. That this achievement was not without opposition in some quarters has already been suggested. A further example from the Springfield (Mass.) *Republican* of March 14, 1835 may serve to indicate the contrary climate of opinion:

> . . . The Kentucky Legislature has conferred upon Messrs. Van Doren's Institution for Young Ladies in Lexington the charter rights and standing of a college. . . . A Diploma and the honorary degrees of M. P. L. (Mistress of Polite Literature), M. M. (Mistress of Music), and M. I. (Mistress of Instruction) may be given.

And then the editor leveled his literary wit against the innovation,

> Other degrees suggested from this quarter may be M. P. M. (Mistress of Pudding Making), M. D. N. (Mistress of the Darning Needle), M. S. B. (Mistress of the Scrubbing Brush), and (above all) M. C. S. (Mistress of Common Sense).[17]

Of course, today this does not appear to be very amusing; however, in the first half of the nineteenth century it was, and this indicates the progress made toward an equality in intellectual treatment to the sexes. However, sex equality actually had appeared before 1835 in higher education. Emma Willard had founded Troy Seminary in 1821. Oberlin opened its doors to coeducation in 1833 and Mary Lyon established Mount Holyoke at South Hadley in 1837.[18] The district school permitted mingling of the sexes from the first although it was felt that the female brain might be damaged by contact with certain subjects, e.g., arithmetic. In the first half of the century the academy gave recognition to advanced female education and, as the public high school developed, coeducation eventually came into its own.

State Organization

Two developments which at first glance do not contribute to the uniqueness of Amerian education but rather to administration and professionalization occurred also in the 1830's and '40's. These are the creation of State school offices and State supervision and the organizing of teachers into State professional groups. The significance of both is that each had the power to control or modify the curriculum; also to set standards of various types, thus being in the position to affect the education of every child or adult subject

---

[17] As quoted in Vera M. Butler, "Education as Revealed by New England Newspapers Prior to 1850" (Doctor's thesis, Temple University, 1935), p. 147.

[18] See Thomas Woody, *A History of Women's Education in the United States* (New York: Science Press, 1929), two volumes, for further details.

to instruction in the public schools. A third such factor, believed by some foreign observers to be one of America's most singular educational innovations, was the eventual creation of independent agencies to help standardize and improve education. These private, regional, accrediting associations that were to help with problems of articulation between high school and college, however, did not appear until the latter quarter of the nineteenth century.

The American Public High School

It is a curious fact that in American secondary education each new development has occurred before the preceding institution reached its maximum growth. Thus, the popular academy originated long before the classical grammar school had run its course; the birth of the American public high school antedates the high water level of the academy's progress; and the junior college appeared long before the conventional four-year high school had reached the zenith of its popularity. Especially remarkable is the case of the American public high school.

Noah Webster was 63 years of age when the first public high school in America was founded. Hard at work on his famous dictionary (published in 1828) he perhaps gave the event in 1821 scant notice; yet here at last was a school for the new day, certainly not one suited for class or monarchial purposes. It was American in its very essence. Nevertheless its plebeian features might not entirely have pleased him after all. For many of the factors which were affecting primary education and which, for the time, welcomed the omnibus academy, favored an extension upward of public education. Yet Webster had said, "to continue the form of education . . . that bred an aristocracy and class divisions was to miss the spirit of the Declaration."

The Boston English Classical School was established for the new middle-class America already rising in the Northern half of the republic. It was geared to male occupancy but its twin, the girls' high school, was founded in 1826. In keeping with the simplicity that was supposed to identify it, the name was soon changed to English High School; the name itself seemed not to have been an American idea but an importation from Scotland.

To be completely truthful, the new high school did not differ greatly in its curriculum from the popular academies of the day. It often did not offer foreign languages nor did it prepare for college; otherwise about the only apparent distinction was that it was *public* — that is, in the newer sense, free and tax-supported.

In 1827 the Massachusetts legislature provided by law the requirement that all towns of 500 families offer instruction of such a type that the net result was the establishment of "high schools," although the word itself was not used in the act. Classical languages were not required except in the largest centers of population; thus, like the original English Classical School, these schools were not necessarily propaedeutic. They were established to serve the bourgeois society that was developing rapidly under the impetus of New England industrialism. They could and did sometimes serve the capitalist classes. However, those who could afford private education usually patronized the long established classical academies. The new high school completed the link between the primary or elementary school and a higher education. That it should exist and that it should be free clearly fits the new American concept of a one-track, "single-ladder," democratic system — a concept buttressed by the onward sweep of the American economy itself.

Unique though it was and as indigenous a development, in its conception at least, as has appeared in American education, the high school, except in Massachusetts and a few larger cities as Philadelphia, Chicago, Cleveland, Baltimore, San Francisco, and New Orleans, did not spread as rapidly as might have been supposed. It will be remembered that this period in American educational history marked the heyday of the private academy; not every high school established was perfectly free. Two significant developments were yet to occur in the struggle for the complete one-track pattern mentioned above. These were the passing of public education legislation in states other than Massachusetts and, later, judicial decisions giving clear rights to use public taxation for the new high school.

In the East, Pennsylvania was the first to withdraw the barriers from the so-called pauper school. In 1833 under the inspiration of Thaddeus Stevens, whose classic oration in the interest of the free public school is a landmark in educational history, the example of this citadel of conservatism in providing public education for the multitude created similar demands throughout the north. In the South, the tradition of the private school lingered until long after the Civil War. It has been suggested that a strong reason for the North's success at arms in this "brothers' war" existed in the agencies of free, public education, including the new high school, prevalent north of the Ohio.[19]

The Graded School

Between the years 1840 and 1860 another step was taken in the direction of a better organized and more efficient system of public education. It was also a step toward the development of the high school. This was the "grading" or dividing of the students in the public schools according to their

---

[19] See Kenneth V. Lottich, "The Connecticut Reserve and the Civil War," *History of Education Journal,* Spring, 1957), pp. 92-104.

progress and ability. Thus, those who had reached a certain degree of attainment or proficiency were placed in different rooms, grades, or sections. This supposedly was a great advantage and certainly made the work of the teacher lighter. Prior to this time much of the teaching had been attempted by the oldest methods. A teacher took a roomful of assorted sizes and ages and tried to give each child individual instruction through following some recognized manual or textbook until it was mastered. Sometimes, as chance would have it, several students who were fairly homogeneous might follow this procedure at the same time. Usually, however, everyone was in a different place in the book in progress and often even the textbooks were of different editions or by various authors.

From the standpoint of precedent, grading was not a new idea. Even in America, Cubberley suggests, as early as 1799 "the Code of Regulations recommended for the Middlesex County (Connecticut) Schools, after listing the subjects to be taught, recommended the classification of pupils of equal attainments." Also, the course of study drawn up for the Providence schools in 1800 ordered that "Scholars shall be put into separate Classes according to their several improvements, each Sex by themselves."[20] Nevertheless, the procedure was not adapted generally for some years and it may be doubted that it was much used in the East prior to the middle of the century. It is generally accepted that the first fully graded school was organized by John D. Philbrick, Principal of the Quincy Grammar School in Massachusetts, in 1847.

Under the graded system those more nearly of the same progress were placed in a group and this class passed on to the next higher division as the students' progress might direct (individual students being "retained" as they did not meet the standard of "promotion"). About 1840 five grades began to be generally recognized: (1) primary; (2) secondary; (3) intermediate; (4) grammar; and (5) "high school." Later the number of grades below the "high school" level was doubled and the length of the period of study required increased to 7, 8, or 9 years.

Role of the American Common School

That the American elementary school (or common school as it formerly was called) is of indigenous origin is a controversial point, although one in which definition plays a most significant part.[21] Speaking from the purely

---

[20] Ellwood P. Cubberley, *Public Education in the United States* (Boston: Houghton Mifflin Company, 1934), p. 301.

[21] Two fundamental studies of the common school include Sidney L. Jackson, *America's Struggle for Free Schools* (Washington: American Council on Public Affairs, 1941) and Lawrence A. Cremin, *The American Common School* (New York: Columbia University, Teachers College, 1951).

organizational point of view, it is quite possible that the eight-year school is an importation, European travelers in the 1830's and 1840's being much impressed by the efficiency of the Prussian *Volkschulen*. On the other hand, it is probable that the eight-grade school came through the merely mechanical fashion suggested above, each of the four levels having been divided, for convenience in teaching, into two parts. This certainly is in keeping with the American pragmatic outlook which was already revealing itself in the early decades of the nineteenth century. Moreover, the purpose of the American common school, so vastly different from that of the Prussian example — a school for the lower classes, terminal, and non-propaedeutic — deserves special emphasis.

Although the evolution of the "common school" occurred almost exactly two hundred years later than its celebrated prototype, the New England reading and writing school established in 1647, there is a great deal of the same dedication. At a comparatively late date the inscription "Common Schools the Hope of Our Country" was a shibboleth not taken lightly and suggesting an intuitive realization of the necessity for, and the means whereby, the common culture and politic homogeneity might be appropriately achieved. This school of the people, in its very existence, served too as a focus for republican activity; during the winter months its sanctuary provided a community setting for basket meetings, spelling bees, box socials, political gatherings, and those special ceremonies attendant on the opening and closing of the school itself in which the commonality participated; on the "glorious" Fourth of July its hall became a center for democratic attack on all forms of monarchial prerogative as republican invective filled the air.

The peculiar significance of the elementary school in American life continued long into the nineteenth and partially into the twentieth centuries, spreading its gospel of patriotism and Americanism, group solidarity, and even philanthropic motives until its niche was pre-empted by the development of the likewise unique people's college — the American public high school. The community-civic significance of the elementary school lingers on through the activity of the parent-teacher association or the school council or similar ad hoc bodies; but such organizations and meetings are rather pale copies of the enthusiasm and patriotic fervor of an earlier era.

It was as Secretary of the Massachusetts Board of Education (1837-48), that Horace Mann led in the great struggle to get universal free, public education. He established his *Common School Journal* to push the message of the need for and the power of a common elementary school. It was a long and bitter fight in "enlightened" Massachusetts and it was to be many years before his ideal became the rule for the nation. His annual reports contain some of the best evidences on these and other educational issues of the day. Incidentally, Mann should also be credited for his efforts to get better teachers and for the establishment of the normal school in the country; he recognized that the common school would make a minimal contribution unless competent instructors were provided.

Jacksonianism

In the origins of the high school in many communities in the State of Massachusetts, especially worthy of note is the fact that high school courses existed long before the high school as an institution. The inference here is plain that the American people soon demanded a "higher education" than that of the common school, valuable though this was in welding together the differing economic, social, religious, and ethnic groups that contributed to the American character.

The demand for betterment — for a higher type of education, or at least the appearance of such culture — had been inherent in the success of the popular (and tuition-charging) academy. Yet at the opening years of the new nineteenth century a new current was abroad in the land. Its name was "Jacksonianism" and the origins both of the conception and the name are not difficult to find. That this belief of popular democracy in politics and society should affect education is certainly not surprising. That nothing was to be dragged down was its prime premise; that everything was to be pulled upward was its simple hope. Not necessarily Western (as Arthur M. Schlesinger, Jr., so brilliantly shows in *The Age of Jackson*) it wound roots in the stony soil of New England as well as in the mechanics' and trade associations of the middle Colonies and among the humbler agrarians of the Cotton Kingdom. It too was pragmatic and exemplified the progress of the "new man" as seen in America by de Tocqueville and others of the traveling genus. The conditions and aspirations of the common school and its heir, the new public high school, echoed this movement.

Set over against this quest for everyman's holy grail were the Jeffersonians. It may indeed appear strange that the name of Jefferson has been chosen for this more aristocratic direction although in truth it is an appropriate symbol. As will be remembered, Jefferson too preached for the common man, but he likewise sought the company of the intellectually able who for him comprised the real aristocracy, the elite of brains or talent. Thus, the humanist rather than the moralist tradition, although not that of the Reformation as much as that of the Renaissance, identified this contrary current. That the marks of the Jacksonian-Jeffersonian struggle are still plainly visible is a gross understatement; indeed the battle rages. Both currents are American; but in the early days of the Republic this conflict loomed much larger than it does 175 years later.

Both currents were inherent in the new developing high school. At first

441

it may be alleged the Jacksonian predominated, yet as the high school replaced the academy and indeed gradually moved into the orbit formerly traveled by the frankly traditional school of former days, its complexion became Jeffersonian. At a later time, the legal battles for its continued existence having been fought and won, it became a multi-track organization and, once again, more Jacksonian. Today ideologists are especially brash who strive to contend the merits of the one to the exclusion of worth on the part of the other; but the Jeffersonians again threaten.

The Curriculum

As an illustration in the formation of the public high school, which frequently was the product of evolution rather than devolution, the program of the Prospect Street School, Cleveland, Cuyahoga County, Ohio (circa 1840) may be mentioned. Although the pupils of this school were not divided into "grades" there was an attempt at organization into classes or levels. Moreover, "high school" subjects likewise appear in the schedule of this so-called "elementary" school.[22] The day was divided as follows: [23]

> *Morning Session*
> 1. Scripture reading
> 2. Class in English reader
> 3. Porter's rhetorical reader
> 4. Historical reader
> 5. Angell's No. 2 reader
> 6. First class, Smith's geography
>
> *Recess*
> 7. Second class, Smith's geography
> 8. Parley's history, United States
> 9. Class in Smith's grammar
> 10. Class No. 2 in spelling
> 11. Class No. 3 in spelling
>
> *Afternoon Session*
> 1. Class in historical reader
> 2. Angell's No. 2 reader
> 3. Kirkham's Grammar
> 4. Adam's arithmetic
> 5. First class, Smith's arithmetic

---

[22] Henry Howe, *Historical Collections of Ohio* (Columbus: Henry Howe and Son, 1890-1891), volume I, pp. 142-143.

[23] Andrew Freese, *Early History of the Cleveland Public Schools* (Cleveland: The Board of Education, 1876), pp. 22-23.

Recess
6. Second class, Smith's arithmetic
7. Third class, Smith's arithmetic
8. Class in algebra
9. Class in natural philosophy
10. First class in spelling.

It would appear from the above program that the teacher was obliged to conform his classification, in part at least, to the degree of difficulty of the books in use. Moreover, there was not at that time any uniformity in the use of textbooks in a given school. Neither does it seem that there was an exercise of authority in the matter of textbooks prescribed in the public schools of Cleveland for a number of years after their opening.[24] Nevertheless, from a review of the subjects offered at the Prospect Street School, and from a comparison of them with those offered in the rural schools, as described by Welker,[25] it is quite clear that advanced work was being carried on in the common schools. At least four of the subjects of the academy and later "high school" were being studied: history, grammar, algebra, and natural philosophy. It is readily apparent that there were no definite upper limits to the work offered by the public schools of the third and fourth decades of the 1800's. The tendency was toward a "higher education" than that of the grammar school for a few pupils at least; several more years were to see the separation of these subjects into those of the primary or elementary and those of the secondary or high school. Meanwhile, the "high school" division offered an elastic compartment at the top of the public educational ladder into which those subjects from the academy and formal grammar school could be placed as considered appropriate to the demands of the time.[26]

Religious Ferment

Yet another circumstance lent its emphasis to the demands for a greater freedom and American eclecticism in matters educational. This was the urge to innovation in religion and in social planning. If Jacksonian may be applied to these manifestations, and they do represent a response to the new conditions favoring revision and novelty, then they are but parts of that great

---

[24] Freese, *ibid.*, p. 23.

[25] Martin Welker, "Farm Life in Central Ohio Sixty Years Ago," *Western Reserve Historical Society Tract No. 68,* Vol. IV (1895), pp. 25-85.

[26] A recent study that bears out these democratic origins of the high school as an extension of the common school idea is Thomas N. Barry, "Origins and Development of the American Public High School in the Nineteenth Century" (Doctor's thesis, Stanford University, 1961).

cultural shift of the early 1800's favoring the democratic mode in politics as well as in education and social relations.

Emerson, soon to participate in his own Utopia, had just written to Carlyle, "We are all a little wild here with numberless projects of social reform. Not a reading man but has a draft of a new community in his waistcoat pocket."[27] And with what truth! For the religious reflex of expanding commerce and rising industrialism was indeed comparable to the great religious movement that had accompanied the rise of capitalism in Europe in the day of the Reformation.

Ever since Jonathan Edwards had preached the Great Awakening American evangelism had ignited the frontier by revival and camp meeting. Hand in hand with religious enthusiasm went the new social doctrines which now filled the air, and the call of cheap land in the West that was a magnet both to Americans and Europeans. Eclecticism in religion had already led to the evolution of the Rappites, the Shakers, and the New England Unitarians. In quick succession, likewise were to develop the Latter-Day Saints, Disciples of Christ, and the Seventh-Day Adventists, each an indigenous American religious sect. (Chapter VI traces certain of the activities of these groups.)

The report of a great convention, held in Boston in 1840 to honor "Friends of Universal Peace," makes no distinction between social leaning and theological preference, where

> . . . advocates of the many causes joined in hopeful, friendly congratulations; where Abolitionists saluted Agrarians, Grahamites joined with Millerites, Calvinists met on friendly terms with dubious Unitarians, and the two groups mixed with Vegetarians, Groaners, Come-Outers, Dunkers, and Muggletonians.[28]

Such was the climate into which the new schools for the people made their way.

Creation of the Myth

As the public high school spread, by state legislation, by the method of local election, and by evolution from the common school, so developed the myth or legend of its peculiar American virtues. The edifice itself became a local temple, to be pointed out with pride and even with a quality of awe by those not fortunate enough to have entered its portals in quest of that knowledge which was said to unlock every door to opportunity. Its cere-

---

27 Merle Curti discusses these and other "New Goals for Democracy" in *The Growth of American Thought* (New York: Harper and Brothers, 1943), Chap. XV.

28 Quoted from Constance Rourke, *Trumpets of Jubilee* (New York: Harcourt, Brace and Company, 1927), p. 268.

monies, sometimes of medieval origin but more usually the focus of the national and patriotic sentiments of nineteenth century America, attracted the majority of the community's citizens and the local reputations that were confirmed or made at these exercises emphasized again its Jacksonian origins.

Nor was the opportunity lacking for the implementation of this "American Dream," which frequently began in the public school and, in theory at least, ended in the White House or in the managerial ranks of the new industrialism that followed the Civil War. Since tuition was free, the only real expenses were for books and in the equivalent of the time consumed in attendance. Yet here was the rub. Granted that the scions of the middle class and also those of wealth, were they inclined to attend, could meet these slight conditions, there still was the great group representative of the laboring and farming classes who could not attend. They were unable to do so either because they themselves were needed as contributors to the family welfare or because the return from labor in these rough and tumble days of economic pioneering and agrarian hazard was insufficient to provide such meagre funds. Thus, in terms of the developing ideology of the rights and privileges of American citizens, many could not avail themselves of that which was "free" and actually their birthright.

Nevertheless, these opportunities became a legend, an important one in conditioning allegiance to the American way of life. For, whether one was able to avail himself of this new democratic pattern in education or not, the theory still held good. It was a theory influential both within the national confines and abroad. That, in practice, the magic of the myth had not always been effective, or that the privilege of class had not been entirely eradicated, or that there was indeed not one track for all, was conveniently overlooked.[29] There were, to be sure, other institutions for "public" education; the academy was not entirely dead, and the private successors of the imported classical grammar school were still very much alive. But, all in all, the myth stood; it was part of the American personality that it should; and again, truthfully enough, the spirit itself was not vitiated by the exceptions.

The Courts Take a Hand

These high, democratic, educational principles were recognized by others than those who personally sought to fulfill the "American educational dream." American jurisprudence played a mighty hand in the institutionalization of the motive. Although secondary education of a public nature had been created in Massachusetts as early as 1635, the resulting school was not

---

[29] See Robert Ulich, "The Legend of the 'Single Ladder'," *School and Society,* February 1, 1947, pp. 73-75.

"free" in the modern sense, nor was the education "public" in the contemporary meaning of the word. Neither did the high school legislation of 1827 in Massachusetts, which came closest to the idea of secondary education for the children of all the people, guarantee nation-wide acceptance of this concept. Thus, the influence of the courts was to contribute to the codification of the principle of universal, free, public education on a seondary level.

As previously stated, the spread of the high school, after 1821, had been relatively sluggish except in parts of New England and in the areas where New England influence was strongest, especially the old Northwest. Cubberley, dean of American education writers, is responsible for the much quoted and often misinterpreted statement that ". . . by the close of the second quarter of the Nineteenth Century, certainly by 1860, we find the American public school system fully established, in principle at least, in all of our Northern states."[30] This statement is, of course, not accurate unless so qualified that its specific import is farily whittled away; for the expression *in principle* limits its summarization to not much more than a statement of philosophy. Even this, however, is exceedingly important as it is the basis for the eventual complete acceptance of the People's College.

The key test case questioning the legality of the public high school was brought in the State of Michigan. In 1874, Justice Thomas M. Cooley, in a decision of the highest importance to the American single-track system of free public education, maintained that when the State Constitution . . .

> provided for the establishment of free schools in every school district . . . and for the university . . . the inference seems irresistible that the people expected the tendency towards the establishment of high schools in the primary-school districts would continue until every locality capable of supporting one was supplied . . . (Thus) we content ourselves with the statement that neither in our state policy, in our constitution, or in our laws, do we find the primary-school districts restricted in the branches of knowledge which their officers may cause to be taught, or the grade of instruction that may be given, if their voters consent in regular form to bear the expense and raise the taxes for the purpose.[31]

The legality of the high school, and actually its indispensability, having been sanctioned by public acceptance and by the courts, we may now turn to the creation of the third level of public education in the United States, the college and the state university.

First, however, it should be noted (although the premise must be visible

---

[30] Probably the most thorough study on the origins of the high school is Emit D. Grizzell, *Origin and Development of the High School in New England Before 1865* (New York: Macmillan, 1923).

[31] "Stuart vs. School District No. 1 of the Village of Kalamazoo," 30 *Michigan,* 69.

already) that, as in the Swiss Confederation, there is no federal system of education in the American union; neither is there exercise of federal control except in a few peripheral instances. It has been a matter of endless discussion why, in America, in opposition to almost every other country of the world, education was relegated to the state constitutions and indeed, in practice, to the smallest subdivisions of these — the districts, towns, or counties. Yet when one considers the conditions under which education was provided in the various colonies and especially the aversion to centralization except in the then most urgent areas of finance, war and peace, and international relations, it would have been even more remarkable had a national system been devised. These considerations lead us directly to the development of tertiary education.

Higher Education

The foundations of Harvard, William and Mary, and Yale, the earliest colonial colleges, were laid by religious bodies. The urgencies of the Reformation together with the clerical function inherent in many of the European institutions of the day suggests that this was a not unusual procedure. The plea for Harvard's existence — the dread of an illiterate leadership — was the universal motif (although Pennsylvania was conceived under less sectarian circumstances) and at first the role of each college was much the same. Yet two new conditions were to obtain as the colonies passed from their imperial status to that of independent confederated States. First were the demands of the new embryonic nationalism — the pleas of Webster and Jefferson for new institutions commensurate to the changed circumstances. Secondly, as remarked above, political and social change appeared to entail new modes of religious expression and the religious ferment of the 1800's was to bring demands for indigenous institutions to accompany resultant departures in the ecclesiastical area. Additionally, a later motive included the changing status of women. And then, from the beginning, as America grew and prospered, there was the need for an ever-broadening variety of professionally trained leaders.[32]

The political motive was an immediate outgrowth of the Revolutionary ideology. In Virginia, Jefferson and his friends attempted to transform William and Mary into an institution under the jurisdiction of the State. There were legislative interferences in the organization of Yale, Columbia, and Pennsylvania but "the people" did not succeed in their attempt to gain

---

[32] A recent study that documents the broad purposes of the colonial college is Jerome S. Fink, "The Purposes of the American Colonial Colleges" (Doctor's thesis, Stanford University, 1958).

control here any more than Jefferson had in Virginia. It was, however, in New Hampshire that the matter became most violent.

The charter of Dartmouth College had been granted before the Revolution, in 1769. Operated under Congregational auspices there was little opposition to this ecclesiastical control until the Jeffersonians (i.e., anti-Federalists or Democratic-Republicans) won the legislature in 1816. Reorganizing the college into Dartmouth University, with a State board of control, their thought, no doubt, was to create a true state university in line with the aspirations of Thomas Jefferson in Virginia. This action was, of course, resisted by the former governors of the institution and, in due time, the case reached the United States Supreme Court. Here, in a decision bitterly resented by the Democratic-Republicans, with Chief Justice John Marshall presiding, the court declared for the holder of the original charter, on the grounds of sanctity of contract.

It is a debated point whether this decision aided or curtailed the development of the American state university. That the new legislatures were generally favorable can be maintained and this is shown by the fact that state universities had been chartered in seven of the original States by 1833 and that each of the newly admitted States, beginning with Vermont (1791), made some provision for the establishment of a university.

However, Donald George Tewksbury, in a study of the founding of American colleges, considers that the Dartmouth College decision delayed the development of the state university for many years.[33] And popular universities did not come to New England, New York, and Pennsylvania until the industrialism attendant on the American Civil War had made its appearance. Moreover, the power of vested interests in higher education must also be taken into consideration. In each of the States where the university came late there existed one or more proprietary institutions of immense prestige. (In New York the state university withheld its appearance until 1948!)

Public higher education was stimulated materially by the Morrill Acts of 1862 and 1890. Under the historic provisions, the federal government appropriated 30,000 acres of public land for each of a State's representatives in Congress if the State agreed to provide a liberal yet practical college education for the industrial, mechanical, and agricultural classes. The latter act granted annual supporting appropriations from the national treasury to each college established. In fifteen States where state universities were already organized, the land grant institution was incorporated; but 47 others were established as separate "A & M" schools, including the segregated Negro

---

[33] Donald G. Tewksbury, *The Founding of American Colleges and Universities Before the Civil War* (New York: Teachers College, Columbia University, 1932), pp. 150-151.

colleges set up in the South because of the provisos of the 1890 law. A few private institutions, such as Cornell, were designated by state legislatures as their recipient of the funds. Some of the "cow colleges" became the dominant institution in several States and the great bulk have now become full-fledged universities. The principles back of the Morrill Act were extended by later federal legislation, such as the Smith-Lever (1914) and the Smith-Hughes (1917) Acts. Important adult, vocational, extension, and rural education were all materially promoted by valuable programs resulting from the matched federal and state funds provided under these laws. Again, in the foregoing legislation we have the example of farsighted individuals and groups using their governments to promote the underlying strength of the American dream — the full education of the masses. Intuitively, Jacksonian Americans have pushed toward the upper levels of the goal implied by Jefferson when he claimed: "If a nation expects to be ignorant and free in a state of civilization, it expects what never was and never will be."

The Denominational College

The other organ of popular higher education, although a tuition school like the academy, was the denominational college. Here Tewksbury speaks and there is no dissent:

> . . . The American college was founded to meet the "spiritual necessities" of a new continent. It was designed primarily as a "nursery of ministers," . . . (but) the movement . . . cannot be studied, much less appreciated at its full value, without recognizing the service rendered by the denominational college in the perpetuation of culture as well as of religion on the advancing frontier of American life.[34]

The uniqueness of this mission, while on the one hand reflecting the goal and characteristic of Puritan New England, and on the other, a pragmatic and peculiar American response to the exigencies of the geographical frontier, stamps the denominational institution as a different species from that of the ivy league college or even the state university. Except in certain other colonial settings there appears to exist no parallel for this largely indigenous type of "college."

Its distinctive feature, over and above the rapidity of its spread in most of the 1800's, was its service and, consequently, its durability. For this institution (and it is here that the expression "log college" came into being) served as a stalking horse for civilization. While it may be remonstrated that each denomination cleverly sought to perpetuate itself through the creation of its

---

[34] Tewksbury, *ibid.*, pp. 38, 42.

"colleges," this is much too limited a view. While they were schools for ministers and a sometime focus for ecclesiastical doctrine, their larger role was to provide something of the niceties of culture that had been left behind as the frontier rolled westward. They also sought to preserve as many of the achievements of civilization and tradition as were possible in a new and primitive setting. That these goals were to be furthered within a sectarian framework did not lessen their generality; nor did it follow that competition for "souls" should be a hallmark of these institutions.

Many illustrations could be used to establish the agencies denoted above with their unique devotion to the American culture and government, a special religion, and a desire for individual and general betterment. However, one should suffice. Let us turn to the Pacific Coast for it.

In 1842, 17 years prior to statehood in Oregon, the population of the Willamette Valley (the central section of western Oregon) was small but the pressing need for provision for the proper education of children was already apparent. Alvan F. Waller is found writing to his close friend, the Reverend Fuller Atchison, at Albion, Michigan:

> . . . I want more than anything else a chance to educate my children. And in order to do this I have ventured to pledge two hundred dollars for the erection of an institution of learning in this country.[35]

Waller had not been alone in the desire for this ideal. On February 1, 1842, an interested group including the Methodist Jason Lee and the Independent Congregationalist Harvey Clark had met at the "Old Mission House," a structure built in Salem by Lee and his co-workers eight years earlier. "After a general survey of the ground," goes one account, "it unanimously resolved to establish a collegiate institution and that a log boarding house and school house be built of sufficient size to accommodate the teachers and pupils . . ." Gustavus Hines, one of the committee, leaves this record:

> Whereas it is believed to be highly important to the future welfare of this rising community that a permanent literary institution be established in this valley . . . (to provide) that intellectual and moral training which alone can prepare for respectability and usefulness. . . .[36]

From these humble origins arose Willamette University, the oldest collegiate

---

35 Waller to Atchison, dated Willamette Falls, May 23, 1843. Published in the *Christian Advocate and Journal*, July 3, 1844, p. 186. See Kenneth V. Lottich, "The Oldest University in the West," *School and Society*, March 31, 1951, pp. 193-196 for a description of the founding of the pioneer university in the West.

36 Gustavus Hines, *Oregon and Its Institutions* (New York: Carlton and Porter, (1868), pp. 142-143, 144-149; C. B. Moores, *Oregon Pioneer Wa-Wa* (Portland: The author, 1923), pp. 121-122.

institution west of the University of Missouri; and this is a story that can be duplicated many times over as evidenced in Chapter VI.

To repeat the argument stated above, while denominationalism provided the spark for such like endeavors, the greater significance of the colleges so provided was that they became the civilizing agencies of a frontier society and thus played a unique role in Americanization as well. That they were non-academic is not being suggested. In many cases Latin and Greek became frontier fare, at least for the few enrolled; however, what was learned was not as important as the role of these colleges in the creation of a semi-cultured class whose influence in the development of the societies of which they were a part must be reckoned as exceedingly significant.

College formation was a special hallmark of the early and mid-century 1800's. While the example above was on the Far West (and 21 institutions are reported as having been founded there between the years 1800-1880), by far the greater number were formed in the Midwest, specifically the North Central tier of States, in which 135 denominational colleges and publicly controlled institutions were established. In the South, which after the Civil War comprised a frontier of a special type, 100 colleges and universities were initiated. In the North Atlantic section, the area of greatest population, only 65 such schools were founded during the decades specified.[37]

Other Agencies

There were other educational influences of a popular nature beyond the development of the graded free elementary school and the spread of the new public high school, the urge to establish denominational colleges, and the creation of state universities. To be noted particularly were the work of the "School Societies," philanthropic groups engaged in providing educational agencies largely before the incidence of the free, state-controlled school; the influence of "Infant Schools" and "Sunday Schools"; and the immense vogue in the first half of the century of the schools denominated as Lancasterian or Lancaster-Bell that utilized a monitorial system of instruction, generally under private or philanthropic auspices.[38] These were of British extraction. Even so, it is especially pertinent to note the contribution of each to the intensifica-

---

[37] Based on Reports of the Commissioner of Education, Washington: see table in Edwin G. Dexter, *A History of Education in the United States* (New York: Macmillan, 1904), p. 270.

[38] An interesting description of attempts at Lancasterian instruction is found in Phil E. Hager, "Nineteenth Century Experiments with Monitorial Teaching," *Phi Delta Kappan*, January, 1959, pp. 164-167.

tion of the school effort. Although the agency was private or philanthropic, its labor served to reinforce the American concept of citizenry educated for the form of government based upon the will of the people and their exercise of this in the creation and maintenance of their local institutions. In a word, any and all of the developments cited confirmed to the American citizen his essential need for an education system, universal, public, free, and as nearly as possible following one track or a "Single Ladder" for all. That this system should continue through the university was likewise much more than a pious hope, although the full fruition of this was not to be experienced until approximately a century after Judge Cooley handed down his celebrated pronouncement based on the Kalamazoo case.

American Textbooks for American Schools

With independence and the rise of American nationalism in the first half of the nineteenth century came a corresponding shift in the materials selected for instructional purposes in the schools. Overshadowing the famous hornbooks and the New England Primer was the contribution of Noah Webster. Lest his dour New England manner and visage obscure his real worth to American education, and to America herself, it must be said at once that Webster, as Franklin, was a prophetic figure. He demanded Americanization and more than that set out to bring whatever aid he could muster to the process. While his lectures, no doubt, were tinctured with Federalist irreconciliation, his sentiments did indeed speak wisely: American nationalism, an American language, American political institutions, American schools, and (his personal contribution) American schoolbooks.

The profits from his spellers (The First Part of a Grammatical Institute of the English Language was his extravagant title) allowed him leisure for a 20-year stint on the dictionary. The second and third parts of the "speller" were applied to reading and grammar itself. The books were enormously successful. Moreover, they were "American" in content and arrangement. They breathed patriotism. And the speller fostered the vogue for the "Spelling Bee" — a community manifestation impossible of comprehension at this late date. The creation of this unique focus for group life was hardly planned by Webster. The books and the early American spirit produced a synthesis which led to the rite and a custom that extended well into the twentieth century.

Jeddiah Morse's American Universal Geography likewise had strong national overtones although (as was the custom) it was largely a drill book. Samuel G. Goodrich (who called himself "Peter Parley" in numerous texts) published A History of the United States in 1822, another terrifically successful book. But, after Webster, the most influential textbooks were produced by William Holmes McGuffey, of Oxford, Ohio.[39]

Born in Pennsylvania, McGuffey graduated from Washington and Jefferson College in 1826. Seeking a position in an academy, he presented himself before the board, upon which sat two Yale graduates. Taking a severe examination, in which he was judged a failure by the Yale men, he was refused employment. Later, having accepted the post of Professor of Languages at Miami University, McGuffey conceived the idea for a series of graded readers, to be interspersed with items for penmanship and spelling, and having a high moral content. The first two books, published in Cincinnati in 1836, caught on immediately and others (six altogether) were issued. (McGuffey sold all his rights for $1,000!) It has been estimated that 122 million of the McGuffey books were sold. The morality of these volumes, plus their skill in construction and the worthwhileness and freshness of their materials stimulated the users to the degree that some formed McGuffey clubs to perpetuate the books and the ideals they represented. McGuffey himself spent the last thirty years of his life as Professor of Philosophy at the University of Virginia and goes down in history as the one American name synonymous with school books.[40] The only other books in American publishing history to match the "McGuffeys" are the Horatio Alger American success stories but these, of course, were not school texts.

Equalization of Opportunity

Running like a thread throughout American educational history is the contribution of New England, particularly the idea of public schools and the Puritan concept of morality or "character." This last is an essential ingredient in the contributions of Webster and McGuffey and is not absent in the development of the public high school and the denominational college. Puritan justice or logic likewise permeates many of the legalities which have set the pattern of American education.

Previously considered were the Dartmouth College and Kalamazoo cases. Other court decisions having a significance in the development of the American single track system have involved such items as equal rights, the place of religious instruction in the schools, the existence of parochial education, state and federal relations, and others.

---

[39] A valuable discussion of early American texts, including many insightful quotations and illustrations, is found in John Nietz, *Old Textbooks* (Pittsburgh: University of Pittsburgh Press, 1960).

[40] Of the host of materials available perhaps the most readable, concise, and basically factual is Alice McGuffey Ruggles, *The Story of the McGuffeys* (New York: American Book Company, 1950).

Under the impetus of economic and social conditions the American South for almost sixty years pursued a policy in public education of providing "separate but equal" facilities for members of the white and "colored" races. This position was indeed legalized by the United States Supreme Court decision in the case of Plessy vs. Ferguson in 1896. It was of course no secret, however, that generally speaking the opportunities for a complete education were much less in evidence for Negroes than whites. In 1954 the Supreme Court attempted to reverse the earlier judgment and, in Brown vs. the Board of Education, held that "separate but equal" was "inherently unequal" and not sufficient for the realization of unprejudiced justice to the children of all the people regardless of color or race, saying that "Segregation of white and colored children in public schools has a detrimental effect. . . . A sense of inferiority affects the motivation of the child to learn . . . to retard the educational and mental development of Negro children and to deprive them of some of the benefits they would receive in a racially integrated school system."[41] As an incentive to the implementation of this changed philosophy Southern States were granted a reasonable time in which to comply although a "practical flexibility" was suggested in their compliance with "all deliberate speed."

Fundamental also to the basic concept of American government, although this certainly is not a Puritan doctrine, is the separation of church and state. For those perturbed by the apparent conflict between the dictates of conscience and the secular nature of the school the question of religious instruction in the public schools became an issue. It generally was not expected that public school teachers would be appropriate for sectarian religious instruction, even if this were constitutional; but there were those who felt that students, having been excused from regular school routine, could meet with a counselor of their own faith and thus, with no offense to others or no detriment to the operation of the school program, receive the requisite religious teaching.

While such a procedure seemed quite innocuous to some, to others it created the fear of compartmentalizing the student body as well as subjecting those of no faith at all to an unfair (and unconstitutional) penalization. The latter view was eventually taken in the United States Supreme Court decision in McCollum vs. Champaign, Illinois (1949). Although obviously the Court's finding related only to the protection of individuals under the Constitution, it was roundly criticized as "godless." Devices for allowing release time for religious instruction off campus gained some favor; in fact the court did not seem to hold against this. Yet the principle of separation of church and state, for a long time unique in governmental arrange-

---

[41] "Brown vs. Board of Education," 374 *U.S.* 483 (1954).

ment, is still maintained and certainly is a basic premise that accompanies, and should accompany, universal, free, and public (secular) education.

Consistent with this protection guaranteed by the Constitution is its corollary, the protection of the rights of religious minorities or others who desire to operate schools, at their own expense, within their own private or parochial framework. Thus, when in 1922, the State of Oregon enacted a compulsory education law providing that all children between the ages of eight and sixteen should attend public schools, the high court (in Pierce vs. Society of Sisters of Jesus and Mary) struck the legislation down, saying: "The child is not the mere creature of the State; those who nurture him and direct his destiny have the right, coupled with the high duty, to recognize and prepare him for additional obligations."

The preceding judgments might well stand as the first premise in the American Government's relation to its citizens; although education is not the prerogative of the federal organ, yet it undertakes to protect those on whom a State might in haste or misguided self-interest attempt an enforced conformity. The American attitude toward education, whether lay or in its highest tribunal, avoids statism or, in the case of a single child or group of children, the abrogation of minority rights in the interests of the total society.

Our Pluralistic Culture

Usually, but not invariably, recognized in the American public school is the fact that the American nation, as it has grown to be constituted, represents a pluralistic culture. It is obvious to any thoughtful person that the contributions which have made American culture the mosaic that enhances its originality have come not from Puritan or Cavalier alone, or from even the several leading nations of Western Europe. Here one must, like Thomas Wolfe, offer an extensive catalog of names. The English and the Dutch, Yugoslavs and Czechoslovaks, Spaniards and Italians, the Danish and the Swedish, Estonians and Hungarians, Poles and Ukrainians, the Russians and the Celts, the American Indian and the Eskimo — there is almost no end to the list. When the origins are recognized through folk-day or festival, these builders of our culture are the stars. As Jew undertakes to understand Gentile, the Frenchman the German, the Greek the Turk — this is the origin of true American democracy and here is the best example of democracy in action. (European backgrounds and aspects of these contributions are found in Chapter VII.)

One instance serves to implement this idea: the so-called "Springfield (Massachusetts) Plan." One phase of this plan dealt with identifying the "Contributions of Nationalities to Springfield" — "the Scandinavians organized a singing society in Springfield, the Canadians were a thrifty, industrious

455

people who merged easily with the population of Springfield, many of our fine streets and highways are the product of Italian skill, this description of a Polish wedding was given to me by my mother, all this is a true story of what I experienced when I was living in Worms, Germany, this incident was told me by my mother, who was born in Greece," etc.

During December, Springfield teaches some of its choicest lessons. There comes the Chanukah, the Festival of Lights, in which "Peace on Earth, Good Will to Men" is the guiding motif. The Christmas week program features the "Nativity" and both Jewish and Christian children join in singing the ancient Jewish hymns and the familiar Christmas carols. Three children wrote a letter about their program. The names signed indicated that they probably were Protestant, Roman Catholic, and Jewish. "Our Christmas celebration was very unusual because it was a presentation of a Jewish holiday and the Christmas story. We called it a Festival of Lights because the symbol of the Jewish holiday is the candle and the Christmas symbol is the star. . ."[42]

It would be unrealistic to allege that "one community's total war against prejudice" is a universal tendency in American education. However, the events described harmonize with the deeper convictions and inner realizations of the components of the American way of life. And the American public school has served as a major medium and catalyst for the extension of these ideals. Thus, the schools reflect and embody the spirit which gave rise to the American experiment and which continues to motivate the American dream. If this dream is fading, if principles of democracy can no longer motivate, then the educational system of the United States is failing, and the vaunted effectiveness and originality of the continuing "single track" has become a mere shibboleth.

Expansion of the High School

In the late nineteenth century, as if to provide an agency for the more perfect union, the spread of the American high school proceeded at an increased tempo. Under the impetus of the industrialization following the Civil War and the influence of the Kalamazoo and other such court decisions, public secondary education quickly outpaced the propriety offerings of the academy and the old-line private school. Cubberley reports a total of 321 public high schools by 1860; Dexter lists 116 in cities of 25,000 population by 1880, the greatest increase being in the North Atlantic and the

---

[42] For a complete description of these events see Clarence I. Chatto and Alice L. Halligan, *The Story of the Springfield Plan* (New York: Barnes and Noble, Inc., 1945), pp. 44-47, 60-61.

North Central states.[43] It must be noted that these figures should not be counted as accurate upper limits; problems of definition, reporting, and the existence of high school programs in "elementary" schools complicate the picture enormously. Nevertheless, it can be safely estimated that by 1870 there were approximately 70,000 students in attendance at American high schools; in 1900 the number had reached the astonishing total of 700,000, indicating clearly the desire and demand for this species of free, public, secondary education for the children of all of the people although under fifteen percent of eligible youth attended. Coupled with the rapid growth in numbers were the problems of staff, housing, finance, and administration, to say nothing of curriculum and standards.

Lottich, in a study of curricular offerings, traces the evolution of the high school from an organ interested chiefly in classical and traditional subjects (although this does not necessarily mean college preparatory emphasis) through a period in which scientific or exploratory offerings made their appearance, to the introduction of a more "practical" or vocational curriculum around the turn of the century. The chronological sequence for these developments places the traditional period from 1850 to 1885; the scientific from 1885 to 1910; and the vocational from 1910 through the period of the reorganization of the high school, about 1930.[44] That these dates cannot be accepted as absolute goes without saying; the correlation of these items with the tremendous expansion of the American high school, however, does lend much support to their general validity. Only with developments in these latter periods, however, does the high school finally become a common school for the great bulk of American youth.

The American School Superintendency

The pioneering of American administrative control, especially in cities, was another indigenous development, though not unique now to our educational systems. The key here is the creation of a professional group of managers connected only coincidentally with the business of instruction in the schools.

---

[43] From a *Report of the Commissioner of Education,* 1901, 2; 1912. As quoted in Dexter: *A History of Education in the United States* (New York: Macmillan, 1904), pp. 170-171.

[44] See Kenneth V. Lottich, "Curricular Offerings in the Early High School in Ohio," *The High School Journal,* March-April, 1948, pp. 61-68, for a survey of these developments, including the new subjects and the date of their incidence in this most eastern Midwest State. Some observers believe the period of the vocational high school to be another particularly American achievement — one in which the drive for a practical education was effectively combined for many students with a good general education.

The American school superintendency, in many ways quite analogous to the position of executive or manager in the industrial world, occupies a unique status in the organization and functioning of the school. In its origin it is perhaps one of the most American educational developments, probably arising from the creation of the district system in Massachusetts and Connecticut as described previously.

When this (likewise strictly American) method for handling the needs and wishes of the smallest local school entity was legalized in 1766 in Connecticut and 1789 in Massachusetts, the stage was set for the creation of the new office of superintendent. With the fragmentation of towns due to the advent of industrialism and the increasing population it sometimes happened that as many as ten or twenty such local divisions might exist within a given corporation limit. In order to produce a certain desired uniformity for the town or city it was deemed advisable to place an official over the districts in order to preserve the identity as well as the common purposes of the town or municipality. Such an administrative official, although an educator, did not teach or even associate with the pupils of the various schools as did the headmaster or principal, positions imported from the continental schools. The superintendent's business was that of regularizing and coordinating the activities of those placed under his jurisdiction as well as serving as director of the financial phase of the operation and personnel manager. He acted, of course, in liaison with the Board of Education or the school trustees and was responsible to them.

In the United States, New Orleans is said to have provided such a city "director" as early as 1826. Buffalo, New York, is generally credited with the first city superintendent as of 1837. The date of the establishment of the state school superintendency has been credited to New York (1812) and the first County Superintendent was authorized in Delaware (1829). Louisville and Lexington in Kentucky provided superintendents in 1838 as did Providence, Rhode Island. St. Louis followed suit in 1839 and Springfield, Massachusetts in 1840. The movement spread rapidly, indeed, as remarked above, paralleling its march with that of the great post-Civil War era of new industrial growth.

That this imitation of "big business" (actual or fortuitous) has caused some question, there is no doubt. While on the one hand there is common agreement on the necessity of providing for an efficient and well-articulated method of regularization, on the other there has been some feeling that the schools have become big business themselves and that the contact, at least theoretically valuable, between the parts of the organization are being largely lost. The hierarchical nature of the superintendency with its growing staff and special structure is in some situations viewed as not a real part of the actual educational effort. Conflicts of loyalty are suggested and the superintendent's relationship to the Board of Education does not seem to parallel relationships among the teachers, students, and lesser officials.

Roald F. Campbell, in a recent analysis of this problem of the ambivalent position of the American school superintendency, suggests that the analogy between administration in business and the schools may be somewhat forced. "To the extent that personal needs-disposition are affected by professional values, superior intelligence, and by articulate communication, it seems clear that administration in schools must pay greater attention to personal needs-disposition than administrators in factories; conversely, school administrators can rely less on standard operating procedure than administrators in industrial plants can." This is a welcome diagnosis to those who fear the depersonalization of some forms of business management in the area of public education. Campbell remarks further that this judgment should apply in the case of the schools because they are public rather than private and because an operation "highly visible at all times must be sensitive to its many publics."[45]

Imitation of the Single Ladder

In consequence of the unique developments in American education and because obviously enough the American pattern in public education seemed to correlate well with the image of the democratic society, nations formerly supercilious or aloof, and with education systems anciently derived, grew inclined to investigate the American phenomenon. Starting about the time of the First World War, the American school system was increasingly scrutinized by the newer nations of the world as well as by the directorates of other great powers. Possibly because of American success, militarily and industrially, in providing many of the circumstances of victory and doubtless because of the growing international American hegemony, American educational philosophy and structure gained a respectful attention almost everywhere.

Indeed, what has been called the "Single Ladder" or one-track system in the United States began to find, at least superficially, adherents in many European countries and throughout the world. To illustrate: the French *école unique*, the German *Einheitschule* idea, the Italian *scuola unica*, and one of the underlying purposes in the British reform under the Education Act of 1944 led patently in this direction.[46]

---

[45] Roald F. Campbell, "Educational Administration: Is It Unique?", *The School Review*, Winter, 1959, pp. 461-468, especially pages 465-466; for a complete summary of the rise of school administration as a profession see: Theodore L. Reller, *The Development of the City Superintendent of Schools in the United States* (Philadelphia: the author, 1935), especially pp. 8ff and Table, p. 81.

[46] Arthur H. Moehlman and Joseph S. Roucek, Eds., *Comparative Education* (New York: Dryden, 1952), *passim*.

Again, America's victorious role in the Second World War was credited to a large degree as a result of her system of universal education. Moreover, the protestations of the Atlantic Charter and the well-publicized principles of the lately-born United Nations served to implement these desires and demands for a newer democratic orientation in education throughout the Western World and, to a great and remarkable concurrence, in parts of the Eastern World as well as in rising Africa.

In addition to notions concerning the twelve-year one-track system, American progressivism, too, had come in for scrutiny, and, to a certain extent, emulation. This, for example, had already been true for a time in the Soviet Union; now British, French, and Italian cabinets felt disposed to concede, along with lip service to the single track, that new methods, and even purposes, were the proper concomitants to the demand for broadening the base of popular education. That these methods usually were committed to some sort of pragmatic philosophy which lent itself to mass education was understood. That many Americans and American schools were still highly traditional was, if this was apprehended at all, glossed over.

Among the new patterns expressing the organization as well as the method was that of the comprehensive and "modern" schools in Britain. These new popular secondary schools together with the private and state grammar and technical schools now comprise the alternate routes in the education of adolescents.

In the United States the liberal forces at work in educational theory and practice have herein been designated as Jacksonian for the realistic, vocational, pragmatic, and popular form at its most extreme stage, and Jeffersonian for the more traditional, idealistic, and academic tendency. That pragmatic methods applied especially in the Jacksonian phase (as indeed they did in the British modern school) is a natural conclusion: they had to.

Nor did classically-oriented schools eschew progressivism completely; frequently one found the pragmatic method grafted upon a fairly rigid association of subject matter. Yet circumstances varied, and those conservatives who used the progressive method hardly ever spoke of it as such. In fact, in many quarters, progressivism, for some occult reason, was equivalent to a four-letter word, not to be thought or spoken in polite society.

The Progressive Movement

In order to fathom the development of progressive education one has to consider the history of the late nineteenth century in the United States. It should be crystal clear to every reader that the school not only reflects the culture of which it is a part; indeed, sociologically speaking, to a large extent it *is* the culture. Thus, the unique development of the American States, their independence, their early radical political philosophy, the existence of the frontier, the impact of the industrial revolution and the Puritan ideals and the rugged individualism to which they gave assent — all of these must be considered in their educational perspectives and vice versa.

Progressivism in the schools was but part of that great social and intellectual uplift in American life and culture known historically as The Progressive Movement. Its roots led to the quest for relief of the sweating slum that accompanied the rise of the city, the aspirations of the Knights of Labor, the farmer and his crushing load of indebtedness, municipal politics with its rings and bosses, and even the public common school of the late nineteen hundreds with its lockstep or, as some preferred, "goosestep."

Specifically, American progressive education may be traced to the humanitarianism of Colonel Francis W. Parker, the scientific reevaluation of educational content and method by Doctor Joseph Mayer Rice, and the pragmatic philosophizing of Charles S. Peirce, William James, and John Dewey.[47] Ultimately characterized as essentially a child-centered approach, the liberals also stood for a considerable revolution in school subject matter. While not commonly thought of as a progressive statement, the famous Seven Cardinal Principles, formulated by the Commission on the Reorganization of Secondary Education in 1918, reflected the content concerns of educational reformers.

If John Dewey is one of the better known of the educational prophets of this era, it may be mainly because of his industry as a writer or perhaps because of his personal success in riding the crest of the wave bringing in the new social gospel. Almost invariably Dewey's works bore sociological titles and it may not be at all rash to believe that he carried a few genes of the new doctrine through his contact with George Herbert Mead, the most prominent of the phoenix-raised University of Chicago's interpreters of the new psychology and sociology of learning.[48] In spite of his germinal contributions, as all other educational leaders, Dewey stood on the shoulders of the great thinkers who came before him. A careful study of his works reveals indebtedness to Comenius, Bacon, Locke, Rousseau, Hegel, Herbart,

---

[47] A recent interpretation that attempts to draw together the forces in American education that affected the appearance of this movement is found in Charles J. Brauner, "Education as a Subject of Study" (Doctor's thesis, Stanford University, 1960); an interesting explanation by one of the leaders of the movement is found in Carleton Washburne, *What Is Progressive Education?* (New York: John Day, 1952); the most complete work is Lawrence A. Cremin, *The Transformation of the School* (New York: Knopf, 1961).

[48] Dewey mentions Mead quite affectionately in the Introduction to his *The School and Society* (Chicago: University of Chicago Press, 1899), p. 13.

461

Pestalozzi, Froebel, Spencer, James, Wundt, and Darwin, among others.[49]

Dewey's phrase-making, coupled with constant reference to society and the individual, both intrigued and infuriated. For example, in describing the new methodology relating to child interest, he wrote: "Here individualism and socialism are one. Only by being true to the full growth of the individuals who make it up can society be true to itself."[50] Many of the progressives were tied to accompanying radical developments that marked the first third of the twentieth century. Once the fears of the depression years were capped by the outbreak of the Second World War, progressivism was doomed. However, the movement's pedagogical virility, in spite of the unfortunate misapplications of its views, had permanently permeated all of American education.

Dewey summarized the progressive contributions as including distinct elements of an educational theory that stood for:

> . . . respect for individual capacities, interests and experience; enough external freedom and informality at least to enable teachers to become acquainted with children as they really are; respect for self-initiated and self-conducted learning; respect for activity as the stimulus and centre of learning; and perhaps above all, belief in social contact, communication, and cooperation upon a normal human plane as all-enveloping medium.[51]

To the progressive educational changes there should be added the reorganization of secondary education with junior and senior divisions, the six-three-three plan, and the advent of the public junior college for grades thirteen and fourteen. Viewed in relationship to the "American Dream" as conceptualized by historian James Truslow Adams of New England and to the social and technological revolution of the first half of the twentieth century, it appears that these developments were inevitable. The American people could not but have been powerfully affected by the currents of change and pragmatism which they now saw all about them. That developments in education too would accrue should have been a foregone conclusion. But institutional change is excruciatingly slow and the shadow of the past in education looms particularly large.

Quite probably what Europe saw so vividly was the most evident phase of American nationalism and pragmatism. It squared, however, with the tradition of the American dream and with the glamour of single-track Jack-

---

[49] The definitive work on Dewey's contributions is still to be written; concerned readers would do well to read, in addition to *The School and Society,* his other key works such as *Democracy in Education, The Child and the Curriculum,* and his late restatement of principle, *Experience and Education.*

[50] Dewey, *op. cit.,* pp. 19-20.

[51] John Dewey, "Progressive Education and a Science of Education," *Progressive Education,* July-September, 1928, p. 198.

sonianism in education. Popular method, especially at elementary levels, also seemed to veer almost 180°, except in the citadels of New England privatism where the model of the high British "public school" discouraged innovation. Interestingly, what Europe actually saw in American schools was the first grand scale application of an amalgam of, up to this time, largely isolated ideals and practices that had been promulgated by European educators down through the centuries. The return of some of these conceptions to Europe is traced in the next chapter.

The most intriguing educational experiment of the period between the wars was the Eight-Year Study. Sponsored by the Progressive Education Association, it was the most significant and large-scale attempt of its kind carried out in American education. It aimed to evaluate scientifically the premises of progressive education in the American high school. It thereby brought the new ideology to the attention of the American public at a different level. That the picture presented was a glowing one was not unexpected. Nevertheless, following World War II, something of the bloom was extracted from this flower as certain more critical analyses of the results of the study were given wide publicity. Specifically the results seemed to show: (1) a small statistical advantage in the academic and personal success ratings of the graduates of the progressive schools; (2) that there is no discoverable relationship between the pattern of subjects taken in high school and success in college; and (3) competence in the use of the English language in reading, speaking, and writing is an absolute essential for the satisfactory handling of college and university work (alleging that the traditional high school English seldom developed this ability to a degree commensurate to the predicting of college success).[52]

Before passing from the pre-World War II period in American education, another example of the means by which political ideology entered into educational theory should be offered. We use the words of another commentator in order to capture the flavor of his special emphasis: "During the early 1930's an attempt was made to counter the heavily individualistic emphasis of Progressivism. This was the build-a-new-social-order movement, championed by George S. Counts and that doughty protagonist until then of the 'child-centered school,' Harold Rugg. Wishing to deal with 'man thinking' as well as 'man feeling,' Rugg proposed the derivation of the curriculum by analyzing the ideas of 'frontier thinkers' and in this way he arrived at the content included in his hotly controversial series of social-studies textbooks for the intermediate grades. Support for these ideas was to be elicited through

---

[52] Wilfred M. Aikin, *The Story of the Eight-Year Study* (New York: Harper and Brothers, 1942).

463

classroom instruction and then all march toward the brave new world."[53] That this movement failed is not surprising. Many of the ideas involved are, however, a partial basis for another *ism,* "Reconstructionism," presently being pushed by Theodore Brameld of Boston University.[54]

Controversy and Problems

In the United States following the Second World War an organized opposition to Jacksonianism arose. A whole order of pamphleteers flourished and venerable Harvard herself produced a lengthy study indicating the need for a stemming of the tide of popularism.[55] Among those who sought to indict the popular school, especially the American high school which had in many instances become a comprehensive school, were Albert S. Lynd, Mortimer Smith, John Keats, and Arthur F. Bestor. Lynd's "Quackery in the Public Schools" in a leading periodical, drew a great deal of attention; Smith wrote "And Madly Teach"; John Keats deplored "Schools Without Scholars."

Arthur Bestor, a Professor of History at the University of Illinois, attacked in three directions: [56] (1) what he chose to call the "certification racket" by which he alleged that teachers, because of an unholy alliance between state departments of education and schools of education, were compelled to continue re-training after graduation in order to make work for education professors (who in fact had little to teach anyhow); (2) he viewed with alarm the growing hierarchy of public school officials, and especially the awarding to them of the Doctor of Education degree which he considered non-academic and a plagiarism on the Ph.D.; and (3) he cited instances of slovenly teaching and subject matter dilution.

In the last instance he probably was on the firmest ground. Yet the complaint is a chronic one and represents a questionable tactic by which to condemn any system, educational or political. The point which he and others of his persuasion failed to grasp is that the real wonder resides in the fact that the American schools are as good as they are. A quick thought in the direction of the increased population in the high school (7 million by 1950)

---

[53] Ernest E. Bayles, "The Present Status of Educational Theory in the United States," *School and Society,* January 17, 1959, pp. 5-8.

[54] See his *Patterns of Educational Philosophy* (Yonkers, N.Y.: World Book Company, 1950); and *Cultural Foundations of Education — An Inter-Disciplinary Exploration* (New York: Harper and Brothers, 1957).

[55] *General Education in a Free Society* (Cambridge: Harvard University Press — published by the President and Fellows of Harvard College, 1948).

[56] See his *Educational Wastelands* (Champaign: University of Illinois Press, 1953); and *The Restoration of Learning* (New York: Alfred A. Knopf, 1955).

464

and on the much higher percentage remaining in school should suffice to demonstrate this. In a new age, with the great bulk of American youth in secondary schools, many of the criticisms of the malcontents, well-meaning as they may have been, were at best unrealistic.

The American people were, and are, tremendously proud of their public school system. Single-track or not (reference here is made to the existence of a considerable number of private, academy-type schools in the East, South, and Far West), virtually each high school beyond hamlet-size came to offer a variety of curricula with four majors or interrelated courses being a frequent organization, although usually only one or two of these lead to college preparation. Europe did not err when educational statesmen in Britain, the Netherlands, or France saw something more than quantity and change in the American fetish of universal education. Professor Kenneth Richmond, of the University of Glasgow, finds a uniqueness here that is unparalleled; it is likewise one very proper answer to the ideological dilemma. Concluding a worthwhile study Richmond uses the following happy phrases: "The Jacksonian lion and the Jeffersonian lamb will lie down together and although their natures are opposed, agree, for strange as it seems, the two are of one flesh." [57]

Lest Europeans judge, however, that there no longer are any problems in American education, several supplementary issues in addition to the ideological conflict between the traditionalists and the moderns may be mentioned.[58]

The first deals with class stratification in the United States and consequently in American schools, especially the public high school. The literature here is too voluminous to record although the works of William Lloyd Warner, August B. Hollingshead, Celia Burns Stendler, Robert Havighurst, Allison Davis, and James West (pseudonym) may be consulted with profit. The consensus appears to be that stratification is indeed a reality but the existence of classes need not necessarily nullify the American dream. Mobility still is present and is an important factor in American life; the teacher can act as guide and referee.

A specific and dangerous corollary to stratification, however, exists, for example, in the problem of grading in "culture-fair" terms. The same can be said of certain aspects of grouping and of the testing program, especially intelligence testing. This dilemma presents a real challenge in the search for brainpower although one of the protagonists of revision, Allison Davis,

---

[57] W. Kenneth Richmond, *Education in the U.S.A., a Comparative Study* (New York: The Philosophical Library, 1956), p. 223.

[58] These issues are treated extensively in various texts on the social foundations of education; see, for example, Myles W. Rodehaver, William B. Axtell, and Richard E. Gross, *The Sociology of the School* (New York: T. Y. Crowell Company, 1957), chapter 14.

465

claims to have developed testing programs containing unbiased material. His contention, as stated in one of his many titles, is "Poor People Have Brains Too." Essentially this problem is a part of the growing difficulty of maintaing extended educational opportunities at higher levels for all.

Another sinister development, if current interpretation can be trusted and present conditions judged typical, is a certain retreat in many quarters from the basic values of the American way of life mentioned in connection with the old Puritanism and the development of the early Jacksonian spirit. That this shift concerns largely the young adult population rather more than those of school age is not particularly significant although the existence of the germ cannot safely be ignored. And it is being alleged that, as a creeping malady, the infection has penetrated the entire organism of society.

First brought to attention several years ago by David Riesman, the thesis, simply put, is this: Three stages of value formation may be detected within the past thousand or so years of Western culture. Number one, tradition-centered, lasted until around 1500; it was replaced by an "inner-directed" urge based on individualism and inner-compulsion (this appears to have been the wellspring of the Calvinistic ethos and Puritanism); however, within recent years (and this perhaps was incubated at the depression period between the great wars, and further nurtured in the early post-1945 era at the latest) a third orientation has gained ground; this is "other-directedness," seemingly a reversal of the value formation index of the Protestant ethic and of the builders of the American republic.[59]

That this philosophy, which undoubtedly owed a debt of some kind to one or another of the various existential movements, found favor with younger adults and some adolescents is admitted. The presence of the "world-owes-me-a-living" type, the Beatnik, the "Blackboard Jungle-ite," and the general feeling of "living it up" prevalent in certain sectors of American life in the 1960's seems to corroborate the diagnosis.

That these manifestations are absent to such a degree in other parts of the world is not argued; that "other-direction" is conditioning American schools is not admitted, although a recent vogue for so-called "life-adjustment" curricula may have been a directional step.[60] The dangerous effect of these develop-

---

[59] See David Riesman, Nathan Glazer, and Reuel Denney, *The Lonely Crowd, A Study of the Changing American Character* (New Haven: Yale University Press, 1950); Riesman and Glazer, *Faces in the Crowd* (New Haven: Yale University Press, 1952); Riesman, *Constraint and Variety in American Education* (Lincoln: University of Nebraska Press, 1956).

[60] See *Life Adjustment Education for Every Youth*, Bulletin No. 22, Federal Security Agency, Office of Education (Washington, D.C., 1951). The plan for this shift in curriculum requirements from the more formal program to certain immediate needs was based on the "Prosser Resolution" of May, 1947 which described the usual high school curriculum as "unrelated to the everyday needs of life of 60 per cent of youth."

ments upon teen-agers' values are revealed strikingly by the national poll of adolescents published by the Purdue Youth Survey,[61] the results are of great concern to educators. Even if other-direction is only a tendency, it is a circumstance that, especially as an ingredient in educational philosophy, cannot be passed over lightly. That there are positive connotations within an assumption of other-directedness is not doubted by Riesman. He reports (and this applies in full force to secondary education): "These young people are unwilling to sacrifice the fullness of life for one aspect of life, and this represents in many ways a sounder set of values than that of an earlier generation who would often sacrifice over much for money, respectability, or distinction." [62] That agreement either in respect to secondary education or life would be forthcoming from another generation (or indeed from all members of the generation under consideration) may be questioned; however, our purpose here is to present other-direction as a problem, not necessarily to provide a comprehensive answer.

Unfortunately the dilemmas cited — (1) the continuing conflict between Jeffersonianism and Jacksonians; (2) the problem posed by social stratification in American life; (3) the difficulties in grouping, testing, and measurement in maintaining individualized programs for all; (4) togetherness; and (5) the attrition of the "Puritan" values and the legendary aspect of American national consciousness — are not recognized in every quarter. But a penetrating British observer considers the more positive aspect of American life and education and intimates that we may be over-concerned:

> The United States takes education very seriously, almost too seriously, tacitly assuming that all that is worth learning can be taught — and needs to be taught. . . . The "little red schoolhouse" of American tradition was a New England institution. . . . Next in importance to this tradition was the Jeffersonian [Jacksonian is meant] belief in education as a political necessity for a republican government. Only a literate population could discuss and decide, and so live in freedom.[63]

It is in this motif that we summarize the unique features of the great American educational experiment which indeed has, by the close of the

---

[61] H. H. Remmers and D. H. Radler, *The American Teen-Ager* (Indianapolis: Bobbs-Merrill Co., 1957).

[62] Riesman, *Constraint and Variety*, Part 3, "Secondary Education and Counter Cyclical Policy," pp. 107-154; this quotation, pp. 151-152. Other-direction, especially as applied to the social and business world in the United States, has provided a spate of contemporary novels which deal with these phenomena in realistic fashion. The reader is directed to the offerings of John P. Marquand, William H. Whyte, Sloan Wilson, and others for this contemporary view.

[63] D. W. Brogan, *USA, An Outline of the Country, Its People and Institutions* (second edition) (London: Oxford University Press, 1947), pp. 83-84.

sixth decade of the twentieth century, so transcended the original goals and expectations that it no longer can be considered an attempt or trial. American education lies in the sphere of achievement, an accomplishment increasingly imitated in many respects.

What Is Unique in American Education

First and formost in any catalog of American uniqueness in educational invention or practice stands the fact that the United States is a nation of religious diversity. Although state churches were commonplace until the Revolution and in New England until well after this event, there has never been a national church; nor can there ever be, by strict constitutional prohibition. Yet in any nation, any tribe for that matter, a certain homogeneity or commonality is essential, a fellowship of kindred minds, if that nation or group is to survive. Thus, the free, secular American public school became an agency for that purpose, a special "religion" as it were and one to which the vast majority of American citizens give their allegiance.

This institutionalized concept is charged with the performance of many duties, far more than the average citizen and taxpayer suspects. It has served as the agency for Americanization; in a nation of cultural diversity as well as religious diversity and yet one in which a plurality of cultures is conceded, the school builds a common denominator. If its education in Americanism has sometimes seemed close to chauvinism, perhaps this can be excused on the grounds of "religious" enthusiasm. It is accepted as the school's duty to instill the American myth, which has been for almost 200 years more reality than legend, a pragmatic, practical call to action, having as its ultimate goal the creation of a political innovation, democratic as well as republican, a true "new order for the ages."

The duty of the public school likewise requires the inculcation of the Puritan virtues, simple facts of the American economic enterprise, and the development, when this is possible, of sound bodies and an awareness of the principles of sanitation and personal cleanliness. That the school is also concerned with scholastic values is not debated. But the school has a broad responsibility in the United States. There is no other agency for the accomplishment of those requisites controlled in many States through the institutions of royalty, religion, homogeneous family tradition, or an enforced regimentation under the direction of government ministries or the secret police.

Secondly, the socio-civic as well as the scholastic portion of American education must be contrived within a situation marked by extreme decentralization, an American development of long standing. Indeed, while history and the evolution of the educational pattern clearly reveal the origins of decentralization and can as clearly reveal its limitations, the attachment of

468

the American people is here. The Constitution grants each State primacy in this area; state constitutions, legislation, and precedent grant the major educational rights to the community. That there are democratic values here is sure; that this peculiar manifestation of backwoods Americanism offers its extreme difficulties — financial as well as administrative — cannot be denied. Yet the American people would have it this way; nor do they go unprotected by the courts. The most amazing bugaboo in American education is an outright fear of the higher degrees of centralization and, above all, of the Federal Government itself!

The development of the "single-track" is a third unique and indigenous evolution. The first step towards the system of free, public education from the kindergarten through the university was taken in the Old Deluder Satan Act. Other steps in this evolution were: the eclectic (although private) academy, the demands of nationalists as Webster, the blueprint of Jefferson, the needs of Boston's rising middle class, and ultimately the creation of the state university. Here one should not seek a series of chronologically-related events. The single-track is an idea. It had developed, at least in the North, by approximately the middle of the last century. The Kalamazoo decision did not produce it. The situation produced (and styled) Justice Cooley's argument.

A fourth development in the tableau of American educational evolutionism is, as detailed somewhat earlier, the inception of a new professional class: the scientific and managerial application of the principles of general business practice to the operation of the American school system, the professional superintendency of schools. That dangers exist in an extreme impersonalization of this function has been admitted; nevertheless, distinctive differences exist between educational administration and the management of a tire factory; that the new profession must be conscious of these culturally innate differences is likewise one of the basic tenets of American educational ideology. Furthermore, American administration is justified by the long history of native adaptation to the new climate and environment of the United States.

Fifthly, the American public high school stands as the most conspicuous fruit of the single ladder. Given the framework in which American education was obliged to develop, the high school represents its most significant accomplishment. That the American school is widely copied abroad (and this in the face of traditions of classical and humanist education of centuries' standing) indicates its peculiar attraction. In retrospect it is clear that the high school represented the most natural and fundamental of all our educational institutions. That it evolved historically appears to be true; yet such a development certainly was governed by the genetics of the American culture.

That each educational agency has its own sociology is well understood; yet in the case of the American high school such a seamless web is woven that the casual visitor is hardly aware of its complexity. It is, of course, the American society in miniature and at an adolescent stage. Nevertheless, it taps adult society as well, and there is no clear line of demarcation. Its meanings exist on both levels simultaneously. For the youth, its learning is an achievement; for the parent, he himself is fulfilled, sometimes far beyond his own opportunity. For the adolescent its ritual is a pleasant diversion and frequently meaningful; for the adult, the rites of passage are being consecrated. Athletic contests to the young are pleasurable sublimations; for the adult they are occasions for community or even state glorification.

It is safe to say that the high school in one way or another, consciously or not, touches the lives of each member of the community. It is an institution which sometimes has created the community and it frequently (although naturally in the smaller settings) becomes the community obsession. The building itself, in a sense, is one of the temples of the municipality. It is "the People's College." In the contemporary era, because of the peculiar nature of the American educational system and its unique role in society, the high school in many ways outranks and has superseded the elementary school as the common school of the community.

Moreover, the American high school has frequently assumed a role that is traditionally that of the college or university. Athletics may dominate the scene (although the distribution of scholarships and various other honors in which the community shares the success of the fortunate recipient is becoming more and more another focus for the perpetuation of the conventional image) and in many instances there is no clear line that divides the school from the community. Neither is there the common demarcation between town and gown that so frequently jeopardizes the collegiate contribution. In a word, the development of allegiance and loyalty, produced under the auspices of the American high school, is but a reflection of its basic purpose which actually transcends the relatively minor issues of method and sometimes even of curriculum that may stir the community.

This school imitates the college in numerous instances, yet there is always a linkage between the school and the community which many colleges never achieve. Consider this parallel (an actual instance from the halls of a medium-sized, mid-continent American high school): let us visit the Trophy Room, not a figure of speech but an actual apartment in the school plant. There are the usual glass cases filled with the cups, plaques, banners, and other emblems of victory but, in this little mahogany paneled room there is also a shrine decorated by a marble slab bearing the following inscription:

IN MEMORY OF

———————

1902-1953
For his untiring
efforts in fostering
Scholastic Achievement,
in
Athletic Activities
among the Youth of this
Community, and for his
keen interest in Civic Affairs.

Athletics, scholastic achievement, and civic affairs here represent a triad of interest for both town and gown. A similar effect frequently is achieved through the various oral media contrived for the exaltation of school and community: chants, yells, and especially the school song or "hymn" (as it sometimes is rendered). Consider a few examples:

> In the land of milk and honey,
>   In the central West;
> Stands a school of many virtues,
>   Ranked among the best. . . .
> (Melody: "Far Above Cayuga's Waters")

or
> Cheer for Croydon, Cheer for Croydon,
> Glory to her name;
> Honor, love, and true devotion
> Ever be her fame. . . .
> (An abridgement of "On Wisconsin")

and
> All hail to dear old Newtonville,
>   Hail to the navy and the gold;
> Thy sons and daughters love thee well;
>   Their love and faith will ne'er grow cold. . . .
> (Tune: *University of Louisville National*)

The music for such emotion-arousing fare (and this is said with no thought of denigration) is not the usual, simple, grammar-school, limpid cadence; it must be sonorous, heroic, and majestic, with a stately rhythm and plenty of crashing cymbals. That this music is an effective agency for the creation of a school and community spirit cannot be doubted. It is a peculiar by-product of the American high school.

A third element used in the creation of the high school image is the observance of the school's initiating or culminating activities, the religio-

471

cultural holidays, and the great state and national days of remembrance. While it may be said that these events are not now as symbolic as they formerly were, there still is ample opportunity for the establishment of the school's place — and thereby the role of each individual affected by this institution — in the public life — be it local, state, or national. Indeed upon such occasions it appears that there is little separation of these levels in the general quest for integration.

Much that has been said concerning the unique American secondary school applies to the American college and university, our sixth contribution. Because of its selected clientele, the college represents a third plateau, the final attempt to create the rudiments at least of allegiance to the American civilization and way of life. Here one must rather carefully distinguish between college and university although, in practice, this quite frequently is not done in America. Because of historical circumstances the term university is loosely used in the United States. We are, of course, here concerned primarily with the undergraduate level of "higher education" and do not deal with professional schools, graduate study, or the finer degree of integration or specialization that marks the true university. Nevertheless, the numerous and highly varied college programs that mark many universities and the practical orientation of research and service programs wherein "the boundaries of the university are the boundaries of the state" (a slogan of the University of Wisconsin) characterize the American university as a most important creation of and for democratic progress. Although still in its formative stage, being little more than half a century old, the American junior or community college represents another stage in the evolution of education in the United States that serves a growing multiple function in American society. As discussed in Chapter IX, it serves needs as diverse as those demanded of an evening high school, a technical institute, a pre-engineering or liberal arts college, and an adult education center. Hundreds of thousands are now being served by an extended or continuing public education not available fifty years ago. Thus, another link is being forged in the chain of education indigenous to the American scene and the term "people's college," historically a reference to the high school, promises to take on a new meaning in the generation ahead.[64]

It should be noted that the American college is a unique, nationalistic, and indigenous creation. Historically derived, it may be claimed more a cultural institution than an educational agency per se — although such a statement may produce some shuddering. From its foundation (and here one may conveniently omit the earliest examples which were pure importations)

---

[64] See James E. Thornton, *The Community Junior College* (New York: John Wiley and Sons, 1960).

it was designed to achieve and accomplish ends primarily religious, national, or civilizing. It likewise became one of the earliest status-producing agencies — the college degree — then as now representing entrance into a special circle (regardless of the real worth or standing of the institution). One writer has spoken of the American college as primarily a center "for rating, dating, and mating," and indeed there is some point here.

National Education Association

THE AMERICAN COLLEGE IS A UNIQUE
AND INDIGENOUS CREATION.

Nevertheless, the role of the American college has been considerable. When it is considered that the American national civilization has been produced in a little less than two centuries and that at the same time the

473

advance to the Pacific and to territories beyond the Western shores was consummated; that the political, social, and economic development proceeded until the United States not only survived the holocaust of one of the most terrible Civil Wars but emerged as one of the chief architects of victory in two successive world struggles; when these and many others items are reflected upon, it is clear that the American culture has developed agencies susceptible to the achievement of its ends. Such an integration and even nationalization of culture could have been accomplished only through America's special organs of education, the free public common school, the indigenous high school, the peculiarly American college, and the unique State Universities.

Observers from abroad have sometimes equated college in the United States with their own higher reaches of secondary education and this may be not at all a false judgment when scholastic values alone are involved. However, it has been the purpose of this chapter to show wherein and how the American situation differs from those made the basis for this comparison. Our organs, created indigenously and above all appropriate to our culture and institutions, need bow to none in the efficiency by which they have produced their basic objectives — goals, which in the absence of a state religion or system of ministerial indoctrination, including the agencies of thought control, have been placed squarely, prudently, and successfully in the hands of primary and secondary education.

Bibliography

Adler, Mortimer J. and Milton Mayer, *The Revolution in Education.* Chicago: University of Chicago Press, 1958.

Aikin, Wilfred M., *The Story of the Eight-Year Study.* New York: Harper and Brothers, 1942.

Brogan, D. W., *USA, An Outline of the Country, Its People and Institutions.* Second Edition. London: Oxford University Press, 1947.

Brown, Elmer E., *The Making of Our Middle Schools.* New York: Longmans, Green, 1926.

Butler, Vera M., *Education as Revealed by New England Newspapers Prior to 1850.* Philadelphia: Temple University, 1935.

Butts, R. Freeman and Lawrence A. Cremin, *A History of Education in American Culture.* New York: Henry Holt and Company, 1953.

Conant, James B., *The American High School Today.* New York: McGraw-Hill, 1959.

Cremin, Lawrence A., *The Transformation of the School.* New York: Knopf, 1961.

474

Cubberley, Ellwood P., *Public Education in the United States*. Boston: Houghton Mifflin Company, 1934.

Curti, Merle, *The Social Ideas of American Educators*. New York: Scribner's, 1935.

Davis, Allison, *Social-Class Influences Upon Learning*. Inglis Lecture, 1948. Cambridge: Harvard University Press, 1948.

Dewey, John, *The School and Society*. Chicago: University of Chicago Press, 1899.

General Education in a Free Society. Cambridge: Harvard University Press for the President and Fellows of Harvard College, 1945.

Good, H. G., *A History of American Education*. New York: The Macmillan Company, 1956.

Hollingshead, August B., *Elmtown's Youth, The Impact of Social Classes on Adolescents*. New York: John Wiley and Sons, 1949.

Holmes, Pauline, *A Tercentenary History of the Boston Public Latin School, 1635-1935*. Cambridge: Harvard University Press, 1935.

Hutchins, Robert M., *The Higher Learning in America*. New Haven: Yale University Press, 1936.

Mason, Robert E., *Educational Ideals in American Society*. Boston: Allyn and Bacon, Inc., 1960.

Mead, Margaret, *The School in American Culture*, Inglis Lecture, 1950. Cambridge: Harvard University Press, 1951.

Meyer, Adolphe E., *An Educational History of the American People*. New York: McGraw-Hill, 1957.

Mulhern, James, *A History of Secondary Education in Pennsylvania*. Philadelphia: The author, 1933.

Noble, Stuart C., *A History of American Education*. New York: Rinehart and Co., 1954.

Reisner, Edward H., *The Evolution of the Common School*. New York: The Macmillan Co., 1930.

Reller, Theodore L., *The Development of the City Superintendency of Schools in the United States*. Philadelphia: The author, 1935.

Rice, Joseph M., *The Public-School System of the United States*. New York: The Century Co., 1893.

Richmond, W. Kenneth, *Education in the U.S.A., A Comparative Study*. New York: The Philosophical Library, 1956.

Riesman, David, Nathan Glazer, Reuel Denney, *The Lonely Crowd*. New Haven: Yale University Press, 1950.

Tewksbury, Donald G., *The Founding of American Colleges and Universities Before the Civil War*. New York: Teachers College, Columbia University, 1932.

Thornton, James E., *The Community Junior College*. New York: John Wiley and Sons, 1960.

Ulich, Robert, *A History of Educational Thought*. New York: American Book Co., 1945.

Warner, W. Lloyd, Robert Havighurst, and Martin B. Loeb, *Who Shall Be Educated?* New York: Harper, 1944.

Wertenbaker, Thomas J., *The Puritan Oligarchy*. New York: Charles Scribner's Sons, 1947.

Wesley, Edgar B., *N.E.A.: The First Hundred Years*. New York: Harper and Brothers, 1957.

Woodring, Paul, *A Fourth of a Nation*. New York: McGraw-Hill, 1957.

****

CHAPTER XII

AMERICA AND EDUCATION
IN THE WORLD

Those who have read and pondered what has come before in this book now know that there is little that is "new" in the realm of education. It is seldom that one can say assuredly "This happened here for the first time." Certainly, in the development of American education, it is evident that we are indebted for a rich and varied heritage including some beginnings lost in a past stretching back several thousand years. Do we dare state, as we attempted in the previous chapter, "This is what is indigenous in American education"? Are we brash to attempt to identify and declare "Here are America's educational contributions to the world"? We think not.

Increased numbers of scholars are involved in comparative educational studies. The literature at home and abroad gives us some clear guidance. More educational travelers exchange experiences and opinions each year. As a result we are obtaining increasingly objective and well-rounded views on educational systems, their major characteristics, and key differences. Great variations continue to exist between educational systems and these reflect rightly the considerable differences that are found between cultures. Are there unique aspects of American civilization that can be identified in understanding our educational programs?

477

Recently the historian Arthur M. Schlesinger identified the ten major American contributions to civilization, as follows: [1]

1. The right of revolution
2. The principle of federalism
3. The consent of the governed
4. The status of women
5. The melting pot
6. Freedom of worship
7. The public school
8. Voluntary giving
9. Technology
10. Evolutionary progress

If the above are actually unique and fundamental, they would have to be mirrored in the educational system of a free society as our schools exist to maintain and extend the principles and the values we hold. Actually, American public schools have and do reflect these contributions in the educational aims, programs, organization, approaches, support, and in their very structure and facilities. Each of these basic societal factors, therefore, has its educational implications. Tied to the *right of revolution* are many aspects of our citizenship education programs and our teaching of history; the *principle of federalism* relates to balancing federal and state concerns over education; the *consent of the governed* is tied to ideals of teacher freedom, the democratic school, and local controls; the *status of women* is reflected in our outstanding provisions for their education; the *melting pot* relates to a one-track system for all; *freedom of worship* to separate schools for those who desire them; the *public school* speaks for itself; *voluntary giving* to the unparalleled private and foundational support of American education; *technology* to our rich variety of teaching aids; and the belief in *evolutionary progress* to the spirit and drive that has characterized American education. Of course, a number of additional identifying aspects of American education could be related to each of these ten contributions.

If we accept these ten concepts as fundamentals in the American experience, what if the schools reflect certain of them but weakly or ineffectively? We need then to carefully reexamine the historic concept, the school program as it relates to it, and study our total culture as well, to ascertain why perhaps society apparently turns from the historic value or how the factor has actually been altered. It is believed, however, that the bulk of these forces are evident in our educational system and, indeed, that they serve as sources of strength, providing certain of the unique characteristics of schooling in the United States. As we discuss American educational contributions to the

---

[1] Arthur M. Schlesinger, "Our Ten Contributions to Civilization," *The Atlantic,* March, 1959, pp. 65-69.

world, the reader should keep these historic factors in mind as well as the educational aspects of each. These should be our top exports to the cultural interchange that sweeps the earth.

Prime Factors in the Introduction of America to the World

Old hands at travel who return from Europe these days warn the seeming few who have not squeezed in a foreign sojourn, vacation or assignment, "Go soon; why it is *so* different from just five years ago!" or "In my three trips since 1945 it is disgustingly more American each time!" What the G.I.'s initiated and the growing economic and communications boom has fostered, the now more than four million annual United States overseas travelers promise soon to help conclude — the near final Americanization of much of the world!

Americans undoubtedly take too much credit for the transformation and modernization of the world. Other countries are changing because many aspects of the power saltation and the continuing international revolution that stems from it, though often prodded or supported by examples and funds from the United States, are largely the result of native aspirations. After all, most peoples are today determined to live well, have become more inclined to adjust their ways to the realities of life in the mid-twentieth century, and desire to move more rapidly toward the satisfactory realization of their own personal and national goals.

Institutional change has always been slow but the tempo of existence is so accelerated, with the accompanying geometric progression of technological inventions, that less-favored countries are now skipping entire stages of development that others have experienced in their own industrial and urban revolutions. Why, for example, should a nation undergo a railroad age when it is possible to jump directly into an air age? Why develop power sources with coal-burning machines when radical new sources from atomic to solar energy are available? Even in Western Europe, among our more fortunate friends, where centuries of tradition are still erased quite slowly, the new rings out the old, whether it is the prospect of a political confederation or the ending of the elite-oriented, multi-track educational systems that have persisted. Americans need to remember that it has been difficult, even for young, untraditional, frontier-oriented America to recognize and admit the striking alterations that have rocked its own institutions; that we did not and would not admit that our nation had reached the time of discretion and responsibility that actually arrived over 40 years ago. If we could not recognize the end of our own "age of innocence," [2] what can we expect of

---

[2] Henry F. May, *The End of American Innocence* (New York: Knopf, 1960).

cultures whose comparative history still leaves the United States in the womb?

From supermarkets and sleek skyscrapers to drive-ins and barbeques, even old England changes materially.[3] New styles, launderettes, and American products are but superficial reminders of even more fundamental changes in that nation and others. Most of Europe adjusts to the technology of the new "Atlantic" culture. Because educational institutions are among the less responsive to social change, the alterations in these countries are less rapidly reflected in the schools. However, anyone familiar with world trends in education will emphatically agree that the flux of social, economic, and political life is assuredly being mirrored in increasing educational ferment and concerns.

To recount or attempt to bring a full understanding of the present impact of American leadership, life, institutions, and tools abroad is beyond the scope of this work. Even an attempt to present a fairly complete view of international educational accretions rising from American sources would take a series of volumes. We can, however, attempt to select examples out of the past, primarily the last few decades, that will illustrate the magnitude of the American contribution — a bestowal that now promises, in a relatively short period of time, to equal, perhaps to overshadow, those worthwhile inheritances from which we have benefited in our three hundred years of becoming.

Previous chapters have reviewed the cross-currents in educational exchange that marked earlier American history. Since colonial days Americans going abroad and the Europeans visiting or settling here, along with an exchange of literature, brought a sharing and an amalgam of ideas and practices; but the interchange was largely a one-way transaction with European institutions and experiences being grafted into and adapted to new world conditions. Individual Americans certainly made but limited impressions upon established European educational beliefs and policies and our own domestic challenges were so overwhelming that we had little time or concern for educating the world.

Religious Forces

In our own hinterlands and in the territories we acquired during the last half of the nineteenth century there were souls to be saved and minds and bodies to be properly shaped. From beginnings at home, with native Indians and later with freed Negro slaves, the missionaries moved out in number and soon crossed our boundaries; small groups were working abroad in the early 1800's. With these carriers of God's message went America's

---

[3] Anthony Sampson, "Are the English Being Americanized?" *Saturday Review,* Oct. 17, 1959, pp. 14-15, 63.

first substantial educational legacy to other peoples — an endowment that still looms far greater than many realize and on an increasing basis.

By 1900 there were almost 10,000 Catholic and Protestant missionaries from the United States working in the field; this had increased to approximately 30,000 by 1958. North American Protestant missions are reported to have spent almost $150,000,000 in 1957, with 78 percent of this being used overseas. Catholic missions spent over $45,000,000 on technical assistance type programs alone in 1954. Along with the churches have come thousands of schools from the primary and elementary levels to technical institutes, teacher-training institutions, and colleges. Always accompanying the evangelical work are the inevitable benefits of literacy, hygiene education, social welfare, and like educational efforts.[4] The fact that there may be over fifty different American religious groups sponsoring missions in a single country may be confusing to the potential convert; nevertheless, the total mission expenditures in local assistance throughout the world are second only to United States Government assistance funds expended abroad and are directly and indirectly responsible for multiple educational benefactions in these countries.[5]

American Teachers and Schools Abroad

American mentors have been going overseas for many years, not only as tourists and students, but as tutors and as instructors in schools established on foreign soil. The most famous was probably Anna Leonowens who was employed by the King of Siam during Lincoln's administration. With the growth of American establishments and colonies abroad, American and English language schools have grown considerably in number. It is true that the overseas schools have served mainly English-speaking families, but these have tended to become bi- or multi-lingual. On an increasing basis they have come to draw pupils from the locality, as well as a collection of children from families of diplomatic, military, and business representatives of other nations who also live in the community. Such overseas schools, started as early as 1854 in India, were usually private ventures and many were tied to various church bodies. There were also a few military dependent schools abroad that were authorized by Congress as early as 1821.

---

[4] Most of the facts on missionary contributions presented above were drawn from Harlan Cleveland and others, *The Overseas Americans* (New York: McGraw-Hill Book Co., 1960), Chapter 6.

[5] House Committee on Government Operations, *Government Programs in International Education,* House Report No. 2712, 85th Cong., 2d sess., 1959 (Washington, D.C.: Government Printing Office, 1959), p. 47.

481

After World War I, starting in Switzerland, some of the private schools that had not affiliated with religious groups moved toward the idea of a truly international school and ultimately over 50 joined together in the International Schools Foundation. Located at strategic centers throughout the world, these schools are examples of one of the most important community-centered forces for drawing alien peoples together and in spreading American ideas and culture.[6] The American Council on Education's Inter-American Schools Service, which receives subsidies from the United States Department of State, reports over 270 such American-sponsored schools in Latin America with an enrollment of over 100,000.[7] The greatest development of this type of multi-lingual schools has occurred in that region of the world. U. S. educational influence abroad has probably been greater in Latin America than in any other large area of the globe.

The earliest large-scale movement of bona fide teachers from the United States to service abroad came with the determination of American authorities to teach English to 7 million Filipinos following the Spanish-American War and the Philippine Insurrection. The teachers in this group were called "Thomasites" because a large group of 600 men and women arrived at Manila on the U. S. Army Transport *Thomas* in 1901; it is estimated that over 4,000 American teachers served in Philippine school systems during the subsequent 40 years.[8] The investment of this group can only be estimated but in addition to helping produce some 40,000 English-speaking native teachers during this time, they made a personal contribution in their close contacts with the Filipino people that is one of the main reasons that the Philippines are so democratic, advanced, and westernized today. For example, by 1940 about 27 percent of the population could speak English, with the great bulk who could not, being children under school age or adults over forty. The broad contribution of the original Thomasites and those who followed included developing public schools, coeducation, cultural progress, and the building of morale, as well as the factors previously cited.[9]

---

[6] See their descriptive brochure *International Schools Around the World: New Links in Understanding and Cooperation* (Washington, D.C. and Geneva, Switzerland: The International Schools Foundation and the International Schools Association, 1957). A recent observer, however, feels that most such overseas schools are "wrapped in cellophane" with too much insulation between groups in the schools as well as between school and local culture; see F. L. Redefer, "The Care and Feeding of Provincials," *Saturday Review,* Oct. 22, 1960, pp. 13-14, 39-40.

[7] *International Schools Around the World, op. cit.,* p. 29.

[8] Harold Van Winkle, "Building Better Than They Knew," *Phi Delta Kappan,* June, 1955, p. 331.

[9] These contributions have been documented by Amparo Lardizabal, "Pioneer American Teachers and Philippine Education" (Doctor's thesis, Stanford University, 1956).

American teachers and leadership in the Philippines also contributed to the community school idea that has done so much to improve local living conditions, to modernize the Islands, and to unify its diverse cultures. Just as the community school in rural America has combined basic education, agricultural education, technological education, and hygiene instruction for adults as well as youth, such community schools in underdeveloped nations have served rich purpose. They act as centers of community life wherein American knowledge and ideals are fused with local traditions and purposes into effective instruments for economic and social improvement.[10]

The Influence of American Business

The force of American business in spreading American culture is, of course, inestimable. From the American movies seen by millions throughout the world to the growing American business communities stretching from Venezuela to India and from Saudi Arabia to Japan, with all of their products and personal contacts, the impact has been tremendous. The total American business population abroad at this date, including wives and children, is well over 100,000. In the mines, plantations, dam building projects, retail stores, service agencies, and the like, administered by American concerns, local native employees often run twenty to each American involved, and through these people the spread of American knowledge and principles is materially forwarded.

We have come a long way from the early Yankee Clippers and the China trade of the colonial era. It is estimated that direct United States investment abroad rose from $.6 billion in 1897 to $7.9 billion in 1943; striking increases since World War II brought these investments to $25.3 billion in 1957, with increasing amounts going to poorer and underdeveloped portions of the world.[11] These funds reflect primarily the indirect educational influences of business that far outrank direct contributions, as is true in the United States and is outlined in Chapter IX. However, businesses make a number of direct contributions through programs that include schools set up in their foreign holdings and the training programs for foreign nationals who are brought to the United States for technical instruction. We should also not overlook contributions of American corporations to foreign educational enter-

---

[10] See the following sources: Barnardino Vitaliano, *The Philippine Community School* (Quezon City, Philippines: Phoenix Press, Inc., 1958); *The Community School of the Philippines* (Manila: Department of Education, Bureau of Public Schools, 1952); and J. C. Laya, *New Schools for the Little Democracies* (Manila: Inang Wika Publishing Co., 1952).

[11] Cleveland, *op. cit.,* pp. 101-102.

prises and to American and international educational foundations, a major recent corporate activity.

As with our diplomatic corps, American private business personnel overseas have not always blended well with the local culture but just as our government is taking strides to improve the preparation of our foreign service and military personnel for overseas assignments, so has American business responded to the growing recognition of its responsibility for enabling its employees to project a favorable American image in other countries. Along with the American product they represent and other factors, such as American books and magazines, personnel in our overseas businesses are now more satisfactorily reaching some of the warm personal relationships established by many of our missionaries and our students who have lived in foreign homes. In their working and social relationships, these employees are serving to extend American educational views.

Role of Private Organizations and Foundations

Foundations and private organizations have been significant forces in spreading American education in a variety of ways. Again, this is nothing new. Often such organizations have cooperated with or have been tied to religious facilities in setting up schools and such cooperative ventures were responsible for the establishment of schools in Bulgaria as early as the 1860's. Some of these programs and agencies have also been associated with American universities. For example, a few years ago Turkey requested a specialist in education from the University of Florida to survey rural schools and recommend improvements. One of the recommendations that resulted from the visit was that 25 Turkish leaders in rural education be sent for a year of study to American universities. Through the joint financial efforts of the Turkish Government and the Ford and Rockefeller Foundations, the recommendation was carried out. In total, private organizations and foundations have made one of the most effective contributions in extending American influence for they have tended to concentrate on programs that bring students and scholars to America or that support such Americans in their work abroad and that, thereby, tend to strengthen institutional impact.

In 1918 the American Council on Education was founded to coordinate the services that educational organizations and institutions could contribute to the problems facing the nation at the end of World War I. The interests of the Council grew to include a significant number of international activities — for example: work of the Canada-United States Committee on Education established to improve mutual knowledge and understanding in each country through exchanges of speakers and by means of studies; services to the government through the Washington International Center to provide orientation to American life for foreign nationals coming to the United States; its commissions such as the Commission on Education and International Affairs which have published valuable materials; and Council activities carried on in connection with UNESCO. Perhaps most valuable has been its Inter-American Schools Service for which it recruits teachers, provides information, advises on school programs, and gives small grants-in-aid to American-sponsored schools in Latin America.

In 1919 with financial assistance from the Carnegie Foundation for International Peace, the non-profit Institute of International Education was founded with headquarters in New York. The Institute appealed to American universities for scholarships for foreign students and began to solicit the same from other countries for American students. By 1939 the Institute had exchanged over 5,000 students on scholarships. It also extended its work to promote the exchange of professors and technicians and, in total, by 1955 had helped exchange 20,000 students and scholars. In addition to its exchange program, it has published a number of valuable brochures.[12]

Following an international educational meeting sponsored by the NEA in 1922, the World Federation of Educational Associations was established. International meetings have been sponsored throughout the world by this organization on a biennial basis and it was later reorganized as the World Confederation of Organizations of the Teaching Profession. In addition to the conferences, its bulletins and journals serve as valuable evidence of the leadership of professional organizations in the United States in extending American influences, as well as in bringing valuable foreign viewpoints and practices to the attention of educators in the United States.

As early as 1923 Teachers College, Columbia University had about 250 graduate students from all parts of the world. In that year Teachers College obtained a grant of 1 million dollars from the International Education Board founded by John D. Rockefeller, Jr. With this founding grant, Teachers College established its International Institute and down through the years the Institute has made significant contributions not only towards aiding the increasing number of foreign students enrolled but in sponsoring and conducting studies in comparative education and in publishing the results of these investigations. Other universities have also established similar agencies.

It is estimated that the number of official and private organizations in Europe alone, indirectly or directly promoting cultural and student exchanges, totaled over 700 by 1929. In that same year there were over 115 similar

---

[12] See its helpful series of news bulletins; interested readers are also referred to Committee on Educational Interchange Policy, *Twenty Years of United States Government Programs in Cultural Relations* (New York: The Committee, Institute of International Education, 1959) as an example of one of the helpful publications developed by one of the committees the Institute has established.

groups in the United States promoting the exchange of students and teachers.[13] In the years between the two World Wars a number of the European countries and many American and Asian countries signed cultural agreements establishing provisions for the interchange of scholars and students. During this same period the number of American foundations active in the field of international education increased; included were several foundations established prior to the first World War but which had not carried on extensive work in this area until this time. The Carnegie Corporation of New York began to expend large sums of money for educational purposes in the British Commonwealth; the American-Scandinavian Foundation provided for the exchange of fellows between the United States and Scandinavian countries; the Commonwealth Fund contributed to the Institute of International Education and began to support the Salzburg Seminar in American Studies; the Rockefeller Foundation made significant grants for research and fellowships in many countries; and the W. K. Kellogg Foundation provided aid to educational institutions in Latin America, Canada, and Europe.

Although founded in 1936 the Ford Foundation did not embark upon its huge national and international program for the advancement of education until 1950. It has provided rich opportunities for American scholars to study in all parts of the world and has developed strong educational assistance programs in several foreign countries. In Burma it has promoted agricultural and industrial teacher training and rural adult education; in Indonesia it has supported similar programs and an English-training program for teachers; in India it has assisted in improving secondary education as well as rural education; and in addition to these activities, in Pakistan it has also provided funds to develop home economics education.[14]

Many other nongovernmental organizations interested in international education have developed since World War II such as the American-Korean Foundation, the Asia Foundation, the United States Book Exchange, and commissions and committees of other societies. Many small but significant programs have been carried on for a number of years, typical of which is the World University Service. This organization is the direct descendant of a relief organization set up in Europe after World War I and it now has 41 national committees, being an international organization rather than an

---

[13] *Government Programs in International Education, op. cit.,* p. 32; many of the foregoing and subsequent items of information on international education activities are drawn from this helpful booklet. See also *Time,* June 30, 1961 for a list of 56 private agencies that spent almost $300 million abroad in the previous year on relief, rehabilitation, educational, and health projects.

[14] Paul R. Hanna and Sidney C. High, Jr., "Education in the Far East," *Phi Delta Kappan,* June, 1956, p. 436; this issue of the journal contains a valuable series of studies and articles devoted to recent trends in world education.

American one. Major support, however, comes from cooperating American institutions and citizens. This organization has carried on such varied projects as restoring the libraries in Tokyo after the 1923 earthquake; aiding Chinese students, victims of Japanese aggression in the 1930's; and, in more recent years, building student dormitories in Greece and Korea; establishing a student TB sanitarium in Tokyo, bringing 1,000 Hungarian student refugees to study in American colleges, and providing a scholarship fund for Algerian refugees. The private and nongovernmental institutions and agencies identified in the above paragraphs have promoted American educational ideals and democratic ways in a variety of approaches from the revision of textbooks to include material conducive to international understanding to the establishment of institutions for advanced international study. Their total impact cannot be measured and has never been adequately assessed.

In spite of recent emphases, the roots of American interest in and support of foreign educational activities go back well over a century in many parts of the world. We have selected the Near East to detail somewhat the manner in which the United States has provided educational leadership in a given foreign area. This story, with variations, could be duplicated in a number of other places; it serves to underscore the extent to which rather direct American influences, particularly at higher educational levels, have made their substantial but unostentatious mark.

The United States and Near Eastern Education

In 1820 two American missionaries reached Beirut. They were the first of thousands who, during the next 139 years, built an educational system from kindergartens to medical and engineering schools that spread throughout the Middle East. The total amount of money Americans contributed over this period approaches 400 million dollars.[15]

The missionaries soon learned to transcend their original objectives and also to emphasize social and educational activities. Learning Arabic, some of them became the first modern scholars of the Middle East and contributed to the foundation of a whole scientific vocabulary in Arabic. The Mission Press (first established at Malta) was moved to Beirut in 1834. The translation of the Bible into Arabic by Eli Smith and Cornelius Van Dyck appeared in 1864. Their, then newly designed, print is universally known as American Arabic.

Between 1834 and 1960, American philanthropists, just in Syria and Lebanon, had founded more than 33 primary and secondary schools. At one

---

[15] Dalton Potter, "American Education in the Middle East," *Arab World*, August, 1959, pp. 11-12.

time in the nineteenth century there were 123 schools, mostly elementary schools and vocational institutions. The oldest school was founded in 1830 by the wife of one of the first philanthropists, Mrs. Eli Smith. It has grown steadily (with only two interruptions) to be the American School for Girls in Beirut with 500 students. Many of the girls go on to the Beirut Women's College, founded in 1924 and one of the newest American schools in the Middle East.

In addition in the Near Eastern area a host of varied missions and related church schools were founded through the years by expanding American missionary groups. American Jews have also contributed in no small manner to the revitalization and life in Israel. A number of other private schools have been founded in the region since 1903 that conduct elementary and/or secondary instruction, such as the influential American Community School at Beirut, Cairo American College at Cairo, the American Community School at Athens, and others.

In spite of losses in American prestige in the Near East in recent years, the reputation of American educational contributions to that area remains high. We have particular reference here to six American colleges and one University in that region, one of these having operated over ninety years. These schools are Robert College, The American College for Girls, The American University of Beirut, International College, Athens College, and Anatolia College. In addition, the work and existence of Damascus College, which suspended its operation in 1957, and The American College of Sofia, which was a member of the Near East College Association from its founding in 1925 until it was closed by the Communist regime in Bulgaria, should also be noted.

Although all these institutions are non-sectarian and have never been church affiliated, all except Athens College had their roots in missionary work. Until World War I, each of the institutions functioned independently, administering its affairs in the Middle East and in the United States. Because it was difficult for the colleges to keep in touch with their business affairs and boards of trustees in the United States, the Near East College Association was formed in 1919 to coordinate the administrative work in America. Today, each institution is still independent, with its own administration and board of trustees. The Association exists solely to give administrative help to its member colleges; it does not determine policy or academic procedure for them. It recruits teachers, acts as purchasing agent, aids in raising funds for endowment, scholarships and operations, and acts as a connecting link between the boards of trustees and their institutions.

These institutions represent the largest private American educational effort outside the United States; together they serve almost 10,000 students of many nationalities. In Greece, Turkey, Syria, and Lebanon and other countries of the Near East these schools are universally respected and trusted and their leadership in this area is a vital factor in promoting democratic ideals.[16]

Only two of these schools carry their educational program through to graduate degrees: Robert College in Istanbul and the American University of Beirut. The latter is by far the larger, with a medical and an engineering school plus a number of professional fields including teaching. Robert College is older and includes a preparatory school as well as an engineering school. In addition, the American University at Cairo, founded in 1919, was the first modern university in Egypt and pioneered in professional journalism and teacher training. Its school of oriental studies has become a recognized center for scholarship in Islamic studies.

Robert College. It was a boatload of fragrant bread crossing the Bosphorus during the Crimean War that aroused the curiosity of Christopher Robert, merchant of New York, and led to the founding of the college! The baker of the bread was Cyrus Hamlin, American educator and missionary, and he was taking the bread to the patients in the British hospital at Scutari. From the meeting of these two men came the plans for an American College in Turkey that resulted in the opening of Robert College in 1863 under a charter from the State of New York.[17]

Since then, the College has survived cholera epidemics, an earthquake, two world wars, the rule of the Sultans, and economic crises, and witnessed the birth of the Republic. Enrollment has increased from 72 in 1871 to more than 1,000 students; its present plant includes a superb campus of 118 acres with 25 buildings, playing fields, and homes for faculty members. Thousands of graduates have played a vital part in the development of modern Turkey.

The faculty of more than 100 includes Americans and Europeans but nearly half are Turkish citizens. The student body is largely Turkish by citizenship and mother tongue, and many of the Turkish students are the sons of former Robert College graduates. The College has three main divisions: the Academy (boys at the age of 12 for a five-year preparatory course), the School of Arts and Sciences with a four-year course leading to a B.A. or B.S.; and the Engineering Schools, granting degrees in mechanical, electrical, and civil engineering. The entire program is integrated with the Turkish national educational program and operates under the general regulations of the Turkish Ministry of Education while the Board of Trustees is in the United States.

---

[16] *Near East College Association* (New York: The Association, n.d.).

[17] Cyrus Hamlin, *My Life and Times* (Boston: Pilgrim Press, 1924), gives the background of mission work and records of the early years of the College.

489

The American College for Girls. This well-known institution began as a high school in 1871 with three students and one American teacher. The original school at Scutari on the Asiatic side of the Bosphorus was a pioneer venture in every sense of the word.[18] Even in the United States, higher education for women was still in its early stages and in Turkey women were especially isolated from public and social life. In spite of every obstacle, the school started growing and its influence spread to neighboring countries. In 1890, under a charter from the Commonwealth of Massachusetts it became the first college for women in the Middle East. In 1914 the College was moved to its present site on the European shore of the Bosphorus. In 1932, the American College for Girls and Robert College were united under one administration with a joint President but with separate Boards of Trustees. Today, admission is eagerly sought and the College is able to accept only about one-third of the qualified applicants; 95 percent of its more than 650 students are Turkish. But until the founding of the Republic and the granting of full franchise to women, Turkish graduates were few. Halide Edip Adivar, probably the most widely known Turkish woman writer, is one of the graduates. Of some 1,500 graduates, a number are doctors, lawyers, legislators, and university professors. Women from neighboring countries who graduated from this institution have founded private schools and hospitals and have achieved prominence in social welfare.

The American University of Beirut. In 1871, Daniel Bliss, first President of the Syrian Protestant College, laid the cornerstone of the first building on what is now the campus of the American University at Beirut. Just as other American schools grew out of mission work in many countries, the University had its start in missionary activities in Syria and Lebanon. By 1920, the college which had started in a small house with 16 students had progressed beyond its name and attained university standards.[19]

Today the University campus rises above the sea in the new Beirut residential area, looking over the red roofs of the old city and the famous St. George's Bay to the towering Lebanon Range. The campus stretches to the Mediterranean and the more than 50 buildings which serve the various schools are surrounded with famous gardens.

---

[18] Mary Mills Patrick, *Under Five Sultans* (New York: Century, 1929) is the memoirs of the President of the College from the time it attained college status in 1890 until 1924.

[19] Stephen B. L. Penrose, *That They May Have Life, The Story of the American University of Beirut, 1866-1941* (New York: The Trustees of the American University of Beirut, 1941) is the history of the American University at Beirut by the late President of the University from 1948 until 1954. Bayard Dodge, *The American University of Beirut* (Beirut: The University, 1958) brings the history up to date and is written by the President of the University from 1923 to 1948.

The Institution is one of the largest and most modern educational centers in the Middle East with an average attendance of 3,000 students and over 300 yearly graduates. Teaching is in English and degrees are granted in Arts and Sciences, Medicine, Pharmacy, Public Health, Nursing, Engineering, and Agriculture. A graduate program leads to the Master's degree. The University is chartered by the State of New York and degrees are registered with the Board of Regents of the University of the State of New York. It has been coeducational since 1924. Its 12,000 graduates have created an ever-widening sphere of influence through their leadership in varied fields. The students represent over 50 different nationalities and 20 religious groups; they come from varying social and economic backgrounds. It is claimed that the University's great achievement is that its campus is a practicing and successful little United Nations. Many of the student activities are involved in social service dealing with problems of illiteracy, sanitation, and delinquency in the city and the surrounding area. But the University allows no political or sectarian societies on the campus.

While over half of the faculty personnel are Lebanese and Syrians (many graduates of the American University), 19 other nationalities are represented; American faculty members usually number about 125. The influence of the faculty extends to surrounding areas. It serves as a very important medium in spreading information, good will, and an exchange of ideas between officials and educators in the Mediterranean area. Especially valuable here have been the Near Eastern seminars sponsored by the University. Faculty members serve on many Lebanese committees and are regularly called upon by nearby governments and institutions for advice and assistance as their services are valued far beyond the borders of the campus. They have made special contributions through "leading their students in agricultural experiments, village clinics, slum clearance, in public health education, and nursing. They welcome to the University their colleagues from all parts of the Near East, sharing their knowedge and facilities and encouraging a cooperative approach to the needs of the area."[20]

International College. Originally this institution was a vocational high school in Izmir, Turkey, under the auspices of the American Board of Commissioners for Foreign Missions. By 1903, when it received its charter from the Commonwealth of Massachusetts, it had become a recognized institution, due in large measure to the resourceful leadership of its founder, the Reverend Alexander MacLachlan.

The year 1936 was a turning point in the history of the college. At this time it moved to its present site on the campus of the American University of Beirut and combined its program with the former primary and secondary

---

[20] Near East College Association, *op. cit.*, p. 11.

programs of that institution. Today more than 1,500 students attend the three schools of International College. The Elementary Schools take students through the sixth grade and classes are taught in Arabic. The Preparatory Section gives a five-year course preparing students for the Lebanese Government examinations and entrance to the freshman class of the university; emphasis is placed on proficiency in English. In the Section Secondaire (French Section) classes are taught in French and Arabic and students are prepared for the Lebanese and French baccalaureate and for entrance to the sophomore class of the University. The students represent 38 nations and 18 religious groups. "The fundamental aim of International College is to develop in the Middle East, citizens and leaders of high moral character. The college believes that the Middle East can find its own brand of democracy in combining the experience of America and the West with the rich heritage of the Eastern Mediterranean."[21]

The Athens College. The Athens College was founded in 1925 by a group of leading Greeks who were convinced that America could make a definite contribution to Greek curriculum with American principles and methods while retaining the best of the Greek educational system. A number of prominent Americans helped found the school. The college is administered by two governing bodies, with a Greek board in Athens and an American board in the United States, and positions of administrative responsibility are shared by Greeks and Americans.

The College slowly increased its first enrollment of 15 Greek boys and initial endowment of $10,000. In 1930 Homer Davis, a school teacher from the United States, became President. Under him the school tenaciously survived the Metaxas dictatorship (1936-41), successive occupations by Italians, Germans, and British, and a difficult post-war rebuilding. In 1959 President Davis retired, being succeeded by Charles Rice who had been director of admissions and head of the English department at Choate School in Connecticut.

The school that Rice took over had 1,050 students, a healthy endowment of $1.6 million (contributed mostly by Greek-Americans and by some Athenian Greeks), and a spectacular 35-acre mountain campus. Teaching is carried on in Greek and English and follows roughly the curriculum prescribed by the nation's Ministry of Education, including instruction in the Greek Orthodox religion. Athens College has two divisions with a lower and upper school offering a rigorous 10-year program. However, the school is not an austere learning factory as is true of so many Greek academies and the approaches used do much to lead students to independent thought. In April, 1959, the Ford Foundation announced that it would give Athens Col-

---

[21] *Ibid.,* p. 13.

lege $250,000 for scholarships and for salaries of Americans who teach at the Academy. Many of the alumni have given "distinguished service to both the Greek Government and American agencies in Greece. The prestige of the College is so great that it can accept only 25 percent of the qualified candidates."[22] A number of graduates have come to the United States to complete their higher education.

Anatolia College. The College was originally established in Merzifon, Turkey and taught Greeks and Armenians in that area since 1886. Its charter as a college was granted by the Commonwealth of Massachusetts in 1894.[23] In 1924 the College moved to Salonika at the invitation of Premier Venizelos during the Greco-Turkish exchange of populations. In 1933 the Girls' Mission School in Salonika was placed under its direction. During World War II the plant was requisitioned but classes were continued by the Greek staff members in whatever quarters could be found. Since the War, Americans and Greeks restored the institution and provided new buildings and equipment. The co-educational programs now enroll 700.

The course of study is largely prescribed by Greek law and the special contribution of American education is made by combining the best traditions of the classical Greek academy with the techniques of modern teaching. Students enter after completion of six years of Greek elementary schools and the seven-year course of the College equals the completion of an American junior college education. The study of English is an important part of the curriculum and begins in the first year of instruction. Special stress is placed upon the teaching of the classics; the program approximates a liberal arts course. American methods, especially laboratory methods, characterize the teaching of science and home economics in the technical program.

One of the most popular college projects has been the "adoption" of the villages of Levkohori by the alumni and Mavrorachi by the students. Both of these bodies have cooperated in rehabilitating these destroyed villages and in developing a program of training and recreation. This worthy and practical experience in public service, a part of every student's training, has had a far-reaching result beyond the sense of responsibility for others engendered in the individual student.

American influences at the eastern end of the Mediterranean have been multiple, as evidenced in the above examples and many others could be documented. American relationships with Turkey have been particularly

---

[22] *Ibid.,* p. 17.

[23] George E. White, *Adventuring With Anatolia College* (Grinnell, Iowa: Herald-Register Publishing Co., 1940) presents a history covering the background of the mission work of the institution and its removal to Greece at the time of the exchange of populations with Turkey; the author was associated with the College from 1890 until 1933, and served as its President for many years.

close and, for example, the dean of education at U.C.L.A. recently served the Turkish Ministry of Education by conducting a survey of schools throughout the country and then heading a team of Turkish educators who made a world trip to visit outstanding school systems. Even women are reaching prominence in education as evidenced by the current activities of Dr. Kalliniki D. Antonakaki who serves as adviser to the Greek Minister of Education. She received her doctorate from Teachers College, Columbia University, and developed a successful progressive school in Greece that enabled a group of orphan boys who for three years had failed their entrance exams for the classical high schools to outdo traditionally educated students. She was responsible for drafting the 1959 Greek Educational Reform Bill that promises to revolutionize the Greek public school system from top to bottom. When charged by opponents for promoting "alien American influence," she explained, "In ancient Greece education taught only the pursuit of the esthetic ideals of truth and beauty. Now that society has changed, education must change too."[24]

Cooperative Governmental and Private Programs

Many American efforts in international education have included the cooperation and support of the Federal Government working in conjunction with public and private universities, foundations, foreign governments, and international and regional organizations, such as UNESCO and the Organization of American States. Several examples may be cited. During 1958, almost 3 million dollars in foreign currencies which accrued from the sale of surplus agricultural commodities under the Agricultural Trade Development and Assistance Act of 1954 (P.L. 480, 83d Congress) were used to assist American-sponsored schools in Europe, the Near East, and in other American Republics. Through the International Educational Exchange Program, under the Fulbright Act (P.L. 584, 79th Congress) U.S. Government grants have also been made to bi-national, non-profit, non-sectarian American-sponsored schools in foreign countries to supplement the salaries of teachers from the United States, for the acquisition and improvement of school buildings, and for general educational services and supplies. Over $670,000 was expended between 1955 and 1958, benefiting more than 250 schools. The currencies accruing from the sale of surplus agricultural commodities are also used to supplement the overseas information program of the United States under USIA, in financing book translations and distribution and in aiding in the development of bi-national study and library centers. Fifteen nations have applied to participate in such projects as providing science and technical

---

[24] *Time,* August 10, 1959, p. 56.

texts for Indonesian high schools, texts in American literature for high schools in Iran, and for economic textbooks in Chile. Twenty-four countries wish to have assistance in developing bi-national centers and proposed center projects vary from the construction of an annex to a present center in Colombia to the building of a center for American studies at the University of Bologna.

The U.S. Government and American leaders were also active in the foundation of UNESCO in 1945 whose famed preamble proclaimed: "Since wars begin in the minds of man, it is in the minds of man that the defenses of peace must be constructed." In order for men to be able to construct those defenses of peace, they must be allowed the unrestricted pursuit of objective truth and they must have the means to engage in the free exchange of ideas. The United States Government has held to the stated principle of international cooperation in culture and education stated initially in the U. N. Charter. It has supported UNESCO programs, has supplied leading personnel, and often cooperates with its activities and representatives throughout the world. For example, UNESCO missions and the U.S. International Cooperation Administration (ICA) missions frequently work together on the same project. In Afghanistan, for instance, the teacher-training college program, originally undertaken by UNESCO, has been expanded with the help of ICA.

The United States exerts influence in UNESCO since its policies, like those of the other specialized agencies of the U.N., are formulated by governmental representatives of the member states meeting in general conference. In the 1946 joint resolution by which Congress provided for United States membership in UNESCO, it also established the U.S. National Commission for UNESCO. It is composed of 100 specialists in education, science, and culture, who are appointed by the Secretary of State for three-year terms; 60 of the members represent national voluntary organizations (the AFL-CIO, the U.S. Chamber of Commerce, the National Council of Churches of Christ, the National Education Association, etc.). Twenty-five of the remaining 40 members are drawn from the federal, state, and local governments, while 15 are appointed "at large." The chief function of the U.S. National Commission is to advise the government on American participation in UNESCO activities. Every two years the Commission makes detailed recommendations on the position of the United States at UNESCO's general biennial conference. The Commission serves as a channel of communication between UNESCO and the educational, scientific, and cultural treasure house which is America. Each year, for example, the United States is invited to participate in a myriad of international advisory, consultative, and technical groups; the Commission, through its contacts with professional institutions and associations, recommends qualified Americans to represent the United

States. Through its national conferences and its publications, the Commission has done much to promote an understanding of the objectives of UNESCO on the part of the American people. Equally important are American contacts with representatives of other nations on UNESCO projects.

The government also cooperates with the Organization of American States in extending its educational services and programs. The OAS administers the Rowe Pan American Fund that enables Latin American students to complete courses of study in institutions of higher learning in the United States with loans on an interest-free basis. The OAS has also established a special section to carry out the educational interchange services of the Pan American Union and helps sponsor a fellowship program. The now familiar ICA program of technical cooperation was actually launched initially when the United States began such a program in cooperation with the OAS.

Government Programs

The United States Government has also embarked upon several grand-scale programs of educational reconstruction and re-education that have called for cooperation from many sources. In the following section we will concentrate upon programs that are primarily govenmental. There is not room, however, to more than mention the extensive programs and a host of materials has been made available on the strengths and weaknesses of these projects.[25] We refer here to the attempts to fully revise education in the U.S. zone of Germany and in Japan after the second World War. In both countries the occupation government set basic policies through directives and the Japanese and German officials were expected to carry out the provisions under supervision of United States authorities.

In Germany, under the de-Nazification policy, approximately 65 percent of the elementary school teachers were dismissed and this brought many opportunities for Americans to bring their influence in the revision and enlargement of teacher training in their country. In addition, even before the military government took over, it was recognized that current textbooks would have to be eliminated and new volumes were prepared based primarily on works of the pre-Hitler period. By October, 1945, more than 5 million copies of these texts had been distributed throughout the United States

---

[25] Two governmental reports that present facts but not all the dissenting evaluations of American leadership in reshaping German and Japanese education are: *Post-War Changes in German Education* (Frankfurt: Office of the High Commissioner for Germany, Education Branch of the United States Education and Cultural Relations Division, 1951) and Ronald S. Anderson, *Education in Japan* (Washington, D.C.: U.S. Office of Education, Bulletin 1959, No. 11, 1959).

zone.[26] In addition to content alteration and control, U.S. authorities attempted to introduce new approaches in German education and launched a rich extracurriculum of clubs and activities that were expected to combat traditional German emphases. Through its work in regulating radio broadcasts, providing American educational experts as consultants, its information division, and its documentary film program, among others, the United States further influenced the re-education of Germany.

In Japan, the United States was faced with like problems in terms of screening teachers and reducing ultra-nationalistic tendencies in the schools; it also forbade the dissemination of Shinto doctrines through the schools. It was particularly active in promoting the organization of teachers' associations and unions, and a special United States education mission composed of 27 top educators concluded a study and report that led to a thorough revision of educational organization and of the curriculum in Japanese schools.

The results of these rather complete attempts to alter education in terms of American prototypes while retaining what seemed wise and necessary from the traditional systems have already been considerably modified by the natural backsliding with the passage of time, as well as by the end of American occupational authority in those lands. Nevertheless, United States influence remains substantial; a number of close educational relationships between German and Japanese and American educators, institutions, and agencies continue, and essentials of American educational thought promise to remain.

A third area of massive educational assistance is represented by American efforts in Korea. As it is less known we will examine it in more detail. Although the United States began to aid Korea educationally as early as 1945, the major efforts in that nation were carried out by the United Nations until 1955. However, the 10 million dollars, for example, spent in classroom construction, teacher training, library improvement, etc., just in the three-year period 1952-55, represented a considerable American investment in time and personnel, in addition to the indirect funds expended. Since the latter date major foreign educational efforts in Korea have been concluded under the advice of ICA representatives from the United States.

In 1956-57 almost 8 million dollars were spent in continuing the kinds of efforts indicated above, plus promoting the production of textbooks and the institution of a large-scale vocational education program in the country. A contract was also established with George Peabody College and specialists have been brought from the United States to work on curriculum construction, childhood education, and a number of other areas of educational need. Another ICA contract was signed with the University of Minnesota for

---

[26] *Government Programs in International Education, op. cit.;* see pp. 40-45 for more details on the German and Japanese programs.

special help in medicine, agriculture, and engineering education.[27] Between 1949 and 1959 the number of colleges and universities in Korea was increased from 52 to 79, with a great parallel increase in student enrollment; attendance in the middle schools was nearly doubled, and there were also striking increases in educational enrollments in other schools and particularly among women students.[28] In 1960 a full report on the needs in higher education in Korea was prepared by the ICA mission and it promises considerable further change and growth in education at those levels.[29] During the 8 years 1951-59 over 5,000 Korean students have gone abroad for study with almost 90 percent enrolling in institutions in the United States. In addition, under ICA and the Fulbright and the Smith-Mundt Acts, there has been a valuable exchange of leaders and scholars, almost 400 Koreans having been brought to the United States during the same eight-year period.[30] In all, through 1958, the U.S. economic aid program alone has contributed $16.5 million in direct assistance and $21.5 million in counterpart funds to rehabilitate and modernize Korea's educational system. When one adds to these figures U.S. funds spent on promoting audio-education centers and training films and the extensive technical training projects that have been established through other governmental programs, but that have great educational implications, one recognizes the total impact of American educational effort. This is also revealed through many other aspects emerging in Korean education such as the interesting combination of centralized educational authority working closely with the district-level, local, education committees that have been established to democratize educational administration and the growth of the School Supporters Association, the Korean counterpart of the American P.T.A.! Wood concludes that education will play its important part in the future development of Korea as it must in every culture, and explains "The success with which this out-post nation meets the challenge of the frontier may be even more important to the free world today than has been America's progress during past decades."[31]

The large number of American overseas schools supported by the military services are generally closed to all but children of service personnel; there are,

---

[27] C. W. Wood, "Post-Liberation Problems in Korean Education," *Phi Delta Kappan,* December, 1957, p. 117.

[28] *Progress 1959: United States-Korea Cooperation* (Seoul: United States Information Service, 1959), p. 60.

[29] *Report on Survey of National Higher Education in the Republic of Korea — 1960* (Seoul: Ministry of Education, Republic of Korea and United States Operations Mission to Korea, 1960).

[30] *Education in Korea,* Second Edition (Seoul: Ministry of Education, Republic of Korea, 1960), p. 101.

[31] Wood, *op. cit.,* p. 118.

498

however, some exceptions to this rule. In addition, foreign nationals hired in teaching and other capacities on the bases, the American civilians employed to instruct in these schools and, of course, the servicemen and their families are multiple and important means of extending American influence. Enrollment in Army schools alone for 1947-48 was about 7,000; this leaped to 56,000 for these overseas dependents' schools in 1958-59. Such establishments and their required staffs and facilities from France and Germany to Ethiopia and Okinawa total to a significant education program — serving, in all military dependents' schools, over 100,000 children.[32] In 1958-59 the Navy employed 337 teachers in its schools overseas and the Air Force was operating 93 schools. The Defense Department and the Department of the Army also promote further interaction between Americans and foreign nationals by their training programs for foreign military staffs, the enrollment of foreign students in American military academies, the foreign tuition assistance programs that allow personnel to enroll in foreign universities located at their place of duty, provisions for United States officers to attend foreign military schools, and through the Ryukyuan educational exchange programs.[33]

In addition to the military contacts, United States Government civilian employees overseas reached 33,000 in 1958, about one in five being tied to State Department and consular activities. U.S. Department of Agriculture, U.S. Information Service, Department of Health, Education, and Welfare, and International Cooperation Administration employees with others are joining more traditional overseas groups and have made striking contributions through their work and relationships in foreign assignments. We have certainly moved far beyond the unprepared G.I.'s whose main cultural contributions have rather unfairly been indicted as being limited to the introduction of chewing gum and *Kilroy* to the peoples of the world.

Significant government activity in international education and in promoting American educational influence abroad dates from approximately 1936 and President Franklin D. Roosevelt's Good Neighbor Policy. The government signed conventions with a number of Latin American republics to interchange scientific, technical, and educational knowledge and to institute an exchange program of graduate students and professors. Later like agreements were enacted by Congress in connection with Liberia; but not until World War II was concluded did we move into the extensive programs now carried on, based principally upon two acts of Congress — the Fulbright

---

[32] The data presented on military schools comes from personal correspondence from service headquarters and from *The Dependents' Schools Program of the U.S. Army Europe, 1946-1956* (Historical Division, Headquarters, United States Army, Europe, 1958). See also *The Overseas School in Asia, Africa, and Europe* (Washington, D.C.: The International Schools Foundation, 1960).

[33] *Government Programs in International Education, op. cit.,* pp. 78-84.

499

Act of 1946 (Public Law 584, 79th Congress) and the United States Information and Educational Exchange Act of 1948 (the Smith-Mundt Act). The former authorizes the use of foreign currencies and executive agreements to arrange for educational exchanges and the latter broadened the program and provided authority for more varied and specialized exchanges. To date approximately 39 countries have concluded agreements with the United States to participate in this program. Subsequently other special legislation has been passed relating to: educational cooperation with Finland; emergency aid to Chinese and Korean students; the education of Iranian students in the United States; promoting education in Israel; and the use of funds due the United States from the government of India to purchase 60,000 Indian publications for Indian studies in the United States.

Many of the above programs are just beginning to get underway and their full impact will not be felt for a few years. Undoubtedly the major impact from these programs has resulted from the exchange of foreign students and scholars and from the provisions that allow American students and scholars to work in these other nations. Under the International Educational Exchange Program, between 1955 and 1958, over 12,000 foreign nationals from approximately 100 countries came to the United States and more than 5,600 Americans studied, carried on research, taught, and served as consultants in other nations. During the fiscal year 1960 alone, under the Educational and Cultural Exchange Program of the Department of State, 7,234 persons were exchanged between this country and independent and dependent areas of the world. Of these, 2,061 were Americans and 5,173 were foreign visitors.

Some of the most spectacular American achievements in spreading the influence of this nation have been attained through the activities of the International Cooperation Administration (already referred to in several instances) that was established by the Mutual Security Act of 1954. Activities authorized under this law tend to focus on aiding the efforts of people in economically underdeveloped areas to develop their resources and to improve their working and living conditions through a technical assistance program. ICA's education activities tend to fall into four categories: (1) training of foreign nationals in the United States and third countries, (2) providing United States technical advisers to cooperating countries, (3) technical assistance to the educational systems and institutions of cooperating countries, and (4) financial assistance to educational institutions and systems in host countries. In 1958 ICA conducted various types of programs which affected over 60 foreign countries. Almost 7,000 foreign nationals received training in the United States or designated third countries and over 5,000 technical advisers and ICA employees from the United States were active in the field. The United States Government spent about $135 million in this program, and local currency assistance in other nations amounted to about $21 million.[34]

Much of the technical assistance ICA work is carried out through contracts involving American universities. A total of 83 of these contracts were financed in 1957; 30 percent of the contracts were in agriculture and home economics, 25 percent in education, 17 percent in business and public administration, 11 percent in engineering, 9 percent were multi-purpose, 7 percent were in public health and medicine, and 1 percent in audio-visual areas.[35] It is clear that the educational implications of these contracts go far beyond the 25 percent specifically allocated to that field. Almost 60 U.S. universities had ICA contracts in 1958 in 35 foreign countries. Programs under the university contracts are aimed especially to increase the number of people trained in the skills required for economic development and to offer the background education needed as a prerequisite for such development activities. Examples of recent projects include medical education in Thailand, vocational agricultural education in Afghanistan, training of secondary school teachers in India, nursing education in Iraq, English language education in Turkey, industrial education in Bolivia, higher education in Korea, and vocational education in the Philippines. These programs normally include several elements that may involve training of host country personnel in the United States, the provision by the United States of technical advisers to the foreign projects, supplying equipment and other financing of local costs.

Just one example of ICA contract type activities will be detailed to give some indication of the typical educational aspects involved. In 1960 Stanford University brought to a close its second contract with the ICA after a seven-year period of work in the Philippines to help develop courses in vocational education, engineering, business administration, and general college administration for future teachers. During the seven years of these two contracts, 51 Stanford faculty members spent 97 man-years teaching in the Islands. Among the results of these contracts, the University of the Philippines and five vocational colleges in the Islands are now turning out teachers well equipped to help improve the economy of that country. At each of these centers Stanford teams established programs for teacher-education in the agricultural and vocational arts in 80 vocational high schools established jointly by the United States and the Philippines throughout the Islands between 1951 and 1955. More than 500 Asian educators from over the rest of the Far East are now taking advanced work at the University of the Philippines and the other colleges to determine for themselves what

---

[34] *Government Programs in International Education, op. cit.*, pp. 71-72.

[35] Richard A. Humphrey, Ed., *Blueprint and Experience* (Washington, D.C.: Committee on Institutional Projects Abroad, American Council on Education, 1958), p. 38.

similar programs might accomplish in their own countries. Thus the influence of the American contribution spreads. As is typical in many countries, in addition to the Stanford contracts, the University of Michigan and Cornell also had education teams working in the Islands in areas of their specialty (public administration and agriculture), which further strengthened American influences. A detailed case study of the first contract has been prepared for those who are interested in viewing the problems and accomplishments of such a program.[36]

The total activities of ICA mount in their magnitude and, in addition to examples previously cited, a publication is available that includes case examples of the work of over 5,000 technicians who have served in 50 underdeveloped countries. These vary from a five-year development program in establishing bush schools in the outlands of Liberia to a literacy-reading program affecting over 11,000 Iranian gendarmes![37]

As has been indicated previously, the United States Government has a number of other agencies and departments involved in international education, one of the foremost being the United States Information Agency, whose antecedents can be traced back to a committee established in the State Department in 1938. Today the overseas operation (United States Information Service) includes 198 offices in most nations of the world and over 200 information and bi-national centers. Here library collections, lectures, motion pictures, music, exhibits, English teaching services, and other personalized contacts are available to those seeking information about the United States. The USIS missions distribute nearly 100 newspapers and magazines, millions of pamphlets and leaflets, and have helped to distribute some 35 million copies of American books that have been translated and published in 48 languages as part of the Agency's program. Other specialized booklets such as the Agency's *Outline of American History* and its *Facts About the United States* have had more than 5 million copies distributed in a score of languages.[38]

The United States Office of Education conducts a teacher exchange program under the Fulbright and Smith-Mundt Acts and in 1957-58 handled 800 teachers from the U.S. and 55 other countries. It also sponsors an international teacher education program; beginning in 1944 with Latin American teachers, this program has been extended by Congress to a

---

[36] Sidney C. High, Jr., *Vocational Industrial Education in Newly Developing Nations: A Case Study of the Philippines, 1951-1956*, Study No. 1, Comparative Education Series (Stanford: School of Education, Stanford University, 1960).

[37] *Americans on a New Frontier: U.S. Technicians Lend a Hand Abroad* (Washington, D.C.: International Cooperation Administration, Department of State Publication 6921, 1960).

[38] *Government Programs in International Education, op. cit.*, pp. 74-75.

worldwide scope. Several hundred groups of educators have beeen brought to the United States for a program that combines practical community experience, observation, and residence at an American college or university. These groups of approximately 20 educators receive a two-week orientation period in Washington, D.C., a four- to six-week assignment of residence at a college or university, and later an assignment to a State Department of Education and to a local school community. A final period of two weeks is spent in review with the staff of the U.S. Office of Education as the visiting educators prepare their reports for their home country. During 1959, 359 teachers, supervisors, school administrators, and Ministry of Education officials from 53 foreign countries participated in the program. They observed in over 8,000 public and private schools in 40 states and also visited in more than 10,000 American homes.[39] Funds are also used to bring American teachers to summer seminars abroad. The U.S. Office of Education also recruits educational specialists and technicians for foreign assignments and regularly conducts research and prepares educational studies and bibliographies on important topics in international education.

A number of aspects of the Department of State's responsibilities in international education have already been discussed (Fulbright and Smith-Mundt Acts, ICA, etc.); among its other contributions is its Foreign Service Institute which orients State Department employees for foreign service, provides training at later career-levels, and is also used by other government agencies.[40] Only one other of the many governmental divisions involved in extending American educational influence throughout the world will be mentioned — the Library of Congress. Its lists, and its catalog cards used throughout the world are well known. It also carries on a large-scale exchange program of American publications, especially for foreign visitors and scholars in the United States. In addition, it prepares international exhibits and, of course, loans books to foreign libraries. The Library's Photoduplication Service now also makes available to foreign students many source materials and microfilm copies of items on which there are no copyrights.

American governmental influences in education overseas have been substantial and many have been indirect. Some have been misguided and some have backfired. There is every evidence, however, that in the billions expended in foreign aid, increasing amounts will be put into educational efforts, from the Peace Corps to the well conceived East-West Cultural Center at the University of Hawaii where Americans and Asiatics will study together with the help of millions provided under the Mutual Security Act.

---

[39] *Ibid.,* p. 87.

[40] For State Department activities, see also: *The International Cultural Relations of the United States, Policies and Programs, 1955-1958* (Washington, D.C.: Department of State, n.d.).

American Colleges and Universities

More and more, the institutions of higher learning are coming to play a major role in the complex process by which modern nations conduct their relations with one another, and they are of growing importance in determining national policy in respect to international matters. They educate the specialists in international relations and are conducting the bulk of the research on international law, politics and organization, on social psychology and intergroup education and much of the scientific research that is so important to the government in its international relations. Academic personnel are called on an increasing basis into public service to both formulate and implement policy. Clearly, the colleges and universities are deeply involved in many aspects of extending American influence abroad.[41]

Higher education in the United States seems to be recognizing its growing responsibility in international education. Too often in the past, world affairs of a current nature have been almost completely neglected in college programs and there are too many such American schools that come near to reflecting the situation at the Sorbonne where a course in sixteenth century literature is offered under the heading of "Modern French Literature." American schools, however, are moving from the point where world affairs were considered to be the particular province of the department of political science, its courses in international relations, and of concern only to professors and students in that field. In many universities today practically every department or division has courses, programs, activities, or research that relate to this extension of interest.[42] It is reported, for example, that during 1957-58 nearly 7,000 persons from 134 American colleges and universities were engaged in 382 programs in 71 countries on projects whose annual budgets totaled almost $30 million.[43] By 1961 there were over 65,000 persons from all parts of the world in the United States for educational purposes and about three-quarters of them were students in American institutions of higher learning. Many of the others were foreign teachers and researchers on faculties of American colleges and universities. Over 10,000 U.S. students were enrolled in foreign colleges and universities or involved in the growing number of overseas programs conducted by American colleges and universities.

The foreign students and scholars are a very important element in extend-

---

[41] Howard E. Wilson, *American College Life as Education in World Outlook* (Washington, D.C.: American Council on Education, 1956), Introduction.

[42] Richard N. Swift, *World Affairs and the College Curriculum* (Washington, D.C.: American Council on Education, 1959).

[43] *The International Programs of American Universities* (East Lansing: Institute of Research on Overseas Programs, Michigan State University, 1959).

ing American ideals and practices, and authorities in the field have concluded that one of the best ways to modify education in other countries is by such an approach.[44] The foreign students in the United States in 1954-55 came from 129 different nations, dependent areas, trust territories, and international and military government-administered areas. Nearly one-third of the total came from the Far East, with Chinese, Indians, Japanese, Filipinos, and Koreans heading the numerical listing.[45] UNESCO estimated that of near 30,000 Asian students abroad, approximately one-half were studying in the United States.[46] The implications of these figures in the cultural struggle for the future of the world is implicit and all interested Americans should work to extend these figures through the various opportunities that exist or that can well be enlarged, as, for example, has been evidenced by our present growth of concern over cooperating in African education. A number of interesting studies have been conducted in recent years that give clear direction to those who are interested in promoting the greater effectiveness of the programs that bring foreign students to the United States.[47]

With the International Educational Exchange Programs, American professors teaching and carrying on research in foreign institutions is an ever more common experience. Whether it is conducting lectures in American studies at Kabul University in Afghanistan, developing new courses in accounting at the University of Ceylon, developing the teacher training program at the University of Seoul, building social science programs in Norwegian institutions of higher learning, or teaching and developing English language courses at Thai universities, American professors can be found in schools throughout the world. In addition to State Department and govern-

---

[44] John A. Garraty and Walter Adams, *From Main Street to the Left Bank: Students and Scholars Abroad* (East Lansing: Michigan State University Press, 1959), pp. 186-187.

[45] *Open Doors: A Report on Three Surveys: Foreign Students, Foreign Faculty Members, Foreign Doctors in the United States, 1954-55* (New York: Institute of International Education, 1955).

[46] *Government Programs in International Education, op. cit.,* p. 220.

[47] See, for example, Cora DuBois, *Foreign Students and Higher Education in the United States* (Washington, D.C.: American Council on Education, 1956); E. C. Cieslak, *The Foreign Student in American Colleges* (Detroit: Wayne University Press, 1955); Franklin Scott, *The American Experience of Swedish Students* (Minneapolis: University of Minnesota Press, 1956); Richard Lambert and Marvin Bressler, *Indian Students on an American Campus* (Minneapolis: University of Minnesota Press, 1956); and John W. Bennett and others, *In Search of Identity: The Japanese Overseas Scholar in America and Japan* (Minneapolis: University of Minnesota Press, 1958). Some of these cross-cultural viewpoints are recorded in the collection of articles "How Foreign Students See Us," found in *The Annals,* The American Academy of Political and Social Science, Sept., 1954.

mental programs, there are other projects that bring the American professor to leave his home shores. A large group of American teachers, for example, is employed as instructors in the University of Maryland armed forces program in a number of foreign countries; the University of Chicago and Frankfurt University have conducted a continuing exchange of professors in the humanities. The University of Istanbul regularly receives visiting law professors from Columbia and the University of Michigan. Harvard and the Sorbonne exchange one professor each year; in addition, many professors make their own arrangements for working abroad during sabbaticals and periods of leave, and several of the American philanthropic foundations sponsor such assignments and exchanges.[48]

The impact of American professors and their families can be substantial. Not only is their teaching frequently appreciated, but students in foreign universities seem to be particularly pleased with the give-and-take of class discussions and the questions after lecture or class that American professors often promote. In addition to the democratic aspects of American education that these men demonstrate, they have also brought about some changes in teaching methodology at foreign schools and have helped introduce new disciplines, as some of the behavioral sciences, public administration, and American studies, into the curricula of foreign higher education.

Although American students have been going abroad since the beginnings of our country, for many years this was highly limited and almost all travel was a private affair, financed entirely from private sources. Ultimately, foundations realizing the import of international understanding and governmental organizations that came to recognize the American student as a potentially important "ambassador of good will" began to support the movement of students to foreign institutions. Many came to study abroad under the educational provisions of the "G.I. Bill," the Serviceman's Readjustment Act of 1944, and subsequent legislation. In 1953 the passport office of the United States Department of State issued a total of 418,170 passports of which 29,577 stated "student" as being their occupation; undoubtedly a number of these passport holders were merely traveling, but more than 20,-000 others listed "travel" as being their objective for going overseas.[49]

The numerous organizations that sponsor student tours had their origin in the years immediately following World War I. Outstanding among these is the Experiment in International Living which features the arrangements that enable Americans to live in homes abroad and vice versa. The Students' International Travel Association has specialized in foreign language study and, like a number of other programs, offers study tours that carry credit in

---

[48] Garraty and Adams, *op. cit.;* see Chapter 10, "The American Professor in Europe."

[49] Wilson, *op. cit.,* p. 143.

numerous subjects, with crediting arrangements with both foreign and U.S. institutions of higher learning. The International Youth Hostel Federation has members in a host of countries and features simple accommodations for travelers hiking or bicycling in many parts of the world. Church groups, student councils, Y.M. and Y.W.C.A.'s, and other such organizations offer travel programs, including a great variety of work camps, service opportunities, special institutes, and summer study abroad.

It is coming to be recognized that the typical travel experience is not enough to make any worth-while contribution, either abroad or to the insights of Americans involved. Harlan Cleveland has revealed the poor state of readiness of the average young American traveling to Europe through a study conducted by the Maxwell School of Citizenship at Syracuse University.[50] Three-quarters of some 500 students surveyed as they crossed the Atlantic could not name a single Italian artist or novelist; half of the group could name no German writer; 70 percent knew of no country in which Lutheranism is the state church; and only 30 percent were minimally proficient in the use of a foreign language. Even more devastating was their poor orientation to their own country, 50 percent being unable to name an American playwright, 60 percent having no knowledge of the number of Negroes in the United States, etc. Allport has also cited a study where, after a typical educational tour of Japan, students did reveal a remarkable increase in information about that nation in a follow-up test but there was no accompanying change or improvement in their attitudes towards the Japanese people.[51] Undoubtedly, extended travel experiences that include intimate contact with foreign peoples do bring the realization that, in spite of cultural variations, people are more alike fundamentally, than different; that other peoples have much to offer; and that there are hosts of decent people left in the world.

Educational literature is in agreement that more intense foreign experiences are among the best preparations for teachers as social studies personnel who will work in this area of the curriculum. Certainly all teachers would benefit from living a few months or longer in two or more foreign countries. "Such experience enables the visitor to steep himself in the life of another people, learn something of their language in a situation where it is important to know that language, and begin to understand their values and approaches

---

[50] In Roy A. Price, Ed., *New Viewpoints in the Social Sciences,* Twenty-eighth Yearbook of the National Council for the Social Studies (Washington, D.C.: The Council, 1958), pp. 181-182.

[51] Gordon W. Allport, *The Resolution of Intergroup Tensions* (New York: National Conference of Christians and Jews, 1952), p. 16.

to life."[52] Since so many Americans now face international contacts, both the colleges and the lower schools are broadening their general education curricula to help prepare young men and women for a more intelligent approach to the growing number of international situations they will meet. Numerous volumes have appeared in recent years aimed at helping the elementary and high school teacher to interweave international understanding effectively into their programs.[53] From pen pal programs and international service projects, the personal contacts the pupils have with foreign students they have sponsored, and resource visitors from foreign diplomatic and consular offices, there are immediate extensions of American influences to foreign peoples. The most comprehensive system-wide program in international education has been tested in a project at Glens Falls, New York.[54]

It is recognized, however, at the college level, that broadened international emphases in general education and extended courses and offerings in international relations, comparative education and cultures, the development of true world histories instead of western civilization courses, and the like are still not enough — nor are the international relations clubs that have been sponsored since 1924 by the Carnegie Endowment for International Peace and that reached a peak of almost 800 in the United States and Canada by 1940. Today these clubs work closely with the Foreign Policy Association but they reach only a fraction of the students. International houses and "foreign nationality houses," the latter designed as centers for contact and informal language study on a number of university campuses, have undoubtedly done much in aiding foreign students to adjust to American college life, but again have touched but a handful of American students. All such experiences need to be multiplied and the number of contacts considerably broadened to enhance their value.

A major result of the growing concern to prepare American students for an international era has been the post-World War II developments in area-studies programs. Here concentrations of studies are focused upon a group of courses, or even majors, that deal with a given region of the world — the Far East, Africa, the Middle East, Western Europe, the USSR, Latin

---

[52] Leonard S. Kenworthy in Howard R. Anderson, Ed., *Approaches to an Understanding of World Affairs,* Twenty-fifth Yearbook of the National Council for the Social Studies (Washington, D.C.: The Council, 1954), pp. 402-403.

[53] Anderson, *ibid.;* Richard E. Gross and Leslie D. Zeleny, *Educating Citizens for Democracy* (New York: Oxford University Press, 1958), see Chapter 12 and bibliography; Leonard S. Kenworthy, *Introducing Children to the World* (New York: Harper, 1956); and Ralph C. Preston, Ed., *Teaching World Understanding* (New York: Prentice-Hall, 1955).

[54] Aspects of this interesting approach are described by Mabelle McNulty in "Report From Glens Falls," *Social Education.* May, 1961, pp. 224-226.

America, etc. The staff has generally been drawn from many academic disciplines and provides students with a total insight into an area that is not possible from the typical, unrelated election of courses that have had to satisfy students interested in intense work in such an area in the past. During the last decade numerous such institutes have received grants from foundations and over 40 colleges and universities now offer such concentrations. *The Overseas Americans* includes a valuable chart that indicates the colleges and emphases of all such programs in existence in 1959.[55] Over one-half of these concentrate upon Latin America; but there is a growing number of Asiatic programs. In the light of recent developments in the Dark Continent, Africa would seem to be the most overlooked focus for such concentrations.

Another recent development aimed at bringing college students more valuable experiences in a foreign context has been the introduction of international programs that involve the sending of American students and often staff members abroad and the receiving of foreign staff or students. The Junior Year Abroad approach and the actual establishment of branch schools, such as Stanford's foreign campuses near Stuttgart and in Tours, Florence, and Tokyo are examples of this growing interest. Garraty and Adams review the effectiveness of these programs and discuss a number of them in detail.[56] They evaluate such offerings as the Smith College junior year in Paris, Geneva, and Spain; the Hamilton program in Biarritz and Paris; the Sophie Newcomb-University of Dijon arrangement; Fordham's junior year program for honor students in various European centers; and the Johns Hopkins' Bologna center. More than 35 colleges and universities are developing these organized programs and out of them have come valuable lessons for extending the impact of American influences; for example, it is evident that foreign study should be made an integral part of the American institution's bachelor's or graduate program, that regular, full-time staff members of the American schools need to be appointed for leadership duties at the foreign centers, that the program should be integrated with the foreign educational system, and that students should have personal living contacts with foreign students and families.

Another development in other parts of the world that promises to expand and that is a result of the foregoing contacts is the growth of American studies or American civilization courses and programs in foreign institutions of higher learning. A number of these programs have tended to concentrate upon language and literature but offerings are broadening to provide foreign students, attending their own universities, with a fairly complete view of

---

[55] Cleveland and others, *op. cit.*, p. 220.

[56] Garraty and Adams, *op. cit.*, see particularly Appendix evaluations.

American civilization.[57] Such foreign interest in America was never very great until the period after our Civil War and early offerings tended to emphasize American geography, history, constitutional government, and economy. After 1900 increasing numbers of European scholars visited the United States and used their studies and research upon their return, sometimes in the form of new courses. Following World War I and America's growing international economic hegemony, there was considerable impetus to extending American studies in foreign institutions. General school reforms, for example in France and Germany, brought increased and required attention to the United States in the lower school syllabi and universities began to grant academic and permanent status to American studies, often creating specialized chairs. Frequently these efforts were supported by grants from American foundations and American professors were invited in growing numbers to lecture and teach at the American institutes which were founded following World War II. There is every evidence that programs of this nature will be considerably augmented throughout the world in the near future.

The foregoing pages should demonstrate the steadily progressing American influence in other countries throughout the past half-century and the media by which these forces have been brought to other peoples. We have concentrated particularly upon governmental and non-governmental educational programs, with only incidental attention to other impacts that have educational implications which have accrued from the total American involvement in international affairs. The foregoing descriptions have also indicated some of the strong points and weak points of American influence in foreign education and should suggest future steps for strengthening such activities on the part of American citizens, their institutions, and their governmental organizations. In concluding the chapter we now propose to identify the ideals, viewpoints, and practices that are America's special contributions to the education of other peoples in the world.

The Eclectic Synthesis of American Education

This volume gives evidence that it would be possible to claim with justice that the most significant contribution of the United States to international education is its successful synthesis of the educational beliefs and practices of varied persons, systems, and cultures from the history of the world's education. This is no mean accomplishment, for the educational programs that many peoples have attempted to institute have frequently proved unsatis-

---

[57] Sigmund Skard, *American Studies in Europe: Their History and Present Organization* (Philadelphia: University of Pennsylvania Press, 1958).

factory, either because the idea or organization desired would not or could not be so borrowed or because they made the mistake of attempting a full imitation of a favored program from a different culture or nation.

The various chapters of this book, while documenting the great heritage of American education, have also revealed how, with some natural oversights and mistakes, the American people and their educational leaders have made numerous and often most effective applications and modifications of key ideas and established practices in their new environment. No one could expect them to have brought forth a fully original educational system because men in a new territory always build upon what they have experienced and upon what they know. This is especially true when men move into a virgin land or a backward area where there are no satisfactory educational institutions to build upon. In addition, although most Europeans came to America for fresh opportunities in one realm or another, they often did not look upon their settlements as truly "new" lands, but rather as extensions of their own home lands. In the strange and challenging situation in which they found themselves in North America, they undoubtedly hoped to take from their backgrounds all that was good and that was cherished and that gave promise of enabling them to reach traditional goals more satisfactorily.

Thus, what appeared as "new" in most situations resulted from the demands of the fresh environment coupled with a certain amount of unique creativity on the part of the educational forefathers that was, nevertheless, rooted in their past. The "indigenous" developments in American education traced in the previous chapter have their historic antecedents and there is little that we can say that happened for the first time in America. Yet as we have seen, a host of "firsts" are already lost in forgotten or unrecorded individuals, events, or epochs in many distant places, and, except for rather narrow purposes, of what use are such "firsts"? What counts in history is when an idea becomes accepted by enough people or the "right" people and then is applied in sufficient instances to make some difference in education and in society. Therefore, for our purposes, it is nowhere near as important to know that there was a Danish compulsory school attendance law as early as 1739 or that Lutherans established a compulsory attendance law in 1617 in Weimar as it is to perceive when, where, why, and how such an aim was instituted so as to actually affect a significant number of children and then, once the virtue of the theory was indicated in worth-while results, to understand the means by which compulsory attendance was extended and the obstacles that had to be overcome. Now much in the American educational experience is characterized by the adaptive-eclectic-synthesis syndrome. It is very possible that foreign peoples have been led to accept American educational theory and practice to the extent that they have because implicit in it are not only some familiar factors but also because they recognize intuitively

511

in American achievements the attainment of many of their own personal and social educational goals, even though these may remain unstated or obscure in their own society, community, or nation.

Education in the United States, for example, that early brought literacy to the great bulk of citizens was bound to impress other areas of the world with older cultures and established systems of education that had not as yet reached this end. This was particularly true when a people was led to perceive the value of mass education as was evidenced by American progress. This impact can be expected to multiply as a result of the growing international contacts detailed previously in this chapter, because more than half of the world still cannot read! From Latin America, with nearly 70 million illiterates, to certain Asiatic countries where illiteracy runs in some instances to 85 percent, more people, who are being brought to increasing contacts with advanced cultures, almost instinctively recognize that education is the key to the unfortunate differences between underdeveloped and industrialized nations. That these people would seek to emulate the educational programs of modern cultures is to be expected.

In this international situation there exists an often unrecognized advantage for America and the West as they struggle to maintain and to promote their common values throughout the world; this is the degree to which we share our fundamental beliefs with the aspirations of the underprivileged of the globe. Our totalitarian adversaries seem to realize this advantage and are capitalizing upon our lack of initiative in many instances by pouring resources into the contest and by adapting, emasculating, and masquerading behind these values. The tragedy of western history would be the failure of westernized education, now being extended primarily through American resources, to enable other peoples to find in it, with necessary modifications, the means of reaching that better future which they are now ever more determined to attain in this generation. Thus, the eclecticism of American education that draws on varied backgrounds and that has met the needs of as hybrid a group of people as those who have made America should not be overlooked as one of our most potent gifts to others. ⁷

Educational Implications of Our Respect for the Common Man

Fundamental in the American approach to education is an acceptance of the dignity and rights of the common man. Directly related to this value are the principles: that all men (and women) have a right to education; that the responsibility for providing this education, although protecting the rights of families and minorities to maintain their own private educational ventures within the cultural context, is a governmental responsibility; that this aim is best promoted through a universal, single-track, public system of education, which allows for necessary individual group or local variations as it attempts to guarantee the social good. Corollaries here are the recognition that all citizens have something to contribute to the social order and, therefore, that the state is duty bound to offer as many as possible a fitting education — one that promotes the fullest development of the individual and thus, of his communities of concern. Basic too is the wisdom of drawing intelligence from all classes and groups, of opening the doors of education for equal opportunity to all to achieve to their capacity and thereby gaining the maximum from the full cultivation of the nation's talent.

Indicated here also is an extended general education reaching into higher levels as more and more of the country's youth remain in school and accept the opportunities for advanced education that are proffered. Public nursery schools and kindergartens, our common elementary school, the American public high school, the adult and evening school, the host of varied, state-supported schools for special learnings, our emerging community and junior college movement, and the state colleges and land-grant universities, comprise a system of interrelated schools that reflect America's belief in the common man, in his reason, in his aspirations, and in his sovereignty.

At this juncture it is appropriate to indicate several of the unique features of American higher education that are finding increasing acceptance throughout the world as other countries extend their educational systems. President Wells of the University of Indiana suggests as unique, among others, the universities' and colleges' range of curricula, the growing quality of work in different divisions and departments, the methods of teaching, the wide community services, campus life, relationships with alumni, and, most important, the "social-ladder" wherein almost thirty percent of our youth now spend some time in higher education in contrast with under eight percent in any other English-speaking nation and a much lower percentage in other countries.[58] These characteristics are evident at other levels of our educational structure but they serve to highlight the capstone role of the American college and university in fulfilling the American educational dream, a vision we share on an enlarging basis with other peoples who are bent to follow the American trail.

American universities also need to be commended for their sponsoring systematic and wide-spread study of educational problems. Although strong European precedents exist and continue, higher education in the United States provides a valuable example of experimentation, publication, consultant work, the school survey and other phases of their persistent activity toward furthering a science of education.

---

[58] Herman B. Wells, "American Education and the Rising Tide," *Phi Delta Kappan,* June, 1956, pp. 445-446.

Education for Living, A Spectrum of Aims and Emphases

A third dedicated feature of American education that we have exported is our belief that a practical education is important for all. Each does not need the same practical education but everyone should have the opportunity to pursue those learnings that promise to serve purpose in their lives. American education is not just for elite culture, for the working class, for leisure, for health, for intellectual growth, for parenthood, for citizen-soldiers, or for learning how to live with our fellows — it is for all of these and more.

At this juncture in history, in spite of some reaction, American citizens seem to recognize that our long-time push for a broad curriculum, appealing to many needs, is all the more essential in the age of growing interdependent-specialism that confronts them. These aims were not achieved without opposition; however, the public support and extensive acceptance of, for example, the vocational and the performing arts in regular school programs, as well as the citizens' willingness to provide special public schools and offerings where indicated, reflect their realization of the worthwhileness of many learning experiences in a myriad of subjects, as well as the broad purposes that can properly be expected of public education.

In connection with education for living, as with our previous principle of respect for the individual, is the great American example of the education of its women. A far cry from the practices of ancient Athens or of many contemporary nations, the rich educational provisions for women in the United States, along with the sensible and valuable employment of coeducation, is a distinct practice worthy of emulation. In observing American women as students, scholars, professionals, wives and helpmates, and in their other multiple roles, foreigners cannot but be awakened to the tragic loss of talent in their societies when women are deprived of the opportunity to have a more complete life and of thereby contributing directly and indirectly to the progress of their civilization. In just the teaching profession alone, with the great need for expanded numbers of educators, the outstanding example of the United States (with 90 percent of its elementary and 50 percent of its secondary instructors female) stands in contrast to many nations in sore need of educational manpower who have very few women teachers in the classroom.[59]

A broad program of education is also devoted to concern for the individuals in the lower echelons of ability and for the handicapped. Often, as has been proved by the American practice, if these persons are educated wisely, with

---

[59] Alonzo Grace presents some of the varying percentages of female teachers in a number of countries in "Teachers of the World," *Phi Delta Kappan*, June, 1956, p. 402.

proper materials and facilities, they can make enduring contributions to their society.

All of the concerns for a spectrum of offerings are reflected particularly in America's most unique educational creation, the high school, which we have treated in detail in Chapter XI. /The free, universal, comprehensive secondary school is surely America's educational trade-mark abroad. It con- ③ tinues to serve, now in its second century of evolution, as a growing, co-hesive force in our society. /Although at this point we will delimit our dis-cussion of this truly indigenous school, we need to remind ourselves that while some American critics seek a return to the outmoded institution and program of a half-century ago, foreign cabinets and parties are now retained in office on the promise of establishing such schools. Britain pushes its bilateral and comprehensive secondary programs, France and Belgium tend to mod-ify their lycées and collèges, the Soviet Union extends its common school offer-ings into advanced grades and limits upper level classical emphases with voca-tional experiences, and nations consider eliminating the rigid leaving exams from their lower schools that have tended to discourage, eliminate, and "track" far too early — this is what other countries in the world are carrying out in the light of the achievement of a nation that has been able to serve more than three-quarters of its eligible youth through its high schools.

One feature of the high school that calls for special attention is the extensive extra or co-curriculum. Entire books and courses in teacher educa-tion are now devoted to what has been called the "third curriculum."[60] Admit-tedly the enrichment activities in some schools and communities have reached a point where the "tail wags the dog"; however, a healthy readjustment in this situation now marks many schools that have gone too far in this direc-tion. Again, however, such programs serve to highlight the special and broad purposes that the American people want their secondary schools to perform and which, perhaps surprisingly, they so often accomplish so well — fre-quently outshining the achievements of their equivalent private institutions.

The American Economy and Its Technology

Behind many of the achievements of education in the United States have been the financial largess and the industrial and manufacturing resources of the nation. Expenditures on education may remain far short of what they could be but the palace that is the American school is seldom equalled in the world. These institutions, be they a giant technical high school in a metropolis or a modest community-centered elementary school in a rural

---

[60] See, for example, Robert W. Frederick, *The Third Curriculum: Student Activities in American Education* (New York: Appleton-Century-Crofts, 1959).

515

environ, usually leave foreign visitors in awe and with some pangs of desire.

The school plants themselves, however — swimming pools, flexible walls, little theatres, and all — are not what really impress the touring educator from abroad as being most important. What actually strikes the non-American are our textbooks, in all of their glories, as well as the supplementary references, room sets of encyclopedias, charts, maps, globes, and other media of instruction. Nations with centralized systems of education and state production of texts and teaching materials have developed some excellent volumes and related instructional aids; but generally these pale when contrasted with the results of the principle of independent selection and the production of these teaching materials by American private enterprise.

These rich resources, that enable the American teacher to accomplish a number of purposes with considerable ease, now promise to be multiplied by the further extension of the technological revolution into the school. Mere installation of TV sets in the classroom may soon be looked upon as part of educational history with the advances in this area and the electronic teaching machines and other instructional systems that are on the horizon.[61] American mentors may be little better prepared for these innovations than their foreign colleagues but they need to experiment with and test these media rapidly. This is so because once the basic power resources become available in an economy that can support such automation, we can be sure that American automated and self-instructional devices will find their way to the corners of the earth — just as the ubiquitous "Coke" bottle floats the seven seas.

Whether publicly or privately financed and directed, the dramatic American achievements in machine technology are in tremendous demand when so large a part of the world, essentially unprepared, is entering upon the Industrial Age. Here, indeed, is one of the truly symbolic focal points in the American race with the Soviet Union for international prestige. Although many of these attainments and their related skills have not been gained specifically in the United States through typical school programs, the ability to develop individuals who can succeed in technical areas does depend upon a thorough general education as well as specialized schooling. It is easy to understand how less-favored peoples, now groping for a better future, will turn increasingly to American technical "know how" concerned with tractor repairs, automatic milking systems, electronic circuits, complex business machines, and a host of other such skills and products. It would be a mistake to allow these outward material factors to loom as our most important educational export; however, they are the products of American genius and we cannot overlook or underestimate their deep significance in spreading the

---

[61] See the interesting predictions about developments in this area, in James D. Finn, "Technology and the Instructional Process," *Phi Delta Kappan,* June, 1960, pp. 371-378.

influence of the United States and its educational programs and institutions.

Both private and public education in the United States have benefited immeasurably, not only from bountiful public treasuries but also from the economic contributions of foundations, corporations, alumni, and wealthy individuals. Foreign schools have largely missed these important sources of funds and great endowments and the financial drives, particularly of private schools in the United States, are relatively unknown. Whatever can be accomplished to promote such organizations and to gain private financial support in other nations will aid them materially in strengthening their educational programs.

American School Organization and Administration

The district superintendent, the county office, the town board of trustees, and the city Parents' Council for Better Schools are examples of American local control and concern that are not commonly found in other countries. To the student from abroad, these present a very complex interrelationship of a number of systems and agencies; but they represent the manner by which citizens in the United States have attempted to maintain traditional authority and structure in the face of momentous cultural change. It should be admitted that much of this is a patchwork of educational arrangements that should never be nominated for export or emulation. Nevertheless, our district, community, and state organizations with their overlapping yet coordinated responsibilities and programs can serve, with appropriate modifications, as patterns for systems that are facing some of the same problems that beleaguered the evolution of American educational organization. A number of aspects of the American system have been imposed with varying degrees of success in other countries that have used American consultants, particularly since 1945.

It is understood that decentralization of schools in certain countries could do more harm than good and that a gradual shifting of responsibilities to localities is more appropriate. Such developments can be expected in the years ahead in many nations. Just as America has been forced to build compromises between local and state programs and now considers the incorporation of increased federal activities, so too will other nations have to reach agreeable balances between levels of educational authority. A related point here is that American schools are intimately tied to their locality. School and community tend to reinforce one another's educational efforts and many bonds exist. These are evidenced by joint community service projects, part-time work experience arrangements for students, the public use of school shops and other facilities as the auditorium, cafeteria, and athletic stadia.

Another key aspect of American school organization and administration,

517

besides the diverse and unique means of providing financial support, is the lay leadership centered in school boards. Top administrators remain responsible to the people's representatives and are only delegated responsibilities at local levels; fewer powers are granted to education officials at the state level. Lay influences such as citizens' committees and parent-teachers associations are also rare in other nations. The close relationship between parents, school, and locality being adopted in some foreign community schools is a mark of strength in American education that reaches back to colonial times. As America developed, the school began to replace the church as a center of activity and interest and soon came to house everything from the town meeting to the fall festival. Foreign schools that are able to incorporate this American warmth, interest, mutual service, and necessary local variations into their revised systems of education will benefit materially.

Democratic Citizenship Education

All societies use their schools to promote loyalty and patriotism, a form of nationalism, belief in the political system and other civic attributes deemed of vital import to the preservation of the state. The free schools of a democracy are faced with special obligations and problems that reflect their unique role in maintaining and extending the democratic way. If the school should mirror the society and especially its fundamental values, this calls for a clarification of purposes so that all aspects of the program ring true to the societal goals. All persons responsible in the democratic educational process should be alert to maintain a curriculum and learning experiences which are appropriate for the development of the requisite knowledges, skills, and attitudes essential for the free citizen.

Bound up in the American concept of citizenship education that permeates all schools are a variety of factors. The following ideas seem particularly pertinent for dissemination:

INDIVIDUALISM. Democratic education recognizes individualization as essential and this concept brings a variety of provisions. We tend to have less enforcement and supervision by central authorities (or even by building principals) than is typical in other countries. Such an approach capitalizes on the strengths of each instructor, helps preserve the individual personality, and is based upon a faith in his ability. Teachers likewise make accommodations to the pupils in their classes who are not treated as a herd. True dedication to individualization calls for extensive testing, guidance, and counselling services and procedures — still to be attained in many American schools. It demands provisions for the gifted while at the same time the doors of opportunity are kept open for "late-developers" and the handicapped. This belief is founded upon an instructional process that seems to many foreign observers a unique and valuable American practice.

PROCESS AND APPROACH. The give and take of the American classroom, the free play of discussion, the emphasis upon human relations, the small-group work, the cooperative problem-solving approach toward discovering answers and working out solutions, often to contemporary questions, is what we have in mind when we underscore America's concern over process in education. The wish is to insure both the freedom of the teacher to teach and the learner to learn so as to obtain a purposeful and highly motivated educational experience. The aim is to build those competencies whereby children and youth can ultimately contribute to the further development and improvement of their own society.[62] The planned study of controversial issues is usually missing in foreign curricula. Were it necessary to single out the one most important guideline in this area for newly emerging democracies in the world, it is the recognition of the import of democratic *means*. America's message here is that the school must reflect and inculcate above all the freedoms and responsibilities that are essential for what Max Otto called "the democratic way *at* life."[63]

THE SOCIAL STUDIES. Although all aspects of the school program are expected to mirror the democratic approach, including such co-curricular activities as student councils, in the United States the social studies have been developed as the central media for building the civic responsibilities deemed so important. This organization of subject matter is unique to the United States. In other countries the term social studies or social education, if used at all, will refer rather to the extracurriculum or to adult education. Most schools throughout the world maintain strictly divided social science disciplines, and pupils may be found taking three separate courses in geography, government, and history. In spite of the employment since 1900 of this organization of content that attempts to draw upon the different social

---

[62] Many helpful and diverse volumes have appeared that underscore this approach; typical are: Richard E. Gross, Raymond H. Muessig, and George L. Fersh, Eds., *The Problems Approach and the Social Studies,* Curriculum Series No. 9, revised (Washington, D.C.: National Council for the Social Studies, 1960), which is an example of the method in a given subject area; a helpful "general methods" text that best reflects a problems orientation is Ray H. Simpson, *Improving Teaching-Learning Processes* (New York: Longmans, Green and Company, 1953).

[63] See his selected writings in Max C. Otto, *Science and the Moral Life* (New York: The New American Library, 1949); Chapter 3 entitled "Realistic Idealism" presents this view of the democratic process and is selected from his volume *The Human Enterprise* (New York: Appleton-Century-Crofts, 1940).

disciplines in teaching units that are centered upon social problems, dissension remains in America over this approach.[64] Nevertheless, the idea of the social studies fits the conception and needs of education in the United States and merits study by other peoples who desire to modernize their emphases in citizenship education.

National Education Association

IN AMERICA THE SOCIAL STUDIES HAVE BEEN DEVELOPED AS
THE CENTRAL MEDIA FOR BUILDING CIVIC RESPONSIBILITIES.

Other characteristics of democratic civic education could be identified and some are bound up in factors discussed under other American contribu-

---

[64] For a discussion of the issues involved, see: Gross and Zeleny, *op. cit.,* particularly Part I and Chapter 5; a brief contrast of American social studies with foreign offerings is found in Richard E. Gross, "The Social Studies at Home and Abroad," *California Journal of Secondary Education,* February, 1959, pp. 113-117.

tions. For a more extended discussion of such principles of democratic education, readers are referred to Mursell's helpful volume.[65]

Other Contributions — Present and Potential

Numerous additional aspects of education in the United States may be cited that hold promise for other educational systems. Some of these are on the threshold of adaptation; others will be farther off in their foreign appearance.

With the great illiteracy that hampers many of the underdeveloped countries it is to be expected that American achievements in adult education, discussed in previous chapters (current sources list well over 3 million in formal courses and nearly 50 million in other phases of continuing education in the United States) present goals and approaches worthy of emulation. Countries on the verge of modernization dare not depend just on the education of youth but must reach the adult population. Another emphasis that has been indicated previously as being of special importance to these peoples who are still in an agricultural age or just becoming industrialized, is the American programs of rural and vocational education.[66] The significance of our multiple and varied approaches through public sources, and on all educational levels, that incorporate a dignity for practical schooling and that couple it with general and citizenship education is a prime example for other cultures that out of ignorance, isolation, or long colonial dependency believe that a classical education is the best or the only education that is worthwhile.

Other American prototypes from parent-teachers associations and volunteer citizens' committees for better schools to the attainments in audio-visual areas and in school building facilities will some day find their way on a greater scale into the educational setting in other nations. Present experimentation in American education that attempts to maintain the balance of quantity and quality, that is concerned about the individual and the mass, undoubtedly will also serve as a valuable base for similar developments in the increasing

---

[65] James L. Mursell, *Principles of Democratic Education* (New York: W. W. Norton and Company, 1955) identifies ten basic American principles.

[66] For details and highlights of American achievements in these areas, see *The Handbook on Rural Education* (Washington, D.C.: National Education Association, Department of Rural Education, 1961); *Public Vocational Educational Programs* (Washington, D.C.: Department of Health, Education, and Welfare, U.S. Office of Education, Pamphlet No. 117, 1956).

number of countries that are now moving toward the plausibility of such aims and programs.[67]

American Educational Theory

Many of the foregoing characteristics of American education evidence a point of view that has grown in the United States through the years and that finally found firm expression in the works of a group of educational theorists who appeared at the turn of the twentieth century. Their thinking tended to emerge in a set of practices that have been loosely identified under the banner of "progressive education." Foremost among these leaders was John Dewey. As the most influential of American educational philosophers, we shall limit ourselves to indicating his impact, recognizing the exceptions, differences, and variations that existed and that remain in the continuing modification of his pragmatic views as well as the foreign impact of other spokesmen such as Kilpatrick and Washburne.

Dewey studied the origin and the process of ideas and valuation in order to determine their use for the formulation of the future. He conceived life as the steady adjustment of individuals to their environments and appreciated democracy as the experimental method of testing ideas pertinent to the resolution of social issues. For Dewey, the mind evolved as the organism meets and solves problems: thus mind has developed as a tool for dealing with the environment — his "instrumental" theory of mind. On the basis of this belief, action precedes knowledge. Learning comes from acting and experiencing and results in testing activities; as it influences action then, this knowledge changes. Here knowledge is conceived as a social instrument and education is "the process of the reconstruction or reconstitution of experience, giving it a more socialized value through the medium of increased individual efficiency." Dewey taught, therefore, that as one faces a changing environment and makes adjustments to it, he reconstructs experience and learns. The end or aim of education is more education; the aim of education is within the process of education and is not a termination of education. Thus, Dewey equated education with growth and actual living. The school was envisioned as a formal social institution for providing this growth and was to encourage real experiences for the child. Three main ideas are reflected in the above summary that were fundamental in Dewey's educational thought: his theory of experience and learning; his dedication to the method of intelligence; and his belief in democracy in education. These, applied in the typical school, can institute real educational revolution!

---

[67] Elements of some of these recent trends are found in Arthur D. Morse, *Schools of Tomorrow — Today* (New York: Doubleday and Co., 1960), and in J. Lloyd Trump and Dorsey Baynham, *Focus on Change* (Chicago: Rand, McNally & Co., 1961).

Dewey's influences beyond the boundaries of the United States began about the turn of the century. Kandel states that the earliest foreign study of Dewey was a German doctoral dissertation analyzing his theory of interest that was completed in 1901.[68] The first overseas publication of his work in English had appeared in Britain in 1900 (*The School and Society*). The first foreign translation (of the same work) is believed to have been a Czech edition in 1904. Following World War I, as nations rebuilt and often revised in a spirit of reform, the growth of foreign interest in Dewey was "a remarkable occurrence in the educational history of the twentieth century."[69]

To that time foreign interest in American education had been very limited, but the spokesmen for the New Education appearing in Europe found powerful support in Dewey's work. Although there was considerable interest in Britain, Germany seemed most receptive in terms of the amount of literature that appeared and the positive reaction to Dewey. Dewey was honored in Czechoslovakia and particularly in Russia after the 1917 revolution. During the decade from 1922 to 1933, the head of Soviet education was influenced by Dewey and invited him to come to Russia to study educational conditions and make recommendations. After the Trotsky incident, Dewey's Russian influence declined. His 1926 trip to Turkey had important results in that country and later his works had a material impact upon teacher education in New Zealand.[70]

Most students of Dewey's influence believe that his greatest impact outside of the United States came in China. In 1920 and 1921 he lectured in Peking and Nanking as some of his former students had reached positions of educational power in that country. Many of his works were translated and widely circulated throughout the nation. His writings were also given particular attention by Japanese educators during the early twenties. Dewey enjoyed a high reputation in Latin America, particularly in Mexico, Argentina, and Brazil.

Brickman includes a rich bibliography of foreign works that provide strong evidence of Dewey's educational reach from Poland to India and from Catholic to Communist educators. He concludes that Dewey's philosophy had much less impact than his educational approaches which could be applied in educational reform without accepting Dewey's underlying views about nature and man. It is clear that he incorporated significant expressions on education

---

[68] I. L. Kandel, "The Influence of Dewey Abroad," *School and Society,* November 23, 1929, pp. 700-704.

[69] William W. Brickman, "John Dewey's Foreign Reputation as an Educator," *School and Society,* October 22, 1949, p. 258; the writers are indebted to this extensive survey for many of their comments on this topic.

[70] Arthur H. Moehlman and Joseph S. Roucek, Editors, *Comparative Education* (New York: Dryden Press, 1952), pp. 173, 485.

that reached back to great educational theorists and reformers of the past and that he still stands as the "high priest" of the international, contemporary demand for educational improvement. Foreign students of education "may not accept everything suggested by him, and may even disagree profoundly in important respects, but they will agree that whatever he has said is of interest and significance. This is the status of Dewey's relationship to his colleagues in foreign countries. This is the measure of his reputation as an educator all over the world, a reputation that few other pedagogues are able to approach."[71]

Because of the many factors described in this chapter, in the years immediately ahead, new and altered American educational theory will undoubtedly find its way across the waters in increasing amount. Valuable thinking and progress in specialized areas within the field, such as educational psychology and educational sociology should also find an enlarged audience abroad. Such dispersion is particularly important for dangers of misinterpretation and misapplication threaten when aspects of foreign educational programs are discussed or adopted without recognizing and understanding the bases upon which these rest. This also serves as a call to American educational philosophers and other educational authors to meet the challenge of adequately portraying and explaining the complex eclectic synthesis that characterizes education in the United States.

Conclusion

Have we presented too ambitious a view of the impact and the implications of American education upon the world? We believe not. We realize that educational exchange will continue increasingly to be a true two-way street and we would urge Americans in their age of pre-eminence not to neglect to continue to look abroad for fruitful ideas. In fact, as other countries accept, apply, and modify American approaches, we will find increasing value in being informed of developments in their educational systems. Also, with each passing decade, as the peoples of the world grow ever closer, all promise to have more in common and increased use for the interchange of studies, viewpoints, and practices. Indeed, a new type of sociological-comparative education promises to rise to help meet this need. We hope that this volume fills a small niche in this growing area of demand.

A contemporary French scholar recently challenged citizens of the United States by pointing out the great tasks of social, economic, and political exploration that still lie ahead of us. Bruckberger concludes his analysis by warning, "The West would be doomed, and you eternally shamed if today

---

[71] Brickman, *op. cit.*, p. 261.

you proved incapable not only of fulfilling the spendid hope of the Declaration of Independence in your own country but also of bringing that hope to the rest of the world."[72] As education is a prime means by which we make our ideals real, American education will continue to receive intense attention from foreign observers. Many realize the import of a recent editorial in the *London Times*, that was directed at the United States and asked the question that must be in the minds of numerous serious students of our times: "Can a nation whose power and prosperity demand that more and more of its people shall have a scientific, technological, or vocational education, at the same time produce the amount of wisdom needed for the successful leadership of the free world? . . . There can be few great adventures more worth watching than the course of American education. On it may well depend the kind of civilization in which our grandchildren survive."

If American education remains true to its heritage we have no doubt that, with our growing international fellowship, we will rise to successfully meet this challenge of our expanded frontier. It is not the totalitarian nations that necessarily hold the key to the future. Idealistic American teachers and their fellows across the globe may still help attain the aim stated a century ago by William Lloyd Garrison: "My country is the world. My countrymen are all mankind." When and if such a goal is attained it is our belief that it will be gained in large part through education — an education permeated with the values and practices nurtured in the American educational heritage.

Bibliography

Bereday, George and Luigi Volpicelli, Eds., *Public Education in America*. New York: Harper and Bros., 1958.

Bodenman, Paul S., *American Cooperation With Higher Education Abroad; A Survey of Current Programs*. Washington, D.C.: U.S. Office of Education, Bulletin 1957, No. 8, 1957.

Bruckberger, R. L., *Image of America*. New York: Viking Press, 1959.

Cleveland, Harlan, Gerard J. Mangone, and John Clarke Adams, *The Overseas Americans*. New York: McGraw-Hill Book Company, Inc., 1960.

Committee on Educational Interchange Policy, *Twenty Years of United States Government Programs in Cultural Relations*. New York: Institute of International Education, 1959.

Cramer, John F. and George S. Browne, *Contemporary Education: A Comparative Study of National Systems*. New York: Harcourt, Brace and Company, 1956.

DuBois, Cora, *Foreign Students and Higher Education in the United States*. Washington, D.C.: American Council on Education, 1956.

---

[72] R. L. Bruckberger, *Image of America* (New York: The Viking Press, 1959), p. 277.

Garraty, John A. and Walter Adams, *From Main Street to the Left Bank: Students and Scholars Abroad.* East Lansing: The Michigan State University Press, 1959.

Gross, Richard E. and Leslie D. Zeleny, *Educating Citizens for Democracy.* New York: Oxford University Press, 1958.

House Committee on Government Operations, *Government Programs in International Education,* House Report No. 2712, 85th Congress, 2d sess., 1959, Washington, D.C.: Government Printing Office, 1959.

Jones, Howard M., *Education and World Tragedy.* Cambridge: Harvard University Press, 1946.

Kandel, I. L., *The New Era in Education.* Boston: Houghton Mifflin Company, 1955.

King, Edmund J., *Other Schools and Ours.* New York: Rinehart & Co., Inc., 1958.

Lambert, Richard D., Ed., "America Through Foreign Eyes," *The Annals of the American Academy of Political and Social Science.* Philadelphia: The Academy, September, 1954.

Lerner, Max, *America as a Civilization.* New York: Simon & Schuster, 1957.

Mayer, Martin, *The Schools.* New York: Harper and Bros., 1961.

Meyer, Adolphe E., *The Development of Education in the Twentieth Century,* 2d edition. New York: Prentice-Hall, 1949.

Moehlman, Arthur H. and Joseph S. Roucek, Eds., *Comparative Education.* New York: The Dryden Press, 1952.

Mursell, James L., *Principles of Democratic Education.* New York: W. W. Norton & Company, Inc., 1955.

Quattlebaum, Charles A., *Educational and Cultural Relations With Foreign Countries.* Washington, D.C.: The Library of Congress, Legislative Reference Service, Public Affairs Bulletin No. 51, 1947.

Richmond, W. Kenneth, *Education in the USA, A Comparative Study.* New York: Philosophical Library, 1956.

Scanlon, David G., Ed., *International Education: A Documentary History.* New York: Bureau of Publications, Teachers College, Columbia University, 1960.

Swift, Richard N., *World Affairs and the College Curriculum.* Washington, D.C.: American Council on Education, 1959.

Wilson, Howard E., *American College Life as Education in World Outlook.* Washington, D.C.: American Council on Education, 1956.

* Note: Authors and publications listed only in footnotes or chapter bibliographies are not included in this index.